I0822221

GUARDIANS of Ukraine

Guardians
of Ukraine
The Ukrainian Airforce
Since 1992
Babak Taghvaee

First published 2020 by Crécy Publishing Ltd

ISBN 978 190210 9619

A CIP record for this book is available from the British Library

Publisher's Note: Every effort has been made to identify and correctly attribute photographic credits. Any error that may have occurred is entirely unintentional.

Printed in Turkey by Pelikan Print

Crécy Publishing Limited
1a Ringway Trading Estate
Shadowmoss Road
Manchester M22 5LH
www.crecy.co.uk

Front cover top: Two Su-25M1s of the 299th BrTA, 41 Blue in foreground and 45 Blue in background, over Nikolayev on 28 October 2016. 41 Blue was badly damaged after it was hit by MANPADS on 16 July 2014. It was later repaired and returned to its brigade. *Alexander Golz*

Front cover bottom: MiG-29MU1 02 Blue of the 114th BrTA taxiing in front of several Su-27s of the 831st BrTA during a military exercise at Ivano-Frankovsk in September 2013. A few months later, on 7 August 2014, while returning to Dnepropetrovsk after an interdiction sortie, 02 Blue was shot down at 18:40 local time by a Buk-M1 SAM of pro-Russian separatists south of Yenakievo. At that time, the airplane was in service with the 40th BrTA. *Alexander Golz*

Back cover top: On 6 June 2014, An-30B 80 Yellow of the 15th TrAB was shot down by pro-Russian separatists, resulting in the death of six of its eight crew members. *Luca G. Canossa*

Back cover middle left: Tu-22R 29 Red of the 199th OGDRAP making a low pass over Poltava air base during an air show on 22 May 1993. *Sergey Popsuevich*

Back cover middle centre: Su-24MR 17 Yellow releasing flares during an exercise at Rovno gunnery range on 17 September 2007. *Sergey Popsuevich*

Back cover middle right: MiG-25RBS 17 Red, seen after overhaul at Zaporozhye in 1995. *Zaporozhye Repair Plant Archive*

Back cover bottom: Su-17M4R 12 Yellow (c/n 34814) was one of the last 14 Su-17s in service with the 827th ORAE. It was sent to Zaporozhye and its bort number was changed to 12 Blue in 2003. It was kept airworthy while it was waiting to be sold, and can be seen here during one of its last flights at Zaporozhye in 2003. *Zaporozhye Repair Plant Archive*

Back cover profile: Artwork of how An-30B 80 Yellow looked in 2014. *Luca G. Canossa*

Contents

Acknowledgements

I would like to express my gratitude to many people who helped me with the research and pictures for this book, specifically Anton Pavlov (RuAF, ret.), Andrey Pilschikov, Alexander Golz, Guus Ottenhof, Dr. Heinz Berger, Joe Celiberti, Marco Djkshorn and Sergey Popsuevich. There are those whom I am unable to mention due to their requests for anonymity. Further to this, I would like to thank Chris Chennel, Dmitry Shevchuk, Guk Aleksander, Igor Bubin, Sergei Tryuhan and Vladimir Alexandrovich Kalinin for their generous assistance with additional information, the reconstruction of specific events, and sharing photographs from their private collections.

Abbreviations

AB	Air Base
AAM	Air-to-air missile
AvB	Aviation Base
Albatros	Name of L-39 light training jet airplane
APIB	Fighter-Bomber Aviation Regiment
APON	Aviation Regiment for Special Purposes
ARZ	Aircraft Repair Plant (Russian abbreviation)
ARP	Aircraft Repair Plant (English abbreviation)
b/n	Bort Number
BAD	Bomber Aviation Division
BAP	Bomber Aviation Regiment
Backfire	ASCC code for Tu-22M supersonic, variable-sweep wing, long-range strategic and maritime strike bomber
Bear	ASCC code for Tu-95 four-engine turboprop-powered strategic bomber and missile platform
Blinder	ASCC code for Tu-22 supersonic heavy bomber
Blackjack	ASCC code for Tu-160 supersonic, variable-sweep wing heavy strategic bomber
BrTA	Tactical Aviation Brigade
c/n	Construction number
Col	Colonel (military commissioned officer rank)
CSAR	Combat Search-and-Rescue
CHARZ	Chuguyev Aircraft Repair Plant
Crusty	ASCC code for Tu-134 twin-engined, narrow-body, jet airliner
Cub	ASCC code for An-12 medium transport airplane
Clank	ASCC code for An-30 aerial cartography, reconnaissance and transport airplane
ECM	Electronic countermeasures
ELINT	Electronic intelligence
FS	Fighter Squadron
FCF	Functional Check Flight
FMC	Fully Mission Capable (Abbreviation in western logistical system)
Fencer	ASCC code for Su-24 jet fighter-bomber
Fishbed	ASCC code for MiG-21 supersonic and frontline interceptor fighter jet
Flagon	ASCC code for Su-15 twinjet supersonic interceptor fighter jet

Flanker	ASCC code for Su-27 twin-engine air superiority heavy fighter jet
Flogger	ASCC code for MiG-23/27 variable-geometry wing multirole fighter jet
Foxbat	ASCC code for MiG-25 supersonic interceptor and reconnaissance aircraft
Fulcrum	ASCC code for MiG-29 supersonic and frontline interceptor fighter jet
Gen	General (military commissioned officer rank)
GLIC	State Flight Test Center
GLITS	State Flight Test Center
GvBAP	Guards Bomber Aviation Regiment
GvIAD	Guards Fighter Aviation Division
GvIAP	Guards Fighter Aviation Regiment
GvMRAP	Guards Maritime Missile Aviation Regiment
GvSIAP	Guards Mixed Test Aviation Regiment
GvTBAD	Guards Heavy Bomber Aviation Division
GvTBAP	Guards Heavy Bomber Aviation Regiment
GvVTAD	Guards Military Transport Aviation Division
GvVTAP	Guards Military Transport Aviation Regiment
HQ	Headquarters
Hip	ASCC code for Mi-8/17 medium utility helicopter
IAD	Fighter Aviation Division
IAP	Fighter Aviation Regiment
IAI	Israeli Aircraft Industries
ITAP	Transport Test Aviation Regiment
IBAD	Instructor Bomber Aviation Division
IBAP	Instructor Bomber Aviation Regiment
IIBAP	Research Instructor Bomber Aviation Regiment
IIKAP	Instructor-Research Shipborne Aviation Regiment
IISAP	Research Instructor Composite Aviation Regiment
IRIAF	Islamic Republic of Iran Air Force
IIAPIB	Research-Instructor Fighter-Bomber Aviation Regiment
IIMRAP	Instructor-Research Maritime Missile Aviation Regiment
ISTA	Independent Tactical Aviation Squadron (English abbreviation)
Km	Kilometre
KIAP	Shipborne Fighter Aviation Regiment
KnAAPO	Komsomolsk-on-Amur Aircraft Plant
LDARZ	Lviv State Aviation Maintenance Plant
LGB	Laser-Guided Bomb
Lt	Lieutenant (military commissioned officer rank)
Lt Col	Lieutenant-Colonel (military commissioned officer rank)
Maestro	ASCC code for Yak-28U combat training jet airplane
Maj	Major (military commissioned officer rank)
Maj Gen	Major-General (military commissioned officer rank)
MANPAD	Man-Portable Air Defence (light surface-to-air missiles that can be carried and deployed in combat by a single soldier)
MiG	Mikoyan i Gurevich (the design bureau led by Artyom Ivanovich Mikoyan and Mikhail Iosifovich Gurevich, also known as OKB-155 or MMZ' "Zenit")
Midas	ASCC code for Il-78 tanker airplane
MRAP	Maritime Missile Aviation Regiment
MTBO	Meantime Between Overhaul
NARP	Nikolayev Aircraft Repair Plant
NORM	Not Operational Ready for Maintenance (Abbreviation in western logistical system)
NORS	Not Operational Ready for Supply (Abbreviation in western logistical system)
oaeTA	Independent Tactical Aviation Squadron (Ukrainian abbreviation)
OKB	Experimental Design Bureau
OARZ	Odessa Aircraft Repair Plant
OAPVO	Independent Air Defence Army
OSAP	Independent Mixed Aviation Regiment (also sometimes translated as Composite Aviation Regiment)

OAO REB	Aviation Department for the Radio Electronic Combat
OAP REB	Independent Aviation Regiment for Electronic Warfare
ODRAE	Independent Long-range Reconnaissance Aviation Squadron
ODRAP	Independent Long-range Reconnaissance Aviation Regiment
OG(v)DRAP	Independent Guards Long-range Reconnaissance Aviation Regiment
OGSAP	Independent Mixed Aviation Regiment
OG(v)VP	Independent Guards Helicopter Regiment
OG(v)SAP	Independent Guards Mixed Aviation Regiment
OShAP	Mixed Assault Aviation Regiment
OKShAP	Independent Maritime Assault Aviation Regiment
OMShAP	Independent Mixed Assault Aviation Regiment
ORAE	Indpendent Reconnaissance Aviation Regiment
ORAP	Indpendent Reconnaissance Aviation Regiment
OG(v)RAP	Indpendent Guards Reconnaissance Aviation Regiment
OSAE	Independent Composite Aviation Squadron
OSAP	Independent Composite Aviation Regiment
OTAE	Independent Transport Aviation Squadron
OTAP	Independent Transport Aviation Regiment
OVP	Independent Helicopter Regiment
ove REB	Independent Helicopter Squadron for Electronic Warfare
PMC	Partially Mission Capable (Abbreviation in western logistical system)
PVO	Russian term for the Air Defence Force
QRA	Quick Reaction Alert
RAP	Reconnaissance Aviation Regiment
s/n	Serial number
SAD	Composite Aviation Division
SAM	Surface-to-Air Missile
SAR	Search and Rescue
SIGINT	Signals Intelligence
TBAD	Heavy Bomber Aviation Division
TBAP	Heavy Bomber Aviation Regiment
TrAB	Training or Transport Aviation Brigade
TSOU	Ukrainian Association for the Support of the Defence
TsBPKA	Training Centre for Combat Employment Shipborne Aviation
UATsBPLS	Training Aviation Centre for retraining personnel
UAP	Training Aviation Regiment
UAH	Ukrainian Hyrivna
UVP	Training Helicopter Regiment
USD	US Dollar
USSR	Union of Soviet Socialist Republics
USSR	Union of Soviet Socialist Republics
VA	Air Army
VIP	Very Important Person
VMF	literally 'Military Navy Aviation,' the Russian term for the Navy Aviation
VVS	literally 'Military Air Forces,' the Russian term for the Air Force
VTAD	Military Transport Aviation Division
VTAP	Military Transport Aviation Regiment
w/o	Written off
Wfu	Withdrawn from use
ZARZ	Zaporozhye Aircraft Repair

Introduction

When the Soviet Union collapsed in 1991, it was almost unimaginable that Russia and Ukraine would go to war 23 years later. Not only were, and are, their nations historically and closely related but also their armed forces, including their air forces. The Crimea territorial dispute and subsequently the war in Donbass put these former brothers at the edge of full-scale war against each other and resulted in loss and destruction in the east of Ukraine.

The author started writing about the Ukrainian Air Force and its units based in Crimea in December 2013. Since then, he spent an enormous amount of time gathering information about the history of not only Ukrainian but also the Russian Air Force units stationed in Ukraine, Crimea and around. As a result of almost six years research and studies, finally this book was completed in 2019 with the hope that it would be a reference for researchers and analysts who want to know the history of the Ukrainian Air Force and its major role in the war against Pro-Russian separatists in Donbass in 2014.

Ukraine inherited a large portion of the former Soviet Air Force's equipment and infrastructure after its independence: 944 military aircraft, including 137 heavy strategic bombers, were quickly inducted into service with the air force on 17 March 1992, when it was officially established. As the largest inheritor of ex-Soviet air Force aircraft, soon the UkrAF turned into the second most powerful air force in Europe. In 1992, it consisted of four air armies, ten aviation divisions, 49 air regiments, 11 independent squadrons, and training and research centres, totalling 600 military units, 2,800 aircraft in various types and 120,000 personnel.

The financial problems and new defensive doctrine of the country were two principal factors for the decline in combat strength and the expenditure on Ukraine's air force during the past 23 years. According to the official statistics of the Ukrainian Ministry of Defence, in total 137 heavy bombers including 41 nuclear and strategic Tu-95MSs and Tu-160Ss once existed in Ukraine. They soon became the first victims of the broken economy and later became an area of major concern for the US government, who forced the Ukraine to dispose of them in order to prevent the transfer of their technology to China.

With almost 610 fighter jets and 90 ground attack/tactical bombers, Ukraine soon became one of the largest sellers of second-hand fighter jets in the world, disposing of a large number to African countries. Others were scrapped after retirement, resulting in a significant decrease in the number of combat aircraft in the air force. However, the downsized and weakened service wasn't just a shadow of former Soviet airpower as since the mid-2000s the country's aircraft repair plants have inaugurated numerous upgrade projects for the enhancement of the combat readiness of its aircraft and helicopters.

In 2014, when the territorial disputes on the Crimea peninsula started before morphing into to a full-scale war with pro-Russian separatists, the Ukrainian Air Force had a fleet of 66 operational fighter aircraft in service across six Tactical Aviation Brigades, with which a series of interdiction and close air support missions were conducted. However, during the war approximately 14 fighters and bombers of the air force were lost, although its outbreak provided the motivation for its commanders to start rebuilding its combat strength.

As a result of the war and the existing threat of Russian invasion, the Ukrainian government funded the overhaul, restoration and modernisation of all types of aircraft in service with the air force, but mostly fighter jets, resulting in a significant increase in the number of airworthy and operational fighter jets to 155 in 2019 when this book was completed. These consisted of 60 MiG-29s, 28 Su-24(M/MR)s, 32 Su-25s and 35 Su-27s in service with seven Tactical Aviation Brigades at Starokostyantyniv, Vasilkov, Ivano-Frankovsk, Kulbakino, Mirgorod and Ozernoye Air Bases.

This book provides a detailed look at the organisation and combat strength of the air force, and its aircraft and helicopters. Drawing on a wide range of previously unseen photographs and supplemented by specially commissioned colour artwork, *Guardians of Ukraine* covers all types of combat, transport and training aircraft, as well as helicopters previously or currently operated by the Ukrainian Air Force, many of which are supported by captions detailing individual aircraft histories.

About the author

Starting his career in 2005 by anonymously writing articles about the history of the Iranian Air Force for Iranian websites, Babak Taghvaee soon became an aviation journalist, book author, historian and photojournalist by publishing his articles in English and German aviation magazines such as *Air Forces Monthly* and *Combat Aircraft* in 2008 and 2009 respectively. He then co-authored his first book about the Iranian Air Force in 2010. In 2011, he became one of two supervisors of the Iranian Air Force's historical research project 'Historical Identity of IRIAF' to document the history of the force and to write books about the subject. In the same year, he was invited by one of the Iranian defence companies to work as a civilian innovator and advisor to the Iranian Air Force's aircraft upgrade projects while he was a student at two Iranian universities (as well as a journalist for several Iranian aviation magazines).

In September 2012, he was arrested by the Ministry of Information (Intelligence) of Iran's Islamic Regime. After spending four and half months in detention in the notorious Evin prison, he was released in February 2013. He left Iran in August 2013 and just a few months after his exit, was sentenced to 10 years in prison by the Islamic Revolution Court on a false accusation of cooperation with hostile nations by means of writing articles and books in English about the the history of the Iranian Air Force during the Pahlavi-era.

Since 2013, he has written almost 300 articles, news reports and three books about the military aviation industry, counter-terrorism, the war in Donbass, and also the Russian and Ukrainian Air Forces. He has reported on the air war and air operations of the Coalition Forces against ISIL in leading British, French, Greek and Russian military aviation magazines and also for the BBC's Persian service, and the Independent Persian and Globe Post while he was living in exile.

1 Eyes and Ears

An-30s Fleet (1992–Today): The Aerial Surveyors

The Ukrainian Air Force operates the An-30, a special derivation of the An-24 transport aircraft, which is nicknamed 'Clank' by NATO. With a raised cockpit and an extensively glazed nose for the Navigator and his NAVAIDS, and equipped with a maximum of five cameras, the An-30 is dedicated to aerial surveying or photo-mapping operations and has already played a key role in Open Skies Treaty Surveillance Flights and also in the war in Donbass in 2014. The history of the An-30 in Ukraine goes back to the 1970s and 1980s, and after almost 40 years, the aircraft is now the only photo-surveying equipment in the air force used for aerial cartography.

Background

In the early 1960s, the Soviet Air Force was studying the design and manufacture of a special aerial survey aircraft, which finally resulted in the selection of the An-24 as the base aircraft for development of the type in 1965.

Responsibility for the design work was granted to the Beriev Aircraft Company, or No. 49 OKB at Taganrog, which had a long history and experience in design and manufacture of flying boats and amphibian aircraft for the Soviet Navy.

After a year of design work, an An-24B with the c/n 57302003 was chosen for conversion to the prototype at Taganrog. It took almost a year before the work was completed and the prototype, designated An-24FK, performed its first flight piloted by test pilot I. E. Davydovka on 21 August 1967. The aircraft later received the c/n 0101 after the name 'An-30' had been assigned to it.

A new forward fuselage was installed after frame 11 that had a large cabin under the raised flightdeck floor for the navigator and more precise and complex NAVAIDS than those installed on the An-24 to provide a precision flight path during photography. The DISS-013-24FK Doppler navigator system to show the aircraft's true air speed relative to the ground was one of the systems installed.

In the aft fuselage, the An-24FK was equipped with a photo laboratory section with five cameras consisting of one APA-42/100, three AFA-54/50s and a single telescopic A-72, each with its specific camera window at the bottom of the fuselage, which were covered or protected with rolling panels or doors during take-off and landing, storage lockers for film cassettes, the operating panels and seats for the operators, worktables and a toilet, all beside a power supply system for providing electricity for the equipment.

The initial stage of the prototype test flights was completed in Taganrog in July 1968, and then the second stage was carried out by the Soviet Air Force's Flight Research Institute up to June 1970. The aircraft then entered Soviet Air Force service as the An-30, and a year later, in 1971, serial production started at the Kiev Aircraft Manufacturing Plant.

In 1973 eight An-30s were manufactured and in 1974 15 more. The production line remained open until 1979, when the last An-30s manufactured (five aircraft) were delivered to the Chinese Air Force.

On 6 June 2014, this An-30B with 80 Yellow was shot down by pro-Russian separatists, resulting in the death of six of its eight crewmembers. Here it is departing Boryspil airport on 24 August 1995. *Sergey Popsuyevich*

86 Blue had been grounded for years when it was selected for restoration and overhaul in order to be a replacement for the lost 80 Yellow in 2014. Here it is stored at Boryspil on 23 March 2005. *Sergey Popsuyevich*

From the total of 125 An-30s manufactured, 33 were delivered to the Soviet Air Force and these entered service with the 151st ODRAE at Krasnoyarsk (nine aircraft), 86th ODRAE at Chernivtsi (eleven aircraft), 3rd ODRAE at Tiraspol, 5th ODRAE at Bratsk, and 181st OSAE at Irkutsk-1 (ten aircraft), 2nd OTAE Gnip at Semipalatinsk-21 (three aircraft). Later, three more An-30s that belonged to Aeroflot were transferred to the air force as attrition replacement for three and these lost in accidents at Semipatatinsk-21, Etorofu, and Irkutsk on 5 January 1978, 19 October 1979 and 25 January 1980 respectively.

Among the total delivered, 26 were the version B equipped with different IFF, radio altimeters, communication radios and other NAVAIDs to the basic An-30 version, with a weather radar inside a fairing under the Navigator's cabin. They were also modified and wired to carry two Veyer (Fan) chaff/flare dispensers each with 192 26mm PPI-26 magnesium flares via installation under two BDZ-34 pylons, or later in the conformal side ASO-2B dispensers filled with 384 flare cartridges in order to reduce the drag and increase the performance after an upgrade by the Soviet Air Force No. 308 Aircraft Repair Plant at Ivanovo-Severney.

Three An-30Bs of the Soviet Air Force, with 04 Red, 16 Red and 17 Red were used to form the 50th OSAP at Chirchik AB on 12 January 1980, and were forward deployed to Afghanistan in March of that year to be used in the war. They were later replaced by other An-30s including 05 Red which was shot down by a Mujahedin Stinger MANPAD on 11 March 1985. Its pilot, Capt. A. Gorbachev, and co-pilot 1st Lt. V. A. Ivanov, were killed while attempting to make an emergency landing in Kabul when their aircraft stalled and crashed into the Panjshir valley; before that the pilot had ordered four other crewmembers to egress via parachute, and they survived.

With the ability to take pictures in a scale range from 1:3,000 to 1:200, 000 using the different focal lengths of its cameras, the main roles of the An-30 and An-30Bs were visual observation, airborne forward air control, crash site finder (discovering crashed friendly or enemy aircraft wreckages on SAR missions), aerial cartography, and photography for locating the appropriate area for the landing of friendly airborne troops. They were also used for tactical reconnaissance for locating enemy positions and strongholds before and after rocket, artillery and ballistic attacks, and air force fighter air raids.

Not only involved in the war in Afghanistan, the Soviet Air Force's An-30s were used in emergency missions over Chernobyl after the explosion of the No. 4 reactor at the nuclear facility on 26 April 1986. Two An-30Bs of the 86th ODRAE were among 21 aircraft that were used in radioactive survey missions and logged total 92 flying hours between 22 May and 1 June 1986. Both aircraft had been forward deployed to Zhuliany to be operated from there.

In service with the Ukrainian Air Force

After the break-up of the Soviet Union, the 86th ODRAE (the 86th Independent Long-Range Aviation Squadron) was inherited by the newly born UkrAF. The unit, based at Chernivtsi AB, had a total of six An-30s, which were 01 Blue, 02 Blue, 03 Blue, 05 Blue, 06 Blue, and 10 Blue together with a pair of

81 Yellow taxiing at Boryspil airport in the mid-1990s. *Sergey Popsuyevich*

For years, the 15th TrAB kept only two An-30Bs operational, 80 and 81 Yellow. Here, 81 Yellow is at Boryspil in April 2015. *Alexander Golz*

An-30Bs, 80 Yellow and 81 Yellow. Participation of these aircraft in the Afghanistan war is not clear, but at least three sets of An-30 flight crews flew on the 50th OSAP's An-30s in the war between April and June 1982.

All the aircraft were operational in 1992 but gradually their overhaul times arrived and some were worked on at 410th ARP, starting with 01 Blue (c/n 0101), which was the first An-30 (former An-24FK prototype), in 1993. Some examples had been put in storage by the mid-1990s due to the lack of funds for their overhaul; among them two were put up for sale in 2006.

Open Skies

On 24 March 1992, upon the break-up of the Soviet Union, 34 countries signed an Open Skies Treaty in Helsinki, Finland, to establish a programme for performing unarmed aerial surveillance flights over the entire territory of the participants. The concept of the treaty was initially proposed to Soviet Premier Nikolai Bulganin at the Geneva Conference of 1955 by President Dwight D. Eisenhower, but was never accepted by Soviets until 1989, when the initiative was signed by the US President George H. W. Bush.

Within the framework of the initial or first stage of the Treaty, the members allocated special surveillance aircraft from their inventories. Among them, Russia and Ukraine both chose the An-30B. In Ukraine it took several months until a special unit to operate the An-30Bs under the Treaty framework was planned to be established at Boryspil. The 10th Independent Aviation Squadron became operational on 1 September 1992 following the order of the Ukrainian Minister of Defence Gen. K. Morozova.

For several reasons, formation of the 10th OAE, which was later officially named 'Blue Watches', was

An-30B 87 Blue was restored and overhauled by the 410th aircraft repair plant following a 14 million UAH contract and here it is fully operational at Boryspil airport on 3 November 2015. *Alexander Golz*

delayed until 26 October 1992. Two An-30Bs, 80 Yellow and 81 Yellow, together with 10-12 aircrew entered service with the squadron. The start of the squadron's surveillance flights was planned for 14 January 1993. Later, the total staff of the squadron reached 305, including 130 officers, 75 warrant officers, 40 regular soldiers, and 25 female staff and communication officers who were from the 255th OSAE, 86th ODRAE, and the disbanded 228th ove REB (228th independent Helicopter Squadron for Electronic Warfare), all under command of the first commander of the unit, S. Krolenko. As well as the two An-30Bs, the unit received three An-26s from the 46the UAP in Luhansk for use in training and transport duties. They were 82 Yellow, 83 Yellow and 84 Yellow.

In 1996, the 86th ODRAE was disbanded and its remaining six An-30s were relocated to Nezhin. Nezhin was the home base of the 199th OGDRAP (199th Independent Long-Range Reconnaissance Aviation Regiment), which was disbanded in same year. The unit had in total 21 Tu-22PD/K/KD/KPD/RD/RDM/RDK/UDs but four of them (three Tu-22RDs and one Tu-22UD) together with the six ex-86th ODRAE An-30s, were used to form the 18th ODRAE there. In the Soviet era, it had been the plan to form the 18th ODRAE with a surveillance variant of the An-72, the An-71, and the Il-38.

In 1997, four An-30s of the 18th ODRAE, 01 Blue, 03 Blue, 06 Blue, and 05 Blue, were added to the inventory of the 10th OSAE, but before that their bort numbers were changed to 85 Blue, 88 Blue, 86 Blue and 87 Blue respectively. Just two An-30s remained in 18 ODRAE service, 02 Blue and 10 Blue.

For the surveillance missions of the Open Skies treaty, the An-30Bs were modified by Antonov. First of the two was 81 Yellow which was certified for Open Skies treaty flights and for operations until 22 September 1995 by inspectors of the Kirov Test Centre on 14 September 1993. Bort number 81 Yellow was fitted with an A-723 LORAN, an RSBN-2S Svod SHORAN system, a TNL-100 GPS satellite navigation receiver (installed in second half of the 1990s), an RV-18Zh high-range radio altimeter, an RV-UM low-range radio altimeter, a VMF-50 altimeter calibrated in feet, an ARK-11 ADF, a DISS-013-24FK Doppler speed/drift meter, a Grooza-M30 weather radar, an SD-75 DME, a Koors-MP-70 automatic approach/landing system working with VOR/ILS radio beacons, and an SO-72M international ATC/SIF transponder.

It was planned to use only one of the aircraft cameras (usually one AFA-41/10 or AFA-41/20) during surveillance missions of the Open Skies Treaty. Unlike the other An-30s that were mostly overall grey, 80 Yellow and 81 Yellow had been painted in civilian colours and received the special badge of the unit designed by P. Dikim, which consisted of an eagle and a camera.

Between 25 and 29 April 1994, the first Open Skies Treaty surveillance mission of the 10th OAE was performed by 81 Yellow which visited the UK. The aircraft landed at RAF Brize Norton after its aircrew had difficulty finding the airport because it was not familiar with the area and also because it was using 1947 flight charts without GPS. The airfield VOR beacons had been turned-off as well!

In November 1994, the joint surveillance flights were continued, this time over Slovakia, and between March and May 1995, they were carried out over Germany. Between 11 and 16 September 1995, the aircraft was evaluated again by experts, and certified for the second stage of the surveillance flights until April 1997. Then the aircraft performed a long surveillance mission to the USA, landing in Washington D.C. and flying over 13 US states. Before reaching Washington DC, 81 Yellow flew 5,539km and identified 120 strategic military facilities and 220 additional smaller military bases in a 17-hour flight with refuelling stops at Lviv in Ukraine, RAF Mildenhall and RAF Lossiemouth in the UK, Keflavik AB in Iceland, Sanderstorm in Greenland and Goose Bay in Canada.

On 15 August 2015, Ukrainian President Poroshenko officially named An-30B 87 Blue after the hero of Ukraine, Konstantin Mogilko, who lost his life after 80 Yellow was shot-down during the war. During the ceremony the pliot's wife and children were present at the 410th ARZ in Kiev. *the Ukrainian Air Force*

Open Skies flights on behalf of Denmark

No. 15 TrAB's An-30s were not only being used in Open Skies Treaty missions but they were also available for lease to other members of the Treaty.

Between 1994 and mid-October 2012, the 'Blue Watches' carried out 116 surveillance missions (some of them consisted of two or more surveillance sorties) over the territories of 23 European countries as well as the US. These were not only for Ukraine: in several cases Poland and Denmark leased 80 and 81 Yellow for their surveillance sorties over Russia.

On 6 August 2012, an An-30B flew from Boryspil to Aalborg AB in Denmark while carrying representatives of the Office of General Staff Verification of Ukraine headed by the implementation Chief of the 'Open Skies' Treaty, Colonel Yury Andrienko, who met their Danish counterparts to negotiate a leasing agreement.

The Ukrainian Delegation stayed in Denmark for four days and on the second day of their visit their An-30B was used in a demonstration/surveillance

88 Blue is one of two An-30s of UkrAF which are stored at Boryspil. 88 Blue was put up for sale by SkyBirdHeli on 27 May 2006 while it had 4,341 hours and 4,155 cycles left on its airframe. *Alexander Golz*

flight over Denmark for four hours while Royal Danish Air Force personnel were on-board. The aircaft was given an honorary escort by a pair of RDAF's F-16s.

On the fourth day, both sides reached an agreement and the An-30 and the Ukrainian delegation left Denmark on 10 August. Three days later, on 13 August, the surveillance flights began over Russia using one of the An-30Bs equipped with AFA-41/7.5 and AFA-41/10 cameras and these continued until 17 August.

Reorganisation of the An-30 unit

On 22 February 1999, following the Decree No. 242 of Verkhovna Rada of the Ukraine (Supreme Council of Ukraine), the 18th ODRAE was transferred to the Ministry of Emergency Situations and was redesignated as the 300th Special Aviation Squadron MOE. Subsequently, the remaining Tu-22s were retired and the ownership of the remaining two An-30s there, 02 Blue (c/n 0302) and 10 Blue (c/n 1310) was handed over to the Ministry of Emergency Situations. They subsequently received the new bort numbers 12 Blue and 11 Blue respectively. Later, in January 2004, the 10th OAE was disbanded and its six An-30s and three An-26s were absorbed by the 15th TrAB at Boryspil.

In 2003, before the disbandment of the 10th OAE, one of the An-30s was used to fly toward Tuzla to take pictures of where the Russians had illegally started to construct a dam when the island had become the subject of territorial dispute between Ukraine and Russia in October that year. Subsequently the An-30 detected a Russian tugboat *Truzhenik,* which crossed the state border of Ukraine and conducted photo and video surveillance from the island on 21 October; the boat was later captured by the Ukrainian Border Service.

Also, in several cases they were used in disaster relief inside and outside the country. For example, one of 15 TrAB's An-30s was used to take pictures of an area that had been destroyed as a result of a fire and the explosion of 15 tons of expired ammunition in Novobohdanivka ammunition depot. This wounded four Ukrainian soldiers and killed two others, while massively disrupting railways and highways nearby.

On 11 November 2007, while a Russian tanker named *Volgoneft-139* was passing through Kerch strait it entered a storm and as a result 1,300 tons of its total of 4,000 tons of black oil was spilled into the strait, causing an environmental disaster. The 15th TrAB quickly dispatched one of its An-30Bs on a surveillance mission over the strait to measure the extent of the disaster. Subsequently it was reported the oil had covered an area that stretched for 12km (7.46 miles) over the strait, killing 30,000 sea birds and thousands of marine animals. Not only the tanker but five other vessels were damaged or sunk, including a freighter that spilled 6,800 tons of sulphur into the strait.

For the first time, in 2010, the 15th TrAB used one of its An-30s for weather control to ensure a cloudless sky over Kiev during major public holidays including the Victory Day and Independence Day parades. As an example of such missions, in the early morning of 9 May 2012, 80 Yellow was used to prevent rain over

This artwork shows how An-30B 80 Yellow looked in 2014. *Luca G. Canossa*

Kiev during the 67th Anniversary of Great Victory Day parade, following the order of Ukrainian MOD Dmytro Slamatin after the weather forecast from the Ukrainian Hydrometeorological Centre showed a possibility of bad weather.

Blue Watches at war

As a result of the political instability in Ukraine following the aftermath of the 2014 revolution, the Crimea was occupied and then annexed to the Russian mainland via a referendum that encouraged separatists in the east of Ukraine, especially Kramatorsk and Luhansk, to demand the same referendums for independence for the states of the country. Subsequently backed by Russia together with the Russian Army, the separatists began a war with the central government and Ukrainian security forces.

When the war started, the 15th TrAB had just two operational An-30s, 'B' variants 80 Yellow and 81 Yellow, while the other four An-30s were in storage. Two of these, 87 Blue and 88 Blue, had been put up for sale by SkyBirdHeli, an Ukrainian aircraft leasing company, even though both the aircraft still had two years of their calendar life left after their overhauls on 27 May 2006.

On 7 April 2014, separatists stormed SBU offices in Donetsk and Luhansk to seize their weapons and armoury. The next day the separatists declared themselves the People's Republic of Donetsk and Lugansk Parliamentary Republic respectively as a part of Russia's strategic plan for diverting European countries and the US from the consequences of the annexation of Crimea to Russia's territory.

On 8 April, the Ukrainian Armed Forces started mobilizing their troops to the areas that were being claimed as territory under control of the separatists. Hundreds of Special Forces and Airmobile Troops were deployed to the regions to take back the occupied areas. Similar to other units of the Ukrainian Air Force, the 'Blue Watches' squadron of the 15th TrAB was asked to perform dozens of surveillance sorties over the warzone to locate and detect Russian-backed terrorist or separatist strongholds, hideouts and their Russian Army collaborators.

Catastrophe over Sloviansk

On 12 April, separatists stormed SBU and police department offices in Sloviansk, seizing 100 automatic rifles and 100-150 pistols to arm their 150-200 local forces. The next day, the Ukrainian Security Forces arrived in the region and confronted the separatists, and two days later, on 15 April, an Ukrainian Army armoured column established a checkpoint 40km from Sloviansk.

On Sunday, 20 April, separatists raided Bylbasivka checkpoint in the west of Sloviansk and killed three civilians guarding it while losing three of their troops in response. Subsequently, two days later, on 22 April, one of the 'Blue Watches' Squadron An-30Bs was sent on a mission over Sloviansk. It was 80 Yellow, which was damaged by small-arms fire while flying over the rebel-controlled territories of the city, although the crew managed to land the aircraft safely at Boryspil. While 81 Yellow was mostly assigned to the Open Skies treaty surveillance flights, 80 Yellow was being used in most of the surveillance sorties.

When 80 Yellow was grounded for a while after the slight damage, 81 Yellow was used in some of the surveillance flights over Donbass. No. 80 Yellow was returned to the 15th TrAB's flightline after a small repair. Following the lessons learned from the loss of several other aircraft due to small- and large-calibre gun fire, the surveillance sorties were being conducted at higher elevations than before.

While Sloviansk was still in hands of the pro-Russian separatists, the Ukrainian Security Forces were attempting to retake the city and this was only achieved by deployment of more troops and reinforcement of the Ukrainian Army and Airborne Forces around the city. Later, on 3 June, a Ukrainian convoy was attacked en route from Izyum to Sloviansk, which resulted in the death of one soldier while thirteen more troops were wounded. Two days later, on 5 June, the Ukrainian Army deployed several T-64 tanks to protect its checkpoint and troops in the west of Sloviansk as a precaution after the ambush on 3 June.

On 6 June 2014, the 'Blue Watches' squadron was tasked with performing a photography mission from Sloviansk, during which An-30B 80 Yellow, piloted by Lt Col Konstantin Victorvych Mohylko, the squadron commander, and six more aircrew on board was used. But while the aircraft was flying at elevation of 4,050m it was hit in the right engine by an SA-14 MANPADS fired by the separatists over Nikolaevka village. The engine was damaged, and the aircraft commander ordered the other crewmembers to leave the burning An-30.

Although the fire had spread over the right wing, the pilot and co-pilot attempted to perform an emergency landing, but their aircraft stalled and crashed at an 80-degree angle south of the Sloviansk residential area at 5:04pm local time. Just two crewmembers had a chance to jump out while the others were trapped inside after the aircraft entered a spin. On 20 June 2014, President Petro Poroshenko awarded the title of Hero of Ukraine to Lt Col K. V. Mohylko.

After this catastrophe, the UkrAF stopped using the An-30s on surveillance missions over the warzone, and instead used Su-24MRs of the 7th BrTA in July and Tu-143 reconnaissance UAVs in August 2014 for tactical reconnaissance missions.

Attrition replacements

After loss of 80 Yellow, the 'Blue Watches' squadron had only one An-30B operational, 81 Yellow, which was in use in Open Skies treaty flights to Russia until the end of the 2014. Quickly it was planned to restore one of the stored An-30s in Boryspil. The 87 Blue (c/n 1309) was chosen for this programme and soon was transferred from Boryspil to Zhuliany to be restored and overhauled by the 410th ARP. No. 87 Blue had logged its last flight in 2003 and then was placed in storage.

It was almost five months until the aircraft returned to flying condition. Painted in an overall olive drab colour scheme, it performed its first post-overhaul functional check flight on 22 November 2014, but soon returned to the maintenance hangar to be retrofitted with the Open Skies Treaty mission equipment. No. 87 Blue equipped with Groza-M30 radar housed in a fairing under its nose was mistakenly named an An-30B by the media while it was actually an An-30. It was finally redelivered to the 'Blue Watches' squadron during a ceremony in January 2015.

Because of the end of 81 Yellow's MTBO, it was necessary to restore another An-30 and modernise it with Open Skies Treaty mission equipment. No. 86 Blue (c/n 0602) was the second aircraft quickly selected for restoration just five days after 87 Blue made its first flight after overhaul.

The aircraft's wings were dismantled to be towed on the highway from Boryspil to Zhuliany on the night of 27 November. Finally, the aircraft reached its destination, the 410th ARP, in the early morning of 28 November 2014. Its restoration and overhaul lasted seven months, and 86 Blue made its first post-overhaul FCF on 30 June 2015. It then returned to the overhaul facility, this time to be retrofitted with all NAVAIDs and Avionic systems necessary for the surveillance flights of the Open Skies treaty. After modernisation, the aircraft was officially redelivered to the air force and named 'Hero of Ukraine Kostyantyn Mohylko' after the pilot of 80 Yellow, by the President of Ukraine during an official ceremony on 25 August 2015.

In 2015, the Ukrainian Air Force had three An-30s simultaneously operational for not only Open Skies missions but also for photography inside the Ukraine. Earlier, in late 2014, the Ukraine was stopped from performing Open Skies flights over Russia, this ban continuing in 2015 and 2016, and subsequently Russia stopped its surveillance flights over Ukraine.

At the time of writing, UkrAF has three An-30s in service, which will be airworthy for aerial survey operations until 2025–2026. The plan for the sale of two more An-30s in storage, 85 Blue and 88 Blue was cancelled at the start of the war with the separatists and Russia in 2014, and in the case of emergency or loss of any of the current active An-30s, they will be restored and modernised.

Ukrainian Air Force and Air Defence Force An-30s

Version	Previous Bort Number	Current Bort Number	Construction Number	Unit in 1992	Current unit	Year of manufacture	Status in 1992	Current status
An-30	01 Blue	85 Blue	0101	86th ODRAE	15th TrAB	1973	Active	Stored
An-30	02 Blue	12 Blue	0302	86th ODRAE	Ukraine MES	1973	Active	Not in service
An-30	03 Blue	88 Blue	0303	86th ODRAE	15th TrAB	1973	Active	Stored
An-30	06 Blue	86 Blue	0602	86th ODRAE	15th TrAB	1974	Active	Active
An-30B	80 Yellow	80 Yellow	0608	86th ODRAE	-	1975	Active	Wfu/Lost
An-30B	81 Yellow	81 Yellow	0609	86th ODRAE	15th TrAB	1975	Active	Active
An-30	05 Blue	87 Blue	1309	86th ODRAE	15th TrAB	1977	Active	Active
An-30	10 Blue	11 Blue	1310	86th ODRAE	Ukraine MES	1977	Active	Not in service

Abbreviations
ODRAE = Independent Long-Range Reconnaissance Aviation Squadron
TrAB = Training or Transport Aviation Brigade

Il-22M-11 Fleet (1993–1998): The Airborne Command Posts

The Ukrainian Air Force inherited two of the 35 Il-22s of the Soviet Air Force that were in service with the 243rd Independent Mixed Aviation Regiment (243rd OSAP), and 456th Independent Guards Stalingradskiy Red Banner Mixed Aviation Regiment (456th OGSAP) under the organisation of 14th and 24th Air Armies respectively.

The design and development of the new airborne command post aircraft based on the Il-18 started following directive No. 603-215 of the Communist Party Central Committee/Council issued on 7 August 1968. Its high flight endurance, long range (4,000-5,000km) and good operating reliability, especially from short runways in comparison with other platforms such as the Il-62, led to the Il-18D platform being chosen as the basis of the Il-22. Developed by Myasishchev Experimental Machinery Plant (EMZ), the Il-22 (Il-18D-36) became the first aircraft designed as an airborne command post.

The Il-22 was equipped with the new TA-6 APU instead of the older TG-16M APU of the Il-18, which provided more power output for the radio communication and relay systems on-board. The first two prototypes were completed in 1971. After completing their test flights, the aircraft mission equipment including radio relay systems passed state complex tests between 1972 and 1974. The aircraft soon was put into mass production at Moscow Machine-Building (MMZ) Plant. The first mass-produced aircraft, CCCP-75895 (c/n 0393607050), made its first flight on 27 December 1976 and was delivered to 535 OSAP at Rostov-na-Donu Tsentralny to be used by the commander of the North Caucasian Military District.

Thirteen more Il-22s were manufactured up to 1979, and production was continued when the Il-22M-11 was developed. Development of the new Il-22 variant had begun in 1977 under project 11-U to equip the Il-22 with new mission equipment. In 1983, the Il-18 production line at MMZ No. 30 was closed and the jigs and fixtures were removed from the factory to provide space for manufacturing MiG-23s. As a solution, at least six Il-18Ds were used for conversion into the Il-22M-11. Later, one of the 21 Il-22M-11s was upgraded into an Il-22M-15, which entered service with 457 OSAP at Almaty.

Before the USSR collapsed, the 35 manufactured Il-22s served in 30 units of the Soviet Air Force: 17 OSAP, with two examples at Plesetsk; 36th OSAP, with two based at Chita; 50 OSAP, with one based at Minsk-Lipki; 103rd GvVTAP with one at Smolensk; 138th OSAP, with one based at Levashovo; 150th OSAP, with one based at Ulan-Ude; 243rd OSAP, with one based at Lviv; 257th OSAP, with one based at Khabarovsk-Bolshoy; 327th OTAP, with one based at Ostafyevo; 354th APON at Moscow-Chkalovsky, with five Il-22s including two Il-22M-11s in service; 457th OSAP at Almaty, with one Il-22M-15 in service; 535th OSAP at Rostov-on-Don, with one; 15th OSAE at Kalinovka, with one; 245th OSAE, with one at Legnica; 44osae, with one at Smolensk; one in service with 98th OSAE at Vladimir; 102nd OSAE at Orenburg-2, with one; 105th OSAE at Omsk, with one; 137th OSAE at Novosibirsk, with

UR-75918, the sole Il-22M-11 of the Ukrainian Air Force, at Saki in June 1998. *Nikolayev Aircraft Repair Plant archive via airforce.ru*

Ukrainian Air Force Il-20/22s

Type	Bort/Serial Number	Construction Number	Current registration/ serial number	Year of manufacture	Status in 1992	Current Status	Last flight in UkrAF
Il-20 (Il-18D)	07 Red	172011401	TT-WAK	1974	Stored	Sold	1998
Il-22	75896	0393607150	D2-FFR	1977	Airworthy	Sold	1998
Il-22M-11	75918	2964017104	-	1983	Airworthy	Scrapped	1994

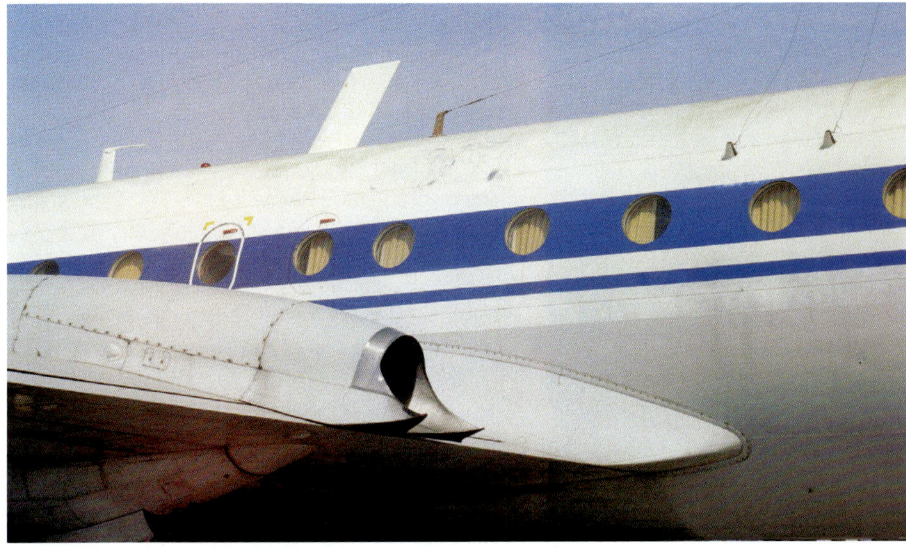

UR-75918 during an open day at Vinnitsa in 1996. *Sergey Popsuevich*

one; one in service with 144th OSAE at Kuybyshev-Bobrovka; 177th OGSAO (later 456th OGSAP) at Vinnitsa, with one; 153rd OSAE at Kishinev, with one; 186th OSAE at Chita, with one; 193rd OSAE at Tbilisi, with one; 245th OSAE at Legnica, with one; 249th OSAE at Riga-Skulte, with one; 300th OSAE at Kala, with one; 349th OTAE at Ermolino, with two; 39th OAO REB, with one Il-22M-11 based at Sperenberg, East Germany; and 929th GLITs at Akhtubinsk with one example, which was later absorbed by one of the above mentioned units.

Among the 35 Il-22s in service with the USSR Air Force, the sole Il-22M-15, CCCP-75915, was inherited by Kazakhstan, while Il-22M-11 CCCP-75916 was taken on by Belarus. Ukraine inherited Il-22 CCCP-75896 and Il-22M-11 CCCP-75918. Finally, Il-22M-11 CCCP-75929 was inherited by Moldova.

Both Il-22s in Ukraine were inherited by the Ukrainian Air Force. In the spring of 1993, the UkrAF started to operate 75918 (c/n 2964017104), which had remained operational in service with 456th OGSAP until it ran out of hours at Vinnitsa in 1994, while 75896, which was with the former 243rd OSAP based at Lviv, took the place of 75918 in 456th OGSAP and remained operational until 1998, when it was converted into an Il-18D during overhaul. Then, 75896 was put up for sale, and the Angolan airline Alada Empresa de Transportes Aeroes procured it in 2001, giving it the civil registration D2-FFR.

While in service, 75896 participated in a dozen international exercises. For example, in 1997, the Il-22 played the role of airborne command post during the exercises Redoubts 97 and Fairway of Peace 97. During Fairway of Peace 97, the Ukrainian Minister of the Defence Army, Gen Oleksander Kuzmuk, together with the Russian Federation's Ministry of Defence, Marshal Igor Sergeyev, flew on board 75896 over the Black Sea in the training area.

The life of the Il-22s in the service of the Ukrainian Air Force was short. After their retirement, the air force did not have an active airborne command post aircraft until the Ukrainian Ministry of Defence decided to restore one of its stored An-26RTs, 22 Blue (c/n 11607), in 2006. The aircraft was converted into an airborne command post by using all the parts of 75918 that had been stored in Vinnitsa. Finally, on 12 June 2014, 75918 was sold to a private company to be scrapped instead of being put in a museum. It had been parked on the civil apron of Gavrishevka airport (Vinnitsa AB) for several years.

As well as the Il-22s, the Ukrainian Air Force inherited another of the Il-18 derivatives, an Il-20. This was the second military derivative of Il-18 and, as a SIGNIT and ELINT aircraft, one of most top-secret aircraft in the Soviet Air Force arsenal. The aircraft was 172011401, which was manufactured in 1974 as the first mass-produced Il-20 delivered to 243rd OSAP and remained in service with the unit until the Soviet Union break-up in 1991. It is reported that it had been converted into Il-18D by 1990. It was inherited by the Ukrainian Air Force but never entered service. It 1998, it was stripped of its remaining military equipment and was fully converted into an Il-18D. It was taken on by Lviv Airlines after years of being stored in Pushkin and later received the civil registration UR-BXD.

Su-17M3/4R Fleet (1992–2004): The Eyes and Ears of Limanskoye

In 1992, the Soviet Air Force had 164 Su-17M3R/M4R tactical reconnaissance aircraft and 54 Su-17UM3/UM3K conversion trainers in service with one Independent Reconnaissance Aviation Squadron (ORAE), eight Independent Reconnaissance Aviation Regiments (ORAP), and two Independent Guards Reconnaissance Aviation Regiments (OGRAP). Of these, 24 Su-17M4R tactical reconnaissance aircraft and six Su-17UM3Ks with the 827th Independent Reconnaissance Aviation Regiment (827th ORAP) found their way into Ukrainian Air Force service and remained active as complementary tactical reconnaissance jets for the air force Su-24MRs until 2004.

Su-17M3R and Su-17M4R in Ukraine

In 1991, the 47th OGRAP from VVS Moscow Military District at Shatalovo, Smolensk Oblast, inducted 12 Su-17M4Rs and in 1992 one more into service with its 3rd Aviation Squadron as replacements for its older Su-17M3Rs. The squadron operated 13 Su-17M3Rs, including 12 ex-101st ORAP examples, between 26 June 1989 and 16 November 1990. Among its new Su-17M4Rs, six with bort numbers 39, 40, 43, 44, 47, 48 Yellow were from the 827th ORAP that were transferred to Shatalovo on 14 January 1991. Its Su-17M4Rs, together with four Su-17UM3s, remained in service with 47th OGRAP until the disbandment of its 3rd Aviation Squadron in September 1993.

According to the USSR Air Force statistics, four Su-17M4Rs of the 827th ORAP had been lost in various accidents on 28 April 1983, 8 June 1985, 12 August 1986, and 8 April 1987. This left 29 Su-17s in service with the unit in November 1990, according to information gathered during the CFE treaty on data exchange. In 1992, the Ukrainian Ministry of Defence said that the Ukrainian Air Force inherited 30 Su-17s in service with the 827th ORAP at Limanskoye, comprising 24 Su-17M4Rs and six Su-17UM3Ks in two Aviation Squadrons (12 Su-17M4Rs and three Su-17UM3Ks in each squadron).

The 827th ORAP based at Limanskoye continued under the UkrAF's 5th Air Army, which was headquartered at Odessa. Its flight activity was reduced to half of the Soviet days. For example, a video recorded on Friday, 4 March 1994 shows ten training sorties on that day by five Su-17M4Rs with bort numbers 05, 21, 23, 29 and 49 Yellow, as well as four Su-17UM3Ks, 62, 64, 65 and 67 Yellow. These sorties included formation flying and reconnaissance training, including taking pictures of each other in the sky.

In May and June 1996, the last reconnaissance MiG-25s were retired by the UkrAF's 48th OGRAP, leaving the regiment with only one squadron of 11 Su-24MRs. Decisions were made to reinforce the 48th OGRAP, which was subordinate to 14th Air Army, with a new Aviation Squadron of Su-17M4Rs from 827th ORAP. Subsequently, the retraining of former MiG-25 pilots on the new reconnaissance jet was started in January 1997, simultaneously with the delivery of 12 Su-17M4Rs and two Su-17UM3Ks (64 and 67 Yellow) from 827th ORAP's 2nd Aviation Squadron.

One of the 48th OGRAP's Su-17M4Rs, 53 Yellow, was lost in an accident on 11 September 1998. On that day, the aircraft was being flown by Col Grigoriy Vasil'yevich Grishchenko, who was an Afghan war veteran with 1,350 hours' flying time, including 1,100 hours on the Su-17. Seventeen minutes after take-off from Kolomiya, the pilot suffered a technical failure in his aircraft's engine at 10,000m (32,808ft) that led to a flame out.

In Afghanistan, the Su-17M3R and Su-17M4R were actively used not only for battle damage assessment but also armed reconnaissance using KKR-1/2 reconnaissance pods with photo, radio, infrared and television equipment. Here a Su-17M3R is seen equipped with a KKR-1/T reconnaissance pod and also armed with iron bombs flying somewhere over Afghanistan in 1985. *Sergey Popsuevich*

Su-17M4R 12 Yellow b/n (c/n 34814) was one of the last 14 Su-17s in service with the 827th ORAE. It was sent to Zaporozhye and its bort number was changed to 12 Blue in 2003. It was kept airworthy while it was waiting to be sold. It can be seen during one of its last flights at Zaporozhye in 2003. *Zaporozhye Aircraft Repair Plant's archive*

Six times he tried to restart but, while the engine still remained shot, he decided to eject over a deserted area at 1,700m (5,577ft) elevation. The aircraft gradually descended toward a city, where it brought its local population to state of shock. Local eyewitnesses said of the accident: 'It silently passed over the bazaar (market area) at an altitude of 15m, then climbed a little, flew over the hospital, and safely hit the ground.' At 14.59 local time the aircraft hit empty ground between two houses and exploded but did not damage the houses nor anyone on the ground. A UkrAF Mi-8 SAR helicopter evacuated the pilot at 16.53 local time and took him to Kolomiya air base. In 2008, Grishchenko became head of the Zaporozhye Aircraft Repair Plant.

The 48th OGRAP lost another Su-17M4R, this time in 2002. During the notorious crash of Su-27UB 42 Blue during an air show on 27 July 2002, the aircraft not only killed 77 people and injured 543 others but badly damaged an Il-76MD and destroyed an Su-17M4R of the 48th OGRAP on the ground. The Su-17 in question was 50 Yellow (c/n 18718), which had been recently overhauled and was one of the best aircraft of the 48th OGRAP's 1st Aviation Squadron stationed in Zaporozhye.

Withdrawal from service

In 2000, the 827th ORAP, which now had become the 827th ORAE, with only 14 Su-17s in its service, was moved to Buyalyk, Odessa Oblast. There it reinforced the local 511th ORAP with 22 Su-24MRs in two Aviation Squadrons, most of which were grounded at the time because they were at the end of their MTBO. In 2003, the 511th ORAP, which had just 16 Su-24MRs in service, was disbanded and its nine airworthy Su-24MRs were moved to Kolomiya between 4 May and 8 July 2003. Seven others that had reached their MTBO moved to Bila Tserkva to be scrapped on 3 September 2003.

The disbandment of the 511th ORAP was accompanied by the end of the 827th ORAE. Some of the last 14 827th ORAP's Su-17s were sent to Odessa to be stored until they were sold. At the time there were just three airworthy examples and the remaining 11 were grounded! One Su-17UM3K, 68 Blue painted in blue and yellow special colours, was kept operational together with another Su-17UM3K 64 Blue from the 48th OGRAP for test pilot training at Zaporozhye Aircraft Repair Plant for a couple of more years until they were both sold to Vietnam. Also, some of the Su-17M4Rs, including 12 Blue (c/n 34814), were kept airworthy in fully mission-capable status in Zaporozhye to be ready for sale to a foreign customer as tactical reconnaissance jets or as fighter-bombers (after being modified to Su-17M4s in case of sale).

After disbandment of the 827th ORAE, the 48th OGRAP was disbanded in 2004. At the time most of its airworthy Su-17M4Rs, including 49 Yellow and

This KKR-1/2 reconnaissance pod belonged to Su-17M4R 12 Yellow (c/n 34814). It is about to be installed on the aircraft on 25 May 2004. *Zaporozhye Aircraft Repair Plant's archive*

Freshly overhauled and painted Su-17M4R 48th OGRAP 49 Yellow before a flight at Zaporozhye in 2003. *Zaporozhye Aircraft Repair Plant's archive*

50 Yellow (c/n 18718) taking off from Zaporozhye in 2001 just a year before its destruction. *Zaporozhye Aircraft Repair Plant's archive*

64 Yellow was one of two Su-17UM3Ks of the 827th ORAE that was kept airworthy by Zaporozhye aircraft repair plant until 2004. *Zaporozhye Aircraft Repair Plant's archive*

50 Yellow as well as Su-17UM3K 64 Yellow, were based at the Zaporozhye Aircraft Repair Plant since their last overhauls had been carried out in 2000 and 2001. After the 48th OGRAP disbanded ten of its airworthy Su-24MRs were sent to Starokostiantyniv to be used by 7th BrTA.

The Last Su-17s for sale

In total, 12 Su-17M4Rs that had been kept in operational status at Zaporozhye or had been stored in good condition at Odessa found a customer in 2003. The government of Yemen finalised a deal to procure the Su-17s, which were modified and delivered as Su-17M4 fighter-bombers to the Yemeni Air Force in 2006 and 2007. They remained in service with 26th Squadron until March 2015, when they were destroyed in air strikes by the Royal Saudi Arabian Air Force at Sana'a International Airport. Before that, in 1994, Ukraine had illegally sold four Su-17s including at least one Su-17UM3K to Yemen and these were delivered to the Yemeni Air Force in 1995.

In 2014, MiGremont had still eight Su-17s in its storage yard waiting for a customer. They were two ex-navy Su-17M3s, an unidentified Su-17UM3 and five Su-17M4Rs with bort numbers 44, 45, 46, 48, and 51 Yellow. Among these aircraft, one Su-17 was sold in 2014, while the rest are still stored in MiGremont. The Su-17M3s were overhauled for the Libyan Arab Air Force following a contract signed in 2004, but because of sanctions and financial reasons they remained at Zaporozhye and were never delivered.

The MiGremont factory, or the Zaporozhye Aircraft Repair Plant, also had the last airworthy Su-17 in Ukraine until 2013. It was 77 Blue (c/n 62918) and it was used for test pilot training and trials of new systems in the repair centre until its MTBO was reached and it was grounded for programme depot maintenance. Its overhaul has remained incomplete since 2014.

At the Odessa aircraft repair plant, there are still seven ex-827th ORAP Su-17s stored waiting to be sold to customers. They are two Su-17UM3Ks, 61 and 63 Yellow/Blue (the Yellow side numbers were painted with Blue after their last overhaul at the Zaporozhye Aircraft Repair Plant in the early 2000s), and five Su-17M4Rs. Of the latter, the identities of two with their KRR-1/54 reconnaissance pods installed are known, which are 02 and 52 Blue (formerly 02 and 52 Yellow).

From almost 70 Su-17s inherited by the Ukrainian Air Force and Navy, just three are on display in various locations in Ukraine: an Su-17M4R with fake bort number 71 Yellow as a monument in Energodar; Su-17UM 80 Blue (c/n 17532351902) in a Soviet Air Force colour scheme in the aviation museum in Zhuliany, Kiev; and an Su-17M3 with the fake identity 50 Yellow (c/n 23503) in the Ukrainian Air Force Museum in Vinnitsa.

68 Blue together with a second Su-17UM3K, was used for Su-17 pilot training and retraining at Zaporozhye until 2004. It was later sold to Vietnam. ***Zaporozhye Aircraft Repair Plant's archive***

Former Su-17M4Rs of the 48th ORGAP were sold to Yemen as Su-17M4 ground attack aircraft in 2003. Here one of them with the serial number 2211 has just completed a test flight at Zaporozhye. ***Zaporozhye Aircraft Repair Plant's archive***

The Ukrainian Ministry of Defence documents show the presence of 40 Su-17M3/UM3s in the inventory of the Ukrainian Navy in 1992. They most likely were from 43rd Fighter-Bomber Aviation Regiment (43rd APIB), Black Sea Fleet based at Gvardeyskoye, Crimean Oblast, which was still part of Russian Navy at that time! Almost half the 43rd APIB's Su-17s had reached the end of their MTBO and were stored in various locations including Saki air base in 1992. They then entered the inventory of the Ukrainian Navy. According to data from the CFE Treaty Data Exchange, the 43rd APIB had 46 Su-17s in November 1990. *Sergey Popsuevich*

In 1997, following an agreement between the Russian and *The Ukrainian Ministry of Defences*, the rest of the 43rd APIB's Su-17s comprising 20 Su-17M3s and three Su-17UM3s, which were mostly grounded, were handed over to the Ukrainian Air Force. They were transferred from Gvardeyskoye to Limanskoye and were later put up for sale at Odessa and Zaporozhye. All three Su-17UM3s together with five ex-UkrAF Su-17UM3Ks were sold to Vietnam in 2004. Deliveries took place after the end of their overhaul at the Zaporozhye aircraft repair plant in 2005 and 2006. *Sergey Popsuevich*

Four of the ex-Navy Su-17M3s were sold to Azerbaijan in 1993, then overhauled by Zaporozhye aircraft repair plant and shipped to Nasosnaya air base in Il-76MDs. They took part in the war with Armenia. This example has just completed a post-overhaul FCF at Zaporozhye in 2003. *Zaporozhye Aircraft Repair Plant's archive*

This Su-17UM3 was one of eight examples sold to Vietnam in 2004. No. 8556 was delivered fully operational but was never inducted into service with the People's Vietnamese Air Force and was used as source of spare parts. *Zaporozhye Aircraft Repair Plant's archive*

77 Blue (c/n 62918) was the last Su-17 flyable in Ukraine. This Su-17UM3K was kept airworthy for experimental and training purposes at the MiGremont facility until 2013, when it was grounded after its MTBO was reached. *Alexander Golz*

Su-24MR Fleet (1992–today): The Recce Fencers

A fleet of eight Sukhoi Su-24MRs are in use by the last tactical reconnaissance squadron of the Ukrainian Air Force as tactical recce jets. They are the surviving examples of a total of 37 inherited from the Soviet Air Force's 14th and 24th Air Armies. This small fleet of Su-24MRs took part in the war in Donbass and was used for reconnaissance missions from Mirgorod, where they had been forward deployed to support the Air Command Centre. One of them, 11 Yellow, was targeted by a Sterla-3 MANPADS of the pro-Russian separatists near Slavyansk on 1 July 2014. It survived the attack and was brought back safely to Mirgorod by its crew, repaired and returned to service in 2015. This incident led to the suspension of the Su-24MR from combat during the war, but despite that the UkrAF is still relying on its small but valuable fleet for tactical reconnaissance.

In Ukrainian Air Force service

In total, 235 Su-24MRs were manufactured and delivered to the Soviet Air Force and Navy between 1983 and 1992; among these, nine were lost in various accidents between 1987 and 1990, leaving 226, of which 214 were in service in 1992. From these 214, only 130 entered service with the Russian Air Force, while the remaining 84 were taken on by Azerbaijan, Belarus, Kazakhstan, Ukraine and Uzbekistan. Twelve with the 39th ORAP were taken over by Kazakhstan, 12 with the 87th ORAP went to Uzbekistan, 11 with the 882nd ORAP were taken over by Azerbaijan, 12 with 10th ORAP went to Belarus, while 37 with the 48th OGRAP (12 examples) and 511th ORAP (15 examples) were taken on by Ukraine.

These 37 Su-24MRs, together with 24 Su-17M4Rs, were the UkrAF assets for tactical reconnaissance. Most of the unit's former Su-24MR pilots who served in both the USSR and Ukrainian days speak about the struggle for survival of the 48th OGRAP and 511th ORAP after the break-up of

This Su-24MR, 31 White, belonged to the 511th ORAP at Buyalyk. Here it has had its UkrAF insignia applied on its red star on the vertical stabiliser during its participation in the Gostomel Air show in 1993. *Alexander Golz*

511th ORAP's 33 Blue which is now based at Starokonstantinov with the side number 15 Yellow, was the first serial-produced Su-24MR in the world, with c/n 0115301. It flew for the first time on 6 June 1983. Here it is at Buyalyk in 2002. *511th ORAP community group*

the Soviet Union. For a short period in 1993 and 1994, the pilots had the opportunity to increase their flying hours, resulting in an improvement in their flight skills, but soon these units faced a decline in flying activity as a result of a financial crisis after the USSR's collapse until 511th ORAP was disbanded in September 2003.

Nine of 511th ORAP's Su-24MRs were absorbed by the 48th ORAP. The first three aircraft flown to Kolomiya were 01, 22 and 28 Blue on 5 April 2003. Then 06 and 10 Blue followed on 28 May, 11 Blue on 4 April, 30 Blue on 4 June and the final two aircraft, 20 and 33 Blue, on 8 July 2003. No. 33 Blue, which is now based at Starokostiantyniv as 15 Yellow, was the first serial-produced Su-24MR in the world (c/n 0115301) and flew for first time on 6 June 1983. No. 15 Yellow was airworthy in 7th BrTA service until the mid-2000s, when its wiring was damaged due to a lightning strike during a flight. Its damaged vertical stabiliser was later swapped with that of ex-511th ORAP's Su-24MR 04 Red, which was stored at Belya Tserkva. No. 15 Yellow is now operational with the 7th BrTA.

Alexander Bidenko, who worked as a technician in the maintenance unit of the 511th ORAP between April 1988 and April 2002, recalled the disbandment of the unit: 'On 3rd September 2003, I was responsible for preparing the Su-24MR with bort number 04 to fly from Buyalyk to Belya-Tserkva [the last aircraft that left Buyalyk]. The heaviest years for the Ukrainian Air Force were 2002 to 2004. Air bases ceased to exist: Limanskoye in 2002, Buyalyk in 2003, Martnovka in 2003 and Kanatovo in 2004. In 2004, the 48th ORAP at Kolomiya also ceased to exist. The 511th ORAP had all its aircraft transferred to other airports after its disbandment. Nine, 01, 06, 08, 10, 20 (former 50 from Voronezh), 22, 28, 30 and 33 Blue (former 49 from Voronezh), were transferred to Kolomiya and six others, 03, 04, 05, 12, 21 and 23 Blue, were transferred to Belya Tserkva, where their valuable parts were removed and then they were all scrapped.'

511th ORAP's Su-24MR 33 Blue (c/n 0115301) was the first Su-24MR overhauled by NARP between 1993 and 1995. It can be seen beside a Ukrainian Navy's Tu-142MR that had received the bort number 33 Red after overhaul at Nikolayev in 1995. *Sergey Popsuevich*

After the 511th ORAP, the 48th OGRAP was disbanded at Kolomiya in 2004. In 1991, the unit had three squadrons equipped with the MiG-25RB (different versions), Su-24MR and Su-17M4R. In 1993, its 3rd Squadron was disbanded and its Su-17M4Rs and Su-17UM3s found their way to another unit. In 1994, the 48th OGRAP received the Su-24MP EW aircraft of the disbanded 118th Independent Aviation Regiment for Electronic Warfare (118th OAPREB) in order to re-form its 3rd Aviation Squadron. In terms of Su-24MR flight

Su-24MR 01 Red b/n waiting for overhaul at the NARP facility on 12 April 1996. *Sergey Popsuevich*

7th BrTA Su-24MR 92 Yellow during the combat phase of the exercise Clear Skies 2006 at Nikolayev on 22 September 2006. *Sergey Popsuevich*

activity, it is claimed that the 48th OGRAP had more opportunities than the 511th ORAP in the early 1990s. In 1996, the Foxbat strategic reconnaissance aircraft were withdrawn from service by the 1st AE. The squadron was re-formed with a group of ex-827th ORAP's Su-17M4Rs and Su-17UM3Ks in January 1997.

As mentioned above, nine of the former 511th ORAP Su-24MRs were absorbed by the 48th OGRAP in 2003 and they gradually had their blue side numbers replaced with new yellow ones. A video recorded only few months before the disbandment of the regiment in Kolomiya shows 12 Su-24MRs still airworthy with the unit, which were 16, 17, 19, 21, 23, 24, 26, 32, 33, 35 and 93 Yellow and 10 Blue. Soon after the disbandment, all the unit's airworthy Su-24MRs were sent to Starokostiantyniv to be used to form a third aviation squadron for the 7th BrTA there, which would operate the air force's last reconnaissance jets.

Su-24MR 17 Yellow releasing flares during an exercise at Nikolayev in September 2007. *Sergey Popsuevich*

At war over Donbass

The number of airworthy Su-24MRs gradually dropped from 12 in 2004 to just four in 2014 just before the Donbass war. The four airworthy examples were 11, 16, 17 and 36 Yellow. The maintenance unit of the 7th BrTA quickly restored three more examples to flying condition, which were 15, 35 and 93 Yellow, in March 2014. In November 2015, the NARP (Nikolayev Aircraft Repair Plant) completed the overhaul of 59 Yellow (c/n 0741612), one of three Su-24MRs delivered to the facility to be overhauled in 2014. No. 60 Yellow (c/n 0741613) was the second Su-24MR, with its overhaul completed in 2018 and delivery in June that year.

Soon after the launch of an anti-terrorism operation in the east of Ukraine, two Su-24MRs with the side numbers 11 and 36 Yellow, together with five Su-24Ms, were forward deployed to the Mirgorod base of 831st BrTA to be operated over the Donbass region. No. 11 Yellow was damaged by MANPADS fired by pro-Russian separatists on 1 July 2014, leaving 36 Yellow as the sole tactical reconnaissance jet available to be used over Donbass. It flew on 2, 9, 15, 18, 22, 23 and 27 July, as well as 1, 3 and 6 August 2014. Its flights were very effective against separatists and Russia; the FSB tried to force its pilot to steal the aircraft and fly it to Russia. He was later arrested by the SBU before he could carry this out.

Following the rise of SAM and MANPADS threats over Donbass, the UkrAF decided to use other means of intelligence gathering for reconnaissance missions. One was the Tupolev Tu-143 Reys unmanned reconnaissance aircraft, which was used frequently over Donbass but with lower-quality pictures than those taken with the state of art BKR-1 reconnaissance suite of the Su-24MR. The separatists managed to shoot down one of the Tu-143s on 1 August 2014. Nowadays, the USAF is supporting Ukraine on intelligence-gathering missions, for which one of two RQ-4B Block 40 Global Hawk UAVs of

19 Yellow, one of the last twelve airworthy Su-24MRs of the 48th OGRAP at Kolomiya, just few months before the disbandment of the regiment in 2003. *511th ORAP community group*

Su-24MRs of the 48th OGRAP during the last days of the existence of the regiment at Kolomiya. *511th ORAP community group*

This ex-511th ORAP Su-24MR, 10 Blue, was one of the few examples that remained airworthy after being absorbed by the 48th OGRAP in 2003. Here it is seen taxiing at Kolomiya in 2003. *511th ORAP community group*

Su-24MR 15 Yellow was one of the participants of the exercise Tight Knot 2005 in September 2005. Here it is seen landing at Nikolayev/ Kulbakino after a reconnaissance mission. *Sergey Popsuevich*

Su-24MR 17 Yellow during an exercise at Nikolayev in March 2012. *Alexander Golz*

Su-24MR 11 Yellow at Starokonstantinov on 17 September 2013. *Alexander Golz*

the 12th Reconnaissance Squadron, 9th Reconnaissance Wing, forward deployed to NAS Sigonella, Italy, is in use for weekly and sometimes daily multi-intelligence gathering missions over the Donbass region.

In April 2019, nine Su-24MRs were airworthy with the 3rd Aviation Squadron of the 7th BrTA: they were 11, 15, 16, 17, 35, 36, 59, 60 and 93 Yellow. Among these, seven were fully mission capable, including the two examples on deployment at Mirgorod. One more Su-24MR (c/n 0741607) was still under major overhaul and lifetime extension at the NARP, with delivery scheduled for 2020.

The other operators of the Su-24MR are the Algerian Air Force, with five examples (in service with 525e Escadron de Reconnaissance et de Guerre Electronique), the Russian Navy with seven and Russian Air Force with 66 airworthy examples. The Russian Air Force units are 799th BAP (12 aircraft), 4th ORAE (12 aircraft), 11th RAP (13 aircraft), 2nd BAP (14 aircraft), 929th Flight Test Centre (2 aircraft) and 98th SAP (13 aircraft). The 43rd OMShAP of the Russian Navy operates seven examples.

Regarding the incident involving 11 Yellow, the aviation journalist Joe Celibirty interviewed the pilot, who had become the commander of the 7th BrTA, in 2016:

'Turmoil in the south-east of the country escalated into an all-out war and on 1 July 2014, Lt Col Bulatsyk Yevhen and his radar systems operator were conducting a reconnaissance flight over the disputed region flying Su-24MR 11 Yellow, call sign 609. The crew launched from a forward operating base closer to the hostilities rather than from their home base in the Khmel'nyts'ka region. Twenty-six minutes into the mission, and while flying at low level, 5 MANPADS were fired towards 11 Yellow.

'Three of them were soon out of range due to the speed of the Su-24MR but the other two were homing straight towards the Ukrainian jet. The pilot, 37-year old Lt Col Bulatsyk Yevhen, an experienced flying officer, flew his Su-24MR further down the valley and managed to avoid the fourth missile by dispensing chaff but the fifth hit his left engine. The stricken jet was 320km away from the forward operating base.

Su-24MR 11 Yellow after being damaged by 9K34 Strela-3 MANPADS of the pro-Russian separatists over Slavyansk on 1 July 2014. *Ukrainian Air Force*

11 Yellow after being painted in overall gunship grey colours after its restoration in 2015. *Alexander Golz*

37-year-old Lt Col Bulatsyk Yevhen, pilot of 11 Yellow when it was hit by MANPADS on 1 July 2014. He is standing beside his repaired bird two years after the event, when he had also become commander of the 7th BrTA. *Joe Ciliberti*

During Ukraine's war in 2014, the Russian Intelligence Service (FSB) contacted Major Yuri Kireev, an Su-24MR pilot of the 7th BrTA, to unsuccessfully try to force him to hijack Su-24MR 36 Yellow and fly it to Russia. *Joe Ciliberti*

'Indications in the cockpit were showing a turbine rapidly losing temperature. First thoughts of the pilot were to nurse the jet back to base but not before Col Yevhen contacted air traffic controllers to bring any recovering aircraft at the airfield to land before him because he expected to block the runway on arrival. He wanted to ensure a clear airfield circuit pattern to address any type of emergency on approach and landing.

'As 11 Yellow was 4km away from the runway threshold and now at a very slow speed, fuel from the damaged engine started burning profusely and at 1km from touch down Lt Col Yevhen's jet was seriously on fire. Notwithstanding the precarious situation, Lt Col Yevhen calmly put his Su-24MR down on the runway, where both engines were then immediately shut down and the crew swiftly exited the burning jet.

'The emergency services attended to the jet and extinguished the fire in a very short time, so much so that the jet was saved and was soon flying after that fateful mission. Today it proudly sits on the ramp together with the rest of the 3rd Squadron of No. 7 Brigade, ready to defend the borders of Ukraine at short notice.

'Not only did Col Yevhen accomplish his reconnaissance mission by bringing back valuable tactical information, but he also brought 11 Yellow to a safe landing. For his bravery, Col Bulatsyk Yevhen was awarded the Order of Bogdan Khmelnytcky III service medal.

'While the author was touring the base and even had lunch at the officers' mess, the pride of the officers in flying the Su-24 in the Ukrainian Air Force service was evident, as was the professionalism of all involved at Starokostiantinov AB. Col K. Mykola's words "We're ready to fight" rang true as ground crew were preparing the jets for the following day's missions while other Su-24s in a pan on the SW corner of the field were undergoing deep maintenance.'

Joe Ciliberti would like to thank the Command of the Ukrainian AF, Col Oleksander Vereschak, Col B. Yevhen and Maj Alexandr Poriadko.

Su-24MR 16 Yellow was one of four airworthy Su-24MRs of the 7th BrTA in February 2014. It is an ex-48th OGRAP aircraft. *Chris Lofting*

Su-24MR 93 Yellow was restored by the 7th BrTA technicians in 2014. *Alexander Golz*

93 Yellow with its wings fully swept banking over Starokonstantinov in May 2014 a few days before the participation of the 7th BrTA in the war in Donbass. *Alexander Golz*

59 Yellow is one of youngest Su-24MRs of the UkrAF and had its overhaul completed by NARP in 2015. It then received this digital camouflage. *Alexander Golz*

This artwork shows 11 Yellow with the mission configuration of the day when it was targeted by pro-Russian separatists on 1 July 2014. It had a pair of PTB-3000 external tanks and also an SRS-14 (M-321) Tangazh ELINT pod. The Su-24MR maximum speed at sea level is 1,320km/h (818mph) with a radius of 650km (403 miles) while carrying a pair of PTB-3000 external tanks under the inboard pylons and 420km (260 miles) without external tanks. *Luca G. Canossa*

Airworthy Su-24MRs in service with the 7th BrTA of the Ukrainian Air Force

Bort Number	Construction Number	Former unit	Manufacture year	Overhaul/Restoration year	Notes
11 Yellow	0415304	511th ORAP	1984	?	Damaged during the war and later restored
15 Yellow	0115301	511th ORAP	1983	?	
16 Yellow	0315304	511th ORAP	1983	?	
17 Yellow	0315302	511th ORAP	1983	?	
35 Yellow	0215303	511th ORAP	1983	2014	Restored by 7th BrTA technicians in 2014
36 Yellow	0415307	?	1984	?	
59 Yellow	0741612	48th OGRAP	1987	2015	Overhauled by NARP in 2015. Painted in digital camouflage
60 Yellow	0741613	48th OGRAP	1987	2018	Overhauled by NARP between 2015 and 2018. Digital camouflage
93 Yellow	0315305	511th ORAP	1983	2014	Restored by 7th BrTA technicians in 2014

MiG-25R Fleet (1992–1996): The Recce Foxbats

The Ukrainian Air Force inherited 16 MiG-25RBFs, RBKs, RBSs, RBTs, RBVs and RUs, which were in service with the 14th Air Army. These different modifications of the reconnaissance MiG-25RB remained in service with the UkrAF's 48th OGRAP until 1996, when the unit was disbanded due to the inability of Ukrainian government to allocate a budget for their costly operation. Some of the MiG-25RBs were kept operational as reserves at the Zaporozhye Aircraft Repair Plant until 2004 with the hope of them being sold to foreign countries, but this never happened and most had been scrapped by 2015.

In service with the UkrAF

The sole Soviet Air Force MiG-25 regiment inherited by Ukraine was 48th OGRAP at Kolomiya. The unit had 16 MiG-25RBS, MiG-25RBF, MiG-25RBT and MiG-25RU in service with its 1st Aviation Squadron, while its 2nd Aviation Squadron had 12 Su-24MRs in service in 1990. Among the MiG-25s of 48th OGRAP, just 13 were in service, while two others – 07 and 08 Red – were in storage.

The first MiG-25s for the 48th OGRAP's 1st AE, which were three MiG-25RUs, 14, 15 and 16 Red, were delivered in September 1973. The next month, five brand new MiG-25RBs, 01 to 05 Red, were delivered. In 1974, four more MiG-25RBs, 06 to 09 Red, arrived, but 07 Red was badly damaged due to pilot error on 6 August 1974. This was sent back to the factory to be repaired, while 08 and 09 Red were delivered to another reconnaissance regiment of the Soviet Air Force in 1975. In the same year, the unit received a new MiG-25RB, 10 Red. In 1976, two more MiG-25RBs were delivered, 11 and 12 Red. In 1982, a single MiG-25RBS, 17 Red (c/n 02045127), entered service.

To replace 08 and 09 Red, the 48th OGRAP received MiG-25RBs 57 and 72 Red after the end of their deployment to Egypt in autumn 1975. Their bort numbers were subsequently changed to 08 and 09 Red! These two aircraft were later lost. First, 08 Red was withdrawn from use after it overran the runway on 31 July 1980, while 09 Red crashed due to technical failure at night on 4 April 1983, although its pilot, V. Yalyashenko, ejected safely. He later resumed flying in summer 1983. It is known

73 Blue was the sole MiG-25RBT serving with the 48 OGRAP when it was inherited by UkrAF in 1992. In 1978, the MiG-25RBT was developed by Gorki plant and it was similar to the MiG-25RBV but with a 'Tangazh' SIGINT pack instead of 'Virazh'. It also had a new IFF unit named 'Parol'. Here it is carrying out one of its last flights from Zaporozhye ARZ in 2003. ***Zaporozhye Aircraft Repair Plant archive***

75 Red was the second MiG-25RBS of the 48th OGRAP. Equipped with SLAR and an SPS-142 ECM pack, the MiG-25RBS was produced until 1977 and was later refitted with a new ELINT system. *Sergey Popsuevich*

that in 1980 01 to 03 Red were MiG-25RB variants; 05, 09 and 10 Red were MiG-25RBVs; 06 Red was a MiG-25RBK, while 11 and 12 Red were MiG-25RBSs.

While the MiG-25RB and its other variants were suitable for high-altitude recce missions, aircraft such as the Yak-28R, then the Su-17M3/4R and finally the Su-24MR were suitable for recce ops at lower altitude. They were complementary aircraft with the recce units. The 2nd Aviation Squadron of the 48th OGRAP received the Su-24MR as replacement for its ageing Yak-28Rs in 1988. There were also plenty of Su-17M3Rs in service with the squadron from 1978, and these were later replaced by Su-17M4Rs.

During the first Independence Day parade of Ukraine on 21 August 1992, a pair of MiG-25RBVs piloted by Yarullin and Voypanyuk, were flying in a formation led by a 48th OGRAP' Su-24MR, flew in the UkrAF flypast over Kiev. On that day, the unit's personnel received a cash prize from the commander of the Ukrainian Air Force's 14th Air Army. Soon, because of the broken economy of Ukraine and the subsequent downsizing programme of the UkrAF, the number of sorties performed by the unit dropped to less than 10% of those during the Soviet Union, but despite that nearly all the unit's MiG-25s, especially the special mission examples, were overhauled by Zaporozhye Aircraft Repair Plant and subsequently the single-seat examples received new bort numbers. Just one MiG-25RBS (17 Red) remained unchanged because its last overhaul had been completed in 1991, a few weeks before the independence of Ukraine.

48th OGRAP had three MiG-25RBVs in service in 1992. In 1978, based on new variants of reconnaissance MiG-25s manufactured by Gorki Aircraft Manufacturing Plant, the older MiG-25RBs were upgraded by replacing their SRS-4A and SRS-4B SIGNIT packs with a more advanced SRS-9 'Virazh'. Their SPS-141 ECM 'Siren' suites were also replaced by SPS-151. The MiG-25RBV had two NA-75 cameras, seen here. *Sergey Popsuevich*

Retirement

Finally, the decision was made to retire the MiG-25 from 48th ORAP service in 1996. All the unit's 13 MiG-25s were placed in storage at the Zaporozhye Aircraft Repair Plant. The transfer of the aircraft to Zaporozhye began on 16 May 1996 when single-seater MiG-25s 73 Blue, 74 Blue, 75 Blue and 76 Red were flown to the facility. Four more MiG-25s were transferred to Zaporozhye on 28 May, followed by another batch of four on 6 June 1996. The last MiG-25 left Kolomiya on 13 June 1996. The bort numbers of the unit's MiG-25s in 1996 were 14, 15, 16 Red, all MiG-25RUs, while the single-seat variants were 06, 11, 17, 18, 19, and 76 Red together with 05, 73, 74 and 75 Blue.

Among the 13 former 48th ORAP MiG-25s at Zaporozhye, four examples – MiG-25RBSs 17 Red and 75 Blue, MiG-25RBF 74 Blue and MiG-25RBT 73 Blue – were kept in reserve condition and were flown regularly until their next overhaul time, which spelled their withdrawal from service. No. 17 Red's last flight was in 2000 and it was then prepared for transfer to Vinnitsa, where it entered the UkrAF Museum in 2001. No. 73 Blue was the last example in service with the UkrAF and remained airworthy until 2004! No. 74 Blue was kept in good condition, unlike other MiG-25s in storage in Zaporozhye, at least until 2010, and it was regularly put on display during the annual open days at the facility.

The MiGremont facility continued performing lifetime extension, modernisation and overhaul of the MiG-25 for foreign customers, including the Algerian, Libyan and Russian Air Forces. Even in 2016, MiGremont was still the contractor for spare part supply, modernisation and overhaul of Algerian MiG-25s. In February 2014, negotiations started between the Azerbaijan and Ukrainian authorities to finalise a deal to re-establish the disbanded Nasosnaya ARZ for the restoration, overhaul and even modernisation of ten out of the 26 MiG-25s of the Azerbaijani Air Force. The Azerbaijani Air Force's commander in chief said they were six MiG-25PDs and four MiG-25RBs (eight MiG-25RBs were procured from Kazakhstan in 1993) but the negotiations ended without a deal and the MiG-25s were scrapped between 2014 and 2016.

A pair of NA-72 cameras in the main compartment of a MiG-25RBT at Zaporozhye Aircraft Repair Plant in 1992. *Sergey Popsuevich*

17 Red (c/n 02045127), built in 1976, was delivered to the 48th OGRAP in 1982. It was kept airworthy in reserve condition in Zaporozhye ARZ after disbandment of the regiment in 1996 until its MTBO was reached. It was flown to Vinnitsa, where it was put on display in the UkrAF museum from 2001. *Zaporozhye Aircraft Repair Plant archive*

Tu-22R/RD/RDM/RDK Fleet (1992–1998): Eyes and Ears of Long-Range Aviation

Not only designed to gather intelligence for Long-Range Aviation in the Soviet Air Force as well as the Soviet Navy, but also having a secondary role as a heavy bomber aircraft with the capability of using nuclear bombs, the reconnaissance variant of the Tu-22 Blinder was one of the most remarkable reconnaissance aircraft ever used by the armed forces of the Soviet Union. In total, 127 Tu-22Rs were manufactured by Plant 22 at Kazan between 1962 and 1967; among these 40 entered service with the Baltic and Black Sea fleets of Navy Aviation (VMF) while the rest entered service with Long-Range Aviation of the Soviet Air Force (VVS). They were intended to remain in service until the 1980s, to be replaced by the more capable Tu-22MR equipped with variable wings, but this never happened due to the financial problems of the Soviet Union. The Tu-22R/RDs not only remained in service until 1992 but also flew in Belarus and Ukraine until 1994 and 1998 respectively and were then retired without being replaced by a heavy reconnaissance jet.

11 Red was a Tu-22RD of the 199th OGDRAP'S 1st Aviation Squadron. According to this photo it had 'The Best Aircraft' sign. *Archive of 199th OGDRAP's Museum*

Retirement by the Ukrainian and Belarusian Air Forces

The retirement of the Tu-22R/RD was projected to take place in the 1980s; however, the delays in the programme to design and develop the Tu-22MR resulted in this being postponed until the 1990s. Without them being properly replaced by the Tu-22MR, the Tu-22Rs were retired by the Russian, Ukrainian and Belarussian Air Forces as well as Russian Navy Aviation between 1993 and 1998. The 199th OGDRAP, which had now been inherited by the Ukrainian Air Force, was the world's last operator of the type and retired its last pair of Tu-22RDs in July 1998.

In 1989, the Soviet Air Force had a total of 40 Tu-22R/RD family aircraft left in service. Among these, 21 – seven Tu-22Rs, 13 Tu-22RDMs and one Tu-22RDK – were in service with the 290th ODRAP at Pribytki in Belarus, which also had three Tu-22PDs and six Tu-22U/UDs. One of its Tu-22RDMs was lost in an accident on 19 January 1990. Later, on 8 August 1991, the 290th ODRAP had eight Tu-22Rs, 12 Tu-22RDMs, three Tu-22A bombers and four Tu-22P/PDs, as well as eight Tu-22U/UDs and a Tu-134UShS in its inventory, all of which were later inherited by Belarus.

The most famous aircraft in service with the 199th OGDRAP was this prototype of the Tu-22RDK with the tactical number 19 Red which remained airworthy in service with the regiment as 09 Red and was grounded in 1996. What makes the Tu-22RDK distinctive from the Tu-22RD/RDM are the antennas of SRS-11 Kub-4 SIGINT system installed on both sides of its front fuselage. *Sergey Popsuevich*

This photograph was most likely taken in May 1992 during the ceremony for taking the oath of allegiance to Ukraine at Nezhyin AB. Three Tu-22RDs are flying in formation while two others are ready for take-off. *Author's collection*

The other 19 Tu-22R/RD/RDKs of the USSR VVS were with the 199th ODRAP at Nezhyin in 1989: they were six Tu-22Rs, 12 Tu-22RDs and a single Tu-22RDK, 19 Red. The 199th ODRAP had also three Tu-22PDs and three Tu-22UDs in service. These 25 Tu-22s were later inherited by the Ukrainian Air Force in 1992.

Suffering from lack of spare parts and without a budget to buy fuel, the 290th ODRAP's activity dropped significantly. Its pilots mainly flew once a month with a handful of serviceable Tu-22s, which were mostly the training Tu-22UD variants. The maintenance squadron of the regiment cannibalised half the Tu-22s for parts, especially the engines on the few serviceable examples.

When the decision were taken to disband the regiment in 1993, Tu-22s were sent from Belarus to Engels AB in Russia to be scrapped there. The unit only had a few serviceable RD-7M2s and engineers had to install the engines for the ferry flights to Russia, then remove them at Engels and send them back to Belarus to be installed on another Tu-22 for its ferry flight.

The last official flight of the regiment took place during its disbandment ceremony when two Tu-22UDs, 10 and 40 Red, performed several flypasts over the base on 17 August 1994. Belarus just kept two aircraft at Zyabrovka, 43 Red and 19 Red, which were a Tu-22R and a Tu-22RD respectively, and these were both scrapped. However, the Russian Air Force kept one of the Tu-22RDMs, 18 Red, which is now displayed at the Long-Range Aviation Museum at Engels-2 AB.

Blinders of Nezhyin

Before the collapse of the Soviet Union, 199th OGDRAP, which was later inherited by Ukraine, had the key mission of intelligence gathering in central and south-west Europe, and also the south of Europe. Once a week, its sole Tu-22RDK was tasked to gather intelligence about NATO's EW radar and SAM sites, while its Tu-22R/RDs regularly photographed NATO's bases and activities in West Germany, Austria, Greece, the Bosporus and the Sea of Marmara, as well as the Black Sea, Turkey

Another rare photo from the archive of 199th OGDRAP's museum in Nezhyin shows a line-up of Tu-22s on Nezhyin's main apron. From front to back, Tu-22RD, Tu-22UD, Tu-22KD (from the 341st TBAP but on assignment to Nezhyin) and a Tu-22RDK with the bort number 19 Red. *199th OGDRAP's museum via Sergey Popsuevich*

This is the first and primary camera package for daylight missions of the Tu-22R/RD, which consisted of four AFA-42/100 cameras mounted on a paired tilting framework. They were capable of operating from a height of 5,000m (16,400ft) to the maximum altitude that the aircraft could fly. *Sergey Popsuevich*

and Iran. In 1992, most of the crews of the 199th OGDRAP had become first-class pilots, but due to lack of spare parts and fuel, flying activity had declined significantly.

However, compared with their sister unit, 290th ODRAP, which was inherited by Belarus, the 199th OGDRAP managed to remain in better combat readiness. In 1995, the regiment had ten Tu-22Rs, one Tu-22RDK, three Tu-22PDs and four Tu-22UDs operational with its three aviation squadrons. However, the situation changed over a period of 18 months and the regiment saw most of its Tu-22s grounded after they reached their MTBO (meantime between overhaul). Then it was reorganised as the 18th Independent Long-Range Reconnaissance Aviation Squadron (18th ODRAE), which had just three Tu-22RDs and one Tu-22UD operational. To fill the gap of caused by the grounding of the Tu-22Rs, six An-30Bs were handed over to the unit in 1996.

Tu-22RD 35 Red during an exhibition at Poltava on 22 May 1993. *Sergey Popsuevich*

Despite shortage of Tu-22Rs, the squadron was tasked with using one of them to patrol over the Black Sea and provide security for the US Navy ships that visited Ukraine for first time in early 1997. Two years before that, one of the Tu-22RDs had suffered the failure of its left engine during one of these flights over the Black Sea and its crew managed to perform an emergency landing with one engine at Odessa airfield.

In their last years of service, UkrAF tried to use its last Tu-22R/RDs for civilian purposes such as cartography and ground mapping, and aerial photography during natural disasters for the Ukrainian Ministry of Emergency Situations. However, the money generated through this activity was not enough to keep the Tu-22s going. Finally, the last two flyable examples were withdrawn from service in July 1998. A few months later, decree No. 242 was issued by the Ukrainian parliament through which the 18th ODRAE was transferred to the Ministry of Emergency Situations and named the 30th Special Aviation Squadron. All the regiment's Tu-22s were scrapped at Nezhyin between 1997 and 2001, while their former aircrews continued flying An-26s and An-30Bs.

As explained before, 40 out of the total 127 Tu-22R/RDs manufactured ended up with the 15th ODRAP and 30th OMRAP of Soviet Navy Aviation (VMF). The 15th ODRAP continued operating them until June 1989, when it started using Su-24M/MRs. This regiment had lost eight Tu-22Rs and one Tu-22U in various accidents and incidents between 1962 and 1982. Its surviving Tu-22R/RDs, Tu-22PDs and Tu-22UDs were later absorbed by the VVS's 199th OGDRAP and VMF's 30th OMRAP (ten, including five Tu-22R/RDs). Due to the fact that only a third of the Tu-22s of the regiment were operational after the fall of Soviet Union, the regiment was reorganised as 198th ODRAE at Saki on 30 December 1993 and continued operating Tu-16s and Tu-22s until 31 August 1995. It remained part of the Russian Navy until its last day of existence.

Tu-22R 29 Red during an air show at Poltava on 22 May 1993. *Sergey Popsuevich*

As a bomber, the Tu-22A Blinder was a failure, but its reconnaissance and electronic warfare variants, as well as missile carrier Tu-22K/KDs, managed to live longer than any heavy tactical reconnaissance, jammer and bomber aircraft in the service of the VVS and VMF simply because of the delays in production of the Tu-22M and its reconnaissance variant, the Tu-22MR. Only ten Tu-22M(3)Rs were manufactured between 1989 and 1991, which together with two Tu-22MR prototypes, entered service with the Russian Air Force. Today, only one of these, 02 Red with the serial number RF-94239, has survived and is now in service with the 6952nd Aviation Group at Belaya, Irkutsk.

Acknowledgement: The author would like to thank former personnel of the 199th Independent Guards Long-Range Reconnaissance Aviation Regiment and also Mr Igor Bubin and Mr Sergey Popsuyevich for their assistance in the preparation of this chapter.

A Tu-22RDM of the 290th ODRAP, 19 Red receiving fuel from a Tu-16N tanker. *Vladimir Alexandrovich Kalinin via Sergey Popsuevich*

2 Fighter Force

MiG-23 Fleet (1992–2001): The Ukrainian Floggers

Once one of the most important multi-role fighter aircraft in use for point air defence and ground attack in both the Soviet Air and Air Defence Forces, the MiG-23ML and MLA, and their more modern version, MiG-23MLD, began to give way to the Fourth Generation MiG-29. However, this process remained incomplete in the European units of the forces, especially in the Socialist Republic of Ukraine, when the USSR collapsed. The Ukrainian Air Force inherited 73 MiG-23ML/MLD/UBs and MiG-27s of the former Soviet Air Force, while the Ukrainian Air Defence Force inherited 117 MiG-23MLA/MLD/UBs of the USSR Air Defence Force after Ukraine's independence. After the collapse of the USSR, the Ukrainian Air Defence Force was the main operator of the type as front-line fighter aircraft until 2001, while this third generation multi-role fighter aircraft was never used by the UkrAF.

In Ukrainian service

The first Soviet Air Force unit that was equipped with the MiG-23 on Ukraine's current soil was the 168th Fighter Aviation Regiment (IAP) subordination of the 24th Air Army's 138th Fighter Aviation Division. The unit, based in Starokostiantyniv, received its first MiG-23Ms as replacements for its ageing MiG-19s in 1972. In 1974, next to the 138th IAP, 14th Air Army's 92nd IAP at Mukachevo received its first MiG-23Ms as replacements for its MiG-21s.

A MiG-23UB of the 894th IAP of the Soviet Air Defence Force over Ozernoye air base in 1988. *Sergey Popsuevich*

As part of the Soviet Air Force's Fighter Aviation Regiments dedicated to air-to-ground missions, the 5th Air Army's 642nd IAP at Voznesensk received the MiG-23B and MiG-23BN as replacements for its Su-7Bs in 1974. Two years later, its ground attack MiG-23B/BNs were replaced by the more capable MiG-27M.

Among the training units located in the current territory of Ukraine, the 701st Training Aviation Regiment of the 17th Air Army's Chernigov Higher Military Aviation School of Pilots received its first MiG-23s, mostly MiG-23UBs, in 1977. The next year, 14th Air Army's 114th IAP based at Ivano-Frankovsk received MiG-23Ms as replacements for its MiG-21SMTs. Also in 1980, the 190th IAP of 24th Air Army's 138th IAD received its first MiG-23s to supersede its MiG-21s.

Furthermore, the six Soviet Air Force's Fighter and Training Aviation Regiments were equipped with MiG-23 fighter aircraft in the Ukrainian territory of the Soviet Union in the 1980s, and the Soviet Air Defence Force had also three of its Fighter Aviation Regiments equipped with the MiG-23M, ML, P and MLA, which were later upgraded into the MLD variant standards in the 1980s. The regiments were the 179th, 894th and 737th IAPs at Stryi, Ozernoye and Chervonoglinsloye respectively. They had been equipped with the MiG-23M and MiG-23MLA since 1978, 1979 and 1981 respectively.

In 1986, deliveries of MiG-29s to the Soviet Air Force's front-line Fighter Aviation Regiments started and gradually the number of active MiG-23s in the air force reduced, while a huge number of MiG-23s were involved in the Afghanistan war. Among the units based on Ukrainian territory, the 92nd IAP was the first unit that received MiG-29s, in 1987, and as a result the number of its MiG-23s reduced. By 1989 all its single-seat MiG-23MLAs had been withdrawn from service or transferred to other units. However, five MiG-23UBs were kept airworthy for conversion training of the unit's pilots until 1990.

84 White was the sole MiG-23UB of the 894th IAP of the UkrADF that had a three-tone brown camouflage. *Sergey Popsuevich*

Next to the 92nd IAP, the 642nd IAP, which had MiG-27Ms, received its first MiG-29s in 1988. According to the exchanged data of the CFE Treaty, the unit still had eight MiG-23UBs for conversion training in November 2011. In the same year, the 701st UAP withdrew all its MiG-23s from service. Two years later, the 114th and 190th IAPs began conversion from the MiG-23 to the MiG-29. The 114th IAP had ten MiG-29s and 26 MiG-23MLD/UBs in October 1990, according to the CFE treaty.

After the independence of Ukraine, 190 MiG-23s of all the above-mentioned units on Ukrainian territory were inherited by the Ukrainian Armed Forces, including 117 MiG-23ML/MLA/MLD/UBs in service with the Soviet Air Defence Force. The

MiG-23MLA 25 Blue c/n 15510 of the 894th IAP was an Afghan war veteran with two mission marks under its canopy. *Sergey Popsuevich*

MiG-23UB with 97 White was in use for pilot training at the Odessa Aircraft Repair Plant in the early 1990s. Here it is seen in 1992. *Sergey Popsuevich*

MiG-23UB 47 Blue is an ex-894th IAP example stored at Odessa Aircraft Repair Plant and has been awaiting a customer for decades after its retirement from UkrADF service. Here it is seen in 2008. *Sergey Popsuevich*

03 Yellow, a MiG-23MLD of the 737th IAP of UkrADF, still with the Soviet Air Defence Force's Red Star insignia on its vertical stabiliser, standing on QRA (quick reaction alert) duty at Chervonoglinsloye air base while armed with an R-23R under the right wing, an R-23T under its left wing and two R-73 missiles under the fuselage. *Sergey Popsuevich*

06 Yellow, another MiG-23MLD of the 737th IAP, standing QRA in 1992 while it was armed with an R-23R, an R-23T and two R-60M IR – guided missiles. In those years, the 737th IAP always had four MiG-23MLDs on QRA duty. *Sergey Popsuevich*

Ukrainian Air Force rarely used the remaining MiG-23UBs in service with the IAPs, which had been kept for conversion training of MiG-23 fighter pilots onto the new MiG-29, because no new MiG-29 pilots were required to be added to the units, especially when they were gradually disbanded during the UkrAF downsizing process. For example, the 92nd IAP was disbanded in 1994.

The newly established Ukrainian Air Defence Force, which inherited six Air Defence Regiments and a single Fighter Aviation Regiment of the Soviet Air Defence Force on Ukrainian territory, became the main operator of the MiG-23 in Ukraine. However, soon the Western Air Defence Region's 179th IAP and Southern Air Defence Region's 737th IAP, which had been equipped with 43 and 36 MiG-23MLA/MLD/UBs respectively in 1992, were disbanded in 1996 and 1998, leaving the 894th IAP as the last operator of the MiG-23 in Ukraine as part of the Ukrainian Air Defence Force's Western Region until 2001.

In 1998, when the 737th IAP was disbanded, there were only around 15 MiG-23s airworthy in its service, including MiG-23MLAs 04, 12, 22, 25, 29, and 44 Yellow and MiG-23UBs 90, 91, 94 Yellow.

In 2001, when the 894th IAP was disbanded and then re-formed as 9th BrTA with ex-62nd IAP Su-27s, it had only five fully mission-capable MiG-23MLDs,

VVS's 642nd IAP received MiG-23BN as replacements for its Su-7Bs in 1974 and these remained in service until late 1970s, when they were replaced with the more capable MiG-27M. Some of them ended up at the Kiev Military Aviation Engineering Academy to be used as training platforms including 67 Red which is seen on 14 September 1994. *Sergey Popsuevich*

An ex- 642nd IAP MiG-27M at the Kiev Military Aviation Engineering Academy on 14 September 1994. *Sergey Popsuevich*

This MiG-23UB, 61 White, was in use by the Kirovskoye State flight test centre (GLIC or GLITS) for test and pilot training. It was also being used for tourist flights when it was photographed in the mid-1990s. *Heinz Berger*

09, 14, 22, 23, and 25 Blue, as well as MiG-23UB 91 Blue. There were also 12 more MiG-23MLDs in good condition (mostly in reserve) but not airworthy, which were 01, 05, 10, 11, 24, 28, 29, 31, 33, 44, 47 and 49 White and Blue, as well as six MiG-23UBs, 61, 80, 81, 83, 84 and 94 Blue and White.

All the airworthy MiG-23s of the 894th IAP, together with some of the stored examples in good condition, were moved to the Odessa Aircraft Plant and joined the former MiG-23BNs, MiG-23UBs and MiG-27Ms of the 642nd IAP stored there. At least one of them, MiG-23UB 91 Blue, was kept airworthy until 2003 in order for it to be ready for sale to any potential customer. According to satellite images, the Odessa Aircraft Plant, with ten MiG-23s and MiG-27s, has had the largest amount of available MiG-23s for sale after the Chuguyev Aircraft Repair Plant, which had 34 MiG-23s stored at its facility in 2016.

According to data about arms transfers from Ukraine to other countries in the archive of the SIPRI, 7 ex-UkrAF's MiG-23s and ten MiG-27s were sold to various countries between 2000 and 2006. Among them, six MiG-23UBs were sold to India in 2002, which were delivered in 2004, while one MiG-23UB and ten MiG-27Ks were sold to Sri Lanka between 2000 and 2006.

A group of the former UkrADF's MiG-23UBs of the 894th IAP, including 61 and 63 Blue, stored at Lviv. *Sergey Popsuevich*

This MiG-27M with construction number 83712538777 was one of ten ex-642nd IAP examples sold to Sri Lanka between 2000 and 2006. This example received the serial number CF735 and then SFS-5302. After retirement of the Sri Lankan MiG-27Ms and the sole MiG-23UB in 2014, this aircraft was put on display in the SLAF museum in Colombo. *Sergey Popsuevich*

MiG-25P Fleet (1992–2004): The Interceptor Foxbats

While it was planned to equip the Soviet Union PVO regiments on Ukrainian territory with the MiG-31 by 1996, this never happened and the MiG-25PDS remained in service with the 146th GIAP and 933rd IAP when they were inherited by the Ukrainian Air Defence Forces on 12 January 1992. The Ukrainian Air Defence Force inherited 80 MiG-25PDSs and MiG-25PUs in service with the PVO's 49th Air Defence Corps. They served until 1996, when the units were disbanded due to financial problems. Some of the MiG-25s, especially various modifications of the reconnaissance MiG-25RB, were kept in reserve at the Zaporozhye Aircraft Repair Plant until 2004 with the hope of selling them to foreign countries, but this never happened and most had been scrapped by 2015.

In service with the UkrADF

After Ukraine's independence, just one of the ten regiments of the Soviet Air Force equipped with reconnaissance variants of MiG-25s and two of the 14 regiments of the PVO equipped with interceptor variants of MiG-25s remained on Ukrainian territory. The PVO units in question were 146th GIAP at Vasilkov and 933rd IAP at Dnepropetrovsk, which respectively had 41 and 40 MiG-25s in service according to the CFE treaty records in 1990. Information released by the Ukrainian MoD in 1992 stated that 80 MiG-25PDS and MiG-25PU had been inherited from these two PVO units in 1992.

In 1992, the Ukrainian Air Defence Forces (PVO) was formed and inherited all Soviet Union PVO units on Ukrainian territory, including the 8th Independent Air Defence Army (8th OAPVO) and its 146th GIAP at Vasilkov and 933rd IAP at Dnepropetrovsk, both under the 49th Air Defence Corps. On 12 January 1992, most of the 933rd IAP took the oath of allegiance to the people of Ukraine, despite being forgotten by the country's leaders and government as they had not received their salaries regularly or salaries received were less than those given to airport cleaners! Despite this, combat readiness of 146th GIAP and 933rd IAP was still high and this was demonstrated during a tactical air defence exercise in November 1992, during which pilots even launched live R-40 and R-60 AAMs against target drones.

On 1 June 1993, 146th GIAP, which defended Kiev, was disbanded and all its airworthy MiG-25PDS/Pus, which had been overhauled by Dnepropetrovsk Aircraft Overhaul Plant in the early 1990s, were absorbed by the 933rd IAP. Their bort numbers were blue, while 933rd IAP's MiG-25 numbers were red. After this transfer some of the MiG-25s bort numbers were repainted red, while most of them, including 36 Blue, remained unchanged.

In 1994, because of the limited amount of kerosene available for the flights of 933rd IAP's MiG-25s and the subsequent decline in the flying hours of the pilots, a new technique was developed to compensate by using six L-39Cs, 16, 42, 47, 65, 68 and 103 Red. This process worked until 1996, when the unit was disbanded. Even in 1996, MiG-25 activities were limited to just combat duties and exercises because the Ukraine could not afford their operational costs.

02 Red, a MiG-25PDS of the 146 GIAP, can be seen departing Vasilkov AB during a joint exercise with the 933rd IAP on 6 October 1993. *Sergey Popsuevich*

UkrADF MiG-25PDS 48 Red belonging to the 933rd IAP during an exercise at Vasilkov AB on 5 October 1993. This aircraft belonged to the 1st Aviation Squadron of the regiment, which was the operator of eight aircraft, while the 2nd and 3rd Squadrons had seven and nine aircraft respectively. *Sergey Popsuevich*

Retirement

In early 1996, at the beginning of the withdrawal of the MiG-25 in Ukraine, it was planned to transfer 933rd IAP to the Ukrainian Air Force's 5th Air Army headquartered at Odessa, but this never happened. Later, in early May 1996, when representatives of the Ukrainian Army Command visited Dnepropetrovsk, personnel from 933rd IAP asked them for a better residential campus for themselves and their families. A few days later, on 15 May, a directive was received by regiment for its disbandment!

On 18 October 1996, 933rd IAP personnel said goodbye to their battle flag and the regiment was totally disbanded. A few days later, its L-39Cs were transferred to the Ukrainian Air Force and served in other units, while the MiG-25s remained at Dnepropetrovsk with an unclear fate. The 1st Aviation Squadron of the regiment had eight MiG-25s in service, the 2nd Squadron had seven, while the 3rd Squadron had nine MiG-25s, although most of them had reached their MTBO before disbandment.

These 24 MiG-25s, together with other stored MiG-25s, were transferred to the Zaporozhye Aircraft

A MiG-25PDS of the 933rd IAP during a joint exercise with 146th GIAP at Vasilkov AB on 13 October 1993. *Sergey Popsuevich*

18 Red (c/n 84046147), a MiG-25PDS, during an air defence exercise at Vasilkov AB in October 1993. *Sergey Popsuevich*

68 Red (c/n 84045211) during an air defence exercise at Vasilkov in October 1993. *Sergey Popsuevich*

36 Blue was a MiG-25PDS of the 146th GIAP but it was transferred to the 933rd IAP in 1993 and remained in its service until December 1996. Here it can be seen at Dnepropetrovsk in 1994. *Sergey Popsuevich*

Line-up of the MiG-25PDS and MiG-25PUs in service with the 933rd IAP at Dnepropetrovsk in 1994. *Sergey Popsuevich*

Repair Plant facility, where the UkrAF's 48th OGRAP MiG-25s had been stored as well. The last fully mission-capable MiG-25PDS of the unit were 09 Red, 18 Red, 69 Red, 77 Red and 78 Red. They left Dnepropetrovsk in December 1996, and were kept in reserve condition at the MiGremont facility for a couple of years.

The personnel of the regiment under the command of A. N. Tarantsev found different fates; only a few of them decided to continue serving the PVO and UkrAF and were subsequently transferred to other bases all over Ukraine. Most decided to remain in Dnepropetrovsk and served in the military units of the Air Force Air Defence Forces around the region after passing various training courses. Some of them even ended up working on the offices of the Ukrainian Ministry of Interior in the city. Some other

MiG-25PDS 28 Red of the 933rd IAP at Zaporozhye ARZ in 1995. It has nine red stars on its left engine air intake, indicating the successful launch of nine air-to-air missiles during the various exercises in which this aircraft participated. *Sergey Popsuevich*

001, the ex-933rd IAP MiG-25PU with c/n 3698, was the test bed for the MiG-25 modernisation project at the Zaporozhye ARZ in 2001. *Zaporozhye Aircraft Repair Plant archive*

officers and non-commissioned officers chose retirement and signed letters of their dismissal.

Zaporozhye State Repair Plant MiGremont was established at the 713th Aircraft Repair Plant in accordance with a Resolution of the Cabinet of Ministers of Ukraine dated 25 January 1996. Zaporozhye State Aircraft Repair Plant's MiGremont name was changed to 'Zaporozhye State Aircraft Repair Plant MiGremont' on 16 February 1998. For years MiGremont attempted to sell the stored and reserved PVO and Air Force MiG-25s.

In the early 2000s, MiGremont unveiled a programme for the lifetime extension and modernisation of the MiG-25, during which ex-933rd IAP MiG-25PU c/n 36981, which had been kept operational for training MiG-25 test pilots at the MiGremont facility, was used as a test bed and the first prototype of the modernisation programme. It received the bort number 001 Blue and was painted in a special colour scheme after modernisation work that included the installation of various avionic systems, including a new digital ADI with the ability to be used as a radar scope, etc. The technology demonstrator or prototype regularly participated in air shows in Ukraine until 2005, when it was finally put in storage.

According to global images, in 2004 65 MiG-25s were stored at Zaporozhye. This was reduced to 51 and 35 in 2005 and 2010 respectively. On 6 August 2008, when the Ukrainian Cabinet of Ministers approved the sale of various aircraft on the inventory of the Ukrainian Ministry of Defence, 33 MiG-25s were put up for sale to any third parties, consisting of a 1976-made MiG-25P in the National Aviation University, Kiev; 16 MiG-25PDSs manufactured between 1977 and 1978, seven MiG-25PUs manufactured between 1977 and 1985, as well as eight MiG-25RBs (various modifications) manufactured between 1974 and 1981 and a single MiG-25RU manufactured in 1977, all stored at MiGremont.

On 13 October 2011, just 19 MiG-25s remained there while the rest had been scrapped. Since 2013 only eight MiG-25s have been left in storage in Zaporozhye. Among the former 933rd IAP's MiG-25s, only 17 Red and 98 Red were lucky enough to be restored and they were put on display in the city of Energodar's Victory Park and one of Zaporozhye's parks respectively. Among the former UkrAF's MiG-25s, just two MiG-25RBS survived, 17 Red in the air force museum in Vinnitsa and 75 Blue in the aviation museum in Lugansk.

36 Blue, the ex-146th GIAP MiG-25PDS that served with 933rd IAP between 1993 and 1996, being disassembled at Zaporozhye ARZ in 2003. *Zaporozhye Aircraft Repair Plant archive*

A group of former UkrADF MiG-25PDSs and UkrAF MiG-25RBS/Ts stored at Zaporozhye ARZ in the 2000s. The nearest aircraft is ex-933rd IAP MiG-25PDS 89 Red. *Sergey Popsuevich*

Two MiG-25PUs of the 933rd IAP participated in a joint air defence exercise with the 92nd IAP at Vasilkov in October 1993. They were 55 and 65 Red; both still had the red star on their vertical stabilisers. *Sergey Popsuevich*

MiG-29 Fleet (1992–today): The Frontliners

The Ukrainian Air Force is now the world's third largest operator of the MiG-29 (after India and Russia) with 117 examples in service with its 40th BrTA, 114th BrTA, and 204th BrTA under the organisation of Air Command Centre, West and South respectively, while at least ten more examples were under overhaul and modernisation in Lviv State Aircraft Overhaul Centre in 2019. Among the Ukrainian MiG-29s, 60 were operational in 2019. These MiG-29s, together with Su-25 ground-attack aircraft, played a key role in close air support, strike and CAP missions during the war in Donbass in 2014.

In Ukrainian Air Force service

In 1988, Soviet Air, Air Defence and Naval Aviation had 300 MiG-29s in service; this number had increased to 815 in 1990. After the collapse of the Soviet Union, almost two-thirds of the entire fleet of Soviet Air Force MiG-29s were outside Russia, consisting of around 20 Fulcrum-As, 30 Fulcrum-Bs and 300 Fulcrum-Cs in service with ten fighter regiments based in Europe! This was because the MiG-29's role a front-line fighter interceptor meant it was mostly stationed in Europe to oppose NATO's fourth-generation fighter aircraft. Many of the fighter regiments were in the republics, which were separated from the Russian mainland and which became independent states.

After Ukraine's independence, four Soviet Air Force regiments with 220 MiG-29s (220 according to the Ukrainian Ministry of Defence and 216 according to unofficial sources) and two Soviet Navy fighter regiments with 35 MiG-29s were inherited by the Ukrainian Air Force and Navy Aviation respectively. Among these, the presence of 155 Fulcrum-Cs (NATO Code name) or izdeliye 9-13 was reported.

Among the inherited USSR air force units was the 85th Guards Fighter Aviation Regiment, which was the first unit of the Soviet Air Force to be equipped with MiG-29s and which therefore had some Izdeliye 9-12 examples in service. Beginning in March 1986, early-variant MiG-29s were delivered to the 85th GVIAP as replacements for its ageing MiG-23Ms. The unit was based in Merseburg, Germany, until 1 July 1991, but soon, due to the withdrawal of Soviet forces from Germany after the country's reunification, they were sent to Falkenberg AB and then totally withdrew from Germany on 15 July 1991. The unit moved to Starokostiantyniv, Khmelnitskiy Oblast, where it was inherited by the Ukrainian Air Force. Up to 1990, the unit had received 33 MiG-29s, but this number had declined to 26 when it was disbanded on 17 March 1992.

On the same date, another MiG-29 unit of the newly formed Ukrainian Air Force was disbanded, which was 642nd GVAPIB in Voznesensk. Most of its Izdeliye 9-13 (manufactured by Lukhovitsy factory before 1989) and MiG-29UBs similar to the 85th GVIAP examples were stored at Aircraft Repair Plant 117 in Lviv in good condition as reserve aircraft, unlike some of 85th GVIAP's Izdeliye 9-12 examples, which had been stored in Starokostiantyniv because they had less value.

The 642nd GVAPIB was mostly a ground-attack regiment and therefore its MiG-29s were painted in a four-tone camouflage scheme (green, light green, cinnamon and sand). After the disbandment of the 642nd GVAPIB, four of its MiG-29s found operational use in service with the Ukrainian Navy Aviation's 100th IAP (the former Soviet Navy 100th KIAP), namely 46, 47, 48 and 49 Blue, but their bort numbers were changed to 26, 27, 28 and 29 Yellow in Navy service. It is believed that some of its MiG-29s were also absorbed by the 161st IAP of the Ukrainian Navy, and also the 86th GVIAP in Moldova.

An ex-642nd GVAPIB MiG-29 Izdeliye 9-13, 43 Blue, in the early 1990s. After the disbandment of the regiment on 17 March 1992, this aircraft was sent to the 562nd ARZ at Odessa. It is still in storage there. *Sergey Popsuevich*

45 Blue was another MiG-29 Izdeliye 9-13 of the 642nd GVAPIB. After the disbandment of the regiment on 17 March 1992, the aircraft was sent to the 117th ARZ at Lviv. Due to the fact that the aircraft had logged its first flight on 30 December 1988 and had six years left until its MTBO, it was kept airworthy and even took part in the Gostomel air show at Kiev in 1993, when it was pictured here. 45 Blue (c/n 2960725858) was one of the examples sold to Azerbaijan. It was overhauled and modernised (navigation system) between 2002 and August 2003 and sold in 2006. It entered service at the AzAF's Nasosnaya air base as 04 Blue. *Sergey Popsuevich*

08 Blue (c/n 2960721909) was another MiG-29 Izdeliye 9-13 of the 642nd GVAPIB that was sent to the 117th ARZ at Lviv after disbandment of the regiment on 17 March 1992. It was overhauled in August 2003 but was never sold. *Sergey Popsuevich*

Former 643rd GVAPIB's 08 Blue, is still in storage at the Lviv State Aircraft Repair Plant today. *LDARZ via the airforce.ru*

с 23 по 29 сентября 1991 г.

Четверг 26	Пятница 27	Суббота 28	Примечание (итоги) 29
На Миг-29 - 7 ед.	средства не будут	97 - замена дв. - нет ИАМ 90 ч 96 - замена КСА 5-7 ч. 92 - нет ИАМ 90 ч 94 - нет ИАМ 90 ч 95 - трещина в ВЗ 91 - АРВ 96 - будет. 77 - замена дв. 76 - вибр. дв 72 - вибр. дв	

№ п. п.	Указания подчиненным командирам (начальникам)	Срок исполнения

After the disbandment of the 642nd GVAPIB on 17 March 1992, one of the four MiG-29UBs of the regiment, 61 Blue (c/n N50903011844), ended up at the 562nd ARZ at Odessa. Then it was used by the flight test centre at Kirovskoye for tourist flights. Late in 2001, it was sent to the 117th ARZ at Lviv to be overhauled and slightly upgraded for sale. In 2006, it was sold to Azerbaijan and received the bort number 10 Blue in service with the 411th Fighter Aviation Squadron of its air force at Nasosnaya AB near Baku. *Heinz Berger*

This document shows the status of the MiG-29s in service with the 100th IAP of the Soviet Navy (AV-MF) in September 1991 before Ukraine's independence. From nine serviceable MiG-29s of the unit only two were airworthy, while the rest were grounded due to various reasons including an engine change requirement for 97 Blue and a structural crack in the air intake of 95 Blue. *www.airforce.ru*

After Ukraine's independence, while the 100th KIAP (subordinated to the 1063rd Centre for Combat Employment Shipborne Aviation) had been left without an aircraft carrier and any plans for the future, half of its personnel, led by the unit commander Timor Apakidze, left the unit and went to Russia to join the Russian Navy Northern Fleet, while the other half, led by the unit's acting commander, O. Artemyev, took the oath and joined the Ukrainian Navy on 5 June 1992. Because of the lack of an aircraft carrier, the unit was renamed the 100th IAP and became a part of the State Aviation Research and Test Centre of Ukraine.

The first batch of four MiG-29 9-12s of the 100th KIAP had been delivered on 16 November 1985, which

A group of MiG-29 9-12s of the 100 IAP that were transferred to Lviv to be stored at the LDARZ facility, seen on 11 July 1995. The nearest aircraft is 09 Yellow. *Sergey Popsuevich*

were 91 to 94 Blue, of which 93 Blue was lost during an accident on 22 September 1988. Also in 1988, the unit received four MiG-29 9-13s, 95 to 98 Blue, and MiG-29UB 99 Blue, which was lost during an accident on 1 August 1990. In 1989 and 1990, the unit was reinforced with a MiG-29 9-12, five MiG-29 9-13s and two MiG-29UBs. In 1991, six to eight of the unit's MiG-29s were in service with the 1st Aviation Squadron of the 3rd Scientific-Experimental Department of the 929th State Flight Test Centre of the Defence Ministry of the USSR, together with four Su-27s, four L-39Cs and four Su-25UTGs, in Kirovskoye.

In September 1991, before Ukraine's independence, out of the unit's nine serviceable MiG-29s, only two were airworthy while the rest were grounded due to various reasons, including an engine change requirement for 97 Blue and a structural crack in the air intake of 95 Blue. This situation was improved after Ukraine's independence for a short period when the unit was reinforced by several MiG-29s of the disbanded 85th GVIAP of the UkrAF, and soon after the withdrawal of Su-27s from 100th IAP service, ten MiG-29 9-12s and a pair of MiG-29UBs were assigned to the unit's 1st AE, while ten MiG-29 9-13s and two MiG-29UBs were in service with its 2nd AE. Later, four of the former 642nd GVAPIB's MiG-29s were added to the unit inventory, which led to the formation of its 3rd AE.

Despite having 28 MiG-29s in service by the end of 1993, the 100th IAP had a short life after

A group of ex-100th IAP MiG-29 9-12s stored at the Lviv State Aircraft Overhaul Centre on 15 February 2007. The nearest aircraft is 94 Blue which later became 02 Yellow. *Sergey Popsuevich*

Ukraine's independence and was disbanded in 1996 when it was under the command of Col A. Telyehin. At the time, most of the unit's MiG-29 9-13s were not operational. Gradually, within two years of its disbandment, all its MiG-29s excepting two out of the total of eight MiG-29s in service with the Kirovskoye State flight test centre (GLIC or GLITS), were transferred to the 62nd IAP as replacements for its Su-15s, which were withdrawn from service in 1996. One of the last MiG-29s of the disbanded unit, which was flown to Belbek in 1998, was the ex-642nd GVAPIB's 26 Yellow.

In Ukrainian Air Defence Force service

As a result of the disbandment of the Ukrainian Air Defence Force's 146th GVIAP on 1 June 1993, the 92nd IAP was moved from Mukachevo to Vasilkov to guard Kiev. The relocation of the unit was completed between 21 July and 1 August 1993 following a Ukrainian Ministry of Defence directive issued on 6 January 1993. At the time, the unit had fewer than ten airworthy 9-12s, including seven with bort numbers 01, 06, 14, 15, 22, 36 and 40 White, which were former 145th IAP examples but had recently been overhauled by LDARZ because most of the 92nd IAP's 9-12 examples had reached their MTBO earlier in 1992. The MiG-29 Fulcrum-As, or Izdeliye 9-12s, looked different to the unit's other machines due to the leopard artwork on their nose sections, which had been added after their participation in an air exercise at Mary gunnery range in 1991. These included 01, 03, 09, 11, 14, 15, 22, 23, and 26 White.

From 1 January 1994, the 92nd IAP became part of the Ukrainian Air Defence Force's 49th Air Defence Corps to fulfil the needs of a fighter unit to protect the Kiev area, and on 1 October 1994 the regiment received its military unit number, A1789. The unit was assigned to the 6th Guards Fighter Aviation Division of the Ukrainian Air Force's 14th Air Corps on 1 June 1996, and several months later, following a reorganisation of the Ukrainian Armed Forces, the 92nd IAP was re-formed as the 207th air base. However, just a year later, on 1 December 1997, the air base was reorganised as the 8th Fighter Regiment.

In 1998, MiG-29 9-12 37 White (c/n 0390502556) from the unit's 2nd AE received the honorary name 'Leonid Bykov' after a Ukrainian actor, film director and script writer, with special markings of carefully painted musical notes on its front fuselage. The aircraft, which had been overhauled in 1993, reached its MTBO and was grounded in early 2000. Between 2003 and 2007, MiG-29 9-13 70 White (c/n 2960728174) was also christened 'Leonid Bykov'.

On 30 December 1999, following an order of the Ukrainian Ministry of Defence, the 92nd IAP became part of the UkrADF for the second time. Almost a year later, on 1 December 2000, the unit

01 White was one of ten MiG-29 Izdeliye 9-12s of the 92nd IAP. Almost all the regiment's MiG-29s had leopard artwork painted on their nose sections. 01 White is seen at Vasilkov AB during a joint exercise with the UkrADF's 933rd IAP on 14 October 1993. *Sergey Popsuevich*

was re-formed as the 40th Fighter Wing, as the main part of the Ukrainian Air Defence Force Tactical Aviation. On 30 October 2002, following issuance of the Ukrainian Ministry of Defence directive No. D-115/1/07, the 40th Fighter Wing was renamed the 40th Fighter Wing Order of Red Banner.

In 2000, the unit had received 12 L-39Cs after the decline of its MiG-29 flights due to financial problems. In October 2001, the 40th Fighter Wing took part in a large UkrAF air exercise, during which ten of its MiG-29s were forward deployed to Kirov. They practised air-to-air and air-to-ground tactics at Opuk gunnery range in the Crimean peninsula, during which they launched live AAMs against VR-3 target drones for first time since Ukraine's independence.

In 2001, the last of the unit's MiG-29 9-12s was withdrawn from service just a year after two MiG-29 9-12s of 92nd IAP had been delivered to the National Aviation University to be used for educational purposes. In 2003, one of the 9-12s, 06 White (c/n 2960505534), was delivered to Ukraine's National Aviation Museum at Zhuliany airport near Kiev.

According to a directive of the UkrADF's chief issued on 25 June 2004, the 40th Fighter Wing was renamed 40th Order of Red Banner Fighter Aviation Brigade. A few months later, on 1 December 2004, the UkrADF was merged with the UkrAF, and the 40th Fighter Aviation Brigade became part of the air force's Air Command Centre. Three years later, following the Ukrainian Ministry of Defence directive No. D-322/1/03 issued on 18 April 2007, the unit was renamed the 40th Order of Red Banner Tactical Aviation Brigade.

A joint exercise of the 92nd and 933rd IAP showing MiG-29 9-12 48 White and MiG-29 9-13 40 White during take-off from Vasilkov AB in October 1993. *Sergey Popsuevich*

92 IAP MiG-29 9-12 48 White had special artwork on its nose that had been painted in 1991 when it was serving with the 145th IAP at Ivano-Frankivsk. *Sergey Popsuevich*

06 White was one of the oldest MiG-29s that served in the Ukrainian Air Defence Force and then the Air Force. This Izdeliye 9-12 aircraft had ventral fins. It is seen during a joint air defence exercise with the 933rd IAP at Vasilkov AB. *Sergey Popsuevich*

22 White, a MiG-29 Izdeliye 9-12, armed with a pair of R-27R semi-active, radar-guided, air-to-air missiles and a pair of R-73 IR-guided air-to-air missiles. It was one of the early production MiG-29s equipped with ventral fins. *Sergey Popsuevich*

MiG-29 Izdeliye 9-13 07 White of the 92nd IAP, with another Izdeliye 9-13, 35 White and Izdeliye 9-51 (MiG-29UB) 50 White in the background, at Vasilkov AB in 1993. *Sergey Popsuevich*

In addition to the leopard artwork, some of the 92nd IAP MiG-29s also received sharkmouth markings in 1991 when they were in service with the 145th IAP at Ivano-Frankivsk, including MiG-29 Izdeliye 9-13 25 White. *Sergey Popsuevich*

MiG-29 Izdeliye 9-13 37 White of the 92nd IAP had distinctive falcon artwork on its nose, seen in June 1994. *Sergey Popsuevich*

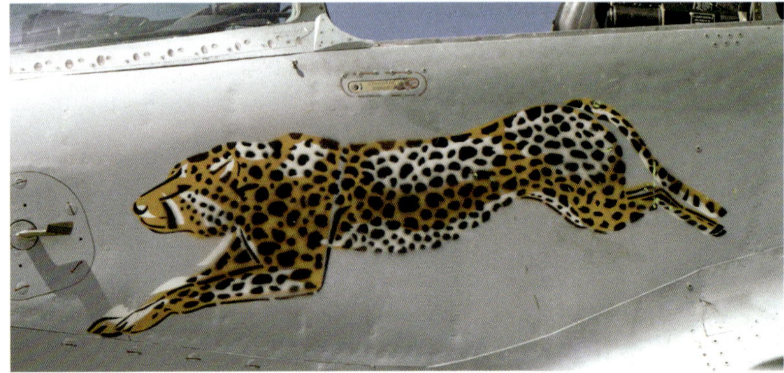

90 White, was one of the 92nd IAP MiG-29UBs. Most of the units MiG-29s had this leopard artwork painted on their nose sections when they were in service with the 145th IAP in 1991. *Sergey Popsuevich*

Fulcrums for sale

After the disbandment of the UkrAF's MiG-29 units, a huge quantity of them were stored in various places, including the LARZ and OARZ, where they were put up for sale by Ukrspetsexport. In the years between 1998 and 2014, the UkrAF succeeded in selling only 22 MiG-29s, including at least five MiG-29UBs, mostly of the former 85th IAP and 642nd IAP stored in the LARZ, to Algeria, Azerbaijan, Chad and Sudan.

The first sale took place in 1998 when a contract was finalised with the Algerian ministry of defence for delivery of five ex-UkrAF's MiG-29s to Algeria after their subsequent overhaul at the LARZ. The MiG-29s, all of which were Izdeliye 9-13s, were delivered to the Algerian Air Force in 2000 and they, together with 25 ex-Belarusian Air Force MiG-29 9-13s and six ex-RuAF MiG-29UBs, entered into service with 193e Escadron de Chasse, 3e Escadre de Défense Aérienne, at Bou Sfer.

The next MiG-29 sale to a foreign country took place in 2005, when Azerbaijan was unable to procure MiG-29s directly from Russia and instead bought 12 MiG-29 9-13s and two MiG-29UBs in a $20 million USD deal with Ukraine, a contract that also included spare parts supply and pilot training. The MiG-29s were slightly modernised by the LARZ, during which their NAVAIDS were replaced with new systems and their radars were supposed to be upgraded to give an increased range of target detection and tracking. However, later leaked information showed that no changes had been made to their radars after the alleged upgrade. This slight upgrade programme initiated the UkrAF's MiG-29MU1 modernisation scheme.

Nine of the MiG-29 9-13s sold to Azerbaijan, which later received the bort numbers 01, 02, 03, 04, 05, 09, 11, 12 and 14 Blue, were former 642nd IAP's machines 16, 21, 48, 45, 32, 09, 10, 47 and 77 Blue, while the remaining three single-seat MiG-29s, which became 06, 07, and 08 Blue, were former 85th IAP machines. In addition, two MiG-29UBs, with Azeri bort numbers 10 and 20 Blue, were the former 642nd IAP's 61 and 63 Blue.

On 29 January 2008, due to low-quality maintenance, 20 Blue, which then was in service with the Azeri Air Force's 411th IAE at Nasosnaya AB, crashed in the Caspian Sea and its pilots, Fakhraddin Asgarov and Afgan Aslanov, were killed. This resulted in the attrition delivery of a third MiG-29UB, 54 White (c/n N50903010194), this time from the UkrAF's 40th BrTA, after modernisation of its NAVAIDS in LDARZ in August 2011. The aircraft had been sold to Azerbaijan for $0.471 million USD in 2009. Today, only four MiG-29 9-13s and two MiG-29UBs of the Azeri Air Force are operational after they received lifetime extensions in 2015.

In 2011, a MiG-29UB was sold to Sudan for $2.75 million USD and it was delivered with the serial number 603 (c/n N80003001048) after overhaul at LDARZ in 2014. Also in 2013, a contract was finalised between Ukrspetsexport and the Chadian Ministry of Defence, and subsequently three MiG-29s, including one MiG-29UB, were sold to Chad with a price of $3 million to $4 million per aircraft, including $1 million restoration and overhaul costs. The first was serialled TT-OAP and its overhaul and slight modernisation was completed by LARZ prior to handover to the Chadian Air Force in April 2014.

As well as the MiG-29 sales for military use, three MiG-29UBs were sold to private companies in the US.

A view of the Lviv State Aircraft Repair Plant. On 15 February 2007, these ex-642nd GVAPIB's MiG-29 Izdeliye 9-13s were being overhauled to be delivered to the Azerbaijani Air Force. *Sergey Popsuevich*

The first was an ex-642nd IAP machine (c/n N50903014896) in February 2006. The aircraft received the civil registration N29UB and the bort number 64 Red in the US. It now belongs to the Historic Flight Foundation, based at Paine Field in Mukilteo. The second and third UkrAF MiG-29UBs to be sold on the civilian market were c/ns N80003003127 and N80003001024, which ended up with Air USA, at the Quincy Regional Airport in Quincy, Illinois, and they received the civil registrations N129XX and N229XX respectively. They are in use for contract training and flight testing.

Guardians of Kiev, the 40th BrTA

The 40th BrTA's history goes back to the 92nd IAP in the Second World War era. On 5 April 1940, the 92nd IAP was formed under the Kiev Special Military District of the Red Army. On 16 May 1940, this regiment was merged with the 38th Aviation Brigade of the Kiev Special Army District. By this time, 57 I-153 and I-16 aircraft, together with a total of 284 flight and ground crew, were in service with the regiment. On 16 June, the name 92nd Fighter Regiment was officially assigned to the unit. Its aircraft and airmen were immediately forward deployed and took part in numerous operations during the war, and had a significant role during the battle to defend Kiev. The 92nd Fighter Regiment was deployed to 47 different places until the end of the war, and its pilots scored 286 aerial victories against Luftwaffe aircraft during 11,285 sorties.

As well as the I-153 and I-16 aircraft in service with the regiment during its establishment in 1940, other warplanes such as the LaGG-3, Yak-7, MiG-3, La-5, La-7 were operated during the war. During the immediate post-war era, the regiment operated piston-engine fighter planes such as the La-7, La-9, La-11, and trainers such as the Po-2 and Yak-11. In 1951 it entered the jet era with the arrival of the first MiG-15s, while three years later the unit converted to the MiG-17. The Yak-12 entered service as a liaison aircraft in 1961 and a year later the MiG-21 interceptor replaced the MiG-17. Following the MiG-21, came the Yak-25 in 1963 and the MiG-23 in 1974.

Following amendments made by President Poroshenko to the No. 1173 directive issued on 30 October 2000, the 40th Order of Red Banner Tactical Aviation Brigade was renamed the 40th Tactical Aviation Brigade on 18 November 2015. As one of two Tactical Aviation Brigades of the UkrAF's

40th BrTA had two of its MiG-29s specially painted in these colours in the occasion of the 60th anniversary of its foundation in April 2000. They were MiG-29 9-13 35 White (c/n 2960728171) and MiG-29UB 50 White. *Sergey Popsuevich*

MiG-29 9-13 70 White (c/n 2960728174) was named after the Ukrainian artist and songwriter Leonid Bykov between 2003 and 2007. It was later sent to Lviv and after being overhauled, it became 19 Blue and was delivered to the 204th BrTA in 2010. It is seen at Vasilkov in 2007. *Sergey Popsuevich*

Air Command Centre, 40th BrTA has not only responsibility to protect Kiev, but also the 40th BrTA is one of two BrTAs of the UkrAF whose fighters play a key role in establishing an air defence barrier in the east of the country following the war in Donbass. Since the beginning of the war in Donbass, at least four of the unit's MiG-29s have always been forward deployed to Dnepropetrovsk to stand as 24/7 QRA fighter-interceptors.

According to information gathered through the CFE treaty data exchange, 92nd IAP had 39 MiG-29 Izdelie 9-12s and Izdelie 9-13s as well as five MiG-29UBs at Mukachevo in November 1990. In the service of the UkrAF, the 92nd IAP was redesignated as the 270th Air Base on 1 December 1996, the 8th IAP on 1 December 1997 and the 40th Order of Red Banner Tactical Aviation Brigade on 1 December 2000.

In August 2008, following the downsizing of the regular force and budget cut programmes, Prime Minister Victor Timoshenko commanded the air force to withdraw 63 of the old Fulcrum As (Izdeliye 9-12) and UBs, among these were ten 40th

MiG-29 9-13s 19 and 21 White of the 40th BrTA, both armed with a pair of R-27ER semi-active radar-guided air-to-air missiles and four R-73 IR-guided air-to-air missiles, flying in formation over Vasilkov AB on 28 March 2008. *Sergey Popsuevich*

A pair of 40th BrTA MiG-29s flying on the wing of 15th TrAB An-26 07 Yellow b/n during a rehearsal over Belya Tserkva on 7 August 2008 prior to the Independence Day parade of that year. The nearest aircraft is MiG-29UB 50 White, while the further is MiG-29 9-13 32 Blue. *Sergey Popsuevich*

BrTA Fulcrum As, including 01, 06, 14, 15, 22 and 36 White and one Fulcrum UB. Most of them had already been grounded due to a lack of spare parts, or maintenance needs such as an airframe overhaul. Only four of them, for example shark-mouthed MiG-29 22 White (c/n: 2960512147), were airworthy after 2005.

The main task of the 40th BrTA is to provide point air defence for the vital infrastructure of Kiev and the east of the country, including nuclear reactors such as Kharkiv TEC-5 (a combined heat and power plant at Podvorky village in the Dergachy District of Kharkiv Oblast). For these important tasks both ground and flight crew combat readiness is kept near to standard levels by means of routine training flights and annual exercises during their deployment to Belbek or Ivano-Frankovsk. Also, as well as the use of the L-39 for maintaining flight

MiG-29MU1 prototype 03 Blue (c/n 2960729011) was formerly in service with the 204th BrTA before being modernised and delivered to the 40th BrTA. It is seen at Belbek AB during the exercise Adequate Response 2011 on 19 September 2011. *Alexander Golz*

skills and the readiness of the pilots to a standard level since the early 2000s, on 17 November 2009 the 40th BrTA received a KTS-21M MiG-29 flight simulator valued at 28 million UAH (£2.15 million).

On 19 and 20 September 2011, MiG-29MU1s 03 and 29 Blue and MiG-29UB 91 Blue from 40th BrTA took part in the research command post exercise Adequate Response 2011 at Belbek AB. Both MiG-29MU1 prototypes were evaluated during the exercise. The upgraded fire control system of the aircraft with extended target detection range was tested on the last day, when its pilot launched an R-27R semi-active AAM against a target drone.

The 40th BrTA was one of four Tactical Aviation Brigades of the UkrAF tasked to protect Ukraine's airspace during the Euro 2012 football tournament. Due to this, a delegation led by the Defence Attaché to the German Embassy, Col Gerhard Hahnerom, visited the 40th BrTA at Vasilkov to discuss the capability and readiness of the unit for Euro 2012.

On 24 April 2012, an anti-terrorism exercise was carried out at Vasilkov air base, during which the 40th BrTA had a key role. During the training, two MiG-29s (19 and 20 White), each armed with two R-27Rs and four R-73s, were used to simulate the interception of a hijacked An-26. An important element of this training was the raising of both the pilots' and ground crews' readiness for the provision of security in Ukraine's airspace during the upcoming Euro 2012. Earlier in January 2012, the 40th BrTA had logged 100 training sorties with MiG-29 9-13s, MiG-29UBs and L-39s to prepare for the exercise. During Euro 2012, which was held between 8 June and 1 July, two MiG-29s and ten crew members were ready 24/7 for QRA.

In February 2014, before the beginning of the Crimea crisis, the 40th BrTA had only six airworthy MiG-29MU1/Cs, 02, 03, 11, 29, 33 Blue and 04 White, together with three airworthy MiG-29UBs 91 Blue and 90 and 99 White, out of its total of 20 MiG-29 9-13s and eight MiG-29UBs. Due to the war, eight MiG-29s in reserve condition were brought back to flying condition after unit-level repair, while more MiG-29s were delivered after overhaul and full restoration at LDARZ, which resulted in the unit having 20 single-seat and four twin-seat examples airworthy in 2019.

The MiG-29MU1s that 40th BrTA received from LDARZ after the war were mostly former 3rd IAP aircraft that had been in storage for years. The last three delivered to the Brigade when this book was completed were 07, 08 and 09 White. Nos 07 and 08 White were delivered during an official ceremony attended by the Ukrainian President Petro Proshonko on 1 August 2018, while 09 White was delivered in 2019. No. 09 White was named 'Leonid Bykov' after the Ukrainian actor, film director and screenwriter on the occasion of the 90th anniversary of his birth on 12 December 2018.

MiG-29 9-13 10 White (c/n 2960721109) was restored by the 40th BrTA in 2014. It still has its high-quality paint scheme applied by the factory in the late 1980s when it was delivered to the 145th IAP and the leopard artwork applied on its nose section when it was at Ivano-Frankivsk in 1991. ***Alexander Golz***

MiG-29UB 91 Blue (c/n N50903017533) is one of four MiG-29s of the 40th BrTA that are painted in Ukrainian Falcons aerobatic demonstration team colours. *Alexander Golz*

40th BrTA MiG-29MU1 11 Blue and MiG-29 35 White during a formation take-off from Vasilkov on 20 April 2016. *Alexander Golz*

MiG-29MU1 9-13 04 White (c/n 2960729036) was delivered to the 40th BrTA after modernisation by the LDARZ in 2013. It was one of nine airworthy MiG-29s of the Brigade in January 2014. When this book was completed, the unit had a total of 24 airworthy and operational MiG-29s. *Alexander Golz*

11 Blue, the second test bed of the MiG-29MU1 modernisation programme, is in service with the 40th BrTA. Here it is armed with a pair of R-27Ers and four R-73s standing QRA at Vasilkov. *Ukrainian Air Force via airforce.ru*

MiG-29MU1 02 Blue of the114th BrTA during a joint exercise with the 40th and 831st BrTAs at Ivano-Frankivsk Air Base in September 2013. This aircraft was later delivered to the 40th BrTA and was lost in the war on 7 August 2014. *Alexander Golz*

40th BrTA MiG-29s in 2019

Model	Construction Number	Bort Number	Colour Scheme	Former Unit	Last Overhaul/ Restoration	Current Fate	Note
MiG-29MU1	2960729011	03 Blue	Ukrainian Falcons	204th BrTA	2011	Operation Ready	
MiG-29MU1	2960728505	11 Blue	Blue/Grey	204th BrTA	2010	Operation Ready	
MiG-29MU1	2960731233	29 Blue	Blue/Grey	204th BrTA	2009	Operation Ready	
MiG-29 9-13	2960731638	31 Blue	Ukrainian Falcons	9th BrTA	2014	Operation Ready	Restored by 40th BrTA engineers
MiG-29 9-13	2960731642	33 Blue	Ukrainian Falcons	9th BrTA	2009	Operation Ready	
MiG-29MU1	?	01 White	Digital	3rd IAP	2016	Operation Ready	
MiG-29MU1	2960731641	02 White	Digital	3rd IAP	2016	Operation Ready	
MiG-29MU1	2960729036	04 White	Digital	114th BrTA	2013	Operation Ready	
MiG-29MU1	?	05 White	Digital	-	2017	Operation Ready	
MiG-29MU1	2960731232	06 White	Digital	3rd IAP	2017	Operation Ready	Delivery on 14/10/2017
MiG-29MU1	2960731222	07 White	Digital	3rd IAP	2018	Operation Ready	Delivery on 01/8/2018
MiG-29MU1	2960731239	08 White	Digital	3rd IAP	2018	Operation Ready	Delivery on 01/8/2018
MiG-29MU1	?	09 White	Digital	3rd IAP	2018	Operation Ready	
MiG-29 9-13	2960721109	10 White	Green/Grey	-	-	Operation Ready	Restored by 40th BrTA engineers
MiG-29 9-13	?	18 White	Blue/Grey	-	2014	Operation Ready	Restored by 40th BrTA engineers
MiG-29 9-13	2960729355	19 White	Blue/Grey	114th BrTA	2014	Operation Ready	Restored by 40th BrTA engineers
MiG-29 9-13	?	20 White	Blue/Grey	-	2014	Operation Ready	Restored by 40th BrTA engineers
MiG-29 9-13	2960728507	21 White	Blue/Grey	204th BrTA	2015	Operation Ready	Restored by 40th BrTA engineers
MiG-29 9-13	?	26 White	Overall Grey	-	-	Stored	
MiG-29 9-13	?	30 White	Blue/Grey	-	-	Stored	

MiG-29UB of the 40th BrTA during a joint air defence exercise with the 114th and 831st BrTAs at Ivano-Frankivsk AB in September 2013. *Alexander Golz*

Model	Construction Number	Bort Number	Colour Scheme	Former Unit	Last Overhaul/ Restoration	Current Fate	Note
MiG-29 9-13	?	32 White	Blue/Grey	-	-	Stored	
MiG-29 9-13	?	33 White	Digital	-	2015	Operation Ready	
MiG-29 9-13	2960728171	35 White	Blue/Grey	-	2015	Operation Ready	Restored by 40th BrTA engineers
MiG-29 9-13	?	42 White	Overall Grey	-	-	Stored	
MiG-29 9-13	2960721096	94 White	Green/Grey	-	-	Grounded	
MiG-29UB	N50903017533	91 Blue	Ukrainian Falcons	-	2010	Operation Ready	
MiG-29UB	N50903003127	37 White	Green/Grey	-	-	Stored	Wfu in 2008.
MiG-29UB	?	50 White	Blue/Grey	114th BrTA	2014	Operation Ready	Restored by 40th BrTA engineers
MiG-29UB	?	51 White	Blue/Grey	-	-	Stored	
MiG-29UB	?	52 White	Green/Grey	-	-	Stored	
MiG-29UB	N50903024156	90 White	Digital	3rd IAP	2012	Operation Ready	Former 111 Blue
MiG-29UB	?	91 White	Blue/Grey	-	2007	Grounded	
MiG-29UB	N50903024178	99 White	Digital	9th BrTA	2013	Operation Ready	Former 52 Blue
MiG-29 9-12	2960515291	01 White	Green/Grey	92nd IAP	-	Stored	Wfu in 2008
MiG-29 9-12	2960515107	11 White	Green/Grey	145th IAP	-	Stored	Wfu in 2008
MiG-29 9-12	0390502260	14 White	Green/Grey	-	-	Stored	Wfu in 2008
MiG-29 9-12	2960505532	15 White	Green/Grey	-	-	Stored	Wfu in 2008
MiG-29 9-12	2960512147	22 White	Green/Grey	-	-	Stored	Wfu in 2008
MiG-29 9-12	2960515111	23 White	Blue/Grey	145th IAP	-	Stored	Wfu in 2008
MiG-29 9-12	2960512111	26 White	Green/Grey	-	-	Stored	Wfu in 2008
MiG-29 9-12	0390502556	36 White	Green/Grey	-	-	Stored	Wfu in 2008
MiG-29 9-12	2960507678	47 White	Green/Grey	-	-	Stored	Wfu in 2008
MiG-29 9-12	?	89 White	Green/Grey	-	-	Stored	Wfu in 2008
MiG-29 9-12	2960512114	09 Green	Green/Grey	-	-	Stored	Wfu in 2008
MiG-29 9-12	2960512118	49 Green	Green/Grey	-	-	Stored	Wfu in 2008

Defender of the West, 114th BrTA

The history of 114th BrTA goes back to 24 September 1940, when a decree was issued for the creation of the 159th Fighter Aviation Regiment. I-16s and MiG-3s entered service in September and December 1940 respectively, and these were later replaced by the P-40 Tomahawk and P-40 Kittyhawk in 1941 and 1942 respectively. During the Second World War, two more fighter types, the La-5 and Yak-9, entered service in December 1942 and April 1945 respectively.

The unit logged 9,000 sorties and its fighters and pilots shot down 387 enemy aircraft during the war, including those piloted by German aces. Because of the courage and bravery of nine pilots of the regiment, it was awarded the title 'Hero of Soviet Union' by the regimental commander, Col Peter Pokryshev. The regiment was also awarded the honorary name 'Tallinskiy' because of its key role in the battle for the capital of Estonia, and also given the Order of the Red Banner because of the important missions carried out by its pilots who fought in the battle for the liberation of the Baltic states.

MiG-29 63 White during an engine change at Ivano-Frankivsk Air Base in 1988. This aircraft was most likely in service with the 114th IAP. *Sergey Popsuevich*

After the war, the Yak-9s were replaced by MiG-15s in 1951, and they were superseded by MiG-17s in 1955, and its successor, the MiG-21, in 1965. In 1978, the MiG-23M entered service with the regiment, which by then had been renamed the 114th IAP, which had been subordinated to the 131st Mixed Aviation Division since 21 July 1972.

After Ukraine's independence, the 114th Tallinskiy Red Banner Fighter Aviation Regiment personnel swore allegiance to Ukraine on 6 January 1992. Soon the regiment's name was simplified to the 114th IAP and it was subordinated to the 14th Air Army's 4th IAD, becoming the largest MiG-29 operator regiment of the force after it absorbed those of the disbanded 145th IAP. It was re-formed as the 114th Tallinskiy Red Banner Fighter Aviation Regiment and six years later, on 5 June 2009, it was reorganised as the 114th Tallinskiy Red Banner Tactical Aviation Brigade. Its name was simplified to the 114th Tactical Aviation Brigade again on 18 November 2015.

On 1 December 2005, the unit became the first fighter aviation brigade of the new air defence system of Ukraine. Soon the unit became a constant participant in the UkrAF's exercises and its aircraft were being forward deployed from Ivano-Frankovsk to various air bases such as Belbek, Limanskoye, Lutsk and Ozernoe.

In September 2006, for first time since 1993, the 114th BrTA joined in an exercise, named Clear Sky 2006, which took place with the participation of the

On 19 and 20 September 2011, the 114th BrTA participated in the Research Command Post exercise Adequate Response 2011, during which two MiG-29 9-13s of the unit, 54 and 55 White, were forward deployed to Belbek AB. 53 White is seen here armed with a pair of R-73 missiles during the first day of the exercise. *Alexander Golz*

MiG-29 9-13 55 White of the 114th BrTA during Adequate Response 2011, in which one of its R-73 missiles was launched on 19 September 2011. Its brake parachute is deployed after landing. *Alexander Golz*

President of Ukraine – the Supreme Commander-in-Chief of the Armed Forces – and demonstrated a satisfactory level of readiness of the air force units to work jointly with the other armed services to fulfil their operational missions. Both in terms of the number and the scope of the practical tasks performed by participating units, this exercise was the largest the air force has staged in several years.

The exercise was held on six firing ranges throughout the territory of Ukraine and on a Russian range, Telemba, where the firing of long- and medium-range anti-aircraft artillery systems, S-200 and S-300, was executed beside a live AAM launch by MiG-29 pilots against Tu-141 and Tu-143 target drones flying 17–24km away. The redeployment of 26 aircraft to the operational airfield, including 14 MiG-29s and Su-27s, six Su-24Ms, two Su-25s, and two Su-24MRs, was practised. In the course of the exercise a total of 129 sorties were flown and 46 training and 96 tactical bombing runs were completed.

In April 2007, the 114th BrTA pilots participated in a gunnery exercise, during which, for the first time in 17 years, they practised bombing and rocketry against ground targets. Three years later, on 23 and 25 November 2010, the 114th BrTA's MiG-29s and their pilots again took part in a large UkrAF exercise, during which three of the unit's MiG-29 9-13s and a MiG-29UB participated in 13 sorties on the first day and night.

On 19 and 20 September 2011, the 114th BrTA took part in the research command post exercise Adequate Response 2011, during which two MiG-29 9-13s, 54 White and 55 White, were forward deployed to Belbek AB, where they, together with three MiG-29s of 40th BrTA – including a MiG-29UB – and five MiG-29s of 204th BrTA, and another MiG-29UB, participated in a series of air-to-air and air-to-ground missions. These included a live R-73 AAM launch against target drones performed by two 114th BrTA pilots. The purpose of the exercise

114th BrTA MiG-29 9-13 55 White departing Belbek to aunch a R-73 IR-guided missile during the second day of exercise Adequate Response 2011. *Alexander Golz*

was to review the level of combat training of the forces, as well as to research the framework of a prospective model of the Ukrainian Armed Forces. Updated techniques and tactics of command and control systems of the armed forces and their future organisational structure were tested.

During Euro 2012, the 114th BrTA was on alert 24/7, with other units, to provide security over Ukraine's airspace. Before that, the unit's personnel had been prepared for their mission via participation in several air exercises and joint training missions. These included the Ukrainian–American–Polish exercise Safe Skies 2011, which was held between 18 and 27 November 2011. During the exercise, the 114th BrTA carried out several CAP missions in the airspace under the supervision of the Air Command West. In order to fulfil the needs of the 114th BrTA for an adequate number of fully mission-capable MiG-29s, two restored and overhauled MiG-29s were handed over to the unit by the Lviv State Aircraft Repair Plant in March 2012. The cost of their overhaul and restoration was 8 million UAH per airframe (equivalent to £630,000).

In February 2014, before the start of the Crimea crisis, the 114th BrTA had only seven airworthy MiG-29 9-13s, 05, 09, 54 and 55 Blue, and 07, 53 and 54 White, together with two airworthy MiG-29UBs, 10 and 20 White, out of its total of 38 MiG-29 9-13s and six MiG-29UBs, while 17 of its 21 MiG-29 9-12s were stored on the main apron and several hardened aircraft shelters (HAS) at Ivano-Frankovsk in 2016. Due to the war, five MiG-29 9-13s in reserve were brought back to flying condition after unit-level repair, while eight more MiG-29 9-13s were delivered after overhaul and full restoration at LDARZ, which resulted in the unit having 18 single-seat and three twin-seat examples airworthy in 2019

114th BrTA MiG-29s in 2019

Model	Construction Number	Bort Number	Colour Scheme	Former Unit	Last Overhaul/ Restoration	Current Fate	Note
MiG-29 9-13	2960728125	05 Blue	Ukrainian Falcons	204th BrTA	2011	Operation Ready	
MiG-29 9-13	2960721110	09 Blue	Ukrainian Falcons	204th BrTA	2009	Operation Ready	Former 09 White
MiG-29 9-13	?	24 Blue	Three tone-Blue	9th BrTA	-	Stored	
MiG-29 9-13	?	32 Blue	Blue/Grey	-	2014	Operation Ready	Restored by 114th BrTA engineers
MiG-29 9-13	2960731234	54 Blue	Ukrainian Falcons	-	2013	Operation Ready	Former 54 White
MiG-29 9-13	?	55 Blue	Ukrainian Falcons	-	2012	Operation Ready	
MiG-29 9-13	?	03 White	Green/Grey	-	-	Stored	
MiG-29 9-13	2960728501	04 White	Green/Grey	-	2014	Operation Ready	Restored by 114th BrTA engineers
MiG-29 9-13	?	06 White	Green/Grey	-	-	Stored	
MiG-29 9-13	2960721108	07 White	Green/Grey	40th BrTA	2012	Operation Ready	
MiG-29 9-13	?	08 White	Green/Grey	-	-	Stored	
MiG-29 9-13	?	09 White	Green/Grey	-	2014	Operation Ready	Restored by 114th BrTA engineers
MiG-29 9-13	?	12 White	Green/Grey	-	-	Stored	
MiG-29 9-13	?	14 White	Green/Grey	-	-	Stored	
MiG-29 9-13	?	25 White	Green/Grey			Operation Ready	Restored by 114th BrTA engineers
MiG-29 9-13	?	27 White	Green/Grey	40th BrTA	-	Stored	
MiG-29 9-13	?	34 White	Green/Grey	-	-	Stored	
MiG-29 9-13	?	36 White	Green/Grey	-	-	Stored	
MiG-29 9-13	?	38 White	Green/Grey	-	-	Stored	
MiG-29 9-13	?	41 White	Green/Grey	-	-	Stored	
MiG-29 9-13	?	45 White	Green/Grey	-	-	Stored	
MiG-29 9-13	?	46 White	Green/Grey	-	-	Stored	
MiG-29 9-13	?	49 White	Green/Grey	-	-	Stored	

Model	Construction Number	Bort Number	Colour Scheme	Former Unit	Last Overhaul/ Restoration	Current Fate	Note
MiG-29 9-13	?	51 White	Green/Grey	-	-	Stored	
MiG-29 9-13	2960731255	54 White	Green/Grey	-	2008	Stored	
MiG-29 9-13	2960731235	55 White	Three-tone Blue	-	2008	Stored	
MiG-29 9-13	2960721111	56 White	Blue/Grey	-	-	Stored	
MiG-29 9-13	?	57 White	Digital	-	2014	Operation Ready	
MiG-29 9-13	2960731240	58 White	Green/Grey	-	2014	Operation Ready	Restored by 114th BrTA engineers
MiG-29 9-13	2960729002	71 White	Digital	-	2015	Operation Ready	
MiG-29 9-13	2960729005	72 White	Digital	-	2016	Operation Ready	
MiG-29 9-13	2960729012	73 White	Digital	-	2015	Operation Ready	
MiG-29 9-13	2960729023	75 White	Digital	-	2015	Operation Ready	
MiG-29 9-13	2960729034	76 White	Digital	-	2015	Operation Ready	
MiG-29 9-13	2960729037	77 White	Digital	-	2017	Operation Ready	
MiG-29 9-13	2960729048	78 White	Digital	-	2017	Operation Ready	
MiG-29 9-13	2960735321	68 YELLOW	Green/Grey	100th IAP	-	Stored	
MiG-29 9-13	2960731267	79 YELLOW	Green/Grey	100th IAP	-	Stored	
MiG-29UB	?	83 Blue	Blue/Grey	-	-	Stored	
MiG-29UB	N50903023325	10 White	Digital	204th BrTA	2013	Operation Ready	
MiG-29UB	N50903021006	20 White	Blue/Grey	-	2009	Operation Ready	
MiG-29UB	N50903024147	30 White	Digital	-	2012	Operation Ready	
MiG-29UB	?	40 White	Green/Grey	204th BrTA	-	Stored	
MiG-29UB	N50303025670	-	Green/Grey	-	-	Stored	
MiG-29 9-12	2960510189	01 White	Grey	-	-	Stored	Wfu in 2008
MiG-29 9-12	2960518085	02 White	Grey	-	-	Stored	Wfu in 2008
MiG-29 9-12	2960518478	08 White	Green/Grey	-	-	Stored	Wfu in 2008
MiG-29 9-12	?	09 White	Green/Grey	-	-	Stored	Wfu in 2008
MiG-29 9-12	2960515122	11 White	Green/Grey	-	-	Stored	Wfu in 2008
MiG-29 9-12	2960518474	15 White	Green/Grey	-	-	Stored	Wfu in 2008
MiG-29 9-12	?	16 White	Green/Grey	-	-	Stored	Wfu in 2008
MiG-29 9-12	2960518066	17 White	Green/Grey	100th IAP	-	Stored	Wfu in 2008
MiG-29 9-12	2960515120	23 White	Green/Grey	-	-	Stored	Wfu in 2008
MiG-29 9-12	2960518763	24 White	Green/Grey	-	-	Stored	Wfu in 2008
MiG-29 9-12	2960520160	28 White	Green/Grey	-	-	Stored	Wfu in 2008
MiG-29 9-12	0390505042	29 White	Green/Grey	-	-	Stored	Wfu in 2008
MiG-29 9-12	2960505544	32 White	Green/Grey	-	-	Stored	Wfu in 2008
MiG-29 9-12	2960515119	35 White	Green/Grey	-	-	Stored	Wfu in 2008
MiG-29 9-12	2960515124	42 White	Green/Grey	-	-	Stored	Wfu in 2008
MiG-29 9-12	2960505530	47 White	Green/Grey	-	-	Stored	Wfu in 2008
MiG-29 9-12	2960510189	01 Yellow	Grey	100th IAP	-	Stored	Wfu in 2008
MiG-29 9-12	2960515121	46 Yellow	Grey	100th IAP	-	Stored	Wfu in 2008
MiG-29 9-12	2960512146	61 Yellow	Grey	100th IAP	-	Stored	Wfu in 2008
MiG-29 9-12	2960512141	62 Yellow	Grey	100th IAP	-	Stored	Wfu in 2008
MiG-29 9-12	0390504005	63 Yellow	Grey	100th IAP	-	Stored	Wfu in 2008

The 40th, 114th and 831st Tactical Aviation Brigades participated in an exercise from Ivano-Frankivsk AB in September 2013. 53 White, a MiG-29MU1 of the 114th BrTA, is parked next to L-39M1 122 Blue of the 114th BrTA on 24 September. *Alexander Golz*

40th BrTA MiG-29UB 90 White and 114th BrTA MiG-29MU1 02 Blue during a formation take-off from Ivano-Frankivsk AB. *Alexander Golz*

A pair of 114th BrTA MiG-29MU1s, 02 BLUE and 53 White carrying out a formation take-off from Ivano-Frankivsk on 25 September 2013. 02 Blue was later transferred to the 40th BrTA. They were both lost in the war, on 7 and 17 August 2014. *Alexander Golz*

73 White is one of the seven MiG-29 9-13s that the LDARZ overhauled for the 114th BrTA after the war. This was delivered to the Brigade in 2015 and can be seen in one of the hardened aircraft shelters at Ivano-Frankivsk AB. *Ukrainian Air Force via airforce.ru*

Top is the MiG-29UB 30 White of the 114th BrTA, above left, which was delivered to the Brigade after its overhaul was completed by LDARZ in 2013, while to the left is MiG-29 9-13 75 White. This was one of eight MiG-29 9-13s that the regiment received from LDARZ after their overhauls between 2014 and 2019. *Ukrainian Air Force via airforce.ru*

Knights of Crimea, 204th BrTA

Belbek air base is located in the Sevastopol region of the Crimea peninsula, which was previously in the southern territory of Ukraine and now is annexed to Russia after the Crimea crisis of 2014. This air base is located on the shores of the Black Sea and due to this strategic location it was one of the important Soviet Navy Black Sea Fleet Air Arm Headquarters during the Soviet era.

The name Belbek derives from the River Belbek, south-west of the Crimea peninsula. During the Second World War, this airport was established with a grass-covered runway and was used for Soviet Army and Navy military transport flights. After the war and during the Cold War in the 1970s, a concrete runway was constructed and Soviet Air Defence Force's Su-15s were forward deployed there several times. Finally, in 1986, the first regiment of Su-15TM aircraft was stationed there, later replaced by Su-27s.

In early 1991, the 8th Air Defence Army based a regiment at Belbek. It was the 62nd Fighter Aviation Regiment with 39 Su-15TMs. In late 1991, an Su-15TM replacement programme with the Su-27 was started but never completed due to the break-up of the Soviet Union, and subsequently the unit had mainly Su-15s in its service when it was inherited by the Ukrainian Air Defence Force in 1992. On 1 July 1998 the unit was reorganised as the 62nd Fighter Aviation Brigade, but became a regiment again on 1 July 2001. Two years later the unit was reorganised as the 204th Fighter Aviation Brigade and became part of the Task Force Crimea of Ukrainian Air Command South. Finally, it was reorganised into the 204th Tactical Aviation Brigade on 24 December 2007.

As explained earlier, the 204th BrTA received its first MiG-29s in 1996 as replacements for its Su-15TMs, which had been retired that year. In total, 26 MiG-29s of the Ukrainian Navy Aviation's 100th IAP were transferred to the 62nd IAP between 1996 and 1998. Also in 2004, after dissolution of the 161st IAP at Limanskoye, some of its MiG-29s were absorbed by the unit in Belbek. In addition to these ex-Navy MiG-29s, the 204th BrTA also took delivery of 12 MiG-29 9-13s and a MiG-29UB of the 9th BrTA that had been based in Ozernoye, Zhitomir between 2007 and 2011. The 9th BrTA was previously designated as the 894th IAP of the Soviet Air Defence Force's 28th Air Defence Corps. The unit was the last operator of the MiG-23MLD in the UkrADF, up to August 2001. In that time the unit was disbanded but quickly re-formed as the 9th BrTA, this time with Su-27s of the 62nd Fighter Aviation Regiment, although it had been planned for it to be equipped with MiG-29s since 1999. But finally, in December 2004, the unit did receive the MiG-29.

In total, 14 MiG-29 9-13s and three MiG-29UBs of the former 161st IAP based at Limanskoye entered service with the 9th BrTA. The single-seaters were 20, 21, 22, 24, 25, 26, 27, 28, 29, 30, 31, 32, 33, and 38 Blue, while the two-seaters were 50, 51, 52 Blue, all later painted in the specific three- and four-tone blue camouflage of the Ozernoye (Lakeside) with stencils and markings painted on them, similar to the Su-27s of the Brigade.

Starting in 2007 with 28 Blue, the Ozernoye-based Fulcrums were mostly transferred to the 204th

Due to the fact that the majority of MiG-29s in the service with the Soviet Navy's 100th IAP were not operational in 1991, several MiG-29 9-13s of the disbanded 85th GVIAP were absorbed by the regiment as replacements in January 1992. Later, following the disbandment of the 100th IAP, two of these ex-85th GVIAP MiG-29 9-13s, 04 and 36 Blue entered service with the 62nd IAP. They are seen at Belbek AB in the early 2000s. *Ukrainian Air Force via airforce.ru*

Just a few months before the disbandment of the 100th IAP, some of its MiG-29s were painted in these 'Crimean Sun' colours in 1997. Several of them, including 27 Blue and 29 White, ended up in the 62nd IAP. 27 Blue is here stored at Belbek in 2012. *Alexander Golz*

9th BrTA MiG-29 9-13 28 Blue prior to the disbandment of its Brigade at Ozernoye Air Base. 28 Blue and ten other MiG-29s of the 9th BrTA ended up with the 204th BrTA after the disbandment of their regiment. 28 Blue is the airworthy and still in these colours. It is seen at Ozernoye Air Base. *Ukrainian Air Force via airforce.ru*

BrTA. In December 2008, MiG-29 operations ended and two more MiG-29 9-13s, 21 and 29 Blue, were handed over to the 204th BrTA. At least six more MiG-29 9-13s and a MiG-29UB (50 Blue) were transferred to Belbek in 2009. Another MiG-29, 51 Blue, was transferred to the 40th BrTA in 2008 and it then moved to the 204th BrTA as 85 Blue after overhaul at LARZ in 2012. The third MiG-29UB, 52 Blue, was delivered to the 114th BrTA in 2009, but later went to LARZ for overhaul in 2013 and was delivered to 40th BrTA as 99 White in January 2014. As well as these ex-Ukrainian Navy's MiG-29s of the 204th BrTA, the unit also received eight more MiG-29s from other units between 2004 and 2014.

MiG-29UB 50 Blue of the 9th BrTA before disbandment of the Brigade. *Ukrainian Air Force via airforce.ru*

The most active MiG-29 operator

The 204th BrTA, as part of the Crimean Task Force of UkrAF's Air Command South, had been known as the most active MiG-29 unit of UkrAF before the Crimea crisis in 2014. The unit's aircrews and ground crews played a crucial role, not only in the air force but also in the navy exercises in the south and in multiple cases in the centre of Ukraine.

In 2008, the Ukrainian Armed Forces held Exercise Naval Knot 2008, the most important exercise of that year. During the Command Post exercise the readiness of the military units for performing their designated tasks, coordination of command and control and the interaction of the naval forces and other armed forces was evaluated.

During the exercise, the 204th BrTA which had inherited the primary role of the Ukrainian Navy Aviation Fighter Aviation Regiments was tasked with defending the Ukrainian Navy ships and the Marine Forces on the shoreline against the imaginary enemy, the role of which was being played by other air force aircraft as well as VR-3 drones. The exercise was held between 25 and 27 September. One of the MiG-29 9-13s of the 204th TAB piloted by 1st Class Col Sergei Afanasiev, commander of the Brigade, shot down a Tu-143/VR-3 aerial target drone three minutes after its launch from Chauda over the Black Sea.

In 2009, another Command Post exercise was held in the Crimea Peninsula, this time on 2 June. During the exercise, which took place in the Donuzlav lake district, 12 aircraft and helicopters alongside 65 armoured and non-armoured vehicles and 700 personnel took part. 204th BrTA with its MiG-29s again had been tasked to carry out CAP missions for the protection of the naval units on the ground.

In first two weeks of September 2010, a group of technicians and engineers from Lviv State Aircraft Repair Plant visited Belbek AB and inspected its MiG-29s. During that time, several MiG-29s were cleared as FMC aircraft after maintenance work to take part in the Strategic Command Post Exercise Cooperation 2010. The exercise was carried out in five military training areas of the Land Forces, in the State Scientific Test Centre Chauda of the Air Force and in ten training ranges of the Naval Forces. During Cooperation 2010, which was held between 6 September and 4 October 2010, UkrAF took part with 18 aircraft comprising MiG-29s of 204th BrTA and Su-27s of 831st BrTA.

Ready for Euro 2012

The 204th BrTA, similar to other Tactical Aviation Brigades of the UkrAF, was involved in the provision of security of Ukraine's airspace during Euro 2012, and for this important mission the unit and its personnel were heavily prepared by participating in exercises in 2011 and 2012. One of the exercises was the American-Polish-Ukrainian exercise Safe Sky 2011, which was held at Mirgorod AB between 18 and 27 July 2011. It was held to increase the expertise and practical skills of the flying crews and command and control points during fulfilling and training tasks before Euro 2012.

During the exercise 204th TAB pilots simulated some aerial combat engagements with USAF Alabama Air National Guard F-16Cs, and also escorted and intercepted transport aircraft which

Before participation in Naval Knot 2008 in September 2008, the 204th TAB demonstrated its quick reaction alert capability on 20 August 2008. 06 Blue, a MiG-29 9-13 of the regiment armed with a pair of R-27Rs and four R-73s, is on QRA that day. *Sergey Popsuevich*

MiG-29 20 Blue (c/n 2960728165) was among the 204th BrTA aircraft that participated in Exercise Safe Sky2011 from Mirgorod AB in July 2011. The Su-27s of the 831st BrTA can be seen in the background during the exercise. *Alexander Golz*

were playing the role of hijacked aircraft. Five of 204th BrTA's MiG-29s consisted of four MiG-29 9-13s with 18, 19, 20, and 40 BLUE together with a single MiG-29UB with 84 BLUE which were deployed to Mirgorod Air Base to participate in simulated air-to-air engagement with a USAF F-16C and a F-16D together with eight Su-27s of the 831st BrTA.

In 2011, the 204th BrTA participated in a second exercise, the research command post exercise Adequate Response 2011. It was held at Belbek AB, Sevastopol, on 19 and 20 September, during which five of the participating MiG-29s were from 204th BrTA. These comprised four MiG-29 9-13s, 18, 19, 20 and 40 Blue, and MiG-29UB 84 Blue, which was flown by Lt Col Vladimir Kravchenko and Col Nahima Musaev.

On 19 September, three R-73 AAMs were launched by pilots of the 204th BrTA's 18, 20, and 40 Blue against three VR-2 drones, while on the

The 204th BrTA participated in a second exercise which was the Research Command Post exercise Adequate Response 2011, with five MiG-29s including this 9-13 example 18 Blue, armed with a pair of R-27ER semi-active radar-guided air-to-air missiles. *Alexander Golz*

MiG-29 9-13 29 Blue from the 204th BrTA, armed with R-27ER missiles taxiing at Belbek AB during Adequate Response 2011. *Alexander Golz*

84 Blue, a MiG-29UB of the 204th BrTA, armed with four flash bombs taxiing prior its departure from Belbek AB during Exercise Perspective 2012 on 25 September 2012. These flash bombs were being used as auditory targets for R-73s launched by MiG-29s and Su-27s during the exercise. *Alexander Golz*

204th BrTA MiG-29 9-13 07 Blue and armed with R-73 IR-guided air-to-air missiles during Perspective 2012 on 25 September 2012. *Alexander Golz*

same day an R-27R was launched from 29 Blue (from 40th BrTA) against a VR-3 and two more R-73s were launched by pilots of two 114th BrTA MiG-29 9-13s, 54 and 55 White. One more R-27R was launched by 18 Blue against another VR-3 on 20 September. During the exercise, while seven MiG-29 pilots practised live AAM firing, two other MiG-29 pilots regained lost flying skills and another pilot completed his type transition to the MiG-29.

On 27 February 2012, the new Ukrainian Minister of Defence, Dmytro Salamatin, visited Belbek AB and inspected and examined the readiness of the unit to provide security under the supervision of Air Command South during Euro 2012. During the tournament in June, the 204th BrTA, commanded by Col Alexei Marchenko, carried out many sorties, including routine training flights and in some cases combat air patrol (during some of the most important matches). Eleven pilots of the 204th TAB, commanded by Col Marchenko, flying three of their best MiG-29 9-13s, 18 Blue (c/n 2960728133), 19 Blue (c/n 2960728174) and 20 Blue (c/n 2960728165), plus two forward deployed MiG-29MU1s (they were originally 40th BrTA aircraft), protected Ukrainian airspace from Belbek during the weeks of the competition. Four fully mission-capable MiG-29 9-13s, each armed with two R-27Rs and four R-73 AAMs, were always ready on QRA. On 9 July, soon after the tournament ended, the Ukrainian MoD visited the 204th BrTA's air base at Sevastopol to examine the unit's combat readiness.

In 2012 the 204th BrTA also took part in exercises including Perspective 2012, held between 18 September and 4 October 2012. Seven of the unit's aircraft, MiG-29 9-13s 01, 07, 18, 19 and 20 Blue and MiG-29UBs 20 White and 84 Blue, participated. In total 20 aircraft, including five An-26s from Vinnitsa and a Mi-8, took part, and 17 of the 36 participating fighter pilots practised a live AAM launch against target drones and gun firing against flying targets during air-to-air missions.

Joint combat maritime exercise in 2013

In February 2013, a joint exercise by the Ukraine Navy and Air Forces was conducted in Sevastopol state. Various aircraft types from four air force bases, consisting of Su-25s of Kulbakino, Su-24MRs of Starokostiantinov, Su-27s of Mirhorod and An-26s of 456th Transport Aviation Brigade, were deployed to Belbek, together with the 204th BrTA's L-39M1s and MiG-29s.

On 19 February, a day after the deployment of the participants in Sevastopol, the exercise began and pilots practised air-to-ground and air combat tactics over the Baltic while the Ukraine Navy corvette *Ternopil* was at sea.

One Su-25 (05 Blue) and an Su-25UBM1 (62 Blue) of 299th BrTA were used to carry out several simulated anti-ship sorties against the corvette, while a MiG-29 9-13 (40 Blue) and a MiG-29UB (85 Blue) of 204th TAB provided top cover for them. A pair of Su-27s (Su-27UB 69 Blue and Su-27 53 Blue) from Ozerne AB were tasked with protecting *Ternopil* against Su-25 attacks and also confronting their escorting MiG-29s.

Digital-camouflaged MiG-29UB 85 White of the 204th BrTA during a formation take-off with MiG-29 9-13 07 Blue from Belbek AB on 19 December 2012. ***Sergey Popsuevich***

Guardians of the Sochi Winter Olympics

For the Sochi Winter Olympics in February 2014, the UkrAF was tasked with providing air defence for the Crimea peninsula and also the eastern shores of the Black Sea. On 3 February, 204th BrTA's pilot Alexander Pokryshkin and his MiG-29 9-13 (01 Blue) practised a conventional enemy interception, and 831st BrTA Su-27UB 74 Blue, piloted by 2nd Class Lt Col Yuri Cholovsky, played the role of the aggressor aircraft.

On 6 February, Myhorod forward deployed two Su-27s (46 and 100 Blue) and two Su-27UBs (69 and 74 Blue) to Belbek to reinforce the QRA capability of the air base as part of the programme for providing security within Ukraine's airspace during the games.

On 7 February, a passenger on a Turkish Airline aircraft hijacked the aircraft en route from Kharkiv to Istanbul, and an Su-27 (100 Blue) piloted by Lt Col Alexander Oksanchenko was scrambled from Belbek to intercept it. The Su-27, armed with five R-27Rs and four R-73 air-to-air missiles, escorted the aircraft as far as Turkey's airspace and then TuAF F-16Cs took over until the aircraft landed safely at Istanbul airport. On 24 February, after the Olympics ended, the mission of the 831st BrTA, the unit being nicknamed 'Galati', ended at Belbek and all four forward deployed Su-27s returned to Mirgorod.

The Russian occupation

In the aftermath of the 2014 Ukrainian revolution that led to the withdrawal of the Russian-backed government of Ukraine led by President Viktor Yanukovych on 22 February 2014, the Russian President Vladimir Putin and his government saw their interests in danger in Ukraine. One of the most important of these were the Russian Navy facilities in the Crimean peninsula, which enabled the country to strongly oppose NATO forces by establishing its hegemony in the Black Sea. Subsequently, hundreds of new Russian Army personnel were deployed to Crimea to occupy the peninsula and prepare the region for a referendum on its so-called annexation to Russia.

All the Ukrainian Army, Air Force and Navy bases were soon occupied by Russian forces between 28 February and 4 March 2014. The UkrAF air bases at Belbek and Kirovskoye, which was the home of the State Flight Test Centre (GLIC), were occupied. Troops from the reconnaissance unit of the Russian Army's 7th Guards Airborne Assault Division were tasked with occupying Belbek base on 28 February.

On 4 March Russian troops fired warning shots over the heads of unarmed Ukrainian soldiers trying to return to work at Belbek. Opposing commanders defused the rising tensions at Belbek without any fighting, according to Reuters. The Ukrainian commander, Col Yuli Mamchur, had said that after hours of negotiations, the Russians agreed to joint patrols of the base, with the Ukrainians remaining unarmed. 'This of, course, isn't what we need,' he said. 'We are still awaiting better results.'

Finally, on Saturday, 22 March 2014, Russian forces in armoured personnel carriers broke onto the air base with bursts of their machine guns and stun grenades, while Ukrainian personnel were only armed with sticks. On the same day, the Russians also attacked Kirvoskoye air base and fired guns at its ground navigation systems. This took place a week after the so-called Russian referendum in Crimea for the annexation of the peninsula to its territory.

In total, 52 aircraft of the 204th BrTA, including four L-39M1s, were confiscated by the Russian occupiers at Belbek, but soon negotiations were started between the Russians and Ukrainians for transferring the captured property of the Ukrainian Armed Forces in the peninsula to Ukraine's mainland. As a result, an initial agreement was reached for the relocation of 204th BrTA and the Kirovskoye test centre property to Ukraine on 10 April.

Quickly, technicians from the 204th BrTA disassembled the first MiG-29, which was the former 9th BrTA 30 Blue. The aircraft was transferred to Kulbakino AB on 11 April. A second group of of 204th BrTA engineering technical staff headed by the Deputy Commander of the A4514 military unit then trained technical teams, who were sent to Belbek and Kirovskoye to prepare the aircraft there to be sent to the Ukrainian mainland; they later transferred

The majority of the 204th BrTA MiG-29s were stored at Belbek when the base was occupied by Russian military forces in 2014. All the stored examples were disassembled and transferred back to Ukraine's mainland in spring and summer 2014. Here they can be seen in September 2012. *Alexander Golz*

MiG-29 9-13 31 Blue of the 204th BrTA during transportation by road from Belbek to Kulbakino/ Nikolayev in spring 2014. *Ukrainian Air Force via www.airforce.ru*

one MiG-29 per day. The aircraft had their vertical and horizontal stabilisers, wings, engines, radars and radomes removed for transporting by trailer.

On 17 May, a team of the technicians from the 39th ISqTA (39th Independent Squadron of Tactical Aircraft) joined the 204th BrTA technicians in Belbek to speed up transfer of the UkrAF inventory left in Crimea to the mainland. As a result, two aircraft were disassembled and transferred per day. On 5 June, the technicians began transferring all AGE (Aircraft Ground Equipment) at Belbek to Kulbakino, and on 6 June, one of the 204th BrTA's L-39M1s, 101 Blue, was transferred to Kulbakino.

After transferring 39 MiG-29s and a L-39M1 of the 204th BrTA to Kulbakino AB, the agreement between Ukraine and the Russian Federation for relocating the remaining 11 aircraft, which consisted of L-39M1s 102, 103, and 104 Blue bort numbers as well as MiG-29UBs 84 and 85 Blue and MiG-29 9-13s 01, 07, 18, 19, 20, 22, and 40 Blue, was suspended. These were the only airworthy 204th BrTA aircraft and the Russians did not let the Ukrainians recover them because of the ongoing war in the Donbass region.

New life for the 204th BrTA

Before the Crimea crisis, the last previous activity of the 204th BrTA were the missions to provide security within Ukrainian airspace during the Winter Olympics at Sochi between 7 and 23 February 2014. Before that, the first training of the unit that year had been on 17 January, during which MiG-29UB 85 Blue and L-39M1 104 Blue carried out flights at night and in adverse weather.

When Belbek AB was occupied, the 204th BrTA had 11 airworthy MiG-29s but among these MiG-29MU1 11 Blue was in service with the 40th BrTA, while MiG-29UB 10 White was with the 114th BrTA. After the Crimea crisis, it took four months until the technicians of the 204th BrTA restored one of the MiG-29s in reserve condition to fly again. This was 9-13 28 Blue (an ex-9th BrTA machine), which logged its first flight after restoration during a special ceremony at Kulbakino on 31 July 2014. On that day it was announced that the 204th BrTA would have a total of six airworthy MiG-29s by the end of 2014.

The first MiG-29UB of the 204th BrTA after reactivation at Kulbakino was 82 Blue, which was restored simultaneously with 28 Blue. In addition to these two, the 204th BrTA received three overhauled MiG-29 9-13s from LDARZ, which were 41, 43 and 46 Blue, in 2014. Of these, 41 and 46 Blue had been stored at LDARZ since 2009. Their post-overhaul and restoration FCFs were carried out at Lviv in October 2014, and they were delivered to 204th BrTA on 6 November 2014. No. 43 Blue was an ex-642nd IAP's aircraft that had been stored in Odessa for years and it is not clear if it was also delivered to the 204th BrTA on the same day as the other two were handed over, but it had entered service by the end of 2014.

In 2015 and 2016, 204th BrTA engineers restored three more MiG-29 9-13s, 10, 16 and 17 Blue. The overhaul of another of the unit's MiG-29Cs,

45 Blue, was also completed by the LDARZ and this was handed over in 2015. The LDARZ also restored MiG-29UB 86 Blue, which performed its first post-overhaul FCF in November 2014 and was then was delivered to the 204th BrTA at a formal ceremony on 5 January 2015.

In 2017, the 204th BrTA received two freshly overhauled MiG-29s from the LDARZ. They were MiG-29 9-13 46 Blue and MiG-29UB 83 Blue. In 2018 and 2019, two more overhauled MiG-29s were delivered to the Brigade, 48 and 49 Blue. In 2019, the 204th BrTA had a total of 12 airworthy MiG-29 9-13s and three MiG-29UBs. After the completion of deliveries to the 204th BrTA and the formation of its 1st Aviation Squadron, the unit will be stationed at a new base, most likely Lutsk.

204th BrTA MiG-29s in 2019

Model	Construction Number	Bort Number	Colour Scheme	Former Unit	Last Overhaul/ Restoration	Current Fate	Note
MiG-29 9-13	2960728500	01 Blue	Blue/Grey	-	2012	Captured	Stored at occupied Belbek AB
MiG-29 9-13	?	02 Blue	Blue/Grey	-	-	Stored	
MiG-29 9-13	2960710097	04 Blue	Green/Grey	85th GVIAP	-	Stored	
MiG-29 9-13	?	06 Blue	Blue/Grey	-	2014	Operation Ready	Restored by 204th BrTA engineers
MiG-29 9-13	2960728502	07 Blue	Blue/Grey	-	2011	Captured	Stored at occupied Belbek AB
MiG-29 9-13	?	09 Blue	Blue/Grey	-	-	Stored	
MiG-29 9-13	?	10 Blue	Blue/Grey	-	2016	Operation Ready	Restored by 204th BrTA engineers
MiG-29 9-13	2960729003	12 Blue	Green/Grey	-	-	Stored	
MiG-29 9-13	?	15 Blue	Green/Grey	-	-	Stored	
MiG-29 9-13	?	16 Blue	Blue/Grey	-	2015	Operation Ready	Restored by 204th BrTA engineers
MiG-29 9-13	?	17 Blue	Three-tone Blue	9th BrTA	2016	Operation Ready	Restored by 204th BrTA engineers
MiG-29 9-13	2960728133	18 Blue	Blue/Grey	-	2010	Captured	Stored at occupied Belbek AB
MiG-29 9-13	2960728174	19 Blue	Blue/Grey	-	2010	Captured	Stored at occupied Belbek AB
MiG-29 9-13	2960728165	20 Blue	Blue/Grey	9th BrTA	2009	Captured	Stored at occupied Belbek AB
MiG-29 9-13	?	21 Blue	Blue/Grey	9th BrTA	-	Stored	
MiG-29 9-13	2960728126	22 Blue	Blue/Grey	9th BrTA	2009	Captured	Stored at occupied Belbek AB
MiG-29 9-13	?	23 Blue	Green/Grey	-	-	Stored	
MiG-29 9-13	?	25 Blue	Grey	9th BrTA	-	Stored	
MiG-29 9-13	?	26 Blue	Three-tone Blue	9th BrTA	-	Stored	
MiG-29 9-13	?	27 Blue	Crimean Sun (Brown)	100th IAP	-	Stored	
MiG-29 9-13	?	27 Blue	Blue/Grey	9th BrTA	-	Stored	
MiG-29 9-13	?	28 Blue	Three-tone Blue	9th BrTA	2014	Operation Ready	Restored by 204th BrTA engineers
MiG-29 9-13	?	30 Blue	Three-tone Blue	9th BrTA	-	Stored	
MiG-29 9-13	?	31 Blue	Blue/Grey	-	-	Stored	
MiG-29 9-13	?	33 Blue	Blue/Grey	-	-	Stored	
MiG-29 9-13	?	34 Blue	Blue/Grey	-	-	Stored	
MiG-29 9-13	?	35 Blue	Blue/Grey	-	-	Stored	
MiG-29 9-13	2960723290	36 Blue	Blue/Grey	85th GVIAP	-	Stored	
MiG-29 9-13	?	37 Blue	Blue/Grey	-	-	Stored	

The 204th BrTA received seven overhauled MiG-29 9-13s from LDARZ between 2014 and 2019. Among them, 43 and 45 Blue can be seen beside R-27ER and R-73 missiles on the main apron of the Kulbakino AB in August 2016. *Ukrainian Air Force via www.airforce.ru*

Model	Construction Number	Bort Number	Colour Scheme	Former Unit	Last Overhaul/ Restoration	Current Fate	Note
MiG-29 9-13	2960515100	38 Blue	Grey	-	-	Stored	
MiG-29 9-13	2960721574	39 Blue	Blue/Grey	-	-	Stored	
MiG-29 9-13	2960731217	40 Blue	Blue/Grey	-	2009	Captured	Stored at occupied Belbek AB
MiG-29 9-13	2960721136	41 Blue	Digital	-	2014	Operation Ready	
MiG-29 9-13	?	43 Blue	Digital	-	2014	Operation Ready	
MiG-29 9-13	?	45 Blue	Digital	-	2015	Operation Ready	
MiG-29 9-13	2960714104	46 Blue	Digital	-	2014	Operation Ready	
MiG-29 9-13	?	47 Blue	Digital	-	2017	Operation Ready	
MiG-29 9-13	?	48 Blue	Digital	-	2018	Operation Ready	
MiG-29 9-13	?	49 Blue	Digital	-	2018	Operation Ready	
MiG-29 9-13	?	50 Blue	?	-	-	Stored	
MiG-29 9-13	?	61 Blue	?	-	-	Stored	
MiG-29 9-13	?	29 White	Crimean Sun	100th IAP	-	Stored	
MiG-29UB	?	80 Blue	Blue/Grey	-	-	Stored	
MiG-29UB	?	81 Blue	Green/Grey	-	-	Stored	
MiG-29UB	?	82 Blue	Blue/Grey	-	2014	Operation Ready	Restored by 204th BrTA engineers
MiG-29UB	?	83 Blue	Digital	-	2017	Operation Ready	
MiG-29UB	N50903018624	84 Blue	Blue/Grey	40th BrTA	2009	Captured	Ex-90 White. Now at Belbek
MiG-29UB	N50903024161	85 Blue	Digital	9th BrTA	2012	Captured	Ex-51 Blue. Now at Belbek
MiG-29UB	N50903018194	86 Blue	Digital	9th BrTA	2014	Operation Ready	Ex-50 Blue
MiG-29 9-12	2960515118	18 Blue	Green/Grey	-	-	Stored	Wfu in 2008
MiG-29 9-12	2960512144	19 Blue	Blue/Grey	-	-	Stored	Wfu in 2008
MiG-29 9-12	2960518099	20 Blue	Green/Grey	-	-	Stored	Wfu in 2008
MiG-29 9-12	2960515100	38 Blue	?	-	-	Stored	Wfu in 2008
MiG-29 9-12	2960515104	04 Yellow	Blue/Grey	100th IAP	-	Stored	Former 84 Blue. Wfu in 2008

The Ukrainian Falcons

As with many modern air forces around the world, the UkrAF had its own aerobatic flight demonstration team, which was once active with a pair of MiG-29s, then renamed the Ukrainian Falcons and equipped with nine MiG-29s. Later, while the country was struggling with financial problems, it was temporarily equipped with L-39Cs. The team disbanded or was dissolved several times, mainly because of safety issues after accidents involving team members.

Soon after the Act of Declaration of Independence of Ukraine was adopted by the Ukrainian parliament on 24 August 1991, a group of Ukrainians living in Canada approached the Ukrainian Ministry of Defence with a proposal for the formation of an aerobatic demonstration team in Ukraine to perform demonstrations in North America to represent the country to the world.

The idea was approved and first aerobatic demonstration pilots of the team were selected, who were Col Vladimir Kondaurova (Deputy Commander of the state centre for aviation test flights at the time); Col Mykola Koval, a test pilot; Lt Col Alexander Golovan; and Lt Col Valery Soloshenko; while the team technical support group was headed by the deputy commander of the 4th Fighter Aviation Division, Col Anatoly Suschevsky. After several weeks of training, on 8 May 1992 the pilots and their aircraft, a MiG-29 9-12 and a MiG-29UB, were loaded aboard an An-124 and left Lviv airport for Canada to perform their first aerobatic display during the 100th anniversary celebration of Ukrainian immigration to America. The An-124 landed at Namao Air Base, in Edmonton, and the MiG-29s were reassembled in a record time of just two days.

On 16 May, they flew for the first time at the same air base (Namao). The team did not have an official name but an aviation magazine named them The Tridents, after the show at London, Ontario because of the trident symbol in the UkrAF's emblem. Later the Ukrainian Tridents became the unofficial name of the team. The team performed 30 displays, during which more than 200 flights were logged in 103 hours in Canada and the USA, and its last display was on 14 September 1992 in Burlington, Vermont. The team and its aircraft flew back to Ukraine on 5 November from Bangor, Maine.

The aircrews and ground crews did their best to perform the most impressive aerobatic demonstrations in Canada and USA to demonstrate the state

28 Yellow was one of the former 100th IAP MIG-29 9-13s stored at Kirovskoye air base until spring 2014 when it and all the other stored MiG-29s were disassembled and transferred to Kulbakino/ Nikolayev by road. *Sergey Popsuevich*

A former 161st IAP MiG-29UB in service at Kirovskoye in the second half of the 1990s. It was in use for tourist flights. *Heinz Berger*

sovereignty and independence of Ukraine and promote the expansion of political and economic ties with these two countries in 1992. In the following year, it was planned to hold a similar tour in North America but due to financial problems and a lack of budget it never happened.

Col Viktor Rososhansky, who was present during most of the Tridents' displays as a member of the UkrAF delegation, had been impressed by the performance of the US Air Force Thunderbirds, US Navy Blue Angels and the Canadian Snowbirds aerobatic display teams that gave displays during the same air shows at which the Tridents appeared. This gave him an idea to create a similar team in the UkrAF, but it took three years before the Ukrainian commanders and the Ministry of Defence authorities were convinced and allocated a budget. The Ukrainian Falcons were formed at Kirvoskoye air base in October 1995.

A display by the 'Ukrainian Falcons' MiG-29 9-13s on 9 May 1997. *Sergey Popsuevich*

In 1996, the team members started training flights on L-39Cs of the 3rd IAP of the State Flight Test Centre at Kirovskoye. However, the team was re-equipped with MiG-29s that year, which led to the real establishment of the Ukrainian Falcons team. In same year, the Test Centre engineers began studying the design and development of a smoke generator system for installation on the flight demonstration team aircraft.

The team leader was Col Viktor Rososhansky, and the other pilots were Col Pavel Korolyov, Col Sergei Dudkin, Lt Col Sergei Kovolyov, Maj Vladimir Toponar and Maj Eduard Sotnikov. Soon an accident occurred during one of the training flights in which two MiG-29s piloted by S. Dudkin and P. Korolyov collided in mid-air, damaging the wing of one and vertical stabiliser of the other during barrel roll training. Both aircraft landed successfully in Kirovskoye. Despite the accident, training continued until the team was ready for shows. On 19 and 20 July 1997, the Ukrainian Falcons took part in the Royal Air Tattoo at RAF Fairford in the UK with five MiG-29 9-13s, 101, 102, 103, 106 and 108 White, as well as MiG-29UB 104 White.

On 26 March 1998, the team lost one of its pilots, Col Sergei Dudkin, who was the GLITS chief pilot and commander of the team. That day he was flying MiG-29 9-13 107 White to practise landing with a high angle of attack for the Paris air show the following year but there was just 1km visibility because of low cloud and he approached the runway with an excessive glide path. It resulted in a

UKrAF Il-76MD UR-76413 in formation with six MiG-29s of the Ukrainian Falcons aerobatic team. *Sergey Popsuevich*

Six-ship arrow formation flight of MiG-29 9-13s of the Ukrainian Falcons over Kiev on 24 August 2001. *Sergey Popsuevich*

hard landing, which cracked the fuselage. Col Dudkin ejected over the runway but due to a malfunction of the ejector mechanism he hit the ground still in the seat and was severely injured. He died of his wounds in Kirov district hospital (according to other sources, on the way to the hospital). The reason for the accident was determined to be the poor organisation of the flight without attention to the weather conditions. The head of the Kirvoskoye operations office was later discharged from office and dismissed from the Ukrainian Armed Forces.

After Col Dudkin's death, the UkrAF authorities decided to force Col Pavel Korolyov to quit the team for health reasons (possibly due to mental stress after the fatality). This caused the cancellation of the team's participation at the Paris Air Show in 1997. However, soon two new pilots joined the Falcons, Lt Col Igor Ovchinnikov and Lt Col Michail Lampik, and team flights restarted in 1998. Two years later, the team aircraft were overhauled by the LDARZ, their paint scheme was changed and their bort numbers were written in blue.

The last flight of the Falcons was logged on 5 October 2001, and in 2002 it was disbanded due to financial reasons and the inability of procuring fuel and spare parts for the team to even perform routine training. In that year Col Viktor Rososhansky, the founder and leader of the team, retired from the UkrAF. After the Falcons were disbanded, its eight MiG-29s – seven Fulcrum Cs, 101, 102, 103, 104, 105, 106 and 108 Blue, and MiG-29UB 111 Blue (formerly 104 White) were stored in Kirovskoye. Among these eight aircraft, just 111 Blue was later recovered and sent to the LDARZ for overhaul. It logged its first post-overhaul FCF on 29 November 2012, and was painted in digital camouflage and renumbered 90 White before delivery to the 40th BrTA.

Six years later, in April 2008, Ukrainian President Victor Yushchenko suggested reforming the Ukrainian Falcons. Almost a year after this announcement, three MiG-29 9-13s and a MiG-29UB of the UkrAF were painted in the Falcons' colours. Two of the Fulcrum Cs, 31 and 33 Blue, together with Fulcrum UB 91 Blue, were from 40th BrTA and were painted at Vasilkov, while the third Fulcrum C, 09 Blue, was painted in the team colours in LDARZ facility when its functional check flights were still ongoing in 2009. Later, 31 Blue was grounded and instead another 114th BrTA MiG-29, 05 Blue, was painted in the team colours after its overhaul at LDARZ in 2011 as a replacement.

Despite the announcement of the Ukrainian President in 2008, and although four MiG-29s being had been painted in Ukrainian Falcons colours, the UkrAF still was struggling with a lack of budget dedicated to the aerobatic flight demo team activities in 2011. A decision was then made to re-form the Ukrainian Falcons, this time with a cheaper option, the L-39. Subsequently five L-39Cs were allocated to this programme, two under overhaul at Odessa Aircraft Plant and three under overhaul at CHARZ. All five – 01, 03, 104, 105 and 106 Blue – were painted in the team's special blue/yellow colour schemes and handed over to the UkrAF in spring 2011. Their first performance was held at the A4465 military base at Kulbakino on 25 May 2011.

Finally, the dream came true at the end of 2011 when a budget was assigned for training the MiG-29 team pilots for several displays in 2012. For this purpose, while one more MiG-29 in team colours had been grounded (33 Blue), one more MiG-29, this time 03 Blue from the 40th BrTA, was painted in the team's scheme after overhaul and modernisation at the LDARZ, while two other MiG-29 9-13s from 114th BrTA, 54 and 55 White, also received the colours and their bort number colour was changed to blue in 2012. The team began performing aerobatic demonstrations during important ceremonies in Ukraine in that year. During one of the performances, on 27 September 2012, MiG-29UB 91 Blue together with three MiG-29 9-13s, 03, 54 and 55 Blue, flew together.

The UkrAF again was unable to get a budget for team performances in the second half of 2013, and the Ukrainian Falcons have not given any displays since 2013. The reason is not only financial problems but also the war in Donbass, which kept nearly all the UkrAF's MiG-29s in the team colour scheme busy on missions for protecting the Ukraine's eastern airspace. Because they are FMC aircraft, they were used in many CAP sorties over the war zones. Also, 33 Blue, which had been grounded since 2011, was restored at Vasilkov and was soon forward deployed to Dnetropetrovsk in May 2014.

The team's original seven MiG-29s 9-13s were captured at Kirovskoye air base by the Russian occupiers during the Crimea crisis in March 2014, but similar to the 204th BrTA aircraft, the Russians permitted the Ukrainians to evacuate all the aircraft from the State Flight Test Centre at the base. Subsequently all seven MiG-29 9-13s, together with six other MiG-29 9-13s – 08 Blue, 32 Blue, 22

All of the ex-Ukrainian Falcons aerobatic display team were transported from Kirovskoye to Kulbakino/ Nikolayev in spring 2014, including this example, 106 Blue. *www.airforce.ru archive*

Yellow, 28 Yellow, 36 Yellow and 38 Yellow – besides two MiG-29UBs, 32 and 82 Yellow, which were ex-Ukrainian Navy Aviation examples from the disbanded 100th IAP at Saki and 161st IAP at Limanskoye, were disassembled and transported by road to Kulbakino AB in April and May 2014. They all were parked on a separate ramp to the 204th BrTA's MiG-29s in the west of Kulbakino air base.

Between December 2015 and October 2016, three of the seven Ukrainian Falcons' MiG-29 9-13s, including 103 Blue, were sent to the Lviv state repair plant for restoration and overhaul. In early March 2017, two more MiG-29 9-13s, this time 104 and 105 Blue, were transported by road to LDARZ for restoration. It is believed that two of these MiG-29 9-13s have already been restored and overhauled, and that they were delivered to 40th BrTA in digital camouflage colour schemes in 2016 with the bort numbers 01 and 02 White.

LDARZ overhauled and even modernised two more MiG-29s of the disbanded 3rd IAP in 2017 and 2018. They were 105 Blue (c/n 2960731222) and 108 White (c/n 2960731239), which were painted in digital camouflage and received the bort numbers 07 and 08 White respectively. They were officially redelivered to the UkrAF during a ceremony attended by President Petro Poroshenko on 1 August 2018. Both aircraft were delivered to the 40th BrTA. LDARZ completed the overhaul and modernisation of a third MiG-29, again ex-3rd IAP, which was named after Leonid Bykov – actor, film director, screenwriter – on the occasion of his 90th birthday on 12 December 2018. The aircraft was also delivered to the 40th BrTA.

3rd IAP MiG-29s stored at Kulbakino in 2016

Model	Construction Number	Bort Number	Colour Scheme	Former Unit	Last Overhaul/ Restoration	Current Fate	Note
MiG-29 9-13	?	08 Blue	?	100th IAP	-	Stored	Stored at Kulbakino AB
MiG-29 9-13	?	32 Blue	Blue/Grey	100th IAP	-	Stored	Stored at Kulbakino AB
MiG-29 9-13	2960731232	101 Blue	Ukrainian Falcons	100th IAP	-	Stored	Stored at Kulbakino AB
MiG-29 9-13	2960731225	102 Blue	Ukrainian Falcons	100th IAP	-	Stored	Stored at Kulbakino AB
MiG-29 9-13	2960731227	103 Blue	Ukrainian Falcons	100th IAP	-	Stored	Stored at Kulbakino AB
MiG-29 9-13	2960731239	108 White	Ukrainian Falcons	100th IAP	-	Stored	Stored at Kulbakino AB
MiG-29 9-13	2960731222	105 Blue	Ukrainian Falcons	100th IAP	-	Stored	Stored at Kulbakino AB
MiG-29 9-13	2960728120	106 Blue	Ukrainian Falcons	100th IAP	-	Stored	Stored at Kulbakino AB
MiG-29 9-13	2960728196	108 Blue	Ukrainian Falcons	100th IAP	-	Stored	Stored at Kulbakino AB
MiG-29 9-13	?	22 Yellow	Green/Grey	100th IAP	-	Stored	Stored at Kulbakino AB
MiG-29 9-13	?	28 Yellow	Crimean Sun	100th IAP	-	Stored	Stored at Kulbakino AB
MiG-29 9-13	?	36 Yellow	Green/Grey	100th IAP	-	Stored	Stored at Kulbakino AB
MiG-29 9-13	?	38 Yellow	Green/Grey	100th IAP	-	Stored	Stored at Kulbakino AB
MiG-29UB	?	37 Yellow	Grey	100th IAP	-	Stored	Stored at Kulbakino AB
MiG-29UB	?	82 Yellow	Grey	100th IAP	-	Stored	Stored at Kulbakino AB

Modernisation programme

Since 2000, the Ukrainian Ministry of Defence and UkrAF commanders had been studying the possibilities of the lifetime extension and modernisation of their MiG-29 fleet, leading to negotiations with Israeli Aircraft Industries (IAI) and then RAC MiG of Russia in 2001. These discussions failed to reach a deal because of Ukraine's financial problems. Therefore, the Ukrainian MoD authorities approached domestic companies, which would be cheaper.

The Lviv State Aviation Maintenance Plant (LDARZ) was selected by the Ministry of Defence in 2007 to modernise and upgrade the aged Ukrainian Fulcrum C and UBs. The cost of the first level of modernisation (MU1 level) was estimated at $5 million per aircraft, which also covered the aircraft airframe overhaul at LDARZ and refurbishment of the RD-33 turbofan engines at Motor Sich. The project was started during the second stage of overhaul of MiG-29 9-13 29 Blue (c/n 2960731233), a 204th BrTA aircraft, in 2009. It became the first trial aircraft for this project and was finally redelivered to 204th BrTA after completion of its post-overhaul and modernisation tests on 20 May 2009.

No. 11 Blue, another MiG-29 from 204th BrTA, became the second test bed and its modernisation work was completed in February 2010. Next to it, 03 Blue (c/n 2960729011) from 204th BrTA became the third and final test bed, and it was delivered to the 40th BrTA in summer 2011. The MiG-29MU1 prototypes flew in service with the 40th and 204th BrTAs to be evaluated by the units during the trials phase, which helped the LDARZ to complete the project and begin modernising more MiG-29s by equipping the aircraft with an upgraded fire control system and new navigational and communication systems. Subsequently, after completion of the R&D stage of the project, two MiG-29 9-13s of 204th BrTA, 01 Blue (c/n 2960729047) and 05 Blue (c/n 2960729049), were selected for modernisation work.

The modernisation was planned to mostly enhance the air combat capabilities of the aircraft by upgrading their radars to the N019U2 designated standard. New low-noise UM-522 transistors, to be used a secondary source of power for the receiver module of the radar, would increase the sensitivity of the radar receiving path, with target detection range increased one-and-a-half times. New upgraded radar also provided the ability to use R-27ET1 missiles manufactured by the Ukrainian Artem company, with a maximum effective range of 95km.

For the communication systems upgrade, a high-frequency radio to NATO and ICAO standards was also installed to replace the old system, and for the navigation upgrade, the CH-3307 satellite navigation system, a GPS/GLONASS navigational system with an accuracy of 30m, was installed during the trials. This increased the independence of the aircraft from ground navigation aid systems and also enabled the aircraft to perform accurate automatic landing without the help of any ground-based SHORAN/ILS systems.

In 2011, the results of the trials revealed a simple failure of some of the upgrade work, which resulted in the first two mass-modernised and lifetime-extended MiG-29 9-13s, which later received the bort numbers 02 Blue and 53 White, receiving just digital camouflage and a new communication system as their modernisation elements! After passing all the flight checks, the former 01 Blue, which had now become 53 White, was handed over to the UkrAF, together with 02 Blue, during a special ceremony at Vasilkov AB on 1 June.

No. 02 Blue (former 05 Blue) was detached to the 114th BrTA on 24 June 2012. The total cost of these two aircraft restorations, overhauls and lifetime extensions was 12 million UAH (equivalent to approximately £950,000). The lifetime-extension work would enable the aircraft to remain in service for the next 20–25 years. These two MiG-29 9-13s were used on missions to protect the Ukraine's airspace during Euro 2012, especially the matches held in Kiev, Kharkiv, Lviv and Donetsk.

The MiG-29MU1 programme totally failed and instead the LDARZ continued the lifetime extension of the fleet with a slight upgrade to the communication systems of the aircraft, which led to the delivery of a third lifetime-extended MiG-29 9-13, 04 White, to the 40th BrTA in 2013. Also, three lifetime-extended Fulcrum UBs – 85 Blue, 90 White and 10 White – were handed over to the 204th BrTA and 40th BrTA on 22 November 2012 and 2 April 2013. All the lifetime-extended Fulcrums were painted in digital camouflage, which decreased their visual detection by 20%. LDARZ used high-quality, French-made aviation paint instead of the older domestic-produced paint that had been used since the early 2000s and in many cases had become worn out after five years.

In 2014, before the beginning of the Crimea crisis, the 40th BrTA received a second lifetime-extended MiG-29UB, 99 White, which was the former 9th BrTA 52 Blue. Soon after the war, as a consequence of the UkrAF's urgent need for more fighter aircraft, the LDARZ speeded up the overhaul and lifetime extension

During the course of work to modernise the first MiG-29 9-13s for the UkrAF in 2011, this non-airworthy MiG-29, 25 Blue stored at the LDARZ was used as a research platform for installation of the Kh-29L laser-guided air-to-surface missile in 2011. *Ukrainian Air Force via airforce.ru*

02 Blue was one of two MiG-29MU1s delivered to the UkrAF after the end of their modernisation at LDARZ in 2013. The aircraft had entered service with the 40th BrTA by the end of 2013. After the eruption of the war in Donbass, 02 Blue was forward deployed to Donetropetrovsk and participated in several air-to-ground missions until it was shot down on 7 August 2014. *Ukrainian Air Force via airforce.ru*

of the MiG-29s, especially after 02 Blue and 53 White were shot down by pro-Russian separatists on 7 and 17 August 2014 respectively, while 85 Blue was captured by the Russians at Belbek AB in June 2014.

On 6 November 2014, two lifetime-extended and overhauled MiG-29 9-13s, 41 and 46 Blue, were delivered to the 204th BrTA, which was in urgent need of aircraft after all its airworthy MiG-29s were confiscated by the Russian occupiers of Belbek AB. On 5 January 2015, the third MiG-29 9-13, 43 Blue, together with MiG-29UB 86 Blue, were handed over to the 204th BrTA after completion of their lifetime extension and overhaul at the LDARZ facility. A fourth MiG-29 9-13, 45 Blue, was delivered to the 204th BrTA in October 2015.

The 114th BrTA, with its FMC MiG-29s, which had been forward deployed to Dnepropetrovsk AB to defend the airspace over the east of Ukraine, was on the priority list with the 204th BrTA to receive its newly overhauled and lifetime-extended MiGs. The unit received MiG-29 9-13 57 White and MiG-29UB 30 White on 5 January and July 2015 respectively. In the following winter the unit received also one more overhauled MiG-29 9-13, 71 White, while the 40th BrTA also received MiG-29 9-13 33 White.

In spring 2016, a $230 million agreement was reached between the Ukrainian MoD and the LDAR for the overhaul of six MiG-29s. Four of the MiG-29s 72, 73, 75 and 76 Shite, belonged to the 114th BrTA and the remaining two, 01 and 02 White, were delivered to the 40th BrTA. It was claimed that 01 and 02 White both had been upgraded to the MiG-29MU1 level but it is not clear whether the upgrade only covered the NAVAIDS or was also for its fire control system.

Fulcrums at war

Following the Crimea crisis and the annexation of the Crimea peninsula to Russia's territory, the Russian authorities decided to support pro-Russian separatists in the east of Ukraine to draw the attention of the Ukrainian Armed Forces from the south to the east because of the possibility of the Ukrainian Armed Forces' attempt to liberate Crimea. Subsequently, on 7 April 2014, just weeks after annexation of Crimea, pro-Russian separatists stormed Ukrainian Security Force offices in Donetsk and Luhansk, taking control of them and accessing their weapon storage.

The Ukrainian Air Force HQ quickly put Air Command West on high alert at this time to protect the airspace in the east of the country while the Air Command Centre had been tasked with dealing with threats from the Crimea side (south) via four of the 831st BrTA's Su-27s that had been forward deployed to Kulbakino AB since late February 2014. Subsequently, 114th BrTA forward deployed two of its best MiG-29 9-13s, 05 Blue and 53 White, each one armed with two R-27R semi-active radar homing AAMs and four R-73 IR-guided AAMs, to Dnepropetrovsk. This deployment was part of the Ukrainian government anti-terrorist operation against the insurgents in Donetsk Oblast.

Pro-Russian militias affiliated with the Donetsk People's Republic captured and occupied numerous government buildings, towns and territories in the region. Despite having many governmental buildings under their control, they failed to occupy Donetsk International Airport until 26 May, when the pro-Russian separatist insurgents captured the

MiG-29MU1 02 Blue was shot down by a Buk-M1 SAM of pro-Russian separatists while carrying out an air interdiction mission over the south of Yenakievo on the evening of 7 August 2014. These pictures were taken on the morning of the next day. *Dmitry Shevchuk's archive*

terminal buildings and blocked the main road to the airport, attempting to force the remaining Ukrainian Armed Forces in the area to withdraw their units.

Having Donetsk International Airport under their full control enabled the insurgents to receive military aid from Russia, similar to what had happened in Crimea when 13 Russian Air Force Il-76MDs transported almost 1,000 fully armed Russian airborne troops to Hvardiyske military airport, from where they were sent to various parts of the Crimea to occupy the Ukrainian Armed Forces bases and governmental buildings on February 2014. Because of this potential use of the airport, the Ukrainian Armed Forces conducted an offensive to liberate the occupied part of the airport just a few hours after the insurgents had occupied it, during which Ukrainian Army Aviation gunship Mi-24s and Mi-8s together with UkrAF's Su-25s under the protection of the MiG-29s provided close air support for the Ukrainian paratroopers' assault on 26 May.

The battle for Donetsk airport began with the most intensive use of Ukrainian air power against the separatists during the war. This operation succeeded and the airport came under the full control of government forces. It remained like that until 21 January 2015, when separatists and Russian troops successfully occupied the airfield, while the UkrAF was unable to carry out any operations over the region because of the danger from the separatists' MANPADS and SAM systems.

Between 2 July and 29 August, the UkrAF lost five of the six Su-25M1s that had been forward deployed to Dnetropetrovsk in May 2014. Three of them were shot down by the separatists' Strela-10 and Grom E2 MANPADS, which had been supplied by Russia in May that year, while the rest fell to more capable Buk M1 SAM systems, which were delivered by Russia in early July. These were also used to shoot down an UkrAF An-26 and Malaysian Airlines flight MH17.

On 2 August, while two MiG-29 9-13s were in a FastCAP mission protecting two UkrAF Su-25s that had bombed the broadcasting antenna of Russian propaganda TV channels in Donetsk, they confronted a pair of RuAF MiG-29s that had violated Ukraine's airspace to shoot down the Su-25s. The Russian MiGs soon changed their heading toward their home base at Millerovo. In those days, due to a lack of an adequate number of airworthy Su-25s with the 299th BrTA, and the fact that just four Su-25s were still available in Dnetropetrovsk, the UkrAF was forced to use MiG-29s for ground-attack missions, especially after the QRA detachment of the Dnetropetrovsk had been strengthened with more MiG-29 9-13s from the 40th BrTA in mid-July.

During the air-to-ground missions, the MiG-29 9-13s were mostly armed with four B-8M1 rocket pods carrying S-8 unguided rockets, and they even dropped OFAB-250-270 bombs during interdiction missions despite having an inaccurate targeting system in comparison with the Su-25M1s. On 9 August, two MiG-29 9-13s armed with B-8M1 rocket pods rocketed a convoy of Russian military vehicles near Antratsyt, which resulted in the destruction of several trucks and armoured carriers. Three days later, on 12 August, two MiG-29 9-13s together with Su-25s were used in an interdiction sortie to attack a group of separatist armoured vehicles near Horlivka. Four days later, two MiG-29 9-13s armed with R-27Rs and R-73s provided FastCAP for another MiG-29 9-13 and an Su-25 that bombed and rocketed the abandoned OJSC Avtoagregat factory at Krasnodon, Luhansk Oblast, which had been used as a base for T-72B3s and BTR-82AM IFVs by the insurgents.

The use of MiG-29s in air-to-ground missions dropped to zero after two MiG-29 9-13s were shot down in August. The first aircraft was the digital camouflaged 02 Blue from the 40th BrTA, which was hit by a Buk-M1 SAM over the south of Yenakievo while returning to Dnepropetrovsk after an interdiction sortie on 7 August at 18.40 local time. The aircraft's left engine was lost and fire spread to the rest of fuselage, resulting in the ejection of the pilot, who was captured by the insurgents.

Ten days later, the second MiG-29 was lost at Krasnodon district on 17 August at 05.40am local time: it was the digital camouflaged 53 White from

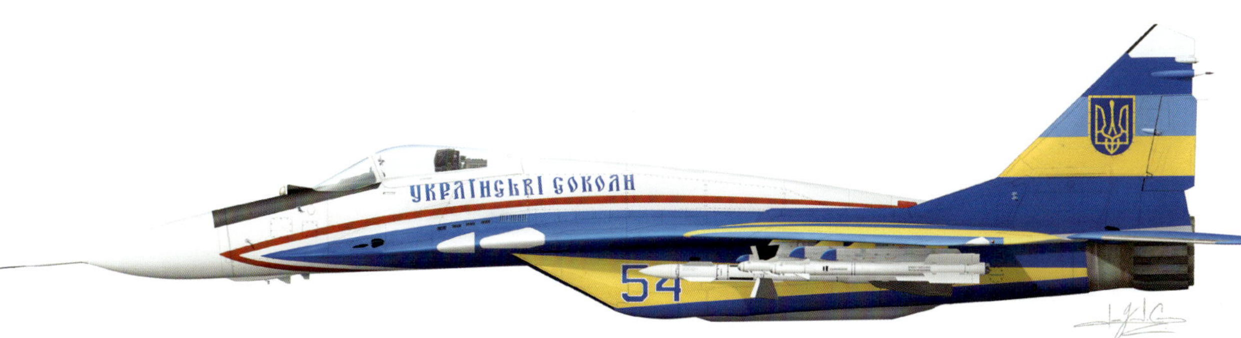

114th BrTA MiG-29 9-13 54 Blue (c/n 2960731234) was among the examples that the regiment had on deployment at Dnepropetrovsk AB to be used for daily combat air patrol missions over the Donbass. Here it can be seen armed with four R-73 IR-guided, short-range, air-to-air missiles and two R-27ER semi-active, radar-guided, medium-range air-to-air missiles. *Luca G. Canossa*

40th BrTA MiG-29MU1 02 Blue (c/n 2960729049) was shot down by a Buk-M1 SAM over the south of Yenakievo while it was returning to Dnepropetrovsk after an interdiction sortie at 18.40 local time on 7 August 2014. On that day it was carrying out a close air support mission and had been armed with four B-8M1 rocket pods and a pair of R-73 missiles. *Luca G. Canossa*

the 114th BrTA. The aircraft had been used to carry out an air strike against the pro-Russian separatists' BM-21 Grad systems located in Sukhodilsk, Luhansk Oblast. A column of three BM-21 'Grad' rocket systems from Russia had passed through the town of Dyakovo in the early hours of that day. Another column of armoured vehicles reached the village of Nizhniy Nagolchik, Luhansk Oblast. After ejection, the pilot hid and navigated 40km on the ground until he found the first outpost of the Ukrainian Armed Forces the next day.

After these accidents, the MiG-29 9-13 flights were reduced to only dedicated to air-to-air missions and the Su-25s were used in ground-attack role again until the loss of another Su-25M1, 08 Blue, on 29 August 2014, which caused the suspension of UkrAF air-to-ground operations over the east of Ukraine due to the presence of Russian Buk-M1 SAM systems. Since that time, the UkrAF has always had a task force that consisted of four Su-25M1/UBM1 aircraft and eight MiG-29 9-13s at Dnetropetrovsk as QRA assets ready for air-to-air and air-to-ground missions in case of emergency. In various cases, the MiG-29 9-13s were scrambled and guided by the UkrAF's ground radar sites to confront Russian Air Force Mi-8 and Mi-35M helicopters, as well as MiG-29s, Su-27s and Su-30s violating Ukraine's airspace after their flights from nearby Millerovo AB.

The UkrAF's two MIG-29 losses during the war weren't the only losses of the type since independence: the UkrAF and Ukrainian Navy lost four other MiG-29s in the 1990s:

- On 15 June 1995, the 114th IAP lost a MiG-29UB and its two pilots, Kozlov AG and Sergey E. Zakhozhiy, during an accident at Bovshev (32km north of Ivano-Frankovsk). The reason for the accident was never discovered due to the destruction of the aircraft's flight data recorder after it crashed
- On 30 July 1996, a 161st IAP (Limanskoye) MiG-29 9-13, 10 Blue (c/n 2960728509), piloted by Vadim V. crashed during aerial combat training between two two-ship MiG-29 formation flights over the Alexandria test site in Mykolaiv Oblast. During the training, the pilot who was flying lower than instructed in his briefing hit the ground and was killed

This MiG-29MU1 of the 40th BrTA, with 29 Blue (c/n 2960731233), logged at least 30 combat sorties from Dnepropetrovsk AB, during which it mostly carried out combat air patrols. Here it is shown armed with a pair of R-27ER semi-active, radar-guided, medium-range, air-to-air missiles and four R-73 IR-guided, short-range, air-to-air missiles. *Luca G. Canossa*

This MiG-29MU1 of the 114th BrTA 53 White (c/n 2960729047) was shot down while its pilot was carrying out an airstrike against BM-21 rocket launchers of the separatists on 17 August 2014. It was armed with a pair of B-8M1 rocket pods for S-8 unguided rockets and had a pair of PTB-1150 (one under each wing) and a PTB-1500 external fuel tank (under the fuselage). *Luca G. Canossa*

- On 31 October 1996, a MiG-29 9-13 of 3rd IAP (Kirovskoye), 42 White (c/n 2960728134), which had previously served at 92nd IAP, piloted by Oleg Kulik fell into the Black Sea after take-off from Kirovskoye airport while flying Dzhankoy–Kirovograd–Vasilkov. This accident occurred 20 minutes after take-off at 10.40 local time. The aircraft was climbing to 10,600m (34,776ft) and changed its heading suddenly by 180 degrees while not responding to radio calls from ground radar sites until it disappeared from radar screens at 3,400m (11,154ft). A fisherman found the pilot's body within 10km of the Yalta coast on 7 November. Eight days later the search team found parts of the aircraft's right wing flap on the shore between Saky and Yevpatoria, but the black box was never found. The cause of the accident was possibly a pilot health issue and technical failure of the ejection seat

- On 26 March 1998, the Ukrainian Falcons team lost one of its MiG-29 9-13s, 107 White, and its pilot Sergei Dudkin due to the crash of the aircraft on the Kirovskoye runway during a training flight of the team in preparation for an appearance at the Paris Air Show the following year. The reason for the accident was human error, including the Test Centre authority's mistake in permitting the aircraft to fly and perform aerobatic demonstration training in bad weather with less than 1km visibility. The technical failure of the pilot's ejector seat led to his death

Post-war activities and the future of the MiG-29 fleet

All Tactical Aviation Brigades except the 204th BrTA took part in an air exercise in Mykolaiv Oblast, during which pilots practised gunnery, rocketry, bombing and live AAM firing from Kulbakino AB before the widespread anti-terrorist operation in May 2014. During one of the days of exercise, on 16 May, four R-73 missiles were launched by pilots of MiG-29 9-13 02 Blue and three MiG-29MU1s, 03, 11 and 29 Blue, from 40th BrTA, together with MiG-29 9-13 09 Blue from the 114th BrTA. Also, two MiG-29UBs, 10 White from 114th BrTA and 90 White from 40th BrTA, dropped eight SAB-250-200 flare bombs on the Kiev-Oleksandrivka gunnery range, marking targets for Su-24s and Su-25s to bomb. This exercise was held instead of the previously planned joint American–Polish–Ukrainian exercise Safe Heaven 2014. Soon after the exercise, MiG-29 and Su-25 pilots, together with their aircraft, were forward deployed to Dnepropetrovsk airport to take part in air operations in the Donbass region.

The next year, on 8 October several recently graduated cadets of the Ukrainian Air Force University practised highway landing using MiG-29UB 91 Blue and L-39M1 102 Blue on the Kiev–Odessa highway. On 14 and 15 October, the Ukrainian Air Force participated in the joint Polish–Ukrainian exercise Safe Skies 2015. During the exercise, which was held in the territory of Air Command West, on 15 October MiG-29 9-13 09 Blue and MiG-29UB 90 White were tasked with intercepting a Polish Air Force C-295, which was playing the role of an aircraft hijacked by terrorists. The exercise was held to increase the cooperation level between air units of the Ukrainian and Polish Armed Forces. The UkrAF took part with the two above-mentioned MiG-29s, while the Polish Air Force participated with three C-295s. The programme for holding this multi-national exercise and the UkrAF's presence had been approved by the Ukrainian President on 6 March 2015.

On 10 August 2016, for the second consecutive year, UkrAF fighter pilots practised take-offs and landings on the Kiev–Odessa road during the first day of exercise Heavenly Shield 2016. This time two MiG-29 9-13s of the 114th BrTA, 71 and 73 White, together with several 7th BrTA Su-24s, landed on the highway strip watched by the first Deputy Chief of the General Staff of Ukraine, Lt Gen Igor Kolesnik, and the Air Force Commander, Lt Gen Sergei Drozdov.

According to the Acting Commander of the Air Command West, Col Alexeu Marchenko, it was the first time that the Air Command West pilots had performed landings and take-offs from roads. On the next day of the exercise, 11 August, Su-24Ms and Su-25M1s carried out a dozen air-to-ground sorties from Kulbakino AB against targets on a nearby gunnery range while being escorted and protected by a pair of Su-27M1s. Two 40th BrTA MiG-29s, 04 White and 35 White, were used to play the role of aggressors and they engaged in aerial combat with the Su-27s.

On 21 October 2016, the 40th BrTA participated in another exercise, the Strategic Command and Staff's Rubezh 2016, and again, similar to the previous year, the Brigade's pilots practised landing on the highway strip with two MiG-29s and an L-39C.

In November 2016, the UkrAF held a two-week gunnery training course for new air force MiG-29 pilots who, together with their eight MiG-29s, were forward deployed to Lutsk Air Base on the afternoon of the 22nd. During the exercise, the 40th BrTA participated with MiG-29UBs 90 and 99 White,

US Air Force Capt Skylar Bautista, a pilot assigned to the 144th Fighter Wing, 194th Fighter Squadron, Fresno Air National Guard Base, California, sits in the back seat of 40th BrTA MiG-29UB 90 White during the exercise Clear Sky at Starokostiantyniv Air Base on 9 October 2018. Clear Sky promoted regional stability and security, while strengthening partner capabilities and fostering trust. ***Tech. Sgt. Charles Vaughn, US Air National Guard***

In November 2016, the UkrAF held a two-week gunnery training course for new MiG-29 pilots who, together with their eight MiG-29s, were forward deployed to Lutsk Air Base. The 114th BrTA participated with three MiG-29 9-13s and a MiG-29UB. One of them was this MiG-29 9-13, 76 White, which is armed with B-8M1 rocket pods at Lutsk on 27 November 2018. *Ukrainian Air Force via airforce.ru*

while the 114th BrTA took part with MiG-29 9-13s 57, 75 and 76 White and MiG-29UB 30 White; and the 204th BrTA flew MiG-29 9-13 43 Blue and MiG-29UB 86 Blue. A Mi-8MT helicopter was also forward deployed to Lutsk to stand alert to fly SAR missions in case of emergency. On 25 November the participants practised bombing with MiG-29UBs, while on 26 November live S-8 rocket firings were performed with MiG-29 9-13s.

Between 8 and 19 October 2018, the UkrAF participated in the exercise Clear Sky 2018, which involved F-15Cs of the 194th FS, 144th FW, of the California Air National Guard. The UkrAF had several of its MiG-29s and Su-27s forward deployed to Starokostiantyniv, from where they participated in the exercise and carried out various air-to-air and air-to-ground missions. Out of the seven MiG-29s participating in the exercise, four – all from the 40th BrTA – had been upgraded to MiG-29MU1 standard with the tactical numbers 05, 06, 07 and 08 White. The four, accompanied by MiG-29UB 90 White, were forward deployed from Vasilkov to Starokostiantyniv AB on 6 October. Next to them, two MiG-29s of 114th BrTA, 71 and 75 Blue, were forward deployed to Starokostiantyniv from Ivano-Frankivsk.

In February 2019, pilots of 114th BrTA had their piloting and navigation skills in bad weather conditions renewed and improved during 36 sorties and eight hours of instrument flight. In March these pilots practised air-to-air missions such as the destruction of UAVs using low-speed flying at low level.

Also in March, Air Command South of the Ukrainian Air Force held a small exercise over the Sea of Azov in response to the provocative actions of Russia in the region. During the exercise, two Su-25M1s of the 299th BrTA, including 15 Blue, participated; each one had a pair of B-8M rocket pods and a pair of PTB-800 external tanks to provide close air support for the Ukrainian Navy ships taking part. They were protected by three MiG-29s of the 204th BrTA, 41, 47 and 49 Blue, each one armed with a pair of R-27R and four R-73s. In addition to these five aircraft, an Su-27P of 831st BrTA that was on QRA duty at Kulbakino flew a mission with them over the sea.

According to the current roadmap of the Ukrainian Ministry of Defence, despite the cancellation and failure of the MiG-29 modernisation programme, the Ukrainian Air Force has plans to keep its fleet airworthy until 2035. The MiG-29s will serve as front-line fighter interceptors with a limited defined air-to-ground role in service with the 40th, 114th and 204th BrTAs of the Air Command East and Air Command West. The 204th BrTA will have the important task of not only defending the east of country against the threat of the Russian Air Force but also of protecting airspace in the south close to the occupied Crimea as well.

Su-15 Fleet (1992–1996): World's Last Flying Flagons

Designed to serve as the successor to the Su-9 and Su-11 fighter-interceptors in the PVO (Soviet Air Defence Force), the Su-15, nicknamed 'Flagon' by NATO, was the deadliest weapon Moscow had to counter the threat of the long-range bombers of the USAF for a short period of the Cold War, but soon gave its place temporarily to the MiG-23P and then permanently to the Su-27P and MiG-31 in the PVO's fighter regiments. The Soviet Union's collapse and the treaty on Conventional Armed Forces in Europe caused the early retirement of the interceptor from the new Russian Air Defence Force in 1993 and 1994, leaving the Ukrainian Air Defence Force as the last operator of the fighter-interceptor in the world until 1996. Ukraine inherited 78 (Ukrainian MoD documents claim 80) Su-15s in service with two former fighter aviation regiments of the PVO. Below is an account of not only their short service life in the UkrADF but also their history in the days of the USSR.

Guardians of Kramatorsk

Since May 1960, the 636th IAP had become the operator of 12 MiG-17Fs, five MiG-17Ps and seven MiG-17PFs as replacements for its MiG-15s. The MiG-17s had been delivered between 1955 and 1960 to take the place of the surviving MiG-15s out of 17 MiG-15bis and one MiG-15UTI delivered between November 1952 and February 1953. Finally, upon delivery of the Su-15s, retraining of the entire MiG-17 crew was started on the Su-7U, then was continued on the brand new Su-15UTIs and Su-15s between February and April 1970. Only a year later, the regiment took part in the tactical exercises of the 9th Air Defence Division with its new Su-15s.

In 1972, the 636th IAP Su-15s flew to Belbek, were they stayed for a week to take part in a joint live-missile firing exercise with the 62nd IAP over the Black Sea. At this time, until 1973, the 1st and 2nd AEs (Aviation Squadrons) of the regiment were equipped with Su-15s, while the third squadron was still operating MiG-17PFs. In 1973, the 636th IAP started to receive its first Su-15TMs, or 'Izdeliye-37Ms', as replacements for the MiG-17PFs of its 3rd AE. The MiG-17PF was the most advanced variant of the MiG-17, equipped with radar and more powerful VK-1F engines and providing a better rate of climb and more acceleration capability in comparison with earlier variants. The MiG-17PFs of the 636th IAP were used in combat just once, on 15 October 1960 when one of them shot down a NATO spy balloon.

The Su-15TM was capable of carrying two UPK-23-250 gun pods, each one with a 23mm GSH-23L

21 Blue was one of the Su-15TMs in service with the 636th IAP at Kramatorsk. It is seen during an exercise in 1983. *Sergey Popsuevich*

23 White was one of 40 Su-15s that were serving in a VVS fighter regiment in the Georgian SSR. This Su-15TM was transferred from Vaziani to Kramatorsk in late 1990. It entered service with the 3rd Aviation Squadron of the 636th IAP. Its colour scheme was distinctive from all the other aircraft in service with the regiment. *Sergey Popsuevich*

76 and 78 Blue, two Su-15TMs of the 62nd IAP during a military exercise at Belbek AB, on 5 October 1995. *Sergey Popsuevich*

28 Blue, an Su-15TM of the 62nd IAP, during landing at Belbek AB during a military exercise over Crimea and the Black Sea on 5 October 1995. *Sergey Popsuevich*

74 Blue, a 62nd IAP Su-15TM armed with two UPK-23-250 gun pods being prepared for participation in the air-to-ground phase of a military exercise on 5 October 1995. *Sergey Popsuevich*

cannon and 250 rounds. Also, it had the capability to carry two FAB-250 bombs or up to two UB-16-57 rocket launchers carrying S-5 unguided rockets or two S-24 unguided heavy rockets for air-to-ground missions. Because of this capability, 14 Su-15TM pilots of the 636th IAP took part in gunnery shooting at ground targets in extremely low altitude at Belbek range in July 1975.

In 1979, the 636th IAP took part in an interception exercise named Dut 79, during which its Su-15s were deployed to Belbek. Two years later, a regimental exercise was held at Krasnovodsk gunnery range, during which Su-15TMs of the 636th IAP armed with gun pods shot down several La-17 target drones. Similar gunnery training with gun pods was held, this time against ground targets, at Old Aidar (Voroshilovgrad area) in June 1983. During each deployment to Belbek, An-12s stationed at Kramatorsk carried ground crews and equipment to Belbek. In the late 1980s, three An-12s always provided logistic support for the 636th IAP.

Between 1988 and 1991, Kramatorsk airfield was used as a refuelling point for fighter aircraft of three Warsaw Pact countries, Czechoslovakia, Poland and East Germany, during summer air defence exercises that were being held at Astrakhan. Among them, the MiG-29 9-12s of the East German Air Force were the most eye-catching visitors.

In 1987, the MiG-25s of the PVO's 933rd IAP were temporarily stationed at Kramatorsk when their airfield's runway at Dnepropetrovsk underwent repair. Similarly, the MiG-25PDS/PDUs of the PVO's 146th GVIAP were temporary stationed there when their airfield at Vasilkov was under refurbishment and repair in summer 1991.

On 10 June 1986, when the 636th IAP had three AEs with 54 Su-15TM/UMs, it became subordinate to the 49th Air Defence Corps (49th KPVO) from the 9th Air Defence Division (9th DPVO). On 1 June 1988, the unit temporarily became part of the 11th DPVO until 15 June 1989, when it joined the 49th KPVO again. This continued after Ukraine independence until 1 June 1992.

On 1 September 1983, Korean Air Lines Flight 007 was shot down by R-98 missiles launched by a Soviet Air Defence Force Su-15. R-98MR, the semi-active radar-homing variant of this medium-range air-to-air missile, is here loaded on Su-15TM 78 Blue of the 62nd IAP with during the second day of a military exercise at Belbek, Crimea, on 6 October 1995. *Sergey Popsuevich*

Su-15 accidents in the 636th IAP

The Su-15 was one of the safest and most reliable fighters to have served in the PVO. Not only were its systems designed on a fail-safe basis but its engines were reliable and maintenance friendly. Despite all this, several Su-15s were lost, mostly due to human factors, including one incident from 636th IAP in 1973 when pilot V. P. Gayzhevskoy burnt all his fuel in an engine flame-out on final approach, causing a loss of altitude and the collision of the nose landing gear with a building at Partizansk village a few miles before reaching the runway at Kramatorsk. The pilot lost control of the aircraft but ejected safely.

On 26 January 1981, another accident occurred to an aircraft of 636th IAP, this time to Su-15UM 20 Blue (the training version of the Su-15TM), killing Maj Alexei Smolkin and injuring Col Ilkevich

Weapon officers of the 62nd IAP loading a R-98MT IR homing, medium-range, air-to-air missile under the left wing of Su-15TM 78 Blue, while a R-60M short-range air-to-air missile can be seen installed under the wing before live missile firing during a military exercise on 6 October 1995. *Sergey Popsuevich*

Su-15UTI 56 Blue of the 62nd IAP can be seen in the main apron at Belbek AB during a military exercise on 5 October 1995. *Sergey Popsuevich*

Constantine (paralysed with spinal injury) during a night flight due to the pilot's mistake on final approach. They approached the airfield at 90 degrees but when they were 60m from landing, the pilot mistakenly released the brake parachute instead of turning the landing lights on! Subsequently, he pulled up the nose, the aircraft lost speed due to the high angle of attack and it stalled and hit the runway threshold.

Two years later, the third and last Su-15 accident to befall the 636th IAP occurred during which two Su-15TMs collided in mid-air above Kramatorsk, destroying the formation leader's aircraft and forcing its pilot, Lt Col Vsevolod Grigorievich Blashov, to eject, while the second Su-15 made an emergency landing. The first Su-15 crashed in the city of Kramatorsk, burning one house and destroying another one but not injuring anyone on the ground. The reason for the accident was never determined due to the destruction of the aircraft's black box. The Su-15's black box was an automatic recorder of flight parameters, model SARPP-12V.

After Ukraine's independence

The 171st IAP from Gudauta, Abkhazskaya ASSR, in 1975, 991st IAP at Besovets, Karelian ASSR, in January 1975, and 57th GVIAP at Besovets, Karelian ASSR, in June 1978 were the last of the Soviet Union PVO's Fighter Aviation Regiments to be equipped with the Su-15TM as replacements for their Yak-28Ps, MiG-17Fs and Su-9s respectively, because these units were located in remote areas and this put them at the end of the queue for the acquisition of the new fighter-interceptor in the PVO. The 700th UAP (Training Aviation Regiment) became the last unit in the PVO to receive the Su-15 as the replacement for its ageing MiG-15s and MiG-17s in 1978!

In the early 1980s, when the Su-15TM was not capable enough to intercept targets at low altitude with the background of the earth because of the weakness of its 'Typhoon-M' radar, which also had +30°/-10° vertical and +/- 70° horizontal angular range, their replacement with more modern fighter-interceptors started across the PVO units. The MiG-23P, which had been inducted into service with the PVO in 1978, was equipped with Sapphire-23P radar with the capability of intercepting low-level targets and several IAPs had replaced their ageing Su-9/11s with the new interceptor. The ageing Su-15s of the 218th UAP at Salsk, Rostov Oblast, were replaced in 1981 and then those of the 28th GVIAP at Andreapol, Tver Oblast, in Tikhoretsk in 1982.

In total, six GVIAPs (Guards Fighter Aviation Regiments), 18 IAPs (Fighter Aviation Regiments), and four UAPs (Training Aviation Regiments) including the 592nd and 594th UAP from the 148th TSBPPLS, operated the Su-15 in the USSR PVO. Five regiments, including the 991st IAP, were disbanded, while Su-15s were replaced by the MiG-23P/MLD in three regiments, Su-27Ps in five regiments and MiG-31/Bs in four regiments between 1978 and 1992. The primary role of four regiments was changed to

60 Blue, another Su-15UTI of the 62nd IAP, departing Belbek AB during a military exercise on 5 October 1995. *Sergey Popsuevich*

ground attack and they started to operate Su-17Ms (976th IAP in 1981), Su-17M3s (156th IAP in 1981), Su-17M4s (302nd IAP in 1982) and Su-25s (90th IAP in 1983) as replacements for their Su-15s.

After the collapse of the USSR, the 166th GVIAP at Mameuli, 62nd IAP at Belbek, 265th IAP at Poduzhemye, 431st IAP at Afrikanda, 611th IAP at Bezhetsk, and 636th IAP at Kramatorsk were the regiments still operating a total of 235 Su-15TM/UMs. Among these, 62nd and 636th IAP with 78 Su-15s were inherited by the Ukrainian Air Defence Force, while the rest remained in Russia. The 166th GVIAP and 431st IAP were disbanded in 1993, while the 265th IAP, the last Su-15 operator unit in Russia, was disbanded on 2 June 1994. The 611th IAP was only unit among them that was completely converted to the Su-27 by 1993.

Retirement of the Su-15 from the USSR PVO was planned to take place in 1992; for this reason the 700th UAP, which had 81 Su-15s in service, was disbanded as the last PVO Su-15 conversion training unit in 1990. While it was planned to disband the 636th IAP in 1992, the unit lived longer, with 39 Su-15s in service with its three AEs after Ukraine's independence. On 21st August 1995, the regiment was reorganised as an independent fighter squadron under the command of Alexander Petrovich, and finally disbanded on 1 January 1997.

The 62nd IAP at Belbek, which was subordinate to the 60th Air Defence Corps, had received its first Su-27s in 1991, and aircrew and ground crew of its 1st and 3rd AEs had undertaken conversion training on the new type in 1991. Later, on 19 January 1992, when personnel of the regiment took the oath of allegiance to the Ukrainian people, the unit had 14 Su-27s beside its 39 Su-15s. The latter served in the unit until 1996, when they were retired and replaced by 26 ex-Ukrainian Navy Aviation's 100th IAP MiG-29s. On 10 December 1996, following a decree issued by the Ukrainian President, the unit became a part of the UkrAF's 5th Air Corps.

Based photographs and videos from both the 62nd and 636th IAPs in their last years of activities, the number of airworthy Su-15s did not exceed 13 in each unit, which was equal to the number of airworthy aircraft in each of their AEs in the days of the Soviet Union! In 1994, the 636th IAP became the sole Su-15 IAP in the UkrADF and painted special markings on one of its Su-15TMs, 41 Blue, in commemoration of the Soviet–Ukrainian actor Leonid Bykov. The aircraft was finally flown from Bila Tserkva airfield, where it had been placed in storage in 1996, to Vinnitsa, where it was displayed in the UkrAF Museum in 2003. It was the last Su-15 flight in Ukraine.

Nearly all the Su-15s were soon sent to Bila Tserkva after the disbandment of their regiments and were intended to be scrapped in 1996, but

Nicknamed 'Maestro' after Leonid Bykov, the Ukrainian actor and songwriter, St-15TM 41 Blue was in service with the 636th IAP of the UkrAF. After disbandment of the regiment, it was stored together with all the unit's Su-15s at Bila Tserkva to be scrapped. But it survived and was sent to the UkrAF museum at Vinnitsa. *Sergey Popsuevich*

'Maestro', Su-15TM 41 Blue of the 636th IAP, can be seen stored at Bila Tserkva in 1996 before being sent to Vinnitsa to be displayed in the air force museum in 2003. *Sergey Popsuevich*

some ex-636th IAP examples survived, including 16 Red (c/n 0915346), which is now on display in the Zhuliany museum. Another Su-15TM found its way to Slovakia when it was gifted to the country by President Leonid Kuchma on 6 June 2001 and it is now preserved in the Kosice aviation museum with the fake bort number 15 Blue. In addition to the Su-15TM in Slovakia, another ex-636th IAP found its way outside the country: 82 Blue (c/n 1015324) was sold by Ukrspetsexport to an aviation museum in Lithuania and was transferred to the country on 31 August 2001. The aircraft had been delivered to the 636th IAP on 26 February 1974.

The fifth surviving ex-636th IAP Su-15TM is 76 Blue, which is now in the closed Lugansk aviation museum. As well as the five above-mentioned Su-15TMs, 56 Blue (c/n 0415319) is the sole surviving Su-15UM in Ukraine and is now in the Poltava aviation museum. The aircraft made an emergency landing at Poltava due to a warning in the hydraulic oil system during a night flight from Kramatorsk in 1995/96. The 636th IAP never recovered the aircraft and just removed its engines.

Su-24s (1992–2001) and Su-24Ms (1992–today) of the Ukrainian Air Force: The Last Tactical Asset

After the retirement of the last Tu-22M3s and MiG-25RBs by the Ukrainian Air Force, a fleet of 24 Su-24M front-line bombers and 12 Su-24MR tactical reconnaissance aircraft became the main strategic assets for long-range strike and reconnaissance missions. These are the remnants of the 283 Su-24s from four different variants in service with an Electronic Warfare Squadron, seven Bomber regiments, two Reconnaissance Regiments of two air armies, a Bomber Aviation Division and a Training Centre of the Soviet Air Force, all inherited by Ukraine after independence in 1991. The remaining fleet of Su-24s took part in the war in Donbass and scored several successful strike and reconnaissance missions until one of the Su-24Ms was lost to enemy fire and an Su-24MR was damaged. Over a period of four years after the Crimea crisis, the Ukrainian Air Force and Nikolayev Aircraft Repair Plant managed to almost double the number of Su-24s in service.

T6-17 with bort number 617 (c/n 0415302) was one of the Su-24 prototypes. It ended up as a training platform for students of Vasilkov Higher Military Technical School. It is seen on 2 October 1995. *Sergey Popsuevich*

Fencer-As in the Ukrainian SSR

In 1976, the 230th BAP from the32nd BAD of the 24th Air Army based at Cherlyani, Lviv Oblast, became the first operator of Su-24 Product-41s as replacements for its Yak-28s, which had been in service since 1968 in the Ukrainian SSR. In total, 30 Su-24s were delivered within a few months to take the place of the Yak-28s in its 1st, 2nd and 3rd Aviation Squadrons. On 10 December 1980, an Su-24 of 230th BAP piloted by V. P. Prudnikov was badly damaged at Cherlyani after skidding off the runway following a high-speed landing.

Next to the 230th BAP in the Ukrainian SSR, the 7th BAP, subordinated to the 32nd BAD, 14th Air Army at Starokostiantyniv, started to receive Su-24 Product-41s as replacements for Yak-28s in its three squadrons from 1 December 1977. The 7th BAP was formed by Lt Col Alexei Bobkov, commander, and chief of staff Maj Vasyl Kalugin on 1 June 1966. At first it was equipped with Il-28s and personnel from various units across the Soviet Union until it converted to Yak-28s on 15 March 1975 (conversion training had started in December 1974). It became subordinate to the 56th BAD until the delivery of its Su-24s, which brought it under the 32nd BAD. Two years after its formation, the regiment took part in Exercise Danube in 1968 and then Vostok in 1969.

The 7th BAP's Su-24s participated in several important exercises, including Granit 78, Karpaty 80, West 81 and Watch 86, and its aircrews and ground crews received good scores, The regiment also took part in Exercise Shield 82 and some of its aircrews flew with Su-24Ms from other units and developed new tactics for combat operations with the new marque. The regiment took part in the war in Afghanistan with 69 personnel, while its Su-24s were flown from the USSR mainland to strike their targets inside Afghanistan.

In the USSR days, 17 of the regiment's crew members lost their lives in various accidents during peacetime. For example, an Su-24 crashed at Starokostiantyniv airfield on 3 April 1979, killing its pilot, A. I. Shipunov, and navigator, V. Buldin. The cause of the accident was pilot error during landing, which caused the loss of control of the aircraft.

In 1977, a third Bomber Aviation Regiment was equipped with Su-24s in the Ukrainian SSR territory of the USSR. It was the 947th Fighter-Bomber

The 29th IBAP, with 62 Su-24 Product-41 types in service in November 1990, was the largest operator of this early variant of the strike bomber in the Ukrainian SSR. This image shows one of its Su-24s, 07 White, after a training mission at Berdyansk in 1991. *Sergey Popsuevich*

Aviation Regiment from the 14th Air Army's 289th Fighter Bomber Aviation Division, an operator of the Su-7B since 1974 at Dubna, Rovno Oblast. By the end of 1988, all the Su-7Bs had been retired or passed to other units, causing a change in the unit's designation to 947th BAP and bringing it under the direct subordination of the 14th Air Army.

In February 1982, the 314th BAP of the 289th Fighter Bomber Aviation Division, 14th Air Army at Cherlyani, Lviv Oblast (the same base at which the 230th BAP was stationed), became another Soviet Air Force unit in the Ukrainian SSR to be equipped with Su-24s. The 314th Fighter-Bomber Aviation Regiment had been established under the 14th Air Army in 1976 and was operating two squadrons of Su-7Bs, each with up to ten aircraft. In 1979, a squadron of Su-17s was added to the regiment while one of its existing Su-7B squadrons converted to the type as well.

A decision was made to equip the unit with just tactical bombers from 21 February 1982, bringing it under the direct subordination of the 24th Air Army from that date. Between 1983 and 1984, 30 Su-24s were delivered to the unit, resulting in the retirement of its last Su-17s in 1984. These changes caused the redesignation of

29 and 54 Red, two Su-24 Product-41s of the 29th BAP, on the main ramp at Berdyansk Air Base in the last year of the regiment's activity in 1996. *Sergey Popsuevich*

28 Red in front and 31 Red at the back on the main ramp of Berdyansk Air Base in 1996. Both aircraft had a pair of PTB-3000 external tanks under their wings and a PTB-2000 external tank under their fuselage. The top image shows the artwork of a man giving a big 'middle finger' drawn by the technicians of the 29th BAP on both sides of 28 Red's radome during an exercise. *Sergey Popsuevich*

the 314th Fighter-Bomber Aviation Regiment into a pure BAP in 1983, while the regiment became subordinate to the 56th Bomber Aviation Division because of the nature of its new capabilities and tasks in 1984. The life of the 314th BAP was short and it was disbanded in 1987. Some of its Su-24s found their way into the neighbouring 230th BAP, while some went to other units.

After 721 Su-24s were built up to 1983, the production lines were switched to Product 44, or the Su-24M. To train aircrews of the rising number of Su-24s in service with the Soviet Air Force, an Instructor Aviation Regiment was equipped with the type for advanced weaponry training purposes at Berdyansk, Zaporozhye Oblast of the Ukrainian SSR in 1987. The unit in question was the 29th Instructor Bomber Aviation Regiment (29th IBAP), which had previously been the 29th Independent Training Aviation Regiment at Sital-Chay, Azerbaijan SSR, and had moved to Berdyansk in 1980.

Within a period of six months, the 29th IBAP converted from the MiG-21 to the Su-24 Izdeliye-41, while still subordinate to the 5th Air Army. From the 222nd Training Course, the officers trained on the Su-24. In September 1990, the unit became a part of the 1270th Training Aviation Centre for retraining personnel, and in November it had a total 62 Su-24s, all previously serving with the 6th BAP at Step, Chita Oblast, and the 733rd BAP at Domna, Chita Oblast (both had been deactivated in July 1987). The 29th IBAP remained as the sole Su-24 Instructor Bomber Aviation Regiment of the USSR Air Force until 1992.

Next to the 29th IBAP, two more regiments were equipped with Su-24 Product-41s in the Ukrainian SSR: they were the 69th Fighter-Bomber Aviation Regiment at Ovruch, Zhitomir Oblast, and the 806th Fighter-Bomber Aviation Regiment at Lutsk, Volynsk Oblast, both subordinate to the 14th Air Army. The Su-24s took the place of Su-17M3s at Ovruch and Su-17M2s at Lutsk, their units changing their names to the 69th and 806th BAPs and bringing them under the control of the 289th Bomber Aviation Division. Each unit received 30 Su-24s, using ten of them in each one of their three aviation squadrons.

Product-41s in Ukrainian Air Force service

In comparison with the Product-44 Su-24M, the Product-41 had restricted combat capabilities with less modern avionics, weapons and targeting systems, and self-defence systems, and more importantly a lack of aerial refuelling capability. Starting from the mid-1980s, some of the Su-24s produced before 1976 began to be retired and this continued on a larger scale after the Soviet Union signed the CFE treaty in November 1990. Despite the treaty, the Ukrainian SSR's Su-24 Product-41s survived until Ukraine's independence. Only the 314th BAP at Cherlyany had been disbanded in 1987, leaving most of its aircraft withdrawn from service while some were absorbed by other air armies.

On 17 January 1992, when the Ukrainian Army held an oath of allegiance to Ukraine, 122 Su-24 Product-41s existed in Ukraine in service with three Bomber Aviation Regiments and one Instructor Aviation Regiment. Among these, 30 were in service with the 806th BAP, 62 with the 29th IBAP and 30 with the 69th BAP.

The 29th IBAP, which still had the primary role of advanced flight and weaponry training for Ukrainian Air Force Su-24 aircrews, was reorganised as the 29th Bomber Aviation Regiment in 1995. By the end of the following year, the 29th BAP had been disbanded at Berdyansk, and some of its airworthy aircraft were delivered to the 69th and 806th BAPs in Cherlyani and Lutsk respectively.

Almost half the 29th BAP aircraft ended up at the 6th Air Base of the Ukrainian Air Force at Kulbakino, where they continued flying as Su-24 pilot and navigator trainers with the 33rd TsBPPLS (33rd Centre for Combat Employment and Retraining of Personnel Aviation) until disbandment of the unit in 2003. In that year the unit had a total 26 Su-24s, although just 22 were kept in service with its 1st and 2nd Aviation Squadrons and only six were operational when the unit disbanded. They were sent to the Nikolayev Aircraft Repair Plant for long-term storage on the south side of the airport, and they were put up for sale in 2008. Nearly all the remaining Su-24 Product-41s of the 6th AB were scrapped between 2005 and 2014.

Su-24 Product-41 with 33 Red bort number armed with a pair of B-8M1 rocket pods and equipped with two PTB-3000 external tanks and a PTB-2000 tank during a military exercise at Berdyansk Air Base in 1996. *Sergey Popsuevich*

29th BAP Su-24 35 Red bort number armed with B-8M1 rocket pods carrying S-8 unguided rockets taxiing towards Berdyansk during the last military exercise in which the 29th BAP participated in 1996. *Sergey Popsuevich*

Su-24 29 Red equipped with multiple ejector racks under its fuselage, taxiing back toward the parking area after a bombing mission during the last exercise in which the 29th BAP participated before its disbandment in 1996. *Sergey Popsuevich*

33 Red, an Su-24 Product-41 of the 29th BAP, seconds before touching down on the runway at Berdyansk Air Base in 1996. Its UkrAF insignia had faded away on its vertical stabiliser, showing the old red star. *Sergey Popsuevich*

With its speed brakes deployed, 53 Red, an Su-24 of the 29th BAP, lands at Berdyansk in 1996. *Sergey Popsuevich*

54 RED, another Su-24 Product-41 of 29 BAP, during landing at Berdyansk Air Base in 1996. *Sergey Popsuevich*

From left to right, 29, 22 and 39 Red, three Su-24 Product-41s of the 29th BAP at Berdyansk in 1996. *Sergey Popsuevich*

Retirement

In 2000, the 69th BAP at Cherlyani was disbanded and its remaining airworthy Su-24s were sent to the 806th BAP at Lutsk, while most of its aircraft, which had been grounded for years as they were due to be overhauled, were sent to the Belya Tserkva storage facility to be scrapped. The 806th BAP, which saw most of its Su-24 Product-41s grounded from the mid-1990s, retired the rest of its flying examples and fully switched to the Product-44 Su-24M in 2001. All its early-variant Su-24s, including the ex-69th BAP examples, were transferred to the Belya Tserkva storage facility to be scrapped. In 2017 seven of them – 02, 06, 02, 20, 34, 36, and 38 White – were present and waiting to be sold as scrap metal. The 29th BAP's Su-24s, which had entered service with the 6th Air Base in Nikolayev, Kulbakino, in 1995, became the last Su-24 Product-41s still in service.

Five Su-24 Product-41s are exhibited in museums and various other locations in Ukraine. No. 74 White

In 1995, several Su-24s of the 29th IBAP were transferred to Nikolayev, where they were used to form the 6th Air Base. 07 White was one of them, seen here on 3 November 1995. *Sergey Popsuevich*

07, 40 and 70 Red, three Su-24s of the 6th AB, at an open day at Nikolayev/ Kulbakino Air Base in 1995. FAB-250M-62 and FAB-500ShL bombs can be seen in front of them. *Sergey Popsuevich*

(c/n 0815306), which was manufactured in the eighth series of Su-24s produced in 1975, previously having served in the 733rd BAP and then the 806th BAP, is now preserved in Lutsk aviation museum. No. 02 Red served in the 6th AB and 29th IBAP and is now preserved at Yuzhnoukrainsk. No. 09 White (c/n 0315309) is at Vinnitsa Air Force museum. No. 56 Red (c/n 0815311), built in 1975, is at the State Aviation Museum at Kiev's Zhuliany airport, and finally 62 Red is at Lugansk, which is now under the control of Russian-backed separatists who are reported to have damaged the aircraft.

Three Su-24 Product-41s, including a flying laboratory, are stored at two airfields in Ukraine to be used for educational purposes by students. Among them, two Su-24 Product-41s, 12 and 69 White, have been stored at Chuguyev airfield since 2000 or 2001, while T-6-21, a former Su-24 Product-41 but converted into flying laboratory for adoption of the Kh-59 air-to-ground missile with the bort number 621 Red (c/n 0815316), is now stored in the Museum of Aviation Equipment of the Lugansk Aircraft Repair Plant at Ostraya Mogila, which is now occupied by separatists.

Product-41s for sale as scrap metal or souvenir

Document No. 1092 of the Cabinet of Ministers of Ukraine, dated 6 August 2008, which gives permission for the sale of surplus Ukrainian Armed Forces military equipment shows that 17 Su-24 Product-41s out of a total of 122 examples inherited by Ukraine were still in good enough shape to be sold and exported.

Among them was an 1974-made example without an engine and many parts, together with six 1978–80 made Su-24s in complete condition with their AL-21F-3 engines installed (the last operational examples at the 6th Air Base, namely 06, 07, 39, 40, 66, and 70 Red), which were stored at the A2488 military base at Nikolayev, and another, 34 Yellow, was stored outside the base inside the city. Two disassembled examples, one manufactured in 1973 and another in 1976, together with seven cannibalised examples all manufactured in 1977 and 1978, were stored at the A1789 military Base at Belya Tserkva. An engineless Su-24 at Kulbakino is reported to have been scrapped in 2014.

05 White on the left and 73 White on the right were the last two Su-24 Product-41s of the 806th BAP to leave Lutsk. They are seen minutes before departure and their flight to Bila Tserkva, Kiev region, in spring or summer 2001. *Vladislav Derebon's archive via www.airforce.ru*

05 White was the last Su-24 of the 806th BAP to leave Lutsk and fly to Bila Tserkva to be stored and then scrapped there in 2001. This image was taken minutes before the last flight. *Vladislav Derebon's archive via www.airforce.ru*

The last flight crew of the 806th BAP, who transferred the last Su-24 of the regiment from Lutsk to Bila Tserkva in 2001. *Vladislav Derebon's archive via www.airforce.ru*

In the past decades, despite the sale of Su-24 spare parts and AL-21F-3A engines to Iran in the 1990s, the Ukrainian Ministry of Defence did not manage to sell all the Su-24 Product-41s declared for sale due to them being expensive to repair as well as old. Only in one case was an Su-24 Product-41 sold, 39 Red to the Estonian Aviation Museum in 2005. Including this aircraft, 33 Product-41s out of 122 inherited by the Ukrainian Air Force survived in 2017.

Fencer-Ds in the Ukrainian SSR

The first serial-produced Su-24M (Product-44, named Fencer-D by NATO) was manufactured at the Novosibirsk aircraft plant in the summer of 1979, but as a result of bureaucratic delays the process to induct the new aircraft into USSR Air Force service was not completed until 1983. In same year, production of the Su-24 Product-41 was stopped, as the avionics and weapon systems had not met the needs of the air force, which required a tactical bomber with similar capabilities to the USAF's F-111E introduced ten years earlier. To familiarise the instructor pilots with the new aircraft, the first Su-24Ms were delivered to the 760th IISAP of the 4th TSBPPLS (4th Centre for Combat Employment and Retraining of Crews VVS) at Voronezh in June 1981. Before that, the 143rd BAP had received the first batch of pre-production but serial-produced Su-24Ms in 1977 to use them for tests at the state research centre at Morozovsk, Rostov Oblast, from September 1978.

The first front-line unit of the USSR Air Force to be equipped with the Su-24M after the 760th IISAP was the 727th Guards Bomber Aviation Regiment (727th GVBAP) in February 1982, when the unit was based in Debrecen, Hungary. Over a period of 18 months, the Su-24Ms replaced the unit's ageing Yak-28s, which had been in service since 1969 after replacing the Il-28. The 727th GVBAP had born as the 804th BAP Debrecen in July 1942 during the Second World War and was redesignated as the 161st GBAP on 5 February 1944 and finally the 727th GBAP on 10 January 1949.

Since its establishment, the unit had been deployed and stationed in various foreign locations such as Sprottaue, Germany, between April and July 1945; Strasshof, Austria, in July 1945–47; Götzendorf, Austria, 1947–January 1952; Zwölfaxing, Austria, January 1952–July 1953; Tököl, Hungary, July 1953–November 1956; Kunmadaras, Hungary, |November 1956–July 1960; and finally Debrecen, Hungary, from July 1960. Finally, on 10 July 1987, the unit, which had 31 Su-24Ms in service with three aviation squadrons, was repositioned to Kanatovo, Kirovograd Oblast, in the Ukrainian SSR.

As one of the most important battle-worthy Bomber Aviation regiments of the air force, the 727th GVBAP developed combat tactics for the Su-24M that were employed by all Su-24 units across the air force over the following years. Participation of the unit in Exercise Shchit 84 and then Granit 85 had a key role in the development of the aerial refuelling system and the aircraft's in-flight refuelling procedure. Despite the adverse effects of the relocation of the unit from Hungary to the Ukrainian SSR in 1987, the unit and its personnel remained the most highly skilled and combat-worthy across all air force Su-24 units. While it was stationed in Hungary, the 727th GVBAP lost three Su-24Ms: the first on 2 April 1984 and next two due to a mid-air collision on 2 July 1985.

In 1987, two more units were equipped with the Su-24M in the Ukrainian SSR, the 7th BAP and 947th BAP, operators of the Su-24 Product-41 at Starokostiantyniv and Dubna since 1977. The 947th BAP had received ten freshly overhauled Su-24s (from the 17th and 18th batches of serial-produced Su-24s) in 1985. These ten product-41s remained in service with the 947th BAP until 1988, when deliveries of its Su-24Ms were completed. The 7th BAP also continued operating one squadron of Su-24 Product-41s until the completion of the delivery of 30 Su-24Ms in 1988.

Su-24M 57 White in the maintenance hangar of the 947th BAP at Dubna Air Base on 26 February 1997. Its 'Orion-A' navigation/attack radar can be seen. It has a detection range for a standard object of 150km with the ability to locate even low-contrast targets against the background of earth and sea and to provide information for the targeting and weapon system to enable the pilot to carry out bombing with much more efficiency than any other third-generation tactical and strike bombers. The second radar (below) is for terrain following. *Sergey Popsuevich*

An Su-24M of the 947th BAP landing at Dubno after using BetaB-500 concrete-piercing bombs during an exercise on 26 February 1997. *Sergey Popsuevich*

The Su-24M turned into the first tactical/strike bomber of the USSR VVS with inflight refuelling capability. The aircraft also could carry the Sakhalin UPAZ-1A aerial refuelling pod to refuel another Su-24M, extending the range of the aircraft to enable deep strike missions within the enemy's territory. Here an Su-24M of the 947th BAP is receiving fuel from another of the type in 1988. *Sergey Popsuevich*

That year, the 230th BAP at Cherlyani began receiving the Su-24M as a replacement for its ageing Su-24s, which had mostly been manufactured in 1975 and 1976. More than 30 Su-24Ms were delivered to the unit in two years. Once the aircrews of its 1st Aviation Squadron gained experience flying the Su-24M, they took part in a large-scale exercise with two other Su-24M units of the 24th Air Army, the 7th BAP and 727th BAP, at Svobodnyy Port gunnery range on the Crimean peninsula in August 1988.

During the exercise, on 31 August one of the 230th BAP's Su-24Ms, crewed by Vyacheslav Konovalov and Vyacheslav Tolmachev (navigator), hit the water and both were killed. The cause of the accident was a mistake by the leader of the formation in executing a dive-bombing manoeuvre at low altitude. He and his wingman dived at 160m instead of 400m, causing the leader of the second formation to dive at just 50m, while Konovalov and Tolmachev dived at a very low altitude and hit the water when they were trying to get the nose up and climb.

During that mission, the four Su-24Ms were accompanied by two Yak-28PPs (providing EW escort) from Chortkov half the way to the gunnery range. According to one of Yak-28PP pilots who flew over Konovalov and Tolmachev's aircraft, they were flying continuously to the left and right of the formation and acting without discipline. Then the Yak-28PPs left the Su-24Ms and flew to Buyalyk. They found out that the No. 4 aircraft had crashed minutes before they landed.

The transition of the 230th BAP to the Su-24M was completed in 1991, just few months before Ukraine's independence. Seventeen of the unit's last Su-24Ms were manufactured in 1990 and 1991. They were the most advanced and newest Su-24Ms in the Ukrainian SSR. In 1989, the last Su-24 Product-41s of the unit were withdrawn from service.

Ukraine's independence and 230th BAP disbandment

Ukraine inherited 119 Su-24Ms in service with four Bomber Aviation Regiments across the country. According to the exchanged data of the CFE treaty, in November 1990, 29 of these were in service with the 7th BAP, 30 with the 230th BAP, 30 in the 727th GVBAP and 30 with the 947th BAP. On 17 January 1992, the Ukrainian Army held an oath of allegiance ceremony at the air bases of the new country, and the oath was taken by all the Su-24 bomber regiments.

One of the 230th BAP's officers at the time recalls that day:

'On 17 January 1992, the army held an oath of allegiance [ceremony] to Ukraine. I also attended

this event. The banners and honorary pennants had been kept secret by the staff of the regiment, all folded in cellophane packages. So, on January 17, the commander told the personnel of the whole regiment to stand on the ramp. A lot of cameramen from news agencies came from Lviv, as well as representatives of the church, and nationalists bringing the yellow and blue flag of Ukraine as a sign of their brotherhood and friendship.

'They [representatives of the church and nationalists] tried to discuss the scenario of taking the oath by the commander. But he [the commander] said that he was still commander there and there was nothing to indicate to him how he should do his job; the regiment with its banner would say goodbye, and then they could do whatever they want [the commander told the regiment].

'The banner was brought in front of the regiment on the right flank. The commander, before the ranks, thanked everyone for their service under this banner, and on our [the personnel's] behalf he kissed the flag. Locals wanted to attach their banner next to the regiment's [banner], but a local Army platoon that was well-known in the city was ordered not to display their banner next to the regiment's. Then we took off our hats. One commander saluted the banner and it was then carried away. Then the commander said those who would take the oath would stay in place and the rest could leave. Soon it become clear that there were very few people left in the regiment who had been born in the territory of Ukrainian SSR, while the others were not originally Ukrainian. It was acceptable that they took the oath to their motherland Ukraine, which had become independent. But in my opinion (I still believe in that), the real officer takes the oath once in a lifetime, which I took inside the walls of DVVAIU [Daugavpils Higher Military Aviation Engineering College] in 1976.

'Before this ceremony, our new commander, V. A. Vasiliev (Belarussian, by the way) came to the base to encourage us to take the oath. But the conversation didn't turn out well because most of the people were not Ukrainian and were loyal to Russia, so the commander left because he was angry. The commander gave ten days' leave to all volunteers after that meeting. And in the course of the argument, our commander, a thoroughbred Don Cossack, V. P. Maleychuk, said that if we were to get it (permission to leave for ten days), then we would fly off to Russia with the whole regiment and he said that he did not want to listen to this nonsense. He said: "Whoever wants to stay, stay, and who does not want to stay, is free." We left the base at the end of the working day. The next day the SBU [Ukrainian Security Service] came from Lviv, they rushed to the base and installed anti-theft security in the cabins of all the aircraft, and the keys were taken to the headquarters, and the fuel was drained from the aircraft, and the personnel were not allowed to enter the parking location, and that was before the oath.'

After the disbandment of the 230th BAP, its aircraft were spread among other units of the 24th Air Army of the VGK in Ukraine, including the 7th BAP. Because they had not been flown for more than two months and been drained of fuel on the orders of the SBU, most of them had damaged tanks. Some were later repaired, while others were withdrawn from service.

Hijack of six Su-24Ms

Although most of the personnel in the 7th BAP at Starokostiantyniv took the oath of allegiance to Ukraine, but some of them decided to flee to Russia, especially after the Russian government set a deadline for those who wanted to remain its citizens to be inside the country, not in Ukraine or elsewhere. Twelve pilots and navigators hijacked six Su-24Ms from the regiment and flew to Shatalovo air base in Russia on 12 February 1992. Together with the aircraft, the flag of the regiment was stolen and transported by car to Russia. The documentation of all six aircraft including their logbooks was left at Starokostiantyniv.

Here is the memory of an unnamed member of the technical staff of the 230th BAP who recalls the details of the hijack:

'Pilots had not flown for weeks due to the security measures carried out by the SMU in Starokostiantyniv. Finally the ban was lifted by the SMU for a flight training mission by nine Su-24Ms on 13 February. After take-off, from these nine, six turned to the north and descended to an altitude of 50m while the remaining three returned to the base. The air base made a radio call and asked the leader of the six aircraft about their position. The leader responded: "We don't know! We will find out after landing." Then they left radio channel and didn't answer the radio calls.

'The chief of staff of the regiment was in the radar control centre of the base and when he saw that the aircraft disappeared from the radar screens, he went to the headquarters, took the banner from its hiding place and went on to Russia by car. Later the Russian press reported the loss of the local banner at the base.

'The twelve pilots and navigators who hijacked the six Su-24Ms had hoped to fly in the Russian Air Force in that base in Shatolovo but they didn't get the opportunity and one of them emigrated to Poland later. Ukraine demanded the six aircraft be returned, while Russia also demanded the return of 17 Su-24Ms with the latest modifications (the six hijacked Su-24Ms were from the first series) in the disbanded 230th BAP. Arguments rose up between the two governments but neither won.'

Russian President Boris Yeltsin had issued a decree on Russian citizenship, stating that 'citizens of Russia are those who were in the country on February 12, 1992' and the rest were not. Later, whoever travelled to Russia after this date had to wait for their documents but it was barely accepted that they were real Russians. This was an important reason behind the hijack of the six Su-24Ms by the 12 pilots and navigators.

During Ukraine's war in 2014, the Russian Intelligence Service (FSB) contacted Maj Yuri Kireev, an Su-24MR pilot of the 7th BrTA, to force him to hijack an Su-24MR, 36 Yellow, and fly it to Russia. According to the SBU, the Russian security forces had detained the pilot's wife and daughter in Moscow and they had also promised him he could continue his career in the Russian Armed Forces as an Su-24 pilot with the rank of colonel, together with housing and a $30,000 bonus. The counter-intelligence department of the SBU finally realised the pilot's intentions in mid-August 2014 and arrested him. On 22 September 2014, the SBU press service told the Ukrainian media that he might receive up to 15 years' punishment. On 6 June 2017, the Khmelnytsky City Court of Khmelnytsky Oblast sentenced him to 12 years in prison.

Downsized Su-24M fleet

The service life of the Su-24M is 20 years (without a lifetime extension); the oldest Su-24M in the UkrAF service was manufactured in 1982 and the youngest in 1991. But even before the end of the service life of many of the Su-24Ms, they were withdrawn from service or retired and their units disbanded due to financial constraints. The 947th BAP of the 14th Air Army was disbanded in 2001, and the 806th BAP from the 14th Air Army and the 44th BrTA (727th BAP until 2003) from the 24th Air Army went in 2004, leaving the 7th Tactical Aviation Brigade at Starokostiantyniv, Air Command West, as the last Su-24 operator at the time of writing.

The 947th BAP's Su-24Ms were manufactured between 1987 and 1988, and the end of their service life was due in 2007 and 2008. After retirement of the nearly 20-year-old Su-24s of the 806th BAP based at Lutsk, less than 50km north-west of Dubna, in 2001, the 947th BAP was disbanded and its Su-24Ms were transferred to the 806th BAP, which remained in Lutsk. Only one squadron comprising ten to 12 Su-24Ms remained active in the 806th BAP until 28 April 2004, when the regiment was totally disbanded. The rest of the 947th BAP aircraft had already been sent to Starokostiantyniv in 2001 and 2002.

The other unit that was disbanded in 2004 was the 44th BrTA based at Kanatovo, Kirovograd Oblast. The unit had 30 Su-24Ms airworthy with its three aviation squadrons in 1991, but when it was disbanded only 11 Su-24Ms were left in service, and just eight of them were airworthy at any one time. The reason was that the unit was the operator of the oldest Su-24Ms in the Ukraine. These had been manufactured between 1982 and 1984, and the end of most of their service lives was in 2003 and 2004, resulting in the disbandment of two of the three aviation squadrons before the regiment's disbandment.

Su-24M with 28 Red was in service with the 6th Air Base for Su-24 pilot and navigator training at Nikolayev in the late 1990s and early 2000s. This was a former 230th BAP machine. *Sergey Popsuevich*

85 White, an Su-24M of the 947th BAP, in the maintenance area of the regiment at Dubna Air Base on 26 February 1997. *Sergey Popsuevich*

A pair of Su-24Ms of 7th BAP (later 7th BrTA) flying in formation with Il-76MD 78820, over Kiev's main Khreshchatyk street during Ukraine's Independence Day parade on 24 August 2001. *Sergey Popsuevich*

947 BAP Su-24M 72 White landing at Dubna AB on 26 February 1997. *Sergey Popsuevich*

After-burner take-off of 947th BAP Su-24M 91 White from Dubna on 26 February 1997. *Sergey Popsuevich*

727th BAP Su-24M 07 White participated in an air show at Poltava Air Base in September 1993. *Sergey Popsuevich*

Participation in annual exercises

For a period of almost two years before the independence of Ukraine, the aircrew of the Bomber Aviation Regiments had faced a decline in the number of flying hours, accompanied by a cut in their monthly salaries, which led to a huge decline in their flying skills and capabilities. In 1992, upon the independence of Ukraine, several aircrew showed a lack of loyalty to the new Ukrainian Air Force, leading to a temporary suspension of flight operations, especially after six Su-24Ms of the 7th BAP were hijacked. But soon, the units resumed their flying activities in late 1992, which required ground crew to restore the Su-24s that had been grounded for a long period of time. As explained above, some Su-24Ms of the 7th BAP had even suffered damaged fuel tanks due to them being grounded for a long period of time.

Following a gradual rise in flying hours in 1993, the Ukrainian Air Force's Lviv Training Centre finally held its first large-scale training exercise and gunnery competition in 1994, during which various Su-24 regiments were involved, including 7th BAP. This was the beginning of a series of annual exercises to keep the skill and efficiency of the UkrAF pilots at a common level. Despite losing some of its best aircrews following the hijack of the Su-24s in 1992, the 7th BAP, which now had 30 Su-24Ms, including ex-230th BAP examples, in service with its three Aviation Squadrons, won the gunnery competition in 1994.

In accordance with the directive of the Minister of Defence of Ukraine, the 7th BAP became part of the 14th Air Army on 16 May 1998. From that time until 2003, when the 7th BAP was reorganised as 7th Tactical Aviation Brigade (7th BrTA), its aircrews were always the best during the gunnery competitions held among the regiments of the 14th Air Army. The unit was officially given the name of 'Petro Franko', a Ukrainian war hero, on 21 August 2008. Being an elite Su-24 regiment in the UkrAF, the 7th BAP and its Su-24Ms took part in flypasts in Ukraine's Independence Day parades in 1997, 1999, 2001, 2008, 2009 and all those after 2010. During the parade on 24 August 2008, four Su-24Ms, 26, 27, 33 and 62 White, flew in formation over Kreshchatik Street, Kiev.

This image, taken at Starokonstantinov Air Base during exercise Reaction 2005 on 7 September 2005, shows 7th BrTA Su-24M the 22 White bort number carrying a KAB-1500L laser-guided bomb, the heaviest precision-guided munition that can be employed by the type. *Sergey Popsuevich*

In 2005, the 7th BrTA had become the last strategic brigade of the UkrAF, especially after a Reconnaissance Aviation Squadron with the last Su-24MR tactical reconnaissance aircraft of the air force was formed within its structure the year before. In 2005, in accordance with the presidential decree for the transition of the Armed Forces of Ukraine to a contractual basis, the 7th BrTA became the first unit within the UkrAF to experimentally comply with this decree and had all its servicemen, including pilots, recruited on a contract basis until 2006.

In 2005, the 7th BrTA took part in two important exercises, Reaction 2005 and Tight Knot 2005. Reaction 2005 was the main training exercise of the Ukrainian Armed Forces; it was an integrated operational–tactical exercise with the Joint Rapid Reaction Forces, at which the Ukrainian president was present. The exercise in September 2005 involved 6,500 servicemen using 590 pieces of weaponry and equipment, including more than 100 tanks and armoured personnel carriers, 20 aircraft, 12 helicopters and nine ships.

During Reaction 2005, a series of tactical flying missions was carried out at Zhytomyr multipurpose gunnery range, while a tactical flying exercise was also conducted by Su-24s and Su-27s at the Kiev-Olexandrivka range, in addition to which air force and airborne troops and their equipment were airdropped from Il-76MDs at the Shyroky range. The

A KAB-500Kr TV-guided bomb, left, installed under a 7th BrTA Su-24M during the exercise Reaction 2005 at Starokonstantinov on 7 September 2005. The right image shows a KAB-500Kr belonging to the 7th BrTA. *Sergey Popsuevich*

7th BrTA Su-24M 28 White with its brake parachute deployed after landing at Starokonstantinov during the Reaction 2005 on 7 September 2005. *Sergey Popsuevich*

A freshly overhauled Su-24M of the 7th BrTA, 30 White, participated in the Gostomel Air show in June 2006. *Sergey Popsuevich*

62 White, an Su-24M of the 7th BrTA, diving over the Shiroky Lan gunnery range during exercise Clear Sky 2006 on 22 September 2006. *Sergey Popsuevich*

7th BrTA's Su-24Ms were used to simulate by air strike from an enemy force after an Su-24MR conducted a recce mission, while airborne troops parachute-jumped from the Il-76MDs, which were escorted by Su-27s.

Between 10 and 25 September 2006, the 7th BrTA took part in the Command Post exercise Clear Sky 2006, with the active phase between 19 and 22 September. The exercise was conducted in the presence of the President of Ukraine – the Supreme Commander-in-Chief of the Armed Forces – and demonstrated a satisfactory level of readiness of air force units to work jointly with the other armed services to fulfil their operational missions. The 7th BrTA's Su-24M pilots had a chance to carry out live precision-guided missile firing and bombing against ground targets at the Kiev-Olexandrivka range. A total of 19 helicopters and 61 aircraft, including six Su-24Ms and four Su-24MRs, took part.

Before Clear Sky 2006, new pilots of the 7th BrTA's Su-24Ms and Su-24MRs took part in the annual tactical training course of the UkrAF at Kulbakino AB in May 2006, during which they logged 15 hours in 22 flights and performed bombing runs using FAB-100 bombs at Povursk airfield, located in the Rivne region. After graduation from this course, they took part in Exercise Tight Knot 2006, during which an Su-24MR identified several targets at the Kiev-Olexandrivka range, which were bombed by six Su-24Ms. A total of 17 flights and 14 flying hours were logged by them during the exercise.

In September 2007, the 7th BrTA took part in the Command Post exercise Artery 2007 (an operational support and logistics exercise) during which, for the first time, the system of comprehensive support for the land force, air force and navy activities was deployed. The number of forces involved in Artery 2007 was three times larger than Clear Sky 2006. Twenty-five helicopters and 75 aircraft, including five Su-24Ms and an Su-24MR, were involved.

Of course, the 7th BrTA aircrews undertook their annual training before taking part in Artery 2007. For example, on 29 March, combat training was held, during which six Tactical Aviation Brigades undertook training flights; among them, 7th BrTA's pilots logged 20 flying hours in 30 sorties bombing

ground targets at the Rivne gunnery range. A few days later, on 17 April, the 7th BrTA took part in another training exercise, during which Su-24MRs flew from Starokostiantyniv to Kulbakino AB, where the Su-24M pilots logged ten hours' flying in ten bombing missions. Two days later, all the Su-24Ms and Su-24MRs and their crews took part in a Joint Ukrainian–Russian command and staff training exercise from Kulbakino and Nikolayev, involving tens of Ukrainian fighter jets and Russian Air Force MiG-29s, MiG-31s, Su-24s and Su-27s.

In September 2008, between 15 and 27 September, the UkrAF took part in the joint command and staff exercise Sea Knot 2008, with 45 aircraft including Su-24M/MRs flying from Nikolayev. As usual, the 7th BrTA aircrews trained before participating in these exercises, the first of which was held in April when 14 Su-24M/MR pilots and navigators had the chance to practise bombing and reconnaissance missions at the Rivne gunnery range from their base at Starokostiantyniv. In that year, the 7th BrTA took part in two several major training exercises, one of which involved formation training with Su-24s on 9 June in order to prepare six pilots to take part in the Independence Day parade that year with two Su-24Ms and an Su-24MR. Another was held on 12 November, during which Su-24 pilots had the chance to practise IFR flight in adverse weather and low visibility during ten sorties from their base. This IFR flight and navigation training was also held on 16 December.

Due to a lack of funding, the combat training activities of the UkrAF decreased and resulted in Ukrainian aircrews fulfilling only 2% of their planned annual flights of 2009 up to 5 February that year. On 4 March, the 7th BrTA, under the command of Lt Col Nikolai Kovalenko, conducted ten training sorties. On 21 April of that year, the pilots of two Su-24Ms from 7th BrTA logged four hours during joint training with 831st BrTA, which also logged

This Su-24M of the 7th Bomber Aviation Regiment, 22 White, was in use by the Kirovskoye Flight Test Centre in the late 1990s. Here it can be seen during a tourist flight during which civilian or military customers paid to fly in the jet for an hour. *Heinz Berger*

Su-24M 22 White taking off from Starokonstantinov AB on 9 June 2011. *Alexander Golz*

7th BrTA Su-24M 26 White bort number during landing at Starokonstantinov on 9 June 2011. *Alexander Golz*

two flying hours at that time. On 27 July, ten Su-24 pilots and navigators had the chance to practise flight and navigation training for eight hours within 16 sorties from their base; this included formation flight training for flypasts for the Independence Day parade. Due to a lack of funds and sufficient training of the UkrAF pilots, no large-scale joint exercise with a large UkrAF presence was held in 2009.

In 2010, enough funds were devoted to the UkrAF to enable the procurement of enough fuel for the 7th BrTA to conduct training exercises for its pilots to prepare them to take part in the joint command and staff exercise Cooperation 2010 between 6 September 6 and 4 October, which involved 18 UkrAF aircraft. On 17 September, the first day of the active phase of the exercise, three Ukrainian Navy Be-12s, two UkrAF Su-24Ms and two Su-25s were used to provide air support for ground troops that had been deployed aboard Ukrainian Navy landing ships in the coastal area. After bombings carried out by Su-24s and Su-25s, a massive artillery strike was conducted from the landing ship *Konstantin Olshansky*, the mid-size landing ship *SDK Kirovograd* and the missile corvette *Prydniprovya*, as well as artillery units of the coastal artillery group of the Coast Guard Centre of the Ukrainian Navy. At the same time, a UkrAF Su-24MR flying from Kulbakino AB carried out a battle damage assessment (BDA) from the areas affected by the artillery attack.

In 2011, the UkrAF and its 7th BrTA from Air Command West took part in the joint command and staff exercise Adequate Response 2011, which involved 36 aircraft including 19 fighter jets, 47 pilots of the air force and 16 helicopters of Army Aviation. The purpose of this exercise was to review the level of combat training of the forces as well as to research directions for developing a prospective model of the Armed Forces of Ukraine. The results of the exercise proved the effectiveness of the command and control system and its ability to function through the chain of command to the

Formation flight of 22 White (leader), 26 White (right wing) and 27 White (left wing of the leader) over Starokonstantinov on 9 June 2011. *Alexander Golz*

General Staff – Operational Command (Immediate Reaction Corps) – Brigade. The prospective combat strength of the Armed Forces was assessed and the new approaches to its application were tested.

The deployment of four Su-24Ms from Starokostiantyniv to Kulbakino AB led by an Su-24MR piloted by Lt Col Victor Poznyakov and Cap Alexander Troshin was carried out under the command of Col Sergei Blyznyuk, commander of the Brigade, on 14 September, two days after the beginning of Exercise Adequate Response 2011. On 19 September, an Su-24MR crew practised a tactical recce mission and identified and located several targets at Opuk gunnery range, which were bombed by Su-24Ms minutes later. Three days later, another tactical reconnaissance sortie was conducted, this time by Su-24MR 36 Yellow directly from Starokostiantyniv, during which the aircrew flew 500km and carried out their mission successfully.

In September 2012, Ukrainian Armed Forces including the UkrAF's 7th BrTA with 50 servicemen, three Su-24Ms (22, 28, 83 White) and an Su-24MR (11 Yellow) took part in the Joint Command Post exercise Perspective 2012 in the Zhytomyr and Bukovina Oblasts. In total 900 servicemen and 145 pieces of equipment were involved in the first phase, during which Mi-8 and Mi-24 helicopters from the Army Aviation and the Su-24s and Su-25s of the UkrAF participated. During the exercise, 600 soldiers, 60 armoured vehicles supported by MiG-29s and Mi-24 helicopters played the role of aggressor forces. The active phase of the exercise involving 1,700 servicemen started after an Su-24MR carried out tactical reconnaissance, which was followed by air strikes by Su-24Ms, Su-25s and Su-27s flying from Kulbakino.

Before participating in Perspective 2012, the 7th BrTA's crews were able to practise for several months. For example, in March, six Su-24M/MRs of the brigade were deployed to the reserve air base, Lutsk, from where they carried out several training flights for a week until they were redeployed back to Starokostiantyniv on 21 March. Between 2 and 6 April, two Su-24M crews consisting of Col Nikolai Kovalenko and Navigator Capt Nikolay Savchuk in the first aircraft and deputy commander of the brigade, Col Sergey Chizh and Navigator Capt Yevgeniy Melnyk, practised bombing at the Povursk gunnery range. It was the first bombing mission for navigators of the Su-24Ms after their graduation from their training course. In addition to the Su-24M flights, an Su-24MR piloted by the senior pilot of the Air Command West headquarters, Maj Yevgeniy Bulatsik, and the navigator Capt Alexander Troshin practised tactical reconnaissance.

Again in 2013, budget cuts resulted in a slight decline in 7th BrTA activity in comparison with the previous year. To keep all Su-24 aircrews up to date, especially when the unit was faced with a lack of flying hours, the UkrAF had specified L-39 advanced jet trainers, by means of which the pilots and navigators were kept current when they had not had enough monthly flying hours on the Su-24. In February 2013, the 7th BrTA began conducting training flights using both the Su-24M and Su-24MR as well as the L-39.

Su-24M 83 White at Starokonstantinov AB on 17 September 2013. This aircraft was lost in an accident in 2014. ***Alexander Golz***

In April 2013, the 7th BrTA participated in the Research Command Training exercise Milky Way 2013. During the active phase of the exercise on 24 April, Su-25s flying from Havryshivka Vinnitsa International Airport acted as SEAD aircraft, destroying enemy air defence. Minutes later, Su-24Ms flying from Starokostiantyniv carried out practice bombing at the Kiev-Oleksandrivsky gunnery range. Finally, an Su-24MR was used for BDA to evaluate the result of the bombings carried out by the Su-24M pilots.

Before participating in the exercise Milky Way 2013, some of the Su-24M/MR pilots had carried out IFR and navigation flight training sorties on 10 April 2013. Also on 2 April 2013, during a joint training exercise with the UkrAF and Ukrainian Army involving nine fighter jets, an Su-24MR piloted by 2nd Grade military pilot Maj Gen Yuriy Kireyev (deputy commander of the Reconnaissance squadron) was used for intelligence gathering, while an Su-24M piloted by 2nd Class military pilot Col Mykola Kovalenko and Navigator 1st Class military pilot Col Sergei Chizha carried out tactical bombing against the targets identified earlier by the Su-24MR at a gunnery range in Zhytomyr Oblast.

In September 2013, a joint command and staff exercise was held, during which Air Command West and its 7th BrTA was involved. During the exercise, which lasted two days, the aircrews of Su-24s and L-39s had the chance to carry out reconnaissance missions and live bombing using iron bombs against ground targets in 32 sorties lasting 40 hours, all from Starokostiantyniv. Before the exercise, participants had the chance to participate in a summer weaponry training course held at Lutsk, where several Su-24M/MRs and L-39s were deployed. Two of the Su-24M pilots had the chance to drop laser-guided KAB-500L bombs for first time after many years.

In action over Donbass

Soon after the end of the new year holidays, the 7th BrTA 'Petro Franko' conducted 12 training sorties (eight in the day and four at night), during which Su-24M and Su-24MR pilots had the chance to practise IFR and navigation flight training with nine hours of flying from Starokostiantyniv. On that day the flights started after Col Nikolai Kovalenko and the deputy commander of the squadron, Maj Alexei Kovalenko, performed a weather check aboard an L-39M1 over the training area at 11.30 local time. Fifteen days later, on 25 January 2014, during a joint training with 831st BrTA, an Su-24M played the role of an aggressor aircraft and flew toward Mirgorod, where an Su-27UB piloted by Maj Igor Dyashishin (front seat) and Lt Col Alexander Mostovoy (back seat) was scrambled to intercept it.

After Viktor Yanukovych, the Russian-backed President of Ukraine, was ousted from power following the Euromaidan Revolution, or the Revolution of Dignity, in February 2014, Russian authorities including President Vladimir Putin felt that their interests, including strategic military bases of the Russian Navy, were in danger of disbandment on the Crimean peninsula. Emergency meetings were held, during which President Putin met his security services chiefs and discussed how to secure the interests of his country in the Black Sea region by taking advantage of the political chaos and weakness of the Ukrainian Armed Forces and how to carry out the annexation of the Crimea peninsula through a combination of a military operation and a referendum.

Four days after the final security meeting of Russian authorities in Moscow, Russian Special Forces occupied the Supreme Council (parliament) of Crimea on 27 February and then captured various strategic sites across the peninsula, including Ukrainian navy and air force bases such as the 204th BrTA at Belbek between 28 February and 4 March. Subsequently, the Ukrainian armed forces, including the air force, were put on high alert from 27 February.

In the beginning of February 2014, the 7th BrTA had only six airworthy Su-24Ms, 02, 22, 27, 28, 66 and 83 White, as well just four airworthy Su-24MRs, 11, 16, 17, and 36 Yellow, two L-39M1s, 71 and 72 Blue, and two L-39Cs, 73 and 74 Blue, in service with two bomber squadrons and a reconnaissance squadron that on paper were supposed to have 24 airworthy Su-24Ms and 12 Su-24MRs. At the time 56 Su-24M/MRs were stored in Starokostiantyniv; among these, 18 had been out of service for more than a decade, including ex-727th BAP Su-24Ms manufactured in 1982. Among them the aircraft that still had time left before the end of their calendar service life were quickly prepared by 7th BrTA technicians and returned to service within two weeks. The first restored aircraft were Su-24Ms 21 and 26 White, as well as Su-24MR 93 Yellow.

Following the extensive military build-up of Russia in Crimea and the annexation of the peninsula through a referendum that was never internationally recognised, the Ukrainian Armed Forces were prepared for a Russian military invasion from the peninsula, resulting in a Joint Staff Command exercise named Spring Thunderstorm 2014 in March 2014 to prepare for large-scale war.

The purpose of the exercise was to test the true state of combat readiness of the Armed Forces, and their level of training and support. Representatives of state and local authorities, other military formations and law enforcement agencies also participated at that time, and all available military training areas were used. This training exercise helped to evaluate the readiness of command and control structures and significantly improved their operational capabilities in the period of crisis.

66 White was one of the Su-24Ms that were forward deployed to Mirgorod AB to take part in the Battle of Donbass. It has 38 iron bombs loaded on seven multiple ejector racks under the fuselage and wings at Starokonstantinov in September 2013. *Alexander Golz*

After almost ten years, several Su-24M pilots of the 7th BrTA were trained and qualified to use Kh-58U anti-radiation missiles during training at Kanatovo in October 2014. 49 White was one of the Su-24Ms that were used during that training. On the left it can be seen equipped with an L-080 Fantasmagoria-A ELINT pod for target acquisition for the Kh-58U. On the right is one of the Kh-58Us in service of the 7th BrTA. *Ukrainian Air Force*

As part of the exercise, the UkrAF increased the readiness of 7th BrTA aircrews via several flight training sorties from Starokostiantyniv on 13 March, during which pilots of Su-24M 22 White, L-39M1 71 Blue and L-39C 73 Blue practised bombing with FAB-100 bombs while pilots of Su-24MR 93 Yellow practised tactical reconnaissance during a battle damage assessment mission after the missions.

Following the start of the war in Donbass, Ukrainian Armed Forces prepared themselves for an anti-terrorist operation by means of holding a Joint Command Post exercise in May. On 16 May, MiG-29s of the 40th and 114th BrTAs, Su-25s of the 299th BrTA and Su-24M/MRs of the 7th BrTA took part and bombed several targets that had been marked via SAB-250-200 flare bombs dropped by MiG-29UBs flying from Vasilkov at Kiev-Oleksandrivka gunnery range. Three Su-24Ms, 22, 28 and 66 White, as well as Su-24MRs 11 and 36 Yellow, were involved in the exercise from Lutsk airfield, where they had been forward deployed. Until 23 May, their aircrews practised using S-8 unguided rockets launched from B-8M1 rocket pods and bombing by means of FAB-100 unguided bombs.

Soon after the exercise, five Su-24Ms and two Su-24MRs were forward deployed to Mirgorod to take part in an anti-terrorist operation against Russian-backed militias in the Donbass region. On 26 May, the first UkrAF missions of this operation were carried out by Su-25s of the 299th BrTA and MiG-29s of the 40th and 114th BrTA, which had been forward deployed to Dnetropetrovsk airport. They took part in the first battle for the liberation of Donetsk airport, providing close air support for Ukrainian Army troops around the airport, while the Su-24s remained on standby at Mirgorod.

Following the loss of an An-30B of the 'Blue Watches' Squadron of the UkrAF to the pro-Russian separatists MANPADS during a photography or aerial surveying mission over Sloviansk on 6 June 2014, the air force decided to carry out tactical reconnaissance missions using Su-24MRs over the battlefield. The speed capability and its adequate self-defence equipment such as chaff and flare dispensers made the tactical reconnaissance jet less vulnerable than the An-30B.

During one of these recce missions, 11 Yellow (c/n 0415304), which was one of four Su-24MRs involved in the Donbass war, was targeted by a 9K34 Strela-3 (SA-14) MANPAD over Slavyansk. The aircraft was damaged in the empennage area and its left engine started to burn; the pilot, Evgeny Bogatanovich Bulatzik, extinguished the left engine fire after he shut off the fuel valve. Bulatzik and his navigator, Troshin Alexander Anatolyevich, decided to stay with their aircraft and continued their flight to Mirgorod 300km away, where they made an emergency landing. Their act of bravery in saving a valuable Su-24MR saw them later awarded the Order of Bogden Khmelnytsky III degree. The Su-24MR was later restored and redelivered to the 7th BrTA in spring 2015.

The majority of the UkrAF combat missions during the anti-terrorist operation in the Donbass region were close air support and air interdiction but on some occasions the Su-24Ms deployed to Mirgorod were used for deep strike missions against high-value targets. It is not known exactly how many of these missions were carried out by the Su-24Ms, but it is known that together with the Su-24MRs they flew 150 missions. At least one of the missions became well known after two Su-24Ms flew from Mirgorod and bombed Antratsit railway station at Lugansk on 9 August 2014.

The Su-24Ms were mostly used where the danger of low-altitude SAM systems, MANPADS and AA guns were present, during which they only used non-precision-guided munitions, mostly FAB-500 iron bombs, from high altitude. These were generally not as accurate as the precision-guided missiles that were available in the arsenal of the 7th BrTA but the majority of the pilots had no experience of using air-to-surface missiles. At least six of the Su-24M pilots passed a retraining course to be qualified

Su-24M 83 White with B-8M1 rocket pods and external tanks, based on images taken during the participation of the aircraft in the exercise before the beginning of the Ukrainian security forces' operation in Donbass. *Luca G. Canossa*

49 White with Kh-58U anti-radiation missile and Fantasmagoria-A as it looked when it participated in a training session for use of the missile during SEAD missions in October 2014. *Luca G. Canossa*

7th BrTA Su-24Ms have had this dragon artwork painted on their engine air intakes since 1990s. The Su-24Ms involved in the Battle of Donbass also had this artwork painted on their fuselages. *Luca G. Canossa*

to use the Kh-58U anti-radiation missile for SEAD operations. Pictures of the retraining course were later leaked and show at least one Su-24M, 49 White, equipped with an L-080 Fantasmagoria-A (Phantasmagoria-A) ELINT pod (ESM with a 222km maximum range for target acquisition of the Kh-58U missile) at Kanatovo airfield in October 2014, but they were never used in the battlefield.

Su-24Ms flying from Mirgorod were used to destroy a fighting position of pro-Russian separatists in Shakhtarsk, east of Luhansk, on 20 August 2014. Su-24s equipped with more powerful ECM and a self-protection suite were not so vulnerable to the surface-to-air missiles of the separatists, and they had been selected for this mission after the loss of several MiG-29s and Su-25s to MANPADS as well as an SA-11 Buk of the Pro-Russian separatists in previous days. The Buk M1 originally belonged to the 53rd Anti-Aircraft Rocket Brigade of the Russian ground forces and was used to mistakenly shoot down Malaysian Airlines flight MH17 on 17 July 2014.

Around 1800 local time on 20 August, when Su-24M 27 White (c/n 0815327) appeared over Shakhtarsk, it was shot down by a Pantsir-S SAM system at an altitude of 6,000m. The aircraft exploded in the air and fell in the vicinity of Novosvitlivka, Luhansk Oblast. The pilot and navigator ejected. The pilot's ejection was unsuccessful and he was badly injured. The navigator found him and helped him to cross the front line and Aidar River, where a UkrAF SAR team rescued them. However, the pilot died due to his severe injuries.

Nine days later, Su-25M1 08 Blue (c/n 25508110284), which had flown from Dnetropetrovsk Airport to take part in a combat mission, was shot down by an 9K33M3 'Osa-AKM' SAM system of the separatists over the Starobeshevsky district, Donetsk region, and its pilot, Vladislav Voloshin, ejected safely. This was the end of the UkrAF's fighter-bomber flights over Donbass during the war.

Despite the fact that the Su-24s no longer flew over Donbass, the UkrAF has kept its detachment of six Su-24s, including an Su-24MR, in Mirgorod. In addition to the Su-24s in Mirgorod, the UkrAF also deployed six Su-24Ms and an Su-24MR to Kanatovo on 3 October 2014, when the air base was officially reopened after the completion of reconstruction work on the runway, taxiway and ramp. The main task of the Kanatovo-based Su-24s was to support Air Command South Operations. They remained on deployment there until the end of 2017. Later, in 2016, when the number of operational Su-24s in service with the UkrAF's 7th BrTA was on the rise, it was planned to reactivate a Tactical Aviation Brigade in Kanotovo using at least 12 Su-24s, but for now it seems the plan is on hold.

Accidents

Su-24M 27 White was not the sole example lost in Ukraine since the birth of the UkrAF, there have been three others that have been destroyed among several accidents. The first loss was between 1995 and 1997 when an Su-24 Product-41 of the 806th BAP was burnt out on the ground at Lutsk air base. The second accident occurred to 44 White (c/n 1615336), another Product-41 of the regiment, on 18 August 1999. On that day the aircraft was under the control of Capt Igor Minenko (pilot) and Lt Sergey Kaverznev (navigator) flying in a training mission. The accident occurred at 10.45am local time within 7km of Lutsk when the pilot lost control while he was banking to the right at 600m (1,968ft) and flying at 550km/h (300 knots). As the aircraft started losing speed and altitude, the crew became confused and decided to eject. Kaverznev ejected first, while the Minenko stayed in the aircraft and directed it away from a village before ejecting safely.

The aircraft, carrying 5.5 tons of fuel, crashed in a swamp within 500m of the village of Lipljani, near the Styr River. This prevented an explosion and the aircraft was left there at a depth of 15m. However, if it had been recovered it would have been found to have been shredded into pieces due to the high-velocity impact. After an investigation, the pilot was fired while the navigator was reprimanded.

The serial disbandment of Su-24 regiments and a decline in the number of sorties by the type had a positive impact on the force, which saw a drop in the number of accidents and incidents involving technical and human factors. No further Su-24 accidents occurred until March 2014, when 7th BrTA sorties had been increased to prepare aircrews for combat following the threat of Russia's invasion from the Crimean peninsula. Subsequently, at 17.15 local time on 21 March 2014, Su-24M 83 White crashed on the final approach of Starokostiantyniv airport due to technical failure. Pilot Lt Col Denis Kochan and navigator Lt Panas Dudnik ejected safely but their aircraft was lost.

One of the last images of 83 White before its crash on 21 March 2014. It is on the main apron of Starokonstantinov AB with a B-8M1 rocket pod on the ground just two days before the crash. *Andrey M. Demidov's archive*

Pro-Russian separatists used the Pantsir S SAM system to shoot down Su-24M 27 White in the vicinity of Novosvitlivka, Luhansk Oblast, on 20 August 2014. It is seen at Starokonstantinov in June 2011. *Alexander Golz*

Su-24 repair and maintenance

After Ukraine's independence there were no aircraft repair plants in Ukraine with the ability to overhaul or carry out depot maintenance on Su-24s. Although the majority of its Su-24M fleet had been manufactured in the late 1980s, the UkrAF needed to keep at least a third of its Su-24 product-41s in service for training purposes for another decade, which made it necessary to overhaul them domestically.

In 1993, the NARP (Nikolayev Aircraft Repair Plant), which was responsible for repairing and overhauling Tu-16s, Tu-95s and Tu-142s of the USSR's Air Force and Navy before the collapse of the USSR, was tasked with developing a major overhaul programme for the UkrAF's Su-24s a year after it joined the repair network of the Ukrainian Ministry of Defence and had been placed under the command of the UkrAF. It took a year until the centre gained enough knowledge and documentation from the Novosibirsk aircraft overhaul centre to carry out mid-life overhauls of the Su-24, with an average rate of three aircraft per year in the 1990s.

Not only restoring and overhauling the UkrAF's Su-24s, the NARP was quickly contracted by the Iranian Ministry of Defence to restore 23 ex-Iraqi Air Force Su-24MKs for the Iranian Air Force (IRIAF) at a price of almost $5 million per aircraft in 1993 and 1994. The Su-24MKs in question had been sent to Iran among almost 140 Iraqi military and civil aircraft to keep them safe from the bombardment of Iraqi air bases during Operation Desert Storm in January 1991. As part of compensation for the costs of the Iran–Iraq war, the Iranian government decided to impound the aircraft and induct them into its air force. NARP was the only solution for Iran to have these aircraft overhauled and restored, especially when Russian President Yeltsin decided not to cooperate militarily with Iran under US pressure. For years, Ukraine remained as the key source of spare parts for Iranian Su-24s.

In the early 2000s, a large number of the Product-41 Su-24s were sent to Belya Tserkva, where they were scrapped. Many others that still had flight time left on their airframes were subject to a resolution for the sale of military equipment approved by the Cabinet of Ministers on 28 December 2000. The items listed for export and sale under this resolution reached their maximum in 2008. According to the final version of the resolution approved by the Ukrainian cabinet headed by Prime Minister Yulia Tymoshenko on 6 August 2008, 70 Su-24s that had been stored at five airfields in Ukraine had been listed as items for sale.

Among the Su-24s listed for sale, 16 were Product-41s, which were six examples manufactured between 1978 and 1980 (all ex-29th BAP examples) that had been stored at Kulbakino air base since the disbandment of the 33rd TSBPPLS, 6th Air Base, in 2003. According to the Ukrainian Ministry of Defence, two of these aircraft were in an almost complete condition and suitable for museums; each were on sale for 11 million UAH (approximately £1.2 million). There was also a seventh example, manufactured in 1974 and without engines or many other parts, which was stored at the NARP facility at Kulbakino and available for 1.3 million UAH (approximately £144,000). Seven disassembled Product-41s manufactured between 1977 and 1978 and two engineless examples built in 1973 and 1976 were on sale for 1.3 to 12.135 million UAH (£144,000 GBP to £1.3 million GBP), all stored at the A1789 military facility at Vasilkov.

Among the 70 Su-24s, 46 were Product-44s or Su-24Ms and included five ex-727th BAP examples, all manufactured in 1983. They were stored complete at Starokostiantyniv and had been priced at 2.6 to 12.3 million UAH each. Twenty-one others manufactured between 1981 and 1987 and mostly ex-727th BAP and ex-947th BAP examples were available for �1.8 to 39.323 million UAH per airframe, all stored disassembled at A1789 at Belya Tserkva. At Lutsk, 20 Su-24Ms that remained from a

83 White, an Su-24M of the 7th BAP at Nikolayev Aircraft Repair Plant, on 3 November 1995. It was one of the first Su-24Ms to be overhauled by NARP. This aircraft was lost in an accident in 2014. *Sergey Popsuevich*

A pair of Su-24MRs under depot level maintenance at the NARP facility in summer 2014. The overhaul of both of them was finished in four years. *Ukrainian Air Force*

total of 30 ex-947th BAP's Su-24Ms that had entered 806th BAP service in 2001 and been put in storage in 2004 were for sale for 1.8 to 9.3 million UAH each.

However, none of these Su-24s were sold and, as mentioned before, Ukraine managed to sell only one Su-24 in total, the Product-41 example 39 Red, which went to the Estonian Aviation Museum in 2005. The aircraft was in good condition and had been in service with the 6th Air Base as a training aircraft until the unit was disbanded in 2005.

In September 2002, the NARP completed the overhaul of two Azerbaijani Air Force Su-24MRs, 110 and 111 Blue, two of five examples that remained in service with the air force's 422nd Reconnaissance Squadron out of 11 that had been seized on 9 June 1992 by Azeri troops at Dallyar Air Base, where they were in with the USSR Air Force's 882nd Independent Reconnaissance Aviation Regiment. These two Su-24MRs were used as bombers until 2010, when they were placed in storage at Kyurdamir air base.

In 2008, the Azeri Air Force prepared the remaining three Su-24MRs at Nasosnaya air base to be sent to Nikolayev, Ukraine, for overhaul. The cost of the work was almost equal to the procurement of the overhauled Su-24Ms of the UkrAF. Therefore, the Azerbaijani government requested Ukrspetsexport to buy four of the surplus Su-24Ms available for sale. The total cost of the aircraft, which were all built in 1986, was 42 million UAH, which also covered their overhaul cost. However, the deal was not finalised and the three disassembled Su-24MRs, 101, 104 and 128 White, remained in Nasosnaya and were robbed of their parts to keep 110 and 111 Blue airworthy at Kyurdamir for another two years.

Lifetime extension by NARP

In 2013, nearly all UkrAF Su-24MRs had reached the end of their 25-year service life, while two-thirds of the Su-24M fleet had also run out of hours. Starting in 2010, the NARP was contracted to carry out not only major overhauls but also lifetime extensions as well as minor upgrades of the Su-24Ms and Su-24MRs, although it took four years before the first aircraft was overhauled. The aircraft in question was an Su-24M with the construction number 1041636 that had been delivered to NARP to undergo a major overhaul on 31 July 2004, almost ten years before its redelivery to the air force!

As mentioned above, the air force had only six Su-24Ms and four Su-24MRs left airworthy out of the total fleet of 114 in the country in February 2014. Most of these, including the Su-24MRs, had been kept airworthy through lifetime extensions, which was possible due to the low flying hours logged on each airframe.

From the NARP point of view, the Su-24M fleet can be conditionally divided into three groups. The first group are those currently operational (which mostly have limited flying hours left until end of their life or their next overhaul), the second are stored examples, and the third are those that have been withdrawn from use and are subject to disposal. Among these, the second group formed the majority of the Su-24M/MRs sent to the NARP for lifetime extension and major overhaul between 2014 and 2018.

Most of the Su-24s of the second group, especially those that had been stored for more than five years, have physical wear due to them being kept outside in an open area affected by cold and

41 White is the first Su-24M that the 7th BrTA received from NARP after completion of its overhaul in November 2014. It received the standard digital camouflage of the UkrAF. Here it is at Starokonstantinov almost five months after redelivery on 16 April 2015. *Alexander Golz*

humid environments, resulting in corrosion damage to metal parts; loss of protective paint, even colour and varnish as well as special coatings for the radome and radio panels; damage to the rubber parts and hoses due to loss of oil; damage to the seals and other rubber material on the fuselage; fatigue and fracture of the bearings and actuators of mechanical parts such as control surfaces due to metal corrosion.

As mentioned above, Su-24M 1041636 was the very first example delivered to NARP to be overhauled on 31 July 2004, when the facility did not have the ability to carry out a major overhaul of the aircraft, and it took almost ten years until it was overhauled and redelivered to the UkrAF's 7th BrTA as 41 White in November 2014. The aircraft also received the service's new digital camouflage pattern paint scheme.

Following a decree signed by the Ukrainian President, the aircraft was officially named after the Ukrainian war hero Alexander Milodichnoy on 25 October 2016.

The second Su-24M (c/n 341605) was delivered to the NARP on 16 July 2012 for a major overhaul and lifetime extension. The work was completed in October 2015 and it was redelivered to 7th BrTA as 20 White in a digital camouflage paint scheme. Finally, in November 2017, a third Su-24M, 44 White, was redelivered to the 7th BrTA also in digital camouflage.

In 2014, three Su-24MRs (c/ns 0741612, 0741613 and 0741607) were delivered to the NARP for overhaul on 15 July, 21 July and 22 July 2014 respectively. Among these, 0741612's standard-level overhaul was completed in 2015 and its first check flight was at Kulbakino AB or Nikolayev on 27 November 2015. The aircraft, 59 Yellow, was also painted in digital camouflage. Next to that, 0741613's overhaul was started under contract No. 343/17, value 19.253 million UAH (about $0.8 million). Redelivery of the second overhauled Su-24MR was scheduled for 10 December 2017 but it was delayed and finally took place in June 2018 due to Russian sanctions and the unavailability of some spare parts. The last Su-24M for which the NARP had completed an overhaul when this book went to press was 08 White. It was painted in digital camouflage colours and redelivered to the 7th BrTA on 16 May 2019.

As well as the standard and major overhauls of the four Su-24Ms and two Su-24MRs by the NARP between 2010 and 2018, the 7th BrTA's maintenance unit has itself restored several Su-24Ms and Su-24MRs since the beginning of the Crimea crisis. As mentioned before, two Su-24Ms, 21 and 26 White, and Su-24MR 93 Yellow, were quickly restored in March 2014. The next Su-24Ms were 06, 27, 33, 38 and 46 White, which together with an Su-24MR (35 Yellow) were restored to mission-ready status between 27 March and 31 September 2014. Finally, four more Su-24Ms, 18, 45, 49 and 77 White, were restored in 2015. In April 2019 the total number of airworthy Su-24Ms and Su-24MRs of the 7th BrTA were 19 and nine respectively and these were at Starokostiantyniv (22) and Mirgorod (six).

After the war

Since September 2014, when the use of combat aircraft in the war in Donbass was stopped due to the huge loss of UkrAF fighter jets to Pantsir-S and Buk M1 SAM systems as well as the MANPADS of Russian-backed separatists, the air force has kept its fleet of Su-24s ready to be used in the event of a Russian invasion. To maintain the standard of the 7th BrTA's aircrews' combat readiness, Air Command

Since the early 1990s, the 7th BAP, which is now the 7th BrTA, has had dragon artwork applied on the engine air intakes of its Su-24Ms. This example, 28 White had its dragon artwork painted during the war in Donbass when it was forward deployed to Mirgorod Air Base. ***Alexander Golz***

West held various annual exercises in which the unit participated alongside the 114th BrTA.

The President of Ukraine, Petro Poroshenko, declared 2016 as the year of the Ukrainian Air Force. During the year, it was planned to restore aviation and air defence combat readiness, and the largest-ever training exercise of 7th BrTA after the Donbass war was held at Lutsk, during which eight Su-24Ms, 18, 20, 22, 28, 41, 46, 66 and 77 White, and two Su-24MRs, 11 and 17 Yellow, as well as L-39s of the unit, took part between 14 April and 3 June 2016.

The key goals of this training were to provide the opportunity for young and new aircrews to fly day and night in all-weather conditions with experienced pilots and instructor pilots on various missions. They also had the chance to practise various flying manoeuvres. This exercise also provided a chance for the training of newly graduated technician and maintenance personnel of the unit under the command of Maj Viktor Voloshchuk, the deputy commander of the engineering and maintenance squadron.

Su-24M 28 White taxiing at Starokonstantinov on 16 April 2015. *Alexander Golz*

45 White is one of the twelve Su-24Ms that the technicians of the 7th BrTA restored between 2014 and 2017. It is seen at Starokonstantinov on 16 April 2019. *Alexander Golz*

A few months later, Air Command South, Centre and West conducted the large-scale exercise Sky Shield 2016 on 11 August. On that day, Su-24Ms 20 and 41 White (both recently overhauled) landed on the Kiev–Odessa highway, which had been closed temporarily to civilian traffic. This was first time in UkrAF history that Su-24s landed on a road. In early 2000s, a pair of MiG-29s had also landed on that section of highway.

On the evening of 11 August, a group of Su-24Ms, including 18 White, and Su-25M1s simulated a strike against an enemy airfield to destroy its medium-range SAM batteries as well as its facilities using iron bombs, S-8 unguided rockets and precision-guided air-to-surface missiles. The strike force were escorted by two Su-27M1s flying from Odessa to provide FORCAP (Force Combat Air Patrol). To simulate the counter air offensive operation of the enemy, a pair of 40th BrTA MiG-29s flew from Vaslikov to intercept the Su-24s and Su-25s and these were confronted by the escorting Su-27s, which were flying at low altitude behind the strike force.

In 2017 and 2018, at least nine more Su-24 pilots and 12 more navigators joined the 7th BrTA after graduation from the 203rd Training Aviation Brigade, which subsequently forced Air Command West to increase the number of training sorties by almost 20%. In June 2017, the Ukrainian Armed Forces held the Joint Staff Command exercise Blue Trident 2017, during which airborne troops and ground forces supported by Army Aviation helicopters played a key role in the simulation of counter-offensive and offensive operations, while air support was provided by the UkrAF including the 7th BrTA and its Su-24s.

In the first stage of the exercise on 16 June, the Su-24Ms destroyed air defence systems, enemy fighting positions and weapon supplies in support of 95 airborne troops who jumped from an Il-76MD and had heavy-duty infantry weapons such as armoured personnel carriers in the Zhytomyr region. The next day, an Su-24M and an Su-27M1 played the role of enemy fighters and these were intercepted by two 40th BrTA MiG-29s. Days later, the 7th BrTA's Su-24Ms took part in another joint exercise, during which two of them flew from Starokostiantyniv air base to simulate an air strike against the runway of Ivano-Frankovsk air base; in response two MiG-29s of the 114th BrTA were scrambled to intercept the Su-24s and also an L-39C, which was simulating the role of an enemy close air support aircraft.

08 White is the fourth Su-24M that the NARP redelivered to the 7th BrTA after completion of its overhaul. The aircraft is seen landing at Starokonstantinov after a ferry flight from Nikolayev on 16 May 2019. It is equipped with an L-081 Fantasmagoria-B ELINT pod. *Ukrainian Air Force*

Su-24Ms in service with the 7th BrTA

Bort Number	Construction Number	Former unit	Manufacture year	Overhaul/ Restoration year	Note
02 White	0715335	?	?	?	
04 White	0815323	?	1985	2016	Was restored by 7th BrTA in 2016
06 White	1041647	?	?	2014	Was restored by 7th BrTA in 2014
08 White	?	?	?	2017–2019	Overhaul by NARP between 2017 and 2019. Digital camouflage
18 White	?	?	?	2015	Was restored by 7th BrTA in 2015
20 White	1341605	230th BAP	1991	2014–2015	Was overhauled by NARP in 2014 and 2015. Digital camouflage
21 White	0315303	?	?	2014	Was restored by 7th BrTA in 2014
22 White	0715347	?	?	?	
26 White	1341606	230th BAP	1991	2014	Was restored by 7th BrTA in 2014
28 White	0815328	7th BAP	1985	2014	Was restored by 7th BrTA in 2014
33 White	0715342	7th BAP	1985	2014	Was restored by 7th BrTA in 2014
38 White	?	?	?	2014	Was restored by 7th BrTA in 2014
41 White	1041636	?	?	2014	Overhaul by NARP in 2014. Digital camouflage
44 White	?	?	?	2015–2017	Overhaul by NARP between 2015 and 2017. Digital camouflage
45 White	?	?	?	2015	Was restored by 7th BrTA in 2015
46 White	?	?	?	2014	Was restored by 7th BrTA in 2014
49 White	1141601	7th BAP	1988	2015	Was restored by 7th BrTA in 2015
66 White	?	?	?	?	
77 White	?	?	?	2015	Was restored by 7th BrTA in 2015

Su-25 Fleet (1992–today): The Stormtroopers

Ukraine inherited 85 Su-25s, comprising 41 from the USSR Air Force and 44 from the Navy; among these, almost 40 are left and 36 of them are in the inventory of the 299th BrTA. Since 2008, MiGremont has modernised them to Su-25M1/UBM1 standard and since 2015 to Su-25M1K/UBM1Ks. The Su-25M1s played a key role in the war in Donbass but paid a high price with the loss of five in combat. Since the beginning of the Crimea crisis and the Donbass war, the Ukrainian MoD has increased the number of operational Su-25s as much as possible and the air force had 32 in service in September 2018.

This historical image shows three Su-25s of the 452 OShAP including 05 and 14 Red during an exercise in 1989. *Sergey Popsuevich*

Stormtroopers of Chortkov, 452nd OShAP

Serial production of the Su-25 and Su-25UB ended in 1992. According to information exchanged following the CFE treaty, almost 390 Su-25s in various variants including Su-25UBs, Su-25UTGs and Su-25BMs were in the service of a Research-Instructor Fighter-Bomber Aviation Regiment, an Independent Assault Aviation Squadron, six Independent Assault Aviation Regiments, a Guards Fighter Aviation Regiment, two Training Aviation Regiments, a Shipborne Fighter Aviation Regiment (Navy), an Independent Shipborne Fighter Aviation Regiment (Navy) and an Instructor-Research Shipborne Aviation Regiment (Navy) in the USSR in November 1990. The Soviet Air Force and Navy statistics showed 415 Su-25s in service at the end of 1990.

452nd OMShAP Su-25UBs 52 Red during an exercise in 1989. *Sergey Popsuevich*

Historical records show that the 760th Research-Instructor Fighter-Bomber Aviation Regiment (760iiapib), part of the 4th Centre for Combat Employment and Retraining of Crews VVS at Lipetsk, was the first air force unit to receive pre-production T-8s and Su-25s for research purposes from 1980. Next to that, the 200th Independent Assault Aviation Squadron of the VVS Transcaucasus Military District based at Sital-Chae, Azerbaijan SSR, became the first combat unit to receive the Su-25 in 1981 and this tested and evaluated them in combat in Afghanistan. The unit was later reorganised as the 80th Independent Assault Aviation Regiment, with all its surviving Su-25s inherited by Azerbaijan in 1992.

The 234th Guards Fighter Aviation Regiment of the 9th Fighter Aviation Division based at Kubinka became another recipient of the Su-25 in 1982. The regiment received at least six serial-produced Su-25s within a year to use them for flight demonstrations in its 4th Aviation Squadron. The following year, the 90th Fighter Aviation Regiment of the VVS Odessa Military District was reorganised as the 90th Independent Assault Aviation Regiment in Artsyz, Odessa Oblast, after receiving Su-25s as replacement for its Su-15s, which had been in service since 1968. To train the Su-25 pilots, the regiment also received L-39 advanced jet trainers, which were replaced by six Su-25UBs in 1987 and 1988. The regiment was disbanded in 1989 and its 40 Su-25s and six Su-25UBs were sent to the 4070 aircraft storage base at Ovruch, but only a few months later they were delivered to the Soviet Union Navy Aviation's 1063rd Training Centre for Combat Employment Shipborne Aviation.

Formed in Alexandria, Kiev, in spring 1987, the 452nd Independent Assault Aviation Regiment became the third operator of the Su-25 in the Ukrainian SSR after the 90th OShAP and 368th OShAP. Because the Alexandria airfield did not have a suitable runway for Su-25 operations, the unit was relocated to Bliznetsy, Kharkiv Oblast, although it was still part of the VVS Kiev Military District. The unit became part of the 17th Air Army in May 1988 and was relocated to Chortkov, Ternopol Oblast, to take the place of the 368th OShAP, which was in the process of complete deployment to East Germany by the end of 1989. The 368th OShAP was the second operator of the Su-25 in the Ukrainian SSR after 1986.

Preparations for the relocation of the 452nd OShAP, which had the new name 'Military Unit 28265', to the new location began on 25 October 1988, with the move starting in January 1989 and ending in February. Between January and March, the first nine Su-25s, 26 to 35 to 42 Red, were adopted by the unit, followed on 24 May by Su-25UBs 54 and 55 Red.

From July until the end of August 1989, the personnel of the 452nd OShAP's 1st Aviation Squadron and some of their 11 Su-25s took part in a military exercise to practise SEAD against 9K331 SA-9 Tor-M1 and Tunguska-M1 2K22M SAM systems at Lutsk gunnery range. This exercise also involved a pair of two new air force Su-25Ts. Eight of the unit's Su-25s, and an Su-25UB, were involved in the exercise and they were forward deployed to Brody airport on 26 July. They were 04, 05, 07, 08, 10, 12, 14 and 15 Red (all single-seater) as well as Su-25UB 51 Red. An An-24 was used to transfer the ground crews and reserve pilots. The next day (27 July), the two Su-25Ts flown by test pilots from the 8th State Red Banner Scientific Research Institute VVS arrived at Brody.

During the exercise, SAM systems had to randomly simulate locking on and shooting down the Su-25s and the Stormtrooper pilots had to evade them by means of combat manoeuvre or deploying IR decoys. During the exercise, small cameras that are usually added to film the cabin during functional check flights were installed to film the pilot's actions during combat manoeuvres. If the SPO-15 'Beryoza' radar warning receiver (RWR) of the aircraft was blinking for more than 30 seconds it meant that the Su-25 was destroyed. It was found that the Tunguska M1 SAM systems managed to score successful hits on all the Su-25s. The 452nd OShAP and 8th Scientific Research Institute investigated the failure of Su-25 pilots to detect the SAM systems locking on before being shot down. It was discovered that the pilots needed more time to destroy the targets (SAM systems). The pilots were spending 35–50 seconds on detection, manoeuvring (dive), aiming and launching their missiles. In contrast, the anti-aircraft missile system Tunguska spent only 18–25 seconds in automatic mode to search and detect the target and launch the missile! Therefore, the Su-25 had already been destroyed in the manoeuvring stage.

In order to make the Su-25s more of a threat to the Tunguska and Tor SAM systems, the air force commanders secretly telephoned commanders of the SAM units involved in the exercise and asked them to give their radio frequency. Then, during the following days of the exercise, when a two-ship formation of Su-25s was simulating an attack against the SAM batteries, the wingman could listen

Four Su-25s of the 452nd OMShAP departing Chortkov Air Base during a military exercise in 1989. *Sergey Popsuevich*

in and monitor the conversation of the SAM operators and inform the leader of formation to do exactly the opposite of what the SAM operators were going to do. As a result of that, the scores of the Su-25s against the SAM systems and vice-versa became equal.

In April 1990, the 452nd OShAP took part in another exercise, this time an air-to-ground one to simulate the destruction of ground targets at Kamenka-Bugskaya gunnery range at night. Night bombings were carried out while the aircraft were flying horizontally (no dive bombing), dropping their FAB-250-270 bombs in one-minute intervals because they were flying within 10km of each other. While all the pilots of the first formations accurately bombed their targets, the leader of the last three-ship formation flight, Capt Khoroshiltsev, carried out his attack with a 15° combat course error, resulting in the bomb being dropped 100–120m from the target in a swamp at Nevryiv.

Flying next to Khoroshiltsev, Capt Volkov (No. 2 in the formation) saw the explosion of the first bomb in the swamp and he also bombed by mistake with a 45° combat course error. As a result, his bomb was dropped within 50m of the observation tower and buildings of the gunnery range and the shockwave resulted in damage to electricity wires and radio antennas. The pilot of the third aircraft, Col G. M. Sokovih, did not receive an order to bomb because the radio antennas of the observation tower had been damaged and the observers could not communicate with him. However, Volkov ordered Sokovih to drop his bomb, which hit a concrete toilet within 50m of the observation post. In total, 11 officers were wounded on the ground, two of them seriously and one of them later died. As a result of the bombing error, the pilots were punished and Capt Volkov was sentenced to eight years in prison.

After independence

Among all the eight combat units of Soviet Air Force operating the Su-25 in 1991, just one was inherited by the Ukrainian Air Force, the 452nd OShAP at Chortkov. The unit had 35 Su-25s and six Su-25UBs in 1992 when the unit was re-subordinated to Ukraine. During the ceremony for taking oath to the allegiance to Ukraine, only 30% of the personnel, mainly those who were Ukrainian by nationality, took the oath while the others who refused left the air force. Col Renat Sadikov was appointed as commander of the regiment after independence.

Due to the shortage of personnel and a fuel crisis, flight activity was stopped, which had an impact on the regiment's combat readiness. In 1993, several of the regiment's pilots flew L-39s to maintain their flight skills. During a training flight in summer 1993, Su-25UB 53 Red (c/n 38220115075) was damaged while taxiing on the apron after it hit a jet blast deflector. The crew were not injured. On 19 August 1992, 452nd OShAP Su-25 25 Red

This Afghan war veteran Su-25 07 previously served in the 90th OShAP. It was among the examples at the Vasilkov Higher Military Technical School for training students. It has nine faded red stars painted under its canopy showing that it had logged 90 combat sorties during the war. It was seen on 25 July 1995. *Sergey Popsuevich*

Raven artwork applied to the nose section of some of the Chortkov-based Su-25s of the 452nd OMShAP in 1989 and 1990. This is 27 Red. *Sergey Popsuevich*

(c/n 25508110275) took part in a Ukrainian Air Force exhibition held at Gostomel airport to celebrate the first anniversary of Ukraine's independence. No. 25 Red was the first of the unit's Su-25s to have UkrAF markings painted on its fuselage.

In 1994, the first large-scale training exercise of the Ukrainian Armed Forces involving the air force was held at the Lviv Educational Centre. During the exercise, a 48th ORAP Su-24MR carried out tactical reconnaissance missions over the gunnery range, transmitting the gathered intelligence in real time to the headquarters. Simultaneously, interceptors flew over the ground forces on a CAP mission. Targets were detected and chosen to be bombed by Su-24M strike bombers of the 947th Bomber Aviation Regiment dropping ODAB-500PM bombs; the leader of their formation was Col Alexey Kotovym. Soon after them, a formation flight of 452nd OShAP Su-25s led by Col Renat Sadikov bombed other targets.

452nd OMShAP Su-25 37 Red over Vinnitsa on 23 March 1996. *Sergey Popsuevich*

The Stormtroopers of Saki, the Navy Su-25s

Following the retirement of the Ya-38 VTOL fighter jet from Soviet Union Navy Aviation service between 1989 and July 1991, as a temporary replacement the Su-25 was used as an assault aircraft by the 279th Independent Shipborne Assault Aviation Regiment and 299th Independent Maritime Assault Aviation Regiment (previously the 299th Instructor-Research Shipborne Aviation Regiment) of the Northern and Black Sea fleets respectively from 1990. The 299th Instructor-Research Shipborne Aviation Regiment had been activated with Yak-38s and Yak-38Us (conversion trainer) as well as MiG-21UMs under the 33rd Centre for Combat Employment and Retraining of Personnel Aviation VMF (Navy Aviation) at Saki, Crimean Oblast, on 17 September 1976.

In December 1988, the unit became part of the 1063rd Training Centre for Combat Employment Shipborne Aviation and in 1990 all its Yak-38s were retired due to safety reasons. A decisions was made to induct the Su-25 attack aircraft as a temporary replacement until the Yak-41M VTOL fighter jet was available. However, the funds for this project were cut in August 1991.

As explained above, the 90th OShAP had all its 40 Su-25s and six Su-25UBs stored at Ovruch and this the best option for the Navy to obtain aircraft to equip the 100th KIAP and 299th IIKAP of the 1063rd Training Centre for Combat Employment Shipborne Aviation. Among these aircraft, 16 found their way into service with the 2nd and 3rd Aviation Squadrons of the 100th KIAP, which also received seven Su-25UTG shipborne (carrier-based) trainer aircraft to train Su-33 pilots. The 100th KIAP's Su-25s were Su-25UBs 11, 16, 18 and 19 Red and 12 Su-25s, 25, 29, 31, 38,40, 41, 43, 48, 49 and 50 Red, which took the place of nine ageing L-39s.

Thirty other ex-90th OShAP's Su-25s reached all three Aviation Squadrons of the 299th IIKAP, which was redesignated as the 299th Independent Maritime Assault Aviation Regiment (299th OKShAP) and came under the command of the Black Sea Fleet. This unit also became the operator of four Su-25UTG carrier-based trainer aircraft that year.

In April 1992, during the official ceremony for the 100th KIAP to declare loyalty to the newly independent Ukraine, 15 personnel, mostly pilots including the commander of the regiment and the chief of the 1063rd Training Centre, Timur Avtandilovich Apakidze, refused to swear the oath and they mostly went to Russia to continue their career in the 279th OKShAP. Apakidze became commander of the unit, which was the sole fighter regiment of Russian Navy Aviation in the early 1990s. On 17 July 2001, while performing manoeuvres in his Su-33 during the air festival of the 85th Anniversary of Russian Naval Aviation, his aircraft crashed and he was killed.

The 100th KIAP became part of the State Flight-Test Centre (GLIC or CLITS) of the 5th Air Army of the UkrAF in 1992. The 3rd Scientific-Experimental Department of the 929th State Flight-Test Centre of the USSR Defence Ministry (GLITS) had been operating eight MiG-29s, four Su-27s, four L-39Cs and four Su-25UTGs of the 100th KIAP at Kirovskoye since 1991. In 1992, the rest of the MiG-29s and Su-27s of the 100th KIAP, which had now become the 100th IAP, were sent to Kirovskoye, while all its Su-25s including the four Su-25UTGs at Kirovskoye, entered service with the 299th OKShAP at Saki in November 1992. In 1996, the 100th IAP was disbanded.

62 Red (c/n 38220123321) was one of the Su-25UBs in service with the 299th OShAP (formerly 299th OKShAP). It still had the Ukrainian Navy flag on its fuselage at Saki in 1995. *Sergey Popsuevich*

Unlike the 100th IAP, the majority of the 299th OKShAP personnel under the command of the regimental commander, Col Yevgeny Kaburov, took the oath of allegiance to Ukraine on 8 April 1992, while the unit became part of the Ukrainian Navy on 17 March 1992. Similar to the 100th KIAP, the 299th OKShAP became part of the State Flight-Test Centre (GLIC or CLITS) of the 5th Air Army of UkrAF. In 1993, the 299th OKShAP was designated the 299th OShAP and became a unit of the Ukrainian Navy, remaining so until 1996. In 1994, the unit exchanged three of its Su-25UTGs with Su-25UB 03 Red of the 279th OKShAP of Russian Navy Aviation. Two other Su-25UTGs of the unit, including the first experimental T8-UTG1, were sold to China in 2007 and the US (through Estonia).

From July 1995, the 299th OShAP became a frequent participant in the large-scale exercises of the Ukrainian Armed Forces, including the Joint Command and Staff training as well as Ukrainian–American peacekeeping exercises. This included Peacekeeping Marine Corps 95, Partnership 97, Fairway of Peace 97 and Sea Breeze 97. The 299th OShAP also took part in joint exercises with the Black Sea Fleet of the Russian Federation Navy including Sea Breeze 98, Autumn 98 and Freewaters of the World 98. From 1999, the unit participated in international exercises with the US again, namely Duel 99, Cooperative Partner 2000, Clear Sky 2000, Fairway of Peace 2001 and Sea Line 2004.

299th BrTA, the sole Su-25 operator

In 1996, the 299th OShAP was moved from Ukrainian Navy Aviation again and became part of the 32nd Bomber Aviation Division (32nd BAD), 5th Air Army, UkrAF. Following the disbandment of the 32nd BAD it became a unit of 5th Air Corps in 2000. In 2002, it was reorganised into the 299th Aviation Base, and in 2003 as the 299th Assault Aviation Brigade. In May 2004, the Brigade was relocated from Saki to Kulbakino, Nikolayev. A satellite image dated 31 August 2004 shows ten of its Su-25s on the main apron at Kulbakino AB.

By the end of 2004, the 452nd OShAP had been disbanded in Chortkov and 22 of its Su-25s and all its active personnel were absorbed by the 299th Assault Aviation Brigade, while 13 other Su-25s were sent to Ivano-Frankovsk AB to be stored and five other Su-25s were sent to the ZARZ (Zaporozhye Aircraft Repair Plant). By May 2005, the relocation of the 299th Assault Aviation Brigade to Kulbakino was complete and the unit was then renamed the 299th Tactical Aviation Brigade under the subordination of air command south. A satellite image dated 9 September 2009 shows 41 Su-25s at Kulbakino AB, which includes the former 452nd OShAP machines.

In 2006, the 299th Tactical Aviation Brigade (299th BrTA) took leadership of the General Staff of the UkrAF during peacekeeping and counter-terrorism operations for the UN. In the same year the unit participated in the joint command and staff exercise of the Ukrainian Armed Forces named Clear Sky 2006, during which the Su-25s were responsible for providing close air support for the ground forces and they practised bombing and also air-to-air missile firing at UAVs. During this exercise, which was held between 25 and 27 July 2006, 61 aircraft, including at least four Su-25s, 01, 02, 24 and 25 Blue, took part.

In 2007, the 299th BrTA participated in the Command Post exercise Artery 2007, which was three times larger than Clear Sky 2006 in terms of number of participants. In total, 25 helicopters and 75 aircraft, including six Su-25s, three Su-25UBs and 200 staff of the 299th BrTA, participated in the exercise in March and April 2007. During the exercise, the nine Su-25s were deployed to Lutsk and Kirovskoye, from where they took part in the operations and demonstrated their high level of professionalism and combat readiness.

Between 15 and 27 September 2008, the 299th BrTA took part in the joint command and staff exercise Sea Knot 2008, this time from its mother base, Kulbakino, at Nikolayev. Forty-five aircraft, including a Be-12 amphibious aircraft of the Ukrainian Navy together with ten helicopters, participated. It is not clear how many Su-25s of the 299th BrTA took part but it is known they provided close air support and maritime attack missions.

In 2009, the number of Command Post exercises decreased one-and-a-half times compared with the previous year. In that year, the 299th BrTA took part with the 72nd Separate Mechanised Brigade of the

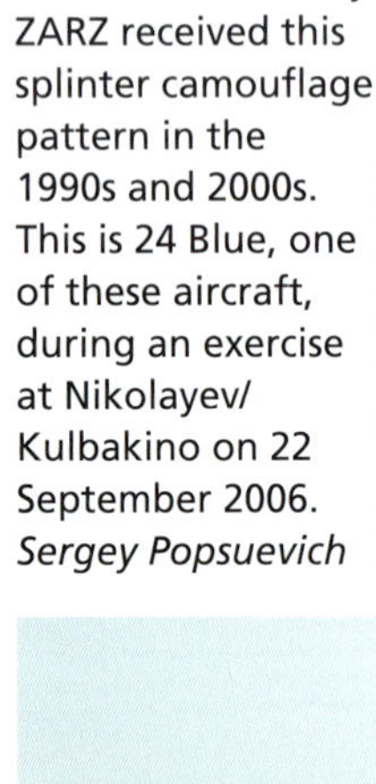

Su-25s of the 299th BrTA overhauled by ZARZ received this splinter camouflage pattern in the 1990s and 2000s. This is 24 Blue, one of these aircraft, during an exercise at Nikolayev/ Kulbakino on 22 September 2006. *Sergey Popsuevich*

27 and 33 Blue, two Su-25s of the 299th BrTA, each armed with a pair of PTB-800 external tanks and B-8M1 rocket pods, during an exercise over the Rovno gunnery range dispensing flares on 17 September 2007. *Sergey Popsuevich*

8th Army Corps with two Su-25s, which employed iron bombs and S-8 rockets during strike missions near Bila Tserkva. Also in September that year, a research exercise was conducted by the Ukrainian Armed Forces involving four 299th BrTA Su-25s, during which the aircraft took part in the training and operational phases of the exercise from Ivano-Frankovsk and Kolomiya air bases respectively.

Earlier in 2009, 299th BrTA also had its own routine training missions to train new pilots and maintain the skill of its combat pilots. For example, on 11 February, 20 sorties were conducted by Su-25s and L-39s. Another series of training flights were carried out in July that year, during which six Su-25s and two L-39s logged 21 hours and 30 minutes in 57 sorties.

On 19 February 2010, an Su-25UB and three Su-25s of thr 299th BrTA were used during an IFR and navigation training exercise, during which their pilots experienced flights in adverse meteorological conditions during the day and night. In total, 11 sorties were conducted in six hours, including several flight check missions during which Su-25 pilots inspected the readiness of S-300 long-range SAM systems in the Nikolayev region.

Later that year, the 299th BrTA took part in the Command and Control exercise Cooperation 2010, held between 6 September and 4 October. The exercise was carried out in five military training areas of the land forces, in the Chauda State Scientific-Test Centre of the Air Force and ten training ranges of the Naval Forces. In total, 18 helicopters and 18 aircraft, among them four Su-25s that included a recently modernised Su-25UBM1, took part. The Su-25s provided fire support for coastal defence.

In 2011, the year started with routine flight training of 40 pilots of the 299th BrTA on the Su-25M1, Su-25UBM1, Su-25UB and L-39 with the key goal of regaining lost pilot skills, including flight capability in bad weather over 144 hours between 17 January and 11 February. In May, 299th BrTA pilots, including those flying the L-39, logged 60 hours of training and retraining in just two days.

On 17 and 18 August 2011, 299th BrTA pilots were prepared for Exercise Adequate Response 2011 in 40 training sorties to improve their piloting and navigation skills, and formation flight at low altitude.

Su-25 14 blue and Su-25UB 60 Blue launching their S-8 unguided rockets at targets on Rovno gunnery range during an exercise on 17 September 2007. *Sergey Popsuevich*

299th BrTA Su-25 33 Blue can be seen launching S-8 rockets from its B-8M1 rocket pods during a military exercise at Rovno gunnery range on 17 September 2007. *Sergey Popsuevich*

Su-25s of the 299th BrTA forward deployed to Vasilkov Air Base on 21 August 2009 to take part in the rehearsal for Ukraine's Independence Day parade. The aircraft taxiing is 33 Blue while 01, 27, 02, 24 and 25 Blue can be seen in the background. Their splinter camouflage had been changed to this jungle design in 2008. *Sergey Popsuevich*

They then took part in the research command post exercise Adequate Response 2011, held between 12 and 30 September. The purpose of the exercise was to review the level of combat training of the forces as well as to research the development of a prospective model of the Armed Forces of Ukraine. Sixteen helicopters and 36 aircraft of the air force took part in this exercise; this included seven Su-25s and an Su-25UB.

During the exercise, a group of three Su-25s from the 299th BrTA together with three Su-24Ms of the 7th BrTA were forward deployed to Kirovskoye airfield in the Crimea for maritime combat training, such as the simulation of anti-shipping missions. From there, Su-25 pilots also carried out rocket attacks using S-8 unguided rockets on ground targets on the Opuk gunnery range, under the command of Col Vladimir Pomogayba.

In 2012, the 299th BrTA resumed activity in the third week of January. On 20 February, the Brigade conducted 14 training sorties, during which two L-39s, an L-39M1, three Su-25/M1s and an Su-25UB were used for day and night flight training. On 12 March, a further series of training missions was carried out, during which pilots practised formation flying and navigation, while on 19 March

299th BrTA Su-25UB 60 Blue armed with six FAB-150-M54 bombs and two R-60M IR-guided missiles at Vasilkov on 28 March 2008. *Sergey Popsuevich*

Su-25 01 Blue during an exercise at Ivano-Frankivsk AB in September 2013. It is equipped with a pair of PTB-800 external fuel tanks and four B-8M1 rocket pods (two under each wing). *Alexander Golz*

02 Blue during the same exercise. It has fired its S-25-OFM unguided heavy rockets, while its OFAB-250-270 bomb has not been dropped. *Alexander Golz*

two Su-25M1s inspected the readiness of air defence sites and the quick reaction alert capability of the 40th BrTA over Poltava. Subsequently, they were intercepted by a pair of MiG-29s.

In the third week of April, the 299th BrTA pilots practised ground-attack missions at the Kiev-Alexandria gunnery range in 24 sorties, including bombing using OFAB-50-75 practice bombs and live OFAB-100-120 bombs and rocketing using S-8 unguided rockets. Later, between 30 July and 3 August, the 299th BrTA took part in the command staff training of Air Command South, carrying out rocketry, gunnery and bombing over 45 hours.

On 5 December, the Ukrainian Ministry of Defence, Dmitry Salamatin, visited Kulbakino AB on the occasion of the delivery of two overhauled and modernised Su-25M1s. On that day, he was accompanied by the Commander in Chief of the UkrAF, Brig Gen Vladimir Zaman. During the official visit, 14 Su-25s and two L-39s flew in four four-ship formation flights. On 19 and 20 December 2012, the two newly delivered Su-25M1s, together with several other Su-25s and L-39s, were used in a training course for retraining the 299th BrTA pilots in 50 sorties over 19 hours.

In April 2013, the 299th BrTA took part in the bilateral research command and staff training exercise Milky Way 2013. During the practical phase of the exercise on 24 April, Su-25M1 06 Blue was flown from Gavryshivka airfield to carry out a SEAD mission. Earlier, between 25 February and 8 March, the 299th BrTA had flown a series of regular training missions in which Su-25 and L-39 pilots had not only maintained and improved their piloting skills but also carried out a number of complex and purely military tasks, such as air interdiction and close air support mission tactics, as well as anti-ship missions over the Black Sea, in 18 sorties within 12 hours.

Between 8 and 12 July, 40 training sorties in 36 hours were carried out by the 299th BrTA in which pilots regained their piloting skills, including formation flying. Between 19 and 23 August another group of other Su-25 pilots restored their flying capability and piloting skills as well as the capability to carry out air-to-surface missions such as cannon firing. Then, between 2 and 6 September they practised rocketry and bombing in another training course in which they logged 40 flying hours in 50 sorties.

The 299th BrTA also took part in two other major events in 2012, first participating in a demonstration of UN peacekeeping forces and then exercise Autumn Cyclone 2013. During the Ukrainian Armed Forces firepower demonstration at the International Centre for Peacekeeping and Security of Ukraine, 20 aircraft took part, among them two pairs of Su-25s that destroyed ground targets firing S-8 unguided rockets. Then, 26 aircraft including at least five Su-25s took part in the bilateral research command post exercise Autumn Cyclone 2013.

299th BrTA Su-25UB 63 Blue was one of the last aircraft of the regiment to be painted in brown camouflage after its overhaul at ZARZ in the early 2000s. It is at Nikolayev/Kulbakino on 22 September 2008. *Alexander Golz*

Maintenance, repair, overhaul and upgrade

Zaporozhye Aircraft Repair Plant (ZARZ), which had the ability to perform depot level maintenance of MiG-25 family jets since 1978 and then Su-27 fourth-generation fighter aircraft since 1993, was contracted by the UkrAF to carry out the overhaul or depot maintenance of 299th BrTA Su-25UB 61 Blue.

After its overhaul the aircraft logged its first Functional Check Flight (FCF) on 6 May 1999 and this was followed by the overhaul of Su-25 17 Blue from same unit, which made its first test flight in 2000. Soon this enabled the ZARZ to profit from the restoration and repair of Su-25s for sale to foreign countries, starting with three Su-25s and an Su-25UB delivered in June 2001 for immediate use by the Macedonian Air Force against the ethnic Albanian National Liberation Army (NLA) militant group.

The second Su-25UB sent to the ZARZ to be overhauled was 54 Red (c/n 38220123321), an ex-452nd OShAP aircraft. After its overhaul, the aircraft remained at the facility to be used as a test bed for the trial of new avionic and navigation systems designed and developed domestically in Ukraine to modernise the Su-25. This work was carried out with the key goal of offering an upgrade programme for the type for domestic and foreign costumers of the repair plant, which was later named MiGremont. In 2007, the ZARZ was contracted to begin modernising UkrAF Su-25s and 54 Red became the first prototype for the project. This aircraft was modernised and returned to its brigade for final operational tests during routine gunnery training missions in 2008.

In late 2008, the air force also allocated funds for the modernisation of a single-seater Su-25 for the 299th BrTA. This example, redesignated as an Su-25M1, was 41 (c/n 25508110281) and it made its functional check flight at Zaporozhye in October 2009, while 54 Red was renamed an Su-25UBM1 and became 62 Blue. Both aircraft completed their flight tests and were officially accepted by the Ukrainian Ministry of Defence on 15 March 2010.

The improvements in the combat and mission capabilities of the Su-25M1/UBM1s after the installation of domestically built equipment by the State Enterprise Orion-Navigation (from the city of Smila in the Cherkassy region) and OJSC Aviakontrol are:

- 30% increased accuracy of the use of unguided weapons for the destruction of ground targets by means of the installation of a new digital targeting sight to replace the old analogue example
- Capability of navigational bombing during horizontal flight without any need to dive if the coordinates are known. This enables the aircraft to carry out bombing at higher altitudes (between 3,000 and 5,000m) and there is also no need for the pilot to see the target (in all weather conditions)
- Increase in the accuracy of aircraft navigation flight on a pre-aligned route from the point of departure until the given point of destination with a deviation of less than 50m by means of GLONASS/GPS NAVSTAR SN-3307-02 satellite navigation systems
- Automatic approach for landing at equipped or unequipped airports by knowing the exact coordinates of the airfield's runway and adding it to the navigation computer by means of the Kurs-93M-V on-board integrated and combined VOR/ILS navigation and landing system
- Ability of automatic flight towards the target with known coordinates by means of the MSD-2000V DME/TACAN receiver
- Ability of the aircraft to fly along a route in complete 'radio silence' mode (without the use of radio)
- Ability to fly an aircraft along international routes using VOR/DME and ICAO-compatible A-511 version 30 transponder
- Ability to fly an instrumental approach with ILS/DME beacons
- Navigation system with the capability to work with the secondary radars of air traffic control (KVS) in different modes
- Recording of all flight parameters such as digital and audio information on the on-board emergency flight data recorder BUR-4-1-10

07 Yellow (c/n 38220115021) was the test bed of the Su-25M1 modernisation programme at ZARZ. It is seen during a test flight over Zaporozhye on 14 June 2012. *Guk Aleksander*

Ex-452nd OMShAP Su-25UB 54 Red but was sent to ZARZ to become the first twin-seater Su-25 to be modernised to Su-25M1 level in 2007. After two years of work, the aircraft was redelivered as 62 Blue to the 299th BrTA in these colours. It is seen at Kulbakino AB on 20 April 2011. *Alexander Golz*

The first Su-25UBM1, 62 Blue (c/n 38220123321) during a joint exercise with Su-27s of the 831st BrTA and MiG-29s of the 114th BrTA at Ivano-Frankivsk on 24 September 2013. *Alexander Golz*

In 2014, the Su-25UBM1 62 Blue was sent back to the factory to receive a series of minor upgrades such as the installation of new chaff/flare dispensers and also to be painted in digital camouflage colours. It is seen at Nikolayev on 28 October 2016. *Alexander Golz*

Su-25M1 03 Blue during a joint military exercise with 40th BrTA MiG-29s on 12 March 2012. Here it is armed with a pair of S-25-OFM heavy rockets and OFAB-250-270 iron bombs. *Alexander Golz*

- Recorded flight data can be used by modern flight information-processing facilities with the use of automated control algorithms through a computer for performing in-depth analysis and advanced diagnostics of the technical condition of on-board equipment, which allows the accumulation of a database to operate the aircraft according to its technical condition

After 41 and 62 Blue, one more Su-25M1, 03 Blue (c/n 25508110278), was delivered to the 299th BrTA in 2010. Following 03 Blue, two more Su-25M1s, 04 Blue (c/n 25508110276) and 05 Blue (c/n 25508110285), were officially handed over to the Ukrainian MoD after being test flown by MiGremont test pilots Gregory Grishchenko and Yuri Yakovunik during a special ceremony at Zaporozhye airfield on 25 November 2011. Both Su-25M1s were flown to Kulbakino AB on 29 November.

In September 2012, the overhaul and modernisation of the fifth Su-25M1 was completed at Zaporozhye and the aircraft, 06 Blue (c/n 25508110121), became the first UkrAF Su-25 to be painted in grey digital camouflage colours. Before that, the Zaporozhye Aircraft Repair Plant, or even the 299th BrTA maintenance Squadron, were painting the Su-25s using low-quality colours, which in some cases was applied over the older paint. Those low-quality paints could easily be washed away by rain and snow within a year, but this time 06 Blue received high-quality and expensive DuPont Helios paints.

The modernisation of two more Su-25M1s, 07 Blue (c/n 25508110131) and 08 Blue (c/n 25508110284), was completed and they were painted in digital camouflage. They were officially handed over to the MoD during a ceremony when the Minister of Defence, Dmytro Salamatin, was present at Zaporozhye on 5 December 2012. During the ceremony, Salamatin told the media: *'The uniqueness of today's event is that for first time in our air force there is a fully staffed squadron* [1st Aviation Squadron of 299th BrTA]. *There are 12 combat aircraft* [Su-25s] *and two training aircraft* [Su-25UBs]. *This is a very significant day. We expect similar days for other brigades in the near future.'*

The Deputy Commander of the Ukrainian Armed Forces, Lt Gen Vasily Nikiforov, also said during the ceremony: *'We have been waiting for this event for a long time. This first brigade today has a full number of 12 combat and 2 training aircraft thanks to the money that was invested for the repair and modernisation of aircraft. This brigade is now ten years old and was underfunded in the beginning. Thanks to the fact that the*

Su-25M1 04 Blue during a gunnery training exercise at Ivano-Frankivsk AB armed with four B-8M1 rocket pods and OFAB-250-270 iron bombs on 25 September 2013. *Alexander Golz*

Su-25M1 41 Blue loaded with four B-8M1 rocket pods during a joint exercise with the 114th and 831st BrTA at Ivano-Frankivsk AB on 25 September 2013. This aircraft dropped two OFAB-250-270 bombs and fired all its S-8 unguided rockets on a gunnery range in Crimea on that day. *Alexander Golz*

Zaporozhye aircraft [repair plant] *repaired these aircraft, we prepared the pilots and showed the Minister of Defence that this brigade is capable of fulfilling all the tasks of its mission in full force.'*

According to Nikiforov, the repair of each Su-25 cost 15–18 million UAH. Each aircraft has a calendar life of eight years (MTBO) or 700 flying hours after overhaul and modernisation.

In November 2013, modernisation of the eighth single-seater Su-25M1 was completed at the MiGremont facility. The aircraft, 40 Blue (c/n 25508110325), was painted in digital camouflage and delivered to the 299th BrTA after its functional check flights at the end of 2013.

Stormtroopers for sale

Ukraine was the third largest seller of second-hand Su-25s after Belarus and Russia. In order to fund the costs of the Ukrainian Air Force, the Ministry of Defence sold 22 of its surplus Su-25s, including five two-seater variants, between 2001 and 2013. As explained above, this started with the sale of four Su-25s, including a single Su-25UB combat training variant, to Macedonia in 2001 and continued with a deal for four more examples, including two two-seaters, to Equatorial Guinea in 2006, with deliveries made after overhaul in MiGremont between 2007 and 2009.

For the first time, on 28 December 2000, the Cabinet of Ministers approved a list of surplus military equipment from the Ukrainian Ministry of Defence for export to foreign countries. An updated list was approved by the Cabinet on 6 August 2008. Seventeen single-seater Su-25s and an Su-25UTG were on the list. Each Su-25 was priced at almost 3 million UAH, while the Su-25UTG was almost 3.1 million UAH.

Two Su-25s, both manufactured in 1984, were available for sale at Nikolayev air base, and nine others, all former 452nd OShAP examples manufactured in 1983, were stored at Ivano-Frankivsk; a 1983 example was available at the National Aviation University of Kiev; three others manufactured between 1985 and 1987 were stored at the State Enterprise 'Evaptoria' Aviation Repair Plant; and two 1984 examples were at the MiGremont facility. The single Su-25UTG, manufactured in 1990, was stored with the military unit A0156 at Kirovskoye (Feodosiya) air base.

In 2008, a contract was finalised for the sale of six Su-25s, including two UB combat training variants, to Chad, and the aircraft were delivered to the Chadian Air Force after restoration and overhaul between 2008 and 2012. A further contract for the sale of four single-seater Su-25s to Chad was finalised in 2012, with deliveries taking place in 2013. In 2012, two more countries, DR Congo and Niger, procured second-hand Su-25s from the Ukraine. Both ordered two aircraft, with deliveries taking place in 2012 and 2013 respectively. Also, the sole Su-25UTG was found a customer in 2008, which was China. After the sale of 22 Su-25s and the Su-25UTG between 2001 and 2013, the disposal of surplus Su-25s was stopped due to the war in Donbass and the need of the 299th BrTA for more aircraft.

Stormtroopers at war

At the beginning of the Crimea crisis in February 2014, Air Command South put the 299th BrTA on high alert, similar to the other air force Brigades. The unit had just 15 of its Su-25s operational, which were four Su-25s, 01, 02, 25 and 27 Blue; Su-25UB 65 Blue; nine Su-25M1s, 03, 04, 05, 06, 07, 08, 38 (delivered in January 2014), 40 and 41 Blue; and Su-25UBM1 62 Blue.

In the third week of January 2014, the first series of flights of the new academic year by 20 student and instructor pilots of the 299th BrTA was carried out at Kulbakino over a total of 21 hours, during which pilots practised flying in difficult weather conditions and low visibility, helping them to restore lost flying skills.

Following the Crimea crisis and the need to increase the combat readiness of the 299th BrTA due to a possible invasion by Russian Armed Forces from Crimea, the brigade's pilots took part in a gunnery competition and carried out bombing and gun firing. They employed Gryazev-Shipunov GSh-30-2 (ГШ-30-2) dual-barrel cannons against ground targets in ten sorties under command of the unit commander, Col Vladimir Pomogayba, at the 235th Combined Arms Brigade gunnery range on 18 February 2014. Lt Col Alexander Dyakov (commander of the brigade) and Maj Viacheslav Ovchinnikov (deputy commander of the 1st Squadron) had the best scores in the competition during six bombing runs and 12 strafing runs by Su-25M1s.

The unit's second training exercise was on 4 April, during which several 229th BrTA pilots practised using OFAB-100-120 bombs and U-8 unguided rockets launched from B-8M1 rocket pods. Two Su-25s, 01 and 02 Blue, four Su-25M1s, 03, 07, 38 and 40 Blue, and Su-25UB 65 Blue were used.

Most of the 299th BrTA pilots were masters of low-level flight, which helped to protect them and their aircraft from the danger of the short-medium and long-range SAM systems of the pro-Russian separatists during the war, especially when they were not carrying an ECM pod. However, this could not protect them against the threat from MANPADS, which resulted in the loss of several Su-25s. Here a 299th TRA Su-25 flies at low level over the shores of the Black Sea in 2013. *Author's collection*

Three days later, on 7 April, Moscow's plan for creating a crisis in the east of Ukraine to divert Kiev's attention from Crimea to Donbass was put into action after a group of pro-Russian activists stormed the SBU offices in Donetsk and Luhansk, taking control of the armoury and arming themselves. Following this, protesters in Donetsk declared the People's Republic of Donetsk and unification with Russia.

Two days later, the Ukrainian Army deployed armoured personnel carriers from Dnepropetrovsk to Luhansk to be used against pro-Russian militias if required, while Russia ordered a retired colonel of Russian military intelligence (GRU) to take over governmental buildings in Sloviansk and to form a militia group, which played a key role in the Crimea crisis and the annexation of the peninsula to Russia. He also tried to repeat the scenario in Donbass. On 12 April his men attacked Ukrainian governmental buildings in Sloviansk including the executive committee building, the police department and the Security Service offices. The next day a group of 150 armed pro-Russians attacked a pro-Ukraine unity rally in Mariupol, nine protesters injured. These actions quickly led to the Ukrainian government launching an anti-terrorism operation in Donetsk Oblast to liberate the government buildings from separatists.

From the beginning of the war against pro-Russian separatists, Ukrainian Army Aviation provided air support for the Ukrainian Army by means of its Mi-24P/VP/R heavy attack helicopters, but soon after the escalation of the war the air force was engaged widely and its fighter jets and bombers took part in strike, interdiction, close air support and combat air patrol missions. The Su-25s and their crews played a key role in the battle and they paid the highest price, which was the loss of five Su-25M1s to air-to-air missiles, MANPADS and SAM systems between 2 July and 29 August.

Before their direct involvement in the Battle of Donbass, the 299th BrTA pilots were prepared in May 2014 for combat by participating in a combat training exercise to qualify them for bombing, gun and rocket firing, as well as air-to-air combat. At the beginning of the exercise on 15 May at Nikolayev, some of the Su-25 pilots used OFAB-100T training bombs while others used live S-8 unguided rockets and OFAB-100-120 free fall bombs against ground targets. The next day, Su-25 pilots launched R-60M IR-guided air-to-air missiles against heat targets. They were not the only participants in the exercise as flight and ground crews of other brigades also took part with their MiG-29s, Su-24Ms and Su-24MRs.

Soon after the exercise, six Su-25M1s were forward deployed to Dnepropetrovsk, where MiG-29s of the 114th BrTA and then the 40th BrTA had been forward deployed earlier to protect Ukraine's airspace over the east of the country. Dnepropetrovsk airport was located within 190, 200 and 310km from Kramatorsk, Donetsk and Luhansk respectively, enabling the Su-25s to target the pro-Russian separatists and their Russian backers in eastern Ukraine.

Following the loss of several UkrAF Su-25M1s to the separatists' MANPADS and also Osa-AKM short-range SAM systems, the 299th BrTA began training pilots to perform their missions at medium altitude while using SPS-141 jamming pods to protect the aircraft from the danger of Buk M1 SAM systems. In the summer of 2014, Su-25M1 05 Blue became the first aircraft to have such a pod installed for training but it was never used in combat. ***Luca G. Canossa***

The first major mission in which the Su-25s played a key role was the first battle at Donetsk airport, during which a pair of Su-25M1s attacked the Vostok Battalion militants in the airport on 26 May 2014. Everything had started after pro-Russian separatist insurgents occupied the terminal buildings at Donetsk International Airport and demanded the withdrawal of government forces from the area at 5.30am local time that morning. This quickly triggered the launch of an assault by Ukrainian Army paratroopers, who were sent there aboard an air force Il-76MD. They quickly joined the Ukrainian Security Forces around the airport.

At 13.00 local time, the Ukrainian security forces gave an ultimatum to the terrorists, told them to surrender and informed them about the consequences if they failed to comply. The terrorists did not lay down their arms and soon were faced with an air strike by two Su-25M1s, which dropped OFAB-100-120 bombs and fired unguided S-8 unguided rockets at the terrorists' positions. This air strike was supplemented by another one carried out by two MiG-29s flying from Dnepropetrovsk. In the course of these air strikes a grounded Yak-40 passenger aircraft, serial UR-MMK, belonging to Ilyich-Avia was destroyed.

Soon after the strikes, the security forces managed to take control of the airport. At 14.40 the Army Aviation's Mi-24 attack helicopters successfully attacked a column of trucks carrying militants near the airport and also two anti-aircraft guns nearby. Despite a counter-attack by the terrorists, the airport remained under the control of the government forces over next few days. In total 35–40 militants were killed and 43 others were wounded in the battle (the majority of them in the air strikes).

The Su-25M1s were involved in other missions, during which two of them bombed several training camps of the pro-Russian militias in the Luhansk district in the last days of May.

On 2 June, two Su-25M1s launched S-8 unguided rockets at the Luhansk Regional State administration building. However, all of them missed and instead hit the square in front of the building, resulting in the deaths of seven civilians and injuries to 28 others while the building remained intact. As a result of this incident, the use of the Su-25s in residential areas was banned and they were only deployed against militants in non-urban areas.

On 5 June, a single Su-25M1 was used to bomb Vostok Battalion militants, resulting in heavy casualties among their forces near the Marinovka border post. According to the Ukrainian Ministry of Defence, during the afternoon the pilot of the Su-25M1 flew near the target over clouds; when he was in the proximity of the target he dived into the clouds and bombed them visually. Fifteen hours later (the next morning), the Mi-24 attack helicopters of Ukrainian Army Aviation engaged the remaining forces while protected by two MiG-29s flying from Dnepropetrovsk.

On the evening of 16 June, an Su-25M1 of UkrAF was used to attack a building under the control of

44 Blue was 01 Blue until 2016. As it was not modernised to Su-25M1 standard this aircraft never took part in the war of Donbass in 2014. Here it is flying over Nikolayev on 28 October 2016. ***Alexander Golz***

Su-25M1 45 Blue (c/n 25508110285) was 05 Blue until 2016. It was one of the 299th BrTA Su-25s that were deployed to Dnepropetrovsk to take part in the Donbass war in, May 2014. The the aircraft is flying near Nikolayev on 28 October 2016. *Alexander Golz*

militants in the city of Horlivka. That air strike caused no death or injuries to anyone. Three days later, on 19 June, Su-25M1s provided close air support for Ukrainian Army Land Forces during a major battle around the village of Yampil after the militants, who were once stationed at Krasnui Lyman, tried to break out of the Ukrainian Army encirclement and escape towards Siversk.

Loss of five Su-25M1s at war

From 1 July, use of the Su-25s in the war was intensified in support of Ukrainian Land Forces' large-scale operations in the north of the Donetsk and Lugansk regions. The Su-25s were used in support of the offensive in the Kramatorsk district as well, using heavy bombs such as 250kg FAB-250M-54s and 500kg FAB-500M-62s rather than light OFAB-100-120s. This also forced Russia to deliver heavy anti-aircraft guns and MANPADS to the separatists to use against the Su-25s, resulting in the loss of several aircraft from 2 July.

The first loss was Su-25M1 06 Blue (c/n 25508110121), which was hit by an anti-aircraft gun on 2 July. The pilot managed to fly his damaged aircraft to Dnepropetrovsk, which was within 300km, but while he was reducing speed to land, the aircraft started banking and he lost control and had to eject. The aircraft crashed close to the runway at 11.20am local time but its pilot, Alexander Dyakiv, was not injured.

Lt Col Diyakiv was the senior navigator of thr 299th BrTA and he had been known as the best airman in the UkrAF in 2013. He logged 130 sorties in 80 hours in 2013. By 13 December 2013, he had logged a total of 500 flying hours during his career on the L-39 and Su-25. On that 2 July, several Su-25M1s were involved in air strikes against militants. One of them targeted an insurgent position near Kondrashovka in the Luhansk district. During the second pass, the pilot mistakenly fired some rockets at the village but there were no civilian casualties.

On 12 July 2014, the Su-25s took part in a series of interdiction and strike missions against pro-Russian forces. The first air strike was carried out against a terrorist base near Lysychansk, resulting in the death of several militants and the loss of their weapons and equipment, including trucks. A second air strike was carried out against another militant base at Golmovsky village, Gorlovsky district, resulting in the destruction of two BM-21 Grad rocket launchers, two ZU-23-2 anti-aircraft guns and six armoured carriers, and the death of 30 militants.

A third air strike was carried out in the vicinity of a concentration of militants near the village of Rovenky, resulting in the death of ten of them, and the destruction of a BM-21 'Grad' rocket launcher and several armoured vehicles, while a fourth strike targeted militants near the village of Torez, resulting in the destruction of at least two of their trucks and some weapons. The fifth strike hit a stronghold of militants near Donetsk where they had parked their armoured combat vehicles and had stored ammunition and weapons. On that day, seven Su-25M1s logged a total of 16 sorties.

On 16 July, the UkrAF conducted 24 combat sorties against the separatists. That day Su-25M1 41 Blue (c/n 25508110281) was targeted by a MANPAD while carrying out a mission against separatists at Gorlovka at 13.00 local time. Its pilot, named Voloshin, managed to continue to fly his damaged aircraft and finally carried out an emergency landing on the grass beside Kramatorsk airport's runway. The aircraft, which had received damage to its vertical and horizontal stabilisers as well as its undercarriage, landed on its belly while its landing gear was retracted. It was later transported to Zaporozhye, where it was repaired and redelivered back to the 299th BrTA in 2015.

On the same day at 18.55 local time, while Su-25M1 03 Blue (c/n 25508110278) was carrying out a combat mission against separatists in the vicinity of Amvrosievka it was shot down by an R-27T IR-guided missile launched by a Russian Air Force MiG-29 from the 6972nd Aviation Base at Millerovo, which was located within 20km from the border with Ukraine. Soon after the missile hit the Su-25, its pilot ejected safely and was evacuated to a safe place by Ukrainian Security Forces. Pro-Russian separatists also claimed to have shot down 03 Blue, perhaps in an attempt to hide the role of the Russian Air Force.

On 23 July 2014, the Ukrainian Air Force lost two more Su-25M1s at 12.30 while the aircraft were attacking pro-Russian separatists along with two more Su-25M1s near the Savur-Mohyla strategic height, south of Snizhne. The first aircraft was 04 Blue (c/n 25508110276), which crashed near Shakhtyorsk, Donetsk Oblast, after its pilot ejected safely, while the second aircraft, 33 Blue (c/n 25508110277), crashed near Dmitrovka (next to the city of Marinovka) after its pilot ejected safely. No. 33 Blue was targeted while flying at 185m (606ft) 15.5km to the west of Savur-Mohyla. Its pilot, Lt Col Yuri Shevtsov Sergeevich, could not find a way to exit the combat area and he stayed hidden until captured by the separatists on 19 August 2014. He was later exchanged with other prisoners and returned to his home in Nikolaev on 9 September 2014.

The loss of 04 and 33 Blue led to an increase in the altitude at which the Su-25s flew during combat missions to protect them from the danger of MANPADS; however, this led to a decline in the accuracy of bombing and rocket firing. It also exposed them to the SAM systems of the separatists, including 9K33M3 'Osa-AKM' (US DoD designation SA-8B Gecko Mod-1). Separatists targeted an Su-25 using this SAM on 2 August, but its pilot managed to bring his damaged aircraft back to Dnepropetrovsk airport.

On 29 August 2014, Su-25M1 08 Blue (c/n 25508110284), was targeted by the Osa-AKM and crashed in the northern outskirts of Starobeshevo at 11.30am local time. Its pilot, Vladislav Voloshin, ejected successfully at 50m (166ft) and reached an abandoned house, where he found civilian clothes. Four days later he managed to pass all the roadblocks and return to the territory under the control of Ukrainian Armed Forces. The loss of 08 Blue on 29 August resulted in the termination of all combat flights by Ukrainian Air Force fighter jets in the war in Donbass.

Su-25M1 06 Blue was the first Su-25 the UkrAF lost in the war. It was shot down on 2 July 2014. Here it has two empty S-25-OFM heavy rocket canisters and OFAB-250-270 iron bombs during a joint exercise with the 114th and 831st BrTAs at Ivano-Frankivsk AB on 25 September 2013. *Alexander Golz*

Su-25M1 08 Blue was the last Su-25 the UkrAF lost in the war. It was shot down by Osa-AKM near Starobeshevo on 29 August 2014. Here it is armed with two S-25-OFM heavy rockets and OFAB-250-270 iron bombs during the same exercise on 25 September 2013. *Alexander Golz*

03 Blue (c/n 25508110278) was one of two UKrAF Su-25M1s that were lost on 16 July 2014. It was shot down by an R-27T IR-guided, medium-range, air-to-air missile fired by a Russian Air Force MiG-29 9-13. Here it is armed with ODAB-500PM air-fuel explosive bombs, which were spotted installed underneath at Dnepropetrovsk a few days before its loss. *Luca G. Canossa*

04 Blue (c/n 25508110276) is one of two Su-25M1s that the UkrAF lost in one day on 23 July 2014. It is not known how the separatists shot it down. It was spotted at Dnepropetrovsk with RBK-500AO-2 cluster bombs loaded and is shown in that configuration a few days before its loss. *Luca G. Canossa*

06 Blue (c/n 25508110121) became the first Su-25M1 to be shot down during the war. On the basis of the wreckage of the aircraft, it had four B-8M1 rocket pods and PTB-800 external fuel tanks (as shown) when it was lost on 2 July 2014. *Luca G. Canossa*

Su-25M1 08 Blue (c/n 25508110284) became the last UkrAF Su-25 to be lost in the war in Donbass. It is reported that it had launched four S-25-OFM heavy unguided rockets against separatists on 29 August 2014 when it was shot down. *Luca G. Canossa*

33 Blue (c/n 25508110277) was shot down on 23 July 2014. On the basis of the images of its wreckage, it had been armed with a pair of B-8M1 rocket pods and two OFAB-250-270 iron bombs. Here it also has R-60M IR-guided missiles. *Luca G. Canossa*

On 16 July 2014, Su-25M1 41 Blue (c/n 25508110281) was targeted by MANPADS of the pro-Russian separatists but its pilot decided to continue flying his damaged aircraft and perform an emergency landing. The aircraft was later restored by the ZARZ. On the day of the accident, 41 Blue had been armed with a pair of B-8M1 rocket pods and had also dropped four OFAB-250-270 iron bombs. *Luca G. Canossa*

Restoration and overhaul of Su-25s after the war

The 299th BrTA took part in the counter-terrorism operations of the war in Donbass with 16 Su-25s, and among them 11 including a two-seater variant had been modernised to M1 level by MiGremont. From these, five Su-25M1s, 03, 04, 06, 08 and 33 Blue, were lost in the war. It was thus necessary to restore and overhaul the 299th BrTA's stored aircraft to maintain the number of operational aircraft for combat missions.

Beginning in March 2014, the maintenance squadron of the 299th BrTA started restoring several Su-25s. These were aircraft that had been grounded due to end of their calendar life but still had flying hours left from their MTBO (Meantime between Overhaul). Thanks to the efforts of the technicians, eight Su-25s and Su-25UBs were restored at the base starting in March 2014. However, these Su-25s could not stay operational for a long time: they were a stopgap solution until the completion of the overhaul of more Su-25s by MiGremont.

The restored Su-25s were 32 and 35 Blue, which had been stored since 2004; 14 and 19 Blue, stored since 2005; 18 Blue, stored since 2007; 16 and 24 Blue, both in storage since 2008; and 10 Blue, which had been stored since 2009. The restored Su-25UBs were 60 and 61 Blue, which were restored in August and May 2014 respectively. One of these was later grounded and sent to MiGremont for modernisation due to the end of its MTBO.

MiGremont repaired a battle-damaged Su-25M1 and overhauled four Su-25s and three Su-25UBs, while also modernising six Su-25s to Su-25M1K standard between 2014 and 2018. This brought the number of total airworthy 299th BrTA Su-25s to 31 by the end of 2018. However, from these aircraft, nine that were restored in Kulbakino and temporarily brought back into in service will need to be sent to MiGremont for overhaul and modernisation within next two years.

In April 2015, the 299th BrTA received four Su-25s from MiGremont. They were two overhauled Su-25s, 09 and 29 Blue, one overhauled Su-25UB, 64 Blue, and also a modernised Su-25M1, 15 Blue. One more Su-25UB, 67 Blue (c/n 38220115021), was also redelivered to the 299th BrTA by MiGremont in November that year. The aircraft was former 07 Yellow, which had previously been in use to test Su-25M1 a systems, including the 'Adros' KUV 26-50-01 multi-calibre flare dispenser, which was eventually procured by the Ukrainian MoD to equip Su-25s. Also in 2015, MiGremont completed the repair of battle-damaged Su-25M1 41 Blue.

In 2016, 299th BrTA received three Su-25s from MiGremont, which consisted of two modernised Su-25M1s, 30 and 39 Blue, and an overhauled Su-25UB, 63 Blue, while in 2017 MiGremont redelivered to the 299th BrTA two overhauled Su-25s, 21 and 31 Blue. No. 31 Blue was redelivered during an official ceremony on 14 October 2017. A year later, in July 2018, the most recently modernised Su-25M1Ks were painted in digital camouflage after the end of modernisation work at MiGremont. The aircraft, 20 and 49 Blue, were delivered to the 299th BrTA by end of that year.

On 16 July 2014, Su-25M1 41 Blue was targeted by MANPADS over Gorlovka but its pilot managed to save his damaged aircraft and bring it back to Dnepropetrovsk, where it carried out a belly landing on the grass beside the runway. It was repaired by ZARZ and redelivered to the 299th BrTA in 2015. It is seen prior its first check flight after the repair in Zaporozhye. *Guk Aleksander*

Part of the damage that 41 Blue sustained after it was hit by MANPADS on 16 July 2014. *Author's collection*

18 Blue was one of the ex-452nd OMShAP Su-25s that had been stored at Nikolayev since 2007 and was restored to flying condition by the technicians of the 299th BrTA in summer 2014 to be an attrition replacement for the lost Su-25M1s. It is seen in the maintenance hangar of the 299th BrTA at Kulbakino/Nikolayev in 2011. *Author's collection*

Ex-452nd OMShAP Su-25 26 Blue in brown camouflage still stored at Nikolayev/Kulbakino. *Author's collection*

The former test bed of the Su-25M1 modernisation programme, 07 Yellow, was later painted in digital camouflage and upgraded to Su-25UBM1K standard with new flare dispensers. It was then was handed over to the 299th BrTA as 67 Blue in 2015. It is seen at Nikolayev on 28 October 2016. *Alexander Golz*

Despite having new KUV 26-50-01 flare dispensers, Su-25 29 Blue was reportedly not modernised during its last overhaul by ZARZ in 2015. It is seen at Nikolayev/Kulbakino AB on 28 October 2016. *Alexander Golz*

Su-25M1K 30 Blue equipped with new KUV 26-50-01 flare dispensers was redelivered to the 299th BrTA in 2016. It is an ex-90th OShAP Afghan war veteran with 900 sorties logged during the war. It is at Nikolayev/Kulbakino AB on 27 October 2016. *Alexander Golz*

Non-upgraded Su-25 of the 299th BrTA at Nikolayev/Kulbakino AB on 25 April 2016. This aircraft was previously 09 Blue, but received this new bort number after its overhaul at ZARZ in 2015. *Alexander Golz*

64 Blue, an Su-25UB of the 299th BrTA with c/n 38220136494, was overhauled by the ZARZ in 2014. It received this new digital camouflage, despite not being modernised to Su-25UBM1K level. *Alexander Golz*

'Adros' KUV 26-50-01

In 2015, the Ukrainian Ministry of Defence procured the 'Adros' KUV 26-50-0 multi-calibre flare dispenser to be added to all airworthy Su-25s in the 299th BrTA. This was two years behind schedule due to the lack of a budget and had led to the loss of four Su-25M1s to the Russian Air Force's IR-guided air-to-air missile and separatists' MANPADS and SAMs during the war. All these losses forced the MoD to procure the flare dispensers, which according to No. 120 resolution of the Cabinet of Ministers dated 20 February 2013 had been developed for use on the Su-25s for self-protection against the danger of IR-guided missiles instead of older types.

The KUV 26-50-0 is operated automatically on energy release mode or manually by a trigger on the flight stick. On each Su-25, four sets of the KUV 26-50 flare launchers are installed; on each one of them ten PRP-50 50mm flare cartridges together with 40 PRP-26 26mm flare cartridges can be found. They can be prepared for launch in 30 seconds (after turning on the launchers), they work with a supply voltage of +27V and have a power consumption not more than 250 watts. They can be operated in temperatures between -50° C and +60° C. The system has to be inspected every 200 hours of flight, while its assigned service life is 2,000 hours or 30 years, or 800 shots per launcher. Each launcher has 24 months' warranty from the date of delivery, or 500 hours or 200 shots.

Su-25m 41 Blue which was damaged over Gorlovka on 16 July 2014 during the Donbass war, was not only repaired by the ZARZ but also received 'Adros' KUV 26-50-01 multicalibre flare dispensers. It is seen over Nikolayev on 28 October 2016. ***Alexander Golz***

62 Blue, an Su-25UBM1 of the 299th BrTA, received the new Adros KUV 26-50-01 flare dispensers at ZARZ in 2015. It is seen at Kulbakino/Nikolayev on 27 October 2016. ***Alexander Golz***

Su-25M1 07 Blue was one of two Su-25s of the 299th BrTA that were used for live firing of Kh-25ML laser-guided missiles in December 2016. Each aircraft carried four Kh-25MLs during the training, which resulted in several Su-25 pilots reacquiring their ability to use this weapon. *Luca G. Canossa*

Precision-guided weapons

As a part of the restoration and raising of the combat readiness of the 299th BrTA, the use of Kh-25ML laser-guided air-to-surface missiles by Su-25s was intended and for this purpose a series of these missiles were overhauled between 2014 and 2016. In December 2016, several 299th BrTA pilots performed live firing of the missile and it was officially readopted by the unit in 2017.

According to the results of tenders in October 2013, the Ministry of Defence agreed a UAH 2.52 million deal with the State Enterprise Kiev Design Bureau Luch to extend the designated life of the KAB-1500L-PR precision-guided bombs and air-to-surface Kh-25ML missiles developed by the Zvezda Design Bureau, produced at the Zvezda-Strela State Scientific Production Centre.

After almost a decade of not using precision-guided munitions, two UkrAF Su-25M1s fired eight Kh-25MLs at Povursky gunnery range in September 2013. However, in June 2014, the State Communal Design Bureau Luch received just UAH 3.354 million for the renewal of the Kh-25ML, which led to a delay in work until 2016.

The Kh-25ML missile with a laser homing sensor is designed to defeat small-sized mobile and static targets. Their illumination can be carried out by ground or on-board target designation stations. The Su-25 attack aircraft uses the Klen-PS laser rangefinder target designator for this; however, this method is ineffective, as seen in a video, since the guidance and search occur visually due to the lack of an optical-electronic station. Therefore, the attack aircraft is forced to enter the target air defence zone, making it vulnerable.

Post-war activities

After the end of the participation by Ukrainian Air Force aircraft in the war, the process of rebuilding the combat capabilities of the 299th BrTA was speeded up. Not only was the number of airworthy Su-25s in the unit increased but also new pilots joined the Brigade, which made it necessary for the Ministry of Defence to procure fuel in order to let them have at least 30 hours' flying training per year as well, as being able to participate in various exercises.

Thanks to the KUV 26-50-01 flare dispensers, the Su-25s could be operated at low altitude again in case of another war. Therefore, the main goal of the training was to increase the level of aircrew readiness to perform tasks at a low altitude. Also, in 2015 the aircrews were prepared for SEAD missions under the enemy's jamming environment while the ground crews gained experience of the deployment of the aircraft to forward operating bases, where they practised arming the aircraft with bombs and rockets.

In September 2015, the Ukrainian Land Forces held a tactical special training involving units of the Operational Command South at the Shiroky Lan training ground in the Nikolayev region. During the final stage of the exercise on 12 September, the participants performed live firing using BM-21 Grad rocket launchers, while Army Aviation Mi-8 and Mi-24 helicopters supported them by launching S-8 unguided rockets. The 299th BrTA Su-25s were also involved at that stage and performed live rocket firing during the simulation of close air support.

However, the increase in the number of flying sorties of the Su-25s increased the chance of accidents and incidents due to technical problems or pilot error. At 09.15am local time on 11 November 2015, Su-25M1 07 Blue was flying a training mission at low altitude less than 40km north of Zaporozhye when it crashed after it hit high-voltage powerlines and its 23-year-old pilot was killed.

The following year, on 14 July, Su-25M1 38 Blue was lost as its pilot took off from the Starokostiantyniv runway at 16.00 local time. The aircraft's nose landing gear collapsed, resulting in damage to the aircraft's nose and fire in its engines. The pilot managed to eject safely using his Zvezda K-36DM ejection seat, while the uncontrolled aircraft exited the runway and was totally burnt out. No. 38 Blue was one of ten UkrAF Su-25s that had been forward deployed to Starokostiantyniv to take part in joint gunnery training with the Su-24M/MRs of the 7th BrTA in July and August 2016.

In addition to the loss of these two Su-25s and five others during the war in Donbass, the UkrAF lost two Su-25s between March 1992 and 1998, and a third one at 12.47 local time on 4 March 2002. The latter Su-25 was 34 Red (c/n 25508110123), which belonged to the 299th OShAP. On that occasion, test pilot Yuri Goodin Genrikhovich was carrying out a functional check flight (FCF) after its overhaul at the Zaporozhye Aircraft Repair Plant. At the end of the flight, the aircraft had to pass over the Zaporozhye runway three times. During the third pass, or minute 34 of the flight, the aircraft collided with the ground and exploded. According to the crash investigation team reports, the pilot had violated flight rules. No. 34 Red had been grounded since 1995 and this was its first flight after restoration.

In 2016, the 299th BrTA and its Su-25s took part in two exercises. The first was Sea Breeze 2016, which was an air, land and marine exercise designed to improve maritime safety, security and stability in the Black Sea. At least two Su-25s took part, playing the role of enemy fighters and performing simulated maritime attacks against US and Ukrainian Navy vessels. The second exercise of the year was another Joint Command and Staff initiative named Heavenly Shield 2016 and involving the units of Ukrainian Land Forces Operational Command South between 13 and 17 August. The Su-25 pilots performed rocketry and bombing at the Shiroky Lan training area in Mykolaiv, simulating the destruction of an enemy airfield.

In June 2017, the 299th BrTA's Su-25s took part in another joint command and staff exercise with the Operational Command South, during which 29 and 45 Blue were flown from Nikolayev air base and their pilots fired live S-8 unguided rockets from their B-8M1 rocket pods in support of Ukrainian Air Assault Forces at the Shiroky Lan training range. A month later, the 299th BrTA's Su-25s were part of 20 aircraft of the UkrAF, Navy Aviation and Army Aviation that took part in the joint Ukrainian–US air, land and marine exercise Sea Breeze 2017. Nos 29 and 30 Blue were spotted taking part on 14 July.

In July 2018, the 299th BrTA participated in Exercise Sea Breeze 2018. During the joint air, land and maritime exercise in which the USMC, Ukrainian Navy, Land, Air and National Guard as well as Georgian and Moldavian Army representatives participated, at least seven Su-25s,

From the front to the end, 44, 22, 41 and 45 Blue on the main apron of Kulbakino Air Base on 28 October 2016. 41 and 45 Blue are Su-25M1s while the other two are not upgraded. *Alexander Golz*

A pair of Su-25M1Ks of the 299th BrTA including 17 Blue flying over Kulbakino AB during an exercise in 2016. *Ukrainian Air Force*

including one Su-25UB and four Su-25M1Ks, took part. They not only provided close air support for land forces during any counter-attack against a possible offensive on the coastline of the Black Sea, they also simulated maritime attack against enemy vessels and enabled the USMC and Ukrainian Navy officers to practise anti-aircraft tactics against them.

In March 2019, the Air Command South of Ukrainian Air Force held a small exercise over the Sea of Azov in response to the provocative actions of Russia in the region. During the exercise, two Su-25M1s of the 299th BrTA, including 15 Blue, participated; each one had a pair of B-8M rocket pods and two PTB-800 external tanks to provide close air support for Ukrainian Navy ships taking part. They were protected by three MiG-29s of the 204th BrTA, with 41, 47 and 49 Blue, each one armed with a pair of R-27R and four R-73s. As well as these five aircraft, an Su-27P of 831st BrTA, which was on QRA duty at Kulbakino, flew a mission with them over the sea.

Today, 36 Su-25s are in the operational cycle of the Ukrainian Air Force, of which 32 are operation ready. There are 16 more Su-25s in the inventory that are withdrawn from service or stored in various places across the country. This includes an ex-452nd OShAP Su-25, 03 Blue, in the Air Force University in Kharkiv. Two Su-25s, 10 Red and 01 Blue, are exhibited in the Lugansk Aviation Museum, while 02 Blue is at the UkrAF aviation museum at Vinnitsa. No. 01 Blue, which was in very bad condition after years without attention, was restored by the separatists and presented as the first combat aircraft of the separatists' air force in a propaganda clip. However, it wasn't flyable due to the absence of hundreds of parts inside its fuselage!

299th BrTA Su-25s in September 2018

Model	Construction Number	Bort Number	Colour Scheme	Former Unit	Year of Overhaul/ Modernisation	Current Fate	Note
Su-25	25508110266	44 Blue	Jungle camouflage	299th OShAP	-	Operation Ready	Its former b/n was 01 Blue until 2016
Su-25	25508110118	22 Blue	Jungle camouflage	299th OShAP	-	Operation Ready	Its former b/n was 02 Blue until 2016
Su-25M1	25508110285	45 Blue	Jungle camouflage	452nd OShAP	2011	Operation Ready	Its former b/n was 05 Blue until 2016
Su-25	25508110125	49 Blue	Digital	299th OShAP	2015	Operation Ready	Its former b/n was 09 Blue until 2016
Su-25	25508103002	10 Blue	Jungle camouflage	299th OShAP	2014	Operation Ready	Afghan war veteran with 600 sorties
Su-25	?	14 Blue	Splinter camouflage	299th OShAP	-	Operation Ready	Restored by 299th BrTA in 2016
Su-25M1K	25508110267	15 Blue	Digital	299th OShAP	2015	Operation Ready	
Su-25	25508110280	16 Blue	1980s camouflage	299th OShAP	-	Operation Ready	Restored by 299th BrTA in 2014
Su-25M1K	25508110283	17 Blue	Digital	299th OShAP	2015	Operation Ready	
Su-25	25508110287	18 Blue	1980s camouflage	452nd OShAP	-	Operation Ready	Restored by 299th BrTA in 2014
Su-25	25508110288	19 Blue	1980s camouflage	452nd OShAP	-	Operation Ready	Restored by 299th BrTA in 2016
Su-25M1K	?	20 Blue	Digital	452nd OShAP	2018	Operation Ready	
Su-25	?	21 Blue	Digital	452nd OShAP	2017	Operation Ready	
Su-25	25508105038	24 Blue	Jungle Camouflage	299th OShAP	-	Operation Ready	Restored by 299th BrTA in 2015
Su-25	25508106009	25 Blue	Jungle Camouflage	299th OShAP	-	Operation Ready	Afghan war veteran with 900 sorties
Su-25	?	26 Blue	1980s camouflage	299th OShAP	-	Stored	
Su-25	25508106029	27 Blue	Jungle Camouflage	299th OShAP	-	Operation Ready	Afghan war veteran with 600 sorties
Su-25	?	28 Blue	1980s camouflage	299th OShAP	-	Stored	
Su-25	?	29 Blue	Digital	299th OShAP	2015	Operation Ready	

22 BLUE, an Su-25 of the 299th BrTA, taxiing at Kulbakino AB on 27 October 2016. *Alexander Golz*

Model	Construction Number	Bort Number	Colour Scheme	Former Unit	Year of Overhaul/ Modernisation	Current Fate	Note
Su-25M1K	?	30 Blue	Digital	299th OShAP	2016	Operation Ready	Afghan war veteran with 600 sorties
Su-25	?	31 Blue	Digital	452nd OShAP	2017	Operation Ready	
Su-25	?	32 Blue	1980s camouflage	452nd OShAP	-	Operation Ready	Restored by 299th BrTA in 2014
Su-25	?	35 Blue	1980s camouflage	452nd OShAP	-	Operation Ready	
Su-25M1K	25508110317	37 Blue	Digital	452nd OShAP	2015	Operation Ready	
Su-25M1K	?	39 Blue	Digital	452nd OShAP	2016	Operation Ready	
Su-25M1	25508110325	40 Blue	Digital	452nd OShAP	2013	Operation Ready	
Su-25M1	25508110281	41 Blue	Jungle camouflage	452nd OShAP	2009	Operation Ready	Repaired by MiGremont in 2014–5
Su-25	?	42 Blue	1980s camouflage	452nd OShAP	-	Stored	
Su-25M1K	?	46 Blue	Digital	?	2018	Operation Ready	
Su-25UB	38220136725	60 Blue	Jungle camouflage	299th OShAP	2015	Operation Ready	
Sy-25UB	38220115092	61 Blue	1980s camouflage	299th OShAP	-	Operation Ready	Restored by 299th BrTA in 2014
Su-25UBM1	38220123321	62 Blue	Jungle camouflage	299th OShAP	2003	Operation Ready	
Su-25UB	?	63 Blue	Digital	299th OShAP	2016	Operation Ready	
Sy-25UB	38220136494	64 Blue	Digital	299th OShAP	2014	Operation Ready	
Sy-25UB	38220123390	65 Blue	Jungle camouflage	299th OShAP	?	Stored	
Su-25UBM1K	38220115021	67 Blue	Digital	452nd OShAP	2015	Operation Ready	Former test aircraft of MiGremont with 07 Yellow bort number

Su-27 Fleet (1992–today): The Ukrainian Flankers

Today, 55 Su-27s form the backbone of the UkrAF's fighter fleet, of which 35 were airworthy in April 2019. This small fleet of air superiority fighter jets are the most viable and valuable assets of the air force to protect Ukraine's airspace by confronting any Russian Air Force fighter jet flying from Crimea or Russia's mainland. These include Su-30SMs of the Russian Navy at Saki, the Su-27SMs and Su-30M2s of the 38th Fighter Aviation Regiment of the Russian Air Force at Belbek and the Su-30SMs of the Russian Air Force's 6972nd AvB at Krymsk. The current fleet of Ukrainian Su-27s are the surviving examples of 67 aircraft that were inherited from the USSR Air Force, Air Defence Force and Navy in 1992.

In service with the Ukrainian Air Force

Out of the 589 Su-27s in service with one VMF, nine VVS and 12 PVO regiments, 126 remained outside Russia's territory and were inherited by Belarus (26), Ukraine (68) and Uzbekistan (32) after the USSR collapsed. The Belarusian Air Force took over all seven Su-27s, 14 Su-27Ps and four Su-27UBs in service with the 61st IAP, together with the 831st IAP's Su-27UB, which was in the 558th Repair Plant in 1992. Uzbekistan took control of 26 Su-27Ps and six Su-27UBs in 9th GIAP service at Andizhan.

Ukraine inherited the largest number of Su-27s out of the total of 589 in the USSR in 1991. Among the 67 examples, 33 Su-27s and four Su-27UBs belonged to the 831st IAP; a single Su-27 was in service with the 3rd Test Centre of the 8th Research Institute of the USSR Air Force in Kirovskoye; 11 Su-27Ps and three Su-27UBs were with the 62nd IAP; and seven Su-27s, two Su-27Ps and seven Su-27UBs were with the 100th KIAP.

After Ukraine's independence, the 62nd IAP, 831st IAP and 100th KIAP became subordinate to the Ukrainian Air Defence Force, Air Force and Navy respectively. Among them, the 100th KIAP was short-lived and was disbanded just five years after independence. The reason for this was the fact that the majority of the unit's fighter pilots refused to swear allegiance to Ukraine. Most of them decided to leave the Navy and some joined Russian Navy Aviation.

The Ukrainian Air Force inherited this valuable prototype of the Su-27, the tenth example known as T-10-10. In 1991 it was in use for training purposes at the Kiev Air Force institute. It is seen there on 5 February 1998. This aircraft was later transferred to Lugansk, where it was put on display in the state aviation museum. It is now under the control of the separatists. *Sergey Popsuevich*

Black Sea Flankers (100th KIAP's Su-27s)

The 100th Shipborne Fighter Aviation Regiment had been formed on 10 March 1986 in accordance with a directive of the General Staff of the USSR Navy dated 24 December 1985. It was equipped with Su-27s (1st AE), MiG-29s (2nd AE), Su-25s (3rd AE) and L-39s (3rd AE) with the key goal of training future Su-33, MiG-29K and Su-25UTG pilots for carrier operations. It was based at Saki Naval Air Station of the Soviet Black Sea Fleet in the Crimean Oblast, where a NITKA aircraft carrier deck simulator was constructed to train pilots in ski-jumping from the deck. At the same NITKA facility there was a landing pad but without arresting cables on which the pilots practised landings with high glide slope angles and high approach speeds.

To simulate carrier landings it was necessary for both the KnAAPO and Irkut Aviation plant to fit the 100th KIAP Su-27s with reinforced landing gears to absorb the stresses of performing touch and gos on the NITKA landing pad. The first four Su-27s so equipped were handed over to the unit together with four MiG-29s on 15 and 16 May 1986. They received the bort or tactical numbers 71 to 74 Blue and began flying in June.

Two more Su-27s, 75 and 76 Blue, were delivered on 6 July 1987, followed by another pair, 77 and 78 Blue, on 21 September 1987. On 24 April 1990, the last pair, which were Su-27Ps (without air-to-ground combat capability) 79 and 80 Blue, were handed over, with their first scheduled flights in May 1990.

Prior to the USSR's collapse, the 100th KIAP received seven Su-27UBs, which had tactical numbers 01 to 07 Blue. No. 01 Blue was delivered on 30 March 1988, 02 and 03 Blue in the first half of 1990, 04 and 05 Blue in May 1991 and 06 Blue in September 1991. According to the directives, it was planned to equip the 1st Aviation Squadron of the 100th KIAP with ten Su-27s and eight Su-27UBs; however, there was no rush to deliver all of them quickly. Before the USSR collapsed, one more Su-27UB, 07 Blue, was delivered to the regiment in November 1991.

Based on a directive of the USSR Navy General Staff dated 13 December 1988, the 1063rd Training

Centre for Combat Employment Shipborne Aviation was formed at Saki and the 100th KIAP became one of its two aviation regiments. Before that, the 100th KIAP was part of the 39th Control for the Test Training Facility of Shipborne Aviation. Subsequently the 1st, 2nd and 3rd Aviation Squadrons of the Regiment were formed.

Before the USSR collapsed, 100th KIAP flying activity dropped, firstly due to financial problems that had led to the inability to procure spare parts for the Su-27s. One of the 100th KIAP veteran pilots remembers that in September 1991, the Su-27s of the 1st Aviation Squadron were mostly worn out and the unit had just three single-seaters flyable out of nine while, five out of seven Su-27UBs were airworthy.

No 77 Blue needed an engine change. No 72 Blue needed an engine change and its other engine had to be checked after reports of vibration, which also affected one powerplant in 76 Blue. Su-27UB 03 Blue needed a landing gear change, while Su-27UB 02 Blue was grounded due to maintenance work on its radar. No. 78 Blue had been left a long time waiting for spare parts under its routine maintenance period. Nos 74 and 75 Blue needed their canopies polished because of the effect of silvering.

In summer 1989, the 100th KIAP lost 71 Blue, its first Su-27, when the afterburner section of its right AL-31F engine started to burn during take-off. The pilot was Sergey Nikolayevich Kornev, who quickly aborted take-off and released the drag chute. His aircraft was fully armed as it was setting off on a gunnery exercise. After the Su-27 came to a halt he opened the canopy, got out and ran. While firefighters were trying to suppress the flames, the ground crew simultaneously removed all the aircraft's ammunition. It took 40 minutes to extinguish the fire. The fire caused major damage to the structure of the aircraft, making it unrepairable. Timur Apakidze, commander of the 100th KIAP, said later that Kornev was lucky to survive because his Su-27 could have exploded at any second.

The Ukrainian Air Force was formed on 17 March 1992, and following that the Navy. During the official ceremony for taking the oath of allegiance to Ukraine, most of the pilots including the commander of the regiment, Apakidze, refused. He said: 'I have sworn an oath to my motherland a long time ago. A military officer doesn't swear for the second time.'

In summer 1989, the 100th KIAP lost this Su-27, 71 Blue. *Author's collection*

Apakidze was later proposed as the commander of the Georgian Air Force, which he refused. He and part of the regiment's staff went to Russia and continued serving in the 279th OKShAP of the Russian Navy Northern Fleet. A few pilots, including the deputy commander of the 100th KIAP, took the oath, remained in Ukraine and flew with Su-27s until 5 June 1992, when a decision was made to transfer all the 1st AE Su-27s to the UKrAF's 831st IAP at Mirgorod, however this was delayed to 1993.

The 100th KIAP was based at Saky, but in April 1992 it had been redesignated the 100th IAP and 14 of its Su-27s were sent to Kirovskoye Air Base near Feodosia to be used by the 3rd State Aviation Test Center. Thirteen of them made the move to Mirgorod in 1993.

Su-27P 56 Red at Vinnitsa, Havryshivka, on 23 March 1996. At the time, this aircraft was in service with the 62nd IAP. It with the 100th KIAP of Soviet Navy Aviation by 1992. *Sergey Popsuevich*

14 Blue is an ex-100th KIAP Su-27S that has been stored at Mirgorod since 2009. It was 72 Blue when it was serving with the 100th KIAP in 1992. *Author's collection*

831st IAP Su-27S 34 Red at an air show in Bratislava in 1995. This aircraft was in service with the 100th KIAP as 73 Blue until 1992. Its bort number was later changed to 34 Blue. It has been in storage at Mirgorod since 2010, when it logged its last flight. *Alexander Golz*

A pair of ex-100th KIAP Su-27UBs of the 831st IAP with bort numbers 70 and 71 Red. They were 05 and 06 Blue when they were in service with the 100th KIAP in 1992. They both went to the 831st BrTA and became 70 and 71 Blue. Both were upgraded to Su-27UBM1 standard. 70 Blue crashed in 2018. They are shown when four F-15E-48-MCs of the USAF's 335th Fighter Squadron based at Seymour Johnson Air Force Base, North Carolina, together with a KC-135R, paid a friendship visit to Mirgorod AB on 12 June 1997. *Sergey Popsuevich*

Defenders of Crimea (Flankers of Belbek)

The 62nd Fighter Aviation Regiment of the PVO's 60th Fighter Aviation Division started the transition from Su-15TMs to Su-27s in May 1991 but this was never completed due to the USSR's collapse. The very first Flanker of the 62nd IAP was an Su-27UB with the construction number 96310425068 that was delivered on 31 May 1991 and received the bort number 40 Blue. The second and third 62nd IAP Su-27UBs were delivered on 13 and 31 June as 41 and 42 Blue respectively, while the fourth and last two-seat Flanker, Su-27UP c/n 96310425070, was delivered on 28 June 1991 and became 43 Blue.

The Su-15TM fighter pilots of the 60th IAP's 1st Aviation Squadron who had completed their transition training on the Su-27s of the 594th Training Fighter Aviation Regiment of the PVO's 148th Centre for Combat Employment and Retraining of Personnel undertook complementary training flights on the Su-27UB and Su-27UP at Belbek until the regiment received its first batch of five Su-27Ps on 4 July 1991, followed by four more on 21 August 1991. The Su-27UP was exchanged with a pair of the 594th Training Fighter Aviation Regiment's Su-27Ps in September 1991. The Su-27Ps received the tactical numbers 01 to 12 Blue.

After the USSR collapsed, the majority of the 62nd IAP's personnel took the oath of allegiance to Ukraine and their regiment, together with its 14 Su-27s and 39 Su-15s, became part of the Ukrainian Air Defence Force. Only 26 of the Su-15s were in service and all 13 Su-15s of the 1st AE were waiting to be sent to the scrapyard. Twenty-eight more Su-27Ps and three more Su-27UBs that were in production at the KnAAPO and Irkut Corporation installations for the 62nd IAP were completed after the Soviet Union's collapsed and entered service with the Russian VVS and PVO.

On 1 July 1998, the 62nd IAP was reorganised as the 62nd Fighter Aviation Brigade, but it became a regiment again on 1 July 2001. Two years later, the unit was reorganised as the 204th Fighter Aviation Brigade and became part of Task Force Crimea of the Ukrainian Air Command South. In October 1997, the 62nd IAP received one of the ex-100th IAP Su-27Ps that had been in 831st IAP service since 1992, and earlier in 1996 the regiment saw all its Su-15s retired and replaced by MiG-29s of the 100th IAP. In 2001, the Su-27s of the 1st Aviation Squadron were sent to Ozernoye, where they entered service with the newly formed 9th Fighter Aviation Brigade (later 9th Tactical Aviation Brigade), ending the Su-27s' career in the unit.

06 Blue (c/n 36911035716) was an Su-27P of the 62nd IAP. Most of the regiment's Su-27s had this insignia of a Crimean Eagle on a un painted on their vertical stabilisers in the early 1990s. This aircraft is now operational as 100 Blue with the 831st BrTA at Mirgorod. Here the aircraft is at Belbek on 5 October 1995. *Sergey Popsuevich*

02 Blue (c/n 36911035612) was another Su-27P of the 62nd IAP, seen landing at Belbek AB on 5 October 1995. This aircraft was transferred to the 9th IAP, where it became 58 Blue at Ozernoye in 2001. It is now modernised to Su-27PM1 standard and is in service with the 831st BrTA. *Sergey Popsuevich*

The shortest-lived Su-27 in Ukraine was this Su-27UB of 62nd IAP, 42 Red (c/n 96310425070). It was transferred to the 9th IAP in 2001 and was involved in the Sknyliv air show disaster on 27 July 2002. *Heinz Berger*

Guardians of Mirgorod

The 831st Fighter Aviation Regiment, which is now the Tactical Aviation Brigade, has been the main operator of Su-27 fighter jets in the Ukrainian Air Force since its birth on 17 March 1992. In 1992, the regiment had a total of 33 Su-27s and four Su-27UBs in service with its three aviation squadrons. The oldest were seven years old, while the youngest was Su-27UB 67 Red (c/n 96310422070) manufactured in 1990.

The history of the 831st IAP goes to November 1941, when it was activated as the 659th Fighter Aviation Regiment. In the beginning it was equipped with the I-15bis, which remained in service until it was replaced by the Yak-1 in April 1942. In October 1942, the regiment became subordinate to the 17th Air Army's 288th Fighter Aviation Division, which had been established on 1 July 1942. In July 1942, the regiment also received the Yak-7b and then in March 1943 the Yak-1b as a replacement for the Yak-1. They were all withdrawn from service or lost in the war until March 1944, when the Yak-9 took their place in the regiment.

In January 1945, the 659th IAP received Yak-3s as replacements for its Yak-9s. Five months later, it was deployed to Yambol, Bulgaria, and remained

11 Blue (c/n 36911014818) was an Su-27S of the 831st IAP. It is seen during a joint air defence exercise with the 62nd IAP at Belbek on 5 October 1995. *Sergey Popsuevich*

This was the 831st IAP insignia, which was applied on the vertical stabilisers of most of the regiment's Su-27s in the early 1990s. It is seen on 11 Blue at Belbek on 5 October 1995. *Sergey Popsuevich*

there until October 1947, when it was transferred to Boryspil, Kiev Oblast, in the Ukrainian SSR. The regiment was renamed the 831st IAP on 20 February 1949 based on a directive issued on 10 January 1949 that also resulted in a change of name of the 228th IAD to the 138th IAD.

While it was based at Boryspil up to 1977, the 831st IAP operated the MiG-15 fighter jet between 1951 and 1954, the MiG-17 between 1954 and 1968 and then the MiG-21PF/PFM between 1968 and 1986. On 9 November 1985, the very first Su-27s of the regiment were delivered and the transition from the MiG-21 to this fourth-generation fighter jet started, being completed in 1986. Before the delivery of the new jets, the fighter pilots of the regiment's 1st Aviation Squadron had theory and practical training on the Su-27 at Lipetsk between March and October 1985. Technicians were trained in Komsomolsk-on-Amur Aviation Plant and the Ufa engine manufacturing company.

On 1 November 1985, first six 831st IAP Su-27s, 01 to 06 Red, were delivered, while a VVS An-12 carried their ground crews. Two factory pilots and four of 60th IAP pilots had to fly them from Komsomolsk-on-Amur to Mirgorod via Belaya, Petropavlovsk, Kamensk, Lipetsk, Petropavlovsk, Kamensk and Kamchatskoye. Due to bad weather and technical issues, just four Su-27s made their way to Mirgorod on 9 November 1985. Two others were delivered in the following days, however, one crashed after delivery.

As a replacement for the lost aircraft, an Su-27 of the 91st Research-Instructor Fighter Aviation Regiment of the 4th Centre for Combat Employment and Retraining of Crews VVS was delivered to the 831st IAP at the end of 1985. Between 11 and 15 February 1986, the second batch of six Su-27s was handed over to personnel of the 2nd Aviation Squadron of the 831st IAP in the KnAAPO factory. The third batch of Su-27s was delivered on 1 April 1986. By that time, the 1st and 2nd Aviation Squadrons had fully transitioned from the MiG-21 to the Su-27, while the 3rd Aviation Squadron's pilots were still undergoing transition flight training, which was completed on 16 May 1986. Practical retraining of all Su-27 pilots of the regiment ended on 27 October 1986, when there was a flight-tactical exercise.

By June 1986, 22 Su-27s had been delivered to the 831st IAP, while six more arrived in October and November. The first Su-27UB combat training jets were delivered in November 1987; they were 60 Red (c/n 96310402006), 61 Red (c/n 96310405008), 62 Red (c/n 96310405010) and 63 Red (c/n 96310407002). A fifth Su-27UB, 64 Red (c/n 96310408025) was delivered in March 1988. Based on the information of the CFE treaty, the 831st IAP had a total of 40 Su-27s on 19 November 1990.

In 1992, when the Ukrainian Air Force was

48 Red, an 831st IAP Su-27S with c/n 36911014411, at Mirgorod AB on 31 May 1996. As 48 Blue, it is now in service with the 831st BrTA. In 2019, the aircraft was still under overhaul at the ZARZ facility. ***Sergey Popsuevich***

08 Blue (c/n 36911013605) was an Su-27S of the 831st IAP, which was overhauled by ZARZ in the mid-1990s and received this splinter camouflage. It is seen during an air show outside Ukraine in 1995. It has been out of service and stored at Mirgorod since 2009/10. *Alexander Golz*

75 Blue (c/n 96310418207), an Su-27UB of the 831st BrTA, previously served alongside 03 Blue with the 100th KIAP of the AV-MF until 1992. It was used for a military tourism programme from the GANIC facility for $6,000 per flight in its back seat between 1993 and 1995. It is seen one or two years after relocation from Kirovskoye to Mirgorod in 2006/07. *831st BrTA Facebook community group*

born, one of the 831st IAP's Su-27UBs, 63 Red, was under depot maintenance at the 558th Aircraft Repair Plant in Belarus. Ukrainian authorities demanded the return of the aircraft, but Belarus refused because Ukraine had not paid for its maintenance costs. The aircraft was later modernised to Su-27UBM1 standard and delivered to the Belarusian Air Force's 61st IAP in 2003. In the late 1990s, in exchange for 63 Red, Belarus gave UkrAF an Su-27S of 61st IAP, 44 Red (c/n 96310427717), which had been stored for a few years. The aircraft was disassembled and transferred by road in 19 boxes. It was later sold to a British company in 2001.

831st IAP accidents and incidents

The 831st IAP was one of the highly active Su-27 operators in the VVS and subsequently had more incidents and accidents compared with other units. It lost ten of its Su-27s between 1986 and 1991!

The first accident was to 44 Red (c/n 36911014003) during a two-hour and 57-minute ferry flight from KnAAPO to Belaya on 29 May 1986. While the aircraft being flown by Vitaliy Alekseevich Baydikov, who was flying at an altitude of 13,000m (42,650ft), a speed of 900km/h (485 knots) and within of 60–70km (37–43 miles) from Belaya, the left engine started to vibrate, which led to the failure of its No. 1 hydraulic system and a subsequent fire that damaged the wiring. The fire spread in the left engine nacelle and the pilot's efforts to restore control of the aircraft were not effective. He ejected safely at an altitude of 6,000m (19,685ft) and speed of 300km/h (161 knots). The pilot was later given an award for his bravery.

In early 1987, 32 Red (c/n 36911015103) sustained serious damage to its landing gear during a test flight and was later withdrawn from service and sent to Vasilkov to be scrapped on 16 March 1987. Two more Su-27s were lost on the same day, 26 November 1987: Su-27 29 Red (c/n 36911013917), flown by of A. Lozovoy, and Su-27UB 60 Red (c/n 96310405008), flown by the commander of the regiment, Vladimir Grigoryevich Kostinevich, and Ebheny Robertovich Dobretsov. The cause of the accidents was icing in the engine air intake and compressor, which resulted in a drop in thrust and the aircraft stalling on final approach. All the pilots survived.

In 1988, three more Su-27s were lost. The first was an accident that again involved the commander of the regiment, Kostinevich, while he was flying Su-27 40 Red (c/n 36911013919) on 31 March 1988. The incident occurred during a formation take-off just four seconds after separation of the aircraft from the runway, when the Su-27 had reached just 30m (98ft) and 290km/h (156 knots). The drag chute was released and reduced the speed to 200km/h (107 knots) and the angle of attack to 26°. The aircraft stalled, touched the runway and bounced 590m before the runway end. The landing gear was broken, the aircraft continued moving on its belly and then caught fire. It was just the thirteenth flight of the aircraft, which had only logged 13 flying hours in its short life.

A member of the ground crew who witnessed the

accident remembered that immediately after the aircraft stopped moving, the pilot opened the canopy, jumped out and quickly ran from the aircraft. Then he stopped, turned around, waved goodbye to the aircraft and then walked away. The base fire truck reached the burning aircraft, but it had a problem with its water pump and so fire engines from the city were called in. However, by the time they arrived the fire had reached the aircraft's cannon rounds, which exploded. After this the aircraft stopped burning.

The pilot suffered spinal injuries and it took him several months to recover. After that he was banned from flying fighter jets and instead was retrained as a Mi-8 helicopter pilot, flying in Chernigov. As a result of this accident some parts of the brake chute release system were redesigned and replaced on all Su-27s with the PVO, VVS and VMF.

On 14 November 1988, Su-27 03 Red (c/n 36911011605), piloted by Lt O. G. Erokhin, and 51 Red (c/n 36911015306), flown by M. A. Moroz, both crashed while on final approach to Mirgorod AB. The cause of the accidents was icing in the engines, which led to a loss of engine thrust and stalling. Both pilots ejected safely and survived. An investigation showed that the flight director and meteorological service had not followed regulations. Because of the loss of two more aircraft due to icing, the 831st IAP and 138th IAD commanders were removed from their positions.

On 26 April 1990, Su-27UB 65 Red (c/n 96310417105) piloted by V. A. Tokar and Alexander M. Sizov suffered a hard landing during a touch and go due to pilot error, which caused the break up of the landing gear and extensive damage to the aircraft's structure. Representatives from the Irkutsk Aviation Plant inspected the aircraft and declared it unrepairable. Squadron commander Lt Col A. Sizov was subsequently removed from office.

In March 1991, Su-27 27 Red (36911013811) was withdrawn from service due to damage sustained during engine run-up. The cause was a mistake by pilot Danilovaky, who started the engines without checking the position of the throttles. They were on afterburner and quickly after engine start, the aircraft's right engine went into afterburner mode, jumped on the wheel chocks, hit the wall of an aircraft hangar and was badly damaged. Neither the technicians nor Danilovaky suffered injury but the aircraft was withdrawn from service and the pilot was forced to pay for part of the damage.

The last USSR-era accident of the 831st IAP occurred to Su-27 25 Red (c/n 36911013813) on 12 May 1991. On that day, test pilot Alexander Posenkov was performing aerobatics. While he was carrying out a loop at an altitude of 1,500m (4,921ft) and a speed of 700km/h (378 knots), the aircraft's right landing gear extended due to unknown reasons. The pilot quickly levelled the aircraft and reduced the speed to 450km/h (242 knots), which was the maximum permitted flying speed of the aircraft with extended landing gear.

He then reported what had happened to the air traffic controllers. On the command of the air base authorities, he extended the landing gear but the right gear light did not come on in the cabin, showing that it was not locked. The pilot decided to perform a landing approach and touch the runway once in order to use the weight of the aircraft to lock the right landing gear. However, upon touch down the right landing gear retracted and the pilot was told to go around. It was not safe for the pilot to land on just two landing gear, therefore the base commander ordered him to fly to the gunnery range at Yareska and then eject. He then ejected after dumping fuel. The aircraft crashed but did not explode and burn due to the small amount of fuel left in its tanks.

The true cause of the accident was never found, but the most probable reason was that after take-off when the landing gear was retracted, the right landing gear lock was not engaged and while the pilot was pulling G during aerobatic manoeuvres it then extended. Lt Col Posenkov continued flying the Su-27 until the collapse of the USSR, when he left the 831st IAP and joined the Belarusian Air Force because he was born in Belarus. He continued flying Su-24s until he retired in 1994.

As mentioned above, the 831st IAP a total of eight Su-27s and two Su-27UBs before the USSR's collapse. However, the aircraft losses continued just a

831st IAP Su-27UB 64 Red (c/n 96310408025) crashed at Mirgorod on 24 April 1992. ***Author's collection***

On 26 May 1997, these two former 100th KIAP Su-27UBs of the 831st IAP collided on the ground due to pilot error. *Sergey Popsuevich*

few weeks after the collapse when the 831st IAP lost an Su-27UB, 64 Red, while being flown by Victor Anatolievich Komelkov and Sergey Mikhailovich Ostanin on 24 April 1992. The accident occurred when Capt Komelkov was performing a Cuban eight aerobatic manoeuvre at an altitude of 1,094m (3,589ft) at a speed of 511km/h (276 knots). The aircraft stalled at that altitude, which was not high enough for it to be recovered. The rear-seat pilot ejected and survived but Komelkov died. The cause of the accident was found later to be pilot error due to him executing the manoeuvre at low altitude.

On 26 May 1997, two Su-27UBs and an Su-27 of the 831st IAP were badly damaged on the main ramp of Mirgorod AB. This incident occurred in the early hours of that day, when the regiment had night flying training. The Division commander, Col A. Titarenko, together with an instructor pilot of the 5th Aviation Corps, N. Kovalom, were tasked to carry out a night flight in 68 Red (c/n 96310418204), which was an ex-100th IAP Su-27UB. During the engine start, they did not check to see if the engine throttles were set in the idle position and the right engine immediately went into afterburner mode. The aircraft, with the pilots in their seats and a technician on a ladder, immediately jumped over the wheel chocks and veered to the left. It hit Su-27 07 Blue (c/n 36911013404) and then struck another ex-100th IAP Su-27UB, 72 Red (c/n 96310424045), breaking its radome and windscreen.

The pilots admitted they were to blame and therefore their remained in their positions, but they were forced to pay for part of the damage. No. 68 Red was repaired and remained in service until 2006, when its MTBO was reached. No. 72 Red was sent to the Zaporozhye Aircraft Repair Plant. The UkrAF could not afford to pay the repair bill after the work had been carried out and therefore it was put up for sale and sold to Eritrea in 2001. The damage to 07 Blue was so great that the aircraft was withdrawn from service. Its fuselage panels were repaired and it was sent to Vinnitsa's air force museum on 2 August 2001.

World's deadliest air show crash

The Ukrainian Air Force lost another Su-27UB with the infamous crash of 42 Blue (c/n 96310425070) on 27 July 2002. It was the newest Su-27UB in

The former 62nd IAP Su-27UB 42 Blue b/n (c/n 96310425070) seen after its left wingtip hit the ground on 27 July 2002. *Sergey Popsuevich*

The pilots can be seen ejecting out of 42 Blue after they lost control. *Sergey Popsuevich*

Ukraine and had been delivered to the 62nd IAP on 21 June 1991. It served in the regiment's 1st Aviation Squadron until 2001, when it was handed over to the newly formed 9th Fighter Aviation regiment at Ozernoye. On the day of the crash the aircraft, flown by Volodymyr Toponar and co-pilot Yuriy Yegorov, crashed due to pilot error during the Sknyliv air show, killing 77 people and injuring 543, among whom 100 were hospitalised. It remains the world's worst air show disaster.

The air show had been held to commemorate the 60th anniversary of the UkrAF's 14th Air Corps and the Su-27UB in question was being flown by two of the most experienced Su-27 pilots, who were performing aerobatic manoeuvres for 10,000 spectators. At 12.52pm local time, it entered a rolling manoeuvre with a downward trajectory at low altitude. It rolled upright once more and was still descending rapidly when the left wing dropped shortly before it hit the ground, at which point the crew ejected. The aircraft skidded over the ground, destroyed an Su-17M4R of the 48th OGRAP and the nose section of an Il-76MD transport aircraft before exploding and cartwheeling into the crowd of spectators. Of the 77 spectators who died, 28 were children.

Ukrainian President Leonid Kuchma publicly blamed the military for the disaster and dismissed the head of the air force, General Viktor Strelnykov. A military court sentenced pilot Volodymyr Toponar and co-pilot Yuriy Yegorov to 14 and eight years in prison respectively on 24 June 2005. The court found the two pilots and three other officials guilty of failing to follow orders, negligence and violating flight rules. In their defence, the pilots stated that the flight map that they had received was different from the actual layout. According to the cockpit voice recorder, one pilot asks, 'And where are our spectators?'

However, the main cause of the accident were the pilot's and air show planners' mistakes, which led to the execution of the manoeuvre at low altitude. Toponar also forgot that his aircraft was heavy due to having 6 tons of fuel on board and when the back seat pilot reminded him of this, it was too late to climb and exit the manoeuvre. Not only were both pilots jailed but two of officials were sentenced to up to six years in prison and the third one received four years. Toponar was ordered to pay 7.2 million Ukrainian hryvnia (US$1.42 million; €1.18 million) in compensation to the families, and Yegorov 2.5 million hryvnia. Yegorov was released in 2008 after President Yushchenko issued a decree reducing his sentence to three and a half years.

Su-22M4R 50 Yellow of the 48th OGRAP with its vertical stabiliser and empennage cut off by the crashing Su-27. *Sergey Popsuevich*

831st BrTA in major exercises

Unlike the 62nd IAP, the 831st IAP's Su-27s participated in various international exercises across Europe and North America in the 1990s. In 1993, for the first time a delegation from the USAF visited the Su-27s of the 831st IAP at Mirgorod after a group of Ukrainian Su-27s had visited the USAF earlier that year. Four years later, in June 1997, four F-15E-48-MCs of the USAF's 335th Fighter Squadron based at Seymour Johnson Air Force Base, North Carolina, together with a KC-135R tanker, paid a friendship visit to Mirgorod.

A year later, the 831st IAP pilot Col I. Chernenko flew to Seymour Johnson in his Su-27UB to perform an aerobatic display. His co-pilot was Lt Col Fedir Ttshchuk, who was also an aerobatic pilot and had performed at various air shows in the Czech Republic, Romania, Austria and Turkey. During the SIAD 2004 air show in Slovakia he was recognised as the best pilot.

In July 1996, an official delegation of the UkrAF headed by its commander-in-chief participated in the Royal International Air Tattoo in the UK and gave the first display in an Su-27 at the annual event. The pilot was Col Nikolai Koval, who won the prize for the best aerobatic display. In 1997, Col I. Chemenko and Maj F. Tishucho gave aerobatic demonstrations at international air shows in Slovakia and the Czech Republic. In 1998, the UkrAF attended the celebration of the 50th anniversary of the Israeli Air Force and 831st IAP pilot M. Koval displayed in his Su-27. In 1999, 831st IAP Su-27s took part in international air shows in Slovakia, Czech Republic and the UK, and in 2000 in Romania and Austria.

Since the creation of the Ukrainian Air Force, the 831st IAP's Su-27s have taken part in various military parades in the country, starting with an aerobatic demonstration for a USAF delegation at Starokostiantyniv air base to mark the first anniversary of Ukraine's independence in 1992. Four years later, 831st IAP pilots took part in the military parade for the fifth anniversary, during which four Su-27s escorted a Tu-160 strategic bomber.

On 1 August 2003, when the 831st IAP had 24 airworthy Su-27s, it was reorganised as a brigade. Two years later, on 25 January 2005, following a decree by the government, the 831st Fighter Aviation Brigade became subordinate to the newly formed Air Command Centre of the air force. Two years later, the 831st Fighter Aviation Brigade was renamed the 831st Tactical Aviation Brigade.

In 2005, Su-27s from Mirgorod took part in two exercises: Peace Shield 2005 and Reaction 2005. Peace Shield was a division-level, computer-assisted command post exercise with unit integration (a battalion-level tactical exercise) that was held in two phases in 11–25 June and 3–17 August. During the second phase, four Su-27s participated in missions at Starokrysmskiy Training Range, Pischana Balka and Feodosiya, the Southern Naval Forces Base of the Ukrainian Navy. Their presence assisted in the training of approximately 400 personnel, including 220 Ukrainian military personnel, to achieve interoperability between land and naval forces.

Reaction 2005 was an integrated operational-tactical exercise with the Joint Rapid Reaction Forces, at which the President of Ukraine was present. The exercise involved 6,500 servicemen using 590 items of weaponry and equipment, including more than 100 tanks and armoured personnel carriers, 20 aircraft, 12 helicopters and 9 ships. At least two Su-27s from Mirgorod took part.

The exercise missions were performed simultaneously at different Armed Forces gunnery ranges. A series of tactical flying missions was carried out at Zhytomyr multi-purpose range; the Black Sea and the Opuk amphibious range was the site of tactical training in amphibious and air landing operations; a tactical flying exercise was conducted

Two of the oldest Su-27s in Ukraine are 01 and 02 Blue, both first flown on 31 July 1985 with delivery to the 831st IAP few days later. They are both stored at Mirgorod AB. 01 Blue (c/n 36911011301) logged its last flight before being put in storage in 2004, while 02 Blue (c/n 36911011302) flew for the last time in 2008. *Vladimir Lazarev via www.airforce.ru*

at the Kiev-Alexandrivka air force range, where the Su-27s flew over; while tactical exercises of airborne and paratroop/airborne elements were carried out at the Shyroky Lan all-services range.

Between May and December 2006, Mirgorod's runway was repaired. During that period, all 14 airworthy Su-27s, including four Su-27UBs, were deployed to Poltava Air Base, 68km south-west of Mirgorod. In July, they took part in Exercise Clear Sky 2006. Units from all three armed services participated and the exercise scenario was implemented simultaneously on land, in the air and in the Black Sea area.

The ability of the air force to perform the tasks assigned to it – working together with land and naval forces – was successfully tested during the exercise. Su-27s of the 831st Fighter Aviation Brigade carried out 20 flights in 14 hours.

The conducting of such exercises along with the participation of Ukrainian units in joint actions (exercises, training and peacekeeping operations) with partner states contributed to an increase in the combat readiness of the Armed Forces and the defence capability of the state.

In January 2007, a delegation of USAF pilots from the California Air National Guard visited the 831st Fighter Aviation Brigade at Poltava to exchange knowledge with its Su-27 pilots. The delegation consisted of Col Gary Taylor, commander of the 144th Operations Group; Col Michael Powel, chief instructor of the 194th Fighter Squadron of the California National Guard; Maj Robert Severtfeger, instructor of the 194th Fighter Squadron; and Capt Dirk Low, Combat Specialist duty on the 144th Fighter Wing. They witnessed the flight operations of the brigade, visited the training complex and participated in high-altitude flights with Su-27 pilots.

In September 2007, the 831st Fighter Aviation Brigade, which had by now been designated a Tactical Aviation Brigade, took part in Command Post exercise Artery 2007. The number of forces involved was three times as large as Clear Sky 2006. During the exercise, the theoretical provisions of the new principles of training and employment of the armed forces were tested in practice – primarily in the employment and comprehensive support of combined task forces, and the current status, capabilities and level of training of Joint Rapid Response Force (JRRF) units. Operational and logistic support units were checked, together with their ability to perform designated missions comprehensively.

The 831st BrTA took part with six of its Su-27s and among them two, together with 21 other air force fighter jets, were deployed to other airfields. During the second stage of the active phase of the exercise on 17 September, 25 fighter jets carried out a variety of air-to-surface missions, including two Su-27UBs dropping bombs at the Rivensky Combined-Arms gunnery range.

Three days later at Novomoskovsk Combined Arms gunnery range (at Dnepropetrovsk Oblast), fighter jets of Air Command Centre carried out a series of missions in support of the 6th Army Corps' operation on the ground. It started with a reconnaissance mission performed by a 7th BrTA Su-24MR to detect positions of the 25th Independent Airborne Brigade on the gunnery range while it was being protected by a pair of 831st BrTA Su-27s. After detecting their position, a series of strike missions were simulated by four Ukrainian Army Aviation Mi-8 helicopters, two Su-27s and two Su-24Ms. Two Su-27Ps provided top cover and they were engaged in dissimilar air combat with a pair of MiG-29s of the 40th BrTA. The Su-27Ps were 52 and 58 Blue (now 100 and

The Ukrainian president Viktor Yushchenko in the back seat of 831st BrTA Su-27UB 74 Blue (c/n 96310425069) prior a flight piloted by Lt Gen Nikiforov, commander of the UkrAF, at Vasilkov Air Base, on 28 March 2008. *Sergey Popsuevich*

The Su-27UB flies President Yushchenko over Vasilkov. *Sergey Popsuevich*

Su-27P 52 Blue (c/n 36911035716) in the maintenance hangar of the 831st BrTA at Mirgorod. This aircraft was in service with the 62nd IAP as 06 Blue until 2001, when the regiment was disbanded. This aircraft was overhauled by ZARZ in 2011 and in 2012, and received new digital camouflage and the bort number 100 Blue. *Poltava Falcons Facebook Page*

101 Blue), both armed with a pair of R-27Rs and R-73s flying from Kramatorsk, while the other Su-27s flew from Belbek, including Su-27UB 70 Blue.

The next month, an Su-27 of the 831st BrTA took part in the international anti-terrorist exercise East Shield 2007 between 29 and 31 October 2007, during which 2,000 Ukrainian Service personnel and two An-26s were involved (one of them was an air ambulance). The exercise was held in Odessa and during it an An-26 played the role of a hijacked aircraft and an Su-27 was scrambled to intercept and escort it. More than 80 representatives from Azerbaijan, Georgia, Moldova, Poland, Romania and the USA witnessed the exercise.

On 28 March 2008, Ukrainian President Viktor Yushchenko visited the headquarters of the UkrAF's Air Command Centre and the 40th BrTA at Vasilkov air base, where he flew in 74 Blue, an Su-27UB of the 831st BrTA. The pilot was the deputy commander of the UkrAF, Maj Gen Vassily Nikoforov, who had some 3,000 flying hours. This 35-minute flight was performed at an altitude of 1,000 to 1,100m (3,280 to 3,608ft) at 600km/h (323 knots).

In September 2008, at least six Su-27s of the 831st BrTA took part in the Command Post exercise Marine Knot 2008, together with almost 40 other air force fighter jets under the command of Lt Gen Vassily Nikiforov, the commander-in-chief of the UkrAF, in support of the forces of the 30th Independent Mechanised Brigade of the 8th Army Corps at Rivnensky combined arms gunnery range. The Su-27s were deployed to Poltava. During both stages of the exercise, the Su-27s provided top cover for the all aircraft participating, rather than joining bombing missions, and flew as escorts for the transportation of airborne troops by Il-76MDs.

On 21 April 2009, a Ukrainian–Russian bilateral joint command and staff exercise was held, during which two UkrAF Su-27s and two Su-24Ms and two RuAF Su-27s and two MiG-29s participated. The exercise was conducted under the direct supervision of Lt Gen Sergey Onishchenko, the acting commander of the UkrAF. Su-24M and Su-27 crews were responsible for playing the role of enemy fighter jets for the Radiotechnical Brigades and Air Defence Rocket Divisions of Ukraine in order to improve the interoperability of air defence forces.

Between 6 September and 4 October 2010, the Command Post exercise Cooperation 2010 was held, during which 18 UKrAF fighter jets including Su-27s took part. On 22 September, Su-27 28 Blue and former Ozernoye Su-27P 39 Blue joined in from Belbek. They flew towards the State Scientific-Test Centre at Chauda, where their pilots performed live air-to-air missile firings against Tu-143/VR-3 Reys drones. On the next day, 39 Blue together with Su-27UB 75 Blue, each one armed with a pair of R-27Rs and a pair of R-73s, provided top cover over the cities of Feodosia and Kerch, launching four more missiles at two more VR-3s.

Preparing for Euro 2012

In 2011, the 831st BrTA took part in two major exercises, Clear Sky 2011 between 18 and 27 July, and Adequate Response 2011 in September. Clear Sky 2011 was a joint exercise in which the UkrAF with 220 service personnel and 15 aircraft, the Polish Air Force with six aircraft and the USAF with 50 service personnel and ten aircraft took part to increase the readiness and practical skills of their pilots and command and control officers in order to be ready to provide security in the airspace of Ukraine and Poland during Euro 2012.

During the exercise, UkrAF MiG-29s and Su-27s intercepted L-39s, which were playing the role of aircraft that had violated Ukraine's airspace. Taking part were five F-16C Block 30s, 86-0326, 87-0271, 87-0276, 87-0283 and 87-0332, as well as F-16D Block 30 87-0379 from the 100th Fighter Squadron, 187th Fighter Wing of the USAF's Alabama Air National Guard, and also another F-16D Block 30, 87-0388 from the Iowa Air National Guard 177th Fighter Wing. All were deployed to Mirgorod and they became the first US Air National Guard aircraft to land in a former Soviet Bloc country, while three C-17As airlifted their ground equipment and ground crews. Their participation in the exercise had been planned in collaboration with the California Air National Guard's 144th Fighter Wing since 2009.

Twelve UkrAF fighter jets took part in the exercise and these included MiG-29 9-13s 18, 19, 20 and 40 Blue as well as MiG-29UB 84 Blue, all from the 204th BrTA. The 831st BrTA took part with seven Su-27s, while three more were reserves. The participating Su-27Ss were 15, 26, 28, 30 and 41 Blue, while the Su-27UBs were 69 and 75 Blue. Loaded with captive training R-73 missiles, the Su-27s engaged in dozens of varied air combat exercises with the UkrAF's MiG-29s and the USAF as well as the Polish Air Force's F-16s in Ukrainian and Polish airspace. In total, 122 air interceptions were carried out and the USAF's F-16s logged 61 sorties.

On 22 July, Maj Gen Don Ralph, the mobilisation assistant to the USAF in Europe, had the opportunity to fly in the back seat of Su-27UB 75 Blue piloted by UkrAF commander-in-chief Maj Gen Vasyl Nikiforov. No. 75 Blue had participated at RIAT 2011 at

Three Su-27s of the 831st BrTA during the exercise Clear Sky 2011 at Mirgorod AB. 27 Blue, an Su-27S with c/n 36911012910, 52 Blue an Su-27P with c/n 36911035716, and 28 Blue an Su-27S with c/n 36911013916. *Sergey Popsuevich*

Fairford in the UK, and had returned to Mirgorod just four days earlier on 18 July. In return, Ukrainian Gen Onyshchenko was granted the opportunity to fly in an F-16D.

During the Safe Sky 2011 closing ceremony on 29 July, Col Scott Patten, 187th Fighter Wing Commander, said: 'Through the hard work of these Air National Guard members, we were able to fly 61 sorties during this event, We were able to provide critical insight into air sovereignty operations; promoting safe skies for the 2012 Euros.'

The ceremony was opened by Maj Gen Nikiforov, who said: 'We have been completely successful in our mission. We have accomplished this historic event, and developed lasting friendships.'

The second major exercise of 2011 in which the Su-27s of 831st BrTA participated was Adequate Response 2011, which was held between 12 and 30 September. Its purpose was to review the level of combat training of the forces as well as to research the development of a prospective model of the Armed Forces of Ukraine. The results of the exercise proved the effectiveness of the command and control system and its ability to function through the chain of command to the General Staff – Operational Command (Immediate Reaction Corps) – Brigade. The prospective combat strength of the Armed Forces was formulated and the new approaches to its application were tested in practice.

In total, 36 UKrAF aircraft took part in the exercise. These included nine Su-27s, comprising five Su-27Ss, 26, 28, 30, 41 and 52 Blue, Su-27P 39 Blue and three Su-27UBs, 69, 74 and 75 Blue. These Su-27s all were forward deployed to Belbek, where more than 11 MiG-29 9-13/UBs also took part. Six more fighter jets comprising three Su-24Ms, two Su-25s and an Su-25UB were deployed to Kirovskoye to be operated from there. One more Su-24M, an Su-24MR and five Su-25s took part from Kulbakino. During the exercise at least 12 Su-27 pilots were involved in live R-27R and R-73 air-to-air missile firing at VR-2 Strizh UAVs over Chauda gunnery range. MiG-29s and Su-27s were also used to test the S-300 and Tor-M1 SAM operators at Chauda.

The last mission of the 831st BrTA during the exercise was carried out on 30 September by Oleg Gesha and Col Oleg Palivoy (commander of the 1st Aviation Squadron) aboard an Su-27UB over the 240th Training Centre near Zhyromyr, while the Chief of the General Staff and the Commander-in-Chief of the Ukrainian Armed Forces and his deputy, as well as commanders of all three forces and their corps, air commands, air force brigades and army regiments, were present. The Su-27UB, together with a MiG-29UB and a MiG-29 9-13, flew from Vasilkov and simulated bombing attacks on the ground troops' positions.

Lt Gen Nikiforov, commander of the 831st BrTA, in the front seat of Su-27UB 75 Blue while the commander of the 100th Fighter Squadron, 187th Fighter Wing of the USAF's Alabama Air National Guard, is sat in the back during Exercise Clear Sky 2011 at Mirgorod AB on 22 July 2011. *Sergey Popsuevich*

USAF F-16 pilots from the 100th FS, 187th FW, had the opportunity to fly in UkrAF Su-27UBs and MiG-29UBs during the exercise Clear Sky 2011. 831st BrTA Su-27UB 75 Blue is departing Mirgorod AB during the exercise. *Sergey Popsuevich*

831st BrTA Su-27UB 75 Blue (c/n 96310418207) taxiing to the runway for take-off during exercise Clear Sky 2011 while seven Su-27s of the regiment, 26, 27, 30, 39, 41 and 43 Blue, as well as MiG-29s of the 204th BrTA, can be seen on the main ramp of the base on 26 July 2011. *Alexander Golz*

Su-27S 30 Blue of the 831st BrTA armed with R-27ET, R-27ER and R-73, departing Belbek AB prior to live missile firing during an exercise with the 204th BrTA on 20 September 2011. *Alexander Golz*

Su-27S 28 Blue (c/n 36911013916) armed with an R-73 IR-guided air-to-air missile taxiing at Belbek AB prior to take-off and live missile firing during a joint exercise with the 204th BrTA on 19 September 2011. *Alexander Golz*

Providing security for Euro 2012

The 831st BrTA was one of four brigades of the Ukrainian Air Force that trained its fighter pilots during the exercises Safe Sky 2011 and Adequate Response 2011 to provide security within Ukrainian airspace during Euro 2012. The football matches were scheduled to take place in stadiums in four cities in Ukraine and four in Poland between 8 June and 1 July. In Ukraine, they were held at the Kiev Olympic Stadium on 11, 15, 19, 24 June and 1 July; at the Donbass Arena, Donetsk, on 11, 15, 19, 23 and 27 June; at the Metalist Stadium, Kharkiv, on 9, 13 and 17 June; and at the Arena Lviv on 9, 13 and 17 June.

In 2011, the Ukrainian Air Force funded the overhaul of four Su-27s to be used exclusively on combat air patrol missions during Euro 2012. The first of them was Su-27S 53 Blue (c/n 36911015411), which was redelivered to the 831st BrTA in April.

The final two aircraft with overhauled airframes and engines were delivered in May and used for patrol missions during Euro 2012. They were a pair of Su-27Ps with 36911035716 and 36911035717 construction numbers, formerly numbered as 52 and 58 BLUE. They both received digital camouflage and new bort numbers, 100 and 101 BLUE respectively. They were handed over to 831st BrTA in late May just days before the championship started.

After these, Su-27UB 73 Blue (c/n 96310425068) was overhauled at the MiGremont facility, with delivery taking place in October or November 2012. It was painted in a digital camouflage developed by specialists at the State Research Aviation Institute, headed by Col Volodymyr Pautinka.

Almost a month before the games, Su-27s began flying from Ozernoye air base, home of the 9th Tactical Aviation Brigade, which operated the former 62nd IAP Su-27s until 2009. Starting on 4 May, three Su-27s of the 831st BrTA were forward deployed to that base to be used later on quick reaction alert in the west of Ukraine in support of the MiG-29s of the 114th BrTA, especially during the games at Lviv. While providing QRA capability in the east of Ukraine, especially during the games at Donetsk, two Su-27s accompanied by an An-26 (carrying ground equipment and ground crew) were forward deployed to Kramatorsk on 11 June.

According to the UkrAF Deputy of Operations, Maj Gen Igor Chehrenko, 42 pilots and ground crews of the 831st BrTA were engaged in missions for the protection of Ukraine's airspace during Euro 2012. In total, 34 combat air patrol sorties were carried out during the games involving at least seven Su-27s. Of these, 12 were conducted from Mirgorod by four Su-27s, 13 from Ozernoye and nine from Kramatorsk, logging a total of 90 flying hours.

Training and retraining of Su-27 pilots with the L-39

The backbone of the Ukrainian Air Force training fleet is the 46 airworthy L-39s surviving among a total of 430 examples inherited from the Soviet Air Force in 1992. Not only are they use for undergraduate pilot training with the 203rd TrAB at Chuguyev, they are also employed for the next stage of training fighter pilots after their graduation from the Kharkiv Air Force University (HUVS), which is named Kozhedub University (after Second World War air ace Ivan Kozhedub). For this purpose, each of the combat units of the air force is equipped with L-39Cs and L-39M1s for advanced pilot training. They not only help the air force to reduce the cost of fighter pilot training but also fill the gap caused by the lack of flying hours available to air force pilots, who can fly the type to maintain flying and navigation skills when their unit receives only a limited budget to procure fuel in peacetime.

On 29 December 2012, the 831st BrTA at Mirgorod received two L-39Cs, 111 and 112 Blue (former 40th BrTA aircraft), both painted in digital colours and which had been overhauled by the Chuguyev Aircraft Repair Plant (CHARZ) in 2012. These two L-39Cs are still in use by the brigade to maintain the flying skills of the unit's Su-27 pilots and train future pilots. As well as the 831st BrTA, another Su-27 operator, the 39th oaeTA (39th Separate Tactical Aviation Squadron) from Ozernoye-Zhytomir, has been operating two L-39Cs, 105 and 106 Blue, which were with the 299th BrTA and 40th BrTA until early 2015, when the Air Command Centre started to re-form the 39th oaeTA.

Su-27 modernisation

In March and August 2012, Su-27S 52 Blue (c/n 36911015408) and Su-27UB 71 Blue (c/n 96310424043) were redelivered to the 831st BrTA after modernisation. They were the first Su-27M1 and Su-27UBM1 prototypes and had received equipment intended to be installed on future modernised Su-27s.

The first Su-27SM1 of the 831st BrTA, 52 Blue (c/n 36911015408), armed with a captive training R-73 missile for DACT against MiG-29s of the 204th BrTA during Exercise Perspective 2012 at Belbek. *Alexander Golz*

The history of the modernisation of the Su-27s in Ukraine goes back to 2007; in that year decisions were made to modernise the fleet, not only to increase their calendar life but also to increase the reliability of their flight and weapon systems and improve their workability, or at least restore their capabilities to a level similar to when they were built by the KnAAPO and Irkut Aviation Plant. But just as other modernisation programmes were delayed, work on the Su-27s was also hit by a lack of budget.

The Ukrainian government funded the modernisation of the first pair of Su-27s in 2010 and 52 and 71 Blue were selected. First, 52 Blue was overhauled, the work being completed in October 2010. After passing all its flight tests, the aircraft was cleared by the quality control officer as fully mission capable and suitable to go into the modernisation programme, which lasted almost a year and was completed in February 2012. The aircraft undertook several test flights until it was redelivered to the 831st BrTA on 26 March 2012. It was named after the former head of MiGremont or Zaporozhye Aircraft Repair Plant, Valentin Kalenov, who died on 8 February 2012.

No. 52 Blue was reclassified as an Su-27M1 after modernisation, while 71 Blue became an Su-27UBM1. Similar to 52 Blue, 71 Blue was modernised after overhaul at MiGremont. It was redelivered to the 831st BrTA on 30 August 2012. Its level of modernisation was higher than 52 Blue, and on several occasions in 2012 and 2013 it flew back to MiGremont to have technical problems in its new systems repaired. It was used heavily to test any technical issues of the newly installed systems and then repair them, with the aim of improving the modernisation programme. No.71 Blue was completely modernised while 52 Blue had only a few of the new systems installed.

No. 71 Blue reached its desired level of reliability and combat capability after several debuggings of its systems at MiGremont in September 2015 and on 14 October 2015 it was handed over to the 831st BrTA during an official ceremony at Zaporozhye while the Ukrainian President was present. B-1831M1, which was the code for the project, was written on its fuselage.

The second fully modernised Su-27 was a 'P' model (air defence), 58 BLUE (c/n 36911035612). It was a former Su-27P of the 62nd IAP that had been transferred to the 9th IAP in 2001. It had been in storage for almost ten years when it was transferred by road to the MiGremont facility in October 2014. The aircraft was first overhauled in 2015 and was then modernised. It was handed over to the UkrAF during an official ceremony together with 71 Blue on 14 October 2015. As they had NAVAIDS with ICAO requirements, these aircraft became regular participants at international air shows because of their ability to fly within international airspace in Europe. They were unveiled for first time during the Skrydstrup air show in Denmark in July 2016.

In 2016, MiGremont partially modernised a second Su-27P, 50 Blue (c/n 36911035611), an ex-

100th KIAP version in 831st BrTA service. The aircraft had been sent to Zaporozhye in September 2015. After modernisation, 50 Blue was named 'Vasily Nikiforov' in honour of the former commander-in-chief of the UkrAF, who died from cancer in 2015. In 2017, MiGremont was contracted to carry out the modernisation of 70 Blue to Su-27UBM1 standard and this was completed in 2018. Next, Su-27S 31 Blue was modernised as an Su-27SM1 between October 2017 and November 2018.

According to MiGremont, the key objectives of the Su-27 modernisation programme were to expand the fighter's combat capabilities and its efficiency in solving combat tasks by increasing by 30% the detection range of air targets and the accuracy of unguided weapons fired at ground targets; expanding the capabilities of the navigation system; ensuring the possibility of flying on international routes; expanding the ability to control and record on-board parameters, increasing flight safety and ensuring the use of modern means of processing flight information.

The following new systems were installed on the modernised Su-27PM1 and Su-27UBM1:

- NAVSTAR CH-3007-02 and GNS-500W GPS and GLONASS navigation systems, which increased the accuracy of navigation along a route, taking the aircraft to a given point with deviation of no more than 50m

- An improved 'EKRAN-02M-3' (ЭКРАН-02М-3) crew alert system was installed, replacing 'EKRAN-02M' in the Su-27PM1, and 'EKRANUB-06M-3 replaced 'EKRAN-UB-06M' in the Su-27UBM1. This new system can issue warning and notification information to the electronic scoreboard of the block 2E-03 airborne onboard recovery system; and record in flight and during ground control on an easily detachable flash cassette of information from the Screen system, the BUR-4-10-01 recorder and the SOK-B objective control system of the weapon control system

- On-board emergency flight data recorder BUR-4-1-10-01 with solid state protective concentrator with the records of voice and video information, with the enhanced folding frequency (512 measurements per second instead of 256mps of parametric information, and 2,048mps instead of 512 [in emergency] of digital information), replacing the 'TESTER-UZ' system. BUR-4-1-10-01 can record data

Ex-62nd IAP Su-27P 58 Blue (c/n 36911035612) became the first Su-27PM1 in the UkrAF in 2015. *Alexander Golz*

This former 100th KIAP Su-27P of the 831st BrTA, 50 Blue (c/n 36911035611), became the second Su-27P to be modernised to Su-27PM1 standard. It was redelivered to its regiment after the upgrade work and was named 'Vasily Nikiforov' after the former commander-in-chief of the UkrAF who died from cancer in 2015. *Alexander Golz*

The name Vasily Nikiforov was written on the fuselage of Su-27PM1 with 50 Blue (c/n 36911035611) in 2016. Nikiforov was the former commander-in-chief of the UkrAF and was also commander of the 62nd IAP. *Alexander Golz*

from the SAVR-27U and Ekran-02M-3 or Ekran-UB-02M-3. Its installation was not planned at the beginning of the modernisation programme but was later incorporated into not only the first Su-27UMB1 but also the first Su-27PM1. To analyse the flight data recorded by the BUR-4-1-10-01 on the ground, the Slavutych-BUR-27 complex was designed and developed. This system entered UkrAF service in accordance with decree No. 468 of the Ukrainian President dated 13 May 2014 as a measure for enhancing the effectiveness of planning in the security and defence sector

- Squawk A-511, designed to operate with national secondary radars (SR) of air traffic control (ATC) systems and to transmit automatically the aircraft number, flight altitude, fuel load and flight path vector information to the ground SR at their request. It ensures additional work with secondary radar systems of ATC RBS with regard to ICAO requirements in modes 'AC' and 'A'. Squawk A-511 has several modes of work: 'ARS', 'ATC', 'P-35', 'READY', 'AC' and 'A'

- Equipment kit of helmet-mounted target detection 'SURA-K', replacing the standard 'ShZUM-1', to improve the use of R-73 IR-guided air-to-air missiles

- Audio and video check system AVCS-27U for the recording to digital videotape (DVT) of video information, shown on IGB-31 with an outside space picture given by on-board video camera as a background. This data could be easily recorded on a flash drive

Later a new U/VHF radio named 'P-800L2' was installed on both the Su-27UBM1 and Su-27PM1 instead of the older L800L1 Lunar-1, providing radio communication capability with other fighter jets and also the command posts. It had all the analogue chips replaced by digital ones, strengthening the signals sent and analysing the received signals better, especially under radio jamming conditions in combat. However, during the exercises when the workload of the radio was high, some errors and technical problems appeared that the manufacturer fixed or is trying to fix. The new radio had a high noise immunity and also a radio encryption capability using T-820 encoding apparatus.

On 24 October 2017, a contract was finalised between the Armed Forces of Ukraine and MiGremont for partial modernisation of ten Su-27s of the 831st BrTA at a cost of 126,840 UAH. As a part of this modernisation, the SAVR-27U audio/video recorder was planned to be installed on the aircraft as a replacement for the obsolete FKP-EU. This system is equipped with two colour video cameras named VK-05 and VK-06, recording the pilot in the cabin and also the head-up display during the flight. Video and audio recorded by the system is transferred to a BUR-4-1-10-01 solid state protected storage drive.

Modernisation of the N001 radar

As well as the installation of these new systems, 71 Blue's Phazotron N001 Myech all-weather/multi-role pulse-Doppler radar was modernised in order to increase the detection range of air targets by 1.3 times, to increase radar noise immunity and improve the reliability and maintainability of the station. This was achieved by means of:

- replacing the standard unit of the high-frequency receiver H019-09 with the unit H019-09R2, which had increased sensitivity and improved noise characteristics

- replacing the regular block of the master oscillator H001-22M with the block H001-22R2 with improved frequency shaping and control modules

- replacing the regular digital processing unit of the BTsO-M with the BTsO-R unit with a high-performance signal processor, which makes it possible to significantly improve the selection of reflected signals

MFI-27 LCD 5in x 4in Multifunction displays were also installed as a replacement for the old CRT radar display on the top right corner of the instrument panel to provide comfortable operator working in any ambient light conditions. Its TFT matrix has high-resolution characteristics and wide viewing angles that allow the display of high-quality graphics even under sunny conditions.

831st BrTA before the war

In September 2012, just a few weeks after their participation in the missions to provide security for Euro 2012, the Su-27s and personnel of 831st BrTA participated in Exercise Perspective 2012 with seven Su-27s, which were Su-27Ss 26, 41, 52 and 53 Blue and Su-27UBs, 69, 74 and 75 Blue. During the exercise on 25 September the pilot of 26 Blue launched two R-73 missiles at SAB-250 flash bombs. Bombing also took place on the same day, during which four Su-27 pilots flew with the three Su-27UBs and dropped a total of 12 SAB-250-200 flare bombs (four by each aircraft). Some of the bombing aircraft were targeted by R-73 IR-guided missiles launched from MiG-29s and Su-27s.

The next day, Su-27UB 74 Blue was used to carry out live firing of two R-27T infrared/passive homing missiles and one R-27R semi-active radar homing missile. Two more R-27Rs and two R-27Ts were launched by another Su-27UB, 69 Blue, in the morning. After 74 Blue returned to base, its R-27 missile launchers were replaced by six pylons to carry six SAB-250-200 flare bombs for another R-73 missile launch, which was carried out in the evening. On the same evening, Su-27Ss 26, 41, 52 and 53 Blue were equipped with captive training R-73 missiles for Su-27 pilots in close air combat and dogfighting.

In January 2013, MiGremont completed the overhaul of Su-27Ss 45 and 46 Blue. Both of them had been stored for almost a decade at Mirgorod and they were transported to Zaporozhye by road in 2010 or 2011. They were both painted in the new blue digital camouflage and handed over to the 831st BrTA on 23 May 2013.

831st BrTA Su-27S 26 Blue (c/n 36911013814) equipped with a captive training R-73 missile landing at Belbek AB after dogfight training during Exercise Perspective 2012 on 26 September 2012. *Alexander Golz*

In September 2013, the 831st BrTA took part in the bilateral research command post exercise Autumn Cyclone 2013 with Operational Commands North and South. That exercise was the main training activity of the Ukrainian Armed Forces in 2013. A total of 26 aircraft and 31 helicopters took part, including five Su-27s comprising Su-27S 53 Blue, Su-27P 39 Blue and Su-27UBs 69, 73 and 74 Blue, all forward deployed to Ivano-Frankovsk. During the exercise they mostly carried out air-to-air missions and provided top cover for the Su-25s and Su-24s.

On 30 October 2013, under the command of UkrAF's commander-in-chief, Lt Gen Yuriy Baidak, a bilateral Ukrainian–Belarusian air defence exercise was held, during which one UkrAF Su-27 and two MiG-29s and three Belarusian Air Force MiG-29s

Su-27UB 74 Blue (c/n 96310425069) armed with a pair of R-27ET (one under each wing) and a single R-27ER under its fuselage landing at Belbek AB during Perspective 2012 on 26 September 2012. *Alexander Golz*

41 Blue (c/n 36911014001), an Su-27S of the 831st BrTA, armed with a captive training R-73 for dissimilar air combat training (DACT) against MiG-29 9-13s of the 204th BrTA at Belbek during Perspective 2012 on 26 September 2012. ***Alexander Golz***

took part. During the exercise the participants had to fly in the airspace of each other's countries and not respond to radio calls. Then two fighter jets were scrambled to intercept and escort them. Based on the requirements of the Chicago Convention on International Civil Aviation, the pilots of the intercepting fighter jets had to approach aircraft in which the pilot was not responsive to radio calls in order to visually identify the aircraft, report its tail number to ground control radar and then visually establish contact with its pilot to direct him to land at an airport.

During the 2014 Winter Olympics held in Sochi, Russia, the 831st BrTA was once again tasked with providing security within Ukrainian airspace, especially in the south over the Crimean peninsula. For this purpose, two of the four Su-27s that had been exclusively overhauled for use during Euro 2012 were deployed to Belbek in Crimea on 6 February 2014 to stand alert 24/7 during the games. They were Su-27S 46 Blue and Su-27P 100 Blue, and both was armed with six R-27R semi-active, radar-homing, medium-range, air-to-air missiles and four R-73 IR-guided, short-range, air-to-air missiles. As well as these two single-seater Su-27s, an Su-27UB piloted by Lt Col Alexander Oksanchenko, commander of the 831st BrTA, was deployed to Belbek. His aircraft was armed with two R-27Rs.

On the evening of Friday, 7 February, a Ukrainian tourist who was a passenger on a Pegasus Airlines flight from Kharkiv to Istanbul and under the influence of alcohol, attempted to hijack the aircraft, which was carrying 110 passengers, by falsely claiming that he had explosives, forcing the pilot to divert to Sochi. This soon resulted in the scramble of Su-27P 100 Blue, piloted by Lt Col Alexander Oksanchenko just a day after his deployment to Belbek. He then escorted the aircraft and patrolled over the border with Russia for one and half hours until Turkish Air Force F-16Cs took over escort duties. The passenger surrendered and the aircraft landed safely at its destination.

One of the first two digital camouflaged Su-27s in the UkrAF, Su-27P 100 Blue, during the Gostomel air show on 27 September 2012. ***Alexander Golz***

Su-27UBs of the 831st BrTA, from front to back, 74, 73 and 75 Blue, at Mirgorod AB in 2013. *Poltava Falcons Facebook Page*

Su-27UB 69 Blue was among the Su-27s of the 831st BrTA that took part in the Bilateral Research Command Post exercise Autumn Cyclone 2013 at Ivano-Frankivsk in September 2013. In the background are MiG-29s of the 114th BrTA. *Alexander Golz*

Su-27UB 73 Blue (c/n 96310425068) during Autumn Cyclone 2013 at Ivano-Frankivsk AB in September 2013. This aircraft later became one of two Su-27UBs in the newly formed 39th ISqTA. *Alexander Golz*

In action in the war in Donbass

The year 2014 started for 831st BrTA with a series of training and retraining missions in the second half of January involving nine Su-27s and Su-27UBs as well as two L-39s. A key goal of the training was to restore the capability of 18 pilots in instrument flight and navigation for day and night in bad weather conditions.

Before participating in the mission during the Sochi games, the 204th BrTA with a MiG-29 9-13 piloted by Col Yuri Cholovsky, flying from Belbek, and the 831st BrTA with an Su-27UB, flying from Mirgorod, took part in an exercise on 3 February, during which they intercepted an An-26 transport that was playing the role of a hijacked passenger aircraft over the Black Sea. They escorted the aircraft until it came over Feodosia, at which point it was forced to land in Kirovskoye. The exercise was held under the direct leadership and supervision of the UkrAF deputy commander, Lt Gen Sergei Drozdov.

On 1 March 2014, just eight days after the end of the 831st BrTA's deployment to Belbek for the Sochi games, 100 and 101 Blue were deployed to Kulbakino to stand on alert following the rise of security issues in the Crimea peninsula.

In March 2014, the Ukrainian Air Force had only 14 operation-ready Su-27s, comprising six Su-27Ss, 17, 41, 45, 46, 52 and 53 Blue, four Su-27Ps, 38, 39, 100 and 101 Blue, and four Su-27UBs, 69, 71 (Su-27UBM1 prototype), 73 and 75 Blue. Among these, two more, 45 and 46 Blue, were deployed to Kulbakino to reinforce the QRA capability there following the increased possibility of Russia's invasion from Crimea. Subsequently, the technicians of 831st BrTA's maintenance squadron began restoring aircraft that still had flying hours left until their next overhaul despite reaching their lifetime limit. The first aircraft that was restored quickly was Su-27UB 74 Blue (c/n 96310425069).

While four Su-27s had been deployed to Kulbakino, the 831st BrTA pilots also took part in several training flights to be ready for battle from Ozernoye, where the 831st BrTA had restarted deploying its Su-27s to re-establish its QRA facility, which it introduced for Euro 2012.

Earlier in January, a group of four Su-27s, an Su-27UB and two L-39s had been deployed to Ozernoye, where they flew 27 training sorties on 30 January totalling 20 flying hours in day and night in bad weather conditions. These aircraft were later dedicated to a separate tactical aviation squadron commanded by 2nd class pilot Col Alexey Zakharchuk. They were deployed to Ozernoye again and performed a similar series of training flights in 20 sorties in just one day in the second week of March.

To increase the number of operation-ready and airworthy Su-27s, the maintenance squadron continued restoring more Su-27s, extending their calendar life for 12 months to provide aircraft for the quick reaction alert facilities at Mirgorod and Ozernoye. As well as Su-27UB 74 Blue, a second Su-27UB, 70 Blue, which had been in storage since 2009 was restored and painted in three-tone blue camouflage in June 2014. Five Su-27Ss were also restored between March and September, namely 06, 27, 28, 30 and 36 Blue. These had been flown for last time in 2008, 2009, 2011, 2011 and 2009 respectively.

The direct participation of the Su-27s in the war in Donbass started with combat air patrols and surveillance missions over the region in mid-April 2014. One of the very first missions was a flight of Su-27S 28 Blue armed with two R-73s and three R-27Rs from Mirgorod on 14 April. On that day the aircraft flew over Sloviansk and Kramatorsk. Three Su-27Ss, 15, 28 and 30 Blue, and Su-27UB 75 Blue were involved in patrol flights between 14 and 17 April based on pictures taken of separatists or Ukrainian security forces on the ground. The main

Su-27S 30 Blue (c/n 36911013918) was in storage at Mirgorod AB but was quickly restored and brought back to flight condition by the technicians and engineers of the 831st BrTA in March 2014. It is seen armed with four R-73 IR-guided, short-range missiles and five R-27ER semi-active, medium-range missiles during an exercise at Nikolayev on 6 May 2014. This exercise was held prior to the anti-terrorism operation of the Ukrainian Security Forces in the Donbass area. 30 Blue was among the Su-27s that carried out CAP over the Donbass during the war. ***Alexander Golz***

Su-27S 27 Blue (c/n 36911012910) was targeted by separatists' MANPADS over Lugansk on 2 June 2014. It was damaged but the pilot managed to bring it back to base and it was later repaired. Here it is armed with a pair of R-73 IR-guided, short-range air-to-air missiles and a pair of B-8M1 rocket pods, which the aircraft were carrying during visual surveillance missions at low altitude over the Donbass. *Luca G. Canossa*

28 Blue, an Su-27S of the 831st BrTA with c/n 36911013916, was restored by technicians of the 831st BrTA in March or April 2014. It was spotted over Lugansk carrying three R-27ERs and two R-73 missiles during CAP missions on 14 April 2014. *Luca G. Canossa*

purpose of these flights over the east of Ukraine was firstly to protect the airspace from the danger of Russian Air Force fighter interceptors and secondly to break the morale of the separatists and increase that of Ukrainian security forces on the battlefield. Four days before that, on 10 April, the 831st BrTA had prepared some of its pilots for combat by carrying out 30 flights within 20 flying hours.

The Russian Air Force fighter jets that were threatening Ukraine's airspace were MiG-29s of the 31st Fighter Aviation Regiment based at Millerovo, 15km from the eastern border with Ukraine. Among the 34 MiG-29s in service with the three aviation squadrons of the regiment, just eight to ten were fully mission capable in March 2014. Four of them, each armed with two R-27Rs and four R-73s, were on 24/7 alert. As a back-up, the RuAF's 19th Fighter Aviation Regiment had four of its eight Su-27s at Millerovo. Each was armed with four R-27Rs and four R-73s but they stayed mostly on the ground and most combat air patrols were carried out by 31st IAP MiG-29s.

The four Su-27s 45, 46, 100 and 101 Blue on deployment at Kulbakino were responsible for dealing with the threat of four Su-27SM3s of the 19th Fighter Aviation Regiment that had been deployed to Gvardeyskoye in Crimea on 20 March 2014 and remained there until 12 September 2014, when they were deployed to Belbek to stand on 24/7 alert. The Russian Aerospace Force had also deployed a pair of S-300PM (5P85Ts) SAM systems at Gvardeyskoye air base between 17 and 22 March 2014. They remained at Gvardeyskoye until were sent to the south of Sevastopol in early 2015.

Before the beginning of major operations by the Ukrainian Security forces in the Donbass region, 831st BrTA pilots again took part in an exercise from Kulbakino, during which all the four Su-27s on deployment there together with two Su-27UBs, 74 and 75 Blue, took part between 13 and 21 May. Nos 74 and 75 Blue arrived on 15 May and the next day they were used for practice bombing using SAB-250-200 flare bombs. These bombs were also used as heat targets to assist live R-73 missile firing practice.

Because of the inaccuracy of the Su-27's targeting system, these flare bombs, which could be used against enemy positions during close air support missions, could potentially be used in the war. On the same day, 46 and 100 Blue carried out live R-73 missile firing. On 17 May, Su-27UBs were again used for bombing during the exercise. Fighter jets from all the UkrAF's brigades except the 204th BrTA took part in the exercise and a total of175 sorties in 220 flying hours were logged. MiG-29 and Su-27 pilots mostly practised air-to-air missions such as similar and dissimilar air combat.

Upon the launch of the major counter-insurgency or terrorism operation of the Ukrainian security

831st BrTA Su-27S 45 Blue (c/n 36911014104) was among the examples which were deployed to Nikolayev/Kulbakino to protect the south of Ukraine during the Crimea crisis in March and April 2014. It was always armed with two R-27ETs, three R-27ERs and two R-73s while it was on QRA duty at Kulbakino. *Luca G. Canossa*

The 831st BrTA Su-27P 100 Blue (c/n 36911035716) was another example deployed to Nikolayev/Kulbakino in March and April 2014 to protect the south of Ukraine in the Crimea crisis. It was also armed with two R-27ETs, three R-27ERs and two R-73s while on QRA duty at Kulbakino. *Luca G. Canossa*

831st BrTA Su-27UB 75 Blue (c/n 96310418207) was spotted in the QRA hangars at Mirgorod AB multiple times in 2013 and 2014. It was usually armed with a pair of R-73 IR-guided, short-range, air-to-air missiles and four B-13L rocket launchers, each one carrying five S-13 unguided rockets as shown here. *Luca G. Canossa*

forces, which included the first battle of Donetsk airport (which started on 26 May), the Su-27s were used regularly to patrol the airspace over Donbass, especially to protect An-30s, MiG-29s and Su-25s from the threat from Russian Air Force fighter jets and also to search for any possible infiltration and incursion of Russian transport and attack helicopters inside Ukraine's territory.

During one of the Su-27 flights over Donbass, 27 Blue (c/n 36911012910) was hit by a MANPAD fired by the separatists while flying at low altitude over Lugansk during a visual reconnaissance mission on 2 June 2014. Its pilot, Yalishev Sergey Aleksandrovich, continued his flight and returned safely to Mirgorod. On 19 July he was awarded the 3rd Class Order of Bogdan Khmelnitsky for his bravery in saving his damaged aircraft, which was later sent to Zaporozhye to be repaired and overhauled by MiGremont. It was eventually redelivered to the 831st BrTA in 2016.

On 29 August 2014, all flights of UkrAF fighter jets were stopped over the Donbass region due to the danger of the Russian Aerospace Force's Buk M1, Osa-AKM and MANPADS in the hands of Russian-backed separatists. This decision was made after the loss of Su-25 08 Blue on that day. This resulted in the end of CAP missions by Su-27s over Donbass.

During the war in Donbass, when the number of operational Su-25s was reduced, the 831st BrTA was ordered to use its Su-27s for air-to-ground missions. However, when the first of these was carried out on 20 July, the results were poor because of the lack of accuracy of the targeting system of the Su-27S when using S-8 unguided rockets and iron bombs. As a result, the Su-27s were not used for close air support and strike missions.

After the war, four Su-27s remained at Kulbakino until the 204th BrTA restored its combat capability and used its own MiG-29 9-13s to provide QRA capability again, which was in early 2015. In September, decisions were made to deploy two Su-27s to Odessa, both armed with R-27Rs and R-73, to stand as QRA fighters there and be a back-up to the four QRA MiG-29s at Kulbakino. The number of the QRA Su-27s at Odessa was increased to three in December. In April 2019, there were still three Su-27s standing on alert at Odessa, each armed with three R-27Rs and two R-73s, while the 39th Tactical Aviation Squadron had two Su-27s on alert duty at Ozernoye and the 831st BrTA had four at Mirgorod.

Maintenance and overhaul

After 29 August 2014, the UkrAF's Su-27s were used to perform routine CAP missions over the east of Ukraine and Donbass but at high altitude and a safe distance from the separatists' Buk M1 SAM system, which had not only shot down a couple of Ukrainian fighter jets but also Malaysian Airlines flight MH17. To keep these missions going and also to reinforce the QRA capability of the air force at Mirgorod and Ozernoye, the 831st BrTA's maintenance squadron was restoring more Su-27s and the Ivan Kozhedub National Air Force University was training more fighter pilots to fly the type.

By the time the war ended, five Su-27Ss and two Su-27UBs had been restored by air force technicians at Mirgorod, of which just one was

04 Blue (c/n 36911011907) became the first UKrAF Su-27 to be overhauled by ZARZ in 1993. It is seen before its first post-overhaul functional check flight at Zaporozhye. ***MiGremont's archive***

Formerly 80 Blue was in service with the 100th KIAP but was transferred to the 831st IAP in 1992 and became 57 Red. This Su-27P, c/n 36911031411, logged its first flight on 11 April 1990. It was painted in these colours to be used by the 831st BrTA for flight displays during air shows. It is seen at Zaporozhye after its overhaul in 2001. *MiGremont's archive*

damaged during the war and sent to MiGremont to be repaired. In total, 20 Su-27s were operation-ready, of which four were deployed at Kulbakino and four others were at Ozernoye. Later, the number of Ozernoye-based Su-27s was increased to six, resulting in the formation of the 39th Independent Tactical Aviation Squadron in 2015.

Before the USSR collapsed, there was no aircraft repair plant with the capability to carry out depot maintenance of the Su-27s in the Ukrainian SSR. The nearest suitable plant was No. 558 ARZ at Baranovichi, Belarus, which in 1990 had been identified as the leading facility in the USSR to perform all types of maintenance and overhaul on the Su-27.

The first aircraft to be delivered to the facility was Su-27UB 63 Red of the 831st IAP, which arrived in October 1991. It remained there after the USSR collapsed and was not handed over to the Ukrainian Air Force after its overhaul. That was because the newborn UkrAF had a limited budget, which was not enough to pay for the work. Even the No. 558 ARZ did not complete the overhaul of 63 Red until its connections with Irkut and KnAAPO were re-established in the late 1990s, enabling it to carry out the work and even modernise the aircraft. No. 63 Red finally flew after overhaul and modernisation in 2003.

Before No. 558 ARZ completed its first Su-27 overhaul, the Zaporozhye ARZ was contracted by the Ukrainian Ministry of Defence to develop a programme for all types of Su-27 maintenance, including depot level. As its result, Su-27S 04 Red (c/n 36911011907) of the 831st IAP, which was manufactured in 1985 and had reached its MTBO, was handed over to Zaporozhye to be put through an experimental semi-PDM, similar to IRAN (Inspect and Repair As Necessary) in the west, in 1993. The aircraft performed its first FCF after the overhaul on 29 August 1994. It was painted in a three-tone light grey, light blue and blue splinter scheme with its bort number colourless to make it distinctive from all other aircraft in Ukraine.

After the USSR's collapse, flying activity at UkrAF Su-27 units declined and this delayed the need for their MTBO. Despite that some Su-27s, especially those manufactured in 1985 including 01 Red (c/n 36911011301) and 02 Red (c/n 36911011302), the first and second Su-27Ss with the 831st IAP, were stored at the end of their MTBO in the mid-1990s. The key reason was the downsizing of the UkrAF and the availability of some younger Su-27S/Ps from the former 100th KIAP of the USSR Navy that had now joined the 62nd IAP and could easily replace the old Su-27Ss of the 831st IAP if required. Based on the pictures available, Su-27S 48 Red (c/n 36911014411) from 831st IAP and Su-27P 57 Red (c/n 36911031411) from the 62nd IAP (ex-100th IAP) were repaired by the Zaporozhye ARZ in the mid-1990s and they participated in international air shows from 1996, including the Royal International Air Tattoo and CIAF.

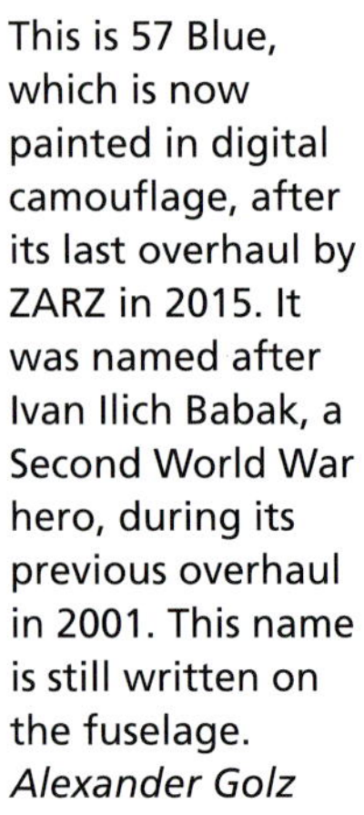

This is 57 Blue, which is now painted in digital camouflage, after its last overhaul by ZARZ in 2015. It was named after Ivan Ilich Babak, a Second World War hero, during its previous overhaul in 2001. This name is still written on the fuselage. *Alexander Golz*

Ex-100th KIAP Su-27S 36 Blue (c/n 36911019614), delivered on 7 June 1987, was overhauled by ZARZ in 1997. It then received this blue splinter camouflage. Here it is undergoing ground checks at Zaporozhye in 1997. *MiGremont's archive*

According to the results of the work carried out on the development of the methodology and technology for the extension of 04 Red's life during the first repair in 1994, and the repair of two other Su-27s, the plant was asked to carry out work on continuing the Su-27's service life, extending the first repair from 12 to 14 years, and in 2000 from 14 to 16 years.

Subsequently, with the expiration of an aircraft's scheduled service life before the first overhaul, the MiGremont jointly with the State Research Centre worked on the specification of the list of restoration work and improving the methods of their implementation, taking into consideration the technical condition of each particular aircraft. The relevant overhaul and maintenance manuals were drafted, the enactment of which authorised the continuation of aircraft overhauls (after performing restoration work) before the first repair from 16 to 17 years (in 2003), from 17 up to 18 years (in 2007) and from 18 to 19 years (in 2009).

Due to end of the MTBO of most of the 831st IAP's Su-27s in the early 2000s, the Ukrainian Ministry of Defence specified funds for the overhaul and lifetime extension of four of its Su-27Ss in 2002. The first two were 06 and 08 Blue, overhauled in 2003, and they remained in service until 2008 and 2009 respectively. After them, 15 and 27 Blue were overhauled between June 2003 and August 2004 and remained in service until 2012 and 2008 respectively.

In 2008, MiGremont overhauled 9th BrTA Su-27P 38 Blue (c/n 36911035509). It was then redelivered to the brigade in January 2009 and remained there until mid-2009 before going to the 831st BrTA. In 2016 it was returned to Ozernoye to serve in the 39th Separate Tactical Aviation Squadron.

Between December 2008 and June 2010, MiGremont fully overhauled and extended the life of Su-27UB 75 Blue of the 831st BrTA. It was actually a former 100th KIAP aircraft with reinforced landing gear, but had served in the State Research Centre at Kirovskoye. There it was used for military tourism, enabling civilians to fly in the back seat for $6,000 an hour. It had been transferred to the 831st BrTA after the end of its MTBO in 2005. No. 75 Blue was still in service in April 2019.

In 2009, 39 Blue (c/n 36911035818), an ex-62nd IAP Su-27P of the 831st BrTA, was overhauled. It then remained in the 831st BrTA's 2nd Aviation Squadron until it was transferred to the newly formed 39th Separate Tactical Aviation Squadron in 2015. Following that, Su-27S 17 Blue (c/n 36911013814) and Su-27UB 69 Blue (c/n 96310418215) were delivered to MiGremont to be overhauled in 2009. Work on the Su-27UB was completed in October 2010, but the aircraft was kept by MiGremont due to the UkrAF owing the company money and it was only redelivered in July

43 Blue (c/n 36911014002), an Su-27S of the 831st BrTA, on Zaporozhye's runway prior take-off for its post-overhaul FCF in 1996 or 1997. *MiGremont's archive*

Su-27UB 74 Blue (c/n 96310425069) was overhauled by ZARZ in 2015. The aircraft is seen prior to its last overhaul dispensing flares over Ivano-Frankivsk AB during the Bilateral Research Command Post Exercise Autumn Cyclone 2013 in September 2013. *Alexander Golz*

2011 when this was paid. No. 17 Blue's overhaul was completed after 69 Blue and the aircraft was redelivered to the 831st BrTA in August 2011.

In 2011, MiGremont was contracted to overhaul and extend the lifetime of Su-27S 53 Blue (c/n 36911019411), Su-27Ps 100 and 101 Blue (c/n 36911035716 and 36911035717) and Su-27UB 73 Blue (c/n 96310425068). They were redelivered to the 831st BrTA between April and August 2012. As mentioned before, MiGremont also completed the first stage of modernisation of the first Su-27SM1 and Su-27UBM1 prototypes, 52 and 71 Blue respectively, in 2012. In the same year, Su-27Ss 45 and 46 Blue (c/ns 36911014104 and 36911014105) were overhauled and redelivered to the 831st BrTA in January 2013.

In 2013, three Su-27s were delivered to MiGremont to be overhauled. Ex-9th BrTA Su-27P 04 Blue (c/n 36911035614) was delivered in April 2013. Its overhaul was completed in November 2014 and it was officially redelivered to the 831st BrTA as 37 Blue during a ceremony on 5 January 2015. Next, in November 2013, two Su-27Ss, 54 Blue (c/n 36911015102) and 33 Blue (c/n 36911015921), were sent to MiGremont by road to be overhauled and have their lifetimes extended. They were both redelivered after the war, in October 2014 and on 5 January 2015 respectively.

In 2014, MiGremont started the overhaul of former 9th BrTA Su-27P 02 Blue (c/n 36911035612), which had been stored by the 831st BrTA for a long time. It was not only overhauled but also became the first single-seat Su-27 to pass the first and second stages of modernisation. It was designated as an Su-27PM1 and was redelivered to the 831st BrTA as 58 Blue together with Su-27UBM1 71 Blue (c/n 96310424043) in October 2015.

In 2015, MiGremont carried out an overhaul and lifetime extension for four more Su-27s: two Su-27Ss, an Su-27UB and an Su-27P, all ex-100th KIAP examples with reinforced landing gear that were in service with the 831st BrTA. The first Su-27S was 28 Blue (c/n 36911021307), which was redelivered after an overhaul as 24 Blue and joined the 39th Separate Tactical Aviation Squadron in December 2015. The other Su-27S was 25 Blue (c/n 36911021308), which was overhauled in 2015 and redelivered to the 39th ISqTA as 55 Blue in May 2016.

The Su-27P was 57 Blue (c/n 36911031411), which since 2001 had been named 'Ivan Ilich Babak', a Second World War war hero. Its overhaul was completed in 2016, with redelivery to the 831st BrTA on 15 October. The Su-27UB was 74 Blue (c/n 96310425069), which had been restored in 2014 and flew for the 831st BrTA until November, when it was handed over to the MiGremont facility to be overhauled. It was redelivered on 14 October 2015.

In 2016, MiGremont overhauled three Su-27s. The first was Su-27UB 67 Blue from the 831st BrTA, which was sent to Zaporozhye by road in the second half of 2015. It was redelivered to the unit after completion of its overhaul in the first quarter of 2017. Next, an ex-100th KIAP Su-27S of the 831st BrTA, 36 Blue (c/n 36911019614), was overhauled in 2016. As with many Su-27s that had been overhauled between 2014 and 2018, it was then delivered to the newly formed 39th ISqTA.

The third Su-27 that MiGremont overhauled in 2016 was 50 Blue (c/n 36911035611), a former 62nd IAP Su-27P. The aircraft had been removed from storage in summer 2014 and was finally sent to Zaporozhye in September 2015. After its overhaul, the aircraft was partially modernised to B-2831M1 (Su-27PM1) level and named 'Vasily Nikiforov' on 10 February 2016 in honour of the former commander of the 62nd IAP who later became commander-in-chief of the UkrAF. Nikiforov had died from cancer on 7 March 2015. He had been awarded the 1st, 2nd and 3rd Class Order of Bogdan Khmelnitsky during his career. He mastered piloting ten types of aircraft, flew nearly all the types in UkrAF service and logged a total of 4,000 hours during his career.

In 2017 and 2018, MiGremont overhauled five Su-27s: 70 Blue (c/n 96310424040), which was not only overhauled but also fully modernised to Su-27UBM1 standard as well in 2018; 27 Blue

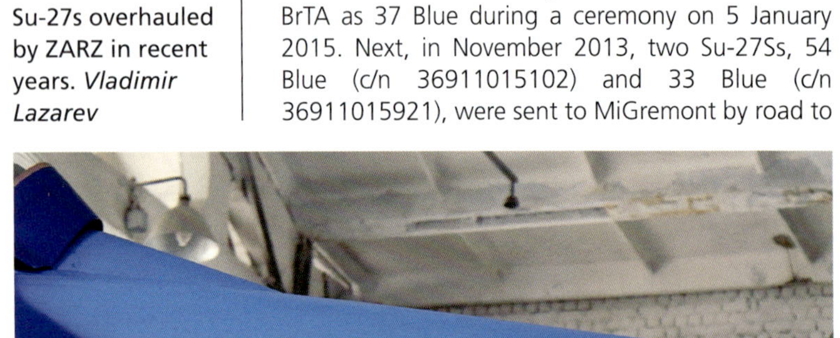

This is the 831st BrTA insignia, which has been painted on almost all the Su-27s overhauled by ZARZ in recent years. *Vladimir Lazarev*

On 5 January 2015, Su-27S 33 Blue (c/n 36911015921), together with Su-27P 37 Blue (c/n 36911035614), were handed over to the 831st BrTA after their overhaul and repair by MiGremont. *Ukrainian Air Force*

(c/n 36911012910), an Su-27S of the 831st BrTA that had been damaged during the war in Donbass and not only had its fuselage repaired but was also overhauled; 21 Blue (c/n 36911013809), a former 9th BrTA Su-27S that was redelivered to the 39th ISqTA after the work was completed in autumn 2018; 23 Blue (c/n 36911015305), another former 9th BrTA aircraft of the 831st BrTA that had been stored since 2002. After completion of its overhaul, it was delivered to the 39th ISqTA. The last aircraft was 31 Blue (c/n 36911019615), an ex-100th KIAP Su-27S of the 831st BrTA.

In November 2017, the 831st BrTA delivered two Su-27s to MiGremont to be restored and overhauled: Su-27S 12 Blue (c/n 36911014820), built in 1986, and 31 Blue (c/n 36911019615), an Su-27S manufactured in 1987 with reinforced landing gear. They had been in storage for almost two decades and had logged very few flying hours compared with other UKrAF Su-27s. Almost a year later, 31 Blue was not only overhauled but it was fully modernised to Su-27SM1 level. It was handed over to the 831st BrTA during a ceremony attended by the Ukrainian President on 1 December 2018.

In total, MiGremont completed the overhaul, lifetime extension and even modernisation of 18 Su-27s between 2014 and 2018. These were nine Su-27Ss, two Su-27Ps, two Su-27PM1s, an Su-27SM1, three Su-27UBs and an Su-27UBM1. Among these, five Su-27Ss and an Su-27P were handed over to the newly formed 39th ISqTA between 2015 and 2018.

Su-27S 15 Blue (c/n 36911011908) was in storage at Mirgorod AB but was restored by the 831st BrTA maintenance squadron in summer 2014. It is seen being painted at the base after the maintenance work. *Dmitry P.'s collection*

Fleet for sale

On 26 May 1997, an accident occurred on the main ramp of Mirgorod AB, resulting in the collision of an Su-27UB with an Su-27S and another Su-27UB of the 831st IAP. The Su-27S was withdrawn from service because it was unrepairable, while the Su-27UBs were repaired by the 831st IAP's maintenance squadron. One of the Su-27UBs, 68 Blue (c/n 96310418204), became operational again while the other, 72 Blue (c/n 96310424045), never flew with the 831st IAP again. It was sold to Eritrea, and was subsequently moved to Zaporozhye on 2 August 2001 to be prepared for delivery to the Eritrean Air Force. After pre-delivery maintenance work and painting, the aircraft was handed over as 609 Black on 25 January 2002.

Six more Su-27s were sold by Ukraine up to 2014, when all plans for the sale of more were cancelled. Following 72 Blue, the sole Su-27S of the 3rd State Aviation Test Centre, 35 Yellow (c/n 36911026310), which was actually a former 100th KIAP machine with reinforced landing gear (as was 72 Blue), was also sold to Eritrea. The contract had been signed in 2001 but the aircraft needed an overhaul prior to delivery. This was completed on 18 August 2003 and it was delivered as 608 Black.

Eritrea had three Su-27Ps on order as well but could not afford to pay for them. Therefore, they were sold to Ethiopia. They were 03 (c/n 36911035613), 05 (c/n 36911035715) and 12 Blue (c/n 36911035510), all former 62nd IAP machines that had been put for sale after its Su-27s were retired or passed to the 9th IAP at Ozernoye in 2001. Nos 03 and 05 Blue were delivered as 1962 and 1963 respectively while 12 Blue was delivered to the Ethiopian Air Force as 1961 on 13 June 2003 following overhaul.

In 2008, an American privately owned company named Pride Aircraft procured a pair of Su-27UBs from Ukraine. They were ex-100th KIAP Su-27UB 61 Blue (c/n 96310408027) with a reinforced landing gear and ex-831st IAP Su-27UB 66 Blue (c/n 96310418210). The airframes and engines of both aircraft were freshly overhauled (zero-timed) by the Zaporozhye ARZ and Motor Sich respectively. They were westernised with new radio and FAA-standard NAVAIDS and all cockpit markings were relabelled in English. The aircraft were equipped with full IFR U.S. instrumentation and avionics. They were painted in two-tone grey splinter camouflage and received the bort numbers 31 and 32 Red. They were licensed by the FAA as N131SU and N132SU.

They were demilitarised before delivery by the removal of the weapon system computers, the wiring for the wing pylons, 30mm Gryazev-Shipunov GSh-30-1 cannon, N001 Mech (Sword) Doppler radar, etc. Pride Aircraft sold 61 Blue for $7.4 million to Meridican Inc, a US company, on 26 September 2008 just four months after it was delivered. No. 66 Blue was sold by Pride Aircraft to Meridican Inc. for $6 million on 10 December 2009. It had only logged 600 flying hours during its 22-year life.

The sale of these Su-27s in the US resulted in Russia ending the delivery of Su-27 spare parts to Ukraine. This resulted in a significant decline in the number of airworthy Su-27s in the country, mainly because it had to buy spare parts at a premium from a third party such as Belarus.

One of three ex-62nd IAP Su-27Ps that were sold to Ethiopia in 2003. It is seen during a post-overhaul FCF at Zaporozhye. *MiGremont's archive*

Su-27S c/n 36911026310 was in use at the 3rd State Aviation Centre in the 1980s and early 1990s. It, together with an Su-27UB, were sold to Eritrea in 2002. It received the bort number 608. *MiGremont's archive*

Formation of 39th IsqTA (Flankers of Ozernoye)

In 2014, the Ukrainian Air Force restarted operating Su-27s from Ozernoye Air Base, which led to the establishment of the 39th Independent or Separate Tactical Aviation Squadron in 2015. For this purpose, almost half the Su-27s overhauled by MiGremont were allocated to the new squadron. The aim was to raise the number of its operational aircraft gradually over a period of three years in order to enable it to properly protect airspace over the west of Ukraine, under control of Air Command West.

In 2001, the 894th Fighter Aviation Regiment operated the MiG-23MLD for air defence at Ozernoye. This regiment belonged to the 120th Fighter Aviation Division of the USSR Air Defence Force (PVO) with a rich history dating back to 9 June 1942, when it was born and equipped with Yak-1 fighters – in the same place in which it was disbanded in 2001. After the 894th IAP's disbandment, the UkrAF formed a new regiment named the 9th Fighter Aviation Regiment, which was renamed the 9th Fighter Aviation Brigade in 2003.

The newly formed unit began operating the Su-27Ps and Su-27UBs of the 62nd IAP, which had now been fully equipped with MiG-29s in Belbek. As well as these, six Su-27Ss of the 831st IAP were sent to Ozernoye to ensure the newly formed unit had at least one fully operational fighter squadron equipped with Su-27s. The 831st IAP's Su-27s that went directly to the 9th IAP in 2001 were 21 Blue (c/n 36911013809), 31 Blue (c/n 36911015102), 36 Blue (c/n 36911019614), 37 Blue (c/n 36911021307) and 55 Blue (c/n 36911021308). Nos 21 Blue and 50 Blue became 03 Blue and 16 Blue respectively at Ozernoye but they were put in storage just a year after delivery. Su-27s 31, 36, 37 and 55 Blue became 17, 21, 28 and 25 Blue respectively at Mirgorod.

In 2015, this Su-27P of the 831st BrTA, 39 Blue (c/n 36911035818), was transferred to the 39th ISqTA at Ozernoye. This aircraft had last been overhauled by ZARZ in 2009. It is seen near Mirgorod on 6 September 2013. *Alexander Golz*

The five 62nd IAP Su-27Ps that ended up in the 9th IAP in 2001 were 11 Blue (c/n 36911035909), 02 Blue (c/n 36911035612), 03 Blue (c/n 36911035613), 04 Blue (c/n 36911035714) and 07 Blue (c/n 36911035717). At least two of them, including 02 Blue, did not remain operational for long and were put in storage. Also, two Su-27UBs ended up at Ozernoye in 2001, one of which was 69 Blue (c/n 96310418215), which was from the 831st IAP, while the other, 42 Blue (c/n 96310425070) was from the 62nd IAP. No. 22 Blue was lost in the crash during the Sknyliv air show on 27 July 2002 that killed 77 people on the ground.

Due to budget shortages, out of the 13 Su-27s that were sent to Ozernoye, five were grounded

Another aircraft that is now in service with the 39th BrTA is Su-27S 53 Blue (c/n 36911019411). It is seen during an exercise at Ivano-Frankivsk AB in September 2013 when it was still in service with the 831st BrTA. *Alexander Golz*

831st Su-27UB 69 Blue (c/n 96310418215). From spring to autumn 2015 it was among several Su-27s that were sent to the 7th BrTA. It was damaged in a hailstorm during deployment but was repaired and returned to Mirgorod, with its routine operations starting in March 2016. It overran the runway during FCF on 30 March 2016. The aircraft was damaged, but the pilot was unhurt, and it was sent to ZARZ for repair in April 2016, being restored in May 2016. *Alexander Golz*

within a period of two years. The number of operational Su-27s dropped steadily until the decision was made to reinforce the unit, which had now been renamed the 9th BrTA, with 14 MiG-29 9-13s and three MiG-29UBs of the former 161st IAP, which had been disbanded in Limanskoye.

These MiG-29s came to fill the gap caused by the lack of operational Su-27s but this improvement did not last long as they met a similar fate to the Su-27s. They were gradually sent to the 204th BrTA at Belbek after their MTBOs were reached, starting in 2007. The last MiG-29s of the 2nd Aviation Squadron of the 9th BrTA left Ozernoye in December 2008, while its last two operational Su-27s were put in storage in August 2009, ending the life of the 9th BrTA.

As explained before, on 4 May 2012, during the Euro 2012 tournament, the 831st BrTA was tasked with the forward deployment of three Su-27s to Ozernoye in order to be used on quick reaction alert in the west of Ukraine in support of the MiG-29s of the 114th BrTA, especially during the games at Lviv on 9, 13 and 17 June. Soon after the end of the tournament, the Su-27s returned to the 831st BrTA.

For two years, Ozernoye was left without any operational fighter jets until the start of the Crimea

This is the second Su-27UB of the 39th ISqTA with the bort number 73 Blue (c/n 96310425068). It is seen armed with four R-73 IR-guided, short-range, air-to-air missiles, two R-27ET IR-guided, medium-range, air-to-air missiles and three R-27ER semi-active, radar-guided, medium-range, air-to-air missiles during a show of force photo exercise at Ozernoye in April 2015. *Alexander Golz*

Su-27Ps 37, 38 and 39 Blue flying with Su-27UB 69 Blue, all belonging to the 39th ISqTA. They are flying over Ozernoye during a photography exercise on 16 April 2015. *Alexander Golz*

crisis and the war in Donbass, when Air Command West needed to reinforce its air defence capability. It is not known exactly when, but a satellite image taken on 4 April 2014 shows that seven Su-27s had been deployed to Ozernoye; five were on the flight line and two had been parked on the north-east part of the base. After 29 August 2014, when the UkrAF's involvement in the war in Donbass ended, there were at least four Su-27s at the base, but after that this dropped to only three, among which just one was on QRA duty24/7, another was a QRA reserve and a third was flown occasionally.

During an official ceremony held at Ozernoye on 5 January 2015, two newly overhauled Su-27s were delivered to the Ukrainian Air Force. They were Su-27S 33 Blue (c/n 36911015921) and Su-27P 37 Blue (c/n 36911035614). No. 37 Blue was a former 9th BrTA aircraft and it ended up serving in a new unit that was finally established at Ozernoye in order to have Su-27s permanently based there. It was named the 39th Independent or Separate Tactical Aviation Squadron. Six (including 37 Blue) of the 15 Su-27s that were delivered to the UkrAF after the end of their overhaul or modernisation in MiGremont were assigned to the 39th ISqTA.

As well as 37 Blue, the other five freshly overhauled Su-27s sent to the 39th ISqTA were all Su-27S – 21, 23, 24, 25 and 36 Blue. In addition, the 831st BrTA delivered seven Su-27s, among them some former 9th BrTA examples, to increase the number of operational Su-27s in the 39th ISqTA from five in 2015 to 13 in August 2017. They were two Su-27Ss, 26 Blue (c/n 36911013814) and 53 Blue (c/n 36911019411); three Su-27Ps, 56 Blue (c/n 36911031310), 38 Blue (c/n 36911035509) and 39 Blue (c/n 36911035818); and two Su-27UBs, 69 Blue (c/n 96310418215) and 73 Blue (c/n 96310425068. As well as these 13 Su-27s serving with the 39th ISqTA, two L-39Cs are also based at Ozernoye.

Pilot training and retraining after the war

Russia's sanctions against the UkrAF's Su-27 fleet had resulted in the air force having only 14 airworthy aircraft when the Crimea crisis started in 2014, but thanks to the maintenance squadron of the 831st BrTA and MiGremont, the number of operational examples in the regiment increased to 22 at the end of summer 2014. Four more Su-27s were redelivered after the completion of their overhauls or modernisation in 2015, followed by four others in 2016, two in 2017 and four in 2018, bringing the total to 36 in mid-2018, from which 23 were in service with the 1st and 2nd Aviation Squadrons of the 831st BrTA and the remaining three with the 39th ISqTA.

Subsequently, the rise in the number of operational Su-27s meant more pilots needed to be trained. Starting from 2014, each year four to six cadets of the Ivan Kozhedub National Air Force University were trained on the Su-27 in the fifth year of their training at the university. Before starting their ten hours' flight training on the Su-27, they have to fly for 90 hours on HAZ-30 ultra-light

An Su-27S of the 831st BrTA, 45 Blue (c/n 36911014104), while it was equipped with a R-73 captive training missile during an exercise at Mirgorod in October 2016. *Alexander Golz*

An Su-27 of the 831st BrTA during a training exercise over Mirgorod AB on 25 October 2016. *Alexander Golz*

primary training aircraft and the L-39C advanced jet trainer (an average of 36 hours in the front seat of the L-39).

To increase the piloting, navigation and combat skills of not only the new pilots but also the more experienced ones, a larger budget was specified for the procurement of jet fuel for the 831st BrTA as well as the 39th ISqTA to allow an increase in annual flying hours from an average of just 30 to 50. Each pilot was also flying an average of 20 hours in the two to three L-39Cs of the 831st BrTA and two others with the 39th ISqTA to keep up their piloting and navigating skills.

In 2015, the 831st BrTA took part in just one major exercise, which was the counter-terrorism Decisive Response 2015. The most significant element of operational training was a Command Post exercise with the military authorities and troops of Ukraine, which was held in September and October with the involvement of the military authorities, units of other military formations and law enforcement agencies. In total, two Su-27s were forward deployed to Kulbakino, from where they took part together with a pair of 299th BrTA Su-25s and two Army Aviation Mi-24Ps. They provided top cover for the ground forces and Su-25s and Mi-24s during the exercise.

While the 39th ISqTA and 831st BrTA did not take a significant part in the major exercises of the Ukrainian Armed Forces in 2015 they were heavily engaged in combat air patrol and surveillance missions over the south and east of the country. Almost 300 CAP sorties were conducted by the Su-27s in 400 flying hours during the year.

In April 2016, for first time, four new Su-27 pilots who had recently graduated from the Air Force University and had trained on the L-39C and Su-27UBs of the 39th ISqTA during their complementary Su-27 type training went solo on Su-27S/Ps at Mirgorod. That year was named as the year of the air force by Ukrainian President Petro Poroshenko, and subsequently a greater budget was assigned for the procurement of fuel for the UkrAF, increasing the number of training and retraining sorties. However, compared with 2015, the number of CAP missions was reduced significantly and the pilots had to take part in routine monthly flights to remain current and retain their combat readiness.

Su-27PM1 58 Blue and Su-27UBM1 71 Blue, both belonging to the 831st BrTA, participated in several air shows across Europe in 2016. Here they are in a formation flight with An-26 44 Blue after the Slovak International Air Fest 2016 in September 2016. *Alexander Golz*

Between 13 and 17 August 2016, the 831st BrTA took part in the joint command and staff exercise Heavenly Shield 2016 with units of the Ukrainian Land Forces Operational Command South. Su-24s of the 7th BrTA and Su-25s of the 299th BrTA, as well as MiG-29s of the 40th, 114th and 204th BrTAs were involved. During the exercise, the Su-25 pilots carried out rocketry and bombing at the Shiroky Lan training area in Mykolaiv, simulating a close air support mission for Ukrainian land forces. Two Su-27s provided top cover for the Su-25s and then engaged in a dogfight with a pair of 204th BrTA MiG-29s that were playing the role of enemy interceptors against the Su-25s.

From 2016, the Ukrainian Air Force's Su-27s returned to international air shows thanks to the ICAO-standard NAVAIDS installed on Su-27UBM1 71 Blue and Su-27PM1 58 Blue. They took part in the Danish International Air Show at Skrydstrup AB between 17 and 19 June 2016 and the Slovak International Air Fest 2016 at Sliač air base on 27 and 28 August. At Sliač, Col Alexander Oksanchenko was awarded a prize by the commander-in-chief of the Slovak Air Force, Miroslav Corba, for the best military aviation display of SIAF 2016.

Col Oksanchenko won similar prizes during air shows in Poland, Romania (Bucharest International Air Show 2016) and the Czech Republic (CIAF 2016) that year. In September, he and his Su-27PM1, 58 Blue, accompanied by Su-27UBM1 71 Blue and an Il-76MD, took part in the Malta International Air Show.

Nos 58 and 71 Blue took part in international air shows within Europe again in 2017, starting with RIAT 2017 between 14 and 16 July. For the Polish International Air Show, which was held between 26 and 28 August, 58 Blue together with two non-upgraded Su-27s, which were Su-27P 56 Blue and Su-27UB 67 Blue, took part. For the Czech International Air Show in September, Su-27PM1 58 Blue and Su-27UB 67 Blue attended.

On 15 and 16 June 2017, the 831st BrTA took part in the command staff training exercise Blue Trident 2017 of the Air Command Centre, during which Su-27 pilots practised similar air combat and air combat manoeuvring while armed with captive training R-73 missiles during the dogfights. As part of the exercise, the Su-27 pilots practised the interception of low-speed and low-altitude targets such as attack helicopters and in the last stage of the exercise, on 17 June, the Su-27s provided top cover and escort for Su-24s and Su-25s and engaged in a dogfight with MiG-29s of the 40th BrTA.

Ten days after this exercise, the 831st BrTA held similar air combat training, during which its pilots practised air combat manoeuvres at night and in bad weather conditions on 27 June 2017. Also, on 15 August of that year Su-27 pilots practised flights at low altitude, during which they gained road navigation experience as well.

In 2018, the 831st BrTA's Su-27PM1 and Su-27UBM1 were involved in various international events to represent the Ukrainian Armed Forces within NATO countries. These started with RIAT 2018, involving 58 and 71 Blue, an Su-27PM1 and an Su-27UBM1 respectively, between 13 and 15 July, then the Polish International Air Show at Radom on 25 and 26 August, which only involved 71 Blue; the Czech International Air Fest on 1 and 2 September involving both aircraft; and finally the Belgium Air Force Days air show on 8 and 9 September. Two instructor pilots of the 831st BrTA, Col Alexander Oksanchenko and Lt Col Yuriy Bulavko, carried out all the aerobatic displays during the above mentioned air shows.

Exercise Clear Sky 2018

One of the most important exercises of the Ukrainian Armed Forces in which the 831st BrTA participated in 2018 was Clear Sky 2018, which was held between 8 and 19 October. It was a joint and multi-national exercise that provided an opportunity for the American F-15C pilots of the 194th FS, 144th FW, of the California Air National Guard to fly with or against the Su-27 and experience air combat with the aircraft in order to improve their knowledge and skill in close encounters with this highly manoeuvrable fighter jet. The exercise involved approximately 950 personnel from nine nations, including Belgium, Denmark, Estonia, the Netherlands, Poland, Romania, Ukraine, the United Kingdom and the United States.

Clear Sky 2018 was held on the 25th anniversary of collaboration between the California Air National Guard and the Ukrainian Air Force, with the participation of six aircraft from the US comprising seven F-15Cs of the 194th FS, 144th FW, serialled 86-0144, 80-0010, 84-0004, 86-0166, 86-0167 and 82-028, as well as a C-130J-30 Hercules of the 115th Airlift Squadron, 146th Airlift Wing, 01-1461. In order to also enable the Ukrainian pilots to experience flying with the F-15, an F-15D-38-MC of the 493rd FS, 48th FW, from RAF Lakenheath in the UK was deployed to Starokostiantyniv. All the F-15s arrived at Starokostiantyniv on 6 October.

56 Blue (c/n 36911031310) was among the 831st BrTA aircraft that participated in Exercise Clear Sky 2018 from Starokonstantyniv air base in October 2018. *Tech. Sgt. Charles Vaughn, US Air National Guard*

F-15C 80-0010 of the USAF's 194th FS taxiing in front of five Su-27s of the 831st BrTA with bort numbers 56, 57, 58, 59 and 71 Blue at Starokonstantyniv during Exercise Clear Sky 2018 on 9 October 2018. *Tech. Sgt. Charles Vaughn, US Air National Guard*

At least four USAF KC-135R tankers also took part in the exercise. Two of them, with the call signs Coder 01 and Coder 02 and serialled 60-0358 and 63-7981 respectively, were from the 108th Air Refuelling Squadron (108th ARS) from the Illinois Air National Guard's 126th Air Refuelling Wing. They refuelled the F-15Cs during their long journey from the US to Starokostiantyniv. Both of them were then deployed to Miroslawiec, Poland, to take part in the exercise from there. They, together with at least a pair of KC-135Rs of the 100th ARS, 57-2605 and 58-0100, provided aerial refuelling capability for the F-15Cs as well as the Polish Air Force's F-16C-52CFs and Romanian Air Force's F-16AMs during the exercise.

Air Command Centre's 831st BrTA participated with Su-27S 21 Blue, three Su-27Ps, 56, 57 and 59 Blue, Su-27PM1 58 Blue, and two Su-27UBM1s, 70 and 71 Blue. All were forward deployed to Starokostiantyniv and equipped with captive training R-73 IR-guided air-to-air missiles.

Air Command West's 7th BrTA, which itself is based at Starokostiantyniv, participated with four Su-24M strike bombers, 20, 41, 44 and 77 White, two Su-24MR tactical reconnaissance jets, 59 and 60 Yellow, L-39C 74 Blue, and L-39M1 71 Blue.

Air Command South's 299th BrTA took part with Su-25M1Ks 20 and 31 Blue and Su-25UBM1K 67 Blue.

Out of the seven MiG-29s that participated, four – 05, 06, 07 and 08 White – had been upgraded to MiG-29MU1 standard, all from the 40th BrTA. Accompanied by MiG-29UB 90 White, they were forward deployed from Vasilkov to Starokostiantyniv on 6 October. Following them, two MiG-29s of 114th BrTA, 71 and 75 Blue, were forward deployed to Starokostiantyniv from Ivano-Frankivsk.

Tragic accident for 70 Blue

As mentioned above, the 831st BrTA sent both its Su-27UBM1s to exercises because they were equipped with the SAVR-27U audio/video recording system that could record every action and manoeuvre of the pilots on the BUR-4-1-10-01 digital and solid state hard drive using a pair of cameras, one installed behind the seat showing the pilot's actions in the cabin and the other just behind the head-up display.

More than ten F-15C pilots of the 194th FS gained the opportunity to fly in the back seat of these Su-27UBM1s and see air interceptions and dogfights from their F-15C's enemy's side. On 16 October, when one of the 194th FS's pilots, Lt Col Seth 'Jethro' Nehring, was flying in the back seat of Su-27UBM1 70 Blue piloted by Col Petrenko Ivan Nikolaevich, an experienced Su-27 pilot from the 831st BrTA and the deputy commander of Air Command East, it crashed during a dogfight at average altitude at night, killing both pilots.

No. 70 Blue had been modernised and lifetime-extended to remain in service for 12 years until 2030, but its life ended after only 20 hours of flight following its last maintenance.

Information recorded on the emergency recording system of the aircraft was used in a crash investigation and showed that human error and vertigo was the cause. The crash occurred during the dogfight with an F-15C when the Su-27 pilot lost orientation due to low visibility.

Forty-four-year-old Nehring was serving as the Operations Officer in the Joint Operations Centre, meaning he was the liaison between the exercise director, Maj Gen Garrison, and all flying operations.

'He was handpicked for this position due to his operational experience and long history with our unit.

831st BrTA Su-27UBM1 70 Blue (c/n 96310424040) prior to a flight from Starokonstantyiniv during the exercise on 9 October 2018. *Ukrainian Air Force*

Jethro has been a member of the 144th family for over 20 years. He began his career here as an enlisted crew chief before being selected for a pilot slot and flew the F-16 Viper for over 15 years and converted to the F-15 Eagle,' reads the report about the crash.

70 Blue (c/n 96310424040) was manufactured for the 100th Shipborne Fighter Aviation Regiment of the USSR Navy in 1990 (one of seven Su-27UBs), with delivery on 30 January 1991 as 05 Blue. Soon after Ukraine's independence and the refusal of the majority of the 100th KIAP pilots to swear allegiance to Ukraine, the regiment's Su-27s were handed over to the 831st Fighter Aviation Regiment at Mirgorod in 1992. After transfer to the new unit, 05 Blue became 70 Red in 1993 and finally 70 Blue in the late 1990s.

No. 70 Blue was in service until 2009, when it was stored at Mirgorod following the end of its MTBO. In 2014, it was restored by technicians of the 831st BrTA's maintenance squadron because of the war in Donbass. A one-year extension kept it flyable until the war was over in 2016 and it was then sent to MiGremont or ZARZ (Zaporozhye Aircraft Repair Plant) to be overhauled and lifetime extended, as well as fully modernised to the Su-27UBM1 standard. Modernisation work was completed in July and the aircraft was delivered to the 831st BrTA.

Just a few months after the loss of 70 Blue, the 39th ISqTA also lost an aircraft. On 15 December 2018 Su-27S 55 Blue piloted by Maj Alexander V. Fomenko crashed near Ozernoye at 15.00 local time.

Future of Ukrainian Flankers

After the loss of 70 during Exercise Clear Sky 2018 and then 55 Blue in October 2018, the UkrAF now has 35 airworthy Su-27s out of its total of 55. They are 20 Su-27Ss, nine Su-27Ps and six Su-27UBs, from which three are fully modernised to Su-27SM1, Su-27PM1 and Su-27UBM1 standard, while there is also a partially modernised Su-27UB, Su-27SM1 and Su-27P among them. Thirteen are in service with the 39th ISqTA at Ozernoye and 22 others are with two squadrons of the 831st BrTA, three of which, including Su-27Ps 100 and 101 Blue, are always on deployment at Odessa Airport to provide 24/7 QRA capability for Air Command South.

In early 2019, two more Su-27s, 12 and 31 Blue, were under overhaul and lifetime extension at MiGremont with their redeliveries to 831st BrTA scheduled for the first half of the year. But they are not the only ones planned to be overhauled. At least two more aircraft will be overhauled in 2019 to bring the number of airworthy Su-27s up to 39, or three aviation squadrons, in 2020. From this total, 11 will be fully modernised (two already are) to Su-27SM1, Su-27PM1 and Su-27UBM1 standard.

Russian sanctions and Ukraine's financial problems to a decline in the number of operational Su-27s from 18 in 2008 to 14 in 2014, but thanks to the efforts of the technicians of the 831st BrTA as well as the MiGremont and the Ukrainian companies that manufactured spare parts that Russian companies no longer provide, 35 Su-27s are now on active duty, protecting the country's airspace alongside its MiG-29s. The Ukrainian Air Force will keep an average fleet of 39 Su-27s operational until 2035, when a replacement for them will be found.

Su-27Ps of the 831st BrTA, each one armed with two R-27ERs, two R-27ETs and two R-73s, on QRA duty at Odessa in January 2016. *Author's collection*

Su-27Ps of the 831st BrTA including 45 Blue (right), each armed with a pair of R-27ERs and two R-27ETs as well as two R-73s, while on QRA duty at Odessa in spring 2015. *Author's collection*

Su-27s inherited by the Ukrainian Air Force and Navy

Model	Construction Number	Bort Number	Previous units	Current unit	Current Status	Last Overhaul	Note
Su-27S	36911011301	01 Blue	831st IAP	831st BrTA	Stored	-	
Su-27S	36911011302	02 Blue	831st IAP	831st BrTA	Stored	-	
Su-27S	36911011907	04 Blue	831st IAP/9th BrTA	831st BrTA	OR	2017	
Su-27S	36911011908	15 Blue	831st IAP	831st BrTA	OR	2017	
Su-27S	36911011909	05 Blue	831st IAP	831st BrTA	Stored	-	
Su-27S	36911011910	06 Blue	831st IAP	831st BrTA	OR	?	Restored by 831st BrTA in 2014
Su-27S	36911012910	27 Blue	831st IAP	831st BrTA	OR	2015–2016	
Su-27S	36911013404	07 Blue	831st IAP	831st BrTA	Wfu	-	
Su-27S	36911013605	08 Blue	831st IAP	831st BrTA	Stored	-	
Su-27S	36911013606	09 Blue	831st IAP	831st BrTA	Stored	-	
Su-27S	36911013607	10 Blue	831st IAP	831st BrTA	Stored	-	
Su-27S	36911013808	20 Blue	831st IAP	831st BrTA	Stored	-	
Su-27S	36911013809	21 Blue	831st IAP/9th BrTA	831st BrTA	Stored	2017	
Su-27S	36911013810	22 Blue	831st IAP	831st BrTA	Stored	-	
Su-27S	36911013812	24 Yellow	831st IAP	831st BrTA	Wfu	-	
Su-27S	36911013814	17 Blue	831st IAP	39th BrTA	OR	2010	
Su-27S	36911013916	28 Blue	831st IAP	831st BrTA	OR	?	
Su-27S	36911013918	30 Blue	831st IAP	831st BrTA	OR	?	
Su-27S	36911014001	41 Blue	831st IAP	831st BrTA	OR	?	
Su-27S	36911014002	43 Blue	831st IAP	831st BrTA	OR	?	
Su-27S	36911014104	45 Blue	831st IAP	831st BrTA	OR	2012	
Su-27S	36911014105	46 Blue	831st IAP	831st BrTA	OR	2012	
Su-27S	36911014206	47 Blue	831st IAP	831st BrTA	NORM	2018–2019	
Su-27S	36911014207	14 Blue	100th KIAP	831st BrTA	Stored	-	

Model	Construction Number	Bort Number	Previous units	Current unit	Current Status	Last Overhaul	Note
Su-27S	36911014308	34 Blue	100th KIAP	831st BrTA	Stored	-	
Su-27S	36911014409	35 Blue	100th KIAP	831st BrTA	Stored	-	
Su-27S	36911014410	42 Blue	831st IAP	831st BrTA	NORM	-	
Su-27S	36911014411	48 Blue	831st IAP	831st BrTA	NORM	2018–2019	
Su-27S	36911014412	49 Blue	831st IAP	831st BrTA	Stored	-	
Su-27S	36911014818	11 Blue	831st IAP	831st BrTA	Stored	-	
Su-27S	36911014820	12 Blue	831st IAP	831st BrTA	NORM	2018–2019	
Su-27S	36911015102	54 Blue	831st IAP/9th BrTA	831st BrTA	OR	2013–2014	
Su-27S	36911015305	23 Blue	831st IAP/9th BrTA	831st BrTA	OR	2017	
Su-27SM1	36911015408	52 Blue	831st IAP	831st BrTA	OR	2010–2012	
Su-27S	36911015921	33 Blue	831st IAP	831st BrTA	OR	2013–2014	
Su-27S	36911019411	53 Blue	831st IAP	831st BrTA	OR	2011	
Su-27S	36911019614	36 Blue	100th KIAP	831st BrTA	OR	2016	
Su-27SM1	36911019615	31 Blue	100th KIAP	831st BrTA	NORM	2017–2018	
Su-27S	36911021307	24 Blue	100th KIAP	831st BrTA	OR	2015	
Su-27S	36911021308	55 Blue	100th KIAP	831st BrTA	OR	2015–2016	
Su-27S	36911026310	35 Yellow	3 НИУ ГНИИ-8	831st BrTA	Sold	-	Sold to Eritrea
Su-27P	36911031310	56 Blue	100th KIAP/62nd IAP	831st BrTA	OR	?	
Su-27P	36911031411	57 Blue	100th KIAP/62nd IAP	831st BrTA	OR	2015-2016	
Su-27P	36911035509	38 Blue	62nd IAP/9th BrTA	39 BrTA	OR	2008	
Su-27P	36911035510	12 Blue	62nd IAP	-	Sold	-	Sold to Ethiopia
Su-27PM1	36911035611	50 Blue	62nd IAP	831st BrTA	OR	2016–2017	
Su-27PM1	36911035612	58 Blue	62nd IAP/9th BrTA	831st BrTA	OR	2014–2015	
Su-27P	36911035613	03 Blue	62nd IAP	-	Sold	-	Sold to Ethiopia
Su-27P	36911035614	37 Blue	62nd IAP/9th BrTA	39 BrTA	OR	2014	
Su-27P	36911035715	05 Blue	62nd IAP/9 BrTA	-	Sold	-	Sold to Ethiopia
Su-27P	36911035716	100 Blue	62nd IAP	831st BrTA	OR	2011–2012	
Su-27P	36911035717	101 Blue	62nd IAP/9 BrTA	831st BrTA	OR	2011–2012	
Su-27P	36911035818	39 Blue	62nd IAP/831st BrTA	39 BrTA	OR	2009	
Su-27P	36911035819	59 Blue	62nd IAP	831st BrTA	OR	2015–2016	
Su-27UB	96310405010	62 Blue	831st IAP	831st BrTA	Stored	-	
Su-27UB	96310408025	64 Red	831st IAP	-	Crashed	-	Crashed on 24 April 1992
Su-27UB	96310408027	61 Blue	100th KIAP/831st IAP	-	Sold	-	Sold to an American Company
Su-27UB	96310418204	68 Blue	100th KIAP	831st BrTA	Stored	-	
Su-27UB	96310418207	75 Blue	100th KIAP/GANIC	831st BrTA	OR	2008–2010	
Su-27UB	96310418210	66 Blue	831st IAP	-	Sold	-	Sold to an American Company
Su-27UB	96310418215	69 Blue	100th KIAP	831st BrTA	OR	2009–2010	
Su-27UB	96310422070	67 Blue	831st IAP	-	OR	2015–2017	
Su-27UBM1	96310424040	70 Blue	100th KIAP/831st BrTA	-	Crashed	2017–2018	Crashed on 16 October 2018
Su-27UBM1	96310424043	71 Blue	100th KIAP	831st BrTA	OR	2010–2014	
Su-27UB	96310424045	72 Blue	100th KIAP/831st IAP	-	Sold	-	Sold to Eritrea
Su-27UB	96310425068	73 Blue	62nd IAP/831st BrTA	39 BrTA	OR	2010–2012	
Su-27UB	96310425069	74 Blue	62nd IAP	831 BrTA	OR	2015	
Su-27UB	96310425070	42 Blue	62 IAP/9th IAP	-	Crashed	-	Crashed on 27 July 2002

3 Military Transport Aviation

An-12 Fleet (1992–1997): Giant Cubs of the Ukrainian Air Force

A large proportion of the inherited transport aircraft from Soviet Military Aviation Transport Command (Komandovaniye voyenno-transportnoy aviatsii [VTA]) were 49 An-12s (53 according to another source), which consisted of four An-12APs with an average age of 30.25 years, one 28-year-old An-12B, ten An-12BPs with an average age of 24.89 years, 25 An-12BKs with average age of 22.52, eight An-12BShs with average age of 28.25 years and one 24-year-old An-12RR.

Soviet background

Among the inherited aircraft, 32 that had been overhauled after 1987 were airworthy and in 1992 they were in service with the 5th Air Army's 112th Independent Mixed Aviation Squadron at Odessa, the 14th Air Army's 243rd Independent Mixed Aviation Regiment at Lviv, the 17th Air Army's 255th Independent Mixed Aviation Squadron at Boryspil, the 24th Air Army's 456th Independent Guards Stalingradskiy Red Banner Mixed Aviation Regiment and Voroshilovgrad Higher Navigators Military Aviation School's 130th Training Aviation Regiment at Mariopol.

Because of the weak state of the economy and also for political reasons, including the Treaty on Conventional Armed Forces in Europe, the Ukrainian Defence Ministry approved plans for the Ukrainian Air Force to operate air force transport aircraft as civil cargo aircraft in association with Ukrainian civilian or MoD-controlled charter airlines.

The day after the independence of Ukraine, personnel including the aircrews of the transport squadrons mostly took the oath and decided to serve in the air force, because of the important opportunity to continue their career and make money by flying as civilian pilots after months of not receiving any income because of the worsening USSR economy.

Subsequently, on the day after the birth of the Ukrainian Air Force, the transport regiments and

Manufactured on 28 December 1961, An-12AP 83 Red (c/n 1400301) was in service with the 243rd Independent Mixed Aviation Regiment of the USSR VVS's 14th Air Army. It was the first An-12 manufactured in Voronezh and had a cabin equipped with 20 seats for the transportation of air force personnel between air bases. It was offered for sale by the Ukrainian privatisation agency in 2005 with a total of 8,073 flying hours and 6,491 cycles. *Sergey Popsuevich*

squadrons started to make money via leasing their aircraft, firstly to Ukrainian airlines. Gradually, a huge number of An-12s were demilitarised for this purpose. The first An-12, An-12AP 02 Blue (c/n 2400802) belonging to the 255th Independent Mixed Aviation Squadron at Boryspil, was sold to the Khors Air Company in March 1992. The aircraft received the civil registration UR-11326.

Following the agreements between the Ministry of Defence and the Ministry of Transport, more An-12s were put up for sale and lease to Ukrainian companies by the air force, which meant more job opportunities for its personnel. Subsequently, in the following year (1993), An-12BK 87 Red (c/n 8345604) of the 243rd Independent Aviation Regiment was leased to Air Ukraine and registered UR-11314; it was sold to Lviv Airlines in 1995.

23 Blue (c/n 1400304) was a 1961-built An-12AP in service with the 255th OSAE. *Sergey Popsuevich*

Maintenance difficulties

Before the collapse of the Soviet Union, just four repair plants were overhauling the An-12, and none of them were in Ukraine, forcing the Ukrainian Ministry of Defence to send UkrAF An-12s abroad. The overhaul plants were the No. 412 ARP at Rostov; 123 ARP, at Staraya, Russia; the 325ARP at Taganrog, Russia, and Fergana in Uzbekistan.

As in the days of the Soviet Union, the 17th Air Army, now part of the Ukrainian Air Force, delivered five An-12s of the 255th Independent Mixed Aviation Regiment that had been deployed to Siberia since 1991 to No. 325 Aircraft repair plant for overhaul at Taganrog, Russia, in 1992.

Because of the confiscation of three Russian Air Force An-124s leased by ASTC in 1992, and Ukraine's debts to NAPO (the Chkalov Aircraft Production Factory in Novosibirsk) for overhaul and spare parts supply of the Ukrainian Air Force's and Army's Mi-6s and Mi-26s (of which 61 and 20 had been inherited from Soviet Air Force and Army respectively), Russia decided to confiscate the five An-12s at Taganrog. These consisted of two An-12BPs, CCCP-11419 (c/n 4342008) and CCCP-11667 (c/n 5343305), and three An-12BKs, which were CCCP-12193 (c/n 9346805), CCCP-12194 (c/n 00347203) and CCCP-12195 (c/n 00347410). The Ukrainians managed to hastily return CCCP-11419, which was not yet under overhaul, in spring 1992. The aircraft was flown to Mariopol, grounded there and cannibalised for parts, including its engines. It was later relocated to Saki air base and stored there in 1999. Later it was sold to a private company. The remaining four An-12s were confiscated while they were under overhaul, and after several years they entered into NAPO service in 1995 and 1997.

CCCP-11419 had an interesting history: it was equipped with seats from Soviet Premier Nikita

This An-12BP with civil registration UR-11302 was in service with Atlant in 2002. It is one of the few ex-UkrAF An-12s still operational in the world. It now belongs to AVFL Logistics Ltd of Limassol (Cyprus) and operated by Cavok Air as UR-CBG. It saw action in the Afghan war and was equipped with ASO-2 flare dispensers. *Sergey Popsuevich*

04 Red (c/n 6344301) was the sole An-12PS in service with the UkrAF in the 1990s. The aircraft was with the 3rd State Research Centre, or GANITs at Kirovskoye. The 'PS' stands for Poiskovo-Spasatel'nyi and the An-12PS is the SAR version of the An-12B with the Istok-Golub emergency UHF homing system and Yorsh (Ruff) or Gagara (Loon) rescue boats, as well as droppable inflatable life rafts and crews for the boats. *Heinz Berger*

Khrushchev's Il-18 in its cargo compartment for his accompanying personnel during his flights when it was based at Zavitinsk. Later it was assigned to Boryspil, where it was in overall grey colours with the old-style flag on its fin. It was also used to carry the Soviet songwriter Alexander Rozenbaum on a tour of Afghanistan in the 1980s.

The approved life limit of an An-12 was 43 years and ten months, or 180,000 hours and 12,000 cycles, which meant that with a fleet of 49 An-12s with an average age of 26.31 years in 1992, the Ukrainian Air Force's An-12s could remain in service until at least 2009. However, the lack of An-12 overhaul permissions/licences for the Ukrainian repair plants as well as budget cuts forced the air force to withdraw them from use gradually after the arrival of their MTBO, which was ten years and seven months in the calendar or 5,000 flying hours and 2,000 cycles according to the logbook.

Fleet for lease and sale

A year after the establishment of the Ukrainian Air Force, the number of operational An-12s dropped from 32 to 25 because of the reasons described earlier, including the inability to fund their overhaul. Subsequently, the flying hours of all operational An-12s dropped significantly; in some cases aircraft were being flown just six hours per month to be kept operational in order to be sold or leased to a cargo airline.

All the UKrAF An-12 units were still carrying out the missions of their Soviet-era days but on a smaller scale in 1993. The single An-12BK of the 112th

UkrAF An-12BK 89 Blue (c/n 6344603) was with the 243rd OGSAP until 1997, when it was retired from service. It was later offered for sale by SkyBirdHeli with a total of 6,841 flying hours and 5,250 flight cycles on 27 May 2006. This aircraft is still in storage at Lviv, as seen here on 11 July 2017. *Alexander Golz*

21 Blue was an An-12BK of the 255th OSAE with the construction number 7345208, manufactured on 30 September 1967. It is seen departing Runway 06 at RAF Lyneham, UK, with the call sign UR09740 at 10.15am on 3 October 1993. It was retired from service and sold to Busol Airline in 1994. *Chris Chennel*

Independent Mixed Aviation Squadron, which had now become the 2nd Independent Mixed Aviation Squadron based at Odessa, was still in use to provide logistic support for the air base as well as the 642nd Guards Fighter-Bomber Aviation Regiment at Martynovka.

In December 1993, one of the last missions ever performed by an air force An-12 took place when the 255th Independent Aviation Squadron was tasked to allocate one of its aircraft to a human relief operation in collaboration with the Red Cross during the Nagorno-Karabakh conflict between Azerbaijan and Armenia. The aircraft carried 5 tons of margarine, bread and soap to Armenia as a part of Red Cross humanitarian aid for the people of Armenia after one refuelling stop at Domodedovo airport in Moscow.

The number of operational An-12s declined again to 17 in 1994 and 13 in 1995. The 243rd Independent Mixed Aviation Regiment was still the major operator of the type, with five examples in 1995 with operational status and several more grounded but for sale at Lviv. Other operators of the type in 1995 were Vinnitsa AB with two, Boryspil with one, Odessa with one, Melitopol with one, and the Ukrainian Parachute Systems Research Institute with one.

In May 1995, following a proposal of the Lviv Regional Council, an agreement was finalised between the Ministry of Defence, Ministry of Finance and Ministry of Transport for transfer of two An-12BKs of the 243rd Independent Mixed Aviation Regiment, 87 Red (c/n 8345604) and 54 Red(c/n 8345702), to Lviv Airlines. No. 87 Red had been demilitarised since 1993 to be leased to Ukrainian Airlines as UR-11314, but it still was on the inventory of the air force when it was delivered to Lviv Airlines. No. 54 Red was in military service in 1994 but grounded for overhaul and demilitarisation in 1995 before delivery to Lviv Airlines in 1996. It was later registered as UR-11346.

Military Unit No. 13786 disbandment

The 130th Training Aviation Regiment, which had seven An-12BShs in service when the USSR collapsed, was faced with the early retirement of some of its aircraft while they still had time and cycles remaining before their next overhaul. They included 87 Red (c/n 3341301), the last overhaul of which had been completed on 27 May 1987, and had logged fewer than 600 flying hours when it was grounded in 1993.

Three other of the unit's An-12BShs, 69 Red (c/n 3341610), 77 Red (c/n 4342007) and 79 Red (c/n 4342405), were withdrawn from service in 1994, although they had flying time left until 28 February 1997. The reason was the disbandment of the regiment, the activity of which had declined significantly since 1991, when three of its An-12BShs were withdrawn for financial reasons.

All the 130th Training Regiment's An-12BShs were stored at Saki-4 Air Base and then put up for

54 Red, A former An-12BK of the 243rd OGSAP, (c/n 8345702). It was manufactured on 31 May 1968 and was in service with the UkrAF until 1995, when it was transferred to Lviv Airlines on 31 May that year and received the civil registration UR-11346 there. It ended up in service with the Sudanese Air Force in 2011. *Sergey Popsuevich*

03 Blue (c/n 8346106) was an An-12BK serving in the 243rd OGSAP until 1999. It was manufactured on 31 December 1968 and retired from service in 2000. It was sold to Aeronord Grup and registered ER-AXZ in 2003. *Sergey Popsuevich*

sale, but because of their training configuration (they had navigator training panels for ten aviator students), they were not attractive to the cargo airlines. Just one of them was lucky: 61 Red (c/n 4342308), which was restored by a private company in 2001 and then leased to Veteran in 2002.

Four years later, on 10 November 2008, while the aircraft was still in use with Veteran as UR-PLV and was en route to Pointe-Noire, it caught fire 80km from the airport. The pilot performed a safe emergency landing. The fire had started in the cargo compartment lining and spread to the wing. The day after the accident a damage assessment team from the Antonov Design Bureau declared the aircraft unrepairable because of the damage to its fuselage (half the wing frames had been burnt). The aircraft was later scrapped on the spot.

After the sale of 61 Red sale, two other of the unit's aircraft were scrapped, which were 79 Red (c/n 4342106) in 2002, and 83 Red (c/n 4342110) in 2013. No. 83 Red's tail section had already been cut off from its fuselage and it was then painted in Aeroflot colours and burnt to depict a crashed aircraft during the filming of the movie *9th Company* in mid-2004.

After the occupation of the Crimean peninsula by Russian forces in spring 2014, the Saki air base came totally under the control of the Russian Navy. Before that, Ukrainian Navy Aviation evacuated their three operational aircraft and four helicopters on 5 March.

Ukrainian Air Force An-12s

Version	Bort Number	Civil Registration	Construction Number	Unit	Year of manufacture	Status in 1992	Year of Retirement/wfu	Year of demilitarisation**
An-12AP	-	UR-11501	1340206	456th OGSAP	1961	Stored	-	1997
An-12AP	83 Blue	-	1400301	243rd OGSAP	1961	Active	1996	-
An-12AP	23 Blue	-	1400304	255th OSAE	1961	Active	1999	-
An-12AP	02 Blue	UR-06175	2400802	255th OSAE	1963	Active	1992	1993
An-12BP	44 Red	-	3341004	?	1963	Active	1997	1997
An-12BSh	78 Red	-	3341301	130th UAP	1963	Active	1993	-
An-12BSh	69 Red	-	3341610	130th UAP	1963	Active	1995	-
An-12B	61 Blue	-	4341710	?	1964	Stored	-	2004
An-12BP	?	UR-11351	4341910	456th OGSAP	1964	Active	1996	1997
An-12BSh	77 Red	-	4342007	130th UAP	1964	Active	1994	-
An-12BP	-	UR-11419	4342008	255th OSAE	1964	Active	1993	-
An-12BSh	79 Red	-	4342106	130th UAP	1964	Stored	-	-
An-12BSh	83 Red	-	4342110	130th UAP	1964	Stored	-	-
An-12BP	84 Blue	UR-11405	4342202	243rd OGSAP	1964	Stored	1994	1997
An-12BP	?	UR-11474	4342207	-	1964	Stored	-	-
An-12BP	?	UR-11313	4342304	?	1964	Stored	-	1997
An-12BSh	50 Red	-	4342306	456th OGSAP	1964	Stored	-	-
An-12BSh	61 Red	-	4342308	130th UAP	1964	Stored	-	2002

Version	Bort Number	Civil Registration	Construction Number	Unit	Year of manufacture	Status in 1992	Year of Retirement/wfu	Year of demilitarisation**
An-12BSh	79 Red	-	4342405	130thUAP	1964	Active	1994	-
An-12BP	86 Blue	-	4342610	243rd OGSAP	1964	Active	1997	1997
An-12BP	-	CCCP-11667***	5343305	-	1965	Active	1993	1994
An-12BK	72 Red	-	5343505	2nd OSAE	1966	Stored	-	-
An-12BP	?	UR-11302/ UR-CBG	6343705	?	1966	Stored	-	1993
An-12BP	?	-	6343707	None*	1966	Active	1995	1998
An-12BP	85 Red	-	6344204	456th OGSAP	1966	Active	1997	-
An-12BK	89 Blue	-	6344603	243rd OGSAP	1966	Active	1993	-
An-12BK	73 Blue	-	6344605	243rd OGSAP	1966	Active	1993	2001
An-12BK	86 Red	-	6344607	2nd OSAE	1966	Active	1996	2008
An-12BK	21 Blue	UR-11348	7345208	255th OSAE	1967	Active	1993	1994
An-12RR	?	UR-11259	?	-	1968	Stored	-	-
An-12BK	87 Blue	UR-11314	8345604	243rd OGSAP	1968	Active	1992	1993
An-12BK	54 Red	UR-11346	8345702	243rd OGSAP	1968	Active	1994	1996
An-12BK	53 Red	-	8345802	?	1968	Stored	-	2003
An-12BK	77 Blue	UR-11347	8346105	255th OSAE	1968	Active	1992	1994
An-12BK	03 Blue	EP-AXZ/UR-CAJ	8346106	243rd OGSAP	1968	Active	1995	2003
An-12BK	77 Blue	UR-11306	9346205	243rd OGSAP	1969	Active	2001	2002
An-12BK	22 Blue	-	9346208	255th OSAE	1969	Stored	-	1997
An-12BK	68 Red	UR-12113	9346309	?	1969	Active	1992	1994
An-12BK	24 Blue	-	9346405	255th OSAE	1969	?	?	1997
An-12BK	-	CCCP-12193***	9346805	-	1969	Active	1993	1994
An-12BK	?	-	9346808	243rd OGSAP	1969	?	?	?
An-12BK	87 Red	-	9346809	243rd OGSAP	1969	Active	1996	1998
An-12BK	05 Red	-	00346907	175th VTAP	1970	Active	1998	2003
An-12BK	20 Blue	-	00347004	255th OSAE	1970	Active	1993	1997
An-12BK	57 Red	-	00347006	456th OGSAP	1970	?	?	1998
An-12BK	71 Red	-	00347107	243rd OGSAP	1970	Active	1993	1996
An-12BK	-	CCCP-12194***	00347203	-	1970	Active	1993	1994
An-12BK	-	CCCP-12195***	00347410	-	1970	Active	1993	1994
An-12BK	01 Red	UR-11305	1347803	?	1971	Active	1996	1998
An-12BK	?	UR-11352	?	456th OGSAP	?	Stored	-	1996
An-12	35 Red	?	?	456th OGSAP	?	Stored	-	-
An-12	38 Red	?	?	456th OGSAP	?	Stored	-	-
An-12	88 Red	?	?	456th OGSAP	?	Stored	-	-

* Parachute Systems Research Institute
** Demilitarisation prior to sale or lease to civilian or military customers
*** Confiscated by Russia as reparations for Russian aircraft confiscated by Ukraine

Abbreviations
UAP = Training Aviation Regiment
OSAE = Independent Mixed Aviation Squadron
OGSAP = Independent Mixed Aviation Regiment
VTAP = Military-Transport Aviation Regiment

This An-12BK registered UR-UCM was in service with Ukraine Cargo Airways when seen in 1999 or 2000. The aircraft was ex-255th OSAE 22 Blue (c/n 9346208) but was retired in 1997 and leased to Volare by the Ukrainian MOD that year. While in service with Ukraine Cargo Airways, it was lost due to a ground incident involving a fire and explosion at an ammunition depot at Ndjili International Airport, Kinshasa, on 14 April 2000. *Sergey Popsuevich*

Later, following an agreement between the countries, the rest of the grounded aircraft including Ka-31 helicopters were disassembled and then evacuated to Kulbakino AB on the Ukrainian mainland. However, the remaining four former 130th Training Aviation Regiment's An-12BShs, 69 Red, 77 Red, 78 Red and 79 Red (the second aircraft of the unit with this code), were left there after almost ten years waiting to be sold to a customer.

Retirement from UkrAF service

In 1997, the MTBO of most of the remaining operational An-12s was reached and the aircraft were grounded. As a consequence, the Ukrainian Ministry of Defence released for sale 20 An-12s including the recently retired examples, leaving the air force with just four operational examples, which were in service at Vinnitsa, Boryspil, Melitopol and Lviv air bases (each with just one operational aircraft).

For these, the Ministry of Defence established Ukrainian Cargo Airways (UCA) to sell or lease air force transport aircraft and helicopters, including the An-12s, in 1997. It was a state-owned company operating charter passenger and cargo services as well as providing aircraft overhaul, leasing and sale services.

In that year UCA sold ten An-12s, of which three were in good condition while the rest had been stored for almost four to five years but restored or overhauled by KARP (Kiev Aircraft Repair Plant 410) prior to delivery to customers in Ukraine, Bulgaria and Moldova.

In 1998 and 1999, two An-12s, one in Odessa (An-12BK 77 Blue) and one in Boryspil (An-12 23 Blue), had been kept operational so they could be sold at a higher price than the grounded ones. However, 23 Blue was grounded in 1999 without finding a customer.

No. 77 Blue was kept in operational condition by ODESAVIAREMSERVIS (Odessa aircraft repair enterprise) until it was leased to a Ukrainian airline in 2002, and then sold to the Angolan Air Force in 2012. Starting from that year, UCA sold many of the former Ukrainian Air Force An-12s that had been leased to Ukrainian airlines including Veteran, Volare and Khors Air, to Ukrainian customers such as Ukrainian Air Alliance and Meridian, or international customers including the Angolan Air Force, the Congo Republic Air Force and the Sudanese Air Force after their overhaul and modernisation at KARP.

The An-12's service life was short with the UkrAF: it was only six years, not only because of financial problems with overhauling the type but also because the An-70 medium transport aircraft (MTA) was under development as a successor to the aircraft for the UkrAF and even RuAF, encouraging the Ukrainian MoD to even use small numbers of operational An-12s in the air force as commercial cargo aircraft. In 1997 the last An-12s were retired while the An-70 was still under development. Nineteen years later, the UkrAF still has no MTA to take on the An-12s' role.

An-12BK 68 Red (c/n 9346309) under depot maintenance or overhaul at the Serial Production Plant at Svyatoshino, Kiev, on 27 July 2005. It was in service with the UkrAF until 1997. *Sergey Popsuevich*

An-24 Fleet (1992–today): The Commander's Flying Limousines

Of the 180 airworthy An-24s in service with the Soviet Air Force, Navy and Border Guard, the Ukrainian Armed Forces inherited just ten aircraft consisting of five An-24BSs, an An-24RV, an An-24T and four An-24RTs. Among the inherited examples, eight belonged to the air force, one An-24T variant to the navy, one An-24RT to the DOSAAF (Volunteer Society for Cooperation with the Army, Aviation, and Fleet) and a single An-24RV to the national guard. Excepting the navy's An-24T, all the remaining nine were enlisted in the Ukrainian Air Force inventory in 1992.

The Commander Carriers

In the Soviet Air Force, the An-24 transport aircraft played three important roles; firstly as a passenger aircraft for transporting air force personnel, secondly as a tactical transport aircraft for carrying small cargo, and thirdly for ferrying the air force's high-ranking officers and commanders between defence districts.

On average, each of the Soviet Air Armies had one passenger version and one 'Saloon' equipped with a VIP cabin, and sometimes an extra aircraft as a reserve for both of versions, in their independent mixed aviation regiments and squadrons (OSAP and OSAE respectively) in order to support the operations of the air armies' headquarters. The Ukrainian Air Force, which consisted of several ex-Soviet Air Force Air Armies, had now inherited three An-24 'Saloon' VIP Aircraft in service with its Mixed Aviation Squadrons and Regiments of the 5th, 14th, and 17th Air Armies.

An-24B 24 Yellow (c/n 87304801) from the 456th OSAP transported the commander-in-chief of the UkrAF and other high-ranking officials from Vinnitsa to Mirgorod when four F-15E-48-MCs of the USAF's 335th Fighter Squadron supported by a KC-135R paid a friendship visit on 12 June 1997. *Sergey Popsuevich*

The An-24BS' (S for 'Saloon' or VIP cabin) were 19 Blue (c/n 87304608), 40 Black (c/n 87304706), and 777 Yellow (c/n 97305306), with the 243rd OSAP at Lviv, 255th OSAE at Boryspil, and 112th OSAE at Odessa respectively with an average age of 25 years of service in 1993.

When it was inherited by the UKrAF, 40 Black had been serving in the Kiev Military District since 1968. Its bort number was changed to 40 Blue in 1996 and then 01 Yellow in 1998 after an overhaul, while it had the civil registration UR-71663 in air force official papers.

Based at Boryspil, 40 Blue was used by the air force commander for air travel inside Ukrainian territory. In the event of 01 Yellow's unavailability, there was one more 'Saloon' An-24 available for use as a VIP aircraft by the commander-in-chief, 777 Blue, which was based at Vinnitsa in the early 1990s but later transferred to Odessa to cover the air force commander's flights in the area under the control of Air Command South. No. 777 Blue was later stationed at Vinnitsa again in 2008, to be

Cargo ramp door-equipped An-24RT with 42 Blue (c/n 9911209) belonging to the 255th OSAE at Boryspil on 10 October 1995. *Sergey Popsuevich*

During Exercise Perspective 2012, this An-24BS of the 456th TrAB transported UkrAF commanders to Belbek AB in September 2012. *Alexander Golz*

used by the air force HQ as the main aircraft of the C-in-C.

The third VIP An-24BS, the air force's 19 Blue, flew less than the other two because its cabin had been converted into the normal An-24B passenger configuration with 48 seats. The aircraft, based at Lviv, was kept as a reserve for the two VIP aircraft, especially when one of them was under overhaul and just one was airworthy. No. 19 Blue was finally withdrawn from service in 2005 and was offered for sale by SkyBirdHeli on 27 May 2006 with a total of 6,392 flying hours and 7,494 cycles.

Based mainly at Vinnitsa, the An-24BSs were not only used as VIP aircraft by the C-in-C but they were also used for training future air force transport aircraft pilots and navigators at Vinnitsa.

As well as the three 'Saloon' aircraft, the air force had two pure passenger versions: two An-24Bs, 24 and 49 Blue, manufactured in 1967 were inherited. No. 49 Blue was in service with the 243rd OSAP at Lviv until 1997, when it was grounded when it reached its MTBO. It was never overhauled, and was offered for sale on 27 May 2006 by SkyBirdHeli when it had a total of 7,090 flying hours and 5,810 cycles.

15th TrAB An-24BS with 01 Yellow (c/n 87304706) being refuelled at Boryspil on 25 March 2005. *Sergey Popsuevich*

Little tactical transporters

The Ukrainian Air Force inherited three An-24RT tactical transports from the original 62 of this variant manufactured for the Soviet Air Force, which were in service with the 243rd OSAP, 255th OSAE and 456th OSAP at Lviv, Boryspil and Vinnitsa respectively. These aircraft, which were jet-boosted, RU19A-300-equipped versions of the An-24T, had specifically been developed for take-off from short fields and hot and high performance.

After the gradual downsizing of the Ukrainian Air Force, these aircraft were retired in the early 2000s. The first aircraft to be withdrawn was 42 Blue (c/n 9911209) at Boryspil in 1999. Its first flight had been on 15 December 1968 and it was delivered to the Soviet Air Force a few days afterwards. Its last overhaul was completed on 28 November 1994, when it was in Ukrainian Air Force service. It was offered for sale by SkyBirdHeli on 27 May 2006 when it had a total of 7,349 flying hours and 8,738 cycles.

After 42 Blue, 16 Blue (c/n 8910801), which was manufactured in 1968, was withdrawn from use in 2000. The aircraft was in service at Vinnitsa and its last overhaul had been completed on 28 November 1995. After retirement it was stored at Vinnitsa until it was offered for sale by SkyBirdHeli in 2006 when it had a total 6,715 hours and 8,245 cycles.

As they were airworthy, both 16 Blue and 42 Blue were declared suitable aircraft for transfer to Ukrainian Cargo Airways, which was under Ukrainian Ministry of Defence management.

Among the three An-24RTs, just one, 47 Blue (ex-23 Blue), which was the youngest An-24 of the force as it was manufactured in 1970, was left operational at Vinnitsa and dedicated to UkrAF missions in collaboration with the State Emergency Service of Ukraine.

Current fleet

Today 777 Blue and 01 Yellow are both still in service with the air force. 01 Yellow is now painted in overall gunship grey with a yellow cheatline and Zbroini Syly Ukrainy/Armed Forces of Ukraine titles following its last periodic maintenance at the Nikolaev Aircraft Repair Plant (NARP) between September and December 2012.

While 777 Blue has GPS/GLONASS satellite navigation equipment, 01 Yellow NAVAIDS has still not been upgraded. Since 2011 there had been a plan to install a CH-4312 GLONASS/GPS aviation receiver in 01 Yellow. This is a highly accuracy flight navigation system for civil aircraft that had been successfully installed and tested in a civilian An-24 by JSC NASVIS in 2010.

01 Yellow, the An-24BS of the 15th BrTA, after its latest overhaul with new paint scheme at Boryspil on 3 November 2016. *Alexander Golz*

456th TrAB An-24RT 47 Blue (c/n 0911405) stored at Vinnitsa AB. *Alexander Golz*

In 2014 the Ukrainian Air Force had still not sold any of its eight An-24s, while ownership of the sole An-24 of the Border Guard and DOSAAF's An-24RT had been transferred in the 1990s. The operational examples are now in service with the 456th TrAB's 1st Aviation Squadron at Vinnitsa and the 15th TrAB at Boryspil.

Although they were intended to be replaced by the An-158 three years ago, 777 Blue and 01 Yellow are still in service as the commander's VIP carriers while the role of their Russian Air Force equivalents have been taken on by the An-140 since 2011.

Ukrainian Air Force An-24s

Version	Bort Number	Construction Number	Unit	Year of manufacture	Current fate	Last flight
An-24BS	19 Blue	87304608	-	1968	Stored	?
An-24BS	01 Yellow	87304706	15th TrAB	1968	Active	-
An-24B	24 Blue	87304801	456th TrAB	1968	Stored	?
An-24BS	777 Blue	97305306	456th TrAB	1969	Active	2013
An-24B	49 Blue	79901310	-	1967	Stored/For Sale	1997
An-24RT	16 Blue	8910801	-	1968	Stored/For Sale	1999
An-24RT	42 Blue	9911209	-	1969	Stored/For Sale	1999
An-24RT	47 Blue	0911405	456th TrAB	1970	Stored/For Sale	2011

Abbreviations
UAP = Training Aviation Regiment
OSAE = Independent Mixed Aviation Squadron
OGSAP = Independent Mixed Aviation Regiment
VTAP = Military-Transport Aviation Regiment

An-26 Fleet (1992–today): The Light Transporters

Derived from the An-24T, but with redesigned front and rear fuselage sections, and equipped with an aft cargo ramp door and a pressurised cargo cabin, the An-26 was designed and manufactured to answer the needs of the Soviet air force for a light transport aircraft with the capability of being used in airdrop missions. Not only was it able to carry out the regular missions of the An-24T, the An-26 had also been designed to meet the needs of Soviet airborne troops, which had been using An-12 and An-22 medium and heavy transports in the 1960s. The Ukrainian Armed Forces inherited almost 60 An-26s from the Soviet Air Force and Navy. Today the UKrAF has 23 An-26s in four main sub-versions in service with three transport regiments and a training regiment.

28 Red, an An-26 of the 223rd OSAP with c/n 10502, carried the Soviet-era Red Star on its vertical stabiliser taxiing at Kiev-Zhuliany airport on 25 September 1992. *Sergey Popsuevich*

Soviet background

The An-26's cabin was spacious enough to load the GAZ-69 four-wheel light truck, ASU-57 airborne tank destroyer/assault gun, D-44 85mm gun, 120mm mortar, and military cargo in ASG-500, SDAP-47 and BAP-1 standard containers. Equipped with more powerful AI-24VT turboprops that had inherited the RU19A-300 APU/booster of earlier versions of the engine installed on the An-24RT (with a cargo ramp door), the An-26 had better STOL capability than the An-24RT and An-24RV and a maximum take-off weight of 24 tons. The aircraft soon took its place in the Soviet Air Armies' Independent Mixed Aviation Regiments and Squadrons, while in some other regiments it played the role of a complementary aircraft for An-24 missions.

Mass production of the An-26 was started at Kiev Aircraft Factory No. 473 in 1968. The first two production An-26s, with construction numbers 0301 and 0302, were delivered to the 606th Training Aviation Regiment of the Soviet Air Force at Balashov in 1970. While test flights of first two prototypes, 831 Black and 830 Black (c/ns 0201 and 0202 respectively), were still ongoing, 14 An-26s were manufactured and most were handed over to the 606th UAP, while a few were delivered to front-line units including the 197th OTAP at Novosibirsk and one to the Soviet Navy in 1970. In the first phase of test flights, 0201 logged 302 hours in 176 flights, and 0202 logged 130 hours and 52 minutes in 83 flights until 21 September 1970.

In total, 1,398 An-26s were manufactured between 1968 and 1986, including 564 examples for the Soviet Armed Forces. They were in service with 13 air armies and three aviation schools (one for airborne commandos, one for pilots and one for navigator training), two air defence armies, two combined arms armies as well as the headquarters of eight air force, air defence and military districts all over the Soviet Union.

This green/brown camouflaged An-26 32 Red, was in service with the 223rd OSAP of the Ukrainian Air Defence Force at Kiev-Zhuliany Airport when seen on 8 September 1992. *Sergey Popsuevich*

223rd OSAP An-26 32 Red had its bort number painted in Blue in 1993. It is seen in its new camouflage at Zhuliany airport on 19 April 1994. *Sergey Popsuevich*

After the Soviet Union's collapse and the birth of the Ukrainian Air Force and Air Defence Force, 60 An-26s were inherited by both forces and these were in service with three Independent Mixed Aviation Squadrons (OSAE), one Training Aviation Regiment (UAP), and three Independent Mixed Aviation Regiments (OSAP) that were under control of the Voroshilovgrad Military Aviation School of Navigators, and the 5th, 14th, 17th and 24th Air Armies.

In service with the Ukrainian Air Force

The Ukrainian Air Force inherited 55 An-26s from the Soviet Air Force and three more from the Soviet Navy in 1992; 48 of them were operational and the rest were grounded waiting for their next overhaul, all in service with the 46th UAP, 112th OSAE, 153rd OSAE, 243rd OSAP, 255th OSAE and 456th OSAP. After the air force, the Ukrainian Air Defence Force inherited eight An-26s of 223rd OSAP of the Soviet Air Defence Force's 8th Mixed Air Defence Army headquartered in Kiev.

In 1993, among the UkrAF's An-26s, 35 were the basic variant, and the rest of the fleet consisted of an An-26B civil cargo variant, three An-26KPA Airfield NAVAIDS testing and calibration aircraft, three An-26RT battlefield communication relay aircraft and 18 An-26Sh navigator trainers.

The An-26 has an MTBO of ten calendar years or 7,800 flying hours and 4,500 cycles, and because of this most UkrAF An-26s had been overhauled in Soviet days, but nearly ten had logged all their MTBO cycles before their calendar time. After independence, as with many other air force units, the flying hours and activity of the Mixed Aviation Regiments and Squadrons of the force dropped and the rest of the airframes reached the end of their MTBOs, most ten years after their last overhaul.

Two of them were 21 years old in 1992, and one of them had already been overhauled before independence. One was manufactured in 1972 and another one in 1973, and their lifetimes ran until 1992 and 1993 respectively. Two were manufactured in 1974, one in 1975, eight in 1976, 15 in 1977, nine in 1978, 13 in 1979, five in 1980, one in 1981 and four had an unknown year of manufacture. According to these manufacture years, the majority of the fleet reached their calendar MTBO in 1997, when the Ministry of Defence was struggling with a budget shortage.

In November 1997, the Ukrainian government accepted an MoD proposal to release air force infrastructure for use in the state enterprise Ukrainian Aviation Transport Company's commercial flights. Among the aircraft earmarked, 15 An-26s –

223 OSAP An-26 30 Blue (ex-30 Red) departing Belbek AB, Crimea on 6 October 1995. It transferred the UkrADF commander in chief and other high-ranking authorities from Zhuliany to Belbek to attend an exercise of the UkrADF's 62nd IAP involving its Su-15TMs and SU-27P/UBs. *Sergey Popsuevich*

One of 18 An-26Shs of the 46th UAP, 24 Blue, taxiing at Belbek AB, Crimea, after a training mission in summer 1996. *Sergey Popsuevich*

including two under overhaul – were selected to be chartered for commercial use. In that year, the air force had 30 airworthy An-26s while the Air Defence Force had three operational examples.

An-26 units

After the establishment of the UkrAF, some An-26 units were disbanded and their aircraft were absorbed by other units. The 46th UAP at Luhansk was disbanded and its 16 An-26Shs, four An-26s and a single An-26B were later absorbed by the 810th Training Aviation Regiment at Chuguyev, near Kiev, which was reorganised into the 203rd Training Aviation Base in 1995.

The single An-26B of the disbanded 46th UAP was used to transfer cadets and student pilots to gunnery ranges, where they were practising bombing by dropping OFAB-100 and FAB-500 bombs installed on BDZ-34 pylons under their An-26Shs.

In 1993, one 46th UAP An-26 together with two An-26s from other units (including the sole example at Starakonstantinov) were transferred to Boryspil to be used for the establishment of the 10th Independent Mixed Aviation Squadron (10th OSAE) beside two An-30Bs of the 86th ODRAE.

At Odessa AB in the south of Ukraine, in the territory under the supervision of the 5th Air Army, the 112th OSAE was redesignated as the 2nd OSAE and absorbed two An-26s of the 153rd OSAE after its disbandment in 1992. This increased the number of An-26s in the 2nd OSAE to six.

In the west of Ukraine, in the area under the protection of the 14th Air Army, the Lviv-based 243rd OSAP had two An-26RTs, with 20 Red (c/n 8302) and 22 Red (c/n 11607), two of a total of 36 An-26 radio relay aircraft manufactured by the Kiev Aviation Plant for the Soviet Air Force to be used for communication between forward and headquarter units.

Both aircraft were in service with the 243rd OSAP, which was one of the major UkrAF An-12 operators until 1996. They were both later transferred to the 456th OSAP at Vinnitsa, with 22 Red becoming 22 Blue and remaining operational while 20 Red, which had become 20 Blue, was grounded. The 456th OSAP, under the organisation of the 24th Air Army VGK, had four An-26 transport variants and one An-26KPA airport NAVAIDS calibration aircraft, 57 Blue.

On 3 May 1985, the 456th OSAP had lost An-26 101 Red (c/n 9506) in a head-on collision with Aeroflot Tu-134A CCCP-65856 while it was in cloud at 3,900m and 6km north-west of Zolochiv while flying between Lviv and Moscow. The crash, which killed the An-26's six crew and nine passengers, was the result of an ATC error.

The 255th OSAE based at Boryspil had two transport An-26s to support military units under supervision of the 17th Air Army around Kiev. Four of its An-26s were operational and the remaining example had been grounded since 1991 after reaching its MTBO.

02 Blue (former 32) with the c/n 8206 was one of eight An-26s in service with the UkrADF's 223rd OSAP (later 223rd OSAE) when seen in basic Aeroflot colours at Zhuliany airport in 2002. It later became 05 Yellow when it joined with the UkrAF's 15th TrAB. *Sergey Popsuevich*

An-26 82 Blue (c/n 8402) was 82 Yellow in service with the 10th Independent Aviation Squadron at Boryspil when it was inherited by the UkrAF. Here it has 'Blakutna Stesha' (Open Skies) titles on its fuselage at Boryspil on 10 October 1995. This aircraft was later transferred to the Ukrainian Navy, where it became 10 Yellow. *Sergey Popsuevich*

Former Soviet Navy's An-26 03 Red was transferred to the Kirovskoye Flight Test Centre after Ukraine's independence. This aircraft was overhauled by the 410th Aircraft Repair Plant in 2018 and 2019. Here it is at Kirovskoye in the 1990s. It also had an artwork of a killer whale painted above its entry door. *Sergey Popsuevich*

An-26 01 Black was in service with 223rd OSAP at Zhuliany in 1999. *Alexander Gol*

'Vita', the air ambulance

Back in 1997, following a request by the Ukrainian Ministry of Defence, an An-26 was converted into a VIP lounge aircraft for the use of the staff and commanders. It was equipped with an air-conditioned and isolated passenger cabin with 12 seats in the front section of the cargo compartment, while the aft section was kept as a cargo area for loading a variety of freight, including cars. The new aircraft was designated an An-26S ('S' for Saloon).

In 2001, when the Ukrainian Armed Force's Military Medical Centre requested an air ambulance, the Odessa Aircraft Repair Plant, 'Odesaviaremservice', was contracted to convert one of the former 46th UAP An-26s. The contract, using An-26Sh 25 Blue (c/n 5406), was completed within a year and it was then certified according to the ICAO standards before handover to the 456th OSAP at Vinnitsa. The unit was later redesignated the 456th Transport Aviation Brigade.

Nicknamed 'Vita' (life), 25 Blue was given an overall white colour scheme with its empennage painted in Ukrainian flag colours and a large badge of the Ukrainian Armed Forces Military Medical Centre applied beside its name on both sides of its fuselage, together with 'Red Cross' signs on both sides of the rear fuselage.

It was equipped with four beds for patients, a defibrillator, a portable ultrasound, cabinets for storing medication, sterile material for dressings, 12 seats for sitting patients each with oxygen mask, nurse call buttons, additional lighting, an artificial respiration machine, an operating table and heart pacemaker. The medical team could carry out in-flight surgery using power generated by the APU.

On 18 February 2009, the Ukrainian MoD put forward 'Vita' for UN peacekeeping operations to NATO representatives visiting Vinnitsa. The medical team and crew members were trained according to NATO standards in mid-April 2009.

'Vita' had saved the lives of 200 Ukrainian Armed Forces personnel up to 2009, and performed hundreds of medical missions afterwards. For example, on 12 August 2009 it was used to transfer two patients who were servicemen in the Ukrainian Navy and Land Force, one with kidney disease and the other with a suspected brain tumour, from Crimea to the Main Military Clinical Hospital on the military side of Boryspil airport.

'Vita' was certified to fly all over the EU and was used in international missions as well; for example, on 6 August 2013 it was used to transport five Ukrainian civilians with brain injuries and fractures suffered in a car accident near Orsha in the Vitebsk region of Belarus to Odessa, Ukraine, a nearly two-hour flight.

An-26 unit changes

Reorganisation of the UkrAF units into brigades started in the mid-1990s. Subsequently, on 17 February 1997,

An-26Sh 25 Blue of the 46th at Dubno on 26 February 1997. This aircraft was later converted into the first 'Vita'. *Sergey Popsuevich*

The cabin layout of the flying hospital 25 Blue. *Alexander Golz*

the 255th OSAE, which had become the 1st OSAP in 1994, was reorganised into the 15th Transport Aviation Brigade at Boryspil.

In 2003, the 25th Guards Military-Transport Aviation Regiment became the 25th Transport Aviation Regiment. It had a single An-26, 21 Blue, to transport its personnel, particularly Il-76 technicians, all over the Ukraine. It also carried spare parts and cargo to support Il-76 operations.

In August 2004, the 203rd Training Aviation Base was reorganised as the 203rd Training Aviation Brigade. From 1 September 2004, it has been enlisted as a part of the Kharkiv Air Force University.

On 1 December 2004, the Ukrainian Air Defence Force was disbanded and its units were merged with the air force. With its HQ still at Vinnitsa and based on the former air force structure, its air armies were reorganised as air commands and its regiments were reorganised into aviation brigades. Almost a year before, the Ukrainian Air Defence Force's 223rd OSAP, based at Vasilkov, which was responsible for supporting the 8th Mixed Air Defence Army HQ, had been disbanded.

The 223rd OSAP had three An-26s in 1999, 22 and 02 Blue operational and another, 75 Blue, grounded. Among them just one, 22 Blue (c/n 7910), remained operational until 2002. Still in the two-tone green camouflage colours of Soviet days and based at Vasilkov, 22 Blue was later transferred to the State Aviation Museum in Kiev. No. 02 Blue was added to the air force inventory and then stored at Boryspil with a new air force bort number, 05 Yellow. It was offered for sale in 2008, but was restored and returned to service in 2014.

After the merger of the two forces, the MoD started to downsize the remaining fleet by reorganising and merging existing regiments and squadrons into the aviation brigades. Thus, the number of personnel and aircraft was reduced.

By the end of 2004, the UkrAF had 22 airworthy An-26s, which were in service with the 15th TrAB (four An-26s) at Boryspil, 25th TrAB (one An-26) at Melitopol, 203rd TrAB (an An-26, an An-26B and five An-26Shs) at Chuguyev, 456th TrAB (seven An-26s, an An-26KPA and an An-26RT) at Vinnitsa, and Kirovskoye Flight Test Centre (an ex-Ukrainian Navy An-26). There were also 20 more examples stored and grounded after reaching their MTBOs.

An ex-112th OSAE An-26. Then unit was redesignated the 2nd OSAP after it received the former 153rd OSAE's An-26s. The regiment was disbanded in 2005 and its An-26s were transferred to the 456th TrAB. An-26 39 Blue (c/n 7509) had its last overhaul completed in July 1998 and it entered service with the 456th TrAB in 2005. It is now 49 Blue and has had its lifetime extended on the basis of a contract signed on 26 April 2019. It is seen in 2006. *Sergey Popsuevich*

15th TrAB An-26 02 Yellow (c/n 8509) taxiing before take-off at Boryspil on 23 March 2005. It is now in overall grey colours with the bort number 02 Blue following its last overhaul in 2016. *Sergey Popsuevich*

The Fleet for sale

Beginning in 1999, a number of the UkrAF's surplus An-26s were sold or transferred to other governmental or security organisations. This started with 39 Red (c/n 5508) and 48 Red (c/n 6107), which had been grounded in 1996 and 1997 after reaching their MTBOs and were overhauled in 1998 and 1999 respectively. They were transferred to the Ukrainian Ministry of Internal Affairs and the Ukrainian State Emergency Service/MNS Ukrayiny (later DSNS) in 1999 and 2000 respectively.

In 2004, An-26Sh 44 Blue (c/n 4709) was transferred to the Ukrainian State Emergency Service, and another An-26, with 35 Red (c/n 5801) was leased to Ukrainian Cargo Airways for four years until in 2009 it was sent for overhaul at No. 410 ARZ and then put for sale.

Between 2006 and 2014, the Ukrainian Ministry of Defence put 18 air force An-26s up for sale. Some of them were sold after overhaul at No. 410 ARZ and some were sold with the understanding that this work would be carried out using the buyer's funds. Among them, just seven examples were demilitarised during their last overhaul to be sold directly or by means of finance leasing to the Ukrainian State Emergency Service, Baltika, Asia Airways, and Meridian.

21 Blue is the sole An-26 in service with the 25th TrAB for transportation of its aircrew and ground crew. A contract for the extension of its lifetime by one year was signed on 26 April 2019. It is seen at Belbek during a military exercise in September 2012. *Alexander Golz*

An-26 units before the war

Since 1992, the Ukrainian Armed Forces have been participating in large-scale exercises in collaboration with other Ukrainian or international armed forces to increase the readiness and skill of flight and ground crews. For example, in January every year the 15th TrAB and 456th TrAB perform navigation sorties between their air bases and other airports in low-visibility conditions to increase the pilots' and navigators' skills for IFR flight in bad weather conditions.

In August every year, after graduation from flight school, the fresh An-26 pilots participate in annual joint training with the UkrAF's Tactical Aviation Brigades at Kulbakino. To train as an An-26 pilot, each cadet flies 12 hours after logging 61 hours on the L-39, while navigators must log 95 hours on An-26Sh navigator trainers at the 203rd TrAB.

The An-26s are also heavily used to train Ukrainian airborne troops, who first use an Mi-8MT before learning to jump from the transport. The jumps from An-26s are usually performed at an elevation of 600m and at 300km/h.

Between 29 and 31 October 2007, during an international counter-terrorism exercise named East Shield 2007, a pair of An-26s were used to carry Ukrainian Army counter-terrorism forces to Odessa air base. The same year, between 9 and 20 June, the

An-26 04 Red (c/n 0909) was in service with the 223rd OSAP of the Soviet Air Defence Force when seen at Ozernoye in 1991. This aircraft was sent to the 410th ARP to be overhauled in 1992 but it never entered in service with the UkrADF and was leased to Busol Airline in 1994. In 2002, it entered service with the UkrAF as a VIP aircraft as UR-26241 but was not used until it was leased to Ukrainian Cargo Airways as UR-UDM in 2004. It was withdrawn from service on 7 July 2011 and sold to Constanta Airlines in April 2019. *Sergey Popsuevich*

UkrAF deployed the An-26 'Vita' and 22 of its personnel, including members of the 'Vita' medical team, to Tbilisi, Georgia, to take part in NATO's international exercise Cooperative Archer 2007 in order to improve the interoperability of the air ambulance medical team with their NATO equivalents.

In 2008, two 456th TrAB An-26s were used in Exercise Decisive Action 2008, and in 2009 the UkrAF participated in the bilateral Ukrainian–Belarus Air Defence Command Post exercise on 20 October with An-26BUS 22 Blue. No. 22 Blue (c/n 11607) had been an An-26RT in 2006, when it was overhauled and modernised at Syvatoshino to become the sole airborne command post in the UkrAF. The former Vasilkov-based aircraft entered 456th TrAB service after conversion.

Between 12 and 29 July 2011, an An-26 and 'Vita', together with two medical teams from the 456th TrAB, participated in the joint Ukrainian–US–Polish exercise Safe Skies 2011 at Mirgorod. The main goal of the exercise was to increase the readiness and coordination of all the participant air forces to provide security for Ukraine's airspace during Euro 2012. During the exercise, a 15th TrAB

This An-26 of the Ukrainian National Guard with bort number 07 Blue (c/n 7005) was a former 46th UAP An-26Sh that was in service with the regiment until 1999, when it was temporarily granted to the Ukrainian Ministry of Internal Affairs to be used for VIP flights. It was later transferred to the National Guard's unit A-2269 at Oleksandriya. It is seen at Boryspil on 3 October 2007. *Sergey Popsuevich*

15th BrTA's An-26 with 07 Yellow b/n (c/n 3907) was escorted by a pair of MiG-29 of 40th BrTA over Kiev in 2008 during Ukraine's Independence Day parade, one of which can be seen here. *Sergey Popsuevich*

An-26BUS 22 Blue of the 456th TrAB (c/n 11607). This aircraft was an An-26RT radio relay aircraft in service with the 243rd OSAP until it was converted into an An-26BUS airborne command post and overhauled and modernised at Syvatoshino in 2006. It was named 'Petro Balabuyev' after the late chief designer of OKB Antonov. It is seen at Vinnitsa in 2010. *Alexander Golz*

flew from Boryspil and was used in an aircraft hijack simulation, being intercepted by a UkrAF Su-27 and an USAF F-16. Three days later, on 24 July, the same aircraft was used in another hijack simulation mission and was intercepted by a pair of UkrAF MiG-29s.

In June 2012, during Euro 2012, the Ukrainian Air Force specified several fighter aircraft including its Su-27s and MiG-29s to be ready 24/7 on QRA shifts to respond to any kind of terrorist attack, including aircraft hijacking in Ukrainian airspace. As well as the fighter aircraft of the three BrTAs, three An-26s (one as reserve) including 'Vita' were also specified to be used, not only in a MEDEVAC or air ambulance role but also by Ukrainian counter-terrorism forces alongside Mi-8 helicopters. In September, Air Command Centre conducted Exercise Perspective 2012, during which 831th BrTA Su-27s were forward deployed to Belbek, Crimea, and a team of their ground crews followed in a 456th TrAB An-26.

In February 2013, the 203rd TrAB's An-26 student pilots and navigators completed their instrument flight training course by performing instrument flights in winter weather in Kharkiv. The next month, three An-26s of the 15th TrAB and 456th TrAB were used by the 8th Separate Special Purpose (Spetsnaz) Regiment for parachute jumping and cargo airdrops in an exercise at Khmelnitsky. Later, during the US–Ukraine exercise Rapid Trident 2013, held between 7 and 19 July 2013, Ukrainian Land Forces including special forces were transported to the exercise area in An-26s and Il-76s.

In 2013, the UkrAF's An-26s completed several international flights, including a medical flight to Belarus performed by 'Vita', and one to Hungary. During its journey to Kecskemet Air Base, Hungary, on 2 August to take part in the Hungarian International Air Show on 3 and 4 August, 15th TrAB An-26 04 Yellow was accompanied by 831st TrAB Su-27UB 69 Blue.

During another international UkrAF mission, An-26 04 Yellow was used to deliver spare parts and

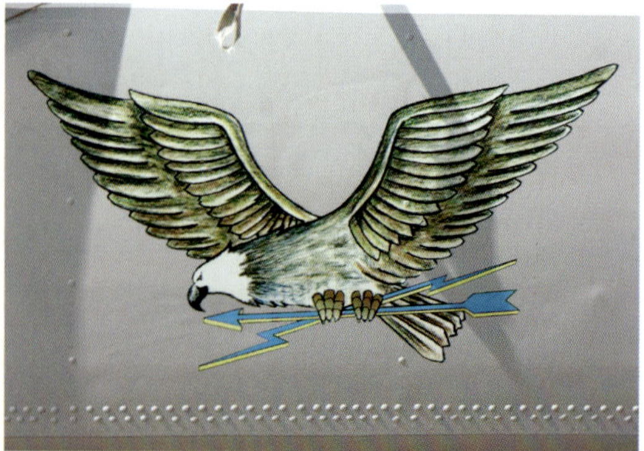

15th TrAB An-26 02 Yellow (c/n 8509) at Boryspil on 4 August 2008. It had this special artwork of an eagle applied on its fuselage as it was in use to transport air force commanders. *Alexander Golz*

ground equipment to Ukrainian peacekeeping forces in Kosovo on 4 December 2013. The flight was from Boryspil to Pristina airport and on its return the aircraft brought back 17 Ukrainian military personnel after completion of their mission in conjunction with KFOR Multi-national Battle Group East.

Ex-255th OSAE An-26 04 Yellow (c/n 8501) is now in service with the 15th TrAB. It participated in the war in Donbass. *Alexander Golz*

An-26s at war

While not facing any threat to the security of the country, and due to years of gradual downsizing of the air force and its resources, the UKrAF had just kept a fleet of seven Il-76s and seven An-26s dedicated for the use of ground and airmobile forces. Among these, just four Il-76s and five An-26s were airworthy! One more An-26, 18 Blue (later 48 Blue) had also been under overhaul at the 410th Aircraft Repair Plant since 2013.

Among the operational An-26s for the tactical transport of cargo and personnel, three were in service with the 15th TrAB, which were 07 Yellow (c/n 3907), 04 Yellow (c/n 8501), and 02 Yellow (c/n 8509), while three others, 09 Blue (c/n 7509), 19 Blue (c/n 9710) and 57 Blue (c/n 6909), were in service with the 456th TrAB and a single An-26, 21 Blue (c/n 10209), was in service with the 25th TrAB.

As well as the seven An-26s dedicated to transport duties, seven more airworthy An-26s were used for special duties and flight training. These were two An-26Shs and an An-26B in service with the 203rd TrAB for navigator and pilot training respectively, three more An-26s consisting of an KPA (airport NAVAIDS calibration), a BUS (airborne command post), and 'Vita' (flying hospital) in service with the 456th TrAB, and a single An-26 in service with the Ukrainian Air Force Research and Test Centre (GANITS) at Kirovskoye, Crimea.

In late January 2014, the Ukrainian Air Command Centre was tasked with increasing the readiness of its units, including the 456th TrAB, to be ready to respond to any security threat in Ukraine's airspace during the 2014 Winter Olympics in Sochi, Russia. During the games, 'Vita' and another An-26 were on alert to participate in any MEDEVAC operation.

After the occupation of all Ukrainian Navy, Air Force and Army bases in the Crimea by Russian forces, and following the possibility of the influx of more Russian forces to the peninsula and an invasion of the Ukrainian mainland, the Ukrainian Air Force was put on high alert. Subsequently, 831st BrTA Su-27s armed with R-27 and R-73 missiles conducted daily CAP sorties over the area under the control of the Air Command Centre. Just a few weeks later, on 7 April, pro-Russian separatists stormed the Ukrainian Security Forces offices in Donetsk and Luhansk, taking

456th TrAB An-26 39 Blue (c/n 7509) was one of only three airworthy examples in service with the 456th TrAB when the war in Donbass began. *Alexander Golz*

Former Soviet Navy's An-26 59 yellow (c/n 5003) in service with the 456th TrAB. 59 Yellow was 03 Red with the Kirovskoye Flight Test Centre. In April 2014 it was forward deployed to Kulbakino, where it participated in an exercise before the launch of ATO's counter-terrorism operation in the Donbass. It is seen at Kulbakino-Nikolayev on 21 April 2014. *Alexander Golz*

control of them and accessing their weapon storage.

Supported by Russia, separatists demanded the Ukrainian government held a referendum for the separation and independence of the regions. While the Ukrainian Armed Forces, including the air force, were on alert to defend the country from the danger of invasion from the south, they were now faced by a new and more potential threat in the east of the country.

Starting from 8 April, all UkrAF transport units were used to transfer ammunition and weapons for the Ukrainian Armed Forces via logistics flights to Dnepropetrovsk airport. From 9 April, the Ukrainian Army conducted an operation to retake the eastern regions and liberate the governmental buildings.

Starting in early May, the seven cargo An-26s joined the Il-76s in the mobilisation of troops and they carried weapon supplies to the eastern regions. In just two months between May and July 2014, seven cargo An-26s logged around 245 combat sorties and airdropped tons of weapons and food supplies to troops on the front line fighting in the counter-insurgency and anti-terrorism operations.

456th TrAB pilots practised bombing 59 Yellow during the exercise at Kulbakino in April 2014. Fifteen bombs were dropped by the aircraft during this time. *Alexander Golz*

From the first day of the Ukrainian Armed Forces' operation in the Donbass region to 19 May, the flying hospital An-26 'Vita' saved the lives of 61 injured troops, including 25 soldiers of the Ukrainian Army. Vital inflight surgery was performed on the severely injured by the medical team on board the aircraft. Not only was the aircraft used in MEDEVAC missions in the east, it was also used to carry two servicemen who had been burned while preparing dinner for troops in a military exercise at Kherson on 13 May.

The years of negligence and decline in the UkrAF meant that the low numbers of fully mission-capable MiG-29s, Su-24s, Su-25s and Su-27s could not meet the surge in demand by Ukrainian ground forces to conduct close air support sorties and the increased need for combat aircraft on ground attack or bombing missions on the eastern front in the Donbass region. The air force HQ ordered all units to concentrate all their available resources on such operations, including any aircraft that could carry and drop bombs. These included the An-26s, which were able to carry a maximum of four bombs via BDZ-34 pylons or bomb racks.

At Kulbakino between 12 and 16 May, the UKrAF conducted an exercise to prepare flight crews for upcoming air operations against Pro-Russian separatists. Three An-26s, 04 Yellow, 19 Blue and 39 Blue, from the 15th and 456th TrABs participated in the exercise, their pilots practising bombing on 15 and 16 May. A week after the exercise, the 15th TrAB, with 04 Yellow, and the 456th TrAB, using 22 Blue (An-26BUS), practised navigation flight training. However, they were never used as bombers during the war.

19 Blue as it appeared during the last days of its service before being shot down over Donbass on 14 July 2014. *Luca G. Canossa*

Tragedy over Luhansk

The 15th and 456th TrABs performed dozens of flights to the front-line airports in the warzone in Donbass, including the airfield at Kramatorsk and Luhansk before they were occupied by separatists. Tons of military equipment, goods and food supplies for military servicemen and in some cases for civilians were airlifted and even airdropped by the aircraft during humanitarian operations.

Not only 'Vita' but also the other An-26s were used to evacuate wounded troops after a series of Ukrainian Army defeats. No. 21 Blue, the sole 25th TrAB An-26, was configured with stretchers racks and holders in its cargo cabin to carry wounded servicemen.

With their STOL capability as well as their cargo airdrop capability, the An-26s were used in in June and July 2014 in a dozen airdrop missions to deliver food and weapon supplies to the Ukrainian Airmobile Forces' Airborne Brigades on the front line, especially where there was no airfield nearby under the control of friendly forces.

On 27 May, Russia delivered military equipment including military vehicles, RPGs, AK-47 machine guns and ammunition to the pro-Russian insurgents in Luhansk to enable them to occupy the whole city. Subsequently, the next day, the militias attacked a Ukrainian military base, while the Ukrainian National Guard was attacked by another unit of the United Armed Forces of Novorossiya's South-Eastern Army in the east of Luhansk.

Because Luhansk airport was still under their control, the Ukrainian Security Forces were able to transfer and mobilise their troops to the city, but it soon became one of the main targets of the separatists and collaborators from the Russian Army. Subsequently, on 14 June 2014 one of three Il-76s of the UkrAF's 25th TrAB carrying a company of 25th Independent Airborne Brigade (40 servicemen), their hardware, ammunition and food was shot down by separatists firing MANPADs when on final approach to Luhansk airport, killing all 49 occupants on board. This accident significantly reduced the number of transport flights to the airport.

On 23 June, militias attempted to besiege Luhansk airport, which was under the control of Ukrainian Forces, forcing the Ukrainian Army to plant landmines outside the perimeter. After the first failed attempt to occupy the airport, it was attacked on 5 July 2015 by Grad rockets, which destroyed several civilian An-2s and damaged the surface of the airport's apron and runways. This made the airport unserviceable and unsafe for logistical flights by UkrAF An-26s. Two days later, while An-26 flights had mostly stopped, pro-Russian separatists used six armoured tanks and an AFV to attack the airport again, while the Ukrainian Armed Forces responded with mortar fire.

The pro-Russian forces surrounding the airport lost two armoured tanks and a single BM-21 Grad rocket launch vehicle after they were rocketed by a pair of 299th BrTA Su-25M1s. This reduced the intensity of the rocket attacks against the airport, but it still was not safe for UkrAF Il-76s and An-26s to land. Five days later, on the evening of 13 July, it was announced that Ukrainian Security Forces had reached the airport on the ground and broken the siege.

The next day, on 14 July, the 456th TrAB was ordered to deliver weapons and ammunition to the besieged Ukrainian ground forces in Luhansk airport at high altitude beyond the range of the separatists' MANPADs and AA guns. An-26 19 Blue (c/n 9710)

456th TrAB An-26 19 Blue (c/n 9710) was shot down by an Osa-AKM SAM (according to other sources a Buk-M1) of the pro-Russian separatists near the border with Russia in Krasnodonsky district on 14 July 2014. It is seen in Mirgorod during Exercise Clear Sky 2011. *Alexander Golz*

An-26Sh 46 Red bort number (c/n 5609) belonging to the 203rd TrAB was overhauled by No. 410 ARP between 2014 and 2016. 46 Red received the new bort number 35 Blue after the work was completed. It was fully converted into a cargo aircraft and transferred to the 456th TrAB. It is seen here at Chuguyev, its previous home base, on 2 August 2018. This aircraft was named 'Dmytro Maiboroda' after the pilot of 19 Blue who lost his life on 14 July 2014. *Alexander Golz*

dropped weapons and food supplies for the armed forces inside and around the airport on its 36th combat mission since the beginning of the war. While it was flying at 6,500m (21,300ft), the aircraft was hit by an SA-11 SAM launched from a Buk-M1 SAM system belonging to the second company of the Russian 53rd Anti-Aircraft Missile Brigade stationed on the Ukrainian–Russian border.

While the aircraft's engines were burning, its pilot, Maj Dmitry Maiboroda, decided to keep it level under his control to give the six other crewmembers time to evacuate using parachutes. The pilot and co-pilot, Dmitry Shkarbunom, remained in the aircraft and lost their lives. Two of the surviving crewmembers were captured by pro-Russian forces, while the rest landed in an area controlled by the Ukrainian Armed Forces. Later, the same Buk-M1 SAM launcher system mistakenly shot down Boeing 777-200ER 9M-MRD on flight MH17 from Amsterdam to Kuala Lumpur while it was flying at 33,000ft.

After the reduction in the airdrop missions to supply the forces at the airport, and after several months of resistance, the Ukrainian forces retreated from Luhansk airport on 31 August 2014. Before leaving they destroyed the airport facility and its NAVAIDS.

On 18 November 2015, following a decree issued by Ukrainian President Petro Poroshenko, one of the 456th TrAB's aircraft, recently overhauled An-26 35 Blue (c/n 5609), was officially named 'Dmytro Maiboroda' after the pilot of 19 Blue who sacrificed his life to save his fellow crewmembers.

05 Yellow, nicknamed 'Vezunchyk' (lucky), became the first An-26 of the UkrAF to be restored by the Wings of Phoenix public association in 2014. *Alexander Golz*

Attrition replacement

Beginning in April 2014, when the danger of a Russian invasion from Crimea and the eastern borders increased, the Ukrainian government and MoD gathered $14 million in donations from the Ukrainian people for the refurbishment of military equipment, including An-26 05 Yellow (c/n 8206) belonging to the 15th TrAB. Some 600,000 UAH was gathered for 05 Yellow's restoration and overhaul by a public association named Wings of Phoenix. Included in this sum was 10,000 UAH allocated by Boryspil city council.

No. 05 Yellow had been overhauled by No. 410 ARP at Zhuliany in 1998 when it was still 32 Red, but it was placed in storage in 2005 and was then put up for sale in 2008. It remained unsold until it was chosen for restoration. Unofficially named 'Vezunchyk' (lucky), it was painted in digital camouflage colours with a large 'phoenix' title on its nose, together with the phoenix emblem. Finally, on 29 August 2014, after four months of volunteer technicians' work, 05 Yellow flew for first time.

According to the deputy commander of military unit A2215 (at Boryspil), Lt Col Alexei Bratus, 05 Yellow had logged just 2,500 hours of its total 15,000 flying hours, therefore after restoration it was able to remain in UkrAF service until 2029.

Later that year, the overhaul of another An-26, 44 Blue (c/n 9603), belonging to the 456th TrAB, was completed by No. 410 ARP at Zhuliany, Kiev. The aircraft was painted in an overall gunship grey colour scheme with a sharkmouth painted under its nose section.

After 05 Yellow, in October 2014 another 15th TrAB An-26, 08 Yellow (c/n 6806), was chosen for restoration and overhaul by the Wings of Phoenix public association via public funds and donations. The overhaul took seven months and the aircraft, which was painted in digital camouflage, was named 'Ryatunchyk' (rescuer) and officially handed over to its unit during an official ceremony at Boryspil on 22 May 2015. The aircraft was modified to be used in MEDEVAC operations and its bort number colour was changed to blue.

15th TrAB An-26 08 Yellow (c/n 6806) under restoration by the Wings of Phoenix public association at Boryspil on 16 February 2015. *Wings of Phoenix*

15th TrAB An-26 08 Yellow (c/n 6806) in digital colours after the completion of its restoration at Boryspil on 19 May 2015. *Wings of Phoenix*

Phoenix artwork applied to the fuselage of 05 and 08 Yellow, the An-26s of 15th TrAB that were restored by the Wings of Phoenix public association. *Wings of Phoenix*

08 Yellow after its post-restoration functional check flight at Boryspil on 24 April 2015. *Wings of Phoenix*

Restoration and modernisation

What happened during the war in Donbass showed how much the An-26s could help the Ukrainian Airmobile Forces' Airborne brigades to mobilise their troops as well as evacuate wounded servicemen to the hospitals in Kiev and Boryspil using 'Vita' and the three other An-26s modified and configured for MEDEVAC missions during the conflict.

Not only the airborne brigades but also the ground forces used the An-26s to transfer their troops to the battle zones, but the 19 Blue catastrophe ended all An-26 flights over territories occupied by Russian Army and pro-Russian separatists, because of the type's vulnerability to MANPADS and SAMs, including the Buk-M1 system.

To solve these problems, the MoD asked the government to allocate a budget for the modernisation of the fleet, as well as for the restoration of the An-26s in storage including those examples for sale. As a part of the modernisation, which was to be performed by No. 410 ARP, the aircraft would be equipped with self-defence sensors and chaff/flare dispensers, as well as given a slight avionic upgrade that included the installation of GLONASS/GPS NAVAIDS. It was also intended to transfer 14 air force An-26s to Army Aviation after the modernisation, which had not happened by 2019.

20 Blue (c/n 8302) belonging to the 456th TrAB, is one of two An-26RTs still in service with the UkrAF. No. 410 ARP restored and overhauled it in 2016 and it was painted in overall gunship grey camouflage. It is seen stored at Vinnitsa in September 2015 just a few months before its restoration. *Alexander Golz*

Two aircraft, 05 Yellow and 08 Blue, were restored and returned to the sky via public funds, while three more aircraft, 46 Red and 44 Blue from the 456th TrAB and An-26Sh 46 Red (c/n 5609) of the 203rd TrAB, were overhauled by No. 410 ARP between 2014 and 2016. An average of 30 million UAH was spent on each airframe and its two engines. No. 46 Red received the new bort number 35 Blue after its overhaul and it was redelivered to the 456th TrAB during a formal ceremony at Vinnitsa on 3 December 2016.

By the end of 2016, No. 410 ARP had restored and overhauled UKrAF An-26RT, 20 Blue. The aircraft was painted in overall gunship grey camouflage. Its first post-overhaul FCF was carried out from Zhuliany airport on 7 December 2016. Before 20 Blue, another of the brigade's An-26RTs, 27 Blue (c/n 11910), had been restored by its maintenance squadron in 2015.

In summer 2016, another An-26 of the 203rd TrAB, 30 Blue, was overhauled by No. 410 ARP and became 50 Blue. After that, the brigade had two more An-26s overhauled by No. 410 ARP. They were 71 Yellow (c/n 5507) and 56 Yellow (c/n 10403), which were redelivered to the regiment after a ferry flight to Chuguyev on 23 June 2017.

The sole UkrAF An-26KPA, 35 BLUE (c/n 6406), which was a laboratory aircraft equipped with KPA-ES-1 'Standart' equipment, was overhauled by No. 410 ARP on 10 December 2017. It became 47 Blue and was redelivered to the 456th TrAB on 6 July 2018.

Current fleet

In 2016, the 15th TrAB had four operational An-26s in service, which increased to five in 2019. The 25th TrAB had one airworthy An-26, the 203rd TrAB had six operational examples (increased to eight in 2019) and the 456th TrAB had eight An-26s (increased to nine in 2019) including the former Kirovskoye flight research and test centre's 59 Yellow. This aircraft's last overhaul was begun by No. 410 ARP in February 2018 and it was finished in mid-2019.

After the loss of 19 Blue in 2014, the number of An-26 missions over the warzone was reduced and then stopped due to the threat from Russian SAM systems. However, the An-26s were used to deliver

One of two An-26RTs of the 456th TrAB, 20 Blue (c/n 8302) was restored and overhauled by No. 410 ARP in 2016. It received overall gunship grey camouflage, as seen at Vinnitsa on 22 June 2017. *Alexander Golz*

An-26RT 27 Blue (c/n 11910) is in service with the 456th TrAB. It was restored after the war but it is not known whether it was still airworthy in 2019. 27 Blue's construction was completed on 29 March 1982 and is the youngest An-26 in UkrAF service. *Alexander Golz*

15th TrAB An-26, 04 Yellow, had its last overhaul completed by No. 410 ARP in October 2017. It was painted in overall grey camouflage and received the bort number 04 Blue. It is seen during an exercise at Korotich on 5 August 2018. *Alexander Golz*

An-26 04 Blue of the 15th TrAB (c/n 8501) during an exercise of the Ukrainian Airmobile Forces at Korotich on 5 August 2018. During the exercise, the An-26s performed cargo airdrops at low altitude and landed on grass fields and unpaved runways. *Alexander Golz*

44 Blue (c/n 4603) was an An-26 of the 456th TrAB and was overhauled by No 410 ARP after the war. Here it is seen at Vinnitsa on 21 April 2016. It received sharkmouth artwork after the overhaul. *Alexander Golz*

49 Blue (c/n 7509) is an ex-112th OSAE An-26 of the 456th TrAB. It was 39 Blue until it had its bort number changed to 49 Blue after its last maintenance in 2015 or 2016. It is seen at Vinnitsa in 2017. *Alexander Golz*

In summer 2016, No. 410 ARP overhauled this An-26 of the 203rd TrAB. It had its bort number changed from 30 Blue to 50 Blue. *Alexander Golz*

food, ammunition and weapon supplies to the front-line units, flying from Kramatorsk and Dnepropetrovsk airports.

In 2014, while the two transport aviation brigades operating An-26s were involved in flights to the front lines, the 203rd TrAB increased the number of training flight sorties for new groups of An-26 pilots and navigators. The Ukrainian airmobile forces also practised parachute jumping and equipment airdrops using An-26s in five exercises in 2014, including the Ukrainian–American exercise Rapid Trident 2014 in the Straychi and Lviv regions during September.

In 2016, the UkrAF had 16 airworthy An-26s, while three more examples including two An-26Shs of the 203rd TrAB were under overhaul at No. 410 ARP. Twenty-four more An-26s were stored at Boryspil (three), Chuguyev (six), Odessa (one), Kulbakino (two), and Vinnitsa (12). There is still no firm plan for the replacement of the ageing An-26s with a new light transport aircraft, but it is most likely that the UkrAF will choose the An-132 for this role in the 2030s. When this book was written in 2019, the UkrAF had 23 operational An-26s in service, among which two were under periodical and depot maintenance.

An-26Sh 76 Yellow of the 203rd TrAB (c/n 5608) at Chuguyev on 7 July 2017. *Alexander Golz*

Ukrainian Air Force and Air Defence Force An-26s

Version	Bort Number	Construction Number	Unit in 1992	Current unit	Year of manufacture	Status in 1992	Current status	Year of Retirement/wfu
An-26	61 Blue	0806	112th OSAE	-	1971	Ground	Scrapped	2008
An-26	34 Blue	0808	112th OSAE	-	1971	Active	Wfu/Stored	2008
An-26	09 Blue	1202	456th OSAP	456th TrAB	1972	Active	Under overhaul	-
An-26	?	1808	RuAF	-	1973	-	Sold	2008
An-26	99 Blue	2005	153rd OSAE	456th TrAB	1974	Active	Ground	-
An-26	50 Blue	2610	?	203rd TrAB	1974	Active	Active	-
An-26	12 Blue	2704	456th OSAP	456th TrAB	1977	Ground	Wfu/Stored	2007
An-26KPA	10 Blue	3205	?	-	1977	Ground	Wfu/Stored	2006
An-26Sh	30 Blue	3209	153rd OSAE	203rd TrAB	1975	Active	Ground	-
An-26	?	3701	?	-	1976	Active	Wfu/Stored	2006
An-26Sh	20 Blue	3902	6th TrAB	-	1976	Active	Wfu/Stored	2008
An-26	07 Yellow	3907	Starakonstantinov	15th TrAB	1976	Active	Active	-
An-26	10 Red	4002	46th UAP	-	1976	Active	Sold	2005
An-26Sh	08 Red	4101	46th UAP	203rd TrAB	1976	Active	StoRed	-
An-26Sh	01 Red	4209	46th UAP	203rd TrAB	1976	Active	StoRed	-
An-26Sh	25 Red	4210	46th UAP	-	1976	Active	Wfu/Stored	2005
An-26Sh	20 Red	4409	46th UAP	-	1976	Ground	Wfu/Stored	2007
An-26Sh	44 Blue	4709	46th UAP	-	1977	Active	Sold	2004
An-26	59 Yellow	5003	GANITS	456th TrAB	1977	Under overhaul	Active	-
An-26	32 Red	5106	46th UAP		1977	Active	Sold	2010
An-26Sh	28 Red	5304	46th UAP	-	1977	Active	Wfu/Stored	2006
An-26	54 Yellow	5305	6th TrAB	-	1977	-	Sold	2006

Version	Bort Number	Construction Number	Unit in 1992	Current unit	Year of manufacture	Status in 1992	Current status	Year of Retirement/wfu
An-26 Vita	25 Blue	5406	46th UAP	456th TrAB	1977	Active	Active	-
An-26Sh	71 Yellow	5507	46th UAP	203rd TrAB	1977	Active	Active	-
An-26	39 Red	5508	?	-	1977	Active	Sold	1999
An-26Sh	76 Yellow	5608	46th UAP	203rd TrAB	1977	Active	Active	-
An-26Sh	46 Red	5609	46th UAP	203rd TrAB	1977	Active	Active	-
An-26Sh	78 Yellow	5710	46th UAP	203rd TrAB	1977	Active	Active	-
An-26	35 Red	5801	?	-	1977	Active	Sold	2004
An-26	75 Blue	5901	223rd OSAP	-	1977	Active	Sold	2009
An-26	?	6102	?	-	1978	Active	Scrapped	2010
An-26Sh	48 Red	6107	46th UAP	-	1978	Active	Sold	2000
An-26	?	6209	?	-	1978	Active	Sold	2007
An-26	?	6401	?	-	1978	Active	Sold	2006
An-26KPA	35 Blue	6406	112th OSAE	456th TrAB	1978	Active	Active	-
An-26Sh	41 Red	6709	46th UAP	-	1978	Ground	Wfu	1999
An-26	08 Blue	6806	Saki	15th TrAB	1978	Active	Active	-
An-26KPA	57 Blue	6909	456th OSAP	456th TrAB	1978	Active	Active	-
An-26Sh	?	7005	46th UAP	-	1978	Active	Transferred	-
An-26	49 Blue	7509	112th OSAE	456th TrAB	1979	Active	Active	-
An-26	20 Blue	7705	223rd OSAP	-	1979	Active	Sold	1997
An-26	22 Blue	7910	223rd OSAP	-	1979	Active	Wfu	2006
An-26	30 Blue	?	223rd OSAP	_	1979	Active	Wfu	?
An-26	32 Blue	?	223rd OSAP	-	1979	Active	Wfu	?
An-26	35 Blue	?	223rd OSAP	-	1979	Active	Wfu	?
An-26	83 Blue	8010	255th OSAE	-	1979	Active	Wfu	2010
An-26	05 Yellow	8206	223rd OSAP	15 TrAB	1979	Active	Active	2008
An-26RT	20 Blue	8302	243rd OSAP	456th TrAB	1979	Active	Active	-
An-26	82 Blue	8402	10th OSAE	-	1979	Active	Transferred	2000
An-26	05 Blue	8405	?	-	1979	Active	StoRed	-
An-26	04 Blue	8501	255th OSAE	15 TrAB	1979	Active	Active	-
An-26	02 Yellow	8509	255th OSAE	15 TrAB	1979	Active	Active	-
An-26	44 Blue	9603	456th OSAP	456th TrAB	1980	Active	Active	-
An-26	19 Blue	9710	456th OSAP	-	1980	Active	Lost in war	2014
An-26	21 Blue	10209	25th VTAP	25th TrAB	1980	Active	Active	-
An-26B	56 Yellow	10403	46th UAP	203rd TrAB	1980	Active	Active	-
An-26	48 Blue	10502	223rd OSAP	456th TrAB	1980	Active	Active	-
An-26BUS	22 Blue	11607	243rd OSAP	456th TrAB	1981	Active	Active	-
An-26RT	27 Blue	11910	456th OSAP	456th TrAF	1982	Active	Active	-
An-26Sh	73 Yellow	?	46th UAP	203rd TrAB	?	Active	Stored	-
An-26Sh	34 Red	?	46th UAP	203rd TrAB	?	Active	Stored	-
An-26	?	?	46th UAP	203rd TrAB	?	?	Stored	-
An-26	?	?	46th UAP	203rd TrAB	?	?	Stored	-

Abbreviations
UAP = Training Aviation Regiment
OSAE = Independent Mixed Aviation Squadron
OSAP = Independent Mixed Aviation Regiment
VTAP = Military-Transport Aviation
TrAB = Training or Transport Aviation Brigade

An-72 Fleet (1992–2002): Cheburashka in Service with the UkrAF

Between 1986 and 1990, 96 An-72s were delivered to the Soviet Air Force, Border Patrol Force, Anti-Radiation Force, Navy and KGB. With its STOL (short take-off and landing) capability, the An-72 had been designed and manufactured by Antonov as a successor to the An-26 in service with the Soviet Armed Forces, but because of the Soviet Union's economic problems in the late 1980s and then its collapse, instead of almost 400 planned, only 56 examples, including an An-72S and an An-72PS, had been manufactured and delivered to the USSR Air Force by 1992. They served in two regiments and two squadrons.

In service with the Ukrainian Air Force

After Ukraine's independence, only three Soviet Air Force An-72s were inherited by the Ukrainian Air Force. The first of them was CCCP-72959 (c/n 36572092858), which had been manufactured in 1990 but had still not been delivered to its unit, the 978th OTAP. The aircraft, serial number 72959, was based at Zaporozhye and was occasionally operated by the Ukrainian Air Force. It had last been operational in 1999, but ran out of hours and was grounded in 2002. In 2004 it was overhauled and delivered to the Ukrainian Border Guard.

The aircraft was painted in white and light grey colours with a blue/yellow cheatline and red stripe on the fin, and it received a Border Guard badge and the bort number 15 Blue but without any titles. It was based at Odesa-Tsentralny. In 2008, its nose wheel collapsed after a hard landing at Kiev-Zhuliany. It was withdrawn from service and put up for sale by the Ukrainian government for €800,000. It was soon was sold, together with a former Ukrainian Border Guard An-72P, to Equatorial Guinea. It was restored and its cabin was reconfigured by No. 410 ARP at Kiev-Zhuliany between May and August 2009. Its first FCF after restoration was on 17 August 2009. It was entered service with Equatorial Guinea's Ministry of Defence as a presidential transport, with the registration 3C-CMN.

An-72s of the Kirvoske Test Centre

The USSR Air Force had three An-72s including an An-72PS with the 929th GLITS of the USSR Ministry of Defence, two of which were inherited by the Ukrainian Air Force.

The An-72PS was a maritime search and rescue aircraft under development for Soviet Naval Aviation. The sole example, with the serial number 08-01 (c/n 36572080775) and civil registration CCCP-71052, was sent to the 168th LIC of the 929th GLITS in Kirovskoye, on the Crimean peninsula. According to historical documents, it was a part of the Soviet Air Force inventory while it was intended to become a Soviet Navy aircraft. The aircraft was designed by a team at the Antonov Design Bureau led by O. J. Tkachenko to locate navy or civilian ships in distress or crashed aircraft and to

The Ukrainian State Aviation Research Centre operated An-72 with 02 Red (c/n 36572060645). This aircraft was used by the UkrAF to transfer ground crews and equipment for the MiG-29s of the Ukrainian Falcons demonstration team during air shows. It also displayed at various shows including RIAT 2000. When it had logged 1,946 flying hours and 1,936, it was put up for sale by SkyBirdHeli on 27 May 2006. It was sold to Asia Airways and received the registration EY-512 in October 2014. It is seen at Kirovskoye on 26 August 2000. *Sergey Popsuevich*

The former UkrAF An-72 UR-72959 while it was leased to Air Ukraine in the 1990s. It remained the property of the UKrAF until it was transferred on 22 May 2004 to the Ukrainian Border Guards, where it received the bort number 15 Blue. Due to the collapse of its nose wheel landing gear during a hard landing at Zhuliany, it was put in storage in 2008 and offered for sale by the Ukrainian government for €800,000 on 17 December 2008, being sold to Equatorial Guinea. *Sergey Popsuevich*

airdrop life rafts and other material, and then to assist rescue teams.

After the Soviet Union collapsed, the Crimean branch of the 929th GLITS or 168th State Flight Test Centre (168th GLIC) became part of the Ukrainian Ministry of Defence, to be used as the sole organisational and testing facility in Ukraine. The unit had experience in supporting the research and development of all types of aircraft equipment and weapons, including anti-ship armaments. It was later named the National Aeronautical Research and Test Centre of the Ukrainian Armed Forces, under the control of the Ukrainian Ministry of Defence, following Order No. 4 of Ukraine issued on 4 February 1992

The sole An-72PS remained at Kirovskoye after Ukraine's independence, received the bort number 15 Blue and did not fly again until it was put up for sale by SkyBirdHeli on 27 May 2006. It had only logged 430 hours and 273 cycles during the short period that it was airworthy between 1988 and 1992! It remained unsold when the Crimea crisis occurred in 2014. Following the occupation of Crimea by Russian armed forces, the test centre and all its stored aircraft, including the An-72PS, remained at the air base. Despite the evacuation of the stored MiG-29s in May 2014, 15 Blue stayed behind and has now been confiscated. Since March 2014, when the last 82 Ukrainian staff at the facility left for the Ukrainian mainland, the test centre has

This view at Kherson in the early 2000s shows the An-72V of the Ukrainian Ministry of Internal Affairs 02 Blue (c/n 36572096912). This aircraft was stored after its overhaul time was reached in 2004. It was overhauled and delivered to the Ukrainian National Guard in 2014. *Sergey Popsuevich*

been part of the Russian State Flight Test Centre, named after V. P. Chkalov,

When the Soviet Union collapsed, two other air force An-72s, 01 Red (c/n 36572030470) and 02 Red (c/n 36572060645), were under test by the 929th GLITS branches in Akhtubinsk (267th LIC) and Kirovskoye (168th LIC) respectively. The second aircraft was inherited by Ukraine and entered service with the air force. In 1998, 02 Red was chosen to transfer ground crew and aircraft ground equipment for the Ukrainian Falcons Aerobatic demonstration team, which was based at Kirvoske, and also for RIAT 1998. Subsequently, the paint scheme was changed from overall dark grey to a white fuselage with a dark blue tail and dark blue/yellow trim and 'Ukraine' titles.

In March 1998, during a Falcons practice flight, Col Sergei Dudkin crashed and died while landing in adverse weather conditions. Subsequently, another team pilot, Col Pavel Korolynov, was forced to quit for health reasons. These events led to cancellation of the team's display programme, although 02 Red, together with Tu-22M3 57 Red and Il-76MD UR-76413, participated at RIAT at RAF Fairford, UK, between 24 and 26 July 1998. Two years later, 02 Red attended RIAT 2000.

On 27 May 2006, 02 Red was offered for sale by SkyBirdHeli, at which point it had logged 1,946 hours and 1,936 cycles. It remained in storage at Kirovskoye until March 2014, when it was sold to Asia Airways. Its restoration took until October 2014. Finally, it was delivered with the civil registration EY-512 on 24 October 2014.

There was a fourth An-72 in Ukraine, which was a former Soviet Air Force aircraft but it never entered service with the Ukrainian Air Force. It was CCCP-72002 (c/n 36572010905), which was the first example to be serial-manufactured by KiAPO, and it had served in the USSR Air Force between 1986 and 1988. During its service it was used for test and evaluation at the 8th State Red Banner Scientific Research Institute (later 929th GLITS). It was later returned to Gostomel and became part of the Antonov Design Bureau inventory, again to be used for test purposes.

In 1989, CCCP-72002 was painted in an overall grey colour scheme and received the bort number 11 Red. After the collapse of the Soviet Union it remained with Antonov until it was sold to an Estonian airline named Enimex and registered ES-NOP. It crashed while attempting to land at Wamena, Indonesia, on 21 April 2002. No one was killed but the aircraft was written off.

Despite Ukraine's success in selling several An-74s to military and civil customers across the world after the Soviet Union collapsed, no new An-72s were manufactured for the Ukrainian Air Force to be used as replacements for the ageing fleet of An-26s, despite what had been planned in the 1970s! Today, two of the three UkrAF An-72s have been sold and the last unsold example has been confiscated by the Russian occupiers in Crimea.

Il-62 Fleet (1992–2014): Presidential Jetliners

The Ukrainian Government has used various jetliners for the VIP flights of Ukraine's presidents; among them two Il-62Ms that were used for more than two decades to transport presidents and other high-ranking officials on domestic and international flights. These were two of the seven Il-62s inherited by the Ukrainian Air Force and Navy. They were flown by Ukrainian Air Force crew members, although they were operated by Ukraine Air Enterprise since 1995. The two Il-62Ms UR-86527 and UR-86528 are now grounded and have been replaced by Airbus A319115X (ACJ319) UR-ABA.

In the Ukrainian Air Force

After Ukraine's independence all seven Soviet Navy Il-62s were inherited and inducted into service with the newly formed Ukrainian Air Force. The Il-62Ms, which had been manufactured in 1980 and 1981 and had been overhauled between 1989 and 1992, were in a good enough condition to be used by the president and other government authorities.

Based in Simferopol with new Ukrainian registrations, UR-86528 (c/n 4038111) and UR-86529 (c/n 4038625) were quickly used for commercial flights after being leased to Atlant-SV in September 1992, while UR-86527 (c/n 4037758) remained in the air force and was used for long-range presidential flights. Three years later, in 1995, Ukraine Air Enterprise (Ukraina Aviapredpriatie) was established to operate UR-86527 on behalf of the Ukrainian government.

The other Il-62s, ex-CCCP-86648, ex-CCCP-86612, ex-CCCP-86451 and ex-CCCP-86666 which now had become UR-86648, UR-86612, UR-86451 and CCCP-86666 respectively, remained airworthy until they were

The Ukrainian President Viktor Yanukovych's motorcade departs the flight line on 11 April 2010 at Joint Base Andrews on his way to the Nuclear Security Summit hosted by President Barack Obama in Washington, DC. He used Il-62M UR-86528 of the Ministry of Interior registration for this trip. *USAF*

Ukrainian Ministry of Interior Il-62M UR-86528 at Zhukovsky airport during MAKS-2007 when the Ukrainian president travelled there on 21 August 2007. *Sergey Popsuevich*

withdrawn from service one by one by 1997. The first aircraft, UR-86648, which was Soviet Premier Leonid Brezhnev's personal aircraft in the Soviet era, remained airworthy with the UkrAF until 1996 but was rarely flown. It was later stored at Kulbakino and then scrapped in the second half of 2002.

Il-62TS UR-86612 registration was used as the personal VIP aircraft of the Ukrainian defence minister Valeri Shmarov until 1996, when the government could no longer afford its operating costs. It was later leased to Atlant-SV and based at Simferopol until it ran out of hours in 2001. Then it was withdrawn from use and stored at Kulbakino until it was put up for sale in 2010. It was transferred by road to Vasilkov in October 2010 to be displayed at a privately owned museum in the south of Kiev.

UR-86451 also remained in service but was not flown regularly until it was leased to Atlant-SV in September 1996. It ran out of hours in 1997 and was put in storage, being scrapped at Kulbakino in 2010. The last Il-62, which was UR-86666, the oldest Il-62 in Ukraine as it was manufactured in 1967, remained in service with the UkrAF until 1993. It was put into storage and had been scrapped at Kulbakino by 1999.

It was not only the air force that withdrew its Il-62s from service but also the number of civilian Il-62s in Ukraine was reduced from 11 to only three between 1993 and 2006.

Retirement of the last Il-62Ms

While operated by Ukraine Air Enterprise, UR-86527 and UR-86528 were overhauled by NARP in 2001 and 2003 respectively to remain in service as the presidential aircraft. Their last overhauls kept them in service until 18 December 2014 and 4 February 2015 respectively.

Because of the high maintenance and operation costs of the Il-62Ms, the Ukrainian government leased

The former Soviet Navy's Il-62M CCCP-86529 was in service with the 278th OTAE of the 33rd TsBP i PLS at Nikolayev-Kulbakino until 1992 when the squadron and the training centre became subordinate to the UkrAF. This aircraft was leased from the UkrAF to Atlant and received the civil registration UR-86529 in 1992. This aircraft remained airworthy until 1995, when it was withdrawn from use. It was put on sale in 2005 by the Ukrainian privatisation agency when it had 5,678 flying hours and 1,804 cycles on its airframe but remains unsold to the present day. *Sergey Popsuevich*

and tested various aircraft for presidential flights, including a four-year-old Airbus A319-133XCJ, F-GSVU, which was leased from Aero Services Executive on 13 January 2004 to be used for short-range domestic and international presidential flights. Not only the Airbus A319 but also Ukrainian-built aircraft such as An-74TK-300Ds and An-140K were used. The An-74TK-300Ds were too small and neither the president nor the prime minister, nor even the king of Sweden, who had evaluated the type as a potential personal transport, were interested in flying in them.

F-GSVU was in service until the Ukrainian Government was faced with the Orange Revolution and the aircraft was returned to France, upon which President Yushchenko moved to the Il-62. However, the government later procured a brand new Airbus A319-115X(CJ) from Jet Alliance in November 2007. The acquisition of the new VIP aircraft had been approved by the Ukrainian cabinet according to Decree No. 728. $50 million was specified for the aircraft, which was finally delivered to Ukraine Air Enterprise as UR-ABA on 12 January 2008.

The small A319, with the capability to carry ten to 39 passengers in various configurations, had both limited cabin space and a limited range in comparison with the Il-62M, which was able to carry 60–70 passengers with a 13,000km maximum range. For example, President Viktor Yanukovych flew directly from Kiev to Washington on board one of the two Il-62Ms during his official visit to the US between 10 and 13 October 2003.

On 2 October 2008, when President Yushchenko was flying in UkrAF Tu-134 UR-65718 from Boryspil to Lviv to take part in an economic summit, an engine failed and it performed an emergency landing at Boryspil. A standby Il-62M, UR-86528, was quickly prepared as a replacement. The aircraft had been intended to be used by the Ukrainian PM, Yulia Tymoshenko, for her flight to Moscow to negotiate a gas deal that day. Also, the second Il-62M, UR-86527, had flown to Sweden to bring the country's king to the summit.

In early 2010, the Ukrainian government ordered two Airbus A340-542s as successors but the deal was quickly cancelled, and it was decided to keep the Il-62Ms in service after the NARP won a government $0.56 million tender for their maintenance and overhaul on 19 April 2011.

UkrAF Il-62TS 86612 was the personal aircraft of the Ukrainian defence minister Valeri Shmarov for a short time. In 1996 it was leased to Atlant-SV and based at Simferopol until it ran out of hours. It was transferred from Kulbakino to Kiev in 2010 and then to the north of the Vasilkov Air Base in 2011 after a member of the public purchased it to put in his garden. Here it is being disassembled prior to relocation from Nikolayev to Kiev. ***Alexander Cheban via Dmitry S.***

After the 2014 Ukrainian revolution, while UR-86527 and UR-86528 still had time left until their next overhaul, they were withdrawn from service. After the overthrow of the Ukrainian President, Viktor Yanukovych, the Ukrainian Ministry of Defence could not afford the monthly costs of 7,451.5 UAH per aircraft just to keep them airworthy. After their withdrawal from service, the Ministry of Defence delivered both aircraft to the Ukrainian Ministry of Education and Science to be used for training aerospace engineering students, probably at the university in Kharkiv. One of President Yanukovych's last flights in an Il-62M was in UR-86528, which he used for a trip to Zurich between 22 and 24 January 2014.

Today, Ukraine Air Enterprise has a fleet of just three aircraft for presidential flights and those of other government authorities. One is UR-ABA while the others are An-74TK-300D UR-AWB, made in

Ukrainian Air Force Il-62s

Serial Number	Construction Number	Last operator before being grounded/stored	Current registration/ serial number	Year of manufacture	Status in 1992	Current Status	Year of Retirement/ wfu/Sale
86666	60201	Ukrainian Air Force	UR-86666	1967	Airworthy	Scrapped	1998
86648	00605	Ukrainian Air Force	UR-86648	1970	?	Scrapped	2002
86612	41804	Ukrainian Air Force	UR-86612	1975	Airworthy	For sale	2010
86451	4521152	Atlant-SV	UR-86451	1977	Airworthy	Scrapped	2010
86527	4037758	Ukraine Air Enterprise	UR-86527	1980	Airworthy	Stored	2014
86528	4038111	Ukraine Air Enterprise	UR-86528	1981	Airworthy	Stored	2014
86529	4038625	Atlant-SV	UR-86529	1981	Airworthy	For sale	2005

Il-62TS 86612 at Nikolayev-Kulbakino before being transferred by road to Kiev in 2009. *Alexander Cheban via Dmitry S.*

2001, and An-148-100B UR-UKR, built in 2010. There are no long-range aircraft in service with the air force or Ukraine Air Enterprise to transport the Ukrainian presidents, although Ukraine International Airlines' Boeing 767-322/33A (ER)s can be chartered as a temporary solution until a new long-range VIP aircraft is procured in the future.

Il-76 Fleet (1992–today): The Heavyweight Champions

In the early 1990s the Ukrainian Air Force was the largest military operator of the Ilyushin Il-76 after the Russian Air Force, but it now has one of the smallest (but still strategic) fleets among the world's air forces. The Il-76 played the role of the main source of income for the Ukrainian Defence Ministry and Armed Forces in the early 1990s, and now they are the sole heavyweight air transport asset in the air force. In 2019, the UKrAF maintains a small fleet of eight airworthy Il-76MDs, despite high operation and maintenance costs and the difficulties in obtaining spare parts.

The UkrAF's Il-76MD 76777 was leased to ATI Airlines in 1998 and operated by it until 2002. The 25th TrAB began operating it again in 2006. It was shot down by pro-Russian Novorossiya separatist forces on a flight from Melitopol to Luhansk on 14 June 2014. *Sergey Popsuevich*

Background

The first production Il-76 built in Tashkent was CCCP-76500 (c/n 033401016), which first flew on 8 May 1973. This example later entered service with the 339th Military-Transport Aviation Regiment (VTAP), which became the first operator of the Il-76 in the Soviet Air Force in May 1974. Later, the 374th VTAP, which became subordinate to the 610th Centre for Combat Employment and Retraining of Personnel VTA in 1975, was equipped with the Il-76. The unit trained the first group of 339th VTAP aircrews at Ivanovo.

By the end of 1991, the Soviet Air Force had 14 of its transport regiments equipped with 456 Il-76s. Not only was the type in service with the Military Transport Aviation Regiments and Guards Military Transport Aviation Regiments, the Soviet Air Force also had Il-76s operating with non-transport regiments such as the 610th TSBPPLS' squadrons at Ivanovo and also the 929th GLITS (929th order of Lenin Red Banner State Flight-Test Centre Defence Ministry USSR) and 409th APSZ (409th Aviation Regiment of tanker aircraft), which increased the total number of Il-76s in the force to 470 by 1991.

The Soviet Air Force's Il-76s played a key role in the Afghanistan war, carrying troops and their supplies as well as military equipment to airstrips and airfields everywhere in the country. Between December 1979 and the withdrawal of the last Soviet troops from Afghanistan in August 1992, Il-76s transported 700,000 tons and 233,500 troops, which was 74% and 89% of total amount of supplies and troops carried forward and back from Afghanistan during the war, while only two Il-76s were lost. This was only achieved via extensive training of the VTA regiments' personnel, including their participation in large-scale exercises, or air exercises of the Soviet Air Force.

In March 1979, during Exercise Voostook 79 (East 79), one Military-Transport Aviation Division airlifted two motorised infantry divisions of the Soviet Army a distance of 6,500km, close to the border with China. During the anti-NATO exercise West 81, 280 aircraft took part, of which 95 were Il-76s! The Il-76s also took part in Exercise Brotherhood in Arms 80, Soyuz 81 (Union 81), and Soyuz 83 (Union 83).

The aircraft could carry up to 145 soldiers with personal weapons in single-deck cabin configuration. In 1986, the Soviet Air Force studied a mass airdrop and parachute jump of 138 pieces of equipment and 5,080 paratroopers from 125 Il-76s simultaneously in combat. The Soviet AF's Il-76s not only participated in the Afghanistan war but were also used during the deployment of Soviet military advisers, troops and their military equipment to African countries such as Angola and Ethiopia. They took part in dozens of humanitarian aid missions such as the evacuation of Soviet citizens after the Chernobyl nuclear plant accident in 1988, and later assisted victims of the catastrophic earthquake in Armenia, during which 312 Il-76s were involved.

Ukrainian inheritance

After the USSR's collapse, the Il-76 regiments were inherited by three countries: Russia, Ukraine and Belarus. Among them, six VTA regiments that were subordinate to the 6th Guards Military-Transport Aviation Division and 7th Military-Transport Aviation Division were inherited by Ukraine. The units were the 37th VTAP at Artsyz, which had 30 aircraft in 1991; the 338th VTAP at Zaporozhye, with 28 aircraft in 1991; the 363rd VTAP at Krivoi Rog with 30 Il-76s in 1991; the 25th GvVTAP at Melitopol with 31 Il-76s in 1991; the 175th VTAP at Melitopol with 30 Il-76s in 1991; and the 369th VTAP at Dhanskoy with 31 aircraft in 1991.

Many sources suggest that Ukraine inherited 180 Il-76s in service with all the six above-mentioned VTA regiments, but further investigation by the author shows that the number in service with each unit was different when they became part of the Ukrainian Air Force in January 1992. Some had already been transferred to other units, including the 610th TSBPPLS at Ivanovo, while others were taken up by the Russian Air Force while on temporary deployment to East Germany or under overhaul in Russia's mainland.

According to the existing documents as well as reports by Ukrainian and Russian spotters in the early 1990s, in total 162 ex-Soviet Air Force Il-76s entered Ukrainian Air Force service. Among them, 26 were in service with the 37th VTAP, 25 in the 338th VTAP, 31 in the 363rd VTAP, 20 in the 25th GvVTAP, 33 in the 175th VTAP, 25 in the 369th VTAP, one in service with the 409th APSZ (409th Aviation Regiment of tanker aircraft) and one further Il-76 was not in service with any Soviet Air Force unit on Ukrainian territory.

For months the personnel of the regiments had not been paid due to the weak economy and the financial problems of the USSR before its collapse, and now their commanders had promised them that if they served in the Ukrainian Air Force they would have the chance to make money from commercial flights with the Il-76s of their units. This encouraged many aircrew and ground crew to stay in Ukraine, taking the oath and becoming a member of the UKrAF in January 1992.

UkrAF's Il-76MDs were frequent visitors to the Royal International Air Tattoos at RAF Fairford as they were carrying the ground equipment and personnel for the UkrAF's fighter jets participating in the 1990s. Here UR-78820 with the call sign UTF76 is landing in RAF Fairford on 18 July 1996. *Chris Chennel*

Making money for the Air Force

Soon after Ukraine's independence and the creation of the air force, Ukrainian President Leonid Kravchuk signed a decree to authorise the operation of VTA assets for the transportation of goods and cargo inside Ukraine's territory. However, it later became clear that using Il-76s on domestic flights was economically disadvantageous and could not compensate for the huge expenses of each of the transport regiments. Soon the military aviators and commanders of the regiments developed an economically viable business plan to use air force military transport aircraft to form cargo airlines for carrying cargo all over the world. This later led to the establishment of several small and large air cargo companies, all authorised by the Ministry of Defence and even directly under the control of the transport regiments.

In 1992, among the inherited 162 Il-76s, 104 were fully mission capable or operational, while the rest were stored or grounded, the latter mostly the early variants including Il-76s (the basic variant model without suffix) and Il-76Ms manufactured in the late 1970s and the first half of the 1980s. They had been mostly overhauled in the Soviet era, but most of them had logged many flying hours and reached their MTBO even before their calendar time. Almost 17 of them were brought out of reserve status at Melitopol and other air bases and

UkrAF Il-76MD UR-76700 at RAF Brize Norton, UK, on 6 September 1996. *Chris Chennel*

Il-76MD UR-76697 of UkrAF's 25th VTAP was used to transfer ground equipment for Su-27s from Mirgorod to Fairford in the UK for the Royal International Air Tattoo in July 1999. *Chris Chennel*

were then withdrawn from service between 1999 and 2014. Nearly all of them were scrapped after no customer could be found to buy them.

Among the airworthy aircraft, the ones that had been manufactured in the second half of the 1980s and still had flying hours and cycles on their airframes and engines were chosen for the government and Ministry of Defence programme to be chartered or leased by Ukrainian cargo airlines under the authorisation of the air force commanders.

In late 1992, three Il-76s, which were UR-76437 from the 37th VTAP, UR-86903 from the 338th VTAP, and UR-78820 from the 175th VTAP, were leased to Atlant-SV and Hungarian–Ukrainian Heavylift Co. Ltd. Atlant-SV was established by late 1991 under the name Atlant Aviation; it was soon renamed as the Atlant-SV Aircompany in 1992 and became the largest Ukrainian paramilitary operator of the Il-76.

Based at Simferopol, Atlant-SV operated almost 44 air force Il-76MDs for its scheduled and charter cargo servicers from Ukraine to Russia and many other European destinations until 1997, when it was disbanded. Atlant-SV had a sister company, the Russian government-owned Atlant-Soyuz Airlines, which was based in Moscow and operated at least nine Il-76MDs of the Ukrainian Air Force on lease.

In the years between 1992 and 2000, almost 135 Il-76s of the UkrAF were leased to 22 Ukrainian airlines or air cargo companies, which were:

- **Aeronavigation and Transport Agency of the Ukraine (ANTAU)** operated eight Il-76MDs of the 25th GvVTAP and 175th VTAP from Melitopol, which were leased to South African Airways between 1992 and 1997
- **Air Service Ukraine** with the IATA code 'CH', which later became Ukraine Airservice Airlines with the code '9G', was among the airlines under UkrAF management with a hub in Kiev. It operated 15 air force Il-76s between 1991 and 2001 when it was disbanded
- **Air Ukraine Cargo** (Grooozovyye Avialinii Ukrainy) was another airline under UkrAF control formed at Krivoi Rog. It operated nine Il-76s of the UkrAF's 363rd VTAP until its disbandment in 1998
- **ATI Airlines** leased 13 air force Il-76s between 1996 and 2002
- **Atlant-SV**, which is also mentioned above, became the largest operator of the UkrAF's Il-76s. It operated 44 examples between 1992 and 1997 until ceasing its operations, due a decision taken by the UkrAF C-in-C
- **Avilpond TAV** with a hub in Simferopol, Feodosiya, in the Crimea peninsula, operated two UkrAF Il-76MDs between 1995 and 1998
- **Azov-Avia aircompany** operated four Il-76s of the 25th GvVTAP between 1996 and 1999
- **Belbek 5P** at Sevastopol operated three Il-76s in 1995 and 1996
- **BSL Airlines** at Kiev operated nine demilitarised Il-78s and one Il-76MD of the 409th APSZ between 1994 and 1998
- **Busol Airline**, also based at Kiev, operated eight 409 APSZ Il-78s, among them three were fully converted into Il-76MDs and flown until the airline's disbandment in 1998

- **Hoseba SIC** based at Kiev-Gostomel operated six Il-76MDs of the 338th VTAP between 1994 and 1998

- **Khors Aircompany** leased 17 Il-76s and 15 are believed to have belonged to the UkrAF between 1993 and 1997

- **Liana Aircompany** based at Krivoi Rog was under the supervision of the 363rd VTAP and used to operate six of the regiment's Il-76MDs between 1992 and 1997

- **Poles'ye Air Transport** based at Zhitomyr leased five Il-76MDs of the 25th GvVTAP in 1996 and 1997

- **Ukrainian Cargo Airways** or the Ukrainian Air Transport Company, which had been established in 1993, became the sole airline or cargo company under the supervision of the Ministry of Defence to operate Il-76s for cargo flights within the EU, Africa and Asia. This airline operated 22 air force Il-76MDs and three Il-78s, with nine airframes among them converted into the Il-76TD. The airline was added to the EU banned list five times on 11 April 2008, 24 July 2008, 14 November 2008, 8 April 2009 and 14 July 2009. The airline's Il-76s were mostly withdrawn from use at Boryspil and Zaporozhye after they reached their MTBO or because of a lack of availability of spare parts for the examples that still had time and cycles left before their next overhaul between 2008 and 2012.

- **Veteran Airlines** based at Dhanskoy was established in 1992. The airline started to lease the UkrAF's 338th VTAP Il-76MDs in 1994; in the same year the 369th VTAP was disbanded and 14 Il-76MDs of the unit were operated by Veteran between 1995 and 1999. The airline operated 17 Il-76s of the air force including one 25th GvVTAP example

UkrAF Il-76MD UR-76413 arriving for RIAT97 at RAF Fairford on 16 July 1997. *Chris Chennel*

- **Volare Aviation Enterprise Joint-Stock Company** was the second airline of the 363rd VTAP. It began to operate one of the regiment's Il-76MDs, registered UR-76620, in 1995, followed by a second aircraft, UR-76576, in 1996. The airline later operated one more ex-363rd VTAP Il-76MD and three ex-369th VTAP Il-76MDs, some of which were converted into Il-76TDs between 1999 and 2002

- **Yuzhmashavia** was formed by Yuzhny mashinostroitel'ny zavod/Southern Engineering Plant in 1985. It operated three UkrAF Il-76MDs. The first was the 363rd VTAP's UR-78786 in 1996, which was later converted into Il-76TD and remains in the airline's service today. The second aircraft was the 338th VTAP's UR-78756, which was operated for a few months in 1997 until it was returned to UCA in 1998. The third aircraft was UR-78785 from the 363rd VTAP, which was procured from the Ministry of Defence, then converted into Il-76TD and is still in service with the airline

UR-76624, an Il-76MD of the 25th GvVTAP, at RAF Lyneham on 23 May 1998. This aircraft was put in storage in 2002 and retired from service at Zaporozhye International Airport few years later. *Chris Chennel*

The UkrAF's Il-76MD 76680 has been in storage at Melitopol since 2002. The aircraft was leased to Bosul Airlines, as can be seen here at Boryspil on 14 October 1994. *Sergey Popsuevich*

- In 1993, an airline **(Air Ukraine [Avialinh Ukrainy]),** leased an Il-76MD, which was UR-76688, from the 25th GvVTAP for the first time. **Air Ukraine** was a Ukrainian flag carrier that leased 11 Il-76MDs from the air force between 1993 and 1998. The freighters were operated by Boryspil's United Flight Detachment based at Kiev-Boryspil and also by L'vov Air Enterprise

- **ECO Patrol environmental organisation** (Mahloye predpriyahtiye Ekopatrool'/Ecopatrol Small Enterprise) operated three Il-76MDs of the 37th VTAP and 25th GvVTAP in the years between 1993 and 1999. While its base was Zaporozhye, its Il-76MDs UR-76437, UR-76438 and UR-78821, which had been leased since 1993 and 1997, were based in Melitopol

- Formed by United Energy Systems of Ukraine/Yedini Energetitsni Sistemi Ukrainy, **UES-Avia**, which was based at Dnepropetrovsk, leased Il-76MD UR-78734 for a short while in 1996

- In 1998, **Yuzhnoe State Air**, a small company, was re-established at Kirvoi Rog and operated the same Il-76MD, UR-78734, that UES-Avia operated in 1996, which was finally procured by the airline

Downsized Il-76 fleet

In 1994–99, the number of air force personnel was reduced from 100,000 to 60,000, in the course of which 22 regiments were disbanded. Disbandment of UkrAF units started in 1994 and three Il-76 regiments went that year. They were the 175th VTAP at Melitopol and 369th VTAP at Dhanskoy, both subordinate to the 7th VTAD, as well as the 37th VTAP at Artsyz subordinate to the 6th GvVTAD. In that year, the units had nine, two and six airworthy Il-76s respectively.

With the disbandment of the 37th VTAP, among its six Il-76s that were still airworthy and in service with the UkrAF one remained at Artsyz, one joined the 25th GvVTAP at Melitopol, two entered service with the 363rd VTAP in Krivoi Rog, one was leased to Atlant-SV and the status of the sixth aircraft is unknown. Ownership of the unit's other Il-76s, which had already been leased to different airlines, was shared between the 25th GvVTAP and 338th VTAP at Melitopol and Zaporozhye respectively.

After the disbandment of the 175th VTAP, all its aircraft were absorbed by the 25th GvVTAP, including seven of its nine airworthy Il-76s that were still in military use, while the 369th VTAP's Il-76s were absorbed by the 25th GvVTAP and 338th VTAP. Due to

This former Melitopol-based Il-76MD with c/n 0053462872 was in service with the UkrAF until it was leased to Khors Air as UR-76651 in 1995. It was eventually sold to Angola as D2-FCN in 2001 to be used in its air force. *Sergey Popsuevich*

the disbandment of the above-mentioned units in 1993, the Ukrainian Air Force had leased 43 of its Il-76s to airlines, mostly Ukrainian, including paramilitary airlines. The number of leased Il-76s surged to 67 and then 91 in 1994 and 1995 respectively, and then 108 and 111 in 1996 and 1997.

Three years later, the 338th VTAP was disbanded at Zaporozhye and its 25 Il-76s became part of the 25th GvVTAP's inventory in 1997. At the time, the unit had only one airworthy Il-76MD in military use, while six more that were still in service with the air force had been kept in reserve condition or had been stored. Also, 12 other of the unit's Il-76MDs had been leased to various airlines.

The huge fleet of UkrAF Il-76s and the An-12s was the main source of income for the country's Ministry of Defence and even its Transport Aviation regiments, permitting them to be compensated for a huge portion of the Il-76's costs including their operation, maintenance and even overhaul. However, the days of Il-76 commercial flights were nearing their end by the end of the 1990s, firstly because of the surge in fuel prices and secondly due to the arrival of the overhaul deadline of the transports, which were mostly still the property of the air force.

In 1997, the Ukrainian Aviation Transport Company was formed under the direct orders of the UkrAF's commander in order to return all 111 Il-76s leased to various airlines to Ministry of Defence control. This was to prevent the harmful consequences of distributing the aircraft to several paramilitary airlines and foreign companies. On 3 November 1997, the Cabinet of Ministers approved the establishment of Ukrainian Cargo Airways (UCA), a state-owned company operating charter passenger and cargo services as well as providing aircraft overhaul, leasing and sale services derived from the air force inventory.

An Il-76MD of the UkrAF with the serial number 78752 seen on 15 October 1996 while leased to Hoseba at Gostomel. It has been stored at Melitopol since 2007. *Sergey Popsuevich*

The number of leased air force Il-76s dropped from 94 in 1998 to 71 in 1999 and then 49 in 2000 as most aircraft reached their MTBO. Subsequently, UCA, which had already started to provide surplus Il-76s for sale, sold one Il-76 in 1997, two in 1998, eight in 1999 and three in 2000. In 2001, the number of leased Il-76s dropped to 39, and subsequently 34 aircraft were put on sale by the Ukrainian privatisation agency, of which six were sold in that year. This sharp rise in the number of the Il-76s for sale was a consequence of the ratification, issuance and then adoption of ICAO Stage 3 noise regulations in Europe in 2000 and 2002.

In 2001, the 363rd VTAP was disbanded when it had 26 Il-76s, although none were in military use. Soon after disbandment its aircraft were assigned to the 25th GvVTAP at Melitopol, which was later reorganised as the 25th TrAB (Training Aviation Brigade). While six of its Il-76s had been leased to various airlines through UCA, 14 others were put up for sale, from which three were sold in 2001; two other airframes had been sold in previous years.

UkrAF Il-76MD 76748 on 10 October 1995 when it was leased to Air Ukraine Cargo at Boryspil. It was demilitarised and sold to Equatorial Cargo as 3C-HAV in 2002 and finally ended up in service with the Equatorial Guinea government as 3C-LGF in 2006. *Sergey Popsuevich*

This Il-76MD with civil registration UR-UCR and Ukraine Cargo Airways colour scheme was in service with the UkrAF's 369th VTAP as UR-76728 but was later leased to Veteran in 1994. In 1998 it was delivered to Ukraine Cargo Airways and then leased to the United Nations in 2001. It is now in storage at Zaporozhye International Airport. It is seen during a demonstration of airdropping humanitarian cargo without a parachute at Chauda gunnery range at Crimea on 14 March 2000 while UN representatives were present. *Sergey Popsuevich*

Serving the Blue Helmets

In the early 1990s, the Ukrainian VTA's aviators developed an economically viable business plan to form a quick response brigade for the UN that consisted of Ukrainian paratroopers that could be deployed to any battle zone in the world for peacekeeping missions in the shortest time using the UkrAF's Il-76s. The Ukrainian government and the UN authorities rejected the proposal. Instead, the Ukrainian Army peacekeeping units acted in collaboration with peacekeeping troops of other nations and the UkrAF's Il-76s were directly and indirectly chartered by the UN to be deployed in various African countries.

In the years between 1992 and 1995, almost 12 Il-76MDs of the UkrAF, mostly from the 25th GvVTAP, were leased to the UN for various periods via paramilitary airlines, while the Ukrainian peacekeepers were deployed on board Il-76s still in military service. For the first time, when Ukrainian troops as part of the former Soviet Armed Forces' contingent, participated in UNPROFOR (United Nations Protection Force) in 1992, the Il-76s of the newly formed air force were used to airlift them and their equipment to Sarajevo, Yugoslavia, on 31 July 1992. This happened after the Supreme Council of Ukraine (Verkhovna Rada) adopted a resolution committing the Ukrainian Armed Forces to UN peacekeeping missions.

During the peacekeeping mission, UkrAF Il-76MDs were used to airlift the 240th Separate Special Battalion (UKRBAT-1), which had been formed following the orders of the Ukrainian Minister of Defence, Konstyantyn Morozov. Soon after it arrived in Sarajevo, the battalion's artillery complex was caught in the middle of a mortar fight between Bosnian Serbs and Bosnian Muslims that killed one soldier and wounded six others. From 5 June 1992, UNPROFOR was responsible for the

With a pair of Su-27s of the 831st BrTA flying on its wing, this Il-76MD of the 25th TrAB, serial number 76732, flew over Kiev during the Independence Day parade of 2008. The aircraft was later stored at Melitopol. It has the large title Ukraine North Pole 2000 written on its front fuselage. *Sergey Popsuevich*

This former 338th VTAP Il-76MD of the UkrAF serialled 76397 was leased to Khors Air while it was still based at Zaporozhye in 1994. It was leased to Ukraine Cargo Airways as UR-UCV in 2001 and then leased to the United Nations, remaining airworthy for a few more years. It is seen at Boryspil on 14 August 2003. *Sergey Popsuevich*

protection of Sarajevo airport as mandated by Resolution 758 for humanitarian purposes and it would run a security corridor for aid convoys between the airport and the city.

After the rise of tension between the Serbs and NATO as a consequence of NATO air raids against the Bosnian Serb Army, the NATO countries preferred to reduce and in some periods stop flights to Sarajevo airport due to the risk of being shot down. Therefore, the UKrAF Il-76s were used mainly for logistical support of UN troops from early 1995. Not only were they carrying troops and delivering equipment, the Il-76s were also used to transport humanitarian aid, medicines, and even governmental delegations. In some cases, even the Il-76s flew in convoys, with seven landing one after the other at Sarajevo airport.

Under the command of those who had experienced flying in the most dangerous areas and conditions in Afghanistan during the war in the 1980s, the UkrAF's Il-76MDs became the most reliable air transport assets of the UN for logistical support of UNPROFOR in Bosnia. Peacekeepers of the 60th and 240th Separate Special Battalions of the Ukrainian Army were picked up from Nikolayev in 25th GvVTAP and 363rd VTAP Il-76s flying from Melitopol and Krivoi Rog. After the flight from Nikolayev, the Il-76s headed towards Ancona, Italy, where NATO had set up a peacekeepers' air base. The next destination was Sarajevo. Unlike the NATO transport aircraft, which were always escorted in Bosnian airspace to protect them from Yugoslav Air Force MiG-29s, the UKrAF Il-76s had no such assistance. The flights to Bosnia and Herzegovina were not always without incident: in September 1994, the fuselage of a 363rd VTAP Il-76MD was pierced by 26 large-calibre cannon rounds fired from a heavy machine gun while it was approaching Sarajevo airport. It then landed safely.

On 15 December 1995, the UN officially invited Ukraine to IFOR operations in Bosnia and Herzegovina in accordance with UN Security Council Resolution No. 1031, which was adopted unanimously on 15 December 1995. The resolution transferred authority from the United Nations Protection Force (UNPROFOR) to the multi-national Implementation Force (IFOR) for implementation of a peace agreement between Bosnia and Herzegovina, Croatia, and the Federal Republic of Yugoslavia. Following the resolution, the Ukrainian Ministry of Foreign Affairs and Ministry of Defence prepared a proposal showing details of the Ukrainian peacekeepers' partnership in IFOR missions, including the allocation of ten UkrAF Il-76MDs to the missions. On 29 December 1995, the Ukraine Cabinet of Ministers accepted the proposal.

Later, after the establishment of Ukrainian Cargo Airways, the company took responsibility for leasing air force aircraft to the UN. However, several times active UKrAF Il-76s were used on UN humanitarian and

The former Melitopol-based UkrAF Il-76MD UR-76681 was leased to Belbek 5P in 1995, then to ATI Airlines in 1996. It was returned to the UkrAF in 1998, retired from service in 2004 and sold. It is seen at Boryspil on 23 March 2005. *Sergey Popsuevich*

During Exercise Ukraine North Pole 2000, 76732 became the first UkrAF aircraft to fly to the North Pole. To mark this occasion, this large title was written on its front fuselage. It is now stored at Melitopol waiting for a budget for its restoration and overhaul. *Alexander Golz*

peacekeeping missions with air force serial numbers and markings. The 25th GvVTAP was the main air force operator and mainly its Il-76s were used. Between 1992 and 2001, the 25th GvVTAP's Il-76s transported no fewer than 10,000 Ukrainian peacekeepers.

In the 2000s, the UkrAF's Il-76s in service with Ukrainian Cargo Airways were used by Ukrainian peacekeepers in the Middle East. In one case, on 7 August 2003, an Il-76MD was used to transport 69 Ukrainian peacekeepers from Boryspil to Kuwait, from where they were later deployed to Iraq.

The participation of UkrAF Il-76s in UN peacekeeping missions continues and the airlifters are used to deploy Ukrainian peacekeepers and their equipment to African countries. For example, in May 2013, an Il-76MD was used to transfer equipment and spare parts for the 56th Helicopter Detachment of the Ukrainian Armed Forces during UN peacekeeping missions in African countries.

The Polar expeditions

In April 2000, the 25th GvVTAP Il-76MD serialled 76732 (c/n 0073476296) was the first UkrAF aircraft ever to fly to the North Pole. This first Ukrainian Arctic expedition occurred during the exercise Ukraine North Pole 2000. On 11 April 2000, this aircraft, flown by chief pilot Col Konstantin Shusharina and five other crew members, flew to the North Pole from Kiev via two refuelling stops at Moscow and then Khatanga for a parachute jump by 22nd Ukrainian Army Parachutists in -50°C temperatures with 8m/s to 10m/s Arctic winds on the ice surface. During the exercise, four other Ukrainian aircraft, which were a Ukrainian Association for the Support of the Defence (TSOU) An-28, a UkrAF An-26 and two Mi-8s, participated.

Nine years after the UkrAF's Arctic debut in 2000, during a Danish–Ukrainian operation named 'Cossacks on ice', new generations of Il-76 pilots and crewmembers showed their capabilities after flying 2,400km from Ukraine to the Pole. This operation was the beginning of joint Danish–Ukrainian Arctic operations, which were repeated in following years. During the operation, USAF and Royal Danish Air Force C-130s together with an UkrAF Il-76MD serialled 78820 (c/n 0093496907) transported about 140,000 gallons of fuel and 17 tons of supplies from Thule Air Base to Station Nord, which is 600 miles away in Greenland, on 26 March 2009. The Ukrainian Ministry of Defence was paid $110,000 by the Danish government for the service, which the UkrAF provided using 78820, an aircraft with the ability to carry 40 tons of fuel in one flight with an operation cost equal with five C-130 sorties each able to carry maximum of 15 tons of fuel in one flight. The money was used to restore a UkrAF An-26 and to overhaul an Il-76.

The next operation, this time named Northern Falcon 2010, was conducted in March 2010. Prior to that, in February a memorandum of understanding concerning the joint military fuel transport operation was signed between the Ministry of Defence of Ukraine and the Ministry of Defence of Denmark.

Before the operation and during the preparation of the Il-76 crew members, they carried out a navigation flight from Zaporozhye to Melitopol in No. 78820. RDAF representatives headed by an officer of the Department of International Military Cooperation, Maj Ove Madsen, as well as the Danish Military attaché in Ukraine, Col Ove Bak Hansen, observed the preparations of the flight crew after a weather reconnaissance An-26 had declared suitable conditions over Melitopol for the mission on the morning of 17 March 2010. The pilot, who was also down to fly to Greenland, was Lt Col Sergey Serdyuk, and he and his crew logged 15 training sorties in 11 hours in

25th TrAB Il-76MD 76699 during parachute jumps with Ukrainian Airmobile Forces in an exercise on 22 September 2006. It was in storage at Melitopol from 2002, then restored during the Donbass war and was seen airworthy for first time at Gostomel in 2014. A contract for the prolongation of its lifetime until 28 August 2021 was signed with NARP on 26 April 2019. *Sergey Popsuevich*

order to be ready to fly 10,000km with 48 tons of payload and land on a 1,700m ice runway.

Because of the duration of Northern Falcon 2010, which lasted 20 days, several sets of crew including a total of 31 personnel including ground crews were prepared during training at Melitopol. Several young pilots were trained by experienced instructor pilots such as Lt Col Vadim Eroshkina. They also practised landing in low visibility and on short runway strips similar to the one at the North Pole under the instruction of IPs such as Lt Col Alexander Pasichenko, Col Dimitry Mymirkova and Lt Col Vladimir Buhalskogo during several touch and goes. The extra training was necessary because of the low flying hours of the UkrAF's Il-76 pilots, who accumulated just 20–30 hours per year, while their instructors had flown 200 a year in the Soviet era.

Finally, operation Northern Falcon 2010 was conducted in April 2010, during which the Ukrainian Il-76MD performed three flights with two sets of crews from the USAF's Thule AFB towards the Danish Nord (North) polar station in Greenland. Under the command of Lt Col Alexander Pasichenka and Lt Col Dmitry Mymrikova they carried 68 tons of fuel within 20 hours in the first week of operation. They experienced flying in harsh Arctic conditions, during which they were faced by rapid weather changes, crosswinds, low visibility, low-altitude clouds and stormy conditions. They could only use GPS for navigation during the flight due to the absence of NAVAIDS at the North Pole as well as the effect on navigation systems from the magnetic field, which can cause deviation in the compass and INS. The crews logged 12 more flights in the second week of operations (two flights per day). During the operations from 6 to 24 April 2010 they logged 40 sorties from Thule and transported 517,000 litres of fuel and 49 tons of cargo to station Nord.

In order to continue the fuel and cargo delivering operations in the North Pole in support of NATO operations, the UkrAF's Il-76MD and its crews had to pass NATO assessment Level II. An agreement was reached with the Danes that they would pay all the costs associated with conducting an operation for NATO Level II assessment. In March 2011, 25th TrAB personnel under the command of Col Dmitry Mymrikova were prepared for Northern Falcon 2011 under the supervision of Danish military officials in Zaporozhye.

During the operation, the crew, using Il-76MD 76413 (c/n 1013407215), first flew to the RDAF's Aalborg AB on 29 March and, after two days of preparation there, on 1 April they flew to Thule to participate in the operation. They transferred 601,141 litres of fuel and lubricants, 30 tonnes of other cargo and dozens of Danish military personnel, despite the presence of RDAF transport aircraft in this NATO exercise.

25th TrAB Il-76MD with 76777 during an exercise of the Ukrainian Airmobile Forces on 22 September 2006. It is seen during an airdrop of a BMD-2 airborne infantry fighting vehicle. *Sergey Popsuevich*

25th TrAB Il-76MD 78820 escorted by a pair of Su-24Ms during the Independence Day Parade over Kiev on 24 August 2001. *Sergey Popsuevich*

Several months after this operation, on 9 June 2011, a delegation from Denmark headed by Frederik, Crown Prince of Denmark, officially visited 25th TrAB personnel and their Il-76s forward deployed to Zaporozhye to honour their professional service. During the visit the Crown Prince stated: 'I am sincerely happy for the Air Force of the Armed Forces of Ukraine, today you are still the only partner country of NATO that has passed NATO's Level II assessment successfully.'

The next year, operation Northern Falcon 2012 was held between 9 and 26 April 2012, during which UkrAF Il-76MD 78820 (c/n 1013407215) transported 460,000 litres of fuel from Thule to the Nord, with two sets of crew flying for 89 hours and 13 minutes from Melitopol to Greenland and back.

In November 2012, the Ukrainian and Danish ministries of defence signed another memorandum of understanding for the joint military transport operation Northern Falcon 2013. The was conducted between 8 and 27 April 2013, during which an Il-76MD containing 29 soldiers and two sets of crew, including four pilots – Col Sergey Artemenko (crew commander), Col Vadim Eroshkin, Vladimir Buhalsky and Maj Alexander Bilyy – transported 570,000 litres of jet fuel from Thule to Nord.

For the sixth time, several Il-76 pilots and crew members prepared for the joint operation Northern Falcon 2014 from 23 January 2014. Danish representatives again visited Ukraine to observe the last stage of the 25th TrAB's pre-operation training that was carried out at Melitopol between 24 and 28 February. Before the operation, the Danish government paid Ukraine $150,000 for fuel, extension of the life of aircraft parts and acquisition of spares.

On 13 March the participants left Melitopol for Aalborg. The operation started on 17 March and continued until 10 April, during which the UkrAF's Il-76MD airlifted 360,000 litres of fuel, 140 passengers and 191 tons of cargo including food, snow trucks, spare parts, supplies and equipment in 40 flights and 90 flying hours. The fuel was transported in 5- to 10-ton containers. In total, the UkrAF earned $3 million during the operation and this was later spent on the overhaul and spare part acquisition for the UkrAF's Il-76 fleet.

On 1 July 2014, a meeting was held at the UkrAF's HQ at Vinnitsa between a UkrAF delegation headed by Col Alexander Kulibaba, the UkrAF's Deputy Chief, and a Danish Armed Forces delegation headed by Col Ove Madsen to discuss the joint operation Northern Falcon 2014. At the end of the meeting, the Ukrainian delegation presented a briefing on the 25th TrAB's participation in the joint Danish–Ukrainian operation.

On 14 October, during a ceremony at the Danish Embassy in Ukraine, the Ambassador of Denmark to Ukraine, Mrs Merete Juhl, officially handed over 15 advanced Garmin GPSMAP 695 Atlantic Aviation GPS Handheld (Atlantic Database) devices to representatives of the UkrAF, to be used in Il-76s and An-26s, as a result of the close Danish–Ukrainian economic and military ties.

On 6 April 2015, according to the memorandum of understanding between the Ministry of Ukraine and Kingdom of Denmark, the seventh joint Danish–Ukrainian operation named Northern Falcon 2015 was launched and lasted until 9 May 2015. A 25th TrAB Il-76MD was again used to transport 500 tons of fuel and 170 tons of cargo in 60 flights (100 hours of flight) from Thule and Aalborg to Nord. During one flight, crew members were faced with the challenge of transporting cargo weighing 30 tons, which consisted of snow vehicles and a fire truck. During the operation, 31 of the Ukrainian aircrew and ground crews qualified for the second level of NATO standards.

In 2016, the UkrAF took part in Northern Falcon 2016. This time the operation started on 1 April and lasted for four weeks until 30 April. During the operation 78820 (c/n 0093496907) took part, and the same aircraft participated in Operation Northern Falcon 2017 between mid-March and mid-April 2017.

Between 3 April and 5 May 2018, the UkrAF participated in the tenth Ukrainian–Danish operation, Northern Falcon 2018, during which Il-76MD 76683 transferred 700,000 litres of fuel and 25 tons of supplies from Thule to Nord in 25 missions and 100 flying hours at a temperature below 50 degrees Celsius and a wind speed of up to 15–20m per second, which was in stormy weather.

Between 14 March and 19 April 2019, the same Il-76MD was used in Operation Northern Falcon 2019, during which the aircraft transported 600 tons of fuel and 20 tons of other supplies in 44 flights and 100 hours. Serhiy Artemenko, the chief inspector-pilot of the Aviation Administration, led the Ukrainian group that year.

Despite its massive fuel consumption, which takes 800 tons of kerosene to airlift 400 tons of jet fuel, the Il-76 is still the best available heavy transport aircraft to meet the needs of the Danish Ministry of Defence for logistic support of its armed forces at the station Nord in Greenland.

Before 2009, Ukrainian Cargo Airways provided the Danish Ministry of Defence with chartered UkrAF Il-76MDs, but from 2009 until today 25th TrAB aircraft have been used for the missions, which has brought income to the Ukrainian Ministry of Defence that helped the unit fund the overhaul of one of its aircraft in 2013.

The RDAF has a fleet of four C-130J-30s in service with its Esk 721, each with a 16,329kg maximum normal payload. They are still not cost effective to be used repeatedly for carrying fuel and heavy cargo shipments to the Nord station, which means the air force will benefit from the availability of the UkrAF's Il-76MDs until 2020 or even later during the annual operation Northern Falcon.

In action during humanitarian and disaster relief operations

As the sole heavy transport aircraft in the Ukrainian Air Force inventory, the Il-76s have always been used for humanitarian and disaster relief operations. Their history goes back to the Armenian earthquake on 7 December 1988, or even before that during the Chernobyl disaster in 1986, when Il-76s of the Soviet Air Force's Transport Aviation brigades, including aircraft later inherited by the Ukrainian Air Force, airlifted tons of relief aid for the victims of the disasters and evacuated hundreds of wounded civilians.

In recent years, Il-76s from the 25th TrAB have always played a key role during humanitarian missions, including transporting relief aid to victims of earthquakes or evacuating Ukrainian citizens from warzones.

In the aftermath of the devastating earthquake in Bam, Iran, in 2003, Ukraine, similar to many other countries, provided aid. On 27 December 2003, the Cabinet of Ministers issued a decree to help Iran conduct search and rescue operations in the affected areas. Subsequently, the Ukrainian Ministry of Emergencies and Ministry of Health were tasked with providing a search and rescue unit and also to establish a mobile hospital in Bam, with enough personnel and medicine to treat 400 patients a day within 30 days. For this purpose a $561,000 budget was specified. A UkrAF Il-76MD transported the Ukrainian search and rescue team and nurses, doctors and surgeons, together with the mobile hospital, to Iran.

Three years later, the UkrAF was involved in another humanitarian relief mission during which a 25th TrAB Il-76MD transported 150 sets of military tents, 1,500 blankets and flannels and 42 sets of portable field kitchens to Chengdu on 31 May 2008 in the aftermath of the Sichuan earthquake, which struck on 12 May.

On 14 July 2011, Il-76MD 78820 of the UkrAF's 25th TrAB transferred ground equipment for 75 Blue, an Su-27UB of the 831st BrTA, during RIAT 2011 at RAF Fairford on 14 July 2011. On 26 April 2019, a contract for its lifetime extension until 30 October 2021 was finalised between the Ukrainian MoD and NARP. *Chris Chennel*

In 2011, following the revolution and subsequent civil war in Libya, the UkrAF's 25th TrAB soon got a direct order from the President of Ukraine to evacuate Ukrainian civilians from Tripoli, Libya. Finally, after several days of delay as a result of the unavailability of the aircraft for the mission, an Il-76MD piloted by Lt Col Vladimir Buhalskym flew to Tripoli under supervision of the Ukrainian Armed Forces commander. The aircraft brought back 185 civilians, including 152 Ukrainian citizens, to Boryspil on 24 February.

In 2012 after the Arab spring revolution had reached Syria, the country became heavily involved in a civil war that involved various rebel groups and terrorist organisations that threatened the lives of Ukrainian citizens in the country. Again, the UkrAF was tasked with carrying out an evacuation mission using an Il-76MD. Lt Col Vladimir Buhalskym again flew the aircraft, which evacuated 177 Ukrainian citizens and 15 Polish citizens from Aleppo on 1 August.

On 25 and 26 April 2015, Nepal experienced powerful earthquakes that caused the death of 8,964 people, injured 21,952 others and made 3.5 million people homeless. Almost 60 countries including Ukraine provided relief aid. In order to evacuate Ukrainian citizens working for various companies in the country, the UkrAF was tasked again by an order of the Ukrainian President Petro Proshenko on 28 April with preparing an Il-76MD and sending it to Nepal for two purposes: firstly to deliver Ukraine's relief aid and then to bring back Ukrainian citizens trapped there.

The 25th TrAB prepared Il-76MD 76683 (c/n 0063468029), which had recently participated in the Danish–Ukrainian Operation Northern Falcon 2015. The aircraft was configured with a double-decked cabin with the capability of carrying 220 passengers, and its planned date for departure from Boryspil was 29 April after it received permission to land in Kathmandu. The runway of Tribhuvan International

Airport, sole airport in the country with the ability to accept heavy aircraft, was damaged and the weather conditions were not good.

The UkrAF's Il-76MD flew to Delhi but due to a lack of coordination between the Ukrainian Ministry of Foreign Affairs and Nepalese officials, the crew members and rescuers waited several hours without any instructions because landing in Kathmandu without permission and without the correct protocols and technical procedures was not possible. Also, the crew had been faced with a technical problem in the fuel system of the aircraft's No. 2 engine during the flight to Delhi. With assistance from the head of the 25th TrAB's engineering branch, Col Valeriy Kalinichenko, the problem was temporarily solved, the thrust of the other engines was set to 81% and the aircraft flew for an hour and 30 minutes in that state. The state enterprise Lutsk Repair Plant Motor, which had overhauled 76683's D-30KP engines, was responsible for the technical problem because the powerplant had two years' warranty until the end of December 2015.

After landing, the technicians cleaned the engine's filter and the problem was temporarily fixed but the fuel flow was not normal at high speed or at maximum thrust. In order to complete the repair a new high-pressure fuel regulator, speed sensor and other equipment were required. The maintenance men sent the information and spare part numbers required for the repair by air on 30 April. Although the 25th TrAB prepared the spare parts by the end of the day to ship them to Delhi, customs officials did not issue permission for their export from Boryspil airport. Finally, after negotiations between the Ministry of Foreign Affairs and customs, the parts were released on 1 May, but they did not reach Delhi until 3 May. The Il-76 technician started to replace the parts on the evening of that day, continuing through the night. The next day, 4 May, ground tests were performed by the crew and three maintenance men.

Finally, the aircraft was certified for the flight to Kathmandu. After delivering the relief aid and picking up the Ukrainian citizens, the aircraft returned to Delhi for refuelling to continue its flight back to Ukraine, with another refuelling stop at Baku. On landing at Delhi one of the 20 tyres burst, which was later replaced. This was probably caused by pieces of concrete on Kathmandu's damaged runway. Finally, after the change of the tyre, the aircraft returned safely to Boryspil. The aircraft transported 25 rescuers, doctors and psychologists as well as representatives of the Ministry of Foreign Affairs of Ukraine to Kathmandu and brought back 196 Ukrainian citizens.

In April 2016, the 25th Airborne Brigade of Ukrainian Air Assault Forces held an exercise, during which its paratroopers performed parachute jumps from An-26s as well as Il-76MD 76683 of the 25th TrAB. *The Ukrainian Ministry of Defence*

Participating in NATO exercises

Since Ukraine's independence the UkrAF's Il-76s have been used in an average of three annual domestic exercises, including those held in conjunction with the Ukrainian Airmobile Forces. These have not only been in the domestic exercises of the Ukrainian Armed Forces, as the strategic heavy transport aircraft of the air force they have always accompanied Ukrainian Army and Airmobile forces during their participation in international exercises including those held by NATO. Ukraine has been actively participating in the NATO's PfP Planning and Review Process (PARP) since 1995. In all, 54 partnership goals were reached during the process for 2004–05, including ten for the Land Forces, ten for the Naval Forces and seven for the Ukrainian Air Force.

PfP's (Partnership for Peace) PARP aims to promote the development of the forces and capabilities of those partners that are best able to cooperate with NATO allies in crisis response operations and other activities to promote security and stability. It provides a structured approach for enhancing the interoperability and capabilities of partner forces that could be made available to the Alliance for multi-national training, exercises and operations. The PARP also serves as a planning tool to guide and measure progress in defence and military development and modernisation. The third phase of the Planning and Review Process (PARP) was completed in 2006, and among the Ukrainian aircraft designated for PARP there were four 25th TrAB Il-76MDs alongside the sole An-26 'Vita' air ambulance.

In 2005, the 25th TrAB took part in three exercises, including those of NATO. These started with Exercise Cooperative Key 2005, which was held in Bulgaria between 25 August and 5 September, during which 9 Ukrainian Air Force personnel, 33 personnel of a combined airborne platoon of the Ukrainian Land Forces and five personnel of the air-drop support group, flew to

During the exercise Rapid Trident 2011, which was hold between 25 July and 5 August 2011, 1,600 personnel of 13 NATO and partnership for peace member nations participated. Canadian paratroopers from the 3rd Battalion, Royal 22e Regiment, jumped from Ukrainian Il-76MD 76413 during this exercise at the International Peacekeeping and Security Centre in Yavoriv, Ukraine, on 26 July 2011. A contract for the prolongation of 76413's lifetime until 28 June 2021 was finalised with NARP on 26 April 2019. It is seen with its tail gun removed during a military exercise on 22 September 2006. *Royal Canadian Army/Cpl Jax Kennedy*

Plovdiv, Bulgaria, in an Il-76MD (serial 78820). There they practised parachute jumping and cargo airdrops with transport aircraft of the Bulgarian, Latvian, Lithuanian, Romanian, and Moldovan air forces, which had all been deployed to Krumovo Air Base. The goal of the exercise was to improve interoperability between the units of NATO members and partner countries during air search and rescue, medical evacuations and air-drops in support of peacekeeping operations.

After the exercise in Bulgaria, Exercise Cossacks Steppe 2005 was held in Poland, in which a UkrAF Il-76MD participated, airlifting 110 military personnel including an airmobile company from the Ukrainian Airmobile Force headed by 1st Lt Igor Yermolai from Ukrainian Western Military Air command. It was a battalion-level tactical exercise, during which 300 paratroopers of the Ukrainian, Polish and British armed forces took part in the simulation of peacekeeping missions. Its main goal was to train the joint operations of combined arms units during peacekeeping, search and rescue and humanitarian operations.

In September another exercise was held, this time on Ukrainian territory, which was named Reaction 2005. It was an integrated operational-tactical exercise with joint rapid reaction forces and became one of the largest held since Ukraine's independence. During the exercise, 6,500 servicemen using 590 items of weapons and equipment including more than 100 armoured tanks and APCs, 20 aircraft including 17 from the air force, 12 helicopters and 9 ships participated between 21 and 23 September.

On the first day of the exercise, 21 September, the crew of a UkrAF Su-24MR of the 32nd Independent Reconnaissance Air Squadron, which had been established at Starokostiantyniv Air Base on 19 May 2004, carried out an aerial reconnaissance sortie to detect the location of a camouflaged command post in the tactical area of Ozernoye. The next day, the 7th TAB's Su-24Ms bombed the region. Then a quick reaction force consisting of 25th Independent Airborne Brigade forces were deployed as peacekeepers using an Il-76MD from Melitopol.

In 2006, the 25th TrAB took part in several NATO international exercises including Brilliant Mariner 2006, a tactical exercise with NATO quick response forces certification that was held between 24 and 27 March. During the exercise on the Danish Military Land Force range in Oxbow, Denmark, 74 Ukrainian Armed Forces personnel took part, consisting of a joint Marine Ukrainian Naval Force Company, a tactical group of the Ukrainian Navy's Independent Special Force unit and eight UkrAF personnel with an Il-76MD, in order to practise interoperability between staff during crisis response operations.

According to the PfP PARP, the UkrAF must have four Il-76MDs simultaneously operational, and for NATO performs annual assessments of the fleet readiness during the international exercises. In the years between 2005 and 2008, NATO performed 16 independent first-level assessments of the Ukrainian Armed Forces. In 2007 and 2008, the UkrAF's Il-76MDs participated in various exercises, during which they provided logistical support for the armed forces while they were being assessed by NATO representatives. For example, during the Ukrainian–American Tactical Training Naval exercise Sea Breeze 2008, the Ukrainian Air Force participated with three helicopters and six aircraft, including two of its five operational Il-76MDs, and passed NATO Assessment Level 1 on 28 July 2008. During the event, 2,000 service members from 16 countries participated in the joint and combined maritime exercise held in the Black Sea and at various land-based Ukrainian training facilities with the goals of strengthening maritime security and stability, sharing information and building teamwork and mutual cooperation. Nine Ukrainian aircraft, including the pair of Il-76MDs, together with eight aircraft from other countries logged 50 sorties, anti-submarine warfare operations and SAR missions, and performed 17 drops of nearly 400 paratroopers.

During 2009, propositions by the Federal Republic of Germany were considered concerning the possible participation of the Armed Forces of Ukraine NCB platoon (Nuclear and Chemical and Biological) with its dosimetric and chemical control section in the 15th rotation of NATO's response forces led by Germany. In addition, in order to ensure the systemisation of means and forces participation in NATO's response forces, one air force Il-76MD joined in the 16th rotation of NATO's response forces.

In 2011, for first time in the history of Ukraine–EU relations, a marine corps unit and a military transport Il-76MD with its crew and a group of Ukrainian Armed Forces officers were involved in operative duty as a part of the EU multi-national battle group HELBROC (Greece, Bulgaria, Romania, Cyprus) in the second half of 2011. During the second half of 2011, Ukraine supplied an Il-76MD with aircrew, ground maintenance and command elements for operational duty with the 17th rotation of NATO response forces.

Between 18 and 27 July, the Ukraine–US–Polish exercise Safe Sky 2011 was held at Mirgorod in preparation for the 2012 Olympics, 2012 Euro football tournament and 2014 Winter Olympics in Europe. During the exercise, the UKrAF participated with 220 service personnel and 15 aircraft, including one Il-76MD that was used for logistic support of the 204th TAB during deployment of its aircraft to Mirgorod.

Between 25 July and 5 August 2011, the Joint Command Post exercise Rapid Trident 2011 was held at Yavoriv International Peacekeeping and Security Training Centre Range in order to fulfil tasks as a part of multi-national military contingent during peacekeeping operations. The purpose of this exercise was to review the level of combat training of the Ukrainian forces as well as to research directions for developing a prospective model of the Armed Forces of Ukraine. From Ukraine, 586 service personnel, four aircraft including one Il-76MD and one helicopter, took part, while 681 service personnel and five aircraft participated from other countries. As part of the multi-national airborne exercise, Canadian paratroopers from 3rd Battalion, Royal 22e Régiment, parachuted out of Ukrainian Il-76 76413 (c/n 1013407215).

The following year, the 25th TrAB again took part in international exercises during the joint Ukrainian–Belarusian–Russian Slavic Commonwealth 2012 at the Shiroky Lan training ground off Ukraine's Black Sea coast between 22 and 27 July. The three countries' airmobile brigades, including Russia's airborne unit of the Southern military district, took part. A joint airborne assault force consisting of 60 paratroopers was dropped from a Russian Air Force Il-76MD as part of the exercise. A UkrAF Il-76MD was used to deploy Ukrainian airmobile troops to the exercise area.

On 2 October, for first time since 2002 Ukrainian Airmobile Forces and the Ukrainian Air Force practised airdrops of military equipment during Exercise Perspective 2012. The operation, at Novomoskovsk tactical training range in the Dnepropetrovsk region, was under the supervision of the Ukrainian Land Force's commander, Gen Gennady Vorobyev. For the first time, domestically manufactured parachutes were used for the airdrop of two BMD-2 airborne infantry fighting vehicles from a UkrAF Il-76MD. On that day 130 paratroopers also carried out jumps from the Il-76MD.

Recent overhauls at Nikolaev Aircraft Repair Plant

In the years since the independence of Ukraine, the State Enterprise Nikolaev Aircraft Repair Plant (NARP) has been responsible for heavy or depot-level maintenance of Ukrainian Il-76 and Il-78s. Established on 29 September 1939, it was based at the aircraft repair workshops of Glavsevmorput flying school, which later became the Air Naval School named after Levanevsky Nikolaev. Between 1939 and 1941, NARP carried repaired U-2, R-5, MBR-6, R-6, R-10 aircraft and M-11, M-17 and M-22 engines that were in service with Soviet Naval Aviation at the time. After the outbreak of the Second World War, the workshop was evacuated and relocated next to the railway station at Bezenchuk, in the Kubyshev region.

Soon after the liberation of Ukraine from occupation by Germany, the workshop was relocated to the village of Stepanovka, in the Kherson region, and stayed there until it was redeployed again to its permanent location at Kulbakino, Nokolaev, in September 1949. After the USSR collapsed in 1992, the NARP joined the repair network of the Ukrainian Ministry of Defence and was put under the command of the UkrAF. Since 1993, the NARP has performed the mid-life repairs of Su-24s, repaired NK-8-2U, D-30KP, AI-8, TA-6A, M-14P, M-14V26 engines, repaired Ukrainian Navy and Air Force Tu-22s, Tu-95s, Tu-142s and repaired civil aircraft such as the Il-62 and Tu-154.

Former 369th VTAP Il-76MD 76683 at the NARP facility at Nikolayev-Kulbakino at the beginning of its overhaul on 24 August 2010. Its overhaul lasted until 2013. *Alexander Golz*

Since 2008 the plant has started to master life-extension procedures (major overhaul with life-extension) for Il-76MD and Il-78 aircraft and mid-life repair of the UPAZ-1refuelling pod. For this purpose a unique UPAZ-1 test rig was made by enterprise experts. The appropriate actions have also been taken to master the major overhaul of DF-30KP (KP-2) aircraft engines.

Since the mid-2000s, the UkrAF has always had four airworthy Il-76MDs in service, among which two are fully mission capable, ready to be used for peacekeeping operations and NATO operations, and the other two are reserves. Its remaining two Il-76MDs are not fully mission capable but are operable for logistic support for the Ukrainian Armed Forces. In 2010, the six Il-76MDs were 78820, 76413, 76683, 76699, 76777 and 76732. Among these, the first two examples did not have the parachute system for BMD-1/2 Airborne IFVs due to budget restrictions during their last overhaul at NARP.

Among the above-mentioned aircraft, 76683 reached its MTBO and was grounded at the end of that year, while 76699 was near the end of its MTBO by 2014. As a result, the Ukrainian Ministry of Defence specified a budget for the overhaul and modernisation of 76683 (c/n 0063468029) at NARP. While NARP performed the airframe overhaul, the state enterprise Lutsk Repair Plant Motor worked on the D-30KP engines. The aircraft overhaul was completed in December 2013 and it was painted in an overall dark grey colour scheme. The first functional check flight was performed by Lt Col Vadim Eroshkina on 20 December 2013, and it was handed over to the UkrAF during a ceremony at Melitopol on 18 January 2014.

During an official ceremony on 30 November 2016, following decree No. 529 signed by the President of Ukraine Petro Poroshenko, 76683 was officially christened 'Colonel Alexander Bely' after the pilot of the Il-76MD that was shot down by pro-Russian separatists during the war in Donbass on 14 June 2014.

Following 76683, a second Il-76MD, 76697, was overhauled by NARP after 2014. The overhaul work was started at Nikolayev after a 48,307,000 UAH contract was signed on 21 November 2017 with a deadline for completion of the work on 10 December 2017. NARP also restored Il-76MD 76698 into flying condition after its lifetime extension in 2016. It was redelivered to the 25th TrAB in 2017.

At war

The war in the Donbass region was started by the insurgency of the pro-Russian activists in Donetsk and Luhansk when they stormed the SBU offices of those two cities on 7 April 2014. Several days later, when the Ukrainian Land Forces including the airmobile units were deployed to the battle zone by road, the Il-76s, which all had been equipped with APP-50 chaff/flare dispensers (since March 2014), were used alongside seven An-26s of the UkrAF to provide logistic support. On 15 April 2014, in accordance with Ukrainian law on fighting terrorism, Ukraine's acting President Olexander Tuchynov announced the start of an 'anti-terrorist operation' against pro-Russian separatists. Prior to that all four airworthy Il-76MDs had been used to transfer airmobile equipment to Dnepropetrovsk airport.

Once the war in Donbass had begun, the 25th TrAB's personnel were prepared for tactical flights and special missions to the east of the country during an air exercise conducted at Kulbakino AB, during which several examples of all combat aircraft types of the UkrAF as well as two Il-76MDs serialled 76777 and 78820 took part. The main purpose of the exercise, which was held in the third week of May, was to increase coordination between the acting aircrews in the battle zone. The 25th TrAB's Il-76MDs and their aircrews had participated in a joint exercise with the airmobile units for practising air delivery and parachute jumping in April 2014.

In early June, Ukrainian land forces were hopelessly trying to recapture Luhansk from pro-Russian separatists who had been very well armed by Russia. While the roads to the city were mostly controlled by the separatists, the airport was the last hope for the Ukrainian security forces to deploy their troops at night, despite the danger of mortar barrages.

Three Il-76MDs were used to transfer a company of the Ukrainian 25th Independent Airborne Brigade, with their hardware, ammunition and food, to Luhansk airport on 13 June 2014. The first aircraft landed safely at 01.00am on 14 June, but the second aircraft, 76777 (c/n 0083482490) with 9 crew members and 40 airborne troops on board, was shot down by a MANPAD (some sources suggest an AA gun) on the final approach, killing all on board. In the aftermath all flights to the airport were stopped.

The bodies of the crew members and the paratroopers were later recovered from the crash zone and sent to Melitopol and their home cities for burial. The nine aircrew were Lt Col Alexander Bely, Maj Michael Diakova, Capt Igor Skachkova, Capt Sergey Telegina, Lt Vladimir Burkavtsova, Lt Alexander Kozoliya, Lt Oleg Pavlenko, Ensign Alexander and Lt Victor Mentusa. Their bodies arrived at Melitopol on board Il-76MD 76683 and were buried in the new town cemetery during an official ceremony on 25 July 2014.

Three days after this catastrophe, the chairman of the Mykolayiv Regional State Administration, Nikolay Romanchuk, announced during a speech on 17 June that he was willing to help the Ukrainian Ministry of Defence restore a new Il-76MD to replace the lost example. Later, the first deputy head of the ATO, Deputy Chief of Staff Viktor Nazarov, was found responsible for the accident through negligence. His arrest warrant was issued by Pechersk District Court and he was later arrested and interrogated, but released on bail. Later, the case was transferred to another court and he received more charges; in 2016 he admitted that his negligence had led to the accident.

Despite the act of terrorism by the pro-Russian terrorists who shot down 76777, the accident was also a result of, firstly, a lack of coordination between the ATO forces and its units, airborne troops, air force and special forces. Second, the decision to approve the flight ignored the evidence from previous wars in Chechen, Georgia, Iraq, Afghanistan and Yugoslavia, during which the threat of MANPADs against transport aircraft had always existed; and third, the decision neglected safety and risked the lives of the soldiers by sending them to areas where the danger of MANPADs existed.

Current fleet

Following the lessons learned from the war in Donbass, the Ukrainian Armed Forces held various joint exercises with 25th TrAB airmobile units, mostly practising airdrops and parachute jumping, in which the Il-76s participated.

On 30 and 31 May 2015, the UkrAF participated in a joint exercise with airborne units and Navy

Named after Oleksander Bielyi, the pilot of 76777, which was lost to the Igla MANPADS of pro-Russian separatists during the Donbass war, 76683 is seen at Boryspil in its latest colours on 18 April 2019. *Alexander Golz*

76777 as it was in the last days of its service in the 25th TrAB before being shot down by pro-Russian separatists on 14 June 2014. *Luca G. Canossa*

Marine Corps in the Mykolayiv region. During the exercise the airborne troops and Marine Corps troops performed parachute jumps from 400–500m both by day and night in limited visibility from a 25th TrAB Il-76MD and a Ukrainian Navy Aviation An-26. During the exercise 76683's BPS-95 parachute system was used to drop BMD-2 airborne IFVs.

In the first week of October 2015, the 25th TrAB provided an Il-76MD for a Strategic Command Post exercise with the Ukrainian Naval Marines, this time in the Kherson region, and again the PBS-95 parachute system was used for the airdrop of military equipment.

In late October, in the Mykolayiv region, 25th TrAB Il-76MD 78820 and a 456th TrAB An-26 participated in an exercise and their air crews practised tactical landings and take-offs in the battle zone under the threat of enemy air defence systems.

Between 19 and 28 October 2015, two UkrAF Il-76MDs took part in NATO's joint exercise Trident Juncture 2015, the largest and most ambitious NATO exercise in recent decades, during which 36,000 soldiers of 30 countries participated and demonstrated the high level of combat readiness of NATO and its ability to respond to new security challenges in the event of war with Russia.

On 25 and 26 April 2016, the 25th Independent Airmobile Brigade, together with Ukrainian Navy Marines, participated in another exercise to practise the airdrop of supplies and parachute jumping from a UkrAF Il-76. On 26 May, the UkrAF participated in another exercise with Il-76MD 76683 and an An-26, this time in the Dnepropetrovsk region, and 25th Independent Airborne Brigade troops performed parachute jumps and the airdrop of artillery equipment during a simulation of an offensive using artillery support against the enemy.

During the Royal International Air Tattoo 2017, Il-76MD 78820 serial number was used to transport ground equipment and crew for Su-27PM1 58 Blue and Su-27UBM1 71 Blue.

Between 27 and 29 September 2018, an Il-76MD participated in the Strategic command staff exercise Cossack Will 2018. During the exercise, at least three of UkrAF An-26s airdropped infantry equipment, heavy weapons and ammunition at low altitude. Immediately afterwards, airborne paratroops of the 25th Independent Airborne Brigade of the Airborne Assault Force performed tactical parachute jumps from the Il-76MD over the area at medium altitude. According to the commander of the assault troops, Lt Gen Mykhailo Zabrodskyi, the airdrop of the equipment and the parachute jumps took place over an unfamiliar area in the Dnepropetrovsk region. Minutes later, Su-25M1s of the 299th BrTA provided close air support for the airborne troops on the ground.

In spring 2019, the Ukrainian Air Force had a fleet of eight airworthy Il-76MDs, which were 76413, 76683, 76732, 76691, 76697, 76698, 76699 and 78820. Among these five were fully mission capable for cargo airdrops or air delivery, while two others were partially mission capable. Among them, one was always in reserve. The Ukrainian Air Force has plans to keep this small fleet airworthy until 2035–40.

76683 is seen on 13 March 2019, the day before it flew to Denmark to take part in Operation Northern Falcon 2019. *The Ukrainian Ministry of Defence*

Ukrainian Air Force Il-76s

Version	Serial Number	Construction Number	Unit in 1992	Current unit	Year of manufacture	Status in 1992	Current status	Year of Retirement/ wfu/Sale
Il-76MD	76651	0053462872	25th GvVTAP	-	1985	?	Sold	2001
Il-76MD	76322	0053462873	25th GvVTAP	25th TrAB	1985	Active	Stored	-
Il-76MD	76655	0053463885	25th GvVTAP	25th TrAB	1985	Active	Stored	-
Il-76MD	76656	0053463891	25th GvVTAP	25th TrAB	1985	Active	For Sale	-
Il-76MD	76657	0053463896	25th GvVTAP	25th TrAB	1985	Active	Stored	-
Il-76MD	76658	0053463902	25th GvVTAP	25th TrAB	1985	Active	For Sale	-
Il-76MD	76659	0053463908	25th GvVTAP	-	1985	Active	Sold	2004
Il-76MD	76666	0053464934	25th GvVTAP	-	1985	Active	Sold	1998
Il-76MD	76672	0063466981	25th GvVTAP		1986	Active	Sold	1999
Il-76MD	76394	0063466989	25th GvVTAP	-	1986	?	Sold	2006
Il-76MD	76688	0063469062	25th GvVTAP	-	1986	?	Sold	2004
Il-76MD	76695	0063470112	25th GvVTAP	-	1986	?	Stored	-
Il-76MD	76699	0063471131	25th GvVTAP	25th TrAB	1985	Active	Active	-
Il-76MD	76703	0063471147	25th GvVTAP	-	1986	Active	Sold	2009
Il-76MD	76706	0063472163	25th GvVTAP	25th TrAB	1986	Active	Stored	-
Il-76MD	76732	0073476296	25th GvVTAP	25th TrAB	1987	Active	Active	-
Il-76MD	76715	0073479394	25th GvVTAP	25th TrAB	1987	?	Stored	-
Il-76MD	76777	0083482490	25th GvVTAP	25th TrAB	1988	Active	Crashed	2014
Il-76MD	76778	0083483502	25th GvVTAP	-	1988	Active	Sold	2008
Il-76MD	76438	0083483513	25th GvVTAP	-	1988	?	Sold	1999
Il-76	86639	073409235	37th VTAP	-	1977	Active	wfu/Scrapped	2014
Il-76MD	76570	0033448427	37th VTAP	25th TrAB	1983	Active	For Sale	-
Il-76MD	76571	0033448429	37th VTAP	-	1983	Active	wfu/Scrapped	2001
Il-76MD	76575	0033449445	37th VTAP	-	1983	Active	wfu/Scrapped	2009
Il-76MD	76585	0043451503	37th VTAP	25th TrAB	1984	Active	Stored	-
Il-76MD	76590	0043452544	37th VTAP	-	1984	Active	Stored	-
Il-76MD	76598	0043453591	37th VTAP	25th TrAB	1984	Active	For Sale	-
Il-76MD	76601	0043454606	37th VTAP	25th TrAB	1984	Active	Stored	-
Il-76MD	76568	0033448420	37th VTAP	-	1983	Active	For Sale	-
Il-76MD	76573	0033449437	37th VTAP	25th TrAB	1983	Active	For Sale	-
Il-76MD	76578	0043449468	37th VTAP	-	1984	Active	Sold	2002
Il-76MD	76579	0043449471	37th VTAP	-	1984	Active	Sold	2002
Il-76MD	76580	0043450476	37th VTAP	-	1984	?	For Sale	-
Il-76MD	76581	0043450484	37th VTAP	-	1984	?	Sold	2005
Il-76MD	76582	0043450487	37th VTAP	-	1984	?	For Sale	-
Il-76MD	76583	0043450491	37th VTAP	-	1984	Active	Sold	2007
Il-76MD	76584	0043450493	37th VTAP	-	1984	Active	Sold	2002
Il-76MD	76588	0043451530	37th VTAP	-	1984	Active	Sold	2000
Il-76MD	76591	0043452546	37th VTAP	-	1984	Active	Sold	1999
Il-76MD	76390	0043453562	37th VTAP	25th TrAB	1984	?	For Sale	-
Il-76MD	76391	0043453568	37th VTAP	25th TrAB	1984	?	For Sale	-
Il-76MD	76392	0043454602	37th VTAP	-	1984	?	wfu/Scrapped	2007
Il-76MD	76602	0043454611	37th VTAP	-	1984	?	Stored	2005
Il-76MD	76603	0043454623	37th VTAP	-	1984	Active	Crashed	2005

Version	Serial Number	Construction Number	Unit in 1992	Current unit	Year of manufacture	Status in 1992	Current status	Year of Retirement/ wfu/Sale
Il-76MD	76437	0083484527	37th VTAP	-	1988	?	Sold	1999
Il-76MD	78755	0083484531	37th VTAP	-	1988	Active	For Sale	-
Il-76MD	76567	0033448390	175th VTAP	25th TrAB	1983	Active	Sold	2001
Il-76MD	76443	0043452534	175th VTAP	25th TrAB	1984	Active	For Sale	-
Il-76MD	76595	0043453571	175th VTAP	25th TrAB	1984	Active	Stored	-
Il-76MD	76596	0043453583	175th VTAP	25th TrAB	1984	Active	For Sale	-
Il-76MD	76597	0043453585	175th VTAP	25th TrAB	1984	Active	For Sale	-
Il-76MD	76393	0043455653	175th VTAP	25th TrAB	1984	?	wfu/Scrapped	2007
Il-76MD	76614	0043455665	175th VTAP	25th TrAB	1984	Active	For Sale	-
Il-76MD	76622	0053457702	175th VTAP	25th TrAB	1984	?	Stored	-
Il-76MD	76624	0053457710	175th VTAP	25th TrAB	1985	Active	Stored	-
Il-76MD	76321	0053457713	175th VTAP	25th TrAB	1985	Active	Stored	-
Il-76MD	76423	0053457720	175th VTAP	25th TrAB	1985	Active	Stored	-
Il-76MD	76317	0053458733	175th VTAP	25th TrAB	1985	Active	Stored	-
Il-76MD	76630	0053458749	175th VTAP	25th TrAB	1985	Active	Stored	-
Il-76MD	76632	0053458756	175th VTAP	25th TrAB	1985	Active	Stored	-
Il-76MD	76633	0053459764	175th VTAP	25th TrAB	1985	Active	Stored	-
Il-76MD	76408	0053460820	175th VTAP	-	1985	?	Sold	2002
Il-76MD	76433	0053460827	175th VTAP	-	1985	?	Sold	2001
Il-76MD	76637	0053460797	175th VTAP	25th TrAB	1985	Active	Stored	-
Il-76MD	76645	0053461834	175th VTAP	25th TrAB	1985	Active	Stored	-
Il-76MD	76660	0053463910	175th VTAP	25th TrAB	1985	Active	Stored	-
Il-76MD	76661	0053463913	175th VTAP	25th TrAB	1985	Active	Stored	-
Il-76MD	76663	0053464922	175th VTAP	25th TrAB	1985	Active	Stored	-
Il-76MD	76664	0053464926	175th VTAP	25th TrAB	1985	?	Stored	-
Il-76MD	76665	0053464930	175th VTAP	25th TrAB	1985	?	Stored	-
Il-76MD	76681	0063467021	175th VTAP	-	1986	Active	Sold	2003
Il-76MD	76323	0063466988	175th VTAP	25th TrAB	1986	Active	Stored	-
Il-76MD	76424	0063470096	175th VTAP	-	1986	Active	Crashed	1998
Il-76MD	76444	0063470113	175th VTAP	25th TrAB	1986	Active	Stored	-
Il-76MD	76705	0063472158	175th VTAP	25th TrAB	1986	Active	Stored	-
Il-76MD	76748	0073479386	175th VTAP	-	1987	Active	Sold	2002
Il-76MD	76749	0073479392	175th VTAP	-	1987	Active	Sold	2002
Il-76MD	78820	0093496907	175th VTAP	25th TrAB	1989	Active	Active	-
Il-76MD	78821	0093496914	175th VTAP	25th TrAB	1989	?	wfu/Scrapped	2003
Il-76MD	86899	0023435030	338th VTAP	-	1982	Active	wfu/Scrapped	2002
Il-76MD	86903	0023436048	338th VTAP	-	1982	Active	Sold	2000
Il-76MD	86904	0023436050	338th VTAP	-	1982	Active	wfu/Scrapped	2001
Il-76MD	86921	0023440161	338th VTAP	-	1982	Grounded	Sold	1999
Il-76MD	86922	0023440168	338th VTAP	-	1982	Active	Stored	-
Il-76MD	86923	0023441169	338th VTAP	-	1982	Active	Stored	-
Il-76MD	86924	0023441174	338th VTAP	-	1982	Active	Stored	-
Il-76MD	76531	0023441181	338th VTAP	-	1982	Active	Stored	-
Il-76MD	76532	0023441201	338th VTAP	-	1982	Active	wfu/Scrapped	2007

Version	Serial Number	Construction Number	Unit in 1992	Current unit	Year of manufacture	Status in 1992	Current status	Year of Retirement/ wfu/Sale
Il-76MD	76534	0023442210	338th VTAP	-	1982	Active	Stored	-
Il-76MD	76535	0023442213	338th VTAP	-	1982	Active	Stored	-
Il-76MD	76536	0023442221	338th VTAP	-	1982	Active	Stored	-
Il-76MD	76537	0033442225	338th VTAP	25th TrAB	1983	Active	Stored	-
Il-76MD	76539	0033442234	338th VTAP	-	1983	Active	Crashed	1996
Il-76MD	76540	0033442238	338th VTAP	-	1983	Active	For Sale	-
Il-76MD	76541	0033442241	338th VTAP	-	1983	Active	For Sale	-
Il-76MD	76395	0033443255	338th VTAP	-	1983	?	Stored	-
Il-76MD	76396	0043451508	338th VTAP	-	1984	?	Stored	-
Il-76MD	76397	0043451517	338th VTAP	-	1984	Active	Stored	-
Il-76MD	78752	0083483519	338th VTAP	-	1988	Active	Stored	-
Il-76MD	76398	0083484522	338th VTAP	-	1988	?	Stored	-
Il-76MD	78756	0083484536	338th VTAP	-	1988	?	Stored	-
Il-76MD	76399	0083485566	338th VTAP	-	1988	Active	Stored	-
Il-76MD	78774	0083488643	338th VTAP	-	1988	Active	Sold	2009
Il-76MD	78775	0083489647	338th VTAP	-	1988	Active	Stored	-
Il-76MD	86914	0023438111	338th VTAP	-	1982	Active	wfu/Scrapped	2015
Il-76MD	86915	0023438116	338th VTAP	-	1982	Active	wfu/Scrapped	1999
Il-76MD	86916	0023438120	338th VTAP	-	1982	Active	Sold	2002
Il-76MD	86917	0023438122	338th VTAP	-	1982	Active	Crashed	2005
Il-76MD	86918	0023438127	338th VTAP	-	1982	Active	wfu/Scrapped	1999
Il-76MD	86919	0023438129	338th VTAP	-	1982	?	Sold	1999
Il-76MD	86920	0023440152	338th VTAP	-	1982	Active	wfu/Scrapped	2007
Il-76MD	76555	0033446325	338th VTAP	-	1983	Active	Sold	2001
Il-76MD	76557	0033446329	338th VTAP	25th TrAB	1983	Active	For Sale	-
Il-76MD	76559	0033446340	338th VTAP	25th TrAB	1983	Active	For Sale	-
Il-76MD	76560	0033446341	338th VTAP	-	1983	Active	For Sale	-
Il-76MD	76561	0033447364	363rd VTAP	-	1983	?	wfu/Scrapped	2001
Il-76MD	76562	0033447365	363rd VTAP	-	1983	Active	Sold	2003
Il-76MD	76563	0033447372	363rd VTAP	-	1983	Active	For Sale	-
Il-76MD	76564	0033447373	363rd VTAP	-	1983	Active	wfu/Scrapped	2001
Il-76MD	76565	0033447382	363rd VTAP	-	1983	Active	For Sale	-
Il-76MD	76566	0033448385	363rd VTAP	25th TrAB	1983	Active	For Sale	-
Il-76MD	76567	0033448390	363rd VTAP	-	1983	Active	Sold	2001
Il-76MD	76574	0033449441	363rd VTAP	-	1983	?	Sold	2003
Il-76MD	76576	0043449449	363rd VTAP	25th TrAB	1984	Active	For Sale	-
Il-76MD	76316	0043454633	363rd VTAP	-	1984	Active	For Sale	-
Il-76MD	76320	0043455686	363rd VTAP	-	1984	Active	For Sale	-
Il-76MD	76618	0043455682	363rd VTAP	25th TrAB	1984	Active	For Sale	-
Il-76MD	76620	0043456692	363rd VTAP	-	1984	?	For Sale	-
Il-76MD	76628	0053458741	363rd VTAP	-	1984	Active	Sold	2002
Il-76MD	76629	0053458745	363rd VTAP	25th TrAB	1985	Active	Stored	-
Il-76MD	78758	0083484551	363rd VTAP	-	1988	?	For Sale	-
Il-76MD	78772	0083487627	363rd VTAP	25th TrAB	1988	?	Stored	-
Il-76MD	78785	0083489691	363rd VTAP	-	1988	?	Sold	1998

Version	Serial Number	Construction Number	Unit in 1992	Current unit	Year of manufacture	Status in 1992	Current status	Year of Retirement/ wfu/Sale
Il-76MD	78786	0083490693	363rd VTAP	-	1988	Active	Sold	2003
Il-76MD	78734	1013409303	363rd VTAP	-	1992	Active	Sold	2006
Il-76	86633	073409256	369th VTAP	-	1977	Active	wfu/Scrapped	2004
Il-76M	86028	083415464	369th VTAP	-	1978	Active	wfu/Scrapped	2007
Il-76M	86029	083415465	369th VTAP	-	1978	Active	wfu/Scrapped	2007
Il-76M	86030	093415475	369th VTAP	-	1979	Active	wfu/Scrapped	1999
Il-76MD	76636	0053459781	369th VTAP	-	1985	?	Sold	2009
Il-76MD	76647	0053461843	369th VTAP	25th TrAB	1985	Active	Stored	-
Il-76MD	76654	0053462884	369th VTAP	-	1985	Active	Stored	-
Il-76MD	76667	0053465941	369th VTAP	-	1985	Active	Crashed	2003
Il-76MD	76671	0063465963	369th VTAP	-	1986	?	Sold	2005
Il-76MD	76676	0063467003	369th VTAP	?	1986	Active	Stored	-
Il-76MD	76677	0063467005	369th VTAP	25th TrAB	1986	Active	Stored	-
Il-76MD	76680	0063467020	369th VTAP	25th TrAB	1986	Active	Stored	-
Il-76MD	76683	0063468029	369th VTAP	25th TrAB	1986	Active	Active	-
Il-76MD	76684	0063468036	369th VTAP	-	1986	?	Sold	2000
Il-76MD	76687	0063469051	369th VTAP	25th TrAB	1986	Active	Sold	1997
Il-76MD	76691	0063470089	369th VTAP	25th TrAB	1986	Active	Active	-
Il-76MD	76697	0063470118	369th VTAP	25th TrAB	1986	Active	Active	-
Il-76MD	76698	0063471123	369th VTAP	25th TrAB	1986	Active	Active	-
Il-76MD	76700	0063471134	369th VTAP	25th TrAB	1986	Active	Stored	-
Il-76MD	76707	0063472166	369th VTAP	-	1986	?	For Sale	-
Il-76MD	76716	0073474211	369th VTAP	25th TrAB	1987	Active	Stored	-
Il-76MD	76717	0073474216	369th VTAP	-	1987	?	wfu/Scrapped	2012
Il-76MD	76727	0073475268	369th VTAP	-	1987	Active	Sold	2009
Il-76MD	76728	0073475270	369th VTAP	-	1987	?	Stored	-
Il-76MD	76729	0073476275	369th VTAP	-	1987	?	Stored	-
Il-76MD	76413	1013407215	409th APSZ	25th TrAB	1991	Active	Active	-
Il-76MD	76678	0063467011	-	-	1986	?	Stored	-

Abbreviations
APSZ = Aviation Regiment of tanker aircraft
GvVTAP = Guards Military-Transport Aviation Regiment
VTAP = Military-Transport Aviation
TrAB = Transport Aviation Brigade

Mi-6 Fleet (1992–1998): The Extinct Flying Dinosaurs

The Ukrainian Armed Forces inherited 64 Mi-6 helicopters, among these only eight helicopters had served in the Soviet Air Force while the remaining 56 were used by the Soviet Red Army's 51st OGvVP and 320th OVP, which both became units of Ukrainian Army Aviation. Based on exchanged data in the CFE treaty in November 1990, the 51st Independent Guards Helicopter Regiment (51st OGvVP) was subordinate to the Kiev Military District with 26 Mi-6s and 29 Mi-8s and the 320th Independent Helicopter Regiment (320th OVP) was subordinate to the Odessa Military District with 30 Mi-6s and 33 Mi-8s in service.

The Mi-6 made its first flight on 5 June 1957 and was the largest helicopter in the world at the time. In 1959, serial production started as the first mass-produced turbine helicopter of the Soviet Union. The main production was at Rostov's Factory No. 168 between 1959 and 1980, by which time 874 had been manufactured. In addition, Factory No. 23 at Moscow-Fili built 50 helicopters between 1960 and 1962, making a total of 924. In 1960, variable-

21 Blue (c/n 0692) was one of the two Mi-22 airborne command posts in service with the 112th OSAE (later 2nd OSAE) that were inherited by the UkrAF. This helicopter had reached its MTBO by 1998 and was sent to the 535th Aircraft Repair Plant at Konotop. It can be seen stored and withdrawn from service there on 9 July 1998. *Sergey Popsuevich*

incidence winglets were mounted on the sides of the 30 pre-series units. These wings provide approximately 20% of the lift required during cruise flight.

As the world's largest helicopter at the time, the Mi-6 set 14 speed records including one for sheer circuit speed at 340km/h (211mph) approved by the International Federation of Aviation (FAI). Four of these records remained unsurpassed until 1983. Even in 2013, the Mi-6 still held the FAI record of the fastest 5-tonne lift over 1,000km, in which it flew at 284km/h in 1962. The short first flight of the first Mi-6 prototype with c/n 0101, which was equipped with TV-2VM engines, was carried out by factory test pilot R. I. Kaprelyan on 5 June 1957, and its first long flight was on 18 June 1957. On 30 October, an international record for lifting a maximum load of 12,004kg to 2,432m was set by the same test pilot.

This is the radio for the communications of the commanders who were flying in this 2nd OSAE Mi-22 with bort number 21 Blue. *Sergey Popsuevich*

In the process of joint tests by the Soviet Air Force and the State Aviation Technology Committee that were held between 1959 and 1963, 16 international records were set. These not only made the Mi-6 the heaviest but also the fastest helicopter in the world. In 1961, the absolute speed record of 320km/h set by I. V. Leshina, Design Bureau Mil, was awarded an international prize named after Igor Sikorsky by the American Helicopter Society 'as recognition of the outstanding helicopter art achievements' in the development of the Mi-6.

The basic military transport version was capable of carrying 70 armed soldiers or up to 90 civil passengers. During medical evacuation missions it could be equipped with 41 stretchers and two seats for two medical workers inside its cabin. Its cargo version could carry up to 12 tonnes of payload. In emergency conditions the helicopter was able to carry a maximum of 150 passengers in its cabin, although it only had 65 folding seats.

The Mi-6A, a new base version of the helicopter, was created in 1971 as a result of numerous improvements carried out during the first ten years of operation. It differed from the Mi-6 mainly in the instrumentation equipment and structural parts with longer service endurance and life. Furthermore, the hydraulic systems had been converted to a single unit. The Mi-6A could carry up to 90 paratroopers and up to 9 tonnes of cargo on an external sling. The maximum take-off weight was increased to 44 tons.

Most of the Mi-6s manufactured for the Soviet Armed Forces entered service with transport helicopter regiments or squadrons of the Soviet Air Force that were subordinate to the Soviet Military Districts. Each of these transport helicopter regiments had three aviation squadrons, two with 40 Mi-8s and one with 20 Mi-6s. The transport helicopter regiments were part of an aviation group that also had a combat-transport helicopter regiment with another 40 Mi-8s and 20 Mi-24s in service. By the end of the 1980s, these helicopter regiments were assigned to the Red Army and Army Corps, and then came under the command of Soviet Army Aviation in 1991.

Although nearly all the manufactured Mi-6 and Mi-6As were in service with Soviet Army Aviation, the Soviet Air Armies continued to operate special variants of the Mi-6 in their composite aviation regiments and independent squadrons as their special purpose assets. These variants were the Mi-6PSS (SAR), Mi-6KVP and Mi-22. The Mi-6KVP, the design and development of which had begun at Aircraft Repair Plant No. 535 at Konotop by the end of 1972, was a command post helicopter equipped with a secure radio communications suite and a war room in its cargo cabin that could be deployed after landing on the battlefield to command and control Soviet Army and Air Army units and their forces.

In total 36 Mi-6As were converted into the Mi-6VKP but just 13 of them are known today. Due to the limited capabilities of the Mi-6KVP, the Mi-6VzPU or Mi-22 airborne command post helicopter was designed by No. 329 Mil Moscow Helicopter Plant and modified under the Yakhont (Sapphire) programme. The helicopter was not only able to be operated as a command post on the ground but also had the capability to perform this function while it was flying. It had also been equipped with SLAR. Twelve examples of the helicopter are known to have been built in 1975 and 1976.

When the Soviet Union collapsed, its air force was operating Mi-6, Mi-6A, Mi-6PSS, Mi-6PSA, Mi-6KVP and Mi-22s in service with the 112th OSAE (Independent Aviation Squadron) at Odessa, 218th OSAE at Alma-Ata, 249th OSAE at Riga-Spilve, 255th OSAE at Boryspil, 302nd ove REB (Independent Helicopter Squadron for Electronic Warfare) at Kobrin, 50th OSAP (Independent Mixed Aviation Regiment) at Machulishchi, 65th OVP (Independent Helicopter Squadron) at Kobrin, 138th OSAP at Levashovo, 150th VTAP (Military-Transport Aviation Regiment) in Ulan-Ude, 243rd OSAP at Lviv, 456th OGSAP (Independent Guards Mixed Aviation Regiment) at Vinnitsa, 457th OSAP at Alma-Ata, 679th ITAP (Transport Test Aviation Regiment) at Priozersk and 344th TsBPPLS (Centre for Combat Employment and Retraining of Personnel).

The cabin of Mi-22 21 Blue of the 2nd OSAE while it was in storage at Konotop on 9 July 1998. *Sergey Popsuevich*

After Ukraine's independence the 112th OSAE, 255th OSAE, 243rd OSAP and 456th OGSAP were inherited by the Ukrainian Air Force:

- 112th OSAE, which was later redesignated as 2nd OSAE, had Mi-6KVP 20 Blue (c/n 0247), which was painted in an overall light grey paint scheme, and two Mi-22s, 21 Blue (c/n 0692) and 22 Blue (c/n 0696), painted in

This Mi-6KVP with construction number 737209V was in service with the 243rd OSAP as 30 Red. After Ukraine's independence, it had its bort number changed to 30 White and remained airworthy until 1994. Here it is seen stored at the Konotop Aircraft Repair Plant in 1998. *Sergey Popsuevich*

Mi-6KVP 61 Red (c/n 0690) was in service with the 456th OGSAP at Vinnitsa until it was retired from service in 1997. It is seen stored at Konotop in 1998. *Sergey Popsuevich*

olive drab/brown camouflage, which remained in service until 1997 and 1998 when their MTBO was reached and they were sent to No. 535 ARZ for overhaul

- 243rd OSAP had just one Mi-6KVP in service, 30 White (c/n 737209V), which was reportedly airworthy up to 1994

- 255th OSAE was in possession of two Mi-6s, 75 Red (c/n 0570) and 77 Red (c/n 0638), which were probably being used for cargo and troop transport before the USSR collapsed, but is not clear whether they were airworthy in the Ukrainian Air Force service or not. No. 77 Red later became 02 Yellow and was assigned to the State Flight Test Centre at Kirovskoye. It was probably a USSR Navy Aviation helicopter before it entered service with the UkrAF

- 456th OGSAP had one Mi-6KVP, 61 Red (c/n 0690), in service at Vinnitsa, which remained airworthy until 1997. This helicopter was barely flown by the Ukrainian Air Force. Also, the unit had Mi-22 12 Red (c/n 0699), which was also reported to have been converted to Mi-22BUS (with VIP cabin configuration) 10 White. It was later withdrawn from service while waiting for an overhaul at Konotop

The last flight of a Mi-6 in Ukraine took place on 12 June 1998. This was 77 Red (c/n 0618), which was an Mi-6A from Ukrainian Army Aviation's Military Unit A1604 (320th OVP) based at Chernobaevka, Kherson Oblast, and its last overhaul had been completed in Konotop on 2 August 1994.

Similar to the Ukrainian Army Aviation Mi-6s, the Ukrainian Air Force retired its last Mi-6 in 1998, which was 22 Blue from the 2nd OSAE (formerly 112th OSAE) while it was waiting for overhaul at Konotop. The helicopter was flown back to Odessa where it, together with Mi-6KVP 20 Blue, were stored until they were scrapped in 2008.

In Konotop most of the UkrAF's Mi-6s were scrapped and just ex-UkrAF 10 White from Vinnitsa survived. This was repainted in greenish-grey colours, received the bort number 12 Yellow and was preserved at the Aviakon overhaul plant at Konotop. However, it was targeted by a pro-Russian separatist's Shmel man-portable rocket launcher during the war in Donbass on 9 August 2014. Now only one Mi-6A, 22 Red, which was the former Ukrainian Army Aviation's 78 Blue (c/n 0562), is preserved in good condition in Ukraine, in the State Aviation Museum in Kiev.

Mi-8 and Mi-2 Fleet (1992–today): The Last Air Force Helicopters

The Ukrainian Air Force inherited 96 Mi-8s in service in seven squadrons and two regiments of the 5th, 14th, 17th and 24th Air Armies of the Soviet Air Force in Odessa, Volynsk, Lviv, Kiev and Vinnitsa Oblasts. Today, after 27 years, 33 of them remain in service with the 15th and 456th Transport Aviation Brigades as well as the 203rd Training Aviation Brigade of the UkrAF at Boryspil, Vinnitsa and Chuguyev respectively. In 2016, Ukrainian Army Aviation, which is the main operator of the Mi-8 family in the country, had a fleet of 35 airworthy aircraft, while the UkrAF had only 11 operational Mi-8 family helicopters in use for SAR, CSAR, VIP transport, cargo transport, pilot training and paratroops training. Today, the UkrAF has 14 operational Mi-8s in service in three brigades.

In service with the Ukrainian Air Force

After the independence of Ukraine, 247 Mi-8s and seven Mi-9s were inherited by Ukrainian Army Aviation, all in service with ten former Soviet Army Aviation regiments:

- 51st OGvVP with 29 Mi-8s subordinate to the Kiev Military District at Aleksandriya, Kirovograd Oblast

- 119th OVP with 15 Mi-8s subordinate to the 13th Combined Arms Army at Brody-North, Lviv Oblast

- 238th OVP with 20 Mi-8s subordinate to the Carpathian Military District at Kalinov, Sumska Oblast

- 287th OVP with 18 Mi-8T/MTVs subordinate to the 14th Combined Arms Army at Raukhovka, Odessa Oblast

- 320th OVP with 33 Mi-8s subordinate to the Odessa Military District at Chernobaevka, Kherson Oblast

- 335th OVP with 24 Mi-8s subordinate to the 38th Combined Arms Army at Kalinov, Sumska Oblast

- 340th OVP with 40 Mi-8s subordinate to the Carpathian Military District at Kalinov, Sumska Oblast

- 441st OVP with 23 Mi-8s subordinate to the 8th Tank Army at Korosten, Zhitomir Oblast

- 442nd OVP with 20 Mi-8s and three Mi-9s subordinate to the 13th Combined Arms Army at Zhovtnevoye, Volynskaya Oblast

- 488th OVP with 25 Mi-8s and four Mi-9s subordinate to the 38th Combined Arms Army at Vapnyarka, Vinnitsa Oblast

The Ukrainian Air Force inherited almost 96 Mi-8s helicopters in service with the following units:

- 112nd OSAE with eight Mi-8s subordinate to the 5th Air Army at Odessa, Odessa Oblast

- 153 OSAE with eight Mi-8Ps, Mi-9s and Mi-8MTs subordinate to the 5th Air Army at Kishinev, Moldovian SSR (returned to Odessa before the Soviet Union's collapse)

- 208th ove REB with 14 Mi-8SMV/PPAs subordinate to the 5th Air Army at Buyalyk, Odessa Oblast

- 294th ove REB with 17 Mi-8PPAs, Mi-8SMVs and Mi-8Ts subordinate to the 5th Air Army at Buyalyk, Odessa Oblast

- 209th ove REB with 11 Mi-8SMV/PPAs subordinate to the 14th Air Army at Lutsk, Volynsk Oblast

- 243rd OSAP with eight Mi-8s subordinate to the 14th Air Army at Lviv, Lviv Oblast

- 228th ove REB with 15 Mi-8SMV/PPAs subordinate to the 17th Air Army at Boryspil, Kiev Oblast

- 255th OSAE with seven Mi-8s subordinate to the 17th Air Army at Boryspil, Kiev Oblast

- 456th OGSAP with eight Mi-8s subordinate to the 24th Air Army at Vinnitsa, Vinnitsa Oblast

As can be seen, four Independent EW Helicopter Squadrons (overeb) were inherited by the UkrAF. This was half of the eight EW Helicopter Squadrons equipped with almost 55 Mi-8SMV and Mi-8PPA airborne jamming platforms across the Soviet Union. In the Soviet Union's organisation, these squadrons had the primary role of jamming enemy communications on the battlefield.

The Mi-8SMV (Izdeliye 80SMV), code-named Hip-J by NATO, was equipped with the R-949 jamming system, which consisted of four on-board jamming transmitters and 32 small, expandable communications jammers droppable in the vicinity of the target communication post, while the Mi-8PPA (Izdeliye 90PP), code-named Hip-K by NATO, was a modernised version of the Mi-8PP that had been developed by KB Mil in 1971. It was an active communications jammer and communication intelligence (COMINT) helicopter, and it entered USSR-AF service in 1982. It was equipped with SPS-63, 66 and 68 equipment; a rectangular container and an array of six cruciform dipole antennas on each side of the cabin; without a Doppler box under its tailboom and its heat exchangers were under the front fuselage.

Under the new defensive doctrine of the UkrAF, and especially due to financial issues, the Independent EW Helicopter Squadrons were disbanded one by one. This started with 294overeb in Buyalyk in late 1992, while in the same year another unit, 209overeb, was disbanded in Lutsk. Apart from four of its Mi-8PPAs, which were absorbed by 208overeb in Buyalyk, its remaining seven helicopters were stored at Lutsk and today four of them can still be found on the air base. By the mid-1990s, 228overeb had been disbanded at Boryspil and in 1998, 208overeb, the last UkrAF EW Helicopter Squadron, was disbanded. Apart from five to six Mi-8PPAs that were absorbed by the 456th OGSAP at Vinnitsa, the rest were sent to the Sevastopol and Konotop aircraft repair plants, where they were put in storage and mostly later scrapped.

Not only the Independent EW Helicopter Squadrons but also the Independent Mixed Aviation Squadrons that operated Mi-8T/Ps were disbanded, with one exception, which was the 255th OSAE at Boryspil. First, the 153rd OSAE was disbanded in 1992, and all its Mi-8s and Mi-9s were absorbed by the 112th OSAE, which was redesignated as the 2nd OSAE. In 1998, the last Mi-8s and Mi-9s of the 2nd OSAE were withdrawn from service and the 15th Transport Aviation Brigade (former 255th OSAE/1 OSAP) as well as the 456th Transport Aviation Brigade (former 456th OGSAP) became the last operators of the Mi-8 family helicopters in UkrAF service.

The first UkrAF exercise was held in June 1992 and its Mi-8s have always participated. For example, in 1996 two air force Mi-8PPAs together with an Army Aviation Mi-8MT and a Mi-24 took part in a large tactical exercise over the Kiev-Olexandrivka gunnery range in which 55 UkrAF aircraft took part. This was one of the last exercises held in which the Mi-8PPAs had a role! Generally, the UkrAF's Mi-8MT and Mi-8MTVs participated on SAR and MEDEVAC missions.

In service with the Ukrainian Army medical system

In 2006, the Ukrainian Ministry of Defence approved a programme for the development of a medical system for the Ukrainian Armed Forces. An important part of the plan was the use of the UkrAF's resources and equipment including the An-26 'Vita' and SAR Mi-8 helicopters. To implement the programme, the Ukrainian Armed Forces, including the UkrAF, took part in several special exercises with their air ambulance aircraft. On 17 April 2007 an aviation SAR group was formed within the 456th TrAB with an An-26 'Vita' and six Mi-8s. Completion of the programme to form the medical organisation was planned for 2011.

In December 2006, the UkrAF participated in Ukraine's first large-scale tactical special exercise with the practical deployment of a military mobile hospital of the Military Medical Centre of the Air Force to Novobohdanivka. During the practical phase for medical evacuation aircraft, the 456th TrAB took part with its sole An-26 'Vita' air ambulance and its only Mi-8MTV, 69 Blue (c/n 95198), both forward deployed to Melitopol. Also during the exercise, the sole Mi-8MTYu of the UkrAF in service with the Ukrainian Air Force Research and Test Centre (GANITS) at Kirovskoye participated after deployment to the exercise area. The Mi-8MTYu carried two divers who jumped into the water to rescue two parachute jumpers after the SAR radar of the helicopter detected their location. A winch operation was then performed to lift all four from the water.

The Mi-8MTYu in question, 75 Yellow (previously 80 Red and 80 Yellow) was the only prototype of a maritime SAR helicopter developed by the St Petersburg OAO 'CSPA' Leninist during project 'Zvezdochka' (Star) IOP-40 with the intention of searching and tracking small surface targets via a nose-mounted radar inside a huge radome, especially the splashdown of a spacecraft into the water. After the Soviet Union collapsed, the helicopter prototype was left at the GANITS facility in Ukraine and later entered service with the UKrAF.

The Mi-8MTYu regularly participated in maritime SAR exercises, during which NATO representatives witnessed a demonstration of its SAR capability, especially its ability to find small subjects the size of a human body on the sea surface. The demonstration was intended to create interest in foreign countries to invest in the development of the helicopter project. It is believed that the last time the helicopter took part in an exercise was in December 2006. At least once a year, this helicopter was used for maritime survival and SAR training of UkrAF pilots and SAR teams at Feodosia. On each training course, almost 30 aircrew carried out parachute jumps into the Black Sea in several flights and then the SAR teams using their SAR boats and the helicopter using its winch recovered them from the water.

80 Red (later 75 Yellow) with construction number 94617, the sole Mi-8MTYu of the UkrAF that was tested by GANiTS until 2007, when it was put in storage. It is seen at Kirovskoye, Crimea, on 14 April 1997. *Sergey Popsuevich*

In 2008, the SAR helicopter units of the 15th and 456th TrAB participated in several SAR exercises across Ukraine to increase the readiness of the SAR teams and aircrews. In following years, as well as participating in on average two annual SAR and MEDEVAC exercises, the SAR Mi-8s of the 15th TrAB and 456th TrAB took part in various UkrAF exercises along with the An-26 'Vita' to keep their crews at the highest level of readiness.

In 2012, the An-26 'Vita', together with four Mi-8MTs and their aircrew, were on alert to be used in any kind of MEDEVAC mission during the Euro 2012. It was the same situation in 2014, during the war in Donbass, when two 456th TrAB Mi-8MTs were forward deployed to eastern Ukraine to be used in CSAR missions alongside Mi-8MTVs of Ukrainian Army Aviation.

Mi-8T 01 Yellow of the 15th TrAB in use for the transportation of UkrAF and Ukrainian Army commanders as well as governmental authorities in the 1990s and 2000s. It is seen flying at Boryspil in 2003. Following the war in Donbass, the Wings of Phoenix public association restored this helicopter and brought it back to life in 2014. *Sergey Popsuevich*

Mi-8s of 15th TrAB

According to global images, the 15th TrAB had nine Mi-8 helicopters, of which eight were airworthy, in 2002. This number was reduced to six airworthy and two grounded Mi-8s in 2013. Today the brigade has two Mi-8Ts, with 01 and 02 Yellow; two Mi-8PSs, 03 and 05 Yellow; an Mi-8MT, 67 Yellow; and an Mi-8MTV, 69 Yellow. Among these, four are airworthy while the Mi-8PSs 03 and 05 Yellow are grounded. Another Mi-8MTV-2, 70 Yellow, flew for the last time in 2007 and was then grounded having reached the end of its MTBO. The State Enterprise Aviakon Konotop Aircraft Repair Plant carried out its depot maintenance between 2014 and 2016.

The brigade's Mi-8T(P)s are dedicated to VIP and transport flights of the Ukrainian Air Force commander and other high-ranking officers, and in some cases governmental authorities. Subsequently, the Zbroini Syly Ukrayiny (Ukrainian Armed Forces) title is written on their fuselages. Since 2008, these two Mi-8T(P)s have been used instead of the pair of Mi-8PSs 03 and 05 Yellow, which have been stored since 2008 and 2007 respectively, but when the war started in Donbass, 01 Yellow was grounded due to a lack of spare parts. The Wings of Phoenix public association made the helicopter airworthy again via a public fund between 10 and 30 September 2014 that helped to procure hydraulic lines and spare parts for its GHS-40PU and GHS-30U generators and avionics.

The brigade's Mi-8MT and Mi-8MTV are dedicated to SAR, CSAR and MEDEVAC missions. Nos 67 and

Another Mi-8T of the 15th TrAB with bort number 02 Yellow (c/n 99047210) at Boryspil on 23 March 2005. *Sergey Popsuevich*

15th TrAB Mi-8PS 03 Yellow (c/n 4267) at Boryspil in the early 2000s. This VIP helicopter is now stored at the airport. *Sergey Popsuevich*

69 Yellow both received two white recognition stripes on their tailbooms in spring 2014. No. 67 Yellow was armed with a pair of B8-V20A rocket pods and participated from Kulbakino in a large-scale UkrAF exercise in May 2014. During the exercise the pilots practised rocketry by launching S-8 rockets as well as CSAR and SAR training. When the war started, 69 Yellow was grounded, but was soon restored and forward deployed to the east of Ukraine (believed to be Dnetropetrovsk) to be used alongside Ukrainian Army Aviation helicopters on CSAR missions to save downed UkrAF pilots on the battlefield.

This Mi-8MT of the 15th TrAB with bort number 67 Yellow participated in Exercise Clear Sky 2011 as a search and rescue helicopter at Mirgorod AB in July 2011. *Sergey Popsuevich*

Mi-8s of 456th TrAB

The 456th TrAB is now the largest operator of the Mi-8 family in UkrAF service with 18 examples, although just seven are airworthy. These are Mi-8PPA 03 Blue (one of four Mi-8PPAs with the 456th TrAB and the last airworthy example in UkrAF service); three Mi-8MTs, 16 Blue, 30 Blue (former 35 Yellow of the Soviet Army's 439th OVP based at Parchim, East Germany between 1990 and 1992) and 36 Blue; Mi-8MTV 69 Blue; and two Mi-9s, 31 and 34 Blue. No. 31 Blue, which was 31 Yellow before it was stored at Vinnitsa from 2012, was restored and became airworthy in 2017.

The Mi-9 is a command post helicopter based on the Mi-8T airframe but equipped with a special radio communication system and radio repeater system for use by the commanders of motorised rifle (tank) and airborne divisions. The Mi-9, which flew for first time in 1977, was the replacement for the Mi-8VKP (Mi-8VzPU) command post helicopter. In 1987 its role was taken over by the Mi-19 command post, which was developed on an Mi-8MT platform. The Mi-19 and Mi-19R (command post helicopter for the commanders of missile divisions) never entered service with the Soviet Army and Air Force units in the Socialist Republic of Ukraine.

In May 2014, during an exercise before the large-scale counter-terrorism operation in Donbass, Mi-8MTV 69 Blue, armed with a pair of B8-V20A rocket pods, was forward deployed to Kulbakino. On 15 and 16 May its pilots dropped P-50T practice bombs, and practised rocketry by firing S-8 unguided rockets, using the 15th TrAB's Mi-8MT 67 Yellow. Also, during the annual gunnery training of the 7th BrTA at Lutsk AB in 2015 and 2016, 69 Blue

69 Blue, a Mi-8MTV-1 of the 456th TrAB during an exercise at Rovno gunnery range on 17 September 2007. The bort number was changed to 36 Black after the war in 2015. *Sergey Popsuevich*

from the 456th TrAB participated in bombing and rocketry alongside 7th BrTA Su-24s and L-39s.

It is not known if 69 Blue was deployed to eastern Ukraine during the war in Donbass, but it is known that in multiple cases, including on 30 August and 4 October 2014, this helicopter was used for civilian parachute jumps at Pivdennyi-Kiev while it had white recognition stripes on its tailboom. In the past two years, while this helicopter was mainly used for transport and parachute jump training, 30 Blue also participated in various SAR and MEDEVAC exercises in the area around Vinnitsa, including an airport major incident exercise at Boryspil on 27 September 2016.

One of the 456th TrAB's responsibilities is to provide air assets to transport UkrAF commanders. Its two Mi-8PSs, 32 Blue and 55 Blue, have not flown since 2007 but are kept in good condition. Between 2009 and 2011, 55 Blue was available for sale while it had only 3,606 total flying hours on its airframe. After the war, the 456th TrAB received one freshly overhauled Mi-8MT helicopter, which was 16 Blue. It was worked on by the State Enterprise Aviakon Konotop Aircraft Repair Plant in 2014 and redelivered to the brigade in 2016.

30 Blue, a Mi-8MT of the 456th TrAB, in use for medical evacuation during an exercise at Vinnitsa on 11 June 2008. *Sergey Popsuevich*

Winch operation by a Mi-8MT of the 456th TrAB during the simulation of a combat search and rescue operation in an exercise at Vinnitsa on 11 June 2008. *Sergey Popsuevich*

31 Blue is one of two Mi-9 command post helicopters in service with the 456th TrAB of the UkrAF. It is seen at Vinnitsa on 22 June 2017. *Alexander Golz*

SAR helicopter of the 456th TrAB, Mi-8MT 30 Blue, hovering above the runway at Vinnitsa on 22 June 2017. *Alexander Golz*

34 Blue is one of two Mi-9 command post helicopters in service with the 456th TrAB of the UkrAF. It is seen at Vinnitsa on 21 April 2016. *Alexander Golz*

The radio jammers

During an official ceremony at Ozernoye air base on 21 December 2018, the UkrAF received two unique electronic warfare Mi-8 helicopters, the only examples of their kind in Ukraine. They were a Mi-8MTPB and a Mi-8MTPI, both having been overhauled at the State Enterprise Aviakon Konotop Aircraft Repair Plant. They were designed and developed to take the place of the ageing Mi-8PPAs in service with the Soviet Air Force and Army Aviation but due to the USSR's collapse just eight examples were produced, and only two were delivered to the units stationed in the Ukrainian SSR in 1991.

The Mi-8MTPB, known as the 'Hip-H EW3' by NATO, is a special modification of the Mi-8MT transport helicopter designed for electronic warfare. It is equipped with Bison-type radio and electronic jammers. It can be equipped with six heat exchanger nacelles under its fuselage just behind the nose landing gear, similar to the Mi-8PPA. It has large hinged (upward) and box-shaped dielectric panels on both sides of the fuselage in front of the main landing gear. A pair of large rectangular flat antenna blocks are attached to the rear fuselage of the Mi-8MTPB, each one with 32 circular segments and arranged in eight to four rows. The UkrAF inherited only one Mi-8MTPB, c/n 95375, manufactured in 1991.

In addition, the UkrAF inherited one of the world's three Mi-8MTPI (Mi-8MTBPI) 'Hip-H EW5' aircraft, c/n 95142. The Mi-8MTPI is equipped with the more modern Ikebana-type jammer system, with two pairs of antenna units located inside flat rectangular containers, the first pair of which are attached on each side of the middle of the fuselage, just in front of the main landing gear struts (each with 14 dielectric panels), and the aft containers are installed on the left and right sides of the tail boom, each one with 28 dielectric panels in a pentagonal shape arrangement of 14 in two rows.

It is known that the calendar life both of the helicopters lasted until 2001 and 2002 but the UkrAF had already stopped operating them due to the complexity of their EW systems and from the mid-1990s preferred to continue operating the older Mi-8PPA. Both helicopters were sent to the Konotop Aircraft Repair Plant in the early 2000s to be overhauled and put up for sale. In August 2008, Ukraine offered them to NATO to be used for research purposes but they were not interested. Finally, during the Donbass war, when the air force

03 Blue is believed to be the last Mi-8PPA of the 456th TrAB. *Dmitry P.'s collection*

Mi-8MTPB 38 Blue at the handover ceremony on 21 December 2018. *UkrOboronProm*

needed to increase its combat capability, their overhaul and upgrade was funded and both of the helicopters were redelivered to the air force on 21 December 2018.

C/n 95375 received the bort number 38 Blue and 95142 became 39 Blue. During the war in Donbass, the Russian Air Force used the latest variant of the helicopter, the Mi-8MTPR-1, to support the operations of pro-Russian separatists and their Russian military counterparts. It is believed that the last of the 456th TrAB's Mi-8PPAs, which was still airworthy until 2014, is now grounded after being replaced by these two newer and more capable helicopters.

Mi-8s of 203rd TrAB

Student helicopter pilots were being trained on Mi-2s and Mi-8s of the 203rd Training Aviation Brigade (203rd TrAB) of HUVS (Kharkiv Air Force University). Before 2011, they had to fly at least 20 hours in the Mi-2 light helicopter during their primary flight training course, while they were flying on average 40 additional hours in the Mi-8MT during their advanced flight training course.

Although it had a relatively large number of operational Mi-8s in early 2000s, the 203rd TrAB now has the smallest airworthy fleet in the UkrAF, with only two airworthy Mi-8MTs, 81 and 87 Yellow, as well as two airworthy Mi-2s, 90 and 91 Yellow. Nine Mi-8Ts, 02, 03, 82, 85, 86, 120, 121 and 135 Yellow and another Mi-2 are stored at the brigade's premises in Chuguyev.

No. 120 Yellow was the last operational Mi-8T of the 203rd TrAB until its MTBO was reached and it was grounded in 2011. Until at least 2008, 120 Yellow in participated of various Ukrainian Armed Forces exercises, including Peace Shield 2005, which was held in Crimea. No. 120 Yellow, together with an Mi-8MT of the brigade (probably 81 Yellow), were deployed to Belbek AB to take part in the exercise from there.

The 203rd TrAB had three Mi-8MTs in its inventory in the late 1990s, but apart from 86 Yellow, the other two, 82 and 85 Yellow, were not airworthy by the second half of the 2000s, and the Mi-8Ts were mostly used for training new helicopter pilots. Later, in 2008, the brigade start to replace its Mi-8Ts with superior Mi-8MTs.

In the spring and summer of 2009 some Mi-8MTs from other units, including Ukrainian Army

Mi-8MTPB 39 Blue at the handover ceremony on 21 December 2018. *UkrOboronProm*

Mi-8MT 81 Yellow of the 203rd TrAB at Chuguyev on 7 July 2017. *Alexander Golz*

Aviation's Mi-8MTV-1 45 Black, which had been previously deployed to Africa on UN peacekeeping missions, were transferred to the UkrAF to be used for pilot training by the 203rd TrAB. In the same year the unit received its first overhauled Mi-8MT, 81 Yellow (c/n 94039), while the other Mi-8MTs had been sent to the overhaul facility to be repaired.

By using 81 Yellow and the Mi-8MTs of the other units, as well as leased Mi-8s from Motor Sich, the HUVS trained new pilots until the delivery of a second Mi-8MT in 2013. The second Mi-8MT, which was actually an Mi-8MTV but without weather radar, was 87 Yellow, painted in the green digital camouflage colour scheme, which was first seen with the 203rd TrAB after its overhaul in April 2013. The 203rd TrAB used to operate these two helicopters to train an average of 15 cadets per year between 2010 and 2014. Before their training course on Mi-8s, the cadets had to first fly in Mi-2s.

Mi-8MT 87 Yellow of the 203rd TrAB during training with the California Air National Guard para-rescuemen and aeromedical evacuation specialists at Vinnitsa during Exercise *Clear Sky 2018* on 10 September 2018. *USAF*

The Mi-2s

The air force had no Mi-2s when it was established in 1992, because nearly all of those inherited by Ukraine were in service with the USSR Voluntary Society for Assistance to the Army, Aviation and Navy (DOSAAF). On 26 September 1991, DOSAAF had been reorganised as the Society for the Defence of Ukraine (TSOU) following a decision by the Ukrainian parliament. It is not clear exactly when, but at least from the mid-1990s around ten Mi-2s were transferred to the air force to be used for pilot training. Three ended up at the 203rd TrAB – 147, 148 and 159 Yellow – but they were gradually grounded when they reached their MTBOs. The last was 147 Yellow, which remained operational until 2010. Three more ex-TSOU's Mi-2s were handed over to HUVS to be used as ground instructional airframes, which were 20, 27 and 46 Yellow.

The last airworthy HUVS Mi-2 was 147 Yellow, which was grounded in 2008 or 2009. After the Mi-2s were grounded, HUVS leased helicopters from civil companies. For example, in 2013 three Mi-2s were leased from Motor Sich and in 2014 an Enstrom 480V was leased from the Rotor Ukraine company. After the start of the war in Donbass, HUVS and volunteer technicians quickly started to restore two of the grounded Mi-2s, which, with new bort numbers 90 and 91 Yellow, returned to service in the new green digital camouflage in 2015 and 2016.

It was also reported that two upgraded Mi-2MSBs were delivered to the 203rd TrAB after 2016. One was heavily damaged after an emergency landing due to a technical malfunction on 28 March 2019. Its crew did not suffer any injuries but the helicopter was withdrawn from service.

Now HUVS's cadets fly on these three Mi-2s in their third-year course, and after completion of their 20 hours flight training on them, they start flying with the Mi-8MT flight simulator before their actual Mi-8MT training flights to save on fuel and other costs. Thus, their flying hours on the Mi-8MT can be reduced to 25 hours, and after ten hours they can take control of the helicopter! The simulator was installed at the university in November 2011, and it has enabled the cadets to carry out 90% of the

Mi-2 90 Yellow of the 203rd TrAB with at Chuguyev on 7 July 2017. *Alexander Golz*

Mi-2MSV 93 Yellow of the 203rd TrAB at Chuguyev on 2 August 2018. *Alexander Golz*

Mi-2 96 Yellow cockpit trainer of the 203rd TrAB at Chuguyev. *Alexander Golz*

manoeuvres that can be performed by the real Mi-8MT. The cost of an Mi-8 flying hour was equivalent to 4,000 UAH ($480) in 2011.

|Between 2011 and 2014, many Mi-8 student pilots completed their course after only after 20 hours' flight! It is believed that because of the use of the simulator to compensate for the lack of flying hours available, the new generation of UkrAF and even Army Aviation Mi-8 pilots are suffering from a lack of flying skill, which was revealed during the counter-terrorism operation in Donbass when in some cases Mi-8s crashed due to a combination of pilot error and enemy artillery.

The future of the UkrAF's last helicopters

In 2019, 13 Mi-8s comprising two Mi-8Ts, six Mi-8MTs, two Mi-8MTVs, a Mi-8MTV-2, a Mi-8MTBP and a Mi-8MTBPI, together with two Mi-9s, remained operational out of a total of 33 Mi-8s and two Mi-9s in the possession of the UkrAF.

In May 2014, following the beginning of the war in Donbass, all units of the UkrAF were put on high alert and their elite pilots were prepared for all types of combat missions during a large-scale training exercise at Kulbakino. At the exercise were ten airworthy Mi-8s, of which six, including both airworthy Mi-8MT/MTVs of the 203rd TrAB, were prepared for combat to be used in strike, interdiction and CAS missions beside their primary SAR, CSAR and MEDEVAC roles in emergency situations.

At least 14 or 15 sets of crews were prepared for combat, including six sets consisting of a pilot, a co-pilot and a flight engineer for combat missions involving rocketry and bombing. The six above-mentioned helicopters were equipped with external pylons, with at least a pair of B8-V20A rocket pods under two of six hardpoints, while the remaining empty pylons were equipped with ejector racks for carrying free fall bombs. Chaff/flare dispensers, side external cabin armour, and engine and APU armour were also installed. Two, which had been forward deployed to the war zone, were also equipped with IR missile warning sensors to protect the helicopters against the threat of MANPADS. The sensors were later dismantled when their ineffectiveness was revealed due to the loss of multiple Mi-8s to MANPADS in 2014.

Despite its involvement in the war, the 203rd TrAB was strengthened by an extra Mi-8MT from the 456th TrAB and an Mi-8MTV from the 15th TrAB to speed up the training of new helicopter student pilots in summer and autumn 2014. Its Mi-8MT 81 YELLOW was also forward deployed to the war zone to be used in CSAR and CAS missions.

In 2015 and 2016, after a decline in military activity by the separatists in the Donbass region and the subsequent drop in the number of Mi-8 combat sorties, the 203rd TrAB's Mi-8s were used alongside Mi-8s from other units in routine annual SAR exercises, parachute training jumps for civilians and military paratroopers. For example, during a large-scale SAR exercise at Boryspil International airport, the 15th TrAB's Mi-8MT 30 Blue participated as a MEDEVAC helicopter.

Mi-8s of the UkrAF in 2019

Model	Construction Number	Bort Number	Colour Scheme	Current Unit	Last Maintenance/ Overhaul/ Restoration	Note
Mi-8T	?	01 Yellow	Two tone green camouflage	15th TrAB	2014	With VIP cabin configuration
Mi-8T	99047210	02 Yellow	Two tone green camouflage	15th TrAB	2015	With VIP cabin configuration
Mi-8PPA	?	03 Blue	Two tone green camouflage	456th TrAB	2004	Status uncertain. Probably grounded
Mi-9	?	31 Blue	Green/grey camouflage	456th TrAB	2017	
Mi-9	98556254	34 Blue	Green/grey camouflage	456th TrAB	2012	
Mi-8MT	95119	67 Yellow	Olive drab/sand camouflage	15th TrAB	2007	
Mi-8MT	95197	87 Yellow	Green digital camouflage	203rd TrAB	2013	Formerly Mi-8MTV with weather radar
Mi-8MT	94039	81 Yellow	Two tone green camouflage	203rd TrAB	2009	
Mi-8MT	94548	36 Blue	Green/brown camouflage	456th TrAB	2015	
Mi-8MT	94648	30 Blue	Green/brown camouflage	456th TrAB	2008	
Mi-8MT	?	16 Blue	Olive drab/brown camouflage	456th TrAB	2014	
Mi-8MTV	95057	69 Yellow	Black/brown/white camouflage	15th TrAB	2007	
Mi-8MTPI	95142	39 Blue	Olive drab/sand camouflage	456th TrAB	2018	
Mi-8MTV	95198	36 Black	Olive drab/sand camouflage	456th TrAB	2007	Had 69 Blue bort number until early 2017
Mi-8MTV-2	95237	70 Yellow	Green/beige/reddish brown 'digital' camouflage	15th TrAB	2016	
Mi-8MTBP	95375	38 Blue	Olive drab/sand camouflage	456th TrAB	2018	

Tu-134AK/B Fleet (1992–today): The Crusty VIP Carriers

The Tu-134AK is one of the most successful VIP aircraft ever produced in the Soviet Union and Russia. Almost 180 Tu-134AKs were manufactured, some of which were former Tu-134A-3s and Tu-134Sh-1/2s converted to the variant. Its military variant served in the air forces of 15 countries and they transported thousands of governmental officials and military commanders across the world. Ukraine inherited six Tu-134AKs, among them three were military variants in service with the 243rd Independent Mixed Aviation Regiment and three others were operated by Aeroflot for Ukrainian SSR government officials.

This Tu-134AK registered CCCP-65718 (c/n 63668) operated for the government of the Ukrainian Soviet Republic. It was operated by the Ministry of Interior for flights of Ukrainian governmental authorities until 2010, when its MTBO was reached and it was stored at Boryspil. It is seen at Boryspil airport in 1991. *Sergey Popsuevich*

Tu-134A-3 CCCP-65782 was used by Boryspil's branch of Aeroflot in the 1980s. After the Soviet Union collapsed, this aircraft was operated by Ukrayina Aviation Enterprise for the Ukrainian Government until 2009. When it reached 16,000 total cycles it was put in storage at Boryspil on 10 January 2012. It was disassembled and transferred by road to the Kiev State Aviation Museum on 29 and 30 November 2014. It is seen at Boryspil in 1991. *Sergey Popsuevich*

The stinger-tails

On 7 February 1981, a Tu-104A of the Soviet Navy with the registration CCCP-42332 (c/n 76600402) crashed immediately after take-off from Pushkin Airport. The aircraft stalled quickly after taking off, banked right at an altitude of 50m and crashed almost inverted, killing six crew members and 44 passengers, who were mostly high-ranking Soviet Navy officials returning to Vladivostok after an exercise in Leningrad. The cause of the accident was the displacement of unsecured cargo in the aft section of the cabin. This moved the aircraft's centre of gravity to the tail and beyond the certified limits of the aircraft.

After the accident to the 24-year-old Tu-104A, the Soviet Air Force and Navy quickly retired the surviving examples of the aircraft and simultaneously replaced them with the Salon and Airborne Command Post (VKP) variants of the Tu-134A-3. The replacement was a military variant of the successful Tu-134AK Salon aircraft that had been operated since 1971 by the 235th OAO (235th Otdel'nyy Aviaotryad – independent flight detachment), the 8th Red Banner Air Division at Vnukovo, to carry Soviet government officials.

The Tu-134AK of the General Secretary of the Central Committee of the CPSU, Leonid Brezhnev, was equipped with a Tatra radio system that enabled the VIP passenger to have operational communication with almost the entire world. The other variant of Tu-134AK, which was in use by the Minister of Defence of the Soviet Union, Andrei Grechko, was equipped with a satellite communications complex, Karpaty, which had higher capabilities than the Tatra.

Compared with the Tu-134A-3 passenger aircraft, the VIP Tu-134AK could be identified by the additional entry door in front of the port engine (which is non-functional if the aircraft has been reconfigured to all-economy seating). The Tu-134AK appeared in both standard ('glass-nosed') and export ('radar-nosed') versions, both of which could be equipped to Tu-134A standard (i.e. with D-30 Srs. 2 engines) or Tu-134A-3 standard (with D-30 Srs. 3 engines). In contrast, the regular Tu-134As that had been built with no rear entry door and converted to VIP configuration were popularly called the Tu-134A'Salon.

The airborne command post Tu-134AK was named 'Balkany' due to the installation of the Balkany F radio complex. It was visually distinguishable from the civilian Tu-134AKs with a stinger tail cone under the exhaust nozzle of its APU. The tail cone housed the HF antenna of the Balkany Radio system. The Tu-134AK (Balkany) is an army staff transport that facilitates the work and communications of the army command and supports the operations of the army headquarters. The aircraft is equipped with a special communications centre enabling operation both on the ground and in flight. Thus, to all intents and purposes the Tu-134 'Balkany' can be regarded as an army-level airborne command post.

The first Tu-134 Balkany prototype was created by converting Tu-134AK CCCP-65980 and it made its maiden flight on 20 February 1986. The state research centre tests of this machine were successfully completed on 30 October 1986. Subsequently, by the early 1990s, around 40 serial Tu-134AKs were converted to Balkany aircraft during their overhaul. The basis of all the Tu-134 Balkanys were the Tu-134AK aircraft from the 50th to 63rd production series, which had been manufactured by No. 135 Kharkiv production plant between 1979 and 1982.

Stinger-tail (Balkany) Tu-134A-3 63957 (ex 01 Yellow) of the UkraAF used to transport Ukrainian Armed Forces commanders. It is een at Vinnitsa on 3 December 2008. *Sergey Popsuevich*

This Tu-134Sh-2 with construction number 93551010 served in the Soviet Navy as 70 Blue at Nikolayev-Kulbakino until 1992. It was then transferred to 456th OGSAP of the UkrAF at Vinnitsa and received the bort number 04 Black. With a VIP cabin for 13 people, it flew as a commander carrier aircraft with the serial number 551010 until it logged its last flight to Boryspil on 15 April 2002 and was offered for sale by SkyBirdHeli with a total of 1,164 flying hours and 1,464 cycles on 27 May 2006. It is still in storage at Boryspil. *Sergey Popsuevich*

The VVS regiments deployed to foreign states were the first to receive the Tu-134AK Balkany. Delivery started with the 226th OSAP (Independent Mixed Air Regiment), 16th VA (Air Army), operating from Sperenberg, East Germany (25 and 36 Red), and then the 201st OSAE based at Tökol, Hungary (Black 50). Subsequently, the other OSAEs or OSAPs began receiving the Balkany, including the 243rd OSAP at Lviv, Lviv Oblast, Ukrainian SSR. By 1991, the 353rd APON (353rd Aviation Regiment for Special Purpose), 8th ADON (8th Red Banner Aviation Division for Special Purpose), became the largest operator of the type at Moscow-Chkalovsky, Moscow Oblast. The Tu-134AK Balkany was unveiled to the public at an open day at Kubinka air base on 11 April 1992.

Three Tu-134AK Balkanys entered service with the 243rd OSAP of the 14th Air Army, which were CCCP-63957 (c/n 63957), CCCP-63960 (c/n 63960) and CCCP-63982 (c/n 63982). They received the bort numbers 01, 02 and 03 Yellow respectively. Among these, 01 and 03 Yellow remained airworthy while 02 Yellow was demilitarised and sold. It received the registration UR-CCG and was sold to UTair in Russia in 2005.

No. 03 Yellow was then demilitarised and turned into a Tu-134A-3 Salon during its overhaul at No. 407 ARZ in December 1998. It was used by the Ukrainian Minister of Defence and because of that it had 'Zbroini Syly Ukrainy' (Armed Forces of Ukraine) titles written on its fuselage. No. 01 Yellow remained in full military condition and is now used by the commanders of the Ukrainian Army, Air Force and Navy. It was painted in overall dark grey at the NARP facility at Mykolayiv-Kulbakino during its last periodical inspection in 2012. Today, 01 Yellow is the last operational Tu-134 in service with the UkrAF as 03 Yellow has not flown since 2005. Both aircraft are now on the inventory of the 15th Transport Aviation Brigade of the UkrAF.

The Governmental Crusty

The Tu-134AK CCCP-65746 (c/n 2351608), the construction of which had been completed on 31 July 1972, was used as a VIP aircraft for the

Ex-Soviet Navy Tu-134Sh-2 Marina Raskova tactical navigator trainer with the serial number 551010 is still stored at Boryspil airport. It is seen there in 2008. The UkrAF have had plans to scrap it since 2012, but it was still in one piece in 2019. *Alexander Golz*

Ukrainian SSR from 1972 to 1984, when it was transferred back to Aeroflot after being replaced by a newer Tu-134AK, CCCP-65556. CCCP-65556 (c/n 66372) was manufactured on 30 August 1984 and remained in use with the Ukrainian Government, operated by the UkrAF, after Ukraine's independence. The aircraft became UR-65556 and was overhauled twice after independence, enabling it to remain airworthy until mid-2013. It was last seen airworthy at Boryspil on 28 February 2013. It is now stored by the 15th TrAB.

As a back-up aircraft for CCCP-65746, a second Tu-134AK, CCCP-65718 (c/n 63668), was used from 1 July 1981. The aircraft had been manufactured on 31 March 1981. After Ukraine's independence, it remained in service and was operated by the UkrAF for the Ukrainian government as UR-65718, receiving depot maintenance after the end of its MTBO in 2001. UR-65718 remained airworthy until August 2010 and upon the end of its calendar MTBO, the aircraft was put in storage at the 15th TrAB.

After Ukraine's independence, the first Tu-134AK of the Ukrainian SSR government, CCCP-65746, which had been returned to Aeroflot in 1984 was transferred to Air Kharkiv, which was originally formed as Aeroflot's Kharkiv division of the Ukraine directorate. It received the registration UR-65746 after Ukraine's independence and remained in service with Air Kharkiv until 13 August 2009.

In addition to the Tu-134AK Salons UR-65718 and UR-65556, which were used by the Ukrainian Government until 2010 and 2013 respectively, a third aircraft – former Aeroflot Tu-134A UR-65782 – was added to the fleet after conversion to Tu-134A-3 Salon in 1993. The aircraft was operated by Ukrayina Aviation Enterprise for the Ukrainian government until 2010. Its C of A expired on 23 June 2011, when the aircraft had logged total 16,000 cycles. It was stored without a registration at Boryspil and was then transferred by road to Igor Sikorsky Kiev International Airport (Zhuliany) on three flat-bed trailers at night on 29 and 30 November 2014. It was later assembled and put on display at the State Aviation Museum in Kiev on 25 May 2015.

15th TrAB stinger-tail (Balkany) Tu-134A-3 63982 (03 Yellow) at Boryspil on 23 March 2005. *Sergey Popsuevich*

Out of the six Tu-134AKs that the UkrAF and the Ukrainian government inherited from the 243rd OSAP of the USSR VVS and Aeroflot respectively, just one stinger-tail Tu-134AK Balkany is left operating with the 15th TrAB. In addition, a Balkany aircraft was sold to UTAir leaving four others, which are now stored at Boryspil.

The Ukrainian Air Force also operated two ex-USSR VVS Tu-154B-2s, one registered CCCP-85445 manufactured in December 1980, and the other, CCCP-85561, built in 1983. The first aircraft was based at Orenburg before the USSR collapsed, while the second had been based in Ukraine since 1983. Both the Tu-154s had a short military life and they were soon leased by BSL Airline for a short period. They received the civil registrations UR-85445 and UR-85561 after Ukraine's independence. Both were withdrawn from service in 2001 and 2002 and they are now stored at Boryspil airport. In the early 2000s, the Ukrainian government ordered a Tu-154M (c/n 97A1017), the production of which was started at the Aviakor plant in Samara on 27 June 2002. Production was delayed due to a shortage of money to pay the factory and the airframe remained unfinished when production of the Tu-154 ceased in February 2013.

A pair of Tu-134A-3s of the 15th TrAB, 63957 and 63982, at Boryspil on 4 August 2008. *Alexander Golz*

Another 15th TrAB stinger-tail Tu-134A-3, 63957, at Boryspil on 4 August 2008. *Alexander Golz*

Previously 01 Yellow and now 63597, this is one of two stinger-tail (Balkany) Tu-134A-3s of the UkrAF's 15th TrAB. It was painted in overall grey camouflage after its overhaul at NARP in 2012. It was seen in storage at Boryspil in April 2019. *Alexander Golz*

85445 is one of two Tu-154B-2s that the UkrAF inherited from the Soviet Air Force. This aircraft, with civil registration UR-85445, was operated by Ukrayina Aviation Enterprise for government flights in the early 1990s. It was also leased to BSL Airline between 1996 and 1998. Manufactured in December 1980, its next overhaul was due in 2000 and it was put in storage at Boryspil few months before that in June 1999. It is still in storage. *Alexander Golz*

4 Long Range Aviation

Il-78 Fleet (1992–2005): The Ukrainian Tankers

During the USSR era a total of 47 Il-78s including two prototypes were manufactured by the Tashkent aircraft production facility between 1983 and 1991. Except for two examples that were used for research and development, the other 45 aircraft were delivered to two Tanker Aviation Regiments of the USSR Air Force. When the Soviet Union collapsed, the 409th Tanker Aviation Regiment had 22 Il-78s in service; just one of them was on the Russian mainland for modification and the others were inherited by the independent Ukraine. Under the Ukrainian Armed Force's defence doctrine, they did not have the role of tanker aircraft but were used in various other roles and then sold to four air forces in Africa and Asia.

Background

The first Il-78 prototype, with civil registration CCCP-76556 (c/n 0033445294) and equipped with two cylindrical tanks with a capacity of 14 tons of fuel each in its cargo cabin, made its first flight piloted by Ilyushin OKB test pilot Vyacheslav S. Belousov at Tashkent on 26 June 1983, almost 15 years after the launch of the heavy tanker aircraft project.

The new tanker was based on the Il-76MD platform and equipped with three Sakhalin UPAZ-1A aerial refuelling systems with increased range and fuel capacity, better reliability and the ability to refuel three fighter aircraft simultaneously. Its desired functionality indicated it was the best candidate to replace the aged and less capable Tu-16Zs, Tu-16Ns, M-4-2s, 3MS-2s and 3MN-2s, which had had the important role of supporting long-range flights of the USSR Air Force's Tu-16s, Tu-22s and Tu-95 strategic bombers in the 1980s.

Mass production began while the prototype's test flights were under way in 1983. These flights as well as the development of the aerial refuelling systems continued until 1984, when the first production Il-78 rolled out of the Ilyushin OKB and was delivered to the USSR's Air Force on 19 June 1984. The aircraft, CCCP-76607 (c/n 0043453559), was later used by the 3rd Research Military-Transport Aviation Squadron of the 610th Centre for Combat Employment and Retraining of Personnel at Ivanovo. The second and third production Il-78s were later delivered to the same squadron on 29 September and 29 December 1984 respectively. The fourth and fifth aircraft, CCCP-76610 and CCCP-76616, were delivered on 29 December 1984 and 31 March 1985.

The first four production Il-78s entered service with the 1st Instruction Military-Transport Aviation Squadron. In 1985, officers at the 610th Centre developed methods for aerial refuelling operations. The Centre trained the first Il-78 pilots and crew members and published all the required flight manual and operation manuals.

On 22 May 1993, probably for first and last time in UkrAF history, an Il-78 was used for a demonstration of inflight refuelling of an air force Tu-95MS during an air show at Poltava. The Il-78 is UR-76742, which is now in service with the Pakistani Air Force as R09-001. *Sergey Popsuevich*

UkrAF Il-78 UR-76415 together with Il-76MD UR-76413 are seen at RAF Fairford during RIAT in the UK on 18 July 1997. This aircraft had had its refuelling equipment removed and was being used for the transportation of ground equipment for the fighter jets of the UkrAF participating in the air show. This aircraft crashed during a flight from Burgas to Asmaraits after exceeding its maximum take-off weight by at least 37 tonnes (which the crew was probably unaware of) when it performed a visual approach to runway 15 at Asmara at night in bad weather. It lost altitude and hit the ground, resulting in the death of all nine crew members and the sole passenger. It was being used by Ukraine Cargo Airways as UR-UCI at the time. *Chris Chennel*

409th Aviation Regiment of Tanker Aircraft (409 APSZ)

On 25 June 1986, when nine Il-78s were available at Ivanovo, two of them (CCCP-76609 and CCCP-76610) were delivered to the 106th Heavy Bomber Aviation Division of the 37th Air Army VGK. The aircraft then served in the 409th Heavy Bomber Aviation Regiment when all its Tu-95MKs had been retired or passed to other units. Later, four more Il-78s were transferred from Ivanovo to Uzyn. They were CCCP-76616, CCCP-76632, CCCP-76646 and CCCP-76653.

The regiment's designation was changed to the 409th Aviation Regiment of Tanker Aircraft (409th APSZ) and its primary role became the provision of aerial refuelling for the Tu-95MSs of the neighbouring 1006th Heavy Bomber Aviation Regiment at the same air base and the 182nd Heavy Bomber Aviation Regiment at Mozdok.

The first mission of an Il-78 in the unit was performed over the Arctic Ocean on 16 July 1986. Gradually that year daily aerial refuelling training flights began with the Su-24Ms and Su-24MRs of Dubno, Chernyahovsk and Dzhida air bases. Also that year, the first experimental aerial refuelling of MiG-31Bs and Su-27Bs was carried out over the Akhtuba area north of the Caspian Sea.

The type was never detached to the GDR, but in 1987 the Il-78s at Uzyn were also tasked with supporting Polish-based Su-24M flights from Zagan.

In February 1987, the first Arctic flights of the Tu-95MSs were performed towards Graham Bell Island and Franz Josef Land, during which Uzyn-based Il-78s accompanied the Bear-Hs and landed at Arctic air bases.

By the end of 1989, the unit had 22 Il-78s, which were widely used to support the base's Tu-95MS on long-range flights. While their primary role was aerial refuelling, half their flights were to carry freight for Uzynand other air bases. A pure cargo Il-76MD, CCCP-78853 (c/n 1013407215), was also available in the regiment at the time.

In service with the Ukrainian Air Force

At the beginning of 1991, half the unit's Il-78s were grounded and the number of flights dropped to a third because of a lack of money and spare parts. In the same year, modification of the tail UPAZ-1A/ORM-1A aerial refuelling system mounts of the unit began with the first aircraft, CCCP-76616, being sent to Tashkent. The aircraft remained there after Ukraine became independent.

After the USSR's dissolution, the 21 Ukrainian Il-78s were no longer active as tanker aircraft, because the aerial refuelling systems of Ukrainian Air Force Tu-22M2s and Tu-22M3s had been removed under the SALT II treaty. Also, the Tu-95s and Tu-160s of the 106th Heavy Bomber Aviation Division were never used by the air force under the new defence doctrine of the force.

After the Ukraine's independence, the 106th Heavy Bomber Aviation Division was demilitarised and all its bombers were stored, while most of their flight crew went to Russia. However, the 409th Tanker Aviation Regiment remained active and a third of its aircraft served as cargo freighters all over the world until they reached the MTBO of their D-30KP engines and were gradually grounded.

In 1992 and 1993, during the Nagorno-Karabakh war, when Armenia was besieged by Azerbaijan and Turkey and it became become impossible for the country to import fuel, Ukrainian Il-78s filled with petrol flew regularly from Mozdok to Yerevan.

In 1993, they smuggled 300,000 litres of fuel from the Krasnodar territory of Russia to Yerevan in nine flights without customs clearance. Later, at Krasnodar on 3 September 1993, when the crew of 76744 were ready to board their aircraft, which was fictionally filled with plums, 28 tons of fuel in two tanks were detected by customs officers. The crew was arrested but released some days later.

Gradually, by 2000 most of the Il-78s had been converted to Il-76MDs to be used by the UkrAF or by semi-private air cargo companies (conversion of an Il-78 to an Il-76MD can take only 6 hours).

The Ukrainian Air Force lost two of its Il-78s in accidents. The first occurred to Il-78 76736 when the wing of another taxying Il-78, 76653, hit its cabin at Uzyn on 25 March 1993. The aircraft was

This UKrAF Il-78 with 76760 serial number was operated by the BSL Airline at Uzyn while it had its refuelling equipment removed between 1995 and 1999. It was returned to the UkrAF and used as a source of spare parts at Melitopol until it was prepared for a ferry flight to Nikolayev-Kulbakino on 27 June 2013 and overhauled by the NARP for the Chinese Air Force between 2013 and 2015. Its delivery flight took place on 26 June 2015. It received the seial number 20642 in the People's Liberation Army Air Force (PLAAF) and is now in use by the 38th Air Regiment at Wuhan-Paozhuwan. It is seen at Luton in February 1995. *Chris Chennel*

later withdrawn from use and scrapped in 2004, while 76653 was later repaired and sold to the Algerian Air Force.

The second accident happened to 76415 in Eritrea on 17 July 1998. The aircraft, registered UR-UCI, had been chartered by a Bulgarian company and its maximum take-off weight had been exceeded by at least 37 tonnes, of which the crew were probably not aware. Due to low visibility when landing at Asmara airport at night, the crew decided to perform an instrument landing on its runway, which was at an elevation of 2,321m/7,618ft. However, due to the aircraft's additional weight it lost elevation and collided with a 2,405m hill (72m above the elevation of the runway) 4.4km from the airport, killing all ten people on board, including nine crew members.

Fleet for sale

In 2000, the last of the stored Tu-95s of the 1006th Heavy Bomber Aviation was scrapped, and the Ukrainian government decided to vacate Uzyn and destroy its runway. Nearly all the remaining Il-78s at the base had become Il-76MDs and they were regularly being leased by air cargo companies all over the world. They were all transferred to Melitopol and joined the Il-76s of the 25th GvVTAP there. Just two Il-78s had been kept with two operational UPAZ-1As under their wings to support UkrAF Su-24M/R flights.

In 1998, negotiations between Algeria and Ukraine on the acquisition of Il-78s began and

UR-76742 (c/n 0073478346) was another Il-78 that spent four years in service with the BSL Airline to carry freight all over the world. In 2006, the Pakistani Air Force procured the aircraft and it was recovered from Melitopol after being kept there in storage for seven years. The aircraft was restored by NARP and received the serial number R09-001, then handed over to the Pakistani Air Force in December 2009. It is seen arriving as flight BSL201 at Ostend on 10 October 1996. *Chris Chennel*

BSL, which existed between 1994 and 1998, was one of the Ukrainian government-owned airlines linked with the Ukrainian Air Force to use its air assets, including its fleet of Il-78s, as cargo freighters. UR-76689 (c/n 0063469066) was one of 11 Il-78s that were used by the airline. The aircraft was stored at Bila Tserkva until 2013, when it was temporarily restored to be relocated to Kulbakino AB for complete restoration and overhaul prior to delivery to the PLAAF in 2015. It is seen here at Sharjah on 1 April 1997. *Chris Chennel*

finally a contract was signed with Ukrspetsexport for the sale of six. The Nikolaev Aircraft Repair Plant (NARP) was contracted to prepare the aircraft for delivery to the Algerian Air Force.

The first two aircraft were UR-76662 and UR-76690, which had been used by Bosnia Airlines and Busol Airlines that year but had many flying hours left before their next overhaul. The aircraft received the Algerian civil registrations 7T-WIS and 7T-WIN respectively and were delivered in 1999 after receiving full Algerian Air Force markings.

The other four aircraft were overhauled at NARP. In 2001, the third Il-78, 7T-WIF, was delivered, and following that 7T-WIL in 2002. The latter had previously served as a cargo aircraft at Melitopol. The last two overhauls and renovations were completed in 2003 and these aircraft were registered 7T-WIH and 7T-WIQ. All six Il-78s entered service with the Algerian Air Force's 374 Squadron at Boufarik.

The Texas Midas

By the end of 2005, another UkrAF Il-78 serialled 76759 was sold to a private US company named North American Tactical Aviation Inc. (NATA). Prior to delivery, the aircraft was overhauled by NARP and painted in an overall gunship grey colour scheme. Nine months later, after delivery of the aircraft, the FAA issued a certificate for its civil registration, N78GF.

The company, based in Newark, Delaware, which had been established by Gary R. Fears in 2005, had planned to use the aircraft as a tanker in contracts with the USAF, but the project was suspended due to the bankruptcy of the company. Fears attempted to sell the Il-78 to the Pakistani Air Force, but when the aircraft and its Ukrainian crew were refuelling at North Texas Wittman Regional Airport and ready to depart for Pakistan, its nine crew members were advised not to leave the US and the aircraft was diverted to Sawyer International Airport, Michigan. It has been owned by the Bank of Utah in Salt Lake City since 2012.

Another UkrAF Il-78, 76767, had been purchased by NATA in 2009 to be used alongside N78GF, and on 1 March 2009, it was registered N78RX. The company received its first order to charter the aircraft from a Middle Eastern customer, but similar to N78GF, it was not allowed to leave the US due to the company's financial problems. The aircraft is now owned by IL78-2 LLC and stored in the US.

Sale to Pakistan

When the sale of the Il-78s was more profitable to the UkrAF than using them as commercial cargo aircraft, they put them up for sale as tanker aircraft. They were aged, and subsequently their maintenance fees had surged. Also, problems with Russia and the Ilyushin OKB had mean that NARP had been having difficulty in

UkrAF Il-78 UR-76412 was used by Ukraine Cargo Airways with the civil registration UR-UCF between 1998 and 2001. *Sergey Popsuevich*

Equipped with just a pair of UPAZ-1A aerial refuelling systems, 7T-WIF is one of two IL-78s of the Algerian Air Force that are still equipped as tankers, while the other four are grounded or being used as cargo aircraft in peace time. Here the aircraft is on its final approach to Boufarik AB on 27 June 2012. *Kingvarg-Algerian Spotters*

sourcing spare parts for them. The fleet's MTBO had been reached and their engines were requiring an overhaul, which was not cost-effective for the air force.

In addition to the sales in Algeria and the US, another Il-78 that had been converted to an Il-76TD was sold to Angola and served in the Angolan Air Force as D2-FEW.

In 2002, the Pakistani Air Force (PAF) became the third military customer for the Ukrainian Il-78s. In that year, for the first time, Pakistan's air force authorities and commanders started studying the acquisition of Il-78 tanker aircraft to support the operations of its JF-17 fighter aircraft as well as its IFR-equipped Mirage IIIs by the end of the 2010s.

The contract for the acquisition of four Il-78s was signed with the state company Ukrspecexport in December 2006. The aircraft were 76675, 76682, 76730, and 76742, which were 19 and 20 years old at the time. The airframes were delivered to NARP between 2007 and 2008 to be overhauled and modernised.

The master life-extension procedure (a major overhaul with lifetime extension) for the first Il-78 of the Pakistani order was started in early 2009, and finally the fully refurbished aircraft rolled out of the facility at Kulbakino in November 2009. The Il-78MP received the serial number R09-001 (c/n 0073478346) and its test flights continued until 4 December.

Without any aerial refuelling systems, Algerian Air Force Il-78 7T-WIN (c/n 0063469080) served as a cargo aircraft. It is now grounded at Boufarik AB and is waiting to be sent abroad for overhaul. It is seen seconds before take-off after sunset at Boufarik AB on 27 December 2011. *Kamel Eddine Djezzar*

The former Il-78 76730 of the Ukrainian Air Force became one of the four examples sold to Pakistan. It is seen in the background with a temporary Ukrainian number 883383BC at NARP on 24 August 2010. This Il-78MP was later delivered to the Pakistani Air Force and received its serial number R10-002 there. *Alexander Golz*

Ukrainian Air Force Il-78s

Serial Number	Construction Number	To	Current registration/ serial number	Year of manufacture	Status in 1992	Current Status	Year of Retirement/ wfu/Sale
76609	0043453597	Algerian Air Force	7T-WIF	1984	Active	Sold	2001
76610	0043454640	Algerian Air Force	7T-WIL	1984	?	Sold	2002
76646	0053461837	Algerian Air Force	7T-WIH	1985	Active	Sold	2002
76653	0053462879	Algerian Air Force	7T-WIQ	1985	Active	Sold	2003
76662	0053464919	Algerian Air Force	7T-WIS	1985	Active	Sold	1999
76670	0063465958	People's Liberation Army Air Force	20644	1986	?	Sold	2016
76675	0063466998	Pakistan Air Force	R11-003	1986	?	Sold	2009
76682	0063467027	Pakistan Air Force	R11-004	1986	Stored	Sold	2011
76689	0063469066	People's Liberation Army Air Force	20643	1986	Active	Sold	2016
76690	0063469080	Algerian Air Force	7T-WIN	1986	Active	Sold	1999
76721	0063471139	National Air Force of Angola	D2-FEW	1987	Active	Sold	2003
76730	0073476277	Pakistan Air Force	R10-002	1987	Active	Sold	2002
76736	0073476317	-	-	1987	Stored	Scrapped	2004
76742	0073478346	Pakistan Air Force	R09-001	1987	Active	Sold	2002
76744	0073478359	People's Liberation Army Air Force	20641	1987	Active	Sold	2014
76760	0073479400	People's Liberation Army Air Force	20642	1988	Active	Sold	2015
76415	0083481440	-	-	1988	Active	Crashed	1998
76414	0083482478	-	-	1988	Active	Stored	-
76759	0083485558	Air Support Syst.	N78GF	1988	Active	Sold	2005
76767	0083487598	N.A. Tactical Avn.	N78RX	1988	Active	Sold	2010
76412	0083488638	-	-	1988	Active	Stored	-

R09-001 (c/n 0073478346) was the first Il-78P to be delivered to the Pakistani Air Force on 4 December 2009, after overhaul and restoration in Ukraine. It is seen delivering fuel to a Mirage 3DP. *Rogier Westerhuis /Aero Image*

The aircraft was finally handed over to the Pakistani Air Force at the end of that year.

The second aircraft, which was serialled R10-002 (c/n 0073476277), performed its first functional check flight in July 2010 and was delivered to the PAF in August, and the work on the third and fourth airframes, which were serialled R11-003 and R11-004, was completed in February and August 2011 respectively. After their test flights, they were delivered to the PAF in July and November 2011.

All four aircraft served in the 10th Squadron at Nur Khan AB at Islamabad International airport, and they quickly saw extensive use in both the tanker and transport role.

Sale to China

The People's Liberation Army Air Force (PLAAF), with almost 1,500 fighters and 120 strategic bombers in its inventory, had always suffered from a lack of tanker aircraft, although just a small percentage of its aircraft were equipped with IFR probes. Only around ten HY-6U tankers were available.

In 2005, it was announced that China intended to purchase 30 Il-76TDs and eight Il-78s from Russia. It was claimed by news agencies that a contract had been signed for the procurement of 34 Il-76TDs and four Il-78s with the Tashkent aircraft production enterprise in September 2005.

The contract was put on hold in 2009 and instead 55 D-30KP2 engines were ordered for the PLAAF, the first deputy head of the Federal Service for Military Technical Cooperation (FSMTC) Aleksandr Fomin told Interfax-AVN on 20 July 2010.

Almost a year later, in December 2011, the PLAAF signed a contract with Ukrspetsexport for the acquisition of three Il-78s after a major overhaul with lifetime extension. The total cost of the aircraft was $44.7 million, which was much less than the $120 million cost of four new Ilyushin JSC Il-78Ms, the contract for which was now cancelled.

The first of the three Il-78s was 76744 (c/n 0073478359), one of two UkrAF Il-78s still airworthy in 2009. The aircraft had been put up for auction from 14 June 2011. Its overhaul was quickly started at NARP in January 2012, and after two years of extensive work it was rolled out of the repair plant in March 2014. After functional check flights it was handed over to the Chinese Air Force at Wuhan-Yangluo on 18 September 2014.

The aircraft, now serialled 20641, entered service with the 38th Air Regiment of the 13th Transport Division. After its arrival, two Su-30MKKs, a J-15 and two J-8Hs were soon equipped with external IFRs and flown to Wuhan so the first group of PLAAF fighter pilots could start aerial refuelling training.

In January 2015, Il-78 76760 (c/n 0073479400) was restored for the Chinese Air Force, and delivered later that year after completion of its overhaul at Kulbakino. It received the Chinese serial number 20642.

The third Il-78 of the Chinese contract, c/n 0063469066, was flown from Bila Tserkva to Kulbakino to be delivered to the NARP for overhaul and rework on 12 July 2013. Its overhaul was completed and it logged its first test flight on 7 April 2016. It was flown to Wuhan in China and handed over to the PLAAF on 7 June 2016. It received the serial 20643 in the PLAAF's 38th Air Regiment.

Today, 48 Il-78s are in service with air forces in Algeria, China, India, Pakistan and Russia. Thirteen of them are former Ukrainian Il-78s.

Tu-22K/KD/KP/KDP Fleet (1992–1996): The Aircraft Carrier Hunters

The Tu-22K was a subtype of the Tu-22A supersonic bomber, known as Blinder by NATO, with a primary mission of destroying NATO's aircraft carrier groups using the Kh-22 large, long-range anti-ship missile with a speed of Mach 4.6 and with the capability of carrying nuclear or conventional warheads. For the US Navy, the Tu-22K/KD and their Kh-22 anti-ship missiles were a serious threat in the 1960s and was why the Grumman F-14A Tomcat and its AIM-54A Phoenix long-range air-to-air missiles were designed and developed, while for NATO's surface-to-air missile battalions, the Tu-22KP/KDP aircraft with its primary mission of SEAD (suppression of enemy air defence) using Kh-22MP anti-radiation missiles was a threat in the 1980s. In all, 76 Tu-22K/KPs as well as Tu-22KD/KDPs were manufactured and served in three Heavy Bomber Aviation Regiments of the Soviet Union Air Force's Long-Range Aviation (USSR VVS D-A) between 1962 and 1991 and later in the Belarusian and Ukrainian air forces between until 1994 and 1997 respectively.

This Tu-22KP with bort number 01 Red (c/n 4467023) served in the 1st Aviation Squadron of the 341st TBAP. It is seen at Ozernoye in 1995. Its documents show it served in the 121st TBAP until 1989, when it was sent to the overhaul centre after its MTBO was reached. The Tu-22KP and its aerial refuelling probe-equipped variant, the Tu-22KPD, carried the Kurs-N SIGINT system to detect enemy radar up to a maximum 350–380km (217–236 miles) range and provide compatibility with the Kh-22P/MP anti-radiation missile. *Sergey Popsuevich*

Last years of service in the VVS

The VVS lost eight Tu-22Ks during various incidents and accidents between 1968 and 1986, half of which were to aircraft of the 341st TBAP. Also, at least two others were damaged in accidents and despite being repaired were never used again. Three years after the last Tu-22K accident, which occurred on 29 August 1986 to a Tu-22K of the 341st TBAP at Ozernoye, the Soviet Air Force had 64 serviceable Tu-22K/KD/KDPs, of which 22 were with the 121st GvTBAP, 21 with the 203rd GvTBAP and 21 with the 341st TBAP.

As had been planned since the 1960s, the VVS had intended to fully replace its fleet of 64 ageing Tu-22K/KD/KDPs with the Tu-22M by the end of the 1980s, however this did not happen and they soldiered on even after the collapse of the Soviet Union in the Belarusian Air Force (121st and 203rd GvTBAPs) and Ukrainian Air Force (341st TBAP) until 1994 and 1997 respectively, while a total of 211 Tu-22M2s and 267 Tu-22M3s were produced until 1991. The Tu-22M2/3 not only had superior flight characteristics but also better combat capability, which included the ability to carry two Kh-22M/MA (with conventional warheads) or two Kh-22N (nuclear) missiles under the wings as well as new Raduga Kh-15 hypersonic aero-ballistic missiles and simultaneously conventional bombs in the bomb bay.

Following START I (Strategic Arms Reduction Treaty I), which was signed by the US and the USSR on 31 July 1991 and which entered into force on 5 December 1994, huge numbers of the heavy bombers of the Belarusian, Russian and Ukrainian Air Forces, including all the Tu-22K/KD/KDPs, became subject to disposal. Even earlier, in 1985, when SALT II (Strategic Arms Limitation Talks II) came into force, the aerial refuelling probes of the Tu-22M2/3s were removed. For the Tu-22 Blinders, this process started with the Tu-22UDs in the same year, but due to the fact that the removal of the IFR probe moved the centre of gravity to the rear and caused difficulty in controlling the aircraft, the probes were retained on the Tu-22KD/KDPs, Tu-22RD/RDK/RDMs and Tu-22PDs, although they were blocked from the inside. Before SALT II came into force, each aviation squadron of the Heavy Bomber Aviation Regiments operating the Tu-22KD/KDP had six to eight pilots qualified to perform aerial refuelling.

The financial problems of the USSR resulted in a lack of fuel and spare parts for all three regiments operating Tu-22K/KD/KDPs in the VVS D-A in 1990 and 1991, and this subsequently resulted in a drop in the number of serviceable airframes when the 121st and 203rd GvTBAPs were inherited by Belarus. There were similar conditions in the 341st TBAP, which was inherited by the Ukrainian Air Force.

In 1994, both the 121st and 203rd GvTBAPs were disbanded and their Tu-22K/KD/KPDs as well as Tu-22P/PD jammer aircraft and Tu-22U/UD training aircraft were transferred to the disbanded 1230th Aviation Regiment for refuelling aircraft at Engels. The regiment was disbanded at Engels and the aircraft were later scrapped, while the personnel became the backbone of the new Russian Air Force's 203rd Guards Tanker Aviation Regiment, which was established on 9 May 1995 with all the Il-78/M tanker aircraft inherited by Russia from the USSR's Air Force.

After the disbandment of the 121st GvTBAP, a new regiment was formed by the personnel of the previous regiment, this time using Tu-160 strategic bombers at Engels. All the Tu-22s of the Belarusian Air Force as well as the Tu-22s of the Russian Navy were scrapped by the 6213th aircraft disposal base

Tu-22K 03 Red was serving in the 1st Aviation Squadron of the 341st TBAP on 30 June 1993. It logged its last flight on 4 February 1996 when it was transferred to the 148th Aircraft Repair Plant at Velaya Tserkov, where it was later scrapped. *Sergey Popsuevich*

at Engels. Among these 104 aircraft, just six survived and are now on display at the Long-Range Aviation Museum of the Russian Air Force at Engels-2.

In Ukraine, the 341st TBAP, of which four of its Tu-22PDs had taken part in the Afghanistan war in January and February 1989, managed to survive for longer. In 1995, 12 Tu-22KDs, six Tu-22KDPs and three Tu-22U/UDs were still operational at Ozernoye but just two years later this number had dropped to just five and the regiment was finally disbanded in 1997. Except for one Tu-22KD, which had been placed as a monument at Ozernoye, all the 341st TBAP's Tu-22s were flown from Ozernoye to Belaya Tserkov and Nezhyin in 1998 and 1999, and they were scrapped by 2001 following START I. The last official flight of the regiment took place when two Tu-22KDs flew to Belaya Tserkov on 4 February 1996.

Today, out of the 76 Tu-22K/KD/KDPs manufactured between 1962 and 1969 only four survive. Two Tu-22KDPs of the 203rd GvTBAP, 77 and 80 Red, are now at Engels-2 Air Base: 77 Red is on display at the Long-Range Aviation Museum while 80 Red is a gate guard. As well as these two in Russia, two more have survived in Ukraine, both former 341st TBAP machines. The first is Tu-22KDP 35 Red on display at the Long-Range Aviation Museum at Poltava, while the second is Tu-22KD 07 Red, on display as a gate guard at Ozernoye air base.

No. 07 Red was serving in the 1st Aviation Squadron of the 341st TBAP when it was damaged in a gear-up or belly landing on the runway at Ozernoye on 29 August 1986. The incident occurred during a training flight by Capt V. I. Zherebtsova. That night he was practising instrument landing and had to make four touch and goes. During the last approach he did not follow the checklist and forgot to check the landing gear lights to see if they were extended and locked. The aircraft's tail hit the runway and it skidded for 650m at a speed of 300km/h (162 knots) and then continued on its belly for an extra 1,800m (1.11 miles). The pilot, co-pilot and the navigator remained unharmed and exited through the emergency hatches but the fuselage was damaged, especially the flaps, landing gear bays and radome. It was repaired and displayed on the gate at Ozernoye a year later.

The first aircraft in the row is 11 Red, a Tu-22KP of the 341st TBAP's 1st Aviation Squadron, which is on the main ramp at Ozernoye air base in 1993. It was the last Tu-22K manufactured and the youngest aircraft serving in the squadron. Its assigned service life was scheduled to end in 2001, but despite that the aircraft logged its last flight piloted by K. K. Kolupayevto at the No. 148 ARP on 4 February 1996. It was later scrapped and recycled there. *Sergey Popsuevich*

341st TBAP Tu-22KP 11 Red with a Kh-22MP anti-radiation missile being installed under its fuselage. The Tu-22KP was equipped with the Kurs-N SIGINT system to detect enemy radars up to a maximum 380km range, enabling the launch of the Kh-22P and Kh-22MP anti-radiation missiles at them during SEAD operations. *Sergey Popsuevich*

Another Tu-22K of the 341st TBAP's 1st AE, 12 Red, at Ozernoye in 1995. *Sergey Popsuevich*

This Tu-22UDs with bort number 30 Red serving with the 341st TBAP's 3rd Aviation Squadron is seen doing a flypast over the base during an air show at Ozernoye on 1 August 1994. *Sergey Popsuevich*

Four Tu-22UDs were known to be in service with the 341st TBAP's 3rd AE after Ukraine's independence. They were 10, 30, 40 and 50 Red. 40 Red is seen at Ozernoye, still with the red star insignia on its vertical stabiliser in 1992. *Sergey Popsuevich*

53 Red served in the 2nd Aviation Squadron of the 341st TBAP. It is seen at Ozernoye in 1995. *Sergey Popsuevich*

56 Red was another Tu-22K that served in the 2nd Aviation Squadron of the 341st TBAP. It is seen at Ozernoye in 1995. *Sergey Popsuevich*

Tu-22KP 61 Red, manufactured in 1968, served with the 2nd Aviation Squadron of the 341st TBAP. It is seen at Ozernoye on 30 June 1993. *Sergey Popsuevich*

In 1988, which was the year of the dragon, an artist from Zhytomyr painted a three-headed dragon on the nose of 61 Red and received an award for it. Here 61 Red is seen at Ozernoye on 30 June 1993. *Sergey Popsuevich*

This Tu-22KP with construction number 5467011 was delivered to the 341st TBAP's 2nd AE when it was put into operation on 2 April 1967. After maintenance work at Dyagilevo, it received the bort number 63 Red in 1987. It became the property of the UkrAF on 17 March 1992 and remained in service until 1996. On 22 March 1996 it was flown to Poltava by Eduard Kolupayev. It is still on display in the Long-Range Aviation Museum there. *Sergey Popsuevich*

Tu-22M Fleet (1992–2000): The Strategic Bombers

The Tu-22M (Tu-26) was designed and manufactured to take the place of the various modifications of the Tu-16K in service with both the Soviet Air Force and Navy following the failure of the Tu-22B, known as Blinder by NATO. After the Soviet Union collapsed, Ukraine inherited 18 Tu-22M2s and 32 Tu-22M3s out of a total of 190 Tu-22M2s and 262 Tu-22M3s in service with the Soviet Navy Aviation (AV-MF) and Air Force (VVS) in 1991. The Ukrainian Air Force Long-Range Aviation had withdrawn its Tu-95MS and Tu-160 strategic bombers from service by the mid-1990s, but the denuclearised Tu-22M3s served until 2002, when their disposal began following a contract with the US government.

The Ukrainian inheritance

Based on data exchanged following the CFE treaty, the VVS had 37 Tu-22M2s and 144 Tu-22M3s in service with ten bomber aviation regiments. The two last operators of Tu-22M2s in the VVS were the 1225th and 1229th TBAP, both subordinate to the 31st TBAD based at Belaya, Irkutsk Oblast. Both regiments had received the last serial-produced Tu-22M2s as replacements for their ageing Tu-16Ks in 1982 and 1983, which is why they were still operating the type in 1991.

The eight VVS regiments operating Tu-22M3s in 1991 were the 185th GvTBAP with 18 Tu-22M3s at Poltava, Poltava Oblast; 840th TBAP with 19 aircraft at Soltsy, Novgorod Oblast; 52nd GvTBAP with 19 aircraft at Shaikovka, Kaluga Oblast; 402nd TBAP with 17 aircraft in Balbasovo, Vitebsk Oblast; 132nd TBAP with 18 Tu-22M3s at Vozdvizhevka, Primorskiy Kray; 200th GvTBAP with 20 aircraft at Bobruisk, Mogilev Oblast; 260th TBAP with 18 aircraft at Stryy, Lvov Oblast and 444th TBAP with 15 aircraft at Vozdvizhenka, Primorskiy Kray.

In the air force, the majority of the Heavy Bomber Aviation Regiments operating Tu-22M2s saw their aircraft replaced with the more modern Tu-22M3 by 1991; in Navy Aviation the majority of the Maritime Missile Aviation Regiments continued to operate the older Tu-22M2s. On the basis of the exchanged data from the CFE treaty, a total of 97 Tu-22M2s and 79 Tu-22M3s were in service with eight regiments of the AV-MF.

Five AV-MF regiments operated the Tu-22M2 in 1991. They were the 540th IIMRAP with 18 aircraft at Nikolayev-Kulbakino, Nikolayev Oblast; the 943rd MRAP with 21 aircraft at Oktyabrskoye, Crimean Oblast; the 568th MRAP with 18 aircraft at Mongokhto (Alekseyevka), Khabarovsk Kray; the 570th MRAP with 20 aircraft at Mongokhto; and the 183rd MRAP with 20 aircraft at Knevichi, Primorskiy Kray. Only three regiments of the AV-MF operated the Tu-22M3 in 1991. They were the 5th GvMRAP with 22 aircraft at Veseloye, Crimean Oblast; the 574th MRAP with 25 aircraft at Lakhta (Katunino), Arkhangelsk Oblast; and the 924th GvMRAP with 32 aircraft at Olenegorsk (Olenya), Murmansk Oblast.

After Ukraine's independence, the Ukrainian Air Force inherited 18 of the 20 Tu-22M3s of the 185th Guards Heavy Bomber Aviation Regiment based at Poltava and all 18 Tu-22M3s of the 260th Bomber Aviation Regiment at Stryy, Lviv Oblast. The Ukrainian Navy inherited 18 Tu-22M2s and two Tu-22M3s, all in service with the 540th Instructor-Research Maritime Missile Aviation Regiment at Nikolayev-Kulbakino, Nikolayev Oblast. Two more Tu-22M3s of the Soviet Air Force were left in the 328th Aircraft Repair Plant (including a Tu-22M3 prototype) which increased the total number of inherited Tu-22M3s to 33. Most of the Tu-22Ms, especially the Tu-22M2s, were not airworthy in 1992, mostly because of the lack of a budget to buy spare parts.

Manufactured on 10 April 1969 and logging its first flight on 30 August 1969, 156 Red is the first Tu-22M prototype, which was used as a ground instructional airframe by Kievskoye VVAIU in the late 1980s. After Ukraine's independence, it was put on display at the State Aviation Museum at Kiev. It is seen at Kiev-Zhulyany airport in 1992. *Sergey Popsuevich*

Disbandment of the 260th TBAP

As mentioned above, half the total of 36 Tu-22M3s inherited by the UkrAF were in service with the 260th TBAP at Stryy, Lviv Oblast in the Ukrainian SSR in 1992. The 260th TBAP was subordinate to the 22nd GvTBAD, headquartered at Bobruisk, Mogilev Oblast. The 260th TBAP started receiving Tu-22M3s as replacements for its ageing Tu-16Ks in 1989. However, despite the delivery of 18 Tu-22M3s by mid-1991, the regiment kept operating Tu-16Ks until 1992. The Tu-16K-26s were still in use for training and retraining purposes in order to reduce the pressure on the Tu-22M3s.

In early 1992, using the excuse of a training flight, the commander of the 260th TBAP, Col A. Ya. Fomin, together with 15 other pilots, eight navigators and eight weapon systems officers, hijacked eight Tu-22M3s of the regiment's 2nd Aviation Squadron and fled to Russia. They went to Bobruisk, where the 200th TBAP, which operated 18 Tu-16Ks and 20 Tu-22M3s, was based. The Ukrainian prosecutor's office opened a criminal case against Fomin, his deputy and Lt Col A.V. Korneychuk, who were later stripped of Ukrainian citizenship. The eight Tu-22M3s were not returned to Ukraine and they together with all the aircraft of the 200th TBAP became part of the Belarussian Air Force. However, under an agreement with Russia the whole regiment and its aircraft were transferred to the Russian Air Force and later based in the Far East.

In 1993, all the Tu-16Ks of the 260th TBAP were officially withdrawn from service and its remaining ten Tu-22M3s were relocated to Priluki, where they entered service with the 184th GvTBAP, which had inherited 19 Tu-160S Strategic Bombers from the Soviet Air Force. In Priluki, a series of Tu-160 pilots were retrained on the Tu-22M3 together with the 260th TBAP aircrews who had decided to swear allegiance to Ukraine. After having no aircraft for five years, the 260th TBAP was officially disbanded in 1998.

185th TBAP Tu-22M3 25 Red (c/n 49103343) departing from Poltava during an air show on 21 June 1997. It was transferred to the 184th GvTBAP, where it became 84 Blue in 1998. It was returned and was put into storage at Poltava after the disbandment of the 184th GvTBAP in 2000. It was scrapped on 6 January 2005. *Sergey Popsuevich*

In service with the 184th GvTBAP

The number of flyable Tu-160s had declined to just four, and even they rarely flew due to budget issues. The 184th GvTBAP operated the Tu-22M3 before becoming the first operator of the Tu-160S in Long-Range Aviation in 1989. The ex-260th TBAP Tu-22M3s gave new life to the 184th GvTBAP, enabling its aircrews to fly sufficient hours and remain combat capable. The operational Tu-160s, which numbered only eight, remained in the 1st Squadron while the ex-260th TBAP's Tu-22M3s joined the 3rd Aviation Squadron of the 184th GvTBAP.

The 2nd Aviation Squadron of the 184th GvTBAP remained the operator of the sole airworthy Tu-134UBL in the regiment, which was used for Tu-160 pilot training and retraining. The 185th GvTBAP Tu-22M3 instructor pilots came to Pryluky and they retrained the Tu-160 pilots on the type.

The 2nd AE of the 260th TBAP had the youngest and newest Tu-22M3s in Ukraine but all of them were hijacked and went to Russia. Among the remaining ten Tu-22M3s in service with the 260th TBAP's 2nd AE, four, 50, 52, 63 and 65 Red, were built in 1988 while six others, 51, 53, 54, 61, 62 and 64 Red, were manufactured in 1989. Among these, 50, 52, 54, 61 and 65 Red remained operational with the 184th GvTBAP until their MTBOs were reached in 1998 and 1999 respectively, and they were then all stored at the base and scrapped two years after the disbandment of the regiment in 2002.

In 1998, 51, 53, 62, 63 and 64 Red, which had fewer flying hours despite having reached the end of their calendar lives, went to the 185th GvTBAP, where they served for a few months until they were stored and then scrapped between 2000 and 2004. Among those that went to Poltava, 62 and 64 Red survived longer than the others. They received Poltava standard bort numbers, 89 and 86 Blue respectively, and remained operational until 2001. They were both scrapped in 2004.

In 1995, the 1st Aviation Squadron of the 184th GvTBAP officially lost its combat capability and only four or five of its Tu-160S Strategic bombers were kept airworthy, to be flown on special occasions, for example during the official visit of the Minister of Defence from Pryluky in May 1997. The last public appearance of the Ukrainian Tu-160s took place during the Independence Day parade on 24 August 1997 and after that the 1st AE of the 184th GvTBAP converted to the Tu-22M3 and nine out of the 11 Tu-22M3s that Ukraine had received from the Russian Navy Black Sea Fleet in 1996 entered service.

The fate of the naval units of the Black Sea fleet and their armament and equipment in the Crimean peninsula was always a topic of dispute between both Russia and Ukraine. To ease the tensions, an interim treaty was signed between the two governments for the establishment of a joint Russo–Ukrainian Black Sea Fleet but under bilateral command and the Soviet Navy flag. However, this did not relieve the tension and finally both countries signed the Partition Treaty on the Status and Conditions of the Black Sea Fleet on 28 May 1997, which became effective on 12 July 1999.

Tu-22M3 55 Red (c/n 19100643) was in service with the Soviet Navy's 943rd MRAP at Oktyabrskoye until 1996, when it was transferred to the UkrAF and passed to the 184th GvTBAP at Priluki. It was put in storage in July 1997 and later transferred to the 185th GvTBAP, where it was operated by the regiment as 88 Red for few years until it was retired and then scrapped at Poltava on 21 October 2004. It is seen armed with a pair of Kh-22M anti-ship missiles during an exercise. *Sergey Popsuevich*

Following the treaty, the aircraft of the Naval Aviation units stationed in the Crimea were divided between the two countries, including the 18 Tu-22M3s of the 943rd Konstantskiy Red Banner Maritime Missile Aviation Regiment at Oktyabrskoye. In 1992, the 943rd MRAP had Tu-22M2s in service. The regiment was the second oldest operator of the type in the Soviet Navy and had received its first Tu-22M2 in September 1974. After the Soviet Union's collapse, the number of airworthy Tu-22M2s of the 943rd MRAP dropped significantly and the last examples were withdrawn from service in 1994.

In 1994, the 943rd MRAP received 18 out of 21 Tu-22M3s from the 5th Guards Maritime Missile Aviation Regiment, which was disbanded on 15 November 1994. The 5th GvMRAP, based at Veseloye, had operated the Tu-22M3 since 1985 and the Tu-22M3s in service with its 2nd AE were produced in 1990. Three Tu-22M3s of the 5th GvMRAP that were built in 1985 remained at Veseloye and were scrapped in April 1997.

The 943rd MRAP was officially disbanded on 31 August 1996, but even before that the division of its property between Russia and Ukraine had begun in February 1996 when 44 Red, built in 1986, was handed over to Ukraine and ended up with the 185th TBAP of the UkrAF at Poltava, where it received the new bort number 94 Blue. By the end of 1996, ten more Tu-22M3s of the regiment had been handed over to the UkrAF; among these eight entered service with the 184th GvTBAP and two more joined the 185th GvTBAP. Among these 11 aircraft, one had been built in 1984, three in 1985, two in 1986, one in 1989 and four in 1990. Out of the remaining seven aircraft, 02, 10, 24 and 54 Red were transferred to the 568th MRAP of the Russian Navy Pacific Fleet based in Mongokhto. The last three aircraft, 04, 06 and 23 Red, remained at Oktyabrskoye and were scrapped in May 1997.

In 1999, a deal was made and the last eight airworthy Tu-160S bombers of the 184th GvTBAP were transferred to the Russian Air Force, going to Engels-2 AB. The last two left Pryluky on 21 February 2001. They had a farewell flypast over the city, during which they banked to the left and right to say goodbye. In that year the regiment prepared for disbandment and its nine airworthy Tu-22M3s were sent to Poltava. They were 51, 53, 55, 60, 62, 63, 64, 66 and 70 Red, which became 61, 63, 88, 60, 89, 62, 86, 66 and 70 Blue at Poltava.

On the basis of the Nunn–Lugar Cooperative Threat Reduction agreement, Ukraine started scrapping its strategic bombers on 16 November 1998. Through the funds received from the US under the programme, the first Tu-160, 24 Red, was scrapped for $1 million. Nine more Tu-160s were scrapped at Pryluky by the end of 2001, leaving just one aircraft, 10 Red, to be displayed in the Long-Range Aviation Museum at Poltava.

On 22 July 2000, the 184th GvTBAP celebrated its 62nd and last anniversary. On 11 August 2000, a farewell ceremony took place in the square of the residential area at Pryluky air base. The regimental flag was transferred to the archive of the Ukrainian Ministry of Defence and the regiment was officially disbanded on 1 December 2000. Before this, the process of scrapping its Tu-22M3s had begun on 2 February 2000. In total, seven Tu-22M3s were scrapped at Pryluky up to 23 April 2002. They were 52, 54, 56, 61, 65, 71 and 72 Red. Its nine other Tu-22M3s, which were transferred to Poltava, were scrapped there between 16 November 2000 and 27 January 2006.

Training Mikolayev Backfires

As mentioned above, the 540th Instructor-Research Maritime Missile Aviation Regiment of the 33rd Centre for Combat Employment and Retraining of Personnel Aviation VMF became a unit of Ukrainian Navy Aviation at Kulbakino air base in 1992. This regiment was the oldest unit operating the Tu-22M in the Soviet AV-MF. It received its first Tu-22M2 in 1973, which most likely was 22 Red (c/n 5115059). Its bort number was changed to 81 Red in the 1980s. Next to that, three more examples were delivered in 1977, followed by five in 1978, three in 1979, one in 1980, three in 1981 and three in 1983.

On 12 April 1989, the 540th IIMRAP lost one of its Tu-22M2s, which was being flown by the deputy chief of the 33rd TsBP i PLS VMF, Col A.I. Bagaev. During take-off, one of the aircraft's outer wings fell off and the aircraft suddenly banked. Before it crashed and exploded, one of the navigators managed to eject safely but the other crew members, including Col Bagaev, the pilot-instructor Maj A. P. Poltavtsev and the navigator-operator Maj A. N. Poliner, remained in the aircraft and died. As a result of this accident, the Tu-22M2 fleet was grounded for months.

In 1992, 18 of the regiment's Tu-22M2s, 01, 02, 05, 06, 07, 08, 10, 11, 15, 18, 20, 24, 25, 28, 29, 71, 73 and 48 Red, together with two Tu-22M3s 56 and 91 Red, were in service with the 540th IIMRAP. Due to the fact that the Ukrainian Navy had not inherited the Maritime Bomber Aviation Regiments operating Tu-22M3s in Crimea, the 33rd TsBP i PLS became part of the Ukrainian Air Force to train Tu-22M3 aircrews in 1992.

Due to a lack of budget, only five 540th IIMRAP Tu-22M2s and two of its Tu-22M3s were operational in 1992. Subsequently, two Tu-22M2s that had reached their MTBOs in 1989 and 1992 were sent to No. 328 ARZ to pass overhaul or depot maintenance in 1992. They were 11 and 71 Red, and both had their repair work completed in 1994. No. 71 Red had logged 830 flying hours and 727 cycles by 1 January 1993, when its overhaul started. These two remained the only operational Tu-22M2s in the unit and continued in service until 1998.

The 540th IIMRAP was later turned into the 6th Air Base of the UkrAF and also operated the ex-29th BAP's Su-24s in its 2nd Aviation Squadron for pilot and navigator training at Kulbakino. Although all its Tu-22M2s were out of service, the unit managed to operate one of its two Tu-22M3s after 1998. In addition, an ex-943rd MRAP Tu-22M3 of the 184th GvTBAP, 73 Red (c/n 10105128), was transferred to the unit, to be used for pilot training in 1999.

Following the Nunn–Lugar Cooperative Threat Reduction agreement, the Ukrainian Air Force scrapped its strategic and medium-sized bombers, including 60 Tu-22M2/3s. The 6th AB saw two of its three Tu-22M3s, 56 Red (c/n 4361937) and 91 Red (c/n 4149756), scrapped on 26 November and 11 December 2002 respectively. Also, 17 of its Tu-22M2s were scrapped after the disbandment of the 6th AB. This started with 81 Red (former 22 Red, c/n 5115059), which was the first Tu-22M2 delivered to AV-MF, and ended with 73 Red, a 1983-built aircraft, on 8 April 2004. Five months later, on 7 September 2004, the 1990-built Tu-22M3 73 Red (c/n 10105128) was scrapped.

Only one Tu-22M2 out of the 18 in service with the 540th IIMRAP survives today and that is 3146253. It is now on display in the State Aviation Museum in Kiev. It had been manufactured in 1981 and rolled out of the factory on 28 April of that year.

This ex-Soviet Navy's Tu-22M2 with bort number 08 Red (c/n 2146939) served with the 540th IIMRAP, 33rd TsBP i PLS. It entered service with the UkrAF in 1992 and remained airworthy until 1994, when it was put into storage. It was finally scrapped on 13 January 2004. *Sergey Popsuevich*

It started its career in the 540th IIMRAP as 07 Red. Its bort number was changed to 24 Red before Ukraine's independence and it became the first Tu-22M2 of the 540th IIMRAP to be demilitarised under the Nunn–Lugar Cooperative Threat Reduction agreement, when it was partially dismantled and sensitive parts such as the new PNA target illumination/ground-mapping radar and targeting system were removed in 1994. It was intended to be fully scrapped in 2003, but before that it was assembled again and transported to Zhuliany airport, where it was restored to be put on static display.

Tu-22M3 with 08 Red served with the 185th TBAP before and after the USSR's collapse. Its bort number was changed to 93 Blue in 2000. After retirement from service, it was scrapped at Poltava on 10 January 2003. It is seen after a flight at Poltava on 25 March 1997. *Sergey Popsuevich*

Tu-22M3s of 185th GvTBAP

The 185th GvTBAP, with a total of 18 Tu-22M3s, became the sole active and operational heavy bomber aviation regiment in Ukraine after its independence. The 185th GvTBAP was one of three regiments of the 13th Guards Suvorov Heavy Bomber Aviation Division subordinate to the 46th Air Army VGK. Budget cuts in the final months prior to the Soviet Union's collapse resulted in the 46th Air Force being unable to buy fuel and spare parts for the regiment. The number of operational Tu-22M3s had dropped to almost half in 1992 when the UkrAF was born. Unlike the 260th TBAP, the majority of the 185th GvTBAP's personnel swore allegiance to the Ukrainian flag in March 1992.

One of the three Tu-22M3s of the regiment that reached their calendar MTBO in 1992 was sent to Nikolayev ARZ to be the first Tu-22M3 to be overhauled after Ukraine's independence. Work on the aircraft, 14 Red (c/n 3146142) was completed in 1994. Not all the regiment's Tu-22M3s were as lucky as 14 Red and many of them were put into storage after reaching their MTBOs. This forced the UkrAF to transfer three out of the 11 Tu-22M3s of the 943rd MRAP, which had been handed over to the UkrAF by the Russian Navy Black Sea fleet following the disbandment of the regiment in 1996.

The ex-943rd MRAP's Tu-22M3s that ended up in the 185th GvTBAP in 1996 were 28, 29 and 44 Red. The first two had been manufactured in 1985 and the last in 1986. At least one was restored and flew again at Poltava before the disbandment of the regiment. No. 28 Red, which later received the bort number 85 Blue at Poltava, was intended to be delivered to the 184th TBAP at Priluki and on paper it had even received the bort number 74 Red. However, due to problems that occurred during the ferry flight (the balancing fuel tank was filled with water instead of fuel, which contaminated the fuel system), the aircraft was forced to land at Poltava and never flew again.

Tu-22M3 14 Red (c/n 3146142) served with the 185th TBAP before and after the USSR collapsed. Its bort number was changed to 57 Blue in 2000. It was scrapped at Poltava after retirement on 10 June 2005. Here it is armed with 68 AB-250-M54 iron bombs (36 under the wings and 32 in the bomb bay) at Poltava on 25 March 1997. *Sergey Popsuevich*

Tu-22M3 15 Red (c/n 1144848) served with the 185th TBAP before and after the USSR's collapse. Its bort number was changed to 80 Blue in 2000 and it received the name 'Oleksander Molodchy' after a famous Second World War bomber pilot and hero of the USSR. It was scrapped at Poltava on 21 April 2005. It is seen at Poltava on 21 June 1997. *Sergey Popsuevich*

Due to the economic crisis in Ukraine during the first half of the 1990s, the intensity of combat training decreased significantly. This was even more severe in the heavy bomber aviation regiments, as running their equipment costs much more than the front-line aviation units. However, the commanders managed to maintain an acceptable level of flight training for the crews and this enabled two 185th TBAP Tu-22M3s to take part in the first large-scale exercise of the Ukrainian Air Force on 1–2 August 1996 at Kiev-Oleksandrivka in the Mykolayiv region. During these exercises, bombers, operating under the protection of Su-27 fighters, carried out carpet bombing of enemy targets at operational strength, dropping 69 FAB-250TS bombs (each Tu-22M2/3 can carry a maximum of 36 FAB-250TSs in its bomb bay).

Later, UKrAF Tu-22M3s were occasionally involved in other exercises. In particular, on 21 August 2000, one aircraft took part in the third stage of the air defence exercises of the Commonwealth of Independent States, Combat Commonwealth 2000, which was held at Asuluk near Astrakhan (Russian Federation). In the course of these exercises, a Tu-22M3 simulated the use of

The 185th TBAP Tu-22M3 40 Red (c/n 3686518) at Poltava on 25 March 1997. Its bort number was changed to 92 Blue in 2000. It was scrapped at Poltava on 24 April 2003. *Sergey Popsuevich*

cruise missiles. It launched one of them, which was intercepted by two Ukrainian Su-27 fighters.

During the exercise, two other Tu-22M3s flew more than 4,000km without landing and one became the first Tu-22M3 to launch a Kh-22 missile in the UkrAF's history on 11 August 2000. Pilot V. Tkachenko, co-pilot V. Savchenko and navigators I. Stratilatov and V. Rysenko launched the missiles successfully over the Barents Sea.

The 185th TBAP's bombers were regular participants at various air shows, both in Ukraine and abroad. In particular, they took part in aviation parades on Ukraine's Independence Day. In early June 2002, 96 Blue, a Tu-22M3 of the 185th GvTBAP, represented the Ukrainian Air Force at the international air show in Bratislava (Slovakia), where it won the prize 'for the most impressive plane'. The aircraft was the last Tu-22M3 overhauled by the NARP in 2000 and because of that had taken part in Exercise Combat Commonwealth 2000.

In mid-1999, the Ukrainian Air Force had about 55 Tu-22M bombers. However, this number was considered excessive for the responsibilities and tasks of the Ukrainian Air Force, and also their maintenance costs were too high for the broken economy of Ukraine. Therefore, in November 2002, when the next stage of the reduction of heavy bombers began, an agreement worth $21 million in allocated funds from the US government was reached between the Threat Reduction Agency of the US Department of Defense and the US company Raytheon Technical Service to scrap the last remaining 31 Tu-22M2/3s in a two-and-a-half-year process. These were the 12 Tu-22M3s of the 185th GvTBAP and the two Tu-22M3s and 17 Tu-22M2s of the 6th Air Base at Kulbakino. Also, as a part of the contract, 225 Kh-22 cruise missiles were destroyed at Ozernoye.

Kh-22Ms installed under the 185th TBAP's Tu-22M3 57 Red (c/n 20106726) during an exercise on 25 March 1997. *Sergey Popsuevich*

On 24 August 2001, a Tu-22M3 of the 185th GvTBAP took part in Ukraine's Independence Day parade on the tenth anniversary of the country's independence. It was the last public appearance of the Tu-22M3 in Ukraine. A Tu-22M3 of the 185th GvTBAP, 96 Blue (c/n 20106726) took part in the SIAD 2002 air show at Bratislava, Slovakia, in August 2002. It was the last time an UkrAF Tu-22M3 took part in an air show. Before that the aircraft had taken part at RIAT in the UK, when it had its old bort number, 57 Red.

The number of operational Tu-22M3s of the 185th GvTBAP had fallen to just four when the type was completely withdrawn from service in late 2002. Soon after that, under pressure from the US government, the 29 remaining Tu-22M3s that had been stored at Poltava were scrapped. On 27 January 2006, the last Tu-22M3 was eliminated in

185th TBAP Tu-22M3 57 Red (c/n 20106726), armed with the Kh-22M at Poltava on 25 March 1997. This aircraft became 96 Blue in 2000 and is now preserved at the UkrAF's Long-Range Aviation Museum at Poltava. *Sergey Popsuevich*

185th TBAP Tu-22M3 90 Red (c/n 3147655) waiting for overhaul at NARP at Nikolayev-Kulbakino on 12 April 1996. *Sergey Popsuevich*

Ukraine. It was 60 Blue, one of the ex-943rd MRAP's Tu-22M3s and the youngest in Ukraine, which had been manufactured in late 1990.

The key reason behind US fears about the existence of these Tu-22M3s was the possibility of their sale to China, forcing the Threat Reduction Agency of the US Department of Defense to put pressure on Ukraine to eliminate them. The 185th GvTBAP had turned into an independent air base after the disbandment of the 13th TBAD in 2000. The regiment continued to exist on paper until 2007 when it was officially disbanded, just a few months after its last Tu-22M3 was scrapped. Subsequently, the airport became a reserve airfield for the 831st Brigade of Tactical Aviation equipped with Su-27s in 2007.

Out of the final 29 Tu-22M3s that were eliminated, two have survived: they are 3686153 and 20106726. No. 3686153 is on display today at the Long-Range Aviation museum at Poltava. It now has the bort number 80 Blue, which was painted over its previous number 94 Blue in memory of the original 80 Blue, which had been named after the Second World War bomber pilot and Hero of the

185th TBAP Tu-22M3 93 Blue (c/n 1568346) in 2000. Its bort number was previously 08 Red. It was scrapped at Poltava on 10 January 2003. *Poltava's Long-Range Aviation Museum*

185th TBAP Tu-22M3 96 Blue (formerly 57 Red) during an air show at Boryspil, Kiev, on 6 June 2002. It was the last public appearance for the UkrAF's Tu-22M3s before their complete withdrawal from service. *Sergey Popsuevich*

USSR, Oleksander Molodchy. The original 80 Blue (c/n 1144848) had been scrapped at Poltava on 21 April 2005. No. 3686153 had all of its sensitive parts removed when the Tu-22M3s were being eliminated but its fuselage was not cut up. It was later assembled again in the museum.

The second preserved Tu-22M3 in Ukraine is 20106726, in the State Aviation Museum in Kiev, and it retains its original bort number, 57 Red. It was carried in pieces from Poltava to the museum on 26 April 2006 and was later assembled in June that year. 57 Red is now one of three Tu-22Ms on display at Zhuliany. The last surviving UkrAF Tu-22M2, c/n 3146253, is also on display with its original number 07 Red.

The third Backfire in the museum is Tu-22M0 156 Red (c/n 5019018). It was the first Tu-22M prototype and logged its first flight as 101 Black on 30 August 1969. It was used by the Tupolev OKB for test purposes and was probably at Belaya Tserva for engine test purposes when Ukraine became an independent country in 1992.

The last out of the 60 Tu-22Ms of the UkrAF to be scrapped was this Tu-22M3, 60 Blue (c/n 40109126), which was scrapped at Poltava on 27 January 2006. It was an ex-Soviet Navy aircraft that ended up in the 184th TBAP in 1996 but was put in storage at Priluki only two years later. It was transferred to Poltava, where it became 60 Blue in 2000. *Sergey Popsuevich*

Ukrainian Tu-16s

After the signing of the Bialowieza Accords on 12 August 1991, Ukraine received a large number of Tu-16s that were originally intended to be fully withdrawn from Soviet Air Force and Navy service by 1995. On 17 March 1992, when the Ukrainian Air Force was founded, 76 Tu-16s in two main variants were in service with four aviation regiments. Six Tu-16P jammer aircraft were in service with the 185th TBAP at Poltava, 27 Tu-16K-10-26s and Tu-16K-26s – which were Raduga KSR-5 missile carrier aircraft – were in service with the 251st TBAP at Belaya Tserkov, 20 Tu-16Ks were with the 540th IIMRAP based at Kulbakino, and 23 Tu-16Ks were in the 260th TBAP based at Stryy.

After the formation of the UkrAF, these Tu-16s never flew but some were maintained in flying condition. By the end of 1993, 19 Tu-16s were in airworthy, while 49 others were stored. All of them were retired and decommissioned officially in 1994; however, the process of scrapping the aircraft had started a year earlier with those in service with the 251st TBAP under the Nunn–Lugar Cooperative Threat Reduction Treaty. The 19 Tu-16s that had been kept in flyable condition were scrapped between 1994 and 1996.

This ex-Soviet Navy's Tu-16K-26 with bort number 35 Red served with the 540th IIMRAP at Kulbakino. It is seen withdrawn from service at Gvardeyskoye, Crimea, on 21 August 1994. *Sergey Popsuevich*

Tu-16P 26 Red served in the 3rd Aviation Squadron of the 251st TBAP. It was operational in 1992 but was never flown after Ukraine's independence. *Poltava's Long-Range Aviation Museum*

40 Red (cn 4200703), a former 251st TBAP Tu-16K, is preserved at Belaya Tserkov. *Sergey Popsuevich*

This Tu-16P with construction number 8204130 became a test bed as the first aircraft of its kind to be modified for use of the RPP-59 Highway-1 anti-radiation missile, which was developed for SEAD operations by OKDB-134 and based on the K-5 air-to-air missile system. Test launches showed that the flight of the missile was dangerous and unstable for the aircraft. This aircraft was sent to the 341st TBAP, where it served as 68 Red with the 3rd AE until 1992. *Sergey Popsuevich*

21 Blue (c/n 1882612) is a Tu-16P of the disbanded the 341st TBAP. It is on display today at Priluki. *Sergey Popsuevich*

Tu-22M0s, Tu-22M2s and Tu-22M3s inherited by Ukraine

Model	C/N	Ex-Bort Number	Bort Number	Manufacture year	Previous Unit	Unit	Date of elimination	Note
Tu-22M0	5019018	101 Black	156 Red	1969	-	Tupolev OKB	-	Preserved as 156 Red at Kiev
Tu-22M2	5115059	22 Red	81 Red	1976	-	540th IIMRAP	09/01/2003	
Tu-22M2	1722634	-	48 Red	1977	-	540th IIMRAP	12/12/2003	
Tu-22M2	4725758	-	18 Red	1977	-	540th IIMRAP	26/03/2003	
Tu-22M2	1827812	-	10 Red	1978	-	540th IIMRAP	23/04/2003	
Tu-22M2	2827351	-	01 Red	1978	-	540th IIMRAP	28/05/2003	
Tu-22M2	3829345	-	02 Red	1978	-	540th IIMRAP	26/06/2003	
Tu-22M3	3829456	-	33 Red	1978	Tupolev OKB	148th ARZ	11/12/2001	Engine test bed at Belya-Tserkva
Tu-22M2	4830623	-	05 Red	1978	-	540th IIMRAP	11/02/2003	
Tu-22M2	4830734	-	06 Red	1978	-	540th IIMRAP	17/07/2003	
Tu-22M2	1932726	-	07 Red	1979	-	540th IIMRAP	27/08/2003	
Tu-22M3	2933534	54 Red	54 Blue	1979	-	185th GvTBAP	03/02/2005	
Tu-22M2	3934935	-	11 Red	1979	-	540th IIMRAP	25/09/2003	
Tu-22M2	3935523	-	15 Red	1979	-	540th IIMRAP	16/10/2003	
Tu-22M3	4936823	-	Unknown	1979	-	Unknown	early 2000s	
Tu-22M2	4936259	18 Red	28 Red	1980	-	540th IIMRAP	12/11/2003	
Tu-22M3	2039919	16 Red	56 Blue	1980	-	185th GvTBAP	17/05/2005	
Tu-22M3	1144848	15 Red	80 Blue	1981	-	185th GvTBAP	21/04/2005	Named 'Oleksandr Molodchy'
Tu-22M2	2146939	-	08 Red	1981	-	540th IIMRAP	13/01/2004	
Tu-22M2	3146253	07 Red	24 Red	1981	-	540th IIMRAP	-	Preserved as 20 Red at Kiev
Tu-22M3	3146142	14 Red	57 Blue	1981	-	185th GvTBAP	10/06/2005	
Tu-22M3	3147655	90 Red	90 Blue	1981	-	185th GvTBAP	08/07/2005	
Tu-22M3	4148536	53 Red	53 Blue	1981	-	185th GvTBAP	30/09/2003	
Tu-22M2	4149923	-	25 Red	1981	-	540th IIMRAP	10/02/2004	
Tu-22M3	4149756	-	91 Red	1981	-	540th IIMRAP	11/12/2002	
Tu-22M3	2252819	95 Red	95 Blue	1982	-	185th GvTBAP	25/03/2005	
Tu-22M3	2253412	59 Red	91 Blue	1982	-	185th GvTBAP	early-2000s	
Tu-22M2	1357614	-	71 Red	1983	568th MRAP	540th IIMRAP	early-2000s	
Tu-22M2	2357742	-	29 Red	1983	-	540th IIMRAP	11/03/2004	
Tu-22M2	3358244	-	73 Red	1983	-	540th IIMRAP	08/04/2004	
Tu-22M3	4361937	-	56 Red	1983	-	540th IIMRAP	14/11/2002	
Tu-22M3	1462458	19 Red	59 Blue	1984	-	185th GvTBAP	12/11/2002	
Tu-22M3	2463931	18 Red	58 Blue	1984	-	185th GvTBAP	12/12/2002	
Tu-22M3	2463750	Unknown	72 Red	1984	943rd MRAP	184th GvTBAP	06/03/2001	
Tu-22M3	1568234	Unknown	56 Red	1985	943rd MRAP	184th GvTBAP	17/01/2002	
Tu-22M3	1568346	08 Red	93 Blue	1985	-	185th GvTBAP	10/01/2003	
Tu-22M3	1569921	28 Red	85 Blue	1985	943rd MRAP	185th GvTBAP	06/02/2003	
Tu-22M3	2569648	92 Red	99 Blue	1985	-	185th GvTBAP	25/03/2003	
Tu-22M3	2570326	29 Red	98 Blue	1985	943rd MRAP	185th GvTBAP	26/08/2003	
Tu-22M3	3686518	40 Red	92 Blue	1986	-	185th GvTBAP	24/04/2003	
Tu-22M3	3686153	44 Red	94 Blue	1986	943rd MRAP	185th GvTBAP	-	Preserved as 80 Blue at Poltava

Model	C/N	Ex-Bort Number	Bort Number	Manufacture year	Previous Unit	Unit	Date of elimination	Note
Tu-22M3	4687857	-	71 Red	1986	943rd MRAP	184th GvTBAP	18/12/2001	
Tu-22M3	1895714	-	50 Red	1988	260th TBAP	184th GvTBAP	23/04/2002	
Tu-22M3	4898857	63 Red	62 Blue	1988	260th TBAP	184th GvTBAP	24/06/2003	
Tu-22M3	4899215	-	52 Red	1988	260th TBAP	184th GvTBAP	21/02/2002	
Tu-22M3	4899423	03 Red	52 Blue	1988	260th TBAP	184th GvTBAP	30/05/2003	
Tu-22M3	4899548	-	65 Red	1988	260th TBAP	184th GvTBAP	22/05/1998	
Tu-22M3	19100912	53 Red	63 Blue	1989	260th TBAP	185th GvTBAP	16/11/2000	
Tu-22M3	19100734	51 Red	61 Blue	1989	260th TBAP	185th GvTBAP	30/08/2004	
Tu-22M3	19100643	55 Red	88 Red	1989	943rd MRAP	184th GvTBAP	21/10/2004	
Tu-22M3	19100556	64 Red	86 Blue	1989	943rd	184th GvTBAP	24/09/2004	Became 86 Blue at Poltava in 2000
Tu-22M3	19101415	-	54 Red	1989	260th TBAP	184th GvTBAP	14/03/2002	
Tu-22M3	29101328	-	61 Red	1989	260th TBAP	184th GvTBAP	04/04/2002	
Tu-22M3	29101851	62 Red	89 Blue	1989	260th TBAP	184th GvTBAP	10/12/2004	Became 89 Blue at Poltava in 2000
Tu-22M3	49103343	25 Red	84 Blue	1989	-	185th GvTBAP	06/01/2005	
Tu-22M3	10105019	51 Red	51 Blue	1990	-	185th GvTBAP	28/02/2005	
Tu-22M3	10105128	-	73 Red	1990	943rd MRAP	184th GvTBAP	07/09/2004	
Tu-22M3	10105257	55 Red	55 Blue	1990	-	185th GvTBAP	27/09/2005	
Tu-22M3	10106313	66 Red	66 Blue	1990	943rd MRAP	184th GvTBAP	28/10/2005	Became 66 Blue at Poltava in 2000
Tu-22M3	20106726	57 Red	96 Blue	1990	-	185th GvTBAP	-	Preserved as 57 Red in Kiev
Tu-22M3	20106654	70 Red	70 Blue	1990	943rd MRAP	184th GvTBAP	Late 2005	Became 70 Blue at Poltava in 2000
Tu-22M3	40109126	60 Red	60 Blue	1990	943rd MRAP	184th GvTBAP	27/01/2006	Became 60 Blue at Poltava in 2000

Tu-95MS Fleet (1992–2000): The Nuclear Bombers

Ukraine inherited 30 Tu-95 strategic bombers, including two Tu-95MS-6s and 25 Tu-95MS-16s, out of a total of 84 in service with the USSR VVS D-A in 1991. The 25 Tu-95MS-16s of the 1006th TBAP entered service with the UkrAF, but soon due to budget shortages and the lack of spare parts and staff, the number of airworthy aircraft in the regiment dropped to seven. This led to its disbandment due to safety concerns in 1994. On the basis of the Nunn–Lugar Cooperative Threat Reduction agreement, 23 of these, including two Tu-95K-22s, two Tu-95MS-6s and 19 Tu-95MS-16s, were scrapped between 1999 and 2001. Among the remaining seven, three Tu-95MS-16s were sold to Russia, one Tu-95MS-16 ended up in a museum, the sole inherited Tu-95M was preserved at Uzin airfield and two other Tu-95MS-16s were sold to private companies and scrapped between 2014 and 2018.

On 22 May 1993, probably for the first and last time in UkrAF history, an Il-78 was used to demonstrate inflight refuelling of an air force Tu-95MS during an air show at Poltava. The Il-78 is UR-76742, which is now in service with the Pakistani Air Force as R09-001 while the Tu-95MS was 05 Red from the 1st Aviation Squadron of the 1006th TBAP. *Sergey Popsuevich*

On 22 May 1993, this Tu-95MS of 1006th TBAP 05 Red (c/n 30108) during the flyover at Poltavia. *Sergey Popsuevich*

In Ukrainian Air Force service

After the collapse of the USSR, 67 out of a total of 84 Tu-95MSs of the VVS D-A remained in Kazakhstan and Ukraine. While Russia managed to evacuate the 40 Tu-95MSs (from the 1023rd TBAP and 1226th TBAP) from Kazakhstan without informing its leaders, the Ukrainian commanders of the 106th TBAD decided to keep the 25 Tu-95MS-16s in service with the 1006th TBAP at Uzin. In addition, two ex-1226th TBAP Tu-95K-22s as well as two Tu-95MS-6s were under heavy depot maintenance or were waiting for it at No. 148 ARZ at Bila Tserkva in 1991. They all remained in Ukraine in 1992. The Tu-95MS-6s returned to Russia's jurisdiction by the end of 1992. As well as these, the UkrAF inherited an ex-409th TBAP Tu-95M that was preserved at Uzin air base.

After 24 August 1991, the Russian military and political leadership did not want to give up on the loss of the 1006th TBAP's Tu-95MSs and decided to repeat the scenario that they had used in Kazakhstan to transfer all 40 Tu-95MSs of the 1023rd and 1226th TBAPs to Russia without getting approval from the Kazakhstan government. The Commander of the Air Force of the Russian Federation, P. Deinekin, received an order from the Russian government to carry out this mission on 13 February 1992. The commander of the 106th Bomber Aviation Division, M. Bashkirov, and other senior officers resisted the order and prevented the departure of 25 Tu-95MSs from Uzin. To achieve this, Shilka anti-aircraft gun systems were positioned on the runway at Uzin!

The operation of the Tu-95MSs was complicated for the Ukrainians due to a lack of staff, spare parts and budget to buy fuel for routine training and retraining missions. As a result, the serviceability of the fleet was reduced and the decision was made to disband the regiment in January 1994, when it had only seven airworthy aircraft.

On 17 April 1998, the National Security and Defence Council of Ukraine made a final decision to phase out the strategic Tu-95MS and Tu-160 strategic cruise missile aircraft. The cost of their elimination was financed through funds allocated by the US government under an agreement for providing assistance to Ukraine to destroy strategic nuclear weapons and prevent the proliferation of weapons of mass destruction that had been signed between Ukraine and the United States on 25 November 1993. The decision was taken to destroy 40 of the 44 bombers, leaving two in museums and converting two into reconnaissance aircraft.

Before starting the elimination of the Tu-95s, an agreement was signed between Ukraine and Russia

One of the luckiest Tu-95MS-16s to serve with the 1006th TBAP was 01 Red (c/n 1732191). It was not scrapped but put on display in the Long-Range Aviation Museum at Poltava on 31 May 2000. It is seen at Poltava in 1991. *Sergey Popsuevich*

1006th TBAP Tu-95MS-16 08 Red (c/n 2937345) was one of the three examples sold to Russia in 1999, with the delivery taking place in January 2000. It entered service with the 184th GvTBAP of the RuAF at Engels-2 and received the bort number 27 Red in 2001. The regiment was redesignated as the 6950th AvB in late 2009 and the aircraft received the serial number RF-94117 and named 'Izborsk' after a medieval fortress west of Pskov. *Sergey Popsuevich*

in Yalta on 6 October 1999, which included the transfer of eight Tu-160s to Russia, as well as three Tu-95MS and 240 cruise missiles in exchange for writing off Ukraine's energy debt of $275 million. The three Tu-95MSs, which were in the last batch of serial-produced Bear H-16s, had the capability to use Kh-55SM missiles.

These three Tu-95MSs were 10, 96 and 08 Red, which were completed on 22 January 1990, 26 March 1991 and 3 October 1991. They were all ferried to Engels between 6 November 1999 and January 2000, and they received the bort numbers 19, 28 and 27 Red respectively when in service with the RuAF's 184th GvTBAP. Today they are serialled RF-94123, RF-94116 and RF-94117 and are in service with the 6950th AvB. On 19 November 2016, RF-94116 was one of two Tu-95MSs that launched Kh-101 cruise missiles at ISIL and Jabhat al-Nusra targets in Syria.

One of the 1006th TBAP's Tu-95MS-16s, 01 Red (c/n 32191) was chosen to be preserved in the Long-Range Aviation museum at Poltava. It was ferried there on 4 June 2000 and was decommissioned and put on display on 6 November. Two other Tu-95MSs, 95 and 31 Red, were handed over to NARP (formerly No. 328 ARZ), to be converted into environmental monitoring aircraft, but the plan was cancelled and they were both earmarked for sale in 2011. The Ukrainian MoD sold them to Spetstekhnoeksport on 10 June 2013, and they were then sold on to Avto Trade Ukraina on 12 June. No. 95 Red had been scrapped by April 1994 and 31 Red was offered for sale on eBay for $3 million but was later dismantled and scrapped at NARP in March 2017.

The 19 remaining Tu-95MSs of the 1006th TBAP were scrapped between 31 January 1999 and 17 May 2001. Before the disbandment of 1006th TBAP, five of its Tu-95MSs had been transferred to Bila Tserkva after the end of their MTBOs. They were scrapped there while the remaining 14 were scrapped at Uzin. They were 02, 07, 24, 34 and 41 Red, which together with two other Tu-95MSs, 15 and 25 Red (at Bila Tserkva since 1991) and two Tu-22K-22s, 02 and 05 Red, were scrapped between 7 November 1999 and 8 December 2000. The engines and other valuable parts of the scrapped Tu-95MSs were sold to Russia, some of which were scrapped and recycled there while others were used on the RuAF's Tu-95MSs.

Since April 1956, the Tu-95 strategic bombers have always been one of the greatest symbols of the Cold War. Over the years, they have been used as an important component in stabilising the international policies of the Russian government by threatening the security of the US and its allies. Today, 58 Tu-95MSs from the original 88 manufactured are still in service with the Russian Air Force and almost 40 of them are always kept operation-ready at three aviation bases of the force. Their two main bases are Engels-2 (Энгельс-2) and Ukrainka, while three are operated for training purposes from Ryazan.

This is one of two 1006th TBAP Tu-95MSs, 95 and 31 Red, that were handed over to NARP (formerly the 328th ARZ) to be converted into environmental monitoring aircraft but the plan was cancelled in 2000. *Sergey Popsuevich*

The other aircraft of the two Tu-95MSs of the 1006th TBAP that were handed over to NARP at Nikolayev-Kulbakino in 2000. *Sergey Popsuevich*

One of the two Tu-95MS-6s of the Russian Air Force waiting for overhaul at No. 148 ARP at Bila Tserkva. It is seen there on 14 May 1996. It was scrapped in 2000. *Sergey Popsuevich*

Tu-22K-22 20 Red was in service with the 1226th TBAP at Dolon, Semipalatinsk, in the 1980s. It was sent to 148 ARZ at Bila Tserkva to be overhauled in 1991. It was still under Russian jurisdiction in 1992 and was scrapped on 8 December 2000. *Sergey Popsuevich*

Tu-95K-22 06 Red served with the 1226th TBAP at Dolon, Semipalatinsk, in Kazakhstan, and can be seen with a Kh-22M missile loaded under its fuselage. *Sergey Popsuevich*

The ex-1006th TBAP Tu-95M 51 Red, manufactured on 28 February 1958, is the only Tu-95 preserved in Uzin, where it is seen on 20 August 1990. *Sergey Popsuevich*

This Tu-95MS-16 of the Russian Air Force with serial number RF-94123 and bort number 19 Red is one of three ex-1006th TBAP Tu-95MSs that were sold to Russia in 1999. In service with the 6950th AvB, the aircraft was named 'Krasnoyarsk'. It was 10 Red in UkrAF service. It is seen at Ryazan on 2 August 2012. *Chris Lofting*

Ex-1006th TBAP Tu-95MS-16 01 Red (c/n 1732191) on display at Poltava's Long-Range Aviation Museum. *Sergey Popsuevich*

UkrAF's Tu-95s

Type	Tail Number	Construction Number	Manufacture Date	Fate
Tu-95M	51 Red	7800503	28/02/1958	Preserved at Uzin
Tu-95K-22	02 Red	62M52503	30/11/1962	Ex-1226th TBAP in 148th ARZ at Bila Tserkva. Was scrapped on 07/12/2000
Tu-95K-22	05 Red	63M52602	28/02/1963	Ex-1226th TBAP in 148th ARZ at Bila Tserkva. Was scrapped on 08/12/2000
Tu-95MS-6	15 Red	16204	Unknown	Was waiting for depot maintenance at 148th ARZ in 1992. Scrapped on 04/12/2000
Tu-95MS-6	25 Red	4424550	Unknown	Was waiting for depot maintenance at 148th ARZ in 1992. Scrapped on 28 and 29/11/2000
Tu-95MS-16	24 Red	15119	Unknown	1006th TBAP aircraft waiting for PDM in 148th ARZ. Scrapped btw 21/10/1999 and 07/11/1999
Tu-95MS-16	41 Red	21744	Unknown	1006th TBAP aircraft waiting for PDM in 148th ARZ. Scrapped on 07/11/1999
Tu-95MS-16	02 Red	29561	Unknown	1st AE of 1006th TBAP. Scrapped at 148th ARZ in Bila Tserkva on 11/12/1999
Tu-95MS-16	03 Red	29732	Unknown	1st AE of 1006th TBAP. Scrapped in Uzin between 24 and 26/03/2000
Tu-95MS-16	04 Red	29843	Unknown	1st AE of 1006th TBAP. Scrapped in Uzin on 17 and 18/04/2000
Tu-95MS-16	05 Red	30108	Unknown	1st AE of 1006th TBAP. Scrapped in Uzin between 25 and 27/05/2000
Tu-95MS-16	06 Red	30183	Unknown	1st AE of 1006th TBAP. Scrapped in Uzin on 29 and 30/06/2000
Tu-95MS-16	07 Red	30203	Unknown	1st AE of 1006th TBAP. Scrapped at 148th ARZ in Bila Tserkva on 01/12/1999
Tu-95MS-16	20 Red	30235	Unknown	2nd AE of 1006th TBAP. Scrapped in Uzin on 25 and 26/08/2000
Tu-95MS-16	21 Red	30306	Unknown	2nd AE of 1006th TBAP. Scrapped in Uzin on 27 and 28/08/2000
Tu-95MS-16	22 Red	30309	Unknown	2nd AE of 1006th TBAP. Scrapped in Uzin between 04/10/2000 and 06/10/2000
Tu-95MS-16	23 Red	30419	Unknown	2nd AE of 1006th TBAP. Scrapped in Uzin on 31/01/1999
Tu-95MS-16	24 Red	31135	Unknown	2nd AE of 1006th TBAP. Scrapped in Uzin on 06 and 07/11/2000
Tu-95MS-16	25 Red	31198	Unknown	2nd AE of 1006th TBAP. Scrapped in Uzin on 15 and 16/12/2000
Tu-95MS-16	90 Red	31249	Unknown	3rd AE of 1006th TBAP. Scrapped in Uzin on 15 and 16/01/2001
Tu-95MS-16	91 Red	31370	Unknown	3rd AE of 1006th TBAP. Scrapped in Uzin on 12/03/2001
Tu-95MS-16	92 Red	31483	Unknown	3rd AE of 1006th TBAP. Scrapped in Uzin on 26 and 27/03/2001
Tu-95MS-16	93 Red	31509	Unknown	3rd AE of 1006th TBAP. Scrapped in Uzin on 16 and 17/04/2001
Tu-95MS-16	94 Red	32179	Unknown	3rd AE of 1006th TBAP. Scrapped in Uzin between 7/05/2001 and 17/05/2001
Tu-95MS-16	01 Red	1732191	Unknown	1st AE of 1006th TBAP. Preserved in long-range aviation museum at Poltava from 31/05/2000
Tu-95MS-16	95 Red	1732386	1987	3rd AE of 1006th TBAP. Transferred to NARP on 28/11/2000. Scrapped in 2014
Tu-95MS-16	31 Red	2733144	1987	2nd AE of 1006th TBAP. Transferred to NARP on 28/11/2000. Scrapped in 2018
Tu-95MS-16	10 Red	4936177	22/01/1990	1st AE of 1006th TBAP. Delivered to the RuAF on 06/11/1999. Now 19 Red/RF-94123
Tu-95MS-16	96 Red	4037187	26/03/1991	3rd AE of 1006th TBAP. Delivered to the RuAF in January 2000. Now 28 Red/RF-94116
Tu-95MS-16	08 Red	2937345	03/10/1991	1st AE of 1006th TBAP. DeliveRed to the RuAF in January 2000. Now 27 Red/RF-94117

Tu-160 Fleet (1992–2000): The White Swans

RuAF Tu-160S RF-94100, named 'Nikolai Kuznetsov', was in service with the UkrAF's the 184th GvTBAP as 10 Red until 6 November 1999, when it was transferred to Engels-2 AB as the first out of eight Tu-160s sold to Russia. Here it has been intercepted by a pair of French Air Force Mirage 2000-5 fighter interceptors. *Armée de l'air*

Designed and developed as a Soviet answer to the American B-1 bomber, the Tupolev Tu-160 Blackjack became the largest and fastest variable-wing aircraft in the world and is now the most capable nuclear bomber in the Russian Air Force. Due to the financial problems of the Soviet Union caused by the adverse effects of huge military expenditure and the costs of Soviet intervention in the Afghanistan war, only a few Tu-160s were serial produced before the USSR collapsed and all went into service with the 184th GvTBAP at Priluki, Ukraine SSR.

After Ukrainian independence, the regiment and its 19 Tu-160s became part of the newly formed Ukrainian Air Force, leaving almost no Tu-160s for the Russian Air Force. Under economic pressure, Ukraine could not operate the bombers and they were finally withdrawn from service in 1997, with eight were sold to Russia in exchange for writing off gas debts. Apart from one that ended up in the Long-Range Aviation Museum, the ten remaining examples in Ukraine were scrapped under US diplomatic pressure by 2 February 2001.

In service with the Ukrainian Air Force

By the end of 1987, the 184th GvTBAP had already received ten aircraft, but Tu-22M3 bombers and Tu-16P jammers still remained in its service. Gradually, the Tu-22M3s and Tu-16Ps were transferred to other regiments, and some of the Tu-16s were dismantled and destroyed following the Treaty on the Reduction of Conventional Arms in Europe. By the time of the collapse of the USSR, two squadrons of the regiment consisted of 21 aircraft. The third squadron consisted of four Tu-134UBLs, which were used to train flight personnel and maintain the flight skills of crews, preserving the life of the Tu-160s.

The USSR's collapse adversely affected the fate of one of the most powerful strategic bombers in the world. On 24 August 1991, the Ukraine parliament transferred all military units on its territory under its control. On the same day, the Ministry of Defence of Ukraine was formed. On the territory of the new independent state, 19 Tu-160 bombers remained, which did not fit into the country's defensive doctrine. In February 1992, Russian President Boris Yeltsin signed a decree for the end of production of the Tu-95MS and suspended that of the Tu-160. After that, the United States stopped building B-1B bombers. However, the Russian proposal was not met with a similar response after the US produced the B-2A stealth bomber and with the collapse of the USSR, Russia was left without new strategic bombers.

In the spring of 1992, Ukrainian military units began to take an oath of allegiance to the republic. On 8 May, about 25% of the flight staff and up to 60% of the technical staff of the 184th GvTBAP took the oath. The aircraft received the national yellow-blue symbol of Ukraine, replacing the usual red star.

184th GvTBAP Tu-160S 10 Red (c/n 84906217) at Poltava on 22 May 1993. This aircraft was sold to Russia and is now in service with the RuAF as RF-94100. *Sergey Popsuevich*

This official photo was taken during START-I negotiations in Uzin in 1990. It shows 12 Red, a Tu-160S of the 184th GvTBAP. It was among the eight examples sold to Russia in 1999. It is now in service with the RuAF as RF-94109 and named 'Alexander Novikov'. *Sergey Popsuevich*

The Ukrainian Air Force had severe financial problems that firstly affected the maintenance of complex and expensive aircraft such as the Tu-160. To fly to its maximum range, a Tu-160 needed 150 tons of fuel and for a simple training mission 40 tons, which was completely unaffordable for the UkrAF. The regiment had its combat readiness reduced and its operational flights stopped because of these problems. However, the manufacturer was obliged to carry out a warranty service on the aircraft for ten years. Due to the lack of fuel, spare parts and qualified flight and technical staff, it was necessary to abandon flying most of the available aircraft.

The oil used in the bomber's NK-32 engines had to be purchased in Azerbaijan, and landing gear parts, tyres and engine parts had to be bought from Russia. By the summer of 1994, only a few pilots were still qualified to fly the Tu-160s in Ukraine and they were being kept current by means of flying only six to eight times a year! In May 1993, the regimental commander, Col Valery Gorgol, had to carry out an emergency landing due to a technical failure in the landing gear. The Tu-160 crews were not combat-ready to take part in military exercises and were only able to fly the aircraft during official events, starting with the first Independence Day parade in Ukraine in 1992 and for last time during the parade over Kiev on 24 August 1997. In a few other cases, during visits of Ukrainian officials including the President and the Minister of Defence they were flown around Priluki.

14 Red during an air show accompanying a USAF B-52H, B-1B and KC-10A at Poltava on 23 September 1994. *Sergey Popsuevich*

Retirement and destruction

In 1997, the Tu-160 was officially withdrawn from UkrAF service while only eight were still airworthy but not fully mission capable. In 1998, their destruction began under the Nunn-Lugar programme. The Ukrainian Tu-160s were the most threatening weapon to the Americans and because of that the US allocated $8 million to eliminate them.

On 16 November 1998, while US senators Richard Lugar and Karl Levin were present, the first Ukrainian Tu-160, 24 Red, which had been manufactured in 1989 and had logged only 466 hours of flight, was scrapped. Next, 14 Red, which had been manufactured in 1990 and had logged fewer than 100 flying hours during its short life, was scrapped on 16 January 1999. The aircraft had participated in the events commemorating the 50th anniversary of Operation Frantic in February 1995. (The operation was a series of seven shuttle bombing missions during the Second World War conducted by American aircraft based in Great Britain and southern Italy that then landed at three Soviet airfields in Ukraine). Following 14 Red, 20 and 21 Red were scrapped on 26 November 1999 and 24 March 2000 respectively.

On 6 October 1999, Ukraine and Russia signed an inter-governmental agreement at Yalta for the transfer of eight Tu-160s, three Tu-95MS and 575 Kh-55SM cruise missiles to the Russian side in return for writing off Ukraine's energy debt of $272 million. Subsequently, the first aircraft, 10 Red, flew from Priluki and landed at Engels on 6 November 1999. Following 10 Red, five more Tu-160s, 16, 15,

12, 17 and 22 Red, were flown to Engels in 1999, while the last two, 11 and 18 Red, were delivered on 21 February 2000.

On 30 March 2000, the last Tu-160 flight in UkrAF history took place when one of the remaining 11 Tu-160s, 26 Red (c/n 81804921) was flown from Priluki to Poltava to be displayed in the Long-Range Aviation Museum of the Ukrainian Air Force. After that, the remaining Tu-160s of the 184th GvTBAP were scrapped, starting with 30 Red on 31 March. Next, 31 Red was scrapped on 25 April 2000; 33 Red on 7 June 2000; 23 Red on 19 October 2000; 25 Red on 1 December 2000; and 32 Red on 2 February 2001.

On 1 December 2000, the 184th GvTBAP was officially disbanded and its Tu-22M3s, which were in use as replacements for its Tu-160s, were scrapped. Ukraine scrapped its Tu-22Ms and Tu-160s under diplomatic pressure from the US government. Without any doubt, if the Tu-160s had not been eliminated, they might have ended up in Russia or in the worst case scenario for Americans, in China, which could have used them to develop and design its own heavy nuclear bombers. Prior to being scrapped, Ukraine had offered an American company two Tu-160s to be used as airborne satellite launch vehicles, but the proposal was rejected due to its high cost.

In Russian Air Force service

While Ukraine inherited all 19 Tu-160Ss in service with the 184th GvTBAP, only two pre-production Tu-160 prototypes and three serial-produced Tu-160s, 86, 87 and 63 Grey, had been left flyable in Russia. Nos 86 and 87 Grey were in use as test beds in Zhukovsky while 63 Grey was used by the Tupolev OKB to be converted into the first Tu-160SK prototype and technology demonstrator (an airborne satellite launch vehicle). There were several incomplete Tu-160s at Kazan in 1991, the first of which, c/n 82007617, was completed after Ukraine's independence and was intended to be the 20th Tu-160 for the 184th GvTBAP. It received the bort number 01 Red and logged its first flight on 30 December 1991.

15 Red (c/n 83905953) at Priluki in the mid-1990s. It was sold to Russia and is now flying as RF-94108, named 'Vladimir Sudets'. It attacked ISIL targets in Syria on 17 November 2015. *Sergey Popsuevich*

In 1991, two Tu-160s were in the final stage of production at Kazan; they were completed in 1992, received the bort numbers 02 and 03 Red and became the first two examples in service with the Russian Air Force. The 1096th TBAP of the 201st TBAD had been intended to be the recipient as the second TBAP of the VVS D-A in 1987. The Tu-160s were intended to replace its ageing Myasishchev 3M bombers, but the delays in the programme and also the lack of budget led to the cancellation of this plan and the disbandment of the 1096th TBAP in December 1989.

After the fall of the Soviet Union, President Yeltsin ordered the formation of a complete regiment of Tu-160s. This old plan came into force again and the 121st GvTBAP, the personnel of which had been transferred from Belarus to Russia, became the first and only recipient of the type in the Russian Air Force on 1 June 1994 after absorbing the remaining personnel and all the facilities and equipment of the disbanded 1096th TBAP. No. 01 (c/n 82007617), 02 (c/n 83007526)

On 9 February 2017, a pair of RuAF Tu-160Ss were intercepted by Royal Air Force Typhoon FGR.4s while flying close to the UK's airspace. RF-94108, seen here, was one of these aircraft. It served in the 184th GvTBAP of the UkrAF as 15 Red until 1999. *Crown Copyright*

A flypast of the 184th GvTBAP Tu-160S 16 Red over Poltava during an air show on 22 May 1993. This aircraft is now in service with the RuAF as RF-94107 and named 'Alexei Plokhov'. *Sergey Popsuevich*

and 03 Red (c/n 83007335) became the first three Tu-160s of the regiment.

On 16 February 1992, 01 Red landed at Engels air base two years before the formation of 121st GvTBAP. In May the same year there were already three Tu-160s at Engels. Many pilots, engineers and technicians of the 184th GvTBAP who had refused to take the second military oath to Ukraine began to be transferred from Priluki to the Saratov region to continue their service in the Russian Armed Forces. Using the facilities of the former 1st Squadron of the 1096th Guards TBAP, the formation of a squadron of heavy missile carriers began and as all ground equipment, simulators and aircraft preparation equipment remained at Priluki, everything had to be built at Engels.

On 29 July 1992, Lt Col A. S. Medvedev, who had moved from Priluki to Engels, performed the first flight of a Tu-160S in the Russian Air Force. On October 22, the 121st GvTBAP regiment commander, Lt Col A. Zhikharev, launched a Kh-55SM over a test range. The next day, Lt Col A. Malyshev's crew conducted the same live missile firing practice. The fourth Tu-160 arrived at Engels in early 1993. Initially, to reinforce the regiment, it was planned to transfer six prototypes and production aircraft that had participated in various tests, which still had some flying time and cycles left, but this never happened.

Thus, despite all the difficulties, the 37th Air Force of the Russian Air Force managed to maintain at least some combat capability with the only two Tu-160s that were mission capable. In May 1993, the Russian Tu-160s took part in the Voskhod 93 exercise, during which their aviators practised when and how to react quickly to a threat to the country's security. A live launch of an upgraded missile with an increased range was made during the strategic nuclear forces exercise on 21–22 June 1994, which was witnessed by President Yeltsin. Production of the Tu-160 was resumed by the Kazan Aircraft Production Association (KAPO) and four more aircraft, the production of which had started before the USSR's collapse, were completed and delivered to the 121st TBAP between 1995 and 1999. They were 04, 05, 06 and 07 Red.

Following the inter-governmental agreement of 6 October 1999, Russia received the last eight airworthy Tu-160s in service with the Ukrainian Air Force. As explained above, these bombers were delivered between 6 November 1999 and 21 February 2000. They were not quickly put into service with the 121st TBAP and before that they were all sent to KAPO to be overhauled and repaired. They, together with a former Zhukovsky-based test bed Tu-160 (87 Grey), were overhauled and delivered to 121st TBAP in 2000 and 2001. This increased the number of combat-ready Tu-160s from seven in 1999 to 16 in 2002; however, 01 Red was later lost in an accident on 30 December 1991.

Today, all eight ex-UkrAF Tu-160S bombers are in service at the 6950th Aviation Base of the RuAF, which has been recently reorganised as a heavy bomber aviation regiment again at Engels. Nos 14 and 10 Red are now RF-94103 and RF-94100, and both are now under overhaul and upgrade at Kazan. Nos 15 and 17 Red, which are now RF-94108 and RF-95110, took part in the war against the ISIL terrorist group in Syria and attacked ISIL targets in Syria on 17 and 20 November 2015 respectively.

184th GvTBAP Tu-160S 18 Red was shown to political and military leaders of the CIS at Minsk-Machulishchi, as seen here on 13 February 1992. It is now RF-94111 with the RuAF. *ITAR-TASS via Sergey Popsuevich*

This ex-UkrAF Tu-160S of the Russian Air Force with the serial RF-94111 (c/n 82006458) is seen being intercepted by Typhoon FGR.4 ZK33 of the II(AC) Squadron over the North Sea near Moray, Scotland, in September 2018. This was 18 Red in UkrAF service. Its name is now 'Andrei Tupolev', after the aircraft designer. *Crown Copyright*

184th GvTBAP Tu-160s

Tail Number	Construction Number	Manufacture Year	Fate
30 Red	84602438	1986	Scrapped at Priluki on 31/03/2000
31 Red	84603712	1986	Scrapped at Priluki on 25/04/2000
32 Red	82703629	1987	Scrapped at Priluki on 02/02/2001
33 Red	83703845	1987	Scrapped at Priluki on 07/06/2000
25 Red	84703453	1987	Scrapped at Priluki on 01/12/2000
26 Red	81804921	1988	Logged the last Tu-160 flight in Ukraine on 30/03/2000 – On display in Poltava Museum
20 Red	82804734	1988	Scrapped at Priluki on 26/11/1999
21 Red	82804547	1988	Scrapped at Priluki on 24/03/2000
22 Red	83804352	1989	Delivered to Russia in 1999 and is now in RuAF service as 14 Red/RF-94103
23 Red	84805813	1988	Scrapped at Priluki on 19/10/2000
24 Red	84805425	1988	Scrapped at Priluki on 14/01/1999
16 Red	82905836	1989	Delivered to Russia in 1999 and is now in RuAF service as 16 Red/RF-94107
17 Red	83905142	1989	Delivered to Russia on 19/01/2000 and is now in RuAF service as 17 Red/RF-94110
15 Red	83905953	1989	Delivered to Russia in 1999 and is now in RuAF service as 15 Red/RF-94108
10 Red	84906217	1989	Delivered to Russia 06/11/1999 and is now in RuAF service as 10 Red/RF-94100
11 Red	84906826	1989	Delivered to Russia 21/02/2000 and is now in RuAF service as 11 Red/RF-94114
12 Red	84906335	1988	Delivered to Russia in 1999 and is now in RuAF service as 12 Red/RF-94109
14 Red	81006741	1990	Scrapped at Priluki on 16/01/1999
18 Red	82006458	1991	Delivered to Russia 21/02/2000 and is now in RuAF service as 18 Red/RF-94111

Tu-160Ss of the 184th GvTBAP mostly grounded at Priluki on 22 July 1998. The nearest aircraft to the camera is 25 Red (c/n 84703453), which was scrapped there on 1 December 1998. *Sergey Popsuevich*

26 Red (c/n 81804921) is preserved in the UkrAF's Long-Range Aviation Museum at Poltava. Its last flight was logged on 30 March 2000, when it was transferred to the museum. *Sergey Popsuevich*

This 1987-built Tu-160S of the 184th GvTBAP carried out nine successful Kh-55 missile launches during military exercises in its USSR days. It is seen grounded at Priluki on 22 July 1998. It was scrapped there on 7 June 2000. *Sergey Popsuevich*

Tu-134UBL Fleet (1992–2001): The Blackjack Pilot Trainers

Designed and developed to train the Tu-22M and Tu-160 pilots of VVS D-A and AV-MF, the Tu-134UBL and its naval variant, the Tu-134UBK, is still serving in the Russian Air Force. Among the 77 examples produced between 1981 and 1983, four machines that were in service with the 3rd AE of 184th GvTBAP in Priluki were inherited by the UkrAF in 1992. These aircraft remained in service until the retirement of the force's Tu-160s and Tu-22M3s. In addition to the four Tu-134UBLs, the UkrAF inherited a single ex-Soviet Navy Tu-134Sh-1, which was a heavy bomber crew trainer (Tu-22M2/3 crew trainer), and a single ex-Soviet Navy Tu-134Sh-2, which was a navigator trainer for the tactical bomber crews at Kulbakino AB. These two aircraft were never used by the UKrAF for training purposes.

Due to the fact that the medium-sized Tu-22M2/3 supersonic strategic bombers had no specific training variant, unlike the Tu-22U for Tu-22 Blinder aircraft family, the Tupolev design bureau was contracted to develop a Tu-22M pilot trainer aircraft based on the Tu-134 on 6 August 1979. The rationale for choosing this type was the similarity of its thrust to weight ratio to the Tu-22M2/3 and Tu-160 and their similar flight characteristics at low speed.

The specialised modification of the aircraft was named the Tu-134UBL and it was manufactured from 1980 as a Tu-134B variant equipped with two D-30 Srs.2 engines. The Tu-134UBL was visually distinguishable by its enlarged radome, which was the size of the Tu-22M2/3 radome housing the Almaz PNA navigation/attack radar (NATO Down Beat) and the ROZ-1 navigation/weather radar of the Tu-22M2/3. It was intended to equip the aircraft with telescopic extension refuelling probes but the plan was cancelled due to the restrictions imposed on the aerial refuelling capability of the Tu-22M2/3s of the VVS and VMF following SALT II.

The first Tu-134UBL prototype, CCCP-64010, was completed at the No. 135 aircraft manufacturing plant at Kharkiv in January 1981. The first stage of Tu-134UBL state research centre tests was soon carried out between May and June 1981 involving the prototype and several serial-produced aircraft. The second stage of the state trials, involving the second prototype CCCP-64020, was started in October 1981 and was completed in June 1982.

By the end of 1983, 77 Tu-134UBLs had been manufactured and handed over to the VVS. The first aircraft for the air force was even handed over before the completion of the state tests, arriving at Engels-2 in April 1981. Starting that month, Tu-134UBLs began to replace the ageing Tu-124Sh-1 and Il-28Us of the 652nd Training Aviation Regiment (UAP) at the Senior Military Aviation School of Pilots (VVAUL) at Tambov. The 652nd UAP was responsible for carrying out the second stage of the state tests while the VVS D-A had simultaneously begun using Tu-134UBLs to train strategic bomber crews at Engels-2.

At the beginning of 1991, a small number of Tu-134UBLs became part of the fleet of the 3rd Squadron, 184th GvTBAP (Guards Heavy Bomber Regiment). Until then, the Tu-134UBL had only been operated by the aviation schools. The 184th GvTBAP operated them from the Ukrainian base at Priluki, where its Tu-160 strategic bombers were based. In the 184th GvTBAP, the Tu-134UBL (Crusty B) was used for pilot training for the Tu-160 (Blackjack A).

Several Tu-134UBLs also became part of the fleet of the 652nd UAP (Flight Training Regiment), operating them from Dyagilevo. The Tu-134UBL was unveiled to the public on 11 April 1992 at an open day at Kubinka air force base. After the collapse of the USSR in 1991, all four Tu-134UBLs of the 184th GvTBAP's 1st AE fell into the hands of the UkrAF. These Tu-134UBLs played a key role in keeping the Tu-160 pilots current, especially when they could only fly the Tu-160 up to four times a year! They also played a key role in retraining Tu-22M3 pilots when the 184th GvTBAP converted to this type again.

The 184th GvTBAP's Tu-134UBLs were all ex-652nd UAP machines. They were coded from 41 to

This Tu-134UBL with bort number 41 Red was one of three examples in service with the 3rd Aviation Squadron of the 184th GvTBAP. This aircraft was declared surplus in 2001 and was later scrapped at Priluki. *Sergey Popsuevich*

43 Red was one of the Tu-134UBLs in service with the VVS's 652nd Training Aviation Regiment in the 1980s. It was transferred to the 184th GvTBAP in 1991. It was overhauled in Belarusia and then transferred to the 185th TBAP after disbandment of the 184th GvTBAP in 2001. *Sergey Popsuevich*

The colour of the bort number of 43 Red turned to Blue after it entered service with the 185th TBAP in 2001. It arrived at the State Aviation Museum at Kiev dismantled on 26 April 2006 and was assembled and put on display from June 2008. It is seen at Poltava's Long-Range Aviation Museum on 26 January 2006. *Sergey Popsuevich*

44 Red. After 44 Red (c/n 64148) reached the end of its MTBO, it was sent to the No. 20 ARZ at Pushkin to be overhauled in May 1998 but due to a lack of budget the aircraft remained there. The Russian Ministry of Defence funded part of its overhaul and also modernisation to Tu-134UBKM standard. The aircraft received the new bort number 11 Red, but never entered RuAF service and remained impounded at Pushkin.

No. 43 Red (c/n 64152) remained in 184th GvTBAP service until mid-1995. It was prepared for a short ferry flight to Poltava in 2001 and four years later it was put on display there at the Long-Range Aviation Museum, later moving to Zhuliany with its bort number painted in blue.

No. 42 Red (c/n 64300) was the last flying UkrAF Tu-134UBL between 1995 and 2001. The aircraft had reached its MTBO and, following the USSR's plans before the state collapsed, it was sent to No. 407 ARZ at Minsk-1 on 9 September 1992. The aircraft completed its overhaul and was seen with a new 'Avialiniyi Ukrayini' logo for the first time on 23 August 1996 outside the overhaul facility at the airport. Ukraine managed to pay its overhaul cost and finally the aircraft was redelivered in March 1998. Following the disbandment of the 184th GvTBAP, 42 Red was transferred to the 185th TBAP, which led to a change in colour of its bort number from red to blue. It was later put on display at the Long-Range Aviation Museum at Poltava.

The fourth 184th GvTBAP Tu-134UBL was not as lucky as the other three. The aircraft, 41 Red, which was reported to be the oldest of the type, was grounded and stored at Priluki in the early 1990s. Declared surplus in 2001, it was scrapped at Priluki.

As well as the four Tu-134UBLs of the 184th GvTBAP, the UkrAF inherited the sole Tu-134UBK produced for Tu-22M2/3 crew training with the USSR VMF. The aircraft, c/n 64728, was the last Tu-134UBL built, in December 1982. It received the pre-delivery registration CCCP-64728 and later became 72 Red, being handed over to the 33rd TsBPiPLS of the USSR VMF at Kulbakino in 1984. The aircraft later received the designation Tu-134UBK and was inherited by the Ukrainian Navy. It was transferred to the air force and kept operational until 1994 when there was no money available for the necessary extension of its calendar lifetime. It was scrapped at Mykolayiv-Kulbakino in September 2013.

The Tu-134UBL has an enlarged radome, which is the size of the Tu-22M2/3's, housing the bomber's Almaz PNA navigation/attack radar (NATO Down Beat) and the ROZ-1 navigation/weather radar for training purposes. *Sergey Popsuevich*

5 Pilot Trainers

L-39 Fleet (1992–today): Ukrainian Albatrosses

The backbone of the Ukrainian Air Force pilot training system in 2019 is a fleet of 46 airworthy L-39s, which are the remnants of 430 L-39s inherited from the Soviet Air Force in 1992. Not only are they used for fighter pilot training by the 203rd TrAB at Chuguyev but also to keep fighter pilots of the Tactical Aviation Brigades current as their flying hours are lower than the standards required due to a lack of budget.

L-39Cs of the Soviet Air Force's 809th UAP in 1990. *Sergey Popsuevich*

Ukrainian L-39s in the 1990s

In 1990, out of 2,175 L-39s in service with the Soviet Air Force and Navy, 506 were in service with the Chernigov Higher Military Aviation School of Pilots (ChVVAUL) and the Kharkiv Higher Military Aviation Order of the Red Star School of Pilots (KhVVAUL), both on Ukrainian territory. ChVVAUL had four training aviation regiments (UAP) and among them the 105th UAP at Konotop, 701st UAP at Chernigov and 703rd UAP at Gorodnya were each equipped with 101 L-39s. Two of the five KhVVAUL regiments were equipped with L-39s, the 443rd UAP at Velikaya and the 809th UAP at Akhtyrka, which had 101 and 102 L-39s in service respectively in 1990, based on CFE treaty data exchange.

L-39C 25 Yellow at Chuguyev in 1999. *Sergey Popsuevich*

L-39C of the 203rd Training Aviation Regiment at Chuguyev in 1999. *Sergey Popsuevich*

After Ukraine got its independence, among the above mentioned 506 L-39s, 430 were airworthy, which all entered service with the Ukrainian Air Force. Following the downsizing of the UKrAF combat aircraft fleet, the number of personnel including pilots reduced significantly and as a result the total of student pilots dropped every year. The fleet of L-39s in service with the air force was also cut and the flight training regiments were disbanded one by one.

In 1994, KhVVAUL was renamed the Kharkiv Institute of Pilots and its 443rd UAP and 809th UAP were disbanded and their aircraft relocated to Chuguyev airfield, which became the 203rd Training Air Base. In August 2004, the 203rd Aviation Base was renamed the 203rd Training Aviation Brigade at Chuguyev and later, on 1 September 2004, it became part of the Kharkiv Air Force University (HUVS), which is named Kozhedub university (after Ivan Kozhedub), established earlier in 2003.

Maintenance hangar at the Chuguyev Air Base with a pair of L-39Cs with bort numbers 44 and 66 Yellow under maintenance in 1999. *Sergey Popsuevich*

On 30 November 1995, ChVVAUL was disbanded following a farewell ceremony and its 701st UAP and 105th UAP (the 703rd UAP had already been disbanded in 1992) became part of the newly established Kharkiv Institute of pilots. The units were merged and formed the 201st Air Base at Chernigov. Finally, the last aviation unit of the former ChVVAUL at 201st Air Base was disbanded in September 2004. On 22 January 2004, an L-39C of the unit, 29 Yellow, piloted by N. V. Vasilkiyev and I. M. Patskan, had to make an emergency landing due to engine failure.

As a result of the massive retirement of a large proportion of the Ukrainian Air Force L-39s, they were put mostly put up for sale to foreign customers. According to documents of the Stockholm International Peace Research Institute (SIPRI), at least 60 L-39s were sold to nine countries, to be operated as advanced flight training jets by their air forces. In 1997, four were sold to Cambodia; in 2003, two went to Armenia; in 2004, two went to Slovakia while 14 were sold to Yemen; in 2005, 12 were sold to Azerbaijan while ten others went to Belarus; in 2006 two were sold to Equatorial Guinea, and eight others went to Georgia; in 2009 four were sold to Armenia and in 2013 two went to Estonia.

Nearly all the sold examples had been in storage for years. Because of that, overhaul of their Ivchenko AI-25TL turbofan engines was carried out before delivery at the Motor Sich Joint Stock Company. The airframes were refurbished at one of two State Enterprises, the Odessa Aircraft Plant or the Chuguyev Aircraft Repair Plant. From the day of finalising the contracts, it took a minimum of six months and a maximum two years for the customer to receive its overhauled or sometimes slightly modernised L-39s.

Not only were L-39s sold to be used in the air forces of various countries but also dozens of Ukrainian examples were sold to civilian operators, mostly in the US, after being overhauled and demilitarised at the Odessa and Chuguev Aircraft Repair Plants (ARP or ARZ). Despite the sale of almost a third of the UkrAF's L-39s by 2008, 93 L-39s were still subject to sale. Among them, two at Military Base ⍰2488 at Nikolaev and three others at Military Base ⍰4104, Chuguyev, were in good condition, requiring just an airframe overhaul prior to delivery. Fifty-two other L-39s at Chuguyev; 21 at A1789, Vasilkov; 14 stored at Odesaviaremservice (SE Odessa Aircraft Plant); and nine others stored at SE Chuguev ARZ, all disassembled in crates, were also available for sale but required heavy overhaul of the airframes and the engines.

L-39C 51 Yellow belonged to the 203rd Training Aviation Regiment but had been assigned temporarily to the State Aviation Test Centre at Kirovskoye in the 1990s. *Heinz Berger*

L-39C 30 Red was used by the State Aviation Test Centre of the UkrAF at Kirovskoye in 2000. *Sergey Popsuevich*

During the 1990s, the UkrAF cadets were still flying L-29s of the TSOU (Association for the Support of the Defence) after completion of their training on Yak-52s. At the end of their training on the L-29, they then continued in the UKrAF L-39Cs. *Sergey Popsuevich*

The UkrAF's L-39s' maintenance and overhaul at CHARZ

Established on 1 September 1938 in the form of Aviation Repair Shops at Chuguyev Military Aviation School in order to repair the U-2, UT-2, UTI-4 and I-16 aircraft as well as M-11 and M-25 engines, it was evacuated to Shymkent, Kazakhstan, following the start of the war. It returned to Chuguyev after the war and took on the repair of the La-5, Yak-7, La-9, UTI La-11, Yak-11, Yak-18 aircraft and AL-82, AL-82FN and AL-21 engines before its transformation into the 536th Aircraft Repair Plant Air Force. The Chuguyev Aircraft Repair Plant soon became one of the Soviet Air Force's facilities that was able to perform all types of L-39 maintenance as well as providing maintenance support for other aircraft, including the MiG-23.

After Ukraine's independence, the plant was transferred to the Ministry of Defence, and in 2003 it was renamed the SOE Chuguyev Aircraft Repair Plant, with the abolition of the pre-existing title the No. 536 ARZ/h 36986. Two years later, on 8 June 2005, the AVIAVOENREMONT factory became part of the group. In the same year, the company was contracted to repair and overhaul ten L-39s before they were sold to Belarus on 20–21 December 2005.

Between 2003 and 2006, CHARZ overhauled 35 L-39s for foreign customers. Some L-39s were also slightly modernised by replacing their ageing SARPP-12 system (System of Automatic Registration of Flight Data) with the BUR-4-1, which increased the number of logged parameters and discrete commands by five times. The new computer was also able to process all data in real time on all three flight axes, which reduced the time for calculation and increased the accuracy of the information processed.

By 2008, CHARZ was not only able to repair and even overhaul L-29s and L-39s but was also able to perform overhaul, repair, maintenance and modernisation of the MiG-23 in all its modifications. In 2010, the factory also introduced a demilitarised version of the L-39C, named L-39D. In those years the CHARZ was also manufacturing ground support equipment for MiG-23s, L-29s and L-39s as well as the Sapphire APU of the L-39.

In 2011, when the decision was made to re-form the Ukrainian Falcons team, this time with L-39s, five L-39Cs were allocated to this programme, two under overhaul at Odessa Aircraft Plant and three under overhaul at CHARZ. All the aircraft, with bort numbers 01, 03, 104, 105 and 106 Blue, were painted in the team's special blue and yellow colour schemes and they were handed over to the UkrAF in spring 2011. Their first performance was at the A4465 military base at Kulbakino on 25 May 2011.

On 20 June 2012, the Ukrainian Ministry of Defence finalised a 46.2 million UAH deal with CHARZ for the overhaul of 12 UkrAF's L-39Cs. Among them two aircraft, 73 and 74 Blue, were delivered to the 7th BrTA. Next, the overhaul of 111 and 112 Blue was completed in December 2012, and they were handed over to the 831st BrTA on 11 January 2013. On 19 March 2014, two other L-39Cs were handed over to the 203rd TrAB. On 8 June 2016, a new contract was signed between CHARZ and the MoD for the overhaul of seven UkrAF L-39Cs.

The UkrAF L-39s' modernisation at OdessAviaRemServis (OARZ)

The aircraft repair shops of the Russian Battalion, commanded by Lt Col Harlampy Stamateva, established on 14 April 1911, were soon transformed into the Anatra Aircraft Factory. The first aircraft manufactured there was flown by pilot Nikolay Kostin on 27 April 1911. Soon the factory became one of the most powerful aviation companies, even producing and assembling foreign aircraft. In 1915, the Anatra D or Anade, which was a two-seat reconnaissance aircraft, was designed by Elysée Alfred Descamps and manufactured by Anatra.

The factory was nationalised in 1920 and received a new name, State Aircraft Factory Number 11, but it soon ceased manufacturing aircraft and was turned into an aircraft repair plant as State Aviation Workshop Number 7 in 1924. During the Second World War, when the plant was part of the 256th Odessa Military District School, it started to repair Red Army I-16s but was relocated east to Armavir at the beginning of October 1941. The plant repaired 546 Soviet-made aircraft, including the I-15, I-16, LaGG-3, La-5, La-7, MiG-3, Yak-1, Yak-3, Yak-9 and Il-2, as well as foreign-made aircraft such as the Bell P-39 and Messerschmitt Bf 109, together with 1,135 aircraft engines and hundreds of vehicle engines. Soon after the war, during the early jet era, the plant started to repair MiG-15s.

After Ukraine's independence, the Odessa Aircraft Repair Plant or No. 562 ARZ//h 36981 of the USSR's Ministry of Defence, was transferred to Ukraine's MOD. Soon it was turned into one of the most important repair plants in the country, with the ability to perform major overhauls and modernisation of the MiG-21, MiG-23, MiG-27, L-39 and Yak-52 as well as undertaking various modifications of An-24 and An-26 transport aircraft and Mi-8 and Mi-17 helicopters, while it also had the ability to overhaul all the above mentioned aircrafts' engines and produce various spare parts.

In 2008, the company began work on the modernisation of the L-39C, which was officially named the L-39M1 by the UkrAF on 8 July 2009. Two years later, the company was listed as one of the Ukroboronprom group companies, and later in

2012 was renamed the Odessa Aircraft Plant. In 2009, the L-39M1 modernisation programme bore fruit with the finalisation of a contract with the Ukrainian MoD for the modernisation of two L-39Cs, which were delivered to the 299th BrTA in 2010 and 2011. In 2012, four more L-39s were modernised to the same 'M1' level and were delivered to the 204th BrTA at Belbek, Crimea, on 1 November and December.

By the end of 2012, the OARZ had completed the modernisation of six L-39s, four of which were delivered to the 204th BrTA and ttwo went to the 7th BrTA. In 2015, four more L-39s were modernised to M1 level and delivered to the 40th BrTA (on 5 December), the 114th BrTA, the 204th BrTA (on 27 November) and the 203rd TrAB.

Details of the L-39M1 modernisation programme

Because of ongoing economic problems, the Ukrainian government has always had problems with providing a sufficient budget for its armed forces. As a result of this shortage, which prevented the Ukrainian government buying an adequate amount of jet fuel for the UkrAF's Tactical Aviation Brigades, the amount of flying hours accumulated by fighter pilots dropped significantly after 2005 and this affected their combat readiness. To solve this problem, two options were available to the Ukrainian Air Force commanders: firstly, to use full-motion flight simulators in the BrTAs instead of the available fixed simulators, or secondly to use L-39s as low-cost combat aircraft to maintain the fighter pilots' flight readiness.

In fact, the L-39M1 mutated to become a flight simulator for the MiG-29, Su-24, Su-25, and Su-27. To fulfil this important role, especially when the Ukrainian Air Force's MiG-29s and Su-25s were going to be upgraded into 'MU1' and 'M1' levels respectively, it was intended that the OdessAviaRemServis would modernise the L-39s before delivery to the BrTAs. Not only the OARZ but also a wide range of aviation enterprise companies in the country were involved in the programme, the details of which were released by the OARZ for the first time during AVIASVIT 2008.

To act as a flying flight simulator, the L-39M1s were equipped with the BTK-39 on-board training complex, and because the L-39C's AI-25TL engines did not have sufficient performance, they were re-engined with a new upgraded powerplant: the AI-25TLSh. This engine gave an increase in thrust of up to 1,850kg (130kg more than the basic version), decreasing acceleration time by half at low and medium altitudes, which enhanced the manoeuvrability of the aircraft, and it was also installed with an exhaust gases temperature regulating unit (BRT) that increased the reliability of the engine.

Three other main improvements of the L-39M1 in comparison with the L-39C were the installation of the flight data recorder BUR-4-1-07 instead of the SARPP-12GM (CHARZ had also performed this upgrade at Chuguyev), extension of the aircraft's assigned calendar service life up to 35 years, and installation of an angle of attack measuring and indication system. Also, the avionics were different to the L-39C, as the L-39M1 benefited from an instrument panel with a gauge arrangement similar to the MiG-29 and Su-27 to make it easier for student pilots to convert from the L-39 to these fighter aircraft.

The reduced flying hours of the UkrAF's fighter aircraft saved fuel, and L-39M1s soon were widely used by the 40th, 114th, 204th, 299th and 831st BrTAs. The use of these flying simulators to maintain

04 Blue was an L-39C used by OdessAviaRemServis for research and development purposes, including tests of the new components of the L-39M1. It is seen at Odessa on 29 July 2011. *Alexander Golz*

the flying skills and combat readiness of fighter pilots reduced the expense of MiG-29 pilot training by four times and Su-27 training by five times.

As well as the above-mentioned changes and technical features of the L-39M1, this aircraft has a new R-863 radio set, item 690 IFF transponder, type A511 air traffic control equipment, air speed transmitters (DAS), DVbP-13 barometric altitude sensor with more accurate and improved parameters, EP-39 electronic instruments, MFI-1 multifunctional display, ILS-39 HUD, BUPR combat modes control panel, CH-3700-03 satellite navigation system, MVP-11V air data unit and SAVR-39 audio/video recording system.

In comparison with the L-39C, the L-39M1 is 50kg heavier, but requires 40m less take-off run on a concrete runway. It has 70km/h higher horizontal flight speed at 1,000m (770km/h), 25km/h higher (780km/h) at 3,000m, and 20km/h higher speed (755km/h) at 10,000m. The acceleration time from 220km/h to 590km/h is reduced from 10 to 6 seconds at 3,000m. The L-39M1's airframe assigned service life per hours has remained unchanged at 4,500, while its calendar service life has been increased from 25 years for the L-39C to 30–35 years for the L-39M1. The MTBO of the L-39M1's airframe in comparison with the L-39C has remained unchanged at 1,500 hours or 16 years.

In comparison with the AI-25TL, the AI-25TLSh has 1,000 hours more assigned service life (5,000 hours), while its calendar TBO has been increased from 8 to 12-14 years with a maximum 1,000 flying hours. The engine thrust has been increased from 1,720kg to 1,850kg at sea level, while its acceleration time has been reduced from 9–12 seconds to 5–6 seconds. The specific fuel consumption has also increased from 0.575 lb/(lbf·h) to 0.593 lb/(lbf·h).

203rd TrAB's L-39s today

Today, the 203rd TrAB is the largest operator of the L-39 with a fleet of 16 airworthy examples and 51 stored aircraft, among which one is an L-39M1 while the rest are L-39Cs. Up to four of the L-39s are usually on deployment to Nikolayev more than six months of the year to be used for weapons training beside the L-39C/M1s of the 299th TrAB.

The UkrAF has the largest number of L-39s stored at Chuguyev, of which the majority are subject to sale by the Ministry of Defence. In 2010, according to global images, 82 L-39s were available at Chuguyev, with 58 L-39s stored together with 24 L-39s still assigned to the 203rd TrAB, while only nine of them – 04, 07, 11, 16, 17, 19, 21, 24, and 27 Yellow – were airworthy.

Six years later, in 2016, the number of airworthy L-39s in service with the 203rd TrAB rose to 16, as mentioned above, but the number of stored L-39s had dropped from 58 to 51 due to the sale of some of them or the scrapping of others, according to the global images. Among the airworthy examples, 11 are usually at Chuguyev while the rest are on deployment to reinforce the units. During the annual exams of the Kharkiv University Students, all the L-39s are usually gathered at the air base.

On 20 July 2006, 107 training sorties were carried out by L-39s at Chuguyev during annual navigation or instrument flight training of the third-year Kozhedub Air Force University cadets. In April 2007, the 203rd TrAB again conducted more training for third- and four-year cadets and they logged 16 hours in 20 sorties. In that year the cost of fighter pilot training from the beginning to the end of the L-39 course was 1.5 million UAH, including 94 hours of training flights with the L-39, which was 852,000 UAH (8,000 UAH per hour). During a one-hour flight of the L-39, 736kg of jet fuel, which costs almost 7,800 UAH, is consumed.

Usually the third-year cadets of the Air Force University fly 15 hours on the Yak-52 and HAZ-30 basic training aircraft, resuming their training on the TKS-L-39 flight simulator. After familiarisation on the simulator, they must perform two compulsory parachute jumps from a height of 300m before being permitted to fly the L-39C. During their flight training with the L-39 in their third year at university, they practise more advanced flight manoeuvres such as loops, dive-loops, half-loops, horizontal barrels and 5/8 loops. Every year the advanced flight training course of third-year HUVS cadets usually starts on 15 May and finishes with an exam on 5 August.

After graduation, based on their scores the cadets are chosen to become fighter, transport or helicopter pilots. Those who are going to become fighter pilot must fly the L-39C for extra months to practise flights in adverse weather conditions and also by night (instrument flight training). The cadets learn a variety of combat manoeuvres and also weaponry training in the final stage of their training on the L-39 prior to becoming fighter pilots.

Following the Crimea crisis, when there was possibility of a Russian invasion of Ukraine, even the 203rd TrAB was put on high alert to prepare the

01 Blue (c/n 934619), an L-39C of the 203rd TrAB at Chuguyev, on 7 July 2017. *Alexander Golz*

fourth-year cadets for combat in March 2014. On 24 March, the cadets launched live S-5 rockets and dropped bombs to complete their course. Similar rocketry and bombing practice was repeated on 6 May 2014.

After the revolution and the Crimea crisis, the Ukrainian government allocated a budget for the overhaul and restoration of six L-39Cs for the 203rd TrAB. The first six, 02, 08, 20, 25, 32 and 33 White, were overhauled by CHARZ and handed over to the training brigade between 2014 and 2016. No. 25 White was later transferred to the 114th BrTA. As well as the above-mentioned aircraft, the 203rd TrAB received five more L-39Cs in 2017 and 2018, increasing the number of its airworthy examples to 18 in 2019.

L-39C cockpit-trainer of the 203rd TrAB at Chuguyev in 2017. *Alexander Golz*

32 White was one of the L-39Cs the 203rd TrAB received after completion of their overhaul in 2014. It is seen at Chuguyev on 7 July 2017. *Alexander Golz*

33 White was another L-39C the 203rd TrAB received after the completion of their overhaul in 2014. It is also seen at Chuguyev on 7 July 2017. *Alexander Golz*

TKS-L-39 flight simulator

HUVS student pilots always complete a L-39 simulator course prior to beginning their flights in the type. Manufactured in the 1980s, the HUVS L-39 simulators were not advanced enough to meet the needs of the university for training cadets in the 2000s. Starting in 2010, two companies, Lviv Aircraft Repair Plant (LARZ) and Market-Mats based in Lviv, began work to develop a new L-39 flight simulator, which finally was completed in 2011 and ordered by the MoD for HUVS. It was handed over to HUVS in June 2012. Installation work took 75 days and it was commissioned on 12 August 2012.

Named TKS-L-39, it was designed to firstly maintain the skills of the crews for piloting, navigation and combat missions in the L-39, including air-to-air and air-to-ground missions. Cadets can perform 85% of flight manoeuvres and 75% of the combat missions of the real aircraft using the new simulator. Its introduction has also reduced the cost of pilot training by reducing flying hours of the third-year cadets to just 61 hours on the type. The simulator itself consists of four main sections, which are the simulator main compartment with instrument panel and controls, imaging system and electronic acoustic devices as well as peripheral controllers; the information computer system; the instructor's working place, and the second pilot's working place. Later, Market-Mats announced a plan to develop the TKD-L-39 dynamic simulator.

L-39 accidents

Since 1992, the UkrAF has experienced at least one major L-39 accident a year but among them just three were fatal. The first fatal incident occurred on 13 August 1996, when an L-39 piloted by Lts Gulchenko and Chichikov crashed during a demonstration flight training exercise before an air show, killing both crew. The next fatal accident was on 26 August 1999, again during training for a demonstration flight before an air show, killing both crew members on board, Col Alexander Shapiro and Lt Col Dmitry Rusin, near Kulbakino, Nikolayev.

The last fatal accident occurred at Chuguyev on 22 September 2012. The cause was an engine fire during the take-off roll, preventing the pilot from gaining enough altitude and causing his aircraft to stall. The L-39C, 04 Yellow (c/n 934637) hit the runway and caught fire, killing its sole occupant, the third course cadet Mykola Nakonechnyi, who was on his 72nd flight.

299th BrTA's L-39s

The 299th Tactical Aviation Brigade, which is based at Kulbakino, has always been the largest operator of the L-39C advanced jet trainers in UkrAF service after the 203rd TrAB. The 299th BrTA's L-39s originally belonged to the 90th OshAP (90th Independent Assault Aviation Regiment) of the USSR Air Force's 5th Air Army at Artsyz, Odessa, which was disbanded in 1989. The 90th OshAP operated Su-25s and the L-39s for advanced weapon training of Su-25 pilots, and it also had a complementary combat role for the Su-25s. In 1989, the 299th BrTA was named the 299th Instructor-Research Shipborne Aviation Regiment (299th IIKAP), subordinate to the Soviet Naval Aviation's 1063rd Training Centre for Combat Employment Shipborne Aviation (1063rd TSBPKA). Soon after conversion from MiG-21 to Su-25, while the L-39s had a complementary role in the unit, it became a combat unit and joined the Black Sea Fleet of the Soviet Navy in 1990.

In 1992, the 299th IIKAP was inherited by the Ukrainian Navy and after a year with the Kirov Test Centre, it was absorbed by the 5th Air Army of the UkrAF in 1993, but it was returned to Ukrainian Navy Aviation in 1994. In 1996 it became a part of the UkrAF again and was renamed the 299th Assault Aviation Regiment, still operating the ex-90th OshAP Su-25s and L-39s. As with the 299th IIKAP, the 555th IIPLSAP (555th Instructor-Research Anti-Submarine Mixed Aviation Regiment) operated the L-39 at Kulbakino. The 555th IIPLSAP was a part of the Soviet Naval Aviation's 33rd TSBPPLS (33rd Centre for Combat Employment and Retraining of Personnel Aviation VMF imeni E.N. Preobrazhenskogo) but its L-39s were absorbed by the UkrAF in 1992.

After Ukraine's independence, the 33rd Centre for Combat Employment and Retraining of Personnel Aviation became part of the air force and the L-39s of the 299th OshAP (later reorganised as the 299th BrTA) were used by the centre for training purposes, together with the ex-555th IIPLSAP's 3rd Aviation Squadron L-39Cs. During Soviet days, ten 555th IIPLSAP L-39s were temporarily used by the 100th Shipborne Fighter Aviation Regiment (100th KIAP), based at Ochakov, Nikolyev Oblast, between 1988 and 1990.

By 2004, the 299th OshAP had been renamed the 299th BrTA, one of the UkrAF's Air Command Centre units, with its headquarters in Odessa. In 2004 the unit had 34 L-39Cs, among which 17 were always kept operational for the 33rd Training Centre and the 299th BrTA, while the rest were in temporary open storage. By 2008, the stored L-39s had been removed from the air base and sent to Odessa, where they were scrapped or stored in the OARZ facility. In 2007, just 14 L-39Cs were airworthy at Kulbakino. These were 05, 33, 36, 63 and 77 Blue, and 05, 06, 08, 11, 12, 14, 15, 16 and 17 Yellow.

In 2008, the 299th BrTA began receiving L-39s that had been overhauled by the Odessa Aircraft Plant. The first aircraft was 75 Blue, painted in two-tone dark green camouflage similar to the Su-25s. In 2010, the first L-39M1, 79 Blue (c/n 934651), modernised by the OARZ was handed over. In 2011, two more L-39Cs were overhauled for the 299th BrTA, which were 77 Blue (c/n 934650) and 78 Blue (c/n 834520). In the same year, the unit received its second L-39M1, which was 80 Blue (c/n 834523).

17 Yellow, an L-39C of the 299th BrTA, during an air show in Gostomel on 17 December 2004. *Sergey Popsuevich*

As explained earlier, in 2011, two L-39Cs under overhaul at the Odessa Aircraft Plant and three others being worked on at CHARZ were painted in Ukrainian Falcons demonstration team colours and delivered to the 299th BrTA. Some of them were originally 203rd TrAB machines. In that year the Ukrainian Falcons team was re-formed, this time with L-39s instead of MiG-29s due to budget shortages; and its first demonstration flight was performed on 13 May 2011. The team's first display with L-39s was held with two aircraft and they performed formation 45-degree and 60-degree rolls, dives, combat turns, loops and half loops at the A4465 military base of the 299th BrTA at Kulbakino on 25 May 2011. The Ukrainian Falcons demonstration team had been established in 1995, but due to safety reasons in the aftermath of the Sknyliv crash, displays by its MiG-29s were stopped in 2002.

Before equipping the Ukrainian Falcons with the L-39, the UkrAF had formed an aerobatic team with eight L-39Cs of the 203rd Training Base back in the 1990s. The aircraft were painted in overall white colours with blue underneath, on the top of the nose section and the surface of the vertical stabiliser. The team's name, Ukrainian Cossacks, was also written on their fuselages, and the aircraft were coded 201 to 208 Yellow. The team soon ceased flying and the last L-39, 206 Yellow, which was in use for training purposes by the 203rd TrAB, remained airworthy in the team's colours until 2004.

During Safe Skies 2011, two 299th BrTA L-39s played an aggressor role against 204th BrTA MiG-29s and 831st BrTA Su-27s, as well as USA F-16s, at Mirgorod on the second day of the exercise on 21 August. Following the Crimea crisis and the blockade of Military Base A4515, which includes Belbek where the 204th BrTA's 49 MiG-29s (only nine were airworthy) and four L-39M1s were based on 28 February 2014, the Russian Armed Forces permitted the UKrAF to evacuate its stored aircraft gradually from April until June. All the airworthy MiG-29s, together with three L-39M1s, remained at Belbek after the war started in the Donbass region. In April 2014, the 204th BrTA was temporarily reformed at Kulbakino with one L-39M1, 105 Blue.

299th BrTA L-39C 78 Blue (c/n 834520) at Nikolayev-Kulbakino on 20 April 2011. *Alexander Golz*

As a result of the Crimea crisis and the occupation of the peninsula, the Ukrainian Air Force's Air Command South was put on high alert and it was reinforced by a forward deployment of the 831st BrTA's Su-27s to Kulbakino. The number of training sorties by the 299th BrTA subsequently surged. Prior to the launch of the air operations against pro-Russian separatists in the Donbass region, the UKrAF held gunnery training at Kulbakino, during which 299th BrTA L-39s armed with UB-16-57UMVP rocket pods practised launching S-5 unguided rockets in April. Between 12 and 16 May, 299th BrTA L-39C/M1s practised dropping iron and smoke bombs.

On 22 July 2016, during the joint Ukrainian–American exercise Sea Breeze 2016, held at Kulbakino, two 299th BrTA L-39Cs, 77 and 78 Blue, flew as aggressor aircraft and simulated air raids against Ukrainian Navy ships. During the exercise, the Ukrainian Navy Aviation, which is based at Kulbakino, participated with one An-2, one An-26, one Ka-27PS and two Mi-14PLs.

7th BrTA's L-39s

Following the air force programme to reduce the Tactical Aviation Brigades' expenses, the 7th BrTA at Starokostiantyniv received four L-39s to use as flight simulators and training platforms to compensate it for the lack of flying hours of the Su-24 pilots. The first two aircraft, 71 Blue (c/n 834516), and 72 Blue (c/n 934658), which had both been modernised during their overhauls at OARZ, were delivered to the 7th BrTA, commanded by Col Nikolai Kovalenko, on 26 June 2012.

Two L-39Cs, 73 Blue (c/n 834511) and 74 Blue (c/n 934643), were delivered to the 7th BrTA during an official ceremony at Starokostiantyniv on 19 September 2012 in the presence of the Ukrainian Minister of Defence, Dmytro Salamatin. By the end of March 2013, two new 7th BrTA Su-24 navigators had completed their training course on the newly delivered L-39s prior to beginning flying in Su-24Ms. One of the 7th BrTA L-39 instructor pilots was Col Sergey Blyznyuk.

On 18 October 2012, during a training flight of L-39M1 71 Blue, which had been deployed to Ivano-Frankovsk, when the pilot lowered the landing gear lever on final approach, the left main gear did not extend. The pilot, deputy commander of Air Command West, Col Alexander Kukharenko (MiG-29 pilot and former commander of 114th BrTA), who was flying that day to restore his piloting skills on the L-39, decided to increase his speed to 350km/h to perform high G turns to open the retracted gear manually, but that did not work. Finally, he closed the remaining landing gear and carried out an emergency landing at 200km/h on a dirt strip alongside the Ivano-Frankovsk concrete runway. The aircraft received minor damage to its fuselage and was returned to 7th BrTA service a few weeks later after repairs.

Following the Crimea crisis, when the Ukrainian Air Force was on high alert to confront any possible strike from Russia, the 7th BrTA was quickly ordered to restore the combat readiness of its Su-24M, and Su-24MR aircrews. Between 17 and 21 March 2014, dozens of navigation flights were logged, including training sorties with the unit's L-39s. On 20 March, two of the unit's L-39M1swere used alongside the Su-24s for night flight training. On 23 April, another series of training exercises were carried out at Starokostiantyniv, during which pilots and navigators performed dozens of navigation training flights in Su-24s and L-39s.

In order to complete the restoration of combat readiness and flight skills of the 7th BrTA pilots, six Su-24s and two L-39s were deployed to Lutsk, where they trained in aerial gunnery between 19 and 21 May. Both L-39s were used to practise bombing on the first two days. On the last day, 71 Blue was equipped with a pair of UB-16-57UD pods, while 73 Blue carried a UB-16-57UMVP, which is mostly used by helicopters, to launch S-5 rockets at a nearby range.

After the war, the 7th BrTA lost one of its L-39M1s in an accident on 29 September 2017. The aircraft, 72 Blue, was flying near Starokostiantyniv at 12.20pm when the incident occurred. Both pilots lost their lives.

7th BrTA L-39M1 72 Blue (c/n 934658) at Starokonstantinov on 16 April 2015. This aircraft was lost in an accident on 29 September 2017. *Alexander Golz*

7th BrTA L-39C 73 Blue (c/n 834511) at Starokonstantinov on 16 April 2015. *Alexander Golz*

40th BrTA's L-39s

Before the introduction of the L-39M1s into UkrAF service in 2009, the 40th BrTA was the first unit operating L-39s to maintain its MiG-29 pilots' flight readiness at Vasilkov. By 2010, the unit was operating five L-39Cs, 111, 116, 119, 125, 129 and 140 Blue. Among these, 116 and 119 Blue remained airworthy until 2012. Before them, 111 Blue, a third L-39C, had been grounded due it to reaching the end of its MTBO. It was sent to CHARZ for overhaul in 2012 and following that was delivered to the 831st BrTA at Mirgorod the following year.

In 2012, to improve the flight skills of the 40th BrTA pilots in 2012, Air Command Centre made flight changes and carried out navigation flight training on 23 and 24 April. Because of the availability of just two L-39Cs, 116 and 119 Blue, two recently overhauled L-39Cs of the 203rd TrAB, 101 and 106 Blue, which had been detached to Kulbakino in Ukrainian Falcons colours, joined the remaining two airworthy L-39Cs at Vasilkov. In June 2012, during an Air Command Centre joint training exercise at Vasilkov, another L-39C, 103 Blue and also in Ukrainian Falcons colours, arrived at the base. It remained in service with the 40th BrTA until it was returned to Chuguyev during the annual exam of the Air Force University's third-year cadets in May 2013.

By the end of 2013, the two remaining airworthy L-39Cs at Vasilkov, 116 and 119 Blue, had run out of time and were put in storage. Subsequently, in 2013, the 40th BrTA began receiving its overhauled L-39Cs. The first two of them were digital-camouflaged examples, 101 and 102 Blue (not to be mistaken with the 204th BrTA's 101 and 102 Blue), overhauled by CHARZ. Following them, in 2015 the unit received three more L-39Cs. One of them was the former 204th BrTA L-39M1 103 Blue (c/n 934672), which had been returned from Belbek in May 2014.

Two digital-camouflaged and modernised L-39M1s, 107 and 110 Blue, were delivered to the unit in December and September 2015 respectively. A third L-39M1, 109 Blue, was delivered to the brigade after the completion of its overhaul and upgrade by the end of 2016.

Today, the 40th BrTA has three L-39Cs and four L-39M1s, which are in use to make up the flying hours of the unit's MiG-29 pilots in order to maintain their combat readiness and flying skills. In the event of more L-39s being needed for annual flight changes or joint training of the 40th BrTA with other Air Command Centre units at Vasilkov, more L-39s are being detached from the 203rd TrAB inventory to Vasilkov.

125 Blue, of the 40th BrTA, at Vasilkov in 2003. *Sergey Popsuevich*

104 Blue, an L-39C of the 40th BrTA, at Vasilkov on 18 October 2001. *Sergey Popsuevich*

119 Blue, an L-39C of the 40th BrTA, at Nikolayev on 20 April 2011. *Alexander Golz*

129 Blue, an L-39C of the 40th BrTA, at Vasilkov on 4 August 2008. *Alexander Golz*

102 Blue, an L-39C of the 40th BrTA, at Vasilkov on 20 April 2016. *Alexander Golz*

114th BrTA's L-39s

For first time, in 2012, when the 7th BrTA received four L-39s, the 114th BrTA was regularly operating at least one L-39M1 as a flying simulator for the 114th BrTA's MiG-29 pilots. This lasted until 2013. On 23 February 2013, during the Defender of the Fatherland Day, the first two 114th BrTA L-39Cs, under the command of Col Sergei Globtsov, were handed over. The aircraft were 121 and 122 Blue, both in digital camouflage colours, which had been overhauled by CHARZ. Seven days later both aircraft started regular flights with the brigade at Ivano-Frankovsk.

Despite them not being L-39M1s, 121 and 122 Blue were used by the 114th BrTA as flying simulators and training platforms for newly graduated pilots from the air force academy who were going to become MiG-29 pilots in the unit. Finally, in 2015, the brigade received three L-39M1s, 08, 20 and 21 White. Two of them had been painted in digital camouflage colours and their maintenance work had started at CHARZ on 14 March 2014. In addition to these, two L-39Cs, 25 White and 123 Blue, were also delivered to the brigade in 2016.

L-39M1 122 Blue of the 114th BrTA during the Bilateral Research Command Post exercise Autumn Cyclone 2013 at Ivano-Frankivsk AB on 25 September 2013. *Alexander Golz*

204th BrTA's L-39s

From 2009, 299th BrTA L-39s were deployed to Belbek in the Crimean peninsula during joint flight changes or training with the 204th BrTA of Air Command South. The unit's MiG-29 pilots were able to restore their flying skills in these trainers. Finally, the decision was made to equip the brigade with L-39s. Subsequently, on 12 March 2012, the first two L-39Cs including, 77 Blue (c/n 934650), which were 299th BrTA aircraft, were temporarily based at Belbek.

The decision was then taken to allocate L-39s exclusively to the 204th BrTA, and for this purpose four L-39M1s were overhauled and modernised by OARZ. The first, 101 Blue (not to be mistaken with the 40th BrTA's 101 Blue), flew for the first time after its modernisation at Odessa on 13 November 2012. A few days later, 101 Blue, painted in digital camouflage, was delivered. In 2013, three more digitally camouflaged L-39M1s, 102, 103 and 104 Blue, were delivered.

After delivery of the unit's L-39M1s, the 299th BrTA's L-39Cs were returned to Kulbakino. The Belbek Albatrosses were used widely, not only as flying simulators but also as aggressor aircraft in various exercises with Air Command South or even the Navy in the Sevastopol and Nikolayev regions. For example, during Exercise Perspective 2012 in

October 2012, two 299th BrTA L-39s were flown by 204th BrTA pilots playing the role of aggressors.

On 28 February 2014, when pro-Russians blockaded the 204th BrTA's personnel around Belbek airfield following Russia's plan for the annexation of this part of Ukraine's territory, of the four L-39M1s at the air base only one was operational, while the remaining three were temporarily grounded awaiting spare parts from OARZ.

On 22 March 2014, the Russian Armed Forces occupied Belbek airfield. In May, the Russian occupiers permitted the Ukrainian Air Force to evacuate some of the 38 stored 204th BrTA MiG-29s and one of the four L-39M1s, while all the nine airworthy MiG-29s as well as three L-39s were confiscated.

When the 204th BrTA was re-formed at Kulbakino in April 2014, its pilots used 299th BrTA L-39s to restore their flying skills and combat readiness until its first Albatross, L-39M1 105 Blue (c/n 934645), was delivered after modernisation and overhaul at OARZ in December 2015. It is now based at Kulbakino.

106 Blue is one of the 40th BrTA L-39Cs that had been assigned to the 39th oaeTA between 2016 (39th BrTA since 2018) and 2019. It is seen at Vasilkov AB on 17 April 2015. *Alexander Golz*

L-39s of 39th oaeTA and 831st BrTA

On 29 December 2012, the 831st BrTA at Mirgorod received two L-39Cs, both painted in digital colours with the bort numbers 111 and 112 Blue (former 40th BrTA aircraft), which had been overhauled by CHARZ. These two L-39Cs are still in use by the brigade to maintain the flying skills of the unit's Su-27 pilots and train their future pilots.

As well as the 831st BrTA, another UkrAF Su-27 operator, the 39th oaeTA (39th Separate Tactical Aviation Squadron) from Ozernoye-Zhytomir, has been operating L-39Cs 105 and 106 Blue, previously with the 299th BrTA and 40th BrTA respectively, since the beginning of the Crimea crisis when Air Command Centre started to re-form the 39th oaeTA.

UkrAF's L-39s in the future

While the L-39s are being replaced with Yak-130 advanced training jets in Russia, in Ukraine the L-39 has found a new life through the modernisation programme. The UkrAF's L-39s will remain as the backbone of the country's training system until 2040 via further upgrades, including the L-39M2 and L-39M3, during which the aircraft will be equipped with two extra MFDs with various modifications and changes. In 2014, 2015 and 2016, the air force received five, seven, two and five overhauled and modernised L-39s respectively, bringing the number of total airworthy examples in service with all six BrTAs, one TrAB and an Independent Fighter Squadron up to 46 in 2019.

One of two L-39Cs of the 831st BrTA, with the bort number 111 Blue, can be seen at Mirgorod AB on 25 October 2016. *Alexander Golz*

UkrAF L-39s in 2019

Model	Construction Number	Bort Number	Colour Scheme	Current Unit	Last Overhaul/ Restoration	Note
L-39M1	834516	71 Blue	Pixel	7th BrTA	2012	
L-39C	834511	73 Blue	Pixel	7th BrTA	2012	
L-39C	934643	74 Blue	Pixel	7th BrTA	2012	
L-39C	934674	106 Blue	Ukrainian Falcons	39th BrTA	2011	Detachment from 40th BrTA
L-39C	934661	105 Blue	Ukrainian Falcons	39th BrTA	2010	Detachment from 299th BrTA
L-39C	934642	101 Blue	Pixel	40th BrTA	2012	
L-39C	934649	102 Blue	Pixel	40th BrTA	2012	
L-39M1	934672	103 Blue	Pixel	40th BrTA	2012	Former 204th BrTA aircraft
L-39C	934654	104 Blue	Ukrainian Falcons	40th BrTA	2010	Detachment from 299th BrTA
L-39M1	934704	107 Blue	Pixel	40th BrTA	2015	
L-39M1	934653	109 Blue	Pixel	40th BrTA	2016	
L-39M1	934673	110 Blue	Pixel	40th BrTA	2015	
L-39M1	?	08 White	Pixel	114th BrTA	2014	
L-39M1	?	20 White	Pixel	114th BrTA	2014	
L-39M1	?	21 White	Pixel	114th BrTA	2014	
L-39C	?	25 White	Pixel	114th BrTA	2014	
L-39C	?	121 Blue	Pixel	114th BrTA	2013	
L-39C	934663	122 Blue	Pixel	114th BrTA	2013	
L-39C	?	123 Blue	Pixel	114th BrTA	2015	
L-39M1	934647	101 Blue	Pixel	204th BrTA	2012	
L-39M1	934645	105 Blue	Pixel	204th BrTA	2015	
L-39C	934650	77 Blue	Green Camouflage	299th BrTA	2011	
L-39C	834520	78 Blue	Green Camouflage	299th BrTA	2011	
L-39M1	934651	79 Blue	Green Camouflage	299th BrTA	2010	
L-39M1	834523	80 Blue	Green Camouflage	299th BrTA	2011	
L-39C	934619	101 Blue	Ukrainian Falcons	299th BrTA	2011	Originally the 203rd TrAB inventory
L-39C	?	111 Blue	Pixel	831st BrTA	2013	
L-39C	?	112 Blue	Pixel	831st BrTA	2013	
L-39C	934622	11 Yellow	Green Camouflage	203rd TrAB	Restored in 2014	
L-39C	934702	30 Yellow	Green Camouflage	203rd TrAB	Restored in 2014	
L-39C	934665	35 Yellow	Green Camouflage	203rd TrAB	Restored in 2014	Was put in storage in 2013 but restored in 2014
L-39C	934662	36 Yellow	Green Camouflage	203rd TrAB	Restored in 2014	
L-39C	934619	01 Blue	Ukrainian Falcons	203rd TrAB	2012	Ex-41 Yellow
L-39C	?	03 Blue	Ukrainian Falcons	203rd TrAB	2016	
L-39C	?	06 Blue	Ukrainian Falcons	203rd TrAB	2017	
L-39C	?	10 Blue	Ukrainian Falcons	203rd TrAB	2017	
L-39C	?	21 Blue	Pixel	203rd TrAB	?	
L-39C	?	103 Blue	Ukrainian Falcons	203rd TrAB	2012	Previously detached to 40th BrTA in 2013
L-39C	?	02 White	Pixel	203rd TrAB	2014	
L-39C	?	08 White	Pixel	203rd TrAB	2015	
L-39C	?	12 White	Pixel	203rd TrAB	2017	
L-39C	?	20 White	Pixel	203rd TrAB	2014	
L-39C	?	22 White	Pixel	203rd TrAB	2017	
L-39C	?	23 White	Pixel	203rd TrAB	2017	
L-39C	?	32 White	Pixel	203rd TrAB	2014	
L-39C	?	33 White	Pixel	203rd TrAB	2014	

MiG-21 Fleet (1992–2003): Ukrainian Fishbeds

On 17 March 1992, the Ukrainian Air Force was established in accordance with the directive of the Chief of the General Staff of the Armed Forces, and nearly all the combat aircraft of two former Soviet Air Force fighter divisions, two front-line bomber divisions, two long-range bomber divisions, three reconnaissance regiments, one electronic warfare regiment and four training centres, as well as transport aviation regiments, in Ukrainian territory were inducted into service – except the MiG-21s!

In 1990, the Soviet Air Force had 377 MiG-21s in service with four Training Aviation Regiments on current Ukraine territory. According to information gathered through the CFE data exchange treaty in 1990, the 228th UAP (Training Aviation Regiment) of the Voroshilovgrad Higher Military Aviation School of Navigators had 36 MiG-21s based at Bagerovo, Krymskaya Oblast, the 702nd UAP of the 1270th Training Aviation Centre for retraining personnel had 136 MiG-21s at Uman, while the 810th UAP and 812th UAP at the Kharkiv Higher Military Aviation School of Pilots had 103 and 102 MiG-21s at Chuguyev and Kupyansk respectively.

In the 1980s, most of the fighter pilots of the Soviet Air Force, Air Defence Force and Navy Aviation were trained on the MiG-21 after graduation from their L-39 course. They were logging 170 hours with L-39s and 110 hours on MiG-21s, including weaponry training. Starting in 1989, the number of airworthy MiG-21s in service with the training aviation regiments declined. For example, the 299th Instructor-Research Shipborne Aviation Regiment of Soviet Naval Aviation withdrew all its MiG-21s, which were being used for training Yak-38 pilots, in August 1989. In 1992, when Ukraine received its independence, there were 240 airworthy MiG-21s in service with four Training Aviation Regiments of the Soviet Air Force in the country. They were mostly MiG-21UM and MiG-21SM but some of them were MiG-21bis.

However, they did not serve in any aviation training regiment of the newly formed UkrAF, but some found their way to the Lviv and Odessa Overhaul Plants, where Ukrainian test pilots used them to remain current and avoid the expiration of their MiG-21 pilot certificate in order to be able to perform post-overhaul functional check flights or test flights of the overhauled MiG-21s at the facilities. Two MiG-21bis, 02 and 55 Blue, together with a MiG-21UM, 02 Outline (c/n 31091) which were airworthy until mid-1990s and 2003 respectively, as well as MiG-21bis 01 Blue (c/n 75041927), which was airworthy until 1995, were used by LARZ test pilots for training, while another MiG-21bis, 02 Blue, was used by the Odessa Aircraft Repair Plant in the 1990s.

A huge number of the MiG-21s were scrapped under the terms of conventional arms control treaties, while those in better condition that had logged fewer flying hours and cycles were put up for sale. Some of them were sold, including eight

142 Yellow, a MiG-21UM of the 810th UAP, at Chuguyev in 1989. *Sergey Popsuevich*

44 Yellow, a MiG-21UM of the disbanded 810th UAP, stored at Chuguyev in 1994. *Sergey Popsuevich*

121 Red, a MiG-21bis of the 810th UAP, stored at Chuguyev in 1994. *Sergey Popsuevich*

MiG-21UMs to India in 1996, which were later delivered after overhaul between 1997 and 2000. India ordered eight more MiG-21UMs in 2003, which were delivered in the same year mostly in non-airworthy condition. Six further MiG-21UMs were sold to Vietnam in 1995 (delivered after overhaul in 1996), while other sales included five MiG-21bis to the Azeri Air Force, which found their way to the Nagorniy-Kharabakh war. Also, in 2005, it was reported by SIPRI that the Odessa Aircraft Plant had sold one MiG-21bis but it is not clear whether it had only been overhauled there or was a former Ukrainian Air Force example.

In 2008, one former Ukrainian Air Force MiG-21SM manufactured in 1969, together with one 1975-built MiG-21UM, were still available for sale by the State Enterprise Odessa aircraft repair company, while the Lviv State Aircraft Repair Plant had four 1972–74-made MiG-21UMs available for sale.

This MiG-21bis with bort number 01 Blue (c/n 75041927) was used by LARZ for pilot training until 1995, when it was put in storage at Lviv. *Sergey Popsuevich*

11, a MiG-21bis of the Odessa Aircraft Repair Plant, was in use for pilot training and test purposes in 1992. It is seen during an air show at Odessa on 7 June 1992. *Sergey Popsuevich*

110, an ex-UkrAF MiG-21UM stored in the Odessa Aircraft Repair Plant, is seen waiting for its overhaul at the facility on 28 September 2010. *Alexander Golz*

The Odessa Aircraft Repair Plant used this MiG-21bis with bort number 55 Blue for pilot training and test purposes in 1990s. It is now stored at Odessa. *Alexander Golz*

Ex-UkrAF MiG-21UM 02 White (c/n 31091) was in use at the Lviv Aircraft Overhaul Plant for pilot training until the early 2000s. When its overhaul was due, it was grounded and the work began but this was then halted due to a lack of budget. *Dmitry S. M.*

6 Radio and Radar Jammers

Yak-28PP Fleet (1992–1994): The Flying Jammers

The Ukrainian Air Force inherited 22 out of the 39 remaining Yak-28PP electronic warfare aircraft of the Soviet Air Force in 1992. They were in service with the 118th Independent Aviation Regiment for Electronic Warfare (118th OAP REB) based at Chortkov, Ternopol Oblast, which had three aviation squadrons, two with the Yak-28s and one with the Su-24MP EW aircraft, subordinate to the 24th Air Army. They stayed in the UKrAF for just two more years until 1994, when the regiment was disbanded and its Yak-28PPs were sent to Ovruch to be stored and then scraped.

Retirement

Some ESM systems of the Yak-28PP had 1950s and '60s technology that was no longer effective against advanced NATO EW radars and SAM systems such as the Patriot PAC-2. Even in the early 1970s, the Soviet Air Force did not see the Yak-28PP as being capable of meeting their needs for an EW aircraft in the following decade, which led to the launch of a project in the early 1970s for the design and development of a new replacement aircraft based on the Su-24 strike bomber.

The SPS-5-28 Fasol noise jammer was technologically backward compared with the equivalent American systems installed on EW aircraft such as the EF-111A Raven of the USAF and the EA-6B Prowler of the US Navy and USMC. The Fasol was operated manually and it could not generate sufficient power. Also, the SPS-5's antenna had to face the enemy radar exactly to effectively transmit its location, so the enemy radar frequency had to be known before the operation.

One of five Yak-28Us of the 118th OAPREB on final approach to Chortkov air base in the mid-1980s. *Sergey Popsuevich*

A Yak-28U of the 118th OAPREB with bort number 37 Blue at Chortkov air base in 1990 or 1991. *Sergey Popsuevich*

Line-up of the Yak-28PPs of the 118th OAPREB at Chortkov airfield in 1990. *Sergey Popsuevich*

02 White was one of five Yak-28Us of the 118th OAPREB inherited by the Ukrainian Air Force in 1992. It is seen at Chortkov in 1990. *Author's collection*

Therefore it was nearly impossible to jam modern radars using the SPS-5 in the battlefield. Even after modernisation of the system, it was still problematic because an increase in its power led to disruption of the aircraft's own communication system and even that of the other aircraft flying in its proximity. It also had a negative effect on the health of the crews and the aircraft's other equipment. The Minister of the Radio Industry of the USSR, V. D. Kalmykov, said of Fasol: 'The only thing it can do is interfere with the work of our ministry.'

Production of the Su-24MP EW aircraft started at the same time as the Su-24MR tactical reconnaissance variant at the Novosibirsk Aircraft Manufacturing Plant in 1983. The restricted mission capability of some of the ESM systems of the first ten serial-produced Su-24MPs in East Germany forced the air force to keep the Yak-28PP in service for a longer period until the Su-24MP gained its desired combat capability or efficiency; however, this never occurred, resulting in 39 Yak-28PPs being kept operational until 1992, when the USSR collapsed.

The aircraft were gradually withdrawn from service from the following units up to 1992: 511th ORAP in 1983, 164th OGRAP in 1984, 11th ORAP in June 1986, 193rd ORAP in 1989, 799th ORAP in 1989 and 931st OGRAP in July 1989, leaving the 118th and 151st OAPREBs as the last operators of the type in the USSR Air Force between 1990 and 1992. Also, the 678th Guards Zabaykalskiy Red Banner Mixed Test Aviation Regiment (678th GVSIAP) had several Yak-28PPs still airworthy in Priozersk, Dzhambul Oblast, for test purposes until 1994.

60 Blue one of the 118th OAPREB's the Yak-28PPs, during Chortkov air base open house in 1990. *Author's collection*

While Ukraine inherited 22 out of the 39 Yak-28PPs in the USSR Air Force, Belarus inherited the rest, which totalled 17 out of 26 in service with the 151st OAPREB based at Schuchin, Grodno Oblast. The remaining nine 151st OAPREB's Yak-28PPs were withdrawn from service or were waiting for overhaul in Russia when Belarus gained its independence. This included 45 Blue, the overhaul of which was completed in 1991 but which was not delivered to the 151st OAPREB due to Belarus becoming independent, and it remained in No. 26 Aircraft Repair plant at Pushkin, Leningrad Oblast. It is seen during an exhibition at Pushkin in 1993. 45 Blue was later put on display at the Irkutsk-2 aviation plant. *Pushkin Aircraft Repair Plant Museum*

The 151st OAPREB, subordinate to the 26th Air Army, remained a part of the Russian Air Force with all its 17 Yak-28PPs in service until January 1993, when it was disbanded. That left the 118th OAPREB, which was now part of the UkrAF, as the last operator of the Yak-28PP EW in the world until 1994, when the unit was moved to Kolomiya and quickly disbanded. Its aircraft flew to Ovruch to be stored and scrapped. In May 1998, 17 Yak-28PPs and five Yak-28Us were still stored at Ovruch. Among the 118th OAPREB's 30 Yak-28s, just two have survived today, which are Yak-28U 03 White (c/n 8931906) on display at the State Aviation Museum in Kiev, and Yak-28PP 59 Blue (c/n 0970807) exhibited at the Ukrainian Air Force Museum, Vinnitsa.

118th OAPREB's history

The Yak-28PP was never tested in combat during the Afghanistan war because the Mujahedin did not have a SAM system or early warning radar. No Yak-28PPs were exported, but using the experience of the Iraqi Air Force in the use of ESM systems against the Iranian Armed Forces during the Iran–Iraq war, the USSR Air Force had the opportunity to improve and develop the EW tactics of the Yak-28PP and Su-24MP in 1983 and 1984. The Yak-28PPs always participated in USSR Air Force exercises in order to play the role of adversary EW aircraft by creating a jamming environment or providing an EW escort for the friendly forces.

While the 151st OAPREB was providing combat training for all units of the USSR Air Force based abroad (East Germany, Poland, Czechoslovakia and Hungary), the 118th OAPREB had a similar responsibility to train bomber and fighter aviation regiments inside USSR territory in Europe, Central Asia or the Far East. Alexei Vaneyev, the 118th OAPREB's test pilot who also served in the UkrAF as a colonel, recalls his service with the unit:

'The regiment was formed with former Yak-28PPs of the 511th ORAP [based at Buyalyk] at Chortkov airfield [Ternopol district] on 25 October 1983 from the 229th ORAE, which was part of the 14th Air Army of the Carpathian Military District. Its first commander was Lt Col Perevalov.

'We were involved in exercises throughout the European part of the USSR. We used passive countermeasures such as chaff and air-launched decoys for training about once a year at the Sotanov training ground [gunnery range]. When we were launching the S-5P rockets our visual sight was blocked until we passed the cloud [of chaff]. The wind was spreading the aluminium foil [chaff] all over the area like snow over a Christmas tree.

'The Yaks [Yak-28PPs] generated powerful active electronic countermeasure [jamming] which even interrupted the work of the Su-24 bombers' radars. They successfully jammed the P-18 and P-37 Early Warning radars, which were playing the role of enemy radars. Also, the civilian population in the jamming zone faced problems caused by the ECM system, for example their TVs began to "blink" and "ripple" (when the "Bouquet" was working) and the radio receivers were "wheezing" (from the "Fasol"). Also, the "Fasol" was unwantedly jamming the [Duga] over-the-horizon (OTH) radar system [used as part of the Soviet anti-ballistic missile early-warning network], after which the personnel of [3rd Independent Missile Attack Early Warning] the Army of Special Designation would contact the pilots and order them to stop jamming.

'In August 1989, the regiment formed a third squadron with Su-24MP aircraft. They had better equipment, designed to suppress modern SAM systems (Patriot and etc.). But despite that, the Yak-28PPs were still preferred to be used in the exercises and the pilots and navigators didn't miss the chance to pin the radars.'

33 and 53 White as well as 60 Blue were Yak-28PPs of the 118th OAPREB in 1991 or 1992. These pictures were taken by Sergei Skrynnikov, the Ukrainian aviation journalist and photographer who lost his life in the crash of the Antonov Design Bureau's An-140 UR-14003 near Isfahan on 23 December 2002. *Ukrainian Air Force museum via Dmitry M.*

The Yak-28PP was remembered by the pilots as an exceptionally reliable vehicle. For example, in the 118th OAPREB there were no accidents or incidents. In total, between 1981 and 1983 three Yak-28PPs were lost in accidents and a fourth one was badly damaged in an incident. Failures were noted only on the hydraulic system, and there were unauthorised leaks of fuel from tanks, which were then searched for. Another positive feature remembered by the mechanics about the aircraft and its equipment was that access to its engines, systems and equipment was easy and convenient, and many maintenance operations could be carried out directly from the ground, even without ladders.

Alexei Vaneyev, a Yak-28PP pilot in the 511th ORAP (in 1982 and 1983) and the 118th OAP REB (between 1984 and 1988), who later worked for the Antonov aircraft manufacturing company, explains the aircraft's manoeuvrability in a book named *Yak-28PP: The Director of Interference* published in 2000:

The last surviviving aircraft of its kind in Ukraine, Yak-28PP 59 Yellow (former 59 Blue) is now on display in the Ukrainian Air Force museum at Vinnitsa. It has the UB-16-57UM rocket pod, which could carry flares for passive countermeasures. *Sergey Popsuevich*

'The Yak-28PP was pleasant to pilot. It had the flight characteristics of a bomber, such as a large turning radius, slow rate of climb (lethargy in pitch). Thanks to its effective ailerons, it was good for barrel rolls. In general, its manoeuvrability was limited and it was designed to withstand less than +3G. But there was an occasion in the 118th OAP REB when an aircraft withstood 10G (maybe more, as the pointer went off and it was calculated only for 10G).

'The pilot had executed a barrel roll in the clouds in bad weather conditions and lost spatial orientation. In an inverted position he pulled the handle toward himself and descended and while he was near to the ground restored his orientation and pulled out of the loop and the aircraft miraculously gained altitude. The navigator couldn't grab the ejection handle due to the overload and they landed together. They tried to hide the incident by destroying the tape recording but technicians visually noticed that the aircraft was overstressed 3–4 times higher than its G-limit.' [After a quick look at the engine air intakes during the post-flight inspection, 2–3cm wide gaps between the engine nacelle and the inner surface of air intakes could be seen as evidence of over-G.]

After the USSR's disintegration, the 118th OAP REB became part of the Ukrainian Air Force. At the beginning of 1992, it had 30 Yak-28s. However, the aircraft was already hopelessly outdated by the time and was among the first types to be removed from the arsenal. In December 1994, the regiment was disbanded. Of the 22 Yak-28s remaining in service, 20 were disposed of and two were flown to Ovruch for storage. The six Su-24MPs of its 3rd Aviation Squadron were used to form a 3rd Aviation Squadron in the 48th OGRAP at Kolomiya in 1994 and they remained in service until 1998, when they were sent to Nikolayev for storage.

Su-24MP Fleet (1992–2002): The Patriot Jammers

The Su-24MP electronic warfare aircraft was designed and developed as the successor to the Yak-28PP with the key goal of jamming NATO's latest generation of EW radars and SAM systems in the 1980s, but it soon turned out to be less reliable than its predecessor. The Ukrainian Air Force inherited seven of the ten serial-produced Su-24MPs from the Soviet Air Force but was soon faced with technical issues in maintaining and supporting the aircraft's sophisticated ECM systems. This resulted in their role being downgraded from an EW aircraft to an Su-24 pilot and navigator trainer in the last years of the aircraft's service, before they were scrapped in the early 2000s.

Technical specifications

Since the late 1960s, the USAF had sought to replace its fleet of ageing and subsonic EB-66 and EB-57 electronic warfare aircraft and finally a special modification of the F-111A bomber was selected in 1972. It was designated EF-111A and known as the 'Electric Fox', flying for the first time on 10 March 1977. In total, 42 F-111As were converted to EF-111s at a total cost of $1.5 billion and they entered USAF service between 1981 and 1985.

The Soviets followed the Americans when developing a replacement for the Yak-28PP supersonic EW aircraft, which had been in service with the USSR Air Force since 1970. The Su-24M platform was selected as the basis for the design and development of the new aircraft, which was later named the Su-24MP. The Sukhoi OKB began research for the new EW aircraft project based on the T6-2I prototype under the designation 'T-6P' in the early 1970s. Due to delays in the development of the Su-24 prototypes, the project had to wait until the first Su-24M was almost ready for test flying. Subsequently, the new EW aircraft design was based on the Izdeliye-44 instead of the Izdeliye-41 platform.

The first prototypes of the aircraft, which had now been designated the T-6MP by Sukhoi, were completed in 1979. The first prototype, 0115304, an ex T-6M-25 converted into the T-6MP-25, flew for the first time in April 1980, followed by the second prototype, a T-6MP-35 (made from a T-6M-35). They received the bort numbers 25 and 35 White respectively. They were both used for state research centre tests until the aircraft's completion in 1982. In November 1982, serial production of the Su-24MP started at the Novosibirsk Aircraft Manufacturing Plant as Product-46 (Izdeliye-46), where the Su-24MR was being manufactured at the same time.

The Su-24MP had the fuselage and structure of the Su-24MR tactical reconnaissance jet and the similar NK-24 navigation complex encompassing the 'Relyef' terrain-avoidance radar and the DISS-7 Doppler navigation radar, which was a simplified small navigation system installed instead of the Su-24M's Orion navigation/attack radar in order to create space in the nose section of the Su-24MP to allow for the installation of the ECM systems.

While the Yak-28PP's Bouquet and Fasol ECM suites were designed to jam the radar systems of 1960s SAM systems such as the Nike Hercules and Hawk I, as well as the era's early warning radars, the Su-24MP's ECM systems were designed to protect front-line bombers, mostly Su-24s, from the danger of new SAM systems such as Patriot long-range missiles and high-altitude SAMs in service with the US Army. It was also designed to jam the new phased-array radars. To achieve these goals it had been equipped with the Landish built-in ECM complex equipped with the SPS-22 jamming system.

As well as Landish, the Su-24MP had the capability to carry an ECM pod under its centreline hardpoint beneath the fuselage. This pod could carry the SPS-5M Fasol or the SPS-6 Los and Mimoza. Instead of an ECM pod, an automatic decoy launcher designed to jam radars could be carried under the centreline hardpoint. Also similar to the Su-24MR, the Su-24MP did not have a strike capability, with no built-in GSh-6-23 (GSh-6-23M) cannon installed under the fuselage. It just had the capability to carry a maximum of two pairs of R-60/M short-range IR-guided air-to-air missiles under the outboard pylons, but usually just two were carried under one pylon while the other outboard pylon carried the ELINT pod.

Fencer-F in service with the 118th OAPREB

Ten Su-24MPs were manufactured; among these five were completed in 1983, two in 1984 and three in 1985. The first two serial-produced examples, with construction numbers 4160464201011 and 4160464201042, entered service with the 455th Bomber Aviation Regiment (455th BAP) of the 4th TsBP i PLS at Voronezh in June 1983. They were intended to be used for research and development of Landish and other ECM suites for the Su-24MP.

In 1983, three Su-24MPs were delivered to the 118th OAPREB to be used by its 1st Aviation Squadron. They received the bort numbers 10, 11 and 12 White. In 1984, two more Su-24MPs, 15 and 18 White, were delivered to the unit, and in

One of the seven Su-24MPs that entered service with the 6th AB in 1998 seen at Nikolayev-Kulbakino. *Sergey Popsuevich*

1985 three more examples, 17, 14 and 16 White, were delivered. A group of former Yak-28PP pilots and navigators of the 3rd Aviation Squadron of the 118th OAPREB were retrained on the new type in 1983. They, together with all their eight Su-24MPs, were deployed to Neu-Welzow, East Germany, in June 1986 to replace the ageing Yak-28PP EW aircraft of the 3rd Aviation Squadron of the 11th Independent Reconnaissance Aviation Regiment.

The Su-24MPs were intended to be operated for test purposes within the 11th ORAP structure in East Germany. They took part in various exercises and it was planned to test their systems against US Arm MIM-104 Patriot SAM systems, which in 1986 the USAFE announced would be deployed to West Germany in 1989. However, due to the financial problems of the USSR, and secondly due to technological backwardness, the Landish ECM suite and its SPS-22 ECM system never reached the maximum combat readiness of the Bouquet ECM suite and its SPS-44 and SPS-55 systems that were installed on the Yak-28PP.

Following the reunification of East and West Germany and the gradual disbandment of the Russian Air Force bases in Germany, the 11th ORAP was transferred with all of its personnel and equipment to Marinovka, Volgograd Oblast, in June 1993. Two years earlier, between 5 and 7 June 1991 when the USSR Air Force still existed, the 3rd Aviation Squadron of the regiment had been disbanded and its eight Su-24MPs redeployed to Chortkov to re-form the 3rd Aviation Squadron of the 118th OAPREB.

A year after their return to Chortkov, the Ukrainian SSR of the Soviet Union gained its independence and the 118th OAPREB became part of the new Ukrainian Air Force. Despite their age and having the outdated technology of the Bouquet ECM system, the 22 Yak-28PPs of the regiment were more reliable than the Su-24MPs, which now were all only partially mission capable due to a lack of spare parts or the knowledge of how to bring their Landish ECM suite to operational status in Ukraine.

When Ukraine gained its independence, six out of the eight Su-24MPs of the 118th OAPREB were at Chortkov. One of two missing Su-24MPs had been sent to the 455th BAP of the 4th TsBP i PLS to be used beside its two other Su-24MPs for research purposes in 1991, while another Su-24MP had mysteriously ended up in Belarus! It is not known how, but example was later repaired and exported to Algeria in 1997, where it received the code KY-51 and entered service with the 525e Escadron de Reconnaissance et de Guerre Electronique (525th ERGE) at the Aïn Oussera air base of the Algerian Air Force.

The number of mission-capable Yak-28PPs of the 118th OAPREB dropped to half in 1994, when the regiment was disbanded and its partially operational Su-24MPs were used to form a 3rd Aviation Squadron within the structure of the 48th OGRAP in Kolomiya. They remained in service until 1998, when they were sent to Kulbakino to enter service with the 33rd TsBP i PLS (33rd Centre for Combat Employment and Retraining of Personnel Aviation). At Kulbakino, they were used to form a second squadron together with the ageing Su-24 Izdeliye-41s of the centre for training Su-24MR pilots and navigators! The six Su-24MPs remained in service as training aircraft until they were withdrawn from service in 2002 and later scrapped. It is believed that some of their parts were sold to Algeria to be used to keep its sole Su-24MP airworthy. The Russian Air Force also continued operating two out of its three Su-24MPs, 52 and 53 Red in service with the 968th Fighter Aviation Regiment (968th IAP) of the 4th TsBP i PLS at Lipetsk, for research purposes until 2008.

41 White was one of the Su-24MPs that served in the Soviet VVS's 11th ORAP at Neu-Welzow until 1991. They later entered service with the 118th OAPREB. The aircraft is landing at Neu-Wekzow on 25 March 1991. *Rob Schleiffert*

Tu-22P/PD Fleet (1992–1996): The Heavy Radar Jammers of the Soviet Union

If suppression of enemy's air defence is not possible prior to an air strike, stand-off jammer or electronic warfare aircraft are required to protect the strike force's tactical or heavy bombers and fighters from the danger of the enemy's radar-guided air-to-air missiles and surface-to-air weapons. In the Soviet Air Force and Navy, while Yak-28PPs or Su-24MPs were used to protect tactical and strike bombers such as Su-17s and Su-24s, Tu-22P/PD heavy jammer aircraft protected the heavy bombers and tactical reconnaissance aircraft. Forty-seven Tu-22P/PD stand-off jammer aircraft were manufactured between 1961 and 1969, and they entered service with seven regiments of the Soviet Union Navy Aviation (AV-MF) and the Long-Range Aviation of the Soviet Air Force (VVS D-A).

A Tu-22PD of the 3rd Aviation Squadron of the 203rd GvTBAP based at Baranovichi Brest Oblast. This example was later inherited by Belarus. *Author's collection*

Retirement from service

Six Tu-22P/PDs were lost in various accidents and incidents between 1968 and 1987. In June 1989, the 15th ODRAP of the AV-MF was converted to the Su-24M/MR and its Tu-22s, including the Tu-22PDs, were absorbed by the AV-MF's 30th OMRAP and VVS D-A's 199th ODRAP. In 1990, 41 Tu-22P/PDs were in service with six regiments of the Soviet Air Force and Navy, comprising eight with thr 203rd TBAP, five with the 290th ODRAP, eight with the 121st GVTBAP, six with the 30th OMRAP, six with the 199th OGDRAP and eight with the 341st TBAP.

While the Tu-22M2/M3s were going to take the place of the ageing Tu-22K/KD/KDPs and the Tu-22M(3) R was being developed to replace the Tu-22R/RD/RDMs in service in the AV-MF and VVS, there was no proper replacement for the ageing Tu-22P/PDs. However, it was intended to use the Su-24MP EW aircraft to support the heavy bomber aviation regiments and also the long-range reconnaissance aviation regiments. The Sukhoi Su-24MP had been designed and developed to take the place of the Yak-28PP EW aircraft, but just ten were produced between 1983 and 1985 and its development and further production was stopped.

Image taken by a navigator of 290 ODRAP shows Tu-22PD with bort number 24 Red in 1989. *Author's collection*

After the collapse of the Soviet Union, the 121st GVTBAP at Machulishchi, 203rd TBAP at Baranovichi, and 290th ODRAP at Zyabrovka, and their 21 Tu-22P/PDs, were inherited by Belarus, while the 199th OGDRAP at Nezhyin and 341st TBAP at Ozernoye and their 14 Tu-22P/PDs were inherited by Ukraine. Just six Tu-22P/PDs in service with the 30th OMRAP of the AV-MF were inherited by the Russian Navy and remained in Russian hands after the collapse of the Soviet Union.

Starting in 1991, the Tu-22 regiments saw the number of serviceable airframes reduced due to a lack of spare parts. Also, a lack of budget for the procurement of fuel resulted a decline in the number of pilot flying hours. In 1992, after the formation of the Belarussian Air Force, the situation became even worse and within just two years all three regiments there were disbanded and their Tu-22s flown to Engels-2 Air Base in Russia to be scrapped.

The situation was better in Ukraine and the Tu-22P/PDs of the 341st TBAP and 199th OGDRAP were in service at least until 1995. In that year, all the 341st BTAP's Tu-22P/PDs retired, leaving the 199th OGDRAP, with three operational Tu-22PDs, as the last operator of the type in Ukraine. Even the 199th OGDRAP saw its last three Tu-22PDs withdrawn from service in 1996. The last operator of the type in Russia was the 30th OMRAP of the AV-MF's Black Sea fleet at Saki, which was disbanded in 1993.

While the Belarussian Air Force's Tu-22s were transferred to Engels-2 AB, where they were stored and later scrapped, the Ukrainian Tu-22s were scrapped at Bila Tserkva (341st TBAP) and Nezhyin (199th OGDRAP). The Tu-22s of the 30th OMRAP were scrapped at Saki, on the Crimean peninsula. Today, only two Tu-22PDs survive, one with the bort number 46 Red (c/n 3578035) equipped with a P2 ECM container on display in the Long-Range Aviation Museum at Engels. It is a former 121st GVTBAP aircraft. The second surviving Tu-22PD is now on display in Dyagilevo Museum. It has the bort number

Tu-22PD 29 Red of the 341st TBAP's 3rd Aviation Squadron at Ozernoye on 30 June 1993. *Sergey Popsuevich*

This Afghanistan war veteran Tu-22PD of the 341st TBAP's 3rd AE with bort number 32 Red carried out 21 missions during its deployment between October 1988 and January 1989. It remained in service with the 341st TBAP of the UkrAF until October 1995. *Sergey Popsuevich*

The famous dragon artwork and 21 mission marks painted on the fuselage of 32 Red. It is seen at Ozernoye in 1992. *Sergey Popsuevich*

51 Red and is a former 203rd TBAP machine that made an emergency landing at Dyagilevo due to the failure of one of its engines while it was flying from Baranovichi to Engels-2 to be scrapped in March 1993. The decision was made to keep the aircraft and display at Dyagilevo instead of scrapping it.

The Tu-22PDs were finally retired from service in the 1990s leaving the heavy bomber aviation regiments of the Russian Air Force without any EW aircraft. However, it is claimed that the self-protection systems of the Tu-22M3s could properly protect them from the danger of enemy SAM systems and air-to-air missiles launched by interceptors, but the loss of one of two serviceable Tu-22M3R heavy reconnaissance aircraft of the Russian Air Force to a Buk-M1 SAM system during the Georgian War in 2008 proved that the type was vulnerable to SAM systems in warzones.

This Tu-22PD of the 341st TBAP's 3rd AE with bort number 35 Red took part in the Afghanistan war and because of that it received dragon artwork on its front fuselage. It is at Poltava on 22 May 1993. *Sergey Popsuevich*

Tu-22PD 35 Red of the 341st TBAP at Poltava on 22 May 1993. The ECM systems of the Tu-22P increased its empty weight to 49 tons compared with the 43.6 tons of the Tu-22R. This had a negative effect on the aircraft's characteristics. Similarly to the Tu-22R, the Tu-22P was equipped with the Rubn-1A navigation-bombing radar, which could scan the terrain and help to find a suitable altitude for the ECM systems. Later, the Rubin-1L navigation-bombing radar was installed in production Tu-22PDs. *Sergey Popsuevich*

Tu-22PD 35 Red of the 341st TBAP at Poltava on 22 May 1993. Because the Tu-22R/RDs of the Independent Reconnaissance Aviation Regiments were performing their missions mostly solo, they needed ECM escort provided by just one Tu-22P/PD in the case of flights within range of the enemy's SAMs or deep inside the enemy's airspace before and after a strike mission (for battle damage assessment). *Sergey Popsuevich*

35 Red was one of the 341st TBAP's Tu-22PDs that took part in the Afghanistan war. In October 1988, the 3rd Aviation Squadron of the 341st TBAP assigned three (some sources claim four) Tu-22PDs to Mary-2, Mary Oblast, where the Soviet Long-Range Aviation had six (later increased to twelve) Tu-22M3s of the 185th GvTBAP (from Poltava) on forward deployment to use for bombing Mujahideen militias. *Sergey Popsuevich*

35 Red was one of the Tu-22PDs of the 341st TBAP that participated in the Afghanistan war. As the Tu-22PD could also carry AFA-42/20 and AFA-42/100 cameras for photo reconnaissance during jamming missions, and as they could easily fly over the border with Pakistan without being harmed by Pakistani fighter jets and SAMs, they also photographed the Mujahideen and Pakistani bases near the border. AFA-42/20 vertical cameras could cover an area 3.2 times the altitude of the aircraft and an along-track distance of 220 times the altitude, while the AFA-42/100 oblique camera covered an area with a width equal to the altitude of aircraft and an along-track distance of 23 times the altitude. These cameras were mounted in the front of the aircraft just behind the nose landing gear. *Sergey Popsuevich*

Bibliography

www.16va.be
www.airforce.ru
www.airhistory.net
www.airwar.ru
www.abaza.ilisso.ru
www.avialp.info
www.aviaforum.ru
www.chvvakush.ru
www.dvvaiu.net.ru
www.foro.rkka.es
www.forum.gp.dn.ua
www.forumavia.ru
www.garnizon.sibirjak.ru
www.mil.gov.ua
www.militaryaviation.in.ua
www.paluba.info
www.russianarms.ru
www.russianplanes.net
www.scramble.nl
www.spotters.net.ua
www.tu22.ru
www.troops.ru
www.uprom.info
www.ww2.dk
www.wing.com.ua
www.warfare.ru
www.wap.shmas.forum24.ru
www.zvitiaga.org
www.atez72.livejournal.com
www.bmpd.livejournal.com
www.diana-mihailova.livejournal.com

Aviation and Time magazine (aviaciya-i-vremya)
Newspaper of Ukrainian Air Force – 2011 to 2016
Ukrainian Ministry of Defence, White Book – 2005, 2006, 2007, 2008, 2009, 2010, 2011, 2013, 2014, 2015, 2016 and 2017
Declassified documents of Ukrainian Air Force
Declassified documents of Ukrainian Ministry of Defence
Declassified documents of Verkhovna Rada of Ukraine
Declassified documents of Soviet Air Force
Evgeny Butsky, Sergey Moroz, *Antonov An-12 Transport Aircraft*, Kazan, 2004
'Systems of technical and technical engineering', 2014, No. 3 (39) ISSN 1997-9568
S. I. Azarov, G.A. Sorokin, 'Military-technical problems'
Archive of the State Aviation Museum at Kiev
Archive of the Long-Range Aviation Museum at Poltava
Archive of the Zaporozhye Aircraft Repair Plant (MiGremont)
Lviv Polytechnic National University Institutional Repository
Field Manual, No. 100-2-3, 'The Soviet Army: Troops, Organisation, and Equipment', Headquarters Department of the Army Washington. DC, 6 June 1991
L Gen V. O. YUDAKOV, Chief of Operations, Deputy Chairman of the General Staff, Ukrainian Armed Forces, 'Participation of Ukrainian Armed Forces in Peacekeeping Operations. Lessons Learned and Prospects'

Index

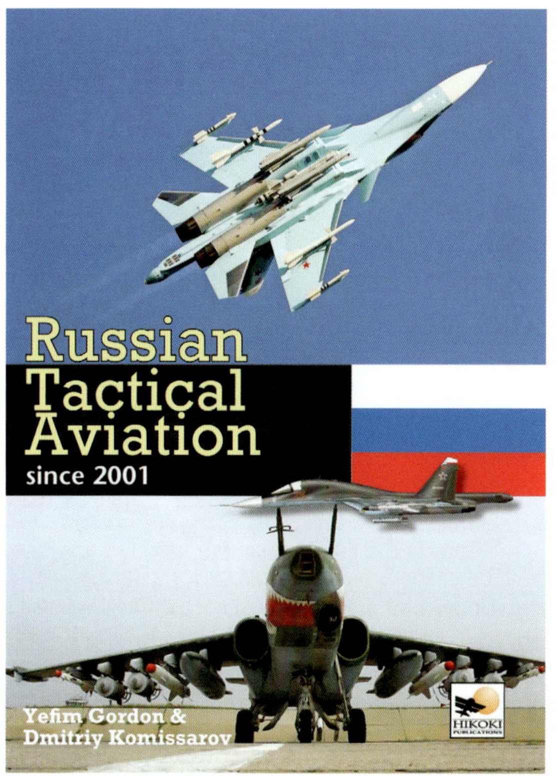

Russian Tactical Aviation since 2001

Yefim Gordon and Dmitriy Komissarov

The Tactical Aviation branch (FA – Frontovaya aviatsiya) has always occupied an important place in the structure of the Soviet, and subsequently Russian Air Force. In the 20-odd post-Soviet years, the Russian Air Force has been repeatedly reformed and in the course of the reforms the importance of Tactical Aviation has risen.

Russian Tactical Aviation illustrates the current state of the Russian Air Force's tactical aviation as well as its recent history in various overseas conflicts. Details are given of the aviation bases (units), their locations and the principal types currently in service. *Russian Tactical Aviation* is illustrated throughout with many previously unpublished photos, including air-to-air shots during Russian Force exercises, as well as colour profiles of Russian tactical aircraft and helicopters operated by various aviation bases.

304 pages, hardback

ISBN: 9781902109527 £34.95

Soviet Strategic Aviation in the Cold War

Yefim Gordon

Born in the 1930s, the Soviet Air Force's long-range bomber arm (known initially as the ADD and later as the DA) proved itself during the Second World War and continued to develop in the immediate post-war years, when the former allies turned Cold War opponents.

Soviet Strategic Aviation in the Cold War shows how the DA's order of battle changed in the period from 1945 to 1991. Major operations including the air arm's involvement in the Afghan War, the Cold War exercises over international waters in the vicinity of the 'potential adversary' and the shadowing of NATO warships are covered together with details of Air Armies, bomber divisions and bomber regiments, including their aircraft on a type-by-type basis.

Over 500 photos, most of which are previously unpublished in the West, are supplemented by 61 colour profiles, colour badges and line drawings of the aircraft and their weapons, making this an essential reference source for the historian and modeller alike.

Pagination: 272 pages, hardback

ISBN: 9781902109084 £34.95